Tragedy

and

Comedy

A Systematic Study and a Critique of Hegel

Mark William Roche

STATE UNIVERSITY OF NEW YORK PRESS

Production by Ruth Fisher
Marketing by Dana E. Yanulavich

Published by
State University of New York Press, Albany

For information, address the State University of New York Press,
State University Plaza, Albany, NY 12246

Library of Congress Cataloging-in-Publication Data

Roche, Mark William.
    Tragedy and comedy : a systematic study and a critique of Hegel /
Mark William Roche.
        p.   cm. — (SUNY series in Hegelian studies)
    Includes bibliographical references and index.
    ISBN 0-7914-3545-8 (hardcover : alk. paper). — ISBN 0-7914-3546-6
(pbk. : alk. paper)
    1. Tragedy. 2. Comedy. 3. Hegel, Georg Wilhelm Friedrich,
    1770–1831—Aesthetics. 4. Hegel, Georg Wilhelm Friedrich,
    1770–1831. I. Title. II. Series.
PN1892.R63   1998   97-986
808.2'512—dc21   CIP

10 9 8 7 6 5 4 3 2 1

For My Mother and Father

CONTENTS

ACKNOWLEDGMENTS

This project began as an introduction to a graduate course on "Tragedy and the Philosophy of Tragedy" in the Winter of 1987. Its development owes a great deal to the response it received in this course and in other graduate courses, where I could present aspects of the topic: "Objective Idealism and the Study of Literature" (Spring 1988); "Selected German Dramas from Lessing to Handke" (Winter 1989); "Poetics, Rhetoric, and Stylistics: An Introduction to the Formal Study of Literature" (Winter 1990); "German Intellectual History from Kant to the Present" (Fall 1993); and "Subjectivity and Intersubjectivity in the Development of German Drama" (Fall 1995). Some of the ideas were also discussed in two undergraduate classes: "Austrian Literature from Grillparzer to Handke" (Fall 1987) and "Modern German Literature in Cultural Context" (Winter 1990). To the students who engaged me in these classes I am extremely grateful.

A project that elevates the concept of intersubjectivity should benefit from various forums of discussion and criticism. Early versions of various sections were presented as papers or lectures over the past seven years. Shorter papers were given at conferences sponsored by the American Philosophical Association, the Hegel Society of America and the World Congress of Philosophy, the Kentucky Foreign Language Conference, the Modern Language Association, the Southeast Conference on Foreign Languages and Literatures, the University of California at Riverside, the University of Florida, the Universität Freiburg, and the University of Louisville. In addition, longer lectures, with correspondingly more thorough discussions, were held at the Istituto Italiano per gli Studi Filosofici in Naples, the University of North Carolina at Chapel Hill, the University of Notre Dame, Wake Forest University, Washington University in St. Louis, and the Universität Zürich. For the resulting discussions—both the encouragement and the criticism— I am indebted to many.

I am also fortunate to have benefited from the advice of three colleagues who share a common intellectual interest and who could therefore offer in-depth criticism. Jan-Lüder Hagens, Vittorio Hösle, and Christoph Jermann commented on an early version of the manuscript, and I am most grateful for their immanent criticism as well as their attention to questions of strategy. Other helpful suggestions were made by the anonymous reviewers for SUNY Press.

A National Endowment for the Humanities Summer Stipend in 1991 and a Study Visit Research Grant from the German Academic Exchange Service during the same year allowed me to concentrate on the manuscript and to consult materials at the Hegel Archives in Bochum, the German Literature Archives in Marbach, and the Univerity Library of the University of Tübingen.

The College of Humanities of the Ohio State University was generous in its support. For a grant-in-aid in 1991 as well as several quarters of released time (Special Research Assignments in the Winter of 1989 and the Fall of 1990 and a Faculty Professional Leave in the Winter and Spring of 1992) I am extremely grateful. This policy of generously supporting research has been consistently pursued by the following current and former officers of the College, David Frantz, Kermit Hall, Isaac Mowoe, G. Michael Riley, Christian Zacher, and Marvin Zahniser. For the funding of a Graduate Research Assistant in the Summer of 1993, I am especially grateful to former Acting Dean David Frantz. During that Summer Carita Zimmerman collected many of the English translations used in this study, checked the work's bibliographical references, and contributed numerous helpful suggestions for felicitous translations from German into English.

During the final months of manuscript preparation, Harold Attridge, formerly George N. Shuster Dean of the College of Arts and Letters at the University of Notre Dame, was gracious and forthcoming. I should also like to thank Associate Dean Roger Skurski and the staff of the Faculty Services Office. Cynthia Miller was kind enough to proofread the manuscript.

Duncan, Karma, and Iona, along with Macbeth, McDuff, and Banquo, have deepened my sense of beauty and balance, of nobility and comedy; I thank them for their inspiriting influence and their patience.

During the writing of this book I am most grateful to Barbara—for her many indirect contributions to the intellectual development of the work and for other gifts beyond words.

For a lifetime of support, encouragement, and love I dedicate this book to my parents.

ABBREVIATIONS, TRANSLATIONS, GENDER

My references, wherever possible, are to sections of texts. For Hegel's *Philosophy of Right* and *Encyclopedia*, for example, I list paragraph numbers. For dramas, I list, wherever possible, Act and Scene numbers or line numbers. Page references for quotations from works such as Hegel's *Aesthetics*, which do not contain section numbers, are in most cases given both for the original and the published translation. Page numbers always refer to the editions listed in the bibliography; whenever two editions are listed in the bibliography and only one page number is given—as is frequently the case with references unaccompanied by quotations, the page number refers to the original rather than the translation. Unless otherwise noted, the use of italics in quoted passages represents the original.

The original German of Hegel is cited for the most part according to the Suhrkamp edition. Because my work does not pretend to be a contribution to Hegel philology, it is less dependent on the newly edited manuscripts. Moreover, the most important text for my purposes, the critical edition of Hegel's *Aesthetics*, which was originally announced for 1985, had not yet appeared in early 1996, as I was completing my text.[1] Finally, the Suhrkamp edition will likely remain for cost reasons the text of choice for students who consult this book.

References to the secondary literature are given simply by way of the author's name. Only when I cite more than one text by a single author does an abbreviated title follow the author's name.

The following abbreviations have been used throughout the text.

A	Hegel, *Aesthetics.*
E	Hegel, *Enzyklopädie der philosophischen Wissenschaften.*
Eng	Refers to English version of the text cited.
ETW	Hegel, *Early Theological Writings.*
Fre	Refers to French version of the text cited.
Ger	Refers to German version of the text cited.
HP	Hegel, *History of Philosophy*
Ita	Refers to Italian version of the text cited.
NL	Hegel, *Natural Law*
PH	Hegel, *Introduction to the Philosophy of History.*
PS	Hegel, *Phenomenology of Spirit.*
R	Hegel, *Grundlinien der Philosophie des Rechts.*
SL	Hegel, *Science of Logic*
VG	Hegel, *Vernunft in der Geschichte.*
WL	Hegel, *Wissenschaft der Logik.*
Z	A 'Z' that follows a section number means that the passage stems not from Hegel's manuscripts but from his oral commentaries or *mündliche Zusätze.*

Wherever possible I have consulted published translations. Unmarked translations are taken from the translations included in the bibliography. Passages that I have altered for accuracy, consistency, or style are marked "translation modified." Translations followed by the predicate "my translation" represent passages for which no published translation exists, passages for which the published translation is seriously inadequate, or passages for which consulting a published translation would have been superfluous.

The translations of Hegel's *Aesthetics*, unless otherwise noted, are by T. M. Knox and are reproduced here by permission of Oxford University Press, which owns the copyright on the 1975 edition of Knox's publication. The translations of Anouilh's *Antigone* are by Barbara Bray and are reproduced here by permission of Reed Books.

A discussion of generic types necessarily creates an inordinate number of pronouns not predetermined by a particular gender. I have answered the problem of gender neutral language by employing male and female forms in various chapters rather than creating stylistically awkward subterfuges or overusing cumbersome hybrids such as "he/she" or "his/her"; the specific gender for each chapter was determined by a binary random number generator.

1

Introduction

How should one approach the subject of genre? The question should perhaps be split into two subquestions: How does one best deal with previous definitions of genre? And how should one define genre today? The two questions address, first, a historical, and second, a systematic field of inquiry. If we believe that previous interpretations of genre have something to offer us today, that they are not entirely wrong, even if much room for improvement remains, and if we believe that our evaluation of previous definitions of genre presupposes a systematic method of evaluation, then the historical and the systematic are ultimately related. Before we view them as one, however, let us first isolate the two, the better to know what it is we may be relating.

Historical Considerations in Generic Studies

Contemporary attitudes toward previous definitions of genre are generally of three kinds: expository, destructive, and critical. In an *expository* analysis the critic employs definitions of genre that have been offered but does not investigate their inner coherence. The power of tradition, rather than argument, determines the categories of genre. One asks questions such as "How did Racine or Lessing define tragedy?" not "Do their definitions make sense in ways that also partially transcend their own works and times?" or "What are the principles of tragedy that allow us to speak of diverse works as commonly tragic?" Critics adopting this approach tend to avoid both generalization and evaluation.

Exposition is by and large a modern technique that arose in tandem with historicism. Studies of classical antiquity up to the mid-

1

nineteenth century, culminating, let's say, in the contributions of
Theodor Mommsen, took the ideas of classical authors seriously
and weighed them for their inner coherence and relevance for contemporary issues. As a consequence of historicism, more recent
classical studies as well as interpretations of other literatures and
ages all too frequently study the past out of a desire to know another culture for its own sake. Hermann Broch's well-known concept of "partial value systems" could help us understand this transition to scholarship for the sake of scholarship, scholarship as a
form of curiosity and pedantry (ch. 44). Critics present a museum
gallery of opinions but often fail to reflect on their inner coherence
or meaning for other spheres. The issues of evaluation and significance vanish in quotation and paraphrase.[1]

Exposition is practiced not merely by historically oriented literary scholars inattentive to questions of literary theory. Gustavo
Firmat, a theorist of genre, draws a distinction between "theoretical genology," which he defines as "the deductive classification of
literary works," and "historical genology," or the "study of genres
from the vantage point of their contemporaries" (279). Firmat
thinks that a theoretical genology is impossible and so calls for the
development of historical genology. Indeed, the former would be
possible only if our theories could be deduced from a comprehensive systematic philosophy: a theoretical genology requires a set of
a priori principles.[2] Historical genology reconstructs a corpus
of works that, according to contemporaries, constituted a genre.
Whereas the former approach would depend on philosophy, more
specifically a form of philosophy no longer viewed as valid, the latter is essentially a form of history. The theoretical approach would
revise our existing typologies and suggest modes of evaluation; the
historical method attempts to recreate the perceptions and evaluations of others without itself being evaluative. Whereas the former
would ask for justification, the latter restricts itself to genesis and
the context of discovery. The former would ask, what constitutes a
genre and what is its value, the latter, denying the possibility of
normative analysis, asks, how did others perceive a genre or, applying the method to an empirical investigation of the present, how
do contemporaries happen to view a genre?

Destructive analyses might be viewed as the logical extension of
expository analyses. Competing views of genre preclude the possibility of one true view; any transcendent concept of genre is thus
ill-conceived and illusory.[3] Because no definition of genre is final,
we should eschew searching for definitions. Beyond the difficulty of

finding a single valid definition, other considerations come into play. Contemporary theorists believe that good literature eludes definition. The best literature not only breaks with established norms, norms are by definition arbitrarily confining. Genre invokes authority and with that repression. The critical elevation of "différance," "altarity," and other neighboring terms has reinforced the tendency to deconstruct the study of genre. Assaults on universals have themselves become almost universal. Just as historicism has passed over into postmodernism, destructive analyses of genre have taken the upper hand in relation to historical analyses. Destructive theorists elevate the particularity and individuality of the artwork; they downplay generic dimensions and in many cases even deny that universal structures or themes exist.[4] As Jean-François Lyotard unmistakably suggests, postmodernism has abandoned the search for metanarratives, for unifying principles and overarching designs. Generic reflections, it is argued, erase, or fail to capture, a work in its difference. Like many traditional forms of inquiry, genre studies miss the distinctive features of literature: ambiguity, indeterminacy, and nonassimilability.

In a *critical* analysis the scholar preserves part of an earlier thinker's analysis while discarding other parts. Proponents of this approach generally proceed by suggesting that the thinker's theory is no longer compatible with positions recognized as valid today. The critical approach argues—in contrast to the destructive approach—that genres do exist and can be defined. In contrast to the expository approach, it suggests that some genres and definitions are better than others. Like the other two, however, the critical approach knows of no theoretical means for establishing the legitimacy of a genre. Instead, it criticizes previous genres only insofar as they deviate from current conventions, norms, or ideology. The measure is derived from consensus, but the consensus has no grounds other than its historical presence.[5] Current theory motivates our criticism or elevation of genres. The question asked is not whether the genre is ultimately coherent, but whether the genre speaks to our current modes of inquiry and practice.

These three approaches to the historical study of genre are insufficient. The first suggests that we employ definitions only insofar as they correspond to views once considered appropriate. A historical genology of this sort is hardly a genology, merely a description of what different people believed at different times. It stems from the devolution of poetics and eschews any attempt to define art or aesthetics. Systematic aesthetics passes over into a literary sociology that merely describes the functions of generic conventions and literary-social institutions. Viewed self-reflexively, its own meta-understanding of genre must be historical and must give way to an alternative. This alternative must by definition be something other than the absolutization of the historical and the avoidance of a priori principles. The theory is internally self-canceling. Moreover, it is of little pragmatic use: genre definitions have no transhistorical validity. This makes it impossible for us to embrace anything but our own historically conditioned and arbitrary definitions, and it gives us no perspective from which to criticize as insufficient *any* generic definition. Rather than allowing for a genuine dialogue with the past, we relegate the past to the past alone and do not take it seriously for the present. Only the rarest of contemporary critics reads Lessing on tragedy not merely to understand Lessing and the eighteenth century but to advance toward an answer to the question, "What is common to all tragedy?"

The principal strength of the historicist approach is its ability to recognize shifts in the definitions and realizations of a genre.[6] The focus on plurality, however, is an advantage only insofar as it is combined with a recognition of overarching unity. We can acknowledge difference without abandoning common elements. A genre will be realized differently in each period, yet every realization will contain certain universal features that transcend the historicity of its epoch. Focus on the latter need not derive from a desire to ignore the former; it can also stem from the intent to reintroduce a moment of universality to a discipline now dominated by historicity and particularity.

The second approach, the abandonment of genre, purports to be modest, recognizing no transcendent categories or genres, but this alleged modesty belies a hidden arrogance: it believes itself sovereign over all previous theories and leaves the determination of genre (or the declaration of non-genre) to the arbitrariness of the individual's will. If the theory is based on the consequence of historical disagreement, its logic is faulty, for even if we cannot agree on what is common to individual tragedies, it does not follow that the tragedies have nothing in common. More frequently, the presupposition is metaphysical. Making the kind of overarching claims it considers invalid, it asserts that aesthetic norms are not possible under any circumstances. Recognizing that not a single aesthetic norm follows necessarily from reason, we are left with no distinction between universal and contingent norms and in effect no coherent arguments against either. If every text is sui generis in this extreme way, literary criticism is nothing more than an imitative echo of the text's poetic properties: it cannot refer to overarching categories, discuss textual similarities, or be judged good or bad.

If, however, every true artwork is a concrete realization of a universal insight, a position I defend below, then reflection on the universal dimensions of a work may strengthen—rather than weaken—its meaning for us. An artwork's strength may well lie in its unique articulation of a universal insight. In addition, works of literature by definition do not only differ, they also resemble one another. If they were only to differ, the words "literature" or "drama" would be unintelligible (and if everything were to differ and only differ, the very concept of "difference" would erase itself). A history of a genre with emphasis on change and difference presupposes a principle of that genre, which alone allows us to view the works as nonetheless comparable.[7] The use of the concept "tragedy" presupposes an identity. Further, the suggestion of similarity within a genre allows us to consider not only internal difference but the constitutive difference of those works belonging to a genre from those that don't. Finally, an overarching conceptual framework does not erase the individuality of a work; it encourages us to see it in its larger context much the way the best historicist criticism offers us a context against which to measure a work's common and distinct features. Even if a large percentage of older genre criticism has refrained from making this criticism productive for the study of individual works, or if in studying individual works, the genre critic has traditionally overlooked what is marginal or what deviates from the norm, these are nonetheless no arguments against genre criticism per se. Instead, they should be viewed as arguments for a more productive and more sensitive genre criticism.

The third approach, insofar as it avoids immanent critique, merely represents reigning opinions that may not be valid. We should not criticize earlier thinkers with the simple assertion: their views are not our views. The issue is, which views are correct? Thus, we shouldn't ask whether Hegel's or another historical thinker's theory of tragedy matches theories that are generally accepted today. Instead, we should inquire whether the arguments these thinkers put forth for their theories are valid or not. Only in this way do we reach an intersubjective ideal: we learn not just about the past, we learn from the past. If we rely solely on consensus and if—adopting a moment of postmodernist theory—we suggest that current paradigms derive their legitimacy from power rather than substantive arguments, then we have no means whatsoever for distinguishing valid from invalid theories. Consensus might dictate anything ranging from the requirement that all good literature mock itself to the stipulation that all good literature be nationalistic or antisemitic. If we simply presuppose that truth is one with our present paradigm, then all the systems of the past must raise themselves to our level of triviality—or be abandoned. Further, if we measure a theory by asking whether it matches what we currently believe, rather than asking whether our current beliefs are more coherent than previous theories, we are destined to learn nothing from alternative paradigms. We are open to what is all around us, but dogmatically closed to what is truly other. Finally, we cannot refute opposing theories in an adequate way. To counter an alternative model by saying that we choose to think differently is not to refute that model. Only an argument that takes the alternative model seriously on its own terms and shows an internal inadequacy or contradiction has achieved a fundamental refutation and true recognition of what is and is not adequate. With a merely external critique we have one dry assurance against another and no means for establishing truth.

The argument against mere consensus does not suggest that we should consider our positions valid without regard to opposing views; on the contrary. Intersubjective exchange of options and thoughts is essential to inquiry, and a consensus that develops out of a genuine exchange—rather than mere power or ad hominem arguments—should help us uncover new insights. Just as frequently as newer theories mark advances, they also represent mere historical transcendence—rather than philosophical refutation—of alternative views. Not all positions taken for granted in the present have been grounded, nor has the alleged outdatedness of alternative views been demonstrated. For a view to appear old-fashioned need not mean that it is wrong. Consensus can help us discover truth; it does not determine truth.

I would like to take a different approach to genre, arguing that within the history of genre some definitions are better than others and that it is indeed appropriate to argue for definitions, even if they cannot claim finality, and to view these in a systematic framework. I am inspired in this attempt by Hegel, though my analysis differs in general and specific ways from his efforts at defining tragedy, comedy, and the drama of reconciliation. Moreover, though my study might be called a critical analysis, the critique is, in contrast to my earlier description of critical analyses, immanent: it criticizes Hegel from within, noting inconsistencies and contradictions in his definitions.

Systematic Considerations in Generic Studies

The most central question in contemporary genre theory revolves around the conflict between an empirical and a rational approach.[8] Do the examples come first, or does the theory? Should one try, empirically, to abstract common features from a large number of works, or should one develop a set of categories from a priori principles? In short, should one approach the subject inductively or deductively?

Let's assume for a moment that the genre critic should proceed *inductively*. We might begin by collecting examples, but what are we collecting examples of? Since we cannot start with a definition, we might commence by collecting similar texts without regard to predetermined categories. Should we look for similarities in terms of style or theme or character-types or period of composition or endings or what? We quickly see that we can catalogue texts in an infinite number of ways and that our principle of selection is random. One can select as the distinguishing feature of a type whatever insignificant qualities one happens to choose. Definitions derived from induction are invariably enumerative: one lists a series of traits without any systematic link or concept (see, for example, Blistein, Charney, and Levin). Or one elevates as the distinguishing feature an arbitrary moment. In a not dissimilar context Hegel made fun of Johann Friedrich Blumenbach, who defined the human being as the animal with earlobes (6:516–17). One could divide literature according to the various foods the heroes eat, but the absurdity of such a view can be shown only by appealing to a system of thought that privileges other matters, for example, types of human relationships, and demonstrates why such matters are of greater importance.

With a purely inductive approach we get everywhere and nowhere; success is a matter of chance. Even if we wanted merely to abstract a general definition from a group of individual works, how would we know that we have selected the right works? With a principle of selection, even one taken at random, we are no longer truly inductive; but without a principle of selection we cannot select at all. In order to determine the elements of a genre empirically, we must first find examples of the genre that most fully exhibit the elements of the genre. Yet in selecting the examples, we are already presupposing what the elements of the genre are, for otherwise we would not know which examples to select. Thus, a purely inductive approach appears impossible. This is no small insight when we consider how many contemporary theories of genre view themselves as inductive.[9] Finally, because a concept of selection is already presupposed, but not grounded, in any inductive approach, the method succumbs to a hidden *petitio principii*, already presupposing what it would prove.

Since it is evident we need a principle of selection, let us experiment, try a few principles, and see where we get. We might call this the *pragmatic* approach.[10] We could begin by calling all works tragedies that have the word "tragedy" in their title. These works, however, appear to share little more than an external name, and it is not difficult to argue that interpreters should not be limited by the author's view of a work. Perhaps we should designate as tragedies whatever the majority of the population deems tragic. But this leads to difficulties as well. Does everyone's vote count equally, that of the informed literary critic and that of the analphabet? Should literary critics merely endorse popular opinion and affirm the status quo, assuming the status quo can be determined?[11] Aren't opinions constantly changing? Even if we restrict consensus to the experts, what do we do about raging controversies over conflicting definitions of tragedy? Because consensus is difficult to determine, perhaps critics should simply offer whatever definitions of tragedy they prefer. They could offer reasons for their definitions, but that would make little sense, since every definition begins with an unfounded and ultimately arbitrary principle. In the rhetoric of Adena Rosmarin, a proponent of the pragmatic approach, every definition is at best a useful illusion.[12]

Rosmarin's account of genre illustrates the inherent arbitrariness of the pragmatic or instrumental approach. Building on Hans Vaihinger, Richard Rorty, and the concept of inevitable error, Rosmarin affirms genre theory as pragmatically useful but, like all theory, inevitably illusory. Our groupings of texts are determined by the texts and the classifier, and no grounds exist for privileging any mode of classification over another. Different critics with varying interests will always group texts differently; thus, the claim that any genre system is valid—beyond its particular purpose—is untenable. Rosmarin embraces "the edifying mistake of classification" (22). The arbitrariness of error enters into play here: "anything can be taken for anything else if our purpose is sufficiently compelling and our standards of acceptance sufficiently tolerant" (21). In consequence, the pragmatic interpretation either engenders its own ideal types—without the rigorous demands of justification—or divides literature into almost as many genres as texts—because it can offer no substantial arguments for lines of demarcation. If all validity derives from the fulfillment of an arbitrary and illusory purpose, no compelling arguments exist for or against any genre system. On what grounds—if indeed no grounds exist—could one legitimately contest the positing of purposes and methods that differ from, or undermine, one's own? Genre criticism becomes a matter of likes and dislikes.

The pragmatic approach was not discovered by postmodernists, even though it receives reinforcement from contemporary theoretical tendencies. Mario Fubini, for example, declared in the 1950s the absurdity of any ontological approach to genre and spoke of the merely instrumental value of generic studies. Genres may be used to order the multiplicity of individual works, but they do not help us understand the individual work, they do not allow us to judge its aesthetic worth, and they cannot be arranged in any hierarchical or normative way.[13] Robert Hume, to take an example from the early 1970s, hopes that his theory might be "thought-provoking" and "useful," though he claims for it "no special theoretical sanctity" (99); he merely wishes that his theoretical constructs and schemes "help us find our way around in the chaos" (100).

The assertion that nondeductive approaches bring insights is not to be contested; on the contrary, we can freely grant this. Every approach—deductive or otherwise—is helpful to the extent that it sheds light on aspects or properties of genre that competing theories overlook or neglect. Nonetheless, a pragmatic typology is incapable of grounding itself, and its merits pass with every change in opinion, even unjustified changes. Some critics, for example Rosmarin, view this affirmation of change as a strength. Yet one can only wonder why—if revision and change are absolutely embraced—one doesn't consider revising the theory that everything is forever to be revised. Also self-contradictory is the principal presupposition of the approach, that is, its negation of all norms. The pragmatic approach presupposes the truth of its own metatheory, namely, that all theories are illusory and untrue.[14] The pragmatic approach does not suggest—as any sensible theory ought to do—that all theories are fallible and must be open to criticism and correction; rather, it asserts—with a beguiling level of arrogance, infallability, and unconscious self-contradiction—that all theories are illusory, untenable, and ungrounded.

We are left with only one alternative, a *deductive* approach.[15] If the typology is to transcend the weaknesses of a major position negated in comedy, the elevation of what is arbitrary,[16] it must be capable of following a logical course. One might object to the elevation of deduction by arguing that the deductive critic inappropriately applies a priori structures to her subject. To which it must be countered, is not this criticism itself from the vantage point of some a priori structure, namely, that a priori structures are not to be applied to a subject? In short, the objection is self-cancelling. One might then modify the argument and claim that a priori structures should not be applied to art: thought is abstract, but art is concrete; thought is deductive, while art follows the freedom of phantasy. Hegel anticipates such an objection when he writes that art is a product of spirit or *Geist* and is not unrelated to thought, which is one of its moments; thought is obliged not only to comprehend itself as thought, in logic, for example, but to grasp its laws in what is external to itself and so to transform the externalization of spirit, even as one recognizes its difference, back into thought (13:18–28). The question is not, should thought reflect on art, but rather, which thoughts should be privileged. Aesthetics is in this sense derivative of logic. Only a study of the coherence of a thought or statement can determine its truth and thus its validity within art.[17]

The deductive approach faces a more fundamental obstacle. Any deductive theory, it is objected, is always hypothetical, deriving its propositions from an unproven axiom: if *p*, then *q*. The theory may claim internal consistency, but nothing more. Thus, an infinite number of competing theories is possible. Unless deduction derives from a first principle, it is essentially one and the same with the pragmatic approach. For any deductive approach to differentiate itself from the pragmatic, a ground is necessary, and if contemporary philosophers and literary critics agree on anything,[18] it is this: there are no absolute grounds.[19] Contemporary philosophy has abandoned the concept of reflexive foundationalism, or self-grounding philosophy, and with it the existence of categorical norms.[20] For contemporary philosophy all norms are hypothetical; they are based on presuppositions. The presuppositions themselves are either axioms or grounded by other propositions, which are themselves grounded by others, leading to an infinite regress or a circle.[21]

The antifoundationalist trilemma that reduces all justification to axioms, infinite regress, or circularity must, according to its own principles, contain a presupposition, which in this case is tautological: accepting as a presupposition that only axiomatic thought is possible, in which by definition no self-grounding knowledge exists, no self-grounding knowledge is possible. Because the impossibility of self-grounding knowledge derives, on its own terms, from a presupposition, under other presuppositions, self-grounding knowledge may be possible. It would be self-contradictory to assert as a presuppositionless truth that no presuppositionless truth exists. Indeed, the proposition, "There is no non-hypothetical a priori truth," is logically equivalent with the blatantly self-contradictory statement, "It is a non-hypothetical a priori truth that no non-hypothetical a priori truth exists." The thesis of the impossibility of self-grounding knowledge, of first principles, must pass over into the thesis of the possibility of self-grounding knowledge. This result, however, is as inconsistent as our starting point: if self-grounding knowledge were merely possible, that is, dependent on presuppositions, then it wouldn't be self-grounding knowledge. Absolute justification is either necessary (positively apodictic) or impossible (negatively apodictic). A possible final foundation is a contradiction in terms. If self-grounding knowledge is possible, it is—in the philosophical sense of the term—necessary. There must be a final, that is, nonaxiomatic, foundation.

While we know, as a result of these brief reflections, that absolute knowledge exists, we appear not yet to know what it is. But we already have an instance of self-grounding knowledge, namely, the insight that a final foundation exists. This insight is itself an example of nonaxiomatic knowledge. The method by which we reached this insight was indirect: recognition of a set of contradictions within the assertion that there is no self-grounding knowledge, that is, the self-cancellation of an untenable proposition. Deduction, we had said, can be based either on dogmatically asserted principles, that is, axioms, or on reflexive arguments, which exhibit the transcendental presuppositions of argumentation. The deductive method I seek to employ in this work is of the latter sort and so might also be called a reflexive or transcendental method.

The expository and inductive approaches introduced above can be viewed as parallel: each describes what is, without searching for or invoking principles of selection or organization, that is, insofar as each remains merely descriptive or merely inductive. The philosophical connection between description and induction has its historical analogue in the fact that the two approaches are frequently united in the same critic, often the same work.[22] Likewise, the destructive approach, which argues that no valid standards of generic classification exist, shares a hidden identity with the pragmatic approach, which argues that all classifications are in principle equally valid or invalid. The different conclusions derive from a shared premise: no tenable grounds exist for the definition of genre. In each theory we speak not of genres but of genre concepts or illusions that do not correspond to objects. Finally, the deductive or transcendental approach correlates to the critical method when taken at its best: each arrives at its answer by way of the immanent refutation of alternative positions.[23] Having shown the untenability of description and induction, of the merely negative and the arbitrarily pragmatic, this study will attempt a critical and deductive analysis of genre. It adopts the unorthodox position—at least for modernity—that true critique and transcendental or systematic thought function in harmony with one another.

Hegel and Intersubjectivity

If we look around to see if indirect arguments for the existence of an absolute, such as those offered above, have ever been presented, we recognize that a similar position has been developed by Hegel.[24] Hegel argues that the absolute derives from the self-contradiction of finite categories, which themselves claim to be absolute—or, in the language of certain categories, proof of the nonexistence of the absolute. His transcendental logic attempts by a series of determinate negations to develop the absolute as the whole of its many parts, a network of categories. The individual categories, in increasing concreteness leading to absolute truth, are themselves moments of absolute truth. Hegel shows that the finite is not absolute but finite and so passes over as a moment into the absolute. This method, the process of making explicit the implicit contradictions in finite positions, is the driving force of his dialectical procedure.

Dialectical logic generally begins with an immediate category of abstract positivity. It is abstract in the sense that it is not yet defined in relation to a contrary; it is abstracted (or separated) from its contextual relation. Its negativity is externally presupposed but not yet recognized. The lack of recognition means an inability to counter the dominance of that term which is presupposed but not set, the negative of itself. The negative, however, as purely negative, denies what it has in common with the positive (in order even to be its opposite), namely the positive itself. The negative thus negates itself (its existence was dependent on the positive that it negated). This self-cancellation of the purely negative means a return to the positive, not, however, to the abstractly positive, which was indifferent to negativity, but to an internally differentiated positive that limits the negative and contains it as sublated. It is concretely positive.

The initial category in any sequence can be called the thesis.[25] Take, for example, finitude or the claim that everything is finite. If everything is finite, then, so too, is the claim that everything is finite. Finitude is itself finite and as such passes over into its other, the infinite. The infinite, viewed as the antithesis, is not an external projection onto the finite but the truth of the finite, the result of the finite having been thought through to its own conclusion. The infinite, however, defined as that which is other than the finite, is not really infinite, for that which exists as something other than another is precisely the definition of the finite. The true infinite then is not other to the finite but contains the finite as a moment within itself; it does not exclude its other and is therefore not finite. We see here, in rather simple terms, the movement from thesis (the finite) to antithesis (the bad infinite or the infinite as the other in opposition to the finite) to synthesis (the true infinite or the infinite that contains the finite). The movement is not linear but dialectic: the synthesis contains both the thesis and the antithesis.

The generating force in the dialectic is contradiction, in particular a form of contradiction that is self-reflexive; the finite, for example, is viewed as itself finite. In order to grasp the dialectic, we must recognize the distinction between analytic and pragmatic contradictions. The former function according to the pattern "*a* and *non-a*" or "It is raining, and it is not raining." More complex are pragmatic contradictions, which are unveiled only through an act of self-reflection. Consider the proposition "There is no truth." The statement denies truth even as it presupposes truth; the contradiction lies in the schism between the proposition's content and its form, between the statement made and what is presupposed in the act of making the statement. We cannot, without refuting ourselves, assert as true the claim that nothing is true. Truth is not in the statement but in the negation of the statement, by way of its self-cancellation and its passage into another, in this case that there is truth, namely the truth of the self-cancellation of the attempt to deny truth; the denial of truth necessarily passes over into an affirmation of truth.

Hegel's dialectical logic consists of a series of such transitions, whereby the finitude of individual categories, viewed as absolute, is recognized and their passage to the next category affirmed. The movement I project between tragedy, comedy, and the drama of reconciliation as well as between the subgenres within these genres functions according to this dialectic. The movement is based not, as is commonly believed (see, for example, Soll), on suspension of the law of noncontradiction but on recognition of contradictions within categories (and genres) otherwise taken to be stable, final, or simply independent of any relation to other categories (or genres). Dialectical logic does not violate the rules of formal logic.[26] Paraphrasing Hegel on Kant, we can say that formal logic simply fails to find *enough* contradictions;[27] in particular it does not recognize self-reflexive or pragmatic contradictions.

The greatest virtue of the dialectic is its ability to criticize positions not by way of external reflection or a position that posits a different set of axioms—as in the weak critical approach mentioned above, but by taking seriously the position presented and undermining it only insofar as it contradicts itself internally. In Hegelian terms, "the absolute method of knowing" is "at the same time the immanent soul of the content itself" (5:17; SL 36–37, translation modified). Hegel views dialectic as the "*positing* of what is already contained in a concept" (E § 88); in another formulation he calls his method "the movement of the concept itself" (6:551; SL 468, translation modified; cf. 4:161 and 5:50). Dialectic is merely a broader term that encompasses what I defined above as immanent critique. This process allows us to develop a network of logical categories, all self-generated and interrelated, rather than an arbitrary projection of whatever categories or genres we happen to deem appropriate.

For Hegel, truth is not in the individual category or genre but in the larger process in which the individual category or genre takes part. Each category is determined by virtue of its relation to other categories, in particular those which pass over into it and those into which it passes. We recognize that each individual position or category is valid but not as absolute, not as final. When discussing individual subgenres, I occasionally suggest that a work contains elements of an earlier subgenre. This derives partly from the sense in which a dialectical sequence not only negates earlier forms, it also preserves them, not as absolute but as moments, in a more comprehensive form. Earlier positions are valid but not as absolute, not as final.

In reading literature (and discussing genre), we necessarily apply categories: identity and difference, closure and openness, reliability and unreliability, stagnation and development, and so forth. These categories can be taken either from whatever happens to be current in discourse or from a system of linked categories that exhibits the interrelation and the hierarchical structure of the individual categories. An advantage of the German Idealist model over both earlier and later theories of genre is its ability to show the systematic interrelation of the various genres. Peter Szondi writes: "the speculative genre poetics of German Idealism differs from the pragmatic-normative of the previous centuries not least in the fact that it does not isolate the individual genres and forms, but rather endeavors to determine their reciprocal relationship: only this speculative poetics establishes in the strict sense a system of poetic forms, while one should speak in the case of earlier theories of genre rather of classifications" ("Von der normativen" 292, my translation). Theories of genre since Hegel have tended to fall back into the realm of mere classification and description. This is true not only of overarching theories but also of analyses of subgenres.[28] Contemporary discourse has the advantage of developing new categories that were previously overlooked or underplayed, yet it often makes the mistake of elevating these categories—even as it denies the viability of any order of rank—at the expense of others and at the expense of the whole. In addition, the reigning categories of an age are frequently viewed uncritically; this is especially ironic today when claims for the nonexistence of the absolute are themselves viewed as unquestionable absolutes.[29]

The reader should not be surprised if at this point I suggest that the most comprehensive and convincing philosophical system of categories ever developed is Hegel's.[30] No other philosopher before or since has produced such a coherent and comprehensive set of terms which not only shed light on each other and on the framework that justifies their existence, but which can also be applied to illuminate structures in spheres as diverse as art, religion, philosophy, politics, and history.

It would be foolish, however, to analyze genre from the standpoint of Hegel, a position rightly viewed as long since overcome. The post-Hegelian world—including the philosophical anthropology of Feuerbach, the social and economic philosophy of Marx, the psychology of Freud, the existentialism of the early Heidegger, the dialogic philosophy of Bakhtin, the universal pragmatics of Habermas and the transcendental pragmatics of Karl-Otto Apel, and a variety of other, often conflicting, philosophies—has developed a multiplicity of categories (of which Hegel never dreamed) that relate to the question of intersubjectivity, the most overarching and dominant category of post-Hegelian philosophy. Intersubjectivity governs the subject-subject (instead of mere subject-object) relations found in friendship, love, and the public sphere. It includes the hermeneutic sphere of reception and communication and the pragmatic sphere of political realization.

Already the early Hegelians (by which I mean collectively the so-called Old and Young Hegelians) recognized deficiencies in Hegel. The last 150 years, moreover, have been informed by a spirit anathema to the Hegelian focus on objectivity and subjectivity. Where Hegel wanted to know truth, his critics wanted to make it real. Where Hegel worked on recognizing objectivity (or the world) and subjectivity (or our consciousness of the world and of consciousness itself), modern philosophers, stressing the preeminent role of language and social environment, focus on the categories of intersubjectivity. But perhaps the neglect of the realization of truth and the role of communicative intersubjectivity does not derive from the Hegelian enterprise per se but stems from contingent weaknesses on the part of Hegel himself. Perhaps the Hegelian focus on objectivity and subjectivity finds its truth in intersubjectivity, such that we can criticize a particular position of Hegel's while holding to the Hegelian method and perhaps even strengthening the fundamental Hegelian claim that the categories of logic are also categories of the world.

A tendency exists at present to abandon earlier thinkers and their ideas by virtue of their finite errors.[31] Truth is dynamic; therefore, there is little reason to seek truth in Plato or Hegel, whose positions are past and in whom we find multiple errors. But perhaps we should be more precise in distinguishing forms of error and forms of truth. There are some uncircumventible and ineliminable—that is, transcendental—categories on which every rational being depends, even the skeptic who attempts to deny them. These structures of thought are valid in principle and a priori. They are those positions that cannot be refuted without self-contradiction and without also necessarily presupposing the position to be refuted. They are structures of thought familiar to us since Plato, and they have resurfaced frequently since then. They involve the method of immanent critique itself as well as such claims as the logical and ontological priority of the concretely positive over both the abstractly positive and the merely negative. Many of these positions can be found in Hegel. Yet beyond the question of transcendental perfection exists a more finite perfection, the sense that within this systematic anchoring is room for improvement, in the sphere of the particular working out of the implications of transcendental perfection, in the noetic relation of the transcendental and the contingent, and in the realization of privileged transcendental categories such as justice or love. If we recognize this distinction between transcendental or systematic perfection and nonformal or finite perfection and view the one as stable, the other as dynamic, then we can—indeed must—separate in our evaluation of Hegel our critique of finite points from our recognition that certain systematic claims remain valid. The critique of the finite may even strengthen our sense of the validity of the systematic. Our understanding of the category of intersubjectivity, for example, may in fact reinforce the systematic claim that the structures of thought correspond to those of reality.

The two most overarching categories in the Hegelian system, as in German Idealism in general, are objectivity and subjectivity. Hegel splits his *Science of Logic*, the nucleus of his entire system, into objectivity and subjectivity. The *Logic* is the center of the system, insofar as it provides the categories, the structures of thought, that are employed in *Realphilosophie*, the philosophical analysis of structures in the real world. Already the claim that the structures of thought and the structures of being are parallel brings us to a major dimension of Hegel's philosophy, namely, the attempt to overcome all dualistic philosophy, in particular the Kantian version, and to assert the identity of subject and object. Aesthetics, as an element of *Realphilosophie*, as truth in sensuous form, employs the categories of objectivity and subjectivity, and it would be useful here to sketch, albeit briefly, what objectivity and subjectivity imply and why, following our earlier reflections on the post-Hegelian turn, a third category, intersubjectivity, is a necessary addition to the earlier two concepts. I shall do so not by elucidating the abstract logical structures of objectivity and subjectivity but by discussing their reigning features as they would be realized in a world view in which one or the other dominates.[32]

Objectivity is a naive position that demands recognition of the good and the true and believes such recognition possible. Knowledge is viewed as objective, not mediated by the particularities of individual subjects, which are seen to be unimportant and accidental. What is, is independently real and enduring. This dogmatism is based on presuppositions that are taken as given, accepted as absolute. Truth is viewed in positive terms; it is eternal and static. Change and dynamism are not acknowledged. This dualism leads to a number of dichotomies: between good and evil, absolute and relative, being and appearance, and so forth, which is not to say that the intricacies of the negative terms are known. On the contrary, viewed like divine oracles, religious and ethical codes are not met with doubt, not compared with alternative models. The objective standpoint has little interest in particular cultures, in persons as particular persons, or in history as the motor of change. The stable institutions of society are endorsed, not criticized; they are viewed as superior to, and transcending, the particularity of the individual subject.

Subjectivity is the negation of objectivity and, as a negative position, has the tendency to divide itself into substages. Its recognition of the deficiencies in objectivity comes gradually. It questions its arbitrary assertions and lack of reflexive foundations. It counters the simplicity and uniformity of objectivity with the richness of concrete alternatives. The process of humanity's recognition of objectivity becomes thematized, culminating in a form of skepticism. Knowledge is viewed as merely subjective; it does not correspond to an objective reality. As a result, everything is called into question. The existence of an absolute is denied. What is secure and foundational is merely one's own subjectivity; subjective will, not objective order, is the motor behind one's evaluations and actions. Recognizing that institutions are not grounded in an absolute, the self turns against them. The state is merely a creation of individual will and can be negated by the same. In the sphere of subjectivity, freedom becomes a dominant concept, first, the freedom from external restraints and, second, the freedom to satisfy one's own particular desires. The categories of subjectivity are negative: difference, otherness, multiplicity, contingency, particularity.

This negativity, however, eventually turns on itself. As mentioned above, even negative propositions presuppose the truth of their own claims (to the nonexistence of truth). Positive categories are evident behind the overwhelmingly negative structures of subjectivity. These positive assertions, however, are not naive but the result of the negation of a negation, the self-cancellation of the negative position. Categories may be subjective, that is, they may arise in the subject, yet they are also objective, that is, they are universal and necessary, found in every thinking being.[33] The subject recognizes its value not in the arbitrariness of its contingent moods but by adhering to recognized laws that are valid for all subjects and in this sense objective. Objectivity as what is universal and necessary takes on a different and richer meaning than in the thesis. The transcendental turn culminates for Hegel in an equation of subjectivity and objectivity, of logic and ontology. It involves a recognition of the positive categories of objectivity, but now as the negation of a negation. We see a synthesis of subjectivity (as a process of thought) and objectivity (as the reestablishment of recognized norms). Self-consciousness as awareness of truth and of the path to truth becomes the final stage of absolute subjectivity.

Absolute subjectivity as the unity of subjectivity and objectivity is a central structure in Hegel's thought, yet it ignores, as we suggested, the dominant category of post-Hegelian philosophy, intersubjectivity. Does this mean that we must abandon Hegel and the claim to an absolute, or can we criticize him in such a way as to reformulate the absolute? Consider in this context the union of subjectivity and objectivity. The two are identical but different. If they are identical, then the relation might best be viewed not as a subject-object but as a subject-subject relation. Here we would thematize not merely objectivity, subjectivity, and self-consciousness, but relations between subjects: the question of language and dialogue, social embeddedness, and the realization of truth as the transcendence of mere knowledge. In an intersubjective sphere the symmetry of subjects is essential. One treats a subject not as an object but as another subject, in principle the same as oneself. Reciprocity, not mastery, becomes the dominant category. Intersubjective structures, the institutions of society, are no longer viewed as an arbitrary extension of the self, a means for self-cultivation, but as ends in themselves, as being of more value than the self alone, owing not to the force of tradition or dogma but to reason. The entire sphere of the social achieves a relevance it did not have when subjectivity alone was dominant. To know the good is no longer enough, one must also attempt to realize it.[34]

Hegel, as we saw, did not introduce the category of intersubjectivity, but it is a truism of philosophical and literary criticism that authors often write more insightfully than they themselves intend, and to suggest that Hegel does not provide us with any particular insights into intersubjectivity would be unfair. His discussion of the master-slave dialectic; his equation of absolute spirit with reciprocal recognition; and his discussion of drama as the synthesis of epic objectivity and lyric subjectivity, as a genre characterized by the interaction of individuated subjects and dialogue between them, are prominent examples. Although Hegel does not spell out for us the category of intersubjectivity as the true synthesis of objectivity and subjectivity, we can see that the development of intersubjectivity is more an explication than a refutation of the Hegelian system. In his important discussion of the dialectic in the *Encyclopedia*, Hegel carefully distinguishes between what he calls the dialectical and the speculative (E § 79–82; cf. E § 32 Z). The dialectical, a mere moment in the dialectic, is negative and antithetical. The dialectic as a whole transcends the merely antithetical and spells out the positive and synthetic, the mirroring unity of opposites, which Hegel terms the speculative. Subjectivity and intersubjectivity, as I would like to view them, are correlative to the dialectical and the speculative. That is, Hegel did not spell out intersubjectivity, but he did give us the structure by which intersubjectivity could and should be recognized. Here, as throughout my study, I would like to criticize Hegel with Hegel, that is, use Hegel to move beyond Hegel himself.

Working with a Hegelian set of categories and enriched by the post-Hegelian concept of intersubjectivity, I would like to present a study of tragic and comic forms that builds on—even as it deviates from—Hegel's aesthetics. This critique of Hegel is precisely what we recognized as a valid form of critical analysis, and it is, in terms of method, Hegelian. Recognizing that there are mistakes in the Hegelian system and consequently mistakes in his theory of genre, we should not follow Hegel slavishly. Moreover, we should not adhere to a theory of genre that, by necessity, takes no account of developments in art during the past 150 years. Nonetheless, Hegel would appear to provide us with a useful orientation point for the interlacing of historical-critical and systematic-deductive analyses. We can with some confidence separate a reflexive-transcendental approach to genre from Hegel's more or less insufficient realization of this approach.

Current interpretations of Hegel's *Aesthetics* tend toward paraphrase (the historicist approach), abandonment (the destructive approach), or the selection of individual topics in relation to contemporary issues, such as postmodernism and the end of art (the weak or extrinsic critical approach). Other dominant approaches, echoing wider trends in the humanities, focus on the *genesis* of Hegel's aesthetics (its various stages, the influence of contemporaries, and so forth) and its *reception* (further dimensions of the historicist approach). Works that attempt to criticize Hegel from within and make him productive for the present are in the minority, although works of this kind belong to the best of contemporary Hegel criticism.[35]

Art and Truth

It would be absurd to argue that art has nothing to do with truth.[36] Even critics who view art as superior to philosophy suggest that truth is in art not in philosophy, and even those who view art as a vehicle for undermining truth view this undermining as an act of truth. Art expresses truth, but it does so in a way that differs from philosophy: art portrays truth not in abstract thought but in sensuous form. Hegel defines beauty as "the sensuous *appearance* of the Idea" (13:151; A 111, my translation). "Idea" refers to the final category of the *Logic* and is to be grasped as the truth of all previous categories.[37] Literature both presupposes and represents the categories of dialectical logic and thus truth.[38] We can employ the term "truth" in our definition of art also insofar as "the Idea" is for Hegel "the unity of concept and objectivity" (6:464; SL 396, translation modified; cf. 6:466–467), the very same definition he gives to truth: "truth means that objectivity corresponds with the concept" (E § 233; cf. E § 24 Z2; E § 91 Z; E § 172 Z; E § 349 Z). Consider, moreover, the opening sentences of Hegel's discussion of "The Idea": "The Idea is the *adequate concept*, the objective truth, or the truth as such. If anything has truth it has it through its Idea; or *something has truth only in so far as it is Idea*" (6:462; SL 395, translation modified). The opening category of the *Logic*, "Being" reaches its truth in the Idea, insofar as "the Idea is the unity of concept and reality" (6:465; SL 397, translation modified).

The appearance of the Idea is not superfluous but—as the logic of Essence tells us—essential: "But *appearance* itself is essential to *essence*. Truth would not be truth if it did not show itself and appear, if it were not truth *for* someone and *for* itself, as well as for the spirit in general too" (13:21; A 8). The truth of art is not the truth of correctness or correspondence to reality, but the truth whereby the artwork sensuously expresses what is conceptually or dialectically true, a coherent array of insights, a being at home with oneself in opposition, a harmony or unity in diversity. We use "truth" in this sense when we say that this or that work is true art, much as we say that someone is a true friend; truth, like the Idea, is a self-accord of reality with its concept or ideal. Finally, the appearance of art is not an appearance in contrast to an essence but an appearance of essence and may therefore contrast with reality, which itself often deviates from the normative ideal it seeks. Thus, the appearance of art may be higher than that of reality: "But it is precisely this whole sphere of the empirical inner and outer world which is not the world of true reality; on the contrary, we must call it, in a stricter sense than we call art, a mere appearance and a harsher deception. Only beyond the immediacy of feeling and external objects is genuine reality to be found. For the truly real is only that which has being in and for itself, the substance of nature and spirit, which indeed gives itself presence and existence, but in this existence remains in and for itself and only so is truly real. It is precisely the dominion of these universal powers which art emphasizes and reveals. In the ordinary external and internal world essentiality also appears, but in the form of a chaos of accidents, afflicted by the immediacy of the sensuous and by the capriciousness of situations, events, characters, and so forth. Art liberates the true content of phenomena from the appearance and deception of this bad, transitory world and gives them a higher reality, born of the spirit. Thus, far from being mere appearance, a higher reality and truer existence is to be ascribed to the phenomena of art in comparison with ordinary reality" (13:22; A 8–9, translation modified).

While we judge philosophy according to its truth, art is evaluated according to its truth *and* its form. We must recognize here the dialectical paradox, first, that truth is conceptual coherence and thus distinguishable from form, and second, that truth is the unity of what art should be, namely a unity of concept and form, with its reality. Great art fulfills both moments of truth: coherence within its concept or statement, which is the principal focus here; and coherence between concept and sensuous matter, which is the truth of art as such.

The categories by which we judge the truth-content of art derive from the philosophical structures sketched above. If we think a work of art is weak because its statement is incoherent, we can attempt to reinterpret the work so as to view its statement differently, or we can argue that incoherence is a valid element of art. The first reaction belongs to literary criticism per se, the second to philosophy. In this sense the literary critic depends on philosophy.

The sensuous dimension of art relates to the expression of truth (partly being shaped by it, partly contributing to its shape). If truth is by definition exclusive and singular, beauty is not; its sensuousness allows for multiple representations of truth. There can be many great tragedies. Nonetheless, we can speak of the extent to which an individual tragedy partakes in truth. Isolating for a moment a work's logical structures or its truth-content, we can argue that a work is more or less truthful. This is analogous to the way in which critics sometimes isolate the style of a work, its language or camera angles, for example, in order to evaluate its formal strengths and weaknesses. Though the two elements influence one another and are ideally codetermining, a definition of art as the sensuous appearance of truth suggests that in discussions of art—as will be the case in what follows—we can for purposes of analysis speak of the truth of a work and its presentation, its content and its form.

My analysis of genre thus implies, in contradistinction to a widely accepted view, that literary texts do have arguments.[39] A work's argument may indeed, as is now popular, be one in favor of the undecidability of meaning, but this is not necessarily the case—and indeed in another context it would be worthwhile to pursue whether such undecidability would strengthen or weaken a literary work and whether the claim of a work's uninterpretability isn't itself an exclusionary interpretation. The arguments in literary works are presented in a literary way, which is not to say—as some critics today might assume—in a necessarily ironic way.[40] Instead, it is to suggest that formal, literary, and material dimensions are significant in the portrayal, constitution, and reception of meaning. The literary dimension is relevant to the theme or argument. Indeed, the form in which an idea is presented often leads to a reevaluation of the idea itself.[41] Content and form are codetermining in the sense that content infuses form with meaning, and form shapes the content. Form is empty unless we give it content; thus the content helps determine the possibilities of form. The Oedipus myth and the Faust story, for example, help determine what tragedy becomes. Yet once placed in a particular form, the content is guided, transformed, transfigured by the autonomous laws of the genre into which it has been placed. An Oedipus or a Faust placed into a comic work becomes transformed—even if the plot line scarcely differs from its earlier tragic development.

In any attempt to define dramatic genre by form or content alone, the two quickly overlap. Take two arbitrary examples: *peripeteia* and *anagnorisis* are formal structures with a particular content; Freytag's pyramid scheme is a formal construct that is defined by the content of each act. Which is then primary in these instances, content or form? Consider an example outside of drama:

Can we define a short story with merely formal criteria, or must
we integrate a moment of content, for example, the loss of didacticism and closure vis-à-vis the *Kalendergeschichte* of earlier centuries? Is the lack of closure a moment solely of content or also of
form? In addition, we can say not only that formal structure helps
shape an idea, but that some themes demand a particular literary
form. In the context of this study, we can say that some themes
may be more appropriately addressed via tragedy or comedy. Correspondingly, this work will reflect on the interaction of philosophical argument and literary form.

Although art is subordinate to philosophy insofar as philosophy
alone can ground itself in a presuppositionless first principle, art
may be said to transcend philosophy in its ability to convey truth
through particular, perceivable events, and one of the tasks of an
aesthetic theory is to comprehend this in the richness of detail.
Therefore, we must complicate our earlier answer to the problem of
genre theory, our elevation of deduction, by recognizing that, although aesthetics is partly the application of philosophically
deduced categories,[42] any theory that fails to immerse itself in
the richness of individual works will remain abstract and empty
(13:39). The way to make sense of the hermeneutic circle is in
terms of *genesis*. One works with particulars, then develops them
in the light of a theory. But induction does not give *validity*. For
Hegel, the literary critic must take as a point of reference a metaphysical stance but enrich this position with illustrations and indeed allow for differentiation within the logical-systematic deductions by drawing on examples: "The philosophical concept of the
beautiful, to indicate its true nature at least in a preliminary way,
must contain, reconciled within itself, both extremes which have
been mentioned, by uniting metaphysical universality with the
precision of real particularity. Only in this way is it grasped absolutely in its truth: for, on the one hand, over against the sterility of
one-sided reflection, it is fertile, since, in accordance with its own
concept, it has to develop into a totality of determinations, and it
itself, like its exposition, contains the necessity of its particularizations and of their progress and transition into another; on the other
hand, the particularizations, to which a transition has been made,
carry in themselves the universality and essentiality of the concept, as the proper particularizations whereof they appear" (13:39–
40; A 22, translation modified). This coupling of deduction and induction, the rational and empirical, is at one with our view of art

as the sensuous appearance of truth,[43] the union of the particular and the universal.[44] As a part of *Realphilosophie*, the philosophy of art has a dual function: to elaborate logical structures or concepts specific to its province and to show to what degree these correspond to the spatio-temporal world. Hegel notes this coupling of concept and experience when he begins his philosophy of nature. Concerning this first sphere of *Realphilosophie* he writes, "we must not only give an account of the object *as determined by its concept* in the philosophical process, we must also name the *empirical* appearance corresponding to it, and we must show that the appearance does, in fact, correspond to its concept" (E § 246, translation modified). Aesthetics mediates between the conceptual-logical and the specific-empirical. The value of any contribution to *Realphilosophie*, including contributions in aesthetics, is determined by the coherence of the categorical framework and its heuristic applicability to a wide range of phenomena.

Art can be grasped systematically, in its relation both to truth and to a system of genres, and as a particular identity, historically conditioned and in its sensuousness unique and contingent. A theory of art cannot replace art. Art does something philosophy cannot; it is in this sense necessary. Art is simultaneously partial (in relation to philosophy) and irreplaceable (in its uniqueness). Hegel mistakenly suggested that philosophy makes art superfluous. The concrete dimension of the artwork itself cannot be ignored or underestimated; indeed the concrete is the defining feature of art as opposed to philosophy, which remains in the realm of the abstract and universal. A theory of art derives its strength not only from its systematic claims but also from its ability to shed light on the artwork itself. If art is the sensuous presentation of truth and offers its viewers a sensuous knowing of truth, then the value of an artwork is to be determined not only by the extent to which it conveys truth, but the extent to which it does so in a formally excellent manner, the degree to which it not only projects issues of common concern but addresses the aesthetic needs of the individual human being. The two are not irrevocably separate: Hegel's definition of the highest content of art, the unity of identity and difference, also defines the richest formal possibilities of art.

One might object to this study by suggesting that it posits a set of truths and then proceeds to measure literary phenomena against these truths. The framework is thus not flexible enough. My procedure, however, is to allow for codetermination of the systematic and the contingent. What we find in literature, in the flux of the concrete, can help us develop our ordering principles, even as these ordering principles shed light on literary phenomena. We must grasp the flux of the world, but this alone does not suffice. We must attempt to grasp it in relation to the activity of reason; otherwise, we are at a loss in evaluating flux.

Granting that art is the unity of form and content, sensuousness and truth, we can immediately draw two consequences: first, the artwork should not deviate from truth, that is, present untenable, self-cancelling claims,[45] though it can of course expand our notion of truth or even undermine what were previously (and mistakenly) viewed as stable truths; second, form and content must function together, such that they act in harmony with one another and no element of the form is inexpressive of the content.[46] If art functions as the form of truth we call beauty, then art should present us with dialectic structures: one moment engenders another, all moments are interrelated, and the work is the complex unity of the unity and difference of its various parts. Ideally, the work is not merely naive, not merely negative, but the speculative synthesis of assertion and negation, a complex harmony. If truth is a complex unity that contains (and overcomes) negativity and is not, as in much of postmodernism, merely negative, then art is to be characterized not as kitsch or as dissonant but as complexly harmonic.[47] It is organic, not arbitrary. Its seemingly arbitrary moments are subsumed in a higher necessity. If form and content function together, then no element of the form can be superfluous; everything must serve the work's meaning. Where form and content appear to be in conflict, this discord must be part of a higher meaning that makes conflict an essential aspect of the work's complex content. Even the dissolution of form must serve the meaning of the work; otherwise, the work is not art. To take an example, Brecht's anti-organic alienation devices are an organic part of a form of art he wishes to privilege. On the whole great art, it remains dialectical, rather than speculative. In another example, the episodic, rather than organic, structure of Schnitzler's *Anatol* organically mirrors the disintegration of the hero's self. Even the negation of form is form. Important is that it serve, and be in harmony with, the work's content and that the content be itself coherent, even complexly coherent, rather than merely contradictory. An artwork that negates meaning and truth is hardly the sensuous representation of truth.

Art and History

The relation of literary form to history is not one in which history determines form, a vulgar Hegelian position. Rather, a particular philosophical position, for example, the denial of harmony or of communication, determines form. History is not the ultimate determining instance. Authors can partially transcend their time in the sense that they can help move history forward. Moreover, to see the forms of genre as determined by external factors alone is mistaken. Genres also have an internal logic, and the germination of a new genre may have as much to do with the internal dynamics of genre, the logical development and transcendence of a previous form, as with contingent psychological, social, economic, and technological factors, a point argued not only by Idealists but also by the Russian Formalists (see, for example, Šklovskij, Eichenbaum, and Tynjanov). The abstract content of art and the general forms in which its content is embedded can develop philosophically. In addition, individual positions in the history of consciousness have been repeated.[48] A particular philosophical argument may not be unique to a specific time period and therefore, though a distinct form—or dissolution of form—may be appropriate to a given idea, the potential of a particular literary form may be realized at different points in history.[49] Thus a particular form of tragedy, let's say the genre I later define as the tragedy of stubbornness, may, despite differences between historical periods, not to mention the individual works themselves, be found in Sophocles, Shakespeare, Schiller, and Brecht. The argument that we should not take artworks by these authors and place them in one subgenre because they derive from different historical periods should be followed with the argument that we should not view them together as art (after all, their historical specificity undermines such transhistorical comparisons). In other words, the argument, taken to its own extreme, is absurd. Even historically entrenched works such as Sternheim's comedies contain fundamental structures that transcend their historical specificity and appeal to audiences of different eras (Arntzen, "Komödie des Irrtums"). In addition, we might consider the transhistorical relevance of certain subjects—for example, Orestes, Oedipus, Antigone, or Medea. What also speaks for transhistorical comparison is the success playwrights have had drawing on historical scenarios to address contemporary issues; one need think only of *The Crucible*, in which Arthur Miller appropriates the

Salem witch trials to address, among other things, some of the injustices perpetrated by the House Committee on Un-American Activities.

One reason for the elevation of historicist criticism is the recognition that works are influenced by extrinsic factors. A full reading of a text takes account of such matters, though the meaning of a work cannot in any substantive way be reduced to its genesis or genealogy.[50] If we take seriously the broader claim that knowledge of influence helps us grasp the full implications of a text, then an account of the synchronic context alone does not suffice. The best historical criticism is diachronic as well as synchronic: it asks, for example, what great works of literary and intellectual history did the author know and draw on? What generic models did she incorporate, adjust, or overcome? A study of generic types contributes in this broad sense to the historical context of a work.

In another complex sense a seemingly ahistorical theory of genre can be said to relate to history. Hayden White defends Northrop Frye against the common attack that Frye is a mere structuralist and formalist, an ahistorical thinker. Developing the implications of Frye's first essay in *Anatomy of Criticism*, "Historical Criticism: Theory of Modes," White argues that the categories of modality (possibility and impossibility, existence and nonexistence, necessity and contingency) are precisely the categories of historical analysis and change. History as the corrective of ideology is graspable only as a system of change. Thus, those critics who insist on historicizing every text in order to show how its meanings are determined by history may be less historically aware than those critics who, instead of simply retelling history, focus on the modalities, the ultimate determining instances, of historical change. If one defines historical consciousness as consciousness of the possibilities for legitimate historical change, then the transcendental thinker may be more sensitive to history than the historicist. As a corollary to this, the structures of tragedy and comedy may offer significant insight into modes of historical change. If this is true, as I argue implicitly in my study, then form may determine history as much as history determines form. White's argument is in some respects a reformulation and extension of the Aristotelean argument that poetry is higher than history, insofar as it reflects not merely on contingencies but on universals. William Desmond ("Hegel, Art, and History") has stressed the similarities between this Aristotelean view and Hegel's assertions that art incorporates not just the sensuous moments associated with materiality but also the universal structures of spirit and truth. These universal structures are also the philosophical and strategic principles of historical change.

We can view the question of the relation between art and history also from a more systematic viewpoint. Vittorio Hösle, one of the most enlightening contemporary critics of Hegel,[51] argues for the superiority of a tetradic system, as in the early Hegel, which would contain logic, nature, subjective spirit, and intersubjective spirit, with the latter consisting of objective and absolute spirit.[52] The task of intersubjective spirit is to know the absolute and to make this knowledge real in the institutions of the world. Both elements of intersubjective spirit, absolute and objective spirit, overcome in various ways the dualism of nature and spirit, object and subject; intersubjective relations, those of subject and subject are essential to each; and each is informed by a history. In this system art has a privileged function in relation to history, a function that relates to its partial transcendence of history. History is the interaction between absolute spirit and objective spirit, and it is the role of art to anticipate history by showing how an idea can be realized in material form. Hegel writes: "Thinking is only a reconciliation between truth and reality within *thinking* itself. A poetic creation and formation, however, is a reconciliation in the form of a *real phenomenon* itself, even if this form is presented only spiritually [eine Versöhnung in der wenn auch nur geistig vorgestellten Form *realer Erscheinung* selber]" (15:244; A 976, translation modified; cf. 15: 437).

Art's transcendence of history (and the absurdity of the purely historicist view) derives from the fact that art realizes what history has yet to realize. What is real in art is for history still a norm. In this sense art transcends its time even as its truth is history. Art, with its prolepsis of philosophy, its sensuous and subliminal recognition of problems and solutions, and its prolepsis of objective spirit, its realization of ideas in sensuous form, helps us to define norms and reassures us, in a symbolic way, that norms can be realized. Art is subordinate to philosophy because of its lack of pure logic, its inability to ground itself and evaluate its prolepses; it gives us truth but not the philosophical grounding or knowing of truth. On the other hand, art transcends philosophy in its ability to deal with the universal by way of concrete objects; it does so in a way analogous to the superiority of a history derived from philosophy over a philosophy that halts before the realization of further history (or for that matter a history that eschews norms and so follows a blind course). Art viewed from the perspective of univer-

sal issues and norms relates to history in a way that art viewed
from the perspective of ideology critique does not. The two are not
mutually exclusive, but the latter is subordinate to the former to
the extent that the former contains the latter, as all reflexive
norms contain the negation of their negation. We shall have recourse to return to some of these issues in the course of our analysis of the partial superiority of comedy over tragedy and of the
drama of reconciliation over comedy.

We have discussed the extent to which art must be grasped in
relation to philosophy and history, but we have also underscored
the extent to which art is an end in itself, not reducible to a means.
Art as an analogue of (and not just a prolepsis of) history may also
tell us something about history that has often been forgotten by
critics who see history as a means to an end and so instrumentalize
the present for the future (Kline). In the Hegelian view—as opposed to the post-Hegelian perspectives of Marx and Nietzsche, for
example—history is not just a bad infinite, an unending progression toward something greater; history has an immanent teleology: it continues to realize new ends without making each moment a mere means. The Hegelian true infinite suggests that we
are constantly realizing perfection in the very process of striving; if
there were no further progress, we would be locked into a stasis
that lacks dynamism, a pseudo-perfection.

Art, too, offers us a perfection that does not exclude further per-
fections; it is an end in itself that can be enjoyed for itself in a
disinterested way (Hegel's appropriation of Kant) even as it also
often motivates us in one sense or another or even changes us (the
Left Hegelian reading of Hegel). A purpose of tragedy is to show
that one-sided and partial perspectives cancel themselves; only
unity prevails. A purpose of comedy is to show—whether directly
or indirectly—that the fulfillment of subjectivity is in a greater
whole. The drama of reconciliation achieves this elevation of harmony directly. Each form is an end in itself, as is any celebration of
wholeness—even as each has ramifications for psychology and
ethics, politics and history. In yet another sense art is both complete and incomplete, for it is a material result and as such an end,
though its significance grows and varies with the future subjects
who interpret it. In this sense, too, art, like history, is both still
and dynamic (Roche, *Dynamic Stillness*). One might thus see a
more elevated analogy between art and history in a Hegelian context than in a reductive historicist context.

Although I do not focus in this study on the relation of past or contemporary history (as opposed to history as the future realization of norms) to particular ideas and their corresponding literary structures, my study encourages—rather than contests—work in this area.[53] My analysis, which might be described as transhistorical rather than antihistorical,[54] focuses on the universal elements of tragedy and comedy and the varieties of ways they are realized in individual works.[55] Some of the historical questions I do not engage, but which one might be inclined to ask after working through my study, are: What are the catalysts for the adoption of a particular idea or structure by a particular author? What differences are there between Aristophanes' comedies of reduction, a genre to be defined below, and those of Schnitzler and Brecht, and how do these differences relate, if at all, to questions of time, nationality, and ideology? Though some genres, despite finite differences, appear throughout history, do other genres surface only in selected historical contexts?[56] Why are there more dramas of reconciliation in Periclean Athens, the Renaissance, and German *Klassik* than in other periods? And why are there so few such dramas in the twentieth century? Should one make subdivisions within subgenres based on historical particularities and the ways in which history influences aesthetic constructs? Do older theories of tragedy, for example, the pyramid model of Gustav Freytag, offer historical variants of the basic structures I delineate, and can such formal theories be applied to each subform of tragedy? If art is both universal and particular, to what extent do national and regional characteristics inform the artwork? To what extent does the focus on the universal versus the particular weaken or strengthen the work?[57] In what ways have historical conditions influenced which views, customs, and actions are considered tragic or comic and how might such differences bring a new diachronic dimension to a systematic typology?[58] Finally, does our development of tragic and comic structures (the roles of collision or subjectivity, for example) help us grasp overarching cultural-historical questions such as why the Indian and Islamic cultures do not have developed traditions of tragedy and comedy?

To grasp the role of succession and history within my study, one might contrast it briefly with the positions of the neo-Hegelians Karl Rosenkranz and Georg Lukács. First, unlike Rosenkranz, I do not merely present a set of aesthetic types. I argue, especially in Chapter 5, that one type *generates* another. My typology has a sequential development. Second, I suggest that the historical patterns of art may partially mirror these sequences, whereas a critic like Rosenkranz never considers the possibility of such a comparison. I recognize, however, that no direct application of logical forms will accurately reflect the development of art, which is highly influenced by contingencies. Unlike Hegel, I would argue that one needs to differentiate a multiplicity of historical subforms—the triad symbolic, classical, romantic is far too undifferentiated—and recognize the possibility of cyclical structures (which also supports a moment of ahistoricity; certain historical forms will recur, if in different guises).

"Historical" accounts of genre such as Lukács's are, perhaps as a result of the complexities of reality, often less historical than they claim to be: what is one to do with the fact that Dickens, whose works belong to Lukács's category of abstract idealism, died more than seventy years after the publication of Goethe's *Wilhelm Meister*, a work that already advances in the direction of a synthesis of abstract idealism and romantic disillusion? Or, to bring the point closer to this study, isn't the global claim that tragedy is no longer possible—as opposed to less frequently written or produced—a gross simplification that ignores complex facets of reality? Such historical accounts must overlook or abandon certain historical facts in order to present a coherent theory. However, an alternative focus on the unique particularities of individual texts combined with the abandonment of overarching narratives or histories is of little universal or general interest. A solution to the dilemma of strained literary histories or the avoidance of overarching histories may lie, as I have suggested, in the recognition of complex, often overlapping, cycles.

Art and Emotions

The three types of aesthetic analysis, corresponding to the genesis, the being, and the effect of art, are production, artwork, and reception aesthetics. Contemporary literary criticism has, to a large extent, moved away from artwork aesthetics and in the direction of production and reception. Production aesthetics focuses on the socio-economic, psychological, and technological prerequisites for the production of art. This rich field of inquiry has led to many insights, but it is not a field of inquiry unique to art, and it can tell us little about art as art. Nonetheless, we hear the refrain that artistic structures should be viewed first and foremost by way of their genesis, as products of particular historical and class settings and corresponding ideological mind-sets.[59] Literary works do have a genesis, but this is true only in the most trivial sense; all intellectual endeavors have a genesis. With this, nothing is said about a work's aesthetic value. Historical conditions help us grasp what authors may have meant to say and why they said what they said or in what ways their positions are (or are not) representative of their times, but the focus on origins does not help us recognize whether what the author said is valid, that is, whether the ideas in the work are true. Historical conditions thus do little to help us evaluate a text's aesthetic worth. The aesthetic dimension, what one understands by the literary structures and philosophical value of the work—which alone determine its universality or lack of universality—is reduced to a genealogical one. Validity, however, should not be determined by genesis. One must distinguish between the conditions that lead to the conception of an idea or the completion of a work and the conditions under which a statement can be true or false, its philosophical presuppositions.[60]

Reception aesthetics likewise has multiple strengths, not least among them its stress on intersubjective factors, the conditions of reception and the possible effects of art. If art speaks not just to the intellect but to viewers' sensuous dimension, their emotions, a full account of genre should also analyze art's emotional reception. Not unlike Kant, Hegel has, in comparison with twentieth-century theorists, an impoverished conception of the emotive life and the effects of art.[61] Nonetheless, the opposite extreme, an overemphasis on reception, also leads to deficiencies, in particular ones analogous to those I noted in my earlier discussion of expository analyses of genre. The history of the philosophy of tragedy, for example—beginning with Aristotle and culminating in the contemporary work of Malcolm Heath—is marred by an overemphasis on reception, by an undue focus on the (emotive) effect of tragedy at the expense of tragic structure.[62] As with production aesthetics, reception studies often arise at the expense of the artwork itself. Such criticism details the predictable or less predictable readings of a given age without evaluating the legitimacy or coherence of those readings. Moreover, as truth is partly transhistorical, partly historical, so too is art; the focus on reception, on contingent and conventional norms, tends to undermine art's transhistoric dimensions and thus fails to explain why a work is of common interest despite historical changes.

In addition, most studies of reception focus on the social and ideological conditions of reception, not on the relationship between a work and the emotions it engenders.[63] The study of art and emotions, however, is an important field of inquiry.[64] Though art cannot ground values philosophically, it can motivate people in a way that philosophy cannot. Logical insight does not always lead to correct action; reason is not unfailing as a motivator. Although knowledge is a necessary condition for the determination of true values, it does not always lead to the realization of these values, and often these values are realized without the guidance of knowledge. Art, not solely intellectual, can motivate where arguments fail. Like religion, art can motivate good deeds intuitively. Moreover, I would accept the critique of Kant first presented by Schiller and developed most thoroughly by Max Scheler that even if the *legitimacy* of a moral code can be grounded only with reason, it is better if our *motivation* stems from reason *and* emotion,[65] and it is indeed perfectly legitimate—or, in a revision of Kantian vocabulary, "moral"— if our motivation stems entirely from emotion.[66] Art can contribute to an atmosphere in which motivation for the good is cultivated and in this sense offers us something that may be said to transcend even philosophy. This is the case from the perspective of not only external effect but also the experience of the artwork itself, which engenders emotions, thus making possible a full experience, whatever the work's (didactic) effects might be.

Not only can emotions help motivate us to do what is good, they can lead us to recognize what is true. Like experiences, emotions can bring us to the point where we have ears for arguments we might otherwise dismiss. Emotions cannot certify themselves, but they can lead us to better judgments. The emotions engendered by literature can thus offer us a broader vision of life and give rise to more nuanced insights into ethical and other issues.

Artwork and reception aesthetics are intimately related. One could go so far as to suggest that a certain idea and form will in turn lead to a certain reception, in particular certain emotions. I accept this as a reasonable theory, as do, I think, most literary critics, but I have nowhere seen it proven. While reception aesthetics generally works with the relatively simple category of causality, asking such questions as, what social and ideological conditions conduce to what kinds of interpretation, there are more complex, more philosophical issues at the center of reception aesthetics, as I would like to see it develop. If Hegel is right in his claim that our emotions cannot be deduced from reason, then it would seem possible that feelings of reception are entirely contingent, to the point that a rational being may experience, for example, sexual feelings during religious exercises or feelings of anger when reading lyrical poetry. Or is it possible that Hegel was mistaken, that, as Scheler attempts to argue, feelings are based on pure intuition, which is neither contingent nor conceptual? Can we deduce a particular emotion from a particular category or intuition (or from a genre of art), or is reception an entirely contingent matter? These are among the most challenging—yet most neglected— issues in reception aesthetics.

Just as critics generally refrain from projecting a hierarchy of aesthetic forms, so do they rarely discuss a hierarchy of emotions. Critics do sometimes evaluate the emotions engendered by art: outrage is to be encouraged or condemned; fear is silly or morbid or justified; joy is superficial or unmotivated or deeply won. Nonetheless, these evaluations are generally proffered without recourse to any coherent system of evaluation or justification. I shall argue below that comedy, occupying an antithetical position, is in principle more advanced than tragedy. This is not to suggest that comedy is in every sense superior to tragedy. As in Schiller's well-known dichotomy of the naive and the sentimental, we can speak of the particular strengths and weaknesses of the individual forms. Whereas comedy questions unreflective adherence to an absolute and appeals to our intellect, tragedy remains superior in its assertion of an absolute. Moreover, tragedy seems higher in the emotions it conveys: admiration (for the hero's greatness), fear (of the possible consequences of tragic greatness), and compassion (for the hero's partly or seemingly undeserved suffering).[67] Compassion, for example, would seem to rank higher than laughter in a hierarchy of emotions. Compassion always derives from an intersubjective feeling of wanting to reduce another's pain; it strives for symmetry. Laughter often originates from a feeling of superiority over another's ineptitude or misfortune; it remains essentially asymmetrical. Comedy primarily evokes laughter; though, in its highest form, it engenders joy. In addition, the intensity of received emotions, including admiration and fear, is generally greater in tragedy than in comedy. The most privileged genre, the drama of reconciliation, effects both tragic and comic emotions, for example, admiration and joy, and is, from the perspective of emotions, as well as from perspectives yet to be articulated, the highest form of drama.

Drama, Novel, and Film

Drama is by definition action between individuals. Theoreticians of drama from Aristotle to the present have reflected on the relative primacy of character and action. Hegel's definition of tragedy high-lights action (or conflict), but he does not neglect character, for not every conflict is tragic; a further condition of tragedy is greatness, which derives from character. Hegel's discussion of ancient tragedy favors action as integral to Greek life. In his discussion of modern tragedy, however, character becomes more prominent. Hegel's discussion of comedy is more equally divided between action and character, partly because comedy already presupposes for Hegel a strong element of subjectivity.

Although various eras as well as different genres and individual works may invite us to stress either action or character, it makes little sense to elevate one to the exclusion of the other. Greatness of character placed in action, that is, in collision with an opposing force, leads to tragic suffering. Both the moment of greatness and the moment of collision are essential. Greatness yields suffering, and so one can speak of character, yet suffering is equally the re-sult of conflict, and so one can speak of action. In comedy an eleva-tion of subjectivity, thus an element of character, leads to a comic sequence of events whereby the subject's original intentions are ironically thwarted. Both the moment of subjectivity or partic-ularity and the ironic development of plot are essential.

Hegel tries to balance action and character both in his overarch-ing evaluations of these categories and in his discussion of specific genres. He argues, for example, not only that collision and the res-olution of collision are essential to drama, but that richness, deter-minateness, and firmness of character are as well. The pathos of individuals is necessary for the movement of action, and, according to Hegel, human individuality is the ideal sensuous representation of the Idea. In a section specifically devoted to action in the *Aesthetics*, Hegel elevates character, writing "character is the proper centre of the ideal artistic representation, because it unifies in it-self the aspects previously considered [the universal powers that form the content and purpose of action and the activation of these powers through the action of individuals], unifies them as factors in its own totality" (13:306; A 236). Yet in a more specific discus-sion of drama, in which he sides with Schiller's critique of Goethe's *Iphigenia*, Hegel highlights action: "What after all is effective in drama is the action as action and not the exposure of the character as such independently of his specific aim and its achievement" (15:501; A 1178).

While still recognizing that in certain subgenres one element may dominate, one can approach the nexus of action and character by suggesting that certain types of characters invite a certain kind of action and are in turn informed by the action around them. Hegel hints in this direction: "What results from an act proceeds from the individual himself and has its repercussion on his subjective character and circumstances. The properly lyric principle in drama is this steady relation of the whole reality to the inner life of the self-determining individual, who is himself the ground of it, even as he absorbs it into himself" (15:478; A 1161, translation modified). Even Aristotle, who defines tragedy as the imitation of an action, does not hesitate to comment extensively on the kind of character appropriate for the genre. Whenever my definitions stress character or consciousness, they also attempt to attend to action, and within that to collision and reversal, those dialectical moments Hegel elevates as well.

Dramatic action is evaluated not only in aesthetic terms (is the action coherent, the motivation convincing, the portrayal and execution commensurate with the content?) but also in moral terms. We ask whether an action is right or wrong, successful or unsuccessful, substantial or insignificant. In my discussion of tragedy and comedy I draw attention to the moral positions that follow from objectivity, subjectivity, and intersubjectivity. Objectivity, as we saw, is the dogmatic assertion of a substantial position deemed valid independently of the hero's private concerns. Subjectivity is the process of reflection that allows us to question a given morality; this allows for both the erasure of the good and consequent development of private and evil interests as well as the valid critique of a false morality and resultant projection of a new morality. Subjectivity also allows for asymmetrical relations, in which one subject treats the other as an object. Thus, master-slave relations and male-female relations frequently surface in comedy, a genre whose dominant category is subjectivity. Intersubjectivity is the realization of a reflexively grounded good in the more private spheres of friendship and love or in a more institutionally embedded public sphere.

When I employ examples to illustrate my categories, I do not restrict myself to tragedy or comedy in their most limited sense.[68] Several reasons support our viewing tragedy and comedy beyond the sphere of drama. First, I would distinguish the tragic and the comic from tragedy and comedy per se, arguing that the former are not merely formal structures; they contain logical and emotional moments not restricted to literature. Most theories of genre transcend the sphere of literature. Even a genre critic like Tzvetan

Todorov, who argues that the criteria by which we define a genre should be entirely literary, does not follow his own precepts; his terms apply not only to literature.[69] Literary genres like tragedy and comedy have noetic as well as purely formal dimensions. If the tragic and the comic transcend literature, they surely transcend drama.

Second, over the ages drama has institutionalized the structures of tragedy and comedy, such that the majority of tragic and comic texts are indeed dramas (Klotz, *Bürgerliches Lachtheater* 10). Conventions have contributed to this development, but so has the very structure of drama with its focus on the conflict and interaction of more than one individualized character and its ability to enact these conflicts before a public. Moreover, drama offers us a succinct and limited action, whereas a meandering genre like the novel rarely offers us the bold and intense action characteristic, for example, of tragedy. Further, the sympathy associated with tragedy is by definition intersubjective and is strengthened by its communal reception. Laughter has been analyzed empirically in the light of its public nature: risibility is more pronounced in public and is often contagious. Moreover, we could argue with Hegel that the interpersonal conflicts central to tragedy and comedy are more appropriately illustrated through the intersubjective medium of drama than in the epic, which is principally concerned with objectivity, and the lyric, which has as its focus subjectivity; nonetheless, the significance of tragedy and comedy and the truth of their essence transcend this one medium. Hegel himself notes, for example, the dramatic and specifically tragic dimensions of the *Song of the Nibelungs* (15:406). The subgenres also occur in the novel, which, unlike the traditional epic, often focuses on the individual, particularly the individual's collisions with society or, in novels more psychologically than sociologically oriented, the individual's search for identity. Such structures provide material for tragedies and comedies, even if the precise development or portrayal differs from what we see in drama (15:393).[70]

I also frequently cite film, a medium that, had Hegel been writing his *Aesthetics* today, would likely have replaced drama as the culmination of aesthetic genres (Hösle, *Hegels System* 638).[71] The same reasons that led Hegel and the early Hegelians to elevate drama above the other arts, its synthesis of the sensuousness of architecture, sculpture, painting, and music with the intellectual content of literature, should lead modern readers to recognize the speculative status of film.[72] Rosenkranz's comments in his review of

Hegel's *Aesthetics* reveal both the validity of his transcendental argument as well as the mistake of his dogmatic equation of the transcendental and contingent: "For with the theatrical realization of drama, which, as Hegel shows very well, lies inherently in its concept, *all arts* band together again to form a sisterly wreath. Music, painting, architecture unite to sustain the actor as a poetically realizing statue that has come to life. Theater is the greatest aesthetic power that is at all conceivable" (388, my translation). Film integrates the strengths of drama, as elucidated by Hegel, but also transcends them. Like drama, film can portray the objectivity of the epic along with the subjectivity of the lyric; moreover, it contains the advanced intellectual structures of literature as well as the concrete sensuous dimensions otherwise associated with nondiscursive artforms such as architecture, sculpture, painting, and music. Film editing combines spatial and temporal dimensions in an unprecedentedly complex and synthetic way. In the richest sense imaginable today, film is the sensuous presentation of truth.

Framework of This Study

If we accept the Hegelian view of aesthetics as a normative discipline, we would still be in a position to improve on Hegel's *Aesthetics*.[73] This could take place in any of four ways: first, one could expand insights that Hegel presents only briefly and cryptically; second, one could develop Hegel's insights in the light of new discoveries in art, individual works that force one to refine one's distinctions or, as in the case of film, the invention of an entirely new medium; third, we could show that Hegel's analyses are flawed insofar as his application of logical categories is inconsistent or inadequate; fourth, we could argue that Hegel's logical structures are themselves partly inadequate and have led to incorrect aesthetic principles.

I plan to improve on Hegel's typology of drama by employing all four techniques. The first technique will be developed in my discussion of tragedy, insofar as Hegel neglects significant subgenres, and throughout my analysis of comedy, for Hegel was extraordinarily cryptic with regard to this genre. I also apply the second approach, insisting that philosophy, though superior to art in its act of grounding itself, can learn from art. Individual artworks lead philosophers to recognize issues, problems, and positions they might otherwise have overlooked. Moreover, those artworks that fall between genres need not refute a typology, nor need they be criticized; rather, they may enrich our understanding of a typology's complexity or encourage us to rethink claims we might earlier have regarded as apodictic.[74] Third, Hegel's discussion of comic forms, which elevates contingency over subjectivity, can hardly be reconciled with the contrasting and valid insights of his *Logic*; they will be revised for this reason. Finally, employing our earlier insight into Hegel's logical neglect of the central category of intersubjectivity, I suggest several comic structures overlooked by Hegel, and I revise Hegel's hierarchy, first, of comic forms, and second, of dramatic forms in general. Hegel concludes his analysis of drama with a discussion of comedy, a mistake that derives from his absolutization of subjectivity and subsequent neglect of intersubjectivity, a mistake that also explains the most undemocratic facets of his *Philosophy of Right*: the extreme elevation of private property and the defense of monarchy (Hösle, *Hegels System* 570). Since the primary focus of my study is not Hegel but the composition, using Hegelian insights, of a systematic typology of tragedy and comedy, my references to Hegel, his strengths and weaknesses, will at times be implicit.[75]

Many contemporary readers, those who believe the Hegelian system irretrievably past and those who are familiar with Hegel doxography (the attempt to do little more than mindlessly paraphrase Hegel—as in the expository approach outlined above), may question the legitimacy of turning back to Hegel. I have tried to defend the approach in a variety of ways, but I would stress two points. First, I do not slavishly adhere to Hegel's systematic or aesthetic insights. I suggest rather a substantial revision of his system and with that his aesthetics; Hegel fails to consider the privileged category of intersubjectivity. The analysis does not hesitate to take Hegel to task in the spirit of his greater insights, nor does it hesitate to expand points that Hegel for one reason or another did not develop. Second, I attempt to question not only the system but the coherence (in the sense of a correspondence) of system and reality. I try to integrate into aesthetics the many developments in art that have taken place since Hegel or of which Hegel was unaware: the dissolution of dramatic form and the intricate combinations of subgenres in modern literature; the increasing sophistication of the novel and of narrative perspective as well as the invention of a new medium such as film. A revision of Hegel by way of these two forms of coherence (internal coherence in the form of noncontradiction and external coherence in the form of a correspondence with reality) can not only provide us with new insights into aesthetics, it promises to give us more foundation than is available in most contemporary criticism. The question, whether one is up-to-date if one analyzes tragedy and comedy from a Hegelian perspective, must be answered negatively if by up-to-date one means according to the newest trends; but the question can be answered affirmatively if by up-to-date one means dealing with current issues in an objective and justified manner. In drawing on Hegel, this study is professedly old-fashioned, but not in a conservative way; it would put pressure on the anti-idealist movement that has assumed the mantle of modernity.

I do not venture into the infinite task of discussing previous attempts to define tragedy and comedy. Ample discussions of this topic exist along with numerous helpful bibliographies.[76] If I were to retread old ground, I would not be serving the reader. Because repetition in the field of genre theory is enormous, discussing the intimate details of each and every theory is best avoided. Moreover, this repetition bodes well for a method that has found few practitioners in this century and so opens up the possibility of presenting—at least to contemporary readers—a novel approach. On the other hand, I occasionally refer to selected theories, for example, those of the earliest students of Hegel, critics such as Christian Weiße, Arnold Ruge, Heinrich Theodor Rötscher, Carl Ludwig Michelet, August Wilhelm Bohtz, Theodor Friedrich Vischer, and Moriz Carriere, who still took Hegel's positions seriously. The immediate post-Hegelian period, insofar as it strove for the critical development of the Hegelian system and was interested in systematic, not merely historical, questions, is richer than much Hegel criticism of the twentieth century. It is attentive to fundamental errors in the macrostructures of Hegel's system. It asks about validity and is not merely interpretive or expository.[77] Unfortunately, an extraordinary percentage of contemporary studies on Hegel—including those discussing his views on drama—exhaust themselves in paraphrase and brief moments of non-rigorous external critique. It is, I believe, no small contribution of this study that it points to the value of these—for the most part—forgotten authors for issues that are still current. One cannot underscore enough that the historical transcendence of a theory is not one and the same with its philosophical refutation. I also engage in dialogue with contemporary critics, Peter Szondi, Elder Olson, Northrop Frye, Robert Heilman, to name a few, who have presented recent, well-received, and challenging readings of the tragic, the comic, or both. In order to justify itself, a new study of genre must confront, if not the entire field of generic criticism, at least its most sophisticated rivals.

Tragedy, comedy, and the drama of reconciliation follow the development from objectivity to subjectivity and intersubjectivity.[78] Within each genre is a micro-development through these three stages. Thus, all three structures are evident in each genre. We can nonetheless say that in tragedy objectivity dominates over subjectivity and intersubjectivity, in comedy subjectivity holds sway over objectivity and intersubjectivity, and in the drama of reconciliation intersubjectivity is primary. Moreover, each genre (or subgenre) not only surpasses earlier ones, it includes moments of these earlier genres in the form of a Hegelian *Aufhebung*. In this sense, the genres become ever more complex.

Hegel's typology of tragedy, however brilliant, appears to exclude all but a dozen or so world tragedies. The true Hegelian may want to assert "so much the worse for the plays," and indeed she would be right in arguing that Hegel's typology, deductive as it is, cannot be refuted by individual dramatic texts. Just because something *is* does not mean that it *should* be. If we accept the priority of what is over what should be, we would fall back into a kind of aesthetic power positivism: whatever is, is valid; norms are by definition untenable. Although examples may serve to enrich a deductive typology, a lack of examples cannot refute one.[79] I could not accept Todorov's claim: "if our deductions fail to correspond to any work, we are on a false trail" (*The Fantastic* 21). Are we to call a theory wrong merely because it accounts for works not yet written? Nonetheless, a typology of tragedy should be in a position to comment intelligently on deviations from the Hegelian model.[80] Moreover, a philosophical typology can benefit from an eye to practice; art can contribute to a philosophy of art, even when its initial precepts are logical and deductive rather than empirical and inductive. My analysis of tragedy attempts to expand on Hegel's definition, while showing strengths and weaknesses of non-Hegelian tragedies, and it holds to the Hegelian claim that just because a work is called a tragedy does not mean that it is a tragedy or deserves to be called one.[81]

The second chapter of this book is thus an expansion of Hegel's very limited definition of tragedy. Here I argue for a dialectic of subforms within the genre: first, the tragedy of self-sacrifice; second, the tragedies of stubbornness and opposition; and third, the tragedy of awareness. The tragedy of self-sacrifice originates from a collision of good and evil; the hero does the good knowing that she will suffer for it. The first antithetical form, the tragedy of stubbornness, is morally less admirable than the tragedy of self-sacrifice but in most cases dramatically richer. Here the hero adopts an untenable position but nonetheless displays formal virtues such as courage, loyalty, or ambition. The second antithetical form, the tragedy of opposition, corresponds to the Hegelian model, the collision of two positions, each of which is justified, yet each of which is wrong to the extent that it fails to recognize the validity of the other position. The synthetic form, the tragedy of awareness, is the Hegelian form insofar as the conflict is synthesized within a single consciousness that recognizes the validity of each good but is unable to grant each its moment of truth; the hero must knowingly violate the good even as she adheres to the good. I also analyze in this chapter the drama of suffering, which only pretends to be tragic. In a drama of suffering the protagonist's position is not necessarily justified, the protagonist exhibits no formal greatness, and there is no philosophical conflict. What we have is simply the portrayal of a character who suffers.

In support of my definitions and in an attempt to weigh strengths and weaknesses of the individual subgenres, I present brief analyses of individual works as well as detailed readings of Schiller's *Don Carlos* and Bolt's and Joffe's *The Mission*, complex works to the extent that they include moments of all four kinds of tragedy as well as the drama of suffering. I attempt to avoid the pitfalls of either treating very few works and so offering no broadly conceived theory or discussing many works superficially but no single work in detail. Throughout the text I have provided ample illustration, for I believe with Hegel that theory should not remove us from the matter at hand but rather allow us a deeper penetration of that matter.[82] Not every reader will be familiar with every example, and in order to appeal to a variety of audiences, my illustrations range from masterpieces of various national literatures to the best works of modern cinema.

Hegel's analysis of comedy is less well known than his discussion of tragedy.[83] His typology, which focuses on the category of subjectivity,[84] suffers not only from its brevity but also from its lack of a rigorous, dialectical pattern. Chapter 3 of this book employs Hegel's general suggestion of the importance of subjectivity in comedy in order to expand his insights, differentiate his typology, and argue for a dialectical sequence within the genre.

The initial position, the comedy of coincidence, is represented by an almost nonexistent subjectivity. The hero, who does not engage in a great deal of reflection, nonetheless succeeds in entering into a communal and harmonic sphere. In the antithetical sphere, which contains a multiplicity of subgenres—reduction, negation, and withdrawal—the hero is obsessed with her own subjectivity. As a result, the hero reduces the universal, mocks the universal, or simply fails to realize it. Finally, in the synthetic form, the comedy of intersubjectivity, the hero passes through error and reaches, owing partially to her own efforts, an intersubjective sphere. Such plays culminate in friendship, love, or social bonds.

The third chapter includes, beyond its brief discussions of many texts, a detailed analysis of Hofmannsthal's *The Difficult Man*, a play that integrates—and to some extent mocks—the various subforms of comedy. In addition, Chapter 3 concludes with analyses of a variety of works that are seemingly difficult to place because they straddle subgenres or contain more than one subgenre.

The comedy chapter is significantly longer than the tragedy chapter. The reason for this lies in the logic of the material itself. Comedy as an antithetical genre lends itself to the development of a multiplicity or plurality of subforms. As a general rule, which we see both in tragedy and comedy, the thesis is defined by undifferentiated unity, the antithesis by difference and multiplicity, and the synthesis by differentiated unity. Form and content thus harmonize whenever a multiplicity of subforms exists within the antithetical position—as in my account of antithetical tragedy and antithetical comedy—or where in the overarching antithesis, in this case comedy, a multiplicity of factors and a wealth of difference come into play. Such diverse figures as Plato, Montaigne, Heine, and Schnitzler have quipped that truth is one and finite, whereas error has a thousand faces and an infinite field. Tragedy and comedy might be viewed in parallel ways. Theories of tragedy are invariably too singular, often accused of obliterating the diversity of genre, whereas theories of comedy are notoriously too decentralized, unable or unwilling to assert a unifying principle. Beyond this, the comic focus on particularity and difference engenders an infinite variety of nuances within the individual subgenres. This antithetical moment—as much as the lack of an authoritative critical tradition, that is, the gap in Aristotle's *Poetics*, or the complex, interdisciplinary investigations of laughter—has led to confusion concerning the nature of the comic.[85] As an antithetical genre, comedy is more complex and difficult than tragedy. The fact that no consensus exists on comedy does not, however, mean that in principle no single, correct definition of the genre is possible.

Following my discussion of comedy, I briefly analyze in Chapter 4 the drama of reconciliation, which is not to be confused with tragicomedy. The drama of reconciliation is not a double plot, one serious and the other comic, nor is it a humorous play that ends tragically. Instead, it involves a serious conflict that ends harmonically. The genre is also analyzed by way of its relation to melodrama and the problem play. For purposes of illustration I analyze one of Hitchcock's greatest, if most underrated, films, *I Confess*. I also argue in this chapter that specific contradictions in Aristotle's *Poetics* and Hegel's *Aesthetics* derive from a failure to clearly distinguish tragedy from the drama of reconciliation.

Chapter 5 demonstrates how tragedy, comedy, and the drama of reconciliation are linked dialectically. It also shows how the various subforms generate one another. In addition, it analyzes interrelations between the tragic and comic subforms and suggests numerous parallel structures that shed light on the overall process of systematic categorization and on individual plays.

Chapter 6 tries to make sense of the contemporary situation, the seeming eclipse of tragedy and the contemporary privileging of comedy, in the light of my typology.

After a final chapter that briefly summarizes the study and points to topics for further inquiry, the work concludes with a set of appendices, in which I list the various definitions and provide a wealth of examples (some of them with brief commentary) for each subgenre.

A Note to the Reader

Some readers, even if they find my typology useful as a heuristic device, will object to the work's highly evaluative tone. In conjunction with the questioning of the canon has arisen a hesitancy to rate individual works as better or worse than others or to allow for principles according to which we might measure a work's merits.[86] Nonetheless, teachers do select texts for their classes, and only the rarest teacher selects them arbitrarily. Those who select works they happen to like and can give no grounds for their selection are not only acting irresponsibly toward their students, they have—following the principle of their own selection—no right to criticize the choices of others.[87] Most teachers do select their texts with care, and most of them select ones they consider good or great. Therefore, evaluations are made, and a hierarchy, even if implicit, is usually present. The criteria for the selection and evaluation of texts, and thus of the structuring of a hierarchy, even if it is complex or tends toward the pluralistic, should be made explicit. We should present arguments for it; only then can we contest either the canon or what might be offered in place of the canon. If a critic wants to argue for the excellence of a particular work, then the critic must also be in a position to privilege certain characteristics or principles and thus certain kinds of works.

Working with a definition of art as the sensuous appearance of truth and assenting to logical claims for the superiority of the speculative over both the naive and the merely negative, I value works that present, in an artistically rich manner, philosophical truth, harmonic works that contain negativity. If beauty presupposes truth, even a formally great work may contain hidden weaknesses. Büchner's *Woyzeck* is formally outstanding but limited by the truth it portrays (it does not integrate a genuine collision) and its episodic, rather than organic, dimensions (Woyzeck's suffering does not derive from his greatness).[88] Other works may make a valid statement but not in a formally great manner. Paul Ernst's mildly epigonal *Prussian Spirit* comes to mind. Only with a synthesis of the two do we find the greatest possible art.

While I believe that such pronouncements, though representative of a minority position, are legitimate, it is equally clear that no discussion of genre can be complete. Completion presupposes full knowledge of the general and particular entities that contribute to a sphere of knowledge, and here, in the sphere of continually developing art, a sphere in which a measure of the individual work's greatness is its inexhaustability, such a task would be impossible; that does not, however, mean that we cannot ground a broad systematic structure that allows for further differentiation or that we cannot recognize individual features that are significant in both a theoretical and practical sense. Hegel employs a set of helpful analogies when discussing the completion of law books: "It is manifestly absurd not to promulgate the law 'Thou shalt not kill' on the grounds that a legal code cannot be complete. Even idle reflection may conclude that every legal code could be improved, for the most glorious, exalted, and beautiful can be conceived of as being still more glorious, exalted, and beautiful. But a large and ancient tree puts out more and more branches without thereby becoming a new tree; yet it would be foolish to refuse to plant a tree just because it might produce new branches" (R § 216 Z, translation modified).

This book is intended for four audiences: literary theorists and philosophers interested in questions of literary categorization and issues of normative aesthetics; Hegel scholars interested in logical structures and their application to individual phenomena; students of drama interested in genre theory and individual plays; and students of German literature, from where many of my examples are taken. Yet another audience, those readers simply interested in the ways in which aesthetic structures shed light on today's world, is sought, if not reached, by every work of literary criticism that deserves the name.

2

A Study of Tragedy

ragedy is an action in which the hero's greatness leads inexorably to suffering. Tragedy contrasts what is substantial and great with the negative consequences of this greatness. By substantial I mean that which is aligned with virtue, both primary virtues such as goodness and justice and secondary or formal virtues such as courage, loyalty, or discipline. The substantial requires that the self abandon limited desires and interests for the sake of what transcends the self, the universal. The contrast between greatness and suffering is evident in all forms of tragedy, as is their organic link.

The various forms of greatness, which can be viewed dialectically, allow us to speak of different types of tragedy.[1] In the initial form we see a tragedy of self-sacrifice: the hero does the good knowing that she will suffer for it. Two antithetical forms follow: first, the tragedy of stubbornness, in which the hero adopts an untenable position but nonetheless displays formal virtues; second, the tragedy of opposition, in which two goods conflict, each of which is partly justified, yet each of which, by rendering itself absolute, transgresses the validity of its counterposition. In the tragedy of opposition the hero is unaware of a collision of goods. In the synthetic form, which is also a collision of goods, the hero knows of the conflict, knows that even as she adheres to the good, she must likewise violate it. The progression takes us from the primacy of objectivity toward subjectivity and a sphere just short of intersubjectivity, or—more precisely—affirmative and symmetrical intersubjectivity.[2] In addition, I distinguish between tragedy and a form of drama that is especially popular in this century, the drama of suffering; in this genre the protagonist suffers not of her greatness but owing to weakness or circumstance.

49

Most readers will already recognize in the final two forms of tragedy variations of the Hegelian concept.[3] The first two forms suggest that other types of tragedy exist, even if they fail to reach the heights of the Hegelian model. Within the Hegelian tragedy of collision I suggest a subdistinction Hegel does not present, and drawing on the insights of Hegel's general definition, I argue that the drama of suffering is so deficient as to be not a tragedy at all.

My definition of tragedy builds not only on Hegel's elevation of collision but also on Max Scheler's concept of the tragic knot: whatever leads to greatness and allows the hero to realize a positive value also engenders suffering and destroys the positive value ("Zum Phänomen" 293–297; "On the Tragic" 22–29). Icarus is the mythological symbol for this: the very glue that holds his wings together melts in the same degree to which he approaches the sun.[4] Scheler took his cue in part from Georg Simmel, but the idea has a long history. Adolf Zeising, for example, defines tragedy as an "objective perfection" coupled with an "objective imperfection" but in such a way that they are one and the same: "The objective imperfection may therefore not be in contradiction with objective perfection; on the contrary, it must prove to be a consequence of the same, indeed one with it" (331, my translation).

Peter Szondi defines tragedy by focusing on the dialectic of reversal, but he doesn't accept the idea that the reversal must stem from the hero's greatness. For Szondi, in contrast to the theory proposed here, *any* reversal of expectations or motives that leads to suffering is tragic (for Szondi's formulation of his definition, see "Versuch" esp. 209 and 213). An American scholar with whom my definition has much in common is Oscar Mandel, an inductive genre critic, who stresses, like few other contemporary theorists of tragedy, the concept of inevitability (23–25). For Szondi, reversal is the *sine qua non* of tragedy; for Mandel, it is organic reversal or inevitable suffering; in this work it is inevitable suffering engendered by greatness or virtue. This definition is shared by Reinhold Niebuhr, who writes: "The word tragic is commonly used very loosely. It usually designates what is not tragic at all but pitiful. In true tragedy the hero . . . suffers because he is strong and not because he is weak. He involves himself in guilt not by his vice but by his virtue" (156). Often critics stress that in tragedy we recognize our finitude; true, the tragic hero comes into conflict with finitude, but it is not finitude alone that makes for tragedy, but the greatness of the hero who would challenge the finitude of her environment.

The transitions between subgenres are partly motivated by the hero's consciousness, revealed to us through speeches and dialogue, as the hero pursues the next step in a dialectic. The hero of the initial tragic form, self-sacrifice, knows only the good. The heroes of the antithetical forms, stubbornness and opposition, know of the strong means to a goal that is the negation of the good—though in opposition it is equally the realization of a good. The hero of awareness, finally, knows of the conflict of two goods and thus of the evil that resides even within the good. Each form develops what is implicit in the previous subgenre. Common to all forms of tragedy is conflict engendered by greatness; different are the forms of conflict and the hero's consciousness thereof.

The Tragedy of Self-Sacrifice (1)

The tragedy of self-sacrifice is a collision of good and evil, whereby the hero, who stands clearly on the side of the good, assumes responsibility for her suffering, and in most cases her death.[5] The hero does the good knowing that she will suffer for it. The tragedy of self-sacrifice is the noblest and most didactic of tragic subforms, although it is dramatically—owing to the simplicity and nonambiguity of the conflict—the weakest. The tragedy of self-sacrifice presents us with a clear conflict. In Hochhuth's *The Deputy* we hear the unequivocal lines: "Either one lives *or* one is consistent" (Act II, my translation). Another passage reads: "A Christian in these times cannot possibly survive if he is consistent" (I.iii, my translation). To preserve a value, its bearer must sometimes perish.

A highly Socratic concept, self-sacrifice teaches that it is better to suffer than to do wrong—the argument being that to suffer wrong is to experience external harm, while to do harm is not only to injure another but also to harm one's inner self. In this spirit Sir Thomas More, "the English Socrates," can say to Richard Rich in Robert Bolt's *A Man for All Seasons*: "I am sorrier for your perjury than my peril" (Act II). The unjust act makes the doer a worse person and in the end less happy (*Republic* 352d). For Socrates, the just life is higher than life itself: "the difficulty is not so much to escape death; the real difficulty is to escape from doing wrong, which is far more fleet of foot" (*Apology* 39a).

The traditional concept of a tragic flaw is not a necessary component of this form of tragedy. The tragic hero of self-sacrifice is more correct in her stance than the theory of tragic flaw or the Hegelian theory of necessary one-sidedness allows. The hero succumbs precisely because she identifies with the universal. In general, I would stress—against what Peter Alexander calls the "hamartians" (53)— that the tragic hero's suffering derives from a virtue, not a fault, or—to cite the insightful discussion of Kurt von Fritz (3–14)—that the concept of *hamartia* is best understood not as a tragic flaw but rather as action according to an immanent necessity that nonetheless leads to catastrophe.

The tragedy of self-sacrifice often introduces a secondary or mild happiness; heroes freely give their lives knowing that to continue to live would be to sacrifice their principles.[6] The hero's misfortune has a kind of peripheral status and does not greatly interfere with her essential moral values and their accompanying emotional essence, the (sometimes submerged) joy associated with willing the good. Schelling writes: "precisely at the moment of *most sublime* suffering the tragic hero enters into the most sublime liberation and most sublime absence of suffering" (Ger 342; Eng 254, translation modified). The conflation of predestination and responsibility, of necessity and free will, which seems to take place in Oedipus's misdeeds, has a richer counterpart in the play's conclusion, where freedom and necessity become not freedom (for evil) and (instinctual) necessity but the freedom to do the good and recognition of the good as law or necessity.[7]

The tragedy of self-sacrifice arises when the hero subordinates herself to the universal; the universal can be realized only in the individual, but the value of the individual is derived from the universal. The hero thus fulfills herself by consistently adhering to the universal. Though the hero dies, the principle of her life survives. Tragedies of self-sacrifice, as, for example, Hebbel's *Agnes Bernauer*, Hochhuth's *The Deputy*, or Duigan's *Romero*, make extensive use of parallels to the Christ story. The Gospel of John elevates self-sacrifice as the highest expression of Christian love: "Greater love has no man than this, that a man lay down his life for his friends" (15:13).[8]

The tragedy of self-sacrifice can be highly inspirational, and plays sometimes thematize the inspiriting reception of self-sacrifice, as, for example, in Kaiser's *The Burghers of Calais*, where Eustache's act of self-sacrifice helps others overcome their lingering desire to be freed of self-sacrifice. A similar structure surfaces in the final act of Arthur Miller's *The Crucible*, where Proctor draws strength from Rebecca's ennobling example. Stanley Kubrik's *Spar-

tacus also evidences the inspirational effects of self-sacrifice. Indeed, the idea of self-sacrifice as inspiration remains today; consider, for example, the staging of *Antigone* within Athol Fugard's South African protest play *The Island*.

Heroes of self-sacrifice ideally trigger transitions in history even as they give their lives for these transitions.[9] The other, often the state, adheres to a principle of the past, yet it still holds power; the tragic hero of self-sacrifice represents the future.[10] Self-sacrificing heroes stand for truths that are too new to have a majority behind them; after the hero's sacrifice the situation will change: "That is the position of heroes in world history generally; through them a new world dawns. This new principle is in contradiction with the previous one, appears as dissolving; the heroes appear, therefore, as violent, destructive of laws. Individually, they are vanquished; but this principle persists, if in a different form, and buries the present" (18:515, my translation).

The tragedy of self-sacrifice may be said to portray in principle less the exception, which must inevitably lead to death, than a universally valid position, which, if it were shared and were the norm, would lead instead to reconciliation. In the tragedy of self-sacrifice a moment of hope surfaces, which relates to the work's overarching didactic function: the hero is singular and an exception, but insofar as her actions are exemplary of greatness, the hero represents a universal norm that should be realized by others as well. Insofar as the techniques for realizing this norm in a universal rather than singular fashion are in many cases not themselves fully developed, we might call the hope impractical, ahistorical, or naive. Nonetheless, its validity as a universal rather than singular ideal can scarcely be called into question.

Moreover, because the structure of tragic self-sacrifice often arises during a historical transition, a paradigm shift, the hero represents a new position that is merely on the horizon. The content of the position should and eventually will be realized for many or for all; it will become common sense in the new paradigm, but what cannot be universalized is the hero's strength of will. This strength of will together with the hero's prolepsis constitutes the moment of greatness. Not only can this not be universalized, it need not be universalized, for the greatness of the hero is to introduce the new norm in such a way that *fighting* for the norm eventually becomes superfluous. The truth of heroic self-sacrifice is the overcoming of the need for heroism; so, for example, the silent heroism of Tom Doniphon in John Ford's *The Man Who Shot Liberty Valance*, which makes possible a transition to the modern state in which heroes are no longer needed (Roche and Hösle). After tragedy follow equilibrium, balance, and harmony. We are reminded of Galileo speaking to Andrea in Brecht's *The Life of Galileo*: "Unhappy the land that needs heroes" (sc. 13).

The tragedy of self-sacrifice is the most frequent form of tragic subplot in drama.[11] This subordination derives mainly from its undramatic and inherently economical character. In the twentieth century, this type of subplot is especially frequent. Consider, for example, Kattrin in Brecht's *Mother Courage*; Athi in Brecht's *Master Puntila und His Servant Matti*; Celia in T. S. Eliot's *The Cocktail Party*; and Lili Tofler in Peter Weiss's *The Investigation*. In these and other twentieth-century works the introduction of a finite tragedy of self-sacrifice derives from the belief, first, that heroic consistency and adherence to virtue are the exception rather than the norm,[12] and second, that the tragic act is accomplished not by the individual at the center of society but by someone on the perimeter. Indeed, Brecht's Athi is such a peripheral figure he never appears on stage. Similarly, though less extreme, the tragic act of Eliot's Celia is only told, not shown.

Self-Sacrifice and Suffering

We must guard against calling tragic a self-sacrifice that does not include suffering or renunciation. In its richest realizations tragic self-sacrifice becomes a kind of collision (the desire to uphold a supreme value versus the desire to live or live comfortably), even as the hero and the viewer recognize that the two poles are not equally weighted. Because something of value is being relinquished (one's life), self-sacrifice is a form of collision, albeit with uneven poles. Even in self-sacrifice, then, there is loss; even when the principles for which the hero dies survive, that singular life is past, gone, irretrievable, and this sense of loss needs to be thematized.[13]

Although self-sacrifice presupposes Socratic principles, to argue that Socrates himself is tragic would be difficult.[14] As we know from the *Apology* and *Crito*, Socrates could have saved himself by compromising his principles, but he recognizes that he must remain true to his ideals. Socrates does what is right and does not regret his actions. He is more serene than suffering. Moreover, he is old and has lived his life; he is not a young Antigone, who relinquishes life at its threshold. Finally, much as in Christianity, for

Socrates truth and reality are in the heavens, precisely where his sacrifice will bring him. Where there is no suffering, tragic experience vanishes.

Consider in this context Corneille's *Polyeuctus*. Paulina and Servinus are the greater tragic heroes in this play. Each sacrifices love for duty. Polyeuctus, on the other hand, sacrifices a life he does not desire. His self-sacrifice is either fulfillment or escape or both. Polyeuctus would die in order to appear great in the eyes of God and the world (thus the moment of suffering disappears) and out of a sense of despair (his will to live is past, and he relinquishes nothing of great value). His disregard for life also blinds him to a possible collision: his martyrdom is coupled with scorn for the value of his wife's love (she is an "obstacle" to him [1144]). The great tragic hero recognizes the value of what her martyrdom forces her to relinquish. Consider, in contrast, Polyeuctus' almost masochistic pronouncements on the suffering he longs to embrace:

> In suffering lies true Christian happiness.
> The fiercest torments are rewards for them.
> God, who repays good deeds a hundredfold,
> Adds persecutions as a crowning bliss. (1535–1538)

In a similar vein, Pauline asserts of the Christians: "Tortures to them are what our pleasures are" (951). Self-sacrifice functions as tragic only when there is some conflict, principally that between self-preservation and moral action; if the conflict becomes too one-sided, with the one pole rendered inferior or non-existent, the tragic structure vanishes—as with Socrates and even more so with Polyeuctus.

The martyr, who differs from the suffering hero of tragic self-sacrifice, experiences no fear of death; on the contrary, she is indifferent to death or even strides to it as to a dance—so a description of John Chrysostom (Migne 50:707). The martyr enters into a kind of fanaticism of death, desiring, and striving toward, demise. Not only does the martyr not fear death, she is free of pain. Such heroes lack in my theory tragic suffering, and they want in the neo-Aristotelean model the quality of awakening sympathy. The transcendence of suffering makes martyrdom possible, but it also renders the hero's action untragic. The only way to render the martyr a tragic hero of self-sacrifice is to focus on the hero's suffering rather than salvation and to portray her as momentarily wavering, fearful of the drastic consequences. Successful in this regard is Dreyer's *The Passion of Joan of Arc*.

Within the tragedy of self-sacrifice I distinguish between befallen and self-inflicted self-sacrifice. In *befallen self-sacrifice* conflict arises without the conscious affirmation of the hero, who asserts strength not in creating the conflict but in choosing the good. An example would be Bolt's *A Man for All Seasons*. In *self-initiated self-sacrifice* the self initiates, wills, and creates the conflict that leads to her demise, knowing from the beginning what the outcome will be. As in Hochhuth's *The Deputy*, it is a matter of asserting one's identity in relationship to an absolute.

A third kind of self-sacrifice, *complex self-sacrifice*, integrates both forms: the hero creates the situation or conflict that makes her sacrifice necessary, though the result appears befallen. Oedipus, for example, wants to help and says, we must search, thus his conflict is self-initiated, though he does not know that the search will come back to himself, thus the moment of befallenness. Oedipus succeeds in his quest (he does find the murderer), but his success is also his undoing (for he himself is that murderer). Francis Fergusson's analysis brings to light Oedipus' ruin as both befallen and self-inflicted: "In one sense Oedipus suffers forces he can neither control nor understand, the puppet of fate; yet at the same time he wills and intelligently intends his every move" (18). His seeking out the murderer reenacts on a higher plane his earlier tragedy, for in going out of his way to avoid the prophecy, he ironically fulfills it: greatness of intention leads in each case to disaster.

Whether befallen, self-initiated, or complex, the most difficult self-sacrifice is one for which the hero receives no recognition. The hero wills the good knowing that others will think that she has weakened. The ending of Michael Curtiz' *Angels with Dirty Faces* realizes this structure with great emotional force. What was once the well-acknowledged courage of stubbornness becomes a much stronger, but unrecognized, courage of self-denial. The objectivity of the deed is present, but it cannot be publicly recognized. The heroine's feigned indifference at the conclusion of Alfred Green's *Dangerous* and Tom Doniphon's heroic silence in John Ford's more complex and beautiful film *The Man Who Shot Liberty Valance* likewise exhibit this structure. It belongs to the idea of the great hero that she act even without being recognized; indeed, the greatest hero avoids recognition.

The suffering of self-sacrifice can be physical, involving torture and death; intellectual, for example, relinquishing one's naive view of the world (a point to be developed below under the rubric of awareness); or intersubjective, for example, experiencing betrayal by one's closest friends and allies. Christ's greatest pain may have been his loneliness in the garden of Gethsemane (Matt. 26.36–46; Mark 14.32–42). A film with several allusions to Christ's self-sacrifice, Elia Kazan's *On the Waterfront*, presents suffering of this sort. After courageously turning against a corrupt union leader, Terry Malloy is temporarily ostracized, without friends, unrecognized and alone. His suffering is less physical or intellectual than it is intersubjective. Ibsen's *An Enemy of the People*, which also alludes to the betrayal of Christ, likewise presents a persecuted and isolated figure, a self-sacrificing hero, who, however, in the spirit of Ibsen, revels in his aloneness: "the strongest man in the world is he who stands most alone" (Act V). The proximity of the martyr drama and the tragedy of self-sacrifice—despite their distinction—helps explain the frequent *imitatio Christi*.

Potential Weaknesses

The greatness of self-sacrifice is its moral legitimacy, its primary weakness the simplicity of conflict. The unambiguous contrast between good and evil often weakens the potential richness of the work, reducing complex art and intricate questions to an almost black and white formula. Not surprisingly, among the tragedies of the greatest dramatist of all time, Shakespeare, we find not a single tragedy of self-sacrifice; his sense of drama was too intense, his view of morality too complex. The audience has unadulterated compassion for the hero of self-sacrifice (there is no awareness of the complexity of action or of moral choice) and clear disdain for the enemy (there is no awareness of the good that sometimes lies hidden behind the facade of evil). Hochhuth's *The Deputy*, considered by many the one tragedy in twentieth-century German literature, is weakened by the clearly evil nature of the other, in this case the Pope. An admirable and a good work, it is nonetheless not great. Modern Britain's most significant contribution to tragedy, Bolt's *A Man for All Seasons*, is likewise a noble but undramatic tragedy of self-sacrifice.

The tragedy of self-sacrifice is clearly less complex than the tragedy of collision. Consider, for example, Brecht's *The Good Person of*

Sezuan. Brecht could have written the play as a simple tragedy of self-sacrifice. Shen Te assists others to the point where her business is ruined, and she can no longer offer help; she remains consistent but goes down in defeat. Overlooked in this scenario would be the implicit conflict of good (doing the good) versus good (surviving so that one can continue to do the good). As written, Brecht's play reflects on the collision of two goods, the idea that a person must in certain circumstances renounce the good in order to realize the good.[15]

Though normally straightforward, tragic self-sacrifice can become complicated and ironic. In Miller's *The Crucible*, for example, the self-sacrifice of Proctor (he tells the truth of his adultery to save his wife) and the self-sacrifice of Elizabeth (she lies to protect her husband) combine in such a way as to destroy both of them: Proctor's confession (to save Elizabeth) is cast into doubt by the testimony of Elizabeth (which is designed to save Proctor). Their self-sacrifice leads only to disaster. In turn, the weakness, dishonesty, and selfishness of the accusers, including Mary Warren, guarantee survival. Were it not for the exceptional acts of those who refused to lie or confess to what was untrue, either about themselves or others, and so died for their honesty, the world of this drama would bear out Proctor's accusation: "God is dead" (Act III). A further, more complex, tragic hero in this play is Hale, who in trying to bring holiness to the village helped destroy it; his recognition of this error places him in the tragic position of having to encourage people to lie to save themselves from earthly justice. The structure is one of awareness, though we might also see in it an element of complex self-sacrifice: Hale is forced to sacrifice his belief that honesty and goodness will triumph.

Several other potential deficiencies can be recognized in the tragedy of self-sacrifice. It can become sentimental and melodramatic because of the weakened conflict and occasional introduction of self-pity. Self-sacrifice can become antidramatic in the additional sense that the hero follows her course with an almost automatic progression.[16] The last-minute frailty and humanness of such tragic heroes as Marquis Posa,[17] Agnes Bernauer,[18] John Proctor,[19] and Riccardo Fontana[20] try to guard against this uncomplicated structure, but the tendency of the subgenre is clearly undramatic.[21] The hero has wisdom and dies, often calmly, out of adherence to a principle, and she attains no further wisdom through suffering.[22] Some critics might even suggest that, since consistency of principle (the moral dimension) so supersedes external reality (the physical dimension), the tragic factor vanishes entirely from self-sacrifice. Self-sacrifice thus transforms into self-magnification: in asserting one's identity with a cause and becoming in effect a martyr, one dissolves the tragic moment. Especially effective is an exposition that portrays the protagonist not as someone aspiring to heroism, but as a fragile person who would prefer to live a normal existence, as, for example, Robert Jordan in Hemingway's *For Whom the Bell Tolls*. Sacrifice necessarily involves pain, but the tragic hero is willing to sacrifice not *because* the action causes pain, which would be masochism, but because the action is just and good; pain is both essential and secondary. The martyr, on the other hand, experiences only fulfillment and bliss.[23]

The mirroring reverse of self-magnification is self-erasure, equally dangerous to tragedy. To extinguish a worthless self is as untragic as to glorify a self in martyrdom. Ford's visually beautiful film *The Fugitive* reflects on both dangers. At the film's opening the priest exhibits pride; he is adored for remaining in the country despite the threat of persecution, and he views himself as a hero and martyr; morally arrogant, he loses grace and courage. Later, the priest does exhibit courage, and he develops humility (including a recognition of nature and the greatness of the priesthood). But the film's conclusion borders on yet another eclipse of genuine self-sacrifice: the priest is so secure and confident in his position that his loss of life is almost insignificant. Pride and glory in self-sacrifice and the erasure of self in self-sacrifice constitute the two extremes that mitigate against *tragic* self-sacrifice.

In addition, the idea of tragic sacrifice has, not surprisingly, been abused ideologically. Consider a National Socialist film such as *Hitler Youth Quex*, a National Socialist drama such as Möller's *The Sacrifice*, or the popularity (and perversion) of Hebbel's *Agnes Bernauer* on the National Socialist stage (Niven 176–184). J. P. Stern devotes a chapter of his book on National Socialism to what he calls the sacrifice syndrome (28–34), and Jay Baird has written an entire book on the National Socialist cult of death. The truly tragic self-sacrificing hero, however, surrenders not to the partial value system of the nationalist state but to a universal idea.

Finally, the tragedy of self-sacrifice can easily be misread to be presenting an inverse power positivism: if you suffer, you are just.[24] The statement is grotesquely false. Instead, the lesson of tragic self-sacrifice is: if you recognize what is just, then you must follow through, even if it means that you will suffer for your actions.

The Tragedy of Stubbornness (2a)

The second form of tragedy is morally less admirable than the tragedy of self-sacrifice but formally and, in most cases, dramatically richer. I call this the tragedy of stubbornness. In self-sacrifice the tragic hero identifies with an absolute and submerges herself in it; in stubbornness more of subjectivity is visible. Stubbornness—or for the general case let us say steadfastness—belongs as a moment to all tragedy.[25] Lukács speaks of a kind of tragic imperative: "the continuance unto death of everything that has begun" ("Metaphysik der Tragödie" 231; "Metaphysics of Tragedy" 161). The greatness of the hero in a tragedy of stubbornness is precisely the consistency with which she adheres to a position, false and one-sided though it may be. For Euripides' Medea, "No compromise is possible" (819). Ibsen's Brand exclaims: "I require All or Nothing. / No half-measures" (Act II). Camus' Caligula resolves "to follow up his ideas to the end . . . to be logical right through, at all costs" (Act I). The adamantine hero of a tragedy of stubbornness pursues an invalid position to the extreme and suffers, or dies, of adherence to a false position.

The hero shows no flexibility, and there is something impressive, heroic, even inspiring, about this intensity and perseverance. Outside forces—in the case of *Ajax*, the urgings of Tecmessa and the chorus—have no compelling effect on the hero. Stubborn heroes will not halt or compromise; they must only accept the consequences of their going forward. Ajax wants the world on his own terms and is willing to destroy himself and others to get it. He cannot function in a world that has nothing as fixed and absolute as himself. Medea would have profited empirically from stilling her anger, but she remains steadfast in her hate, consistent in her desire for vengeance. Coriolanus could have won the favor of all Romans by being flexible, perhaps simply by being mild, but he will not stray from his principles and resoluteness. His honor and pride will not bear it.

Although the stubborn hero's position is invalid, the hero displays formal or secondary virtues, such as loyalty, discipline, or courage,[26] and she pursues an end of objective and not merely private interest. While Hegel does not recognize the tragedy of stubbornness, he is not blind to the "greatness of spirit" in a character such as Macbeth (13:538; A 420), and he presents an insightful description of what is necessary for any successful aesthetic portrayal of evil: "Here above all, therefore, we must at least demand formal greatness of character and a subjectivity powerful enough to withstand everything negative and, without denying its deeds or being inwardly shattered, to accept its fate" (15:537; A 1207, translation modified).[27] The transgression of justice, however important, remains for the viewer less significant than the greatness of the hero's formal virtues. Julius Hermann von Kirchmann comments on tragic heroes who exhibit passion but are not caught in any Hegelian collision: "There is in their case no collision of duties; they more or less violate nothing short of the ethical imperative; but their passion is so heightened as to border on the superhuman, or their person so elevated as to border on the sublime, that the ethical judgment is suspended and the observer is taken in only by the sublimity of the appearance" (1:310, my translation).

We recognize in this form of tragedy the extent to which ambition, will, cunning, and power contribute to the presentation of many tragic heroes, to their formal greatness.[28] Often, heroes of stubbornness equate themselves with gods. Ajax views himself as Athena's equal. Goethe's Faust and Camus' Caligula long to be even greater than divinity. Not only the elevation to the level of the gods but fearless opposition to them—as in Aeschylus' *Prometheus*—is evidence of tragic stubbornness. The stubborn hero defines herself in opposition not only to God but to others and is for that reason also often the isolated hero—a Medea, a Macbeth, a Karl Moor. Indeed, the hero's formal virtues and greatness are underscored when contrasted with the qualities of the hero's opponents or successors, who lack such stature.

Because the stubborn hero elevates herself above others, even above the laws of morality, hubris is frequent. In the antithetical forms, stubbornness and opposition, the hero recklessly and confidently violates an imperative. In self-sacrifice and awareness, on the other hand, hubris is rare: the self-sacrificing hero subordinates her subjectivity to the larger good; in awareness the hero's recognition of the other pole and thus of her guilt keeps the moment of hubris to a minimum.

Stubbornness often introduces a dialectic of self-destruction. Posa's valuation of freedom in Schiller's *Don Carlos*, for example, passes over into despotism. Rudolf's affirmation of inactivity in Grillparzer's *A Fraternal Quarrel in the House of Hapsburg* makes possible the machinations of the assertive individuals Klesel and Ferdinand. Sidney Kingsley's Rubashov, an advocate of the theory that the end justifies the means, himself becomes a victim of instrumentalization. The untenability of the hero's position is often revealed in the act of suicide. Hegel cogently argues that suicide is a transgression against the idea of right (R § 70), yet suicide, in the case of Ajax, for example, reveals a certain courage, strength, and consistency, also a certain arrogance. Ajax, heroically isolated and uncommunicative, is too grand for this life. Coriolanus, likewise a stubborn hero, is "too noble for the world" (III.i.261) and "too absolute" (III.ii.41), but the fault, from the hero's perspective, lies with the world, not the hero's standards. The viewer partially empathizes with the hero's rejection of the status quo. If the stubborn hero is genuinely great in her assertion of formal virtues and if the alternative is mediocre or in some other respect invalid—as in *Coriolanus*, for example—we also recognize in stubbornness a hidden moment of collision.

To speak of "tragic error" in stubbornness as well as in opposition and awareness is much easier than in self-sacrifice. In each antithetical mode the hero violates a good; so, too, the complex hero of awareness. Yet what is interesting about these heroes, what is great about them, and ultimately what is tragic, are not their errors—after all, humans inevitably commit errors—but their extraordinary virtues, which compel them into suffering or disaster. The ideas of fate and necessity we see in such works are most often unveiled not as manifestations of external causality but as the unavoidable consequence of a chain of actions set in motion by human agents. Events seem to take on a life of their own and exceed the hero's control and original expectations, but the ultimate causality is the hero's own action—as, for example, in the escalating murders and chaos triggered by Macbeth's murder of Duncan.

More so in stubbornness than in other forms, except perhaps for the drama of suffering, we see the perpetuation of disaster. One evil deed begets another. Characters try to avenge a wrong but end up duplicating injustice. Violence and psychological disillusion relentlessly follow one another; guilt is perpetuated. This structure is behind the self-cancelling machinations of Christine and Brant and the ways in which Lavinia mirrors Christine and Orin repeats Ezra in O'Neill's *Mourning Becomes Electra*. Any attempt to return to purity and innocence is blocked by a history of guilt, in Orin's words, "guilt which breeds more guilt" ("The Haunted" Act III). Every attempt to break free only perpetuates the pattern from which the hero tries to escape.

In the tragedy of stubbornness the death of a hero is frequent though not necessary. When it does take place, it derives not from the hero's identification with the universal, as in self-sacrifice, but from the self-cancellation of the hero's negation of the universal. The hero boldly transgresses the universal, and the universal reaps its revenge. This is generally represented dramatically. For example, the love that Macbeth and Richard III negate is not there when they require it for survival, and so their actions function as a kind of self-destruction (Vischer 1:331). Some differentiation, however, is in order. Although the hero's inadequacies may inevitably trigger negative consequences, these need not imply death, at least not for the hero.

Indeed, we see an interesting historical development in the tragedy of stubbornness. Whereas in earlier tragedies the hero normally dies, a tendency of modern tragedies is to show the suffering or death not of the protagonist but of others. Stubbornness is linked with firmness of purpose and thus virtue, but this obstinacy can also be a form of stupidity, a lack of awareness that leads to the self-cancellation of a wrongly assumed stance (and in this sense it represents a weakness). The hero can suffer the consequences of a position herself, or—remaining alive—create destruction for others. Consider Master Anton in Hebbel's *Maria Magdalena*, a weak and pathetic hero whose outdated code leads not to his death, but to that of his daughter, or the differences between Ibsen's *The Pretenders* and *The Wild Duck*. Whereas King Skule dies in *The Pretenders*, Gregers, the protagonist of stubbornness in *The Wild Duck*, causes someone else's death. This runs parallel to the diminution of greatness and accountability we see with the emergence of an ever more powerful drama of suffering.[29] Gregers pursues truth blindly. He is well-meaning in his desire to take away others' illusions, but dangerous and impractical, wreaking havoc on others. In destroying Hjalmar's illusions, he also robs him of his contentment. Hjalmar ends up echoing Gregers's language of ideals; he is disoriented and overwhelmed.[30] Most importantly, Hedvig, the daughter, shoots herself as a consequence of the situation into which Gregers has essentially directed everyone. Her innocent death is the end result of the stubborn hero's machinations. The consequences are no longer felt in the mind or body of the stubborn hero.

An ambiguity of Hegel's theory of tragedy can be highlighted in the context of stubbornness. On the one hand, to the nature of the absolute belongs that in order to manifest itself it must take on the definiteness of particularity; tragedy engenders, therefore, a necessary rift in the absolute, which nonetheless in a sense also fulfills the absolute. We see among tragic heroes, however, not only necessary one-sidedness, but also a kind of egocentric one-sidedness: the hero oversteps her bounds in ways that appear to transcend metaphysical necessity. In such cases collision passes over into stubbornness.

Ethical Considerations and Variations

An intellectually necessary, if emotionally undesirable, question arises concerning the tragedy of stubbornness: could a diabolical figure like Hitler be made the hero of such a tragedy? The answer I would give is no. First, an extreme pathological element distinguishes Hitler from figures in the tradition, even evil ones. If Hitler could be made the subject of a tragedy, so too could many unstable individuals who act on their fixations. Even his formal virtues are in this sense deficient. Second, Hitler lacks the slightest moment of truth, and such a moment is necessary even for the hero of a tragedy of stubbornness. The stubborn hero's actions must be justified either by a past transgression or injustice, as with Ajax and Medea, or by a future vision, as with Schiller's Posa and Ibsen's Brand. The hero, whatever intellectual error she may commit, whatever weakness or obsession may sway her, must aspire to act in accordance with virtue. A moment of consistency, if not insight, is equally essential; even Macbeth has the courage to recognize his mistakes and pledge his life for his actions. In his orders of 18 and 19 March 1945, Hitler attempted to destroy Germany, arguing that the remaining Germans were not good enough for him.

Similarly, it would be difficult to imagine as tragic such figures as Shakespeare's Iago or Lessing's Marinelli; the particularity of their claims and their negation of all substance make them melodramatic—or, were the consequences of their actions not so brutal, potentially comic. Even a figure such as Friedrich in Visconti's *The Damned* must be said to spring the tragic mode owing to his lack of substantiality. The more substantial the hero, the greater the tragedy; for this reason, Macbeth, with his sensibility and moral insight, is greater as a *tragic* hero than Richard III.[31]

We can distinguish several different motivations for stubbornness. First, the hero, having been wronged, has justice on her side but is led to incessant rage and thereby oversteps the bounds of justice and moderation. Sophocles' Ajax, Euripides' Medea, Kyd's Hieronimo, and Shakespeare's Timon come to mind. We might call this *retaliatory stubbornness*. Second, the hero seeks a valid goal and so has justice on her side, but in her blind pursuit, she, too, oversteps the bounds of justice and moderation. We think of Goethe's Faust, Schiller's Posa, Ibsen's Brand, or Kingsley's Detective McLeod. This might be referred to as *idealistic stubbornness*. Finally, the hero overreaches not to avenge a wrong or achieve a just goal, but because she has developed a formal virtue either in excess, as with Coriolanus, or in its separation from primary virtues, as with Macbeth; we might call these, respectively, the *stubbornness of imbalance* and the *stubbornness of evil*. In each case tragic stubbornness exhibits the limits and consequences of a virtue isolated from the larger whole in which it should play a mere part.

Although the tragedy of stubbornness always culminates in an untenable action, idealistic stubbornness shows that immoral intentions need not be the source of this action. Indeed, it can arise from the noblest motives; owing to an intellectual deficiency, an inability to perceive the good, or the blind pursuit of a goal, the hero's action is nonetheless immoral. David Lean's *The Bridge on the River Kwai*, one of the most impressive war films ever made, effectively illustrates idealistic stubbornness. Colonel Nicholson is a master of the virtues of pride and dignity, diligence and discipline. He embodies a noble, yet outdated, vision of war. His stress on formal excellence goes so far that he assists the enemy. His goal is in part to overpower the Japanese by impressing them with British knowledge, organization, and thoroughness. Even as Nicholson realizes this dream, however, a new mode of war—less cooperative and more covert—is being introduced and culminates in a mission to destroy the concrete result of Nicholson's vision, the bridge.[32] Nicholson persists until the end, pursuing his view of excellence and of war and almost thwarting the covert mission, but finally recognizing his mistake with his last words: "What have I done?"— a reference not only to his efforts to thwart the attack but to his building of the bridge as well. Colonel Nicholson's act is an obsessive one, full of good intentions, but nonetheless, so the film argues, untenable. The good Nicholson serves is apparent rather than real.

We have distinguished heroes of idealistic stubbornness, whose good intentions have gone awry, from evil heroes of stubbornness, who consciously defy primary virtues. The greater hero of stubbornness is not the hero who has a perverse pleasure in evil but the hero who, owing to an intellectual mistake, follows a position she takes to be valid. On the wrong side, the hero subjectively seeks the good. Another example, taken from narrative, would be Kleist's *Michael Kohlhaas*. The hero's initial position is valid, but when his demands for absolute justice and truth are met with resistance, the hero pursues actions that are the reverse of just and humane action, even as his intentions remain focused on the good. An obsession with justice leading to disaster for all is likewise evident in Otto Ludwig's *The Hereditary Forester*. Frequently in such works we see a valid end corrupted by invalid means. This is the case with Posa's betrayal of friendship in *Don Carlos*. Consider also Brand's extremism, Gregers Werle's fanaticism of truth, or Bull McCabe's obsession with land in Sheridan's *The Field*. The hero of idealistic stubbornness stands closer to collision than the evil hero, for an element of right content is on her side. Nonetheless, both heroes illustrate the subjective moment within tragedy, either the manifest evil of turning from objectivity or the misperception between apparent and real good.

Brecht and the Question of Anagnorisis

Where Brecht criticized the tragedy of self-sacrifice (we should have eyes not for the hero's greatness but for the false material circumstances that cause her tragic suffering), he might have recognized in the tragedy of stubbornness a form of tragedy somewhat in line with his own concept of epic theater, which owes much more to the comic tradition.[33] The tragedy of stubbornness shows us the untenability and dissolution of a particular stance. For the hero the tragedy is final. For the viewer such a tragedy points beyond itself; it is as episodic as the best comedies. Implicit in the dissolution of a stance is the passage to another. The audience distances itself from, as much as identifies with, the hero's actions.[34] Brecht's own *Mother Courage* might be read as a tragedy of stubbornness: the titular hero embraces the war, for it serves her business interests, but it also destroys her family. The play is hardly a simple drama of suffering; Mother Courage—in part against Brecht's intentions—appears to determine or at least codetermine her fate. In contrast to other weaker characters in the play, she excels in secondary virtues. True, however, to Brecht's acknowledged stress on the audience's intellectual distance from the hero, Mother Courage does not recognize, she simply demonstrates, the contradictions in her stance.

The tragic hero of stubbornness may or may not achieve *anagnorisis*. Either the hero is led to recognize the untenability of her position, or the text simply demonstrates the self-cancellation of the hero's stance. If we accept an association of tragedy with objectivity, it follows—for this reason as well—that recognition or self-knowledge is not a requisite element of tragedy. The tension heightens, however, when we do see a moment of insight, a retarding questioning of the hero's position before she acts, a brief consideration of alternatives that may nonetheless be suppressed. Because Philipp in Schiller's *Don Carlos* wants to exert his strength, he is forced to remain aloof from other persons, from those with less power. He thirsts for water, but is given gold, submissive obedience. This denial of symmetry leads to the King's internal destruction, which is all the more severe and wrenching due to his moment of insight and intuitive desire for friendship. With all his might and at the cost of suppressing all intimate relations, the King works to hold together the world he thinks to be right. Posa experiences a last-minute insight into the value of life, which nevertheless does not keep him from making even himself an instrument of his ideal. Adrian Leverkühn, in Mann's tragic novel *Doctor Faustus*, experiences brief moments of human interaction but nonetheless steadfastly affirms his isolation, which he views as both the support and the consequence of his greatness. The moment of insight pushes the tragedy of stubbornness in the direction of a tragedy of collision, much the way the moment of frailty in the tragedy of self-sacrifice places it on the frontier of collision.

Occasionally the stubborn hero's insight leads to a reversal in position.[35] Karl Moor concludes his exploits with reflections on repentance and a return to the court of justice. The insight of King Skule in Ibsen's *The Pretenders* is so great that he supersedes his own tragedy of stubbornness and transforms it into a tragedy of self-sacrifice. Interesting is that the motif of stubbornness can last almost five acts, whereas self-sacrifice is in each case reduced to a single, if magnificent, scene.[36]

Proximity to Collision

One form of tragic stubbornness comes especially close to a concept of collision. I'm thinking of a particular manifestation of what is traditionally called tragedy of character and what I earlier referred to as stubbornness of imbalance. The collision is not of two justified goods, but rather of two formal virtues. In the one instance, a single virtue is stressed at the expense of another, though one is right and the other is not. Electra, for example, chooses revenge over mercy. In the Sophoclean version, Electra's action is just and as such represents tragic awareness. According to Hofmannsthal's portrayal, her behavior is aberrant, and Electra becomes more of a stubborn hero. O'Neill's Electra figure, Lavinia, unambiguously belongs to stubbornness.

In the other—more common—instance, we see two valid formal virtues in tension: an asymmetry arises, with one being cultivated, the other neglected. Here, too, collision is in truth stubbornness, that is, the elevation of a formal virtue. The hero has a particular greatness (one formal virtue in excess) coupled with a weakness (another virtue neglected). Coriolanus, for example, is a great warrior but incapable of peaceful compromise. Romeo sees himself as a lover to the exclusion of his role as son and citizen. Goethe's Egmont exhibits honesty, openness, and trust but is unaware of the need for caution and calculation: he does not flee or restrict his activities, and he freely voices his views to Alba, who does not openly discuss them with him, but rather has him arrested and killed for holding them.[37] Dr. Stockmann in Ibsen's *An Enemy of the People* exhibits the virtues of truth, honesty, and fearlessness at the expense of pragmatism, restraint, and considered action, and so he, too, represents this type of stubborn hero.[38] When Gregers Werle in Ibsen's *The Wild Duck* elevates honesty over sensitivity, he also becomes a tragic hero of stubbornness who exalts one formal virtue at the expense of another. Precisely in these cases greatness stands in a dialectical relationship to the traditional concept of tragic flaw. The hero becomes great by neglecting a contrasting virtue, which is thus the hero's flaw. Even Philipp in Schiller's *Don Carlos* has moments of this structure, as he is torn between the desire for power and the need for symmetry and is eventually forced to settle for power.

The question might be raised: Doesn't the hero of self-sacrifice, much like the hero of stubbornness, embody secondary or formal virtues? The answer is yes, but the secondary virtues are in this case not autonomous. They serve primary virtues to which they remain subordinate; the distinction thus holds: in self-sacrifice we see primary and secondary virtues, in stubbornness only secondary virtues. Moreover, the tragedy of stubbornness becomes more dramatic in the light of the extreme dependence on secondary virtues and the erasure of an uncomplicated good versus evil paradigm.

Though the hero lacks moral content, her formal powers are admirable; we can thus speak, in a modified sense, of a conflict of two goods.

Evil in contrast with goodness does not fully capture the tragedy of stubbornness. A. C. Bradley argues that in tragedy, even one that is not a clear collision of ethical goods as in the Hegelian model, there is "on *both* sides in the conflict . . . a spiritual value" ("Hegel's Theory" 677). Bradley argues that moral evil can so greatly diminish the spiritual value of a tragic personality "that a very large amount of good of some kind is required to bring this personality up to the tragic level" ("Hegel's Theory" 680). In stubbornness this good consists not in the hero's morality, but in one or more of a variety of other factors: the hero's justification, intentions, secondary virtues, or insight. In tragedies of stubbornness positive elements of this kind add power to the evil deed itself, thus reinforcing the viewer's sense of tragedy. This is heightened yet again by the sense that the hero's strengths, not being turned to goodness, are wasted. Indeed, Bradley's definition of tragedy as 'greatness wasted' applies most strongly to stubbornness. Ibsen's *John Gabriel Borkman* provides a fitting example. The sense of waste or loss is extreme because in stubbornness superior intelligence and formal virtues are not united with ethical greatness.

Potential Weaknesses

The primary weakness of stubbornness is the reduction of tragedy to formal greatness: the character adopts an untenable stance and is, therefore, from the standpoint of content hardly admirable. Moreover, since beauty is the unity of form and content, the tragedy of stubbornness, like the tragedy of self-sacrifice, though for a different reason, deviates from this ideal. (The difference of course is the neglect in self-sacrifice of form and in stubbornness of content.)

In addition, in the tragedy of self-sacrifice the hero's suffering, though consequential, nonetheless seems undeserved. In the tragedy of stubbornness, on the other hand, the hero's demise often corresponds to the audience's sense of justice and so runs counter to the incongruity essential to tragedy. What must remain is a sense that the hero's greatness, though misdirected, is nonetheless somehow admirable. The danger exists that the hero's suffering will seem all too justified; we react not to a tragic incongruity but to the symmetry of justice. Thus, Bidermann's *Cenodoxus* can hardly be called tragic. An artist can guard against this danger by stressing the hero's formal virtues, her vitality, ingenuity, and persistence, and by linking the inevitability of demise to this virtue, rather than to a flaw. Moreover, as we have suggested, the most successful tragic heroes of stubbornness show a spark of goodness or legitimacy. This may derive from the hero's having been unjustly wronged, the evocation of a justified telos, or the contemplation of alternatives. Yet another potential problem is the reverse of the first, namely, that only the attraction and not also the untenability of evil is presented. The tragic hero, or the audience, must recognize the untenability of the stubborn hero's position, the death behind the Sirens.

A final, if merely contingent, danger of the tragedy of stubbornness is that one might consider characters who are in no way as objectively great as, let's say, an Ajax or a Brand, tragic heroes simply because they hold on, in their mediocrity, to positions that are untenable, for example, Odoardo in *Emilia Galotti*, Master Anton in Hebbel's *Maria Magdalena*, or Willy Loman in Miller's *Death of a Salesman*. Although such figures may indeed embody a moment of stubbornness, they are also very much protagonists of suffering, whose weaknesses dominate their strengths.

The Tragedy of Opposition (2b)

Hegel on Tragedy

Hegel defines tragedy as the collision of two substantive positions, each of which is justified, yet each of which is wrong to the extent that it fails to recognize the validity of the other position or to grant it its moment of truth: "The original essence of tragedy consists then in the fact that within such a conflict each of the opposed sides, if taken by itself, has *justification*, while on the other hand each can establish the true and positive content of its own aim and character only by negating and *damaging* the equally justified power of the other. Consequently, in its moral life, and because of it, each is just as much involved in *guilt*" (15:523; A 1196, translation modified). The tragedy of collision is the conflict of two goods, two aprioris. What should be a single unity has been split into two—an inevitable consequence of the absolute realizing itself in history. In order to become manifest the absolute must pass over into the particular; this generates conflict within the absolute, to be resolved only with the transcendence (or death) of the particular, which sees itself as the whole of which it is only a part.[39] No matter how the self acts, she will transgress the good.

Not only does the hero refuse to acknowledge the validity of the other position, the other position, or at least the sphere it represents—is also a moment within the hero even as she denies it. This is especially clear in Sophocles' *Antigone*. Not only is Creon stubbornly self-destructive, but Antigone, too, fails to recognize a legitimate conflict of goods and is as single-minded as her nemesis, if nonetheless more valid in her stance.[40] According to Hegel, the action of each hero is shown to be not only destructive of the other but ultimately self-destructive: Antigone is not only a family member but a member of the state, Creon not only a ruler but a father and husband; the tragic heroes transgress "what, if they were true to their own nature, they should be honouring. For example, Antigone lives under the political authority of Creon; she is herself the daughter of a King and the fiancée of Haemon [Creon's son], so that she ought to pay obedience to the royal command. But Creon too, as father and husband, should have respected the sacred tie of blood and not ordered anything against its pious observance. So there is immanent in both Antigone and Creon something that in their own way they attack, so that they are gripped and shattered by something intrinsic to their own actual being" (15:549; A 1217–1218). This sense that opposition is ultimately not only external but also internal helps trigger an eventual transition to awareness.

For Hegel tragic fate is rational. Reason does not allow the individuals to hold on to their positions in their one-sidedness. Because each stance is constituted through its relation to the other, the elimination of one stance leads to the destruction of the other. The human result is death, but the absolute end is the reestablishment of ethical substance. This unity is for Hegel, as for Vischer (1:356–358), the catharsis of tragedy, which takes place in the consciousness of the audience, as it recognizes the supremacy of the whole of ethical life and sees it purged of one-sidedness.[41] Catharsis then is an act of recognition; tragedy gives us ethical insight into the untenability of one-sided positions. Though there is a connection between catharsis and reconciliation (Peter Alexander goes so far as to use "reconciliation" as a translation for the Greek term [85]), a significant difference exists between tragedy and the drama of reconciliation, namely, whether reconciliation takes place in reception, that is, in the consciousness of the audience, or in the object, that is, in the story line itself.[42] If Hegel were to have stressed more clearly the difference between the drama of reconciliation and tragedy, he might not have been led to overstress the reconciliatory moment within tragedy itself.[43]

Hegel writes of this tragic resolution in consciousness: "The tragic complication leads finally to no other end but this: the two sides that are in conflict with one another preserve the justification which both have, but the *one-sidedness* of their claims is stripped away and the undisturbed, inner harmony returns in the position of the chorus, which clearly assigns equal honor to all the gods. The true development consists solely in the cancellation of conflicts as *conflicts* [in dem Aufheben der Gegensätze als *Gegensätze*], in the reconciliation of the powers animating action, which struggled to destroy one another in their mutual conflict. Only in that case does finality lie not in misfortune and suffering but in the satisfaction of the spirit, because only with such a conclusion can the necessity of what happens to the individuals appear as absolute rationality and only then can our hearts be morally at peace: shattered by the fate of the heroes but reconciled fundamentally [erschüttert durch das Los der Helden, versöhnt in der Sache]" (15:547; A 1215, translation modified).[44] The necessity that reigns in tragic drama is both dialectical and speculative. Even when fate is not yet a kind of self-conscious providence, it is nonetheless not blind. "The rationality of fate" refuses to grant permanence "either to the one-sided powers that make themselves independent and thereby overstep the limits of their authority or to the conflicts that follow. Fate drives individuality back within its bounds and destroys it whenever it has become overbearing" (15:547–548; A 1216, translation modified).

The student of Hegel sees in tragedy the workings of *Verstand* or understanding: the hero adheres to a one-sided position, denies the validity of its complementary and contrasting other, and eventually succumbs to the greater process in which it is submerged. Tragic death is the truth of the hero's one-sidedness: "Dialectic . . . is this *immanent* transcending in which the one-sidedness and restrictedness of the categories of understanding display themselves as what they are, namely, as their own negation. Everything finite has as its essence self-cancellation [Alles Endliche ist dies, sich selbst aufzuheben]" (E § 81, translation modified).

Tragedy rarely occurs in an eminently ordered universe, such as the Christian Middle Ages, where suffering is fully rationalized, or in an age such as our own that appears to have lost the notion of an absolute (no transgressions exist, and suffering is not to be explained). More likely it arises when there is partial order and partial disorder, a transition between paradigms, and thus often a collision. The historical importance of paradigm shifts for tragedy may offer an analogue to Hegel's metaphysical stress on collision.

Precisely because tragic opposition frequently arises during paradigm shifts, we recognize the relevance of Hegelian tragedy for historical drama. Its importance has been developed partly under Hegelian influence by the nineteenth-century German dramatist Friedrich Hebbel, who tries to show the clash of values as one norm is pushed aside and another comes into being. Self-sacrifice and stubbornness point toward opposition if the self-sacrificing hero arrives before a new paradigm is set and collides with tradition, or if the stubborn hero holds on to her position long after a new norm has taken shape. Both moments are present in Schiller's *Don Carlos*.

Three consistent and overarching criticisms of Hegel's theory of tragedy have been advanced: first, his restriction of tragedy to only a few works; second, his claim that the protagonists in tragedy, as, for example, in *Antigone*, are equally justified; and third, his argument that despite the suffering and death of the hero, tragedy offers us reconciliation and harmony.[45] We have already discussed the limits of the claim that Hegel's theory is exclusive, even as we have attempted to broaden Hegel's definition. The claim of equal justification we have dealt with, first, by recognizing also unequal collisions (self-sacrifice and stubbornness), and second, by acknowledging the virtues of any tragedy that equalizes the conflict.[46] To a degree, the critics who assert that Hegel overidealizes tragic conflict are right: tragedy is not exhausted by its harmonic resolution; tragedy also suggests the inevitable calamities that result when virtue surfaces in an evil or a complex world. On the other hand, it is equally one-sided to assert, as many contemporary critics do, that tragedy offers us only destruction, uncertainty, and gloom, and that any hidden visions of greatness, harmony, or hope are anathema to the tragic spirit. Tragedy is too multifaceted and complex for an either-or reception.[47]

The logical structure of tragedy and its moment of resolution give Hegel reason to contest a reception of tragedy that focuses on negativity and the particularity of suffering. For Hegel the audience is to fear not external fate but the ethical substance which, if it is injured or reduced, will turn against the tragic hero (15:525). Pity is likewise reinterpreted as sympathy not merely with the suffering hero as sufferer but with the hero as one who, despite her fall, is nonetheless in a sense justified. Fear is most evident in the tragedies of stubbornness and collision; pity surfaces predominantly in the tragedies of self-sacrifice and collision. Hegel's compelling revision of Aristotle reads: "A person can fear, on the one hand, the power of externality and finitude [Macht des Äußeren und Endlichen], or, on the other hand, the power of the Absolute [Gewalt des Anundfürsichseienden]. Now what a person has really to fear is not an external power and oppression by it, but the might of the ethical order, which is a determinant of his own free reason and at the same time the eternal and inviolable, which he summons up against himself if once he turns against it. Like fear, pity too has two kinds of objects. The first concerns ordinary compassion, i.e., sympathy with someone else's misfortune and suffering, which is felt as something finite and negative. . . . The noble and great person does not want to be pitied and deplored in this way. For if it is only the negative aspect, the negative aspect of misfortune, that is emphasized, then the victim of misfortune is degraded. True pity, on the contrary, is sympathy at the same time with the sufferer's moral justification, with the affirmative and substantive aspect that must be present in him. Beggars and rascals cannot inspire us with pity of this kind. Therefore if the tragic character has in his misfortune awakened a tragic sympathy by inspiring in us fear of the power of the ethical order that has been violated, then he must be a person of worth and goodness" (15:525; A 1197–1198, translation modified). We fear the power of an ethical substance that has been violated as a result of collision, and we sympathize with the tragic hero who, despite having transgressed the absolute, also in a sense upholds the absolute. Thus, any intense tragedy of collision has an emotional element: we are torn between the values and destiny of each position; we identify with the character's action but sense the inevitable revenge of the absolute, which destroys the hero's one-sidedness. In opposition we fear for the absolute, but also for the hero, whose greatness has summoned the absolute to avenge itself. We seek the hero's fall not only because we have sympathy with the absolute; poetic justice also involves a purification for the hero, for by falling she is freed from a false path.

As unusual as Hegel's reading is genial, it is also accurate from the perspective of this study. The moment of sympathy can truly enter only into collision. In self-sacrifice we experience admiration for a greater-than-life figure, and sympathy arises only when the hero fears for the value of her life (and self-sacrifice borders on collision). In stubbornness we do not identify with the content of the hero's position, thus shielding us from sympathy, and so our emotions are fixed on the admiration of formal virtues (unless the formal virtues are so great as to trigger a sense of collision, or collision is elicited from the hero's good intentions or the elevation of one formal virtue at the expense of another).

Hegel views Sophocles' *Antigone* as the paradigmatic tragedy of collision. His view has been frequently contested, but if we see in the play a conflict not between Antigone and Creon but between Antigone and the institution of the state, then we could view the work in modified Hegelian terms.[48] Antigone's resistance to the state is based on her adherence to the law of the family, but in following this law she violates the law of the state. Creon's particular law may be unjust (it is not an established law but a subjective decree); nonetheless, it belongs to the idea of the state that its laws be just and that they be obeyed.[49] Creon's decrees are wrong, such that law and justice do not coincide. Thus, the state here is only formally right; in terms of content it is wrong. Antigone's act of resistance is just (and so it belongs to self-sacrifice), yet she collides with the state (and so it is collision), even as the state is weakened by a ruler whose position is untenable (Creon represents stubbornness). With this differentiated model we can understand *Antigone* as a collision perhaps more clearly than Hegel did himself.

Because the tragic hero of collision acts both for and against the good, her nature is as paradoxical as the situation in which she finds herself: she is both great and flawed; indeed, her greatness is her flaw, since greatness comes at the price of excluding what the situation also demands. Not surprisingly, the audience likewise experiences both admiration and despair, pleasure and pain, renewed reconciliation and irretrievable loss.

We can differentiate two forms of collision, viewing one as antithetical and seeing the other as tragedy's version of synthesis: the tragedy of opposition (or external collision) and the tragedy of awareness (or internal collision).[50] In opposition the hero sees only her own perspective and fails to recognize, as the audience does, that her position is as invalid as it is valid.[51] The tragic hero of awareness sees both sides of the conflict. In not differentiating the two types of collision, opposition and awareness, Hegel appears to be overestimating the role of reception. For Hegel the two goods are united in the consciousness of the audience as it sees the death of the hero and her one-sided principle. It makes a great difference, however, whether the hero is aware of the collision; this affects not only the dramatic and in part psychological complexities of the work but also the movement toward reconciliation on the stage itself.

Symmetry and Opposition

In opposition the two goods are not only split as such, they are not yet united in a single consciousness. From the perspective of the hero we see self-sacrifice, from the perspective of the opponent stubbornness. Because each hero believes in the validity of her position, she pursues her end unquestioningly and is ready to sacrifice herself for that end. Self-sacrifice and stubbornness conjoin in each pole.[52] Because of the ambiguities of opposition (each side is right, each is wrong), reception becomes especially interesting. The viewer or reader can take one side or the other, and it is not surprising, therefore, to see the diverse rewritings and performances of Antigone or to find a work like Toller's *Man and the Masses* chastized by some as supporting Bolshevism, by others as being counterrevolutionary. Just as the best tragedies balance opposing forces, so do the best readings avoid one-sidedness.

As if to underline the hidden identity of the two forces, the competing heroes in a tragedy of opposition are often presented, despite their obvious differences, as being in a sense mirror images of one another. Antigone and Creon, we have already suggested, are mirror figures: each pursues justice in a narrow way, each is isolated, stubborn, imperious toward others, and the cause of doom for self and others. A mirroring structure is also evident in Shakespeare's *Julius Caesar*, where the similarities of Caesar and Brutus are presented in parallel and adjoining scenes (II.i and II.ii),[53] and in Büchner's *Danton's Death*, where both Robespierre and Danton compare themselves with Christ and near one another, intellectually, in their soliloquies. Not by chance, *Danton's Death* contains a rich array of allusions to *Julius Caesar*. The ideal unity behind opposition is also apparent in the very title of Shakespeare's and Fletcher's *The Two Noble Kinsmen*, which functions until the final scene as a tragedy of opposition.[54]

The structure of identity can also be viewed from a different angle. Goethe does not present Tasso and Antonio as mirror images of one another, but the focus in *Torquato Tasso* on their difference does bring to light their ideal unity; as Leonore states, they should be one (III.ii). In *Tasso* each pole has an element of validity and an element of success: Tasso's rich inner world captures the sympathy of others; Antonio's clear understanding gains him power in society. Each position is inadequate, however, insofar as it excludes its other. Unlike opposition, stubbornness, which does not present a whole—even in a fractured way—rarely evokes images of totality. The hero of stubbornness can admire only herself and those who resemble her. This partly explains the stubborn hero's admiration of formal virtues in others: courage, heroism, and so forth, as we see, for example, in Camus's *Caligula*.

Hermann Weyl has effectively shown that symmetry is a frequent characteristic of great art. Among tragic genres symmetry is most present in opposition. Yet the dynamism of tragedy results from the inability of both positions to unite; even as there is a symmetry of characters and positions, an asymmetry arises between what each hero must do and does and what she should do or can. Full symmetry is reconstituted only as the hero's fall dissolves her of one-sidedness, and the harmonic whole is restored.

Julius Caesar is a paradigmatic example of opposition. Caesar and his followers are rhetorically gifted, powerful, and good strategists; Brutus, on the other hand, is just and idealistic but lacks the strategic skills necessary for success.[55] Each hero falls owing to his greatness. Caesar is destroyed by virtue of his ambition and boldness ("Danger knows full well / That Caesar is more dangerous than he" II.ii.44–45). Brutus falls victim to his nobility. He refuses to invite Cicero, the great orator, to join his cause; he does not murder Antony ("Let's be sacrificers, but not butchers" II.i.167); and he allows Antony to give a funeral oration, which turns the crowd against him. Brutus suffers, first, because he must sacrifice personal admiration for patriotic honor and, second, because he elevates ethics and honor over brutal and consequential action; he acts of an ideal and holds back because of an ideal, each of which leads to disaster. Especially interesting here are the brutal consequences of Brutus's half-deed. Not going far enough (in killing his enemies), his reticence leads to even worse consequences, more chaos and destruction. Brutus pursues an abstract ethical ideal without fully grasping the context. If Caesar's fearlessness and ambition lead to his ruin, Brutus's demise is the result of idealism and restraint. Caesar lacks Brutus's altruism and caution; Brutus lacks the strategic skills and ruthlessness of Caesar, Antony, and Octavius.

Significant in opposition are intensity and breadth of suffering.

Because Sophocles' *Antigone* is a drama of collision, self-sacrifice and stubbornness are in *each* pole. Antigone is a hero of self-sacrifice, but she is also a hero of stubbornness (she wants to die). Creon is a hero of stubbornness, but he is also a self-sacrificing hero (he is destroyed in the end, both intellectually and in his family ties). The depth of tragedy is greater in any collision where both parties suffer and are destroyed. Thus, in *Antigone, Julius Caesar,* or *Danton's Death* tragic suffering could hardly be greater; in some tragedies of collision, in Goethe's *Tasso,* for example, and often in stubbornness, as for example, in *Macbeth, Fiesco,* or *Egmont,* only one side suffers. An intellectual as well as emotional reason exists for the superiority of a collision in which both poles fall. In any true collision, whichever side succeeds can claim to have right on its side. Thus, the victor gains the false appearance of justice, which from a Hegelian framework would destroy the intellectually reconciliatory moment of tragedy: recognition of the one-sidedness of each pole and its necessary submergence as a mere moment.

Within the tragedy of opposition each character believes in the justice and validity of her position, each scorns the position of the other, extremely and unjustly, though she views herself as fair. Grand in such a conflict is a hero's recognition that the other position, though wrong, carries with it a moment of greatness. Such recognition moves the hero to the brink of tragic awareness, and when both characters recognize the validity of the other, the play moves in the direction of reconciliation—as is intimated, for example, in *Tasso.*

Opposition represents an advance over earlier forms on the axis of complexity and in many instances from the perspective of dramatic intensity as well. In all great dramas of opposition we encounter two forces or characters of legitimacy and stature. Unlike the unequivocal conflicts within self-sacrifice and stubbornness, the presentation of a single great hero, we see here the conflict of two justified and powerful positions.[56] Even Schopenhauer, whose concept of tragedy is diametrically opposed to Hegel's reconciliatory focus, privileges that form of tragedy defined by a collision of goods; it is the most dramatic and most powerful (1:320–321). Our understanding of a tragedy that falls into a simpler subgenre may be enriched by a reading that recognizes in the work submerged moments of opposition. A rereading of Goethe's *Faust,* for example, that stresses moments of opposition (Faust and Mephistopheles) might shed a different and fuller light on the play than a reading that argues merely for stubbornness.

*

In tragic stubbornness the hero violates a good but exhibits formal virtues, in some cases even good intentions. In tragic opposition the hero transgresses a good but also adheres to a good; as in tragic stubbornness, however, the hero fails to recognize the untenability of her actions. Occasionally, recognition arises at the point of death, such that the play borders on the tragedy of awareness, a collision of two positions whereby the hero is aware of the validity and injustice of each.

The Tragedy of Awareness (3)

The final form of tragedy, the tragedy of awareness, is a collision of goods, whereby one individual is aware of both possibilities.[57] The subject brings these together in a single consciousness; it is therefore a synthetic genre. The form is synthetic in a dialectical sense as well. In self-sacrifice the hero knows the good, wills it, and suffers or perishes for her action. In stubbornness the hero, who has formal virtues, is led to violate the good. In opposition two goods collide. In awareness all of these elements are operative. The hero, however, must still choose one position or the other; she must transgress one good in order to preserve another, and so the action remains tragic. In opposition only the audience recognizes the validity of both positions. The tragedy of awareness presents this knowledge in the hero herself. What was in opposition a collision on the object level becomes in awareness a collision on the level of consciousness. To employ a Hegelian phrase, what was in itself is now for itself. The hero synthesizes the two positions even as the split destroys her.

Hegel and the Tragedy of Awareness

In drawing the distinction between ancient and modern tragedy, Hegel stresses the shift from principles to character. Modern tragedy focuses on the passions of characters, not their location in the polis: "But in modern tragedy it is generally the case that individuals do not act for the sake of the substantial nature of their end, nor is it that substance which proves to be the motivation for their passion; on the contrary, what presses for satisfaction is the subjectivity of their heart and mind or the particularity of their character

. . . . The romantic characters . . . stand from the very beginning in
the midst of a wide array of accidental circumstances and conditions within which it is possible to act either this way or that, such
that the conflict, for which the external circumstances do of course
provide the occasion, lies essentially in the *character* to which the
individuals adhere in their passion, not because of any substantial
justification but simply because they are what they are. Even the
Greek heroes, to be sure, act in accordance with their individuality,
but, as I have said, when Greek tragedy is at its height, this individuality is itself of necessity an inherently ethical pathos" (15:
558–560; A 1225–1226, translation modified). Stubbornness, which
stresses subjectivity, often presents this elevation of consciousness;
Richard III and *Macbeth* are paradigmatic examples. Any tragedy
of opposition that focuses more on character than conflict also fulfills this model. Consciousness is most fully developed in awareness, where the hero sees her dilemma but has no means to overcome it. A predominantly modern phenomenon, the tragedy of
awareness arises with the development of subjectivity and coincides with what Lionel Abel calls "metadrama." The tragic dimension deepens, the more conscious the hero becomes, because with
the level of consciousness rises the level of innermost suffering.

Although awareness represents an advance insofar as it allows a
single individual to become conscious of the collision, the danger
arises that the hero will simply waver back and forth between one
pole and the other, thus destroying the hero's resolve and any unity
of character, and that this indecisiveness, not the substance of the
poles, will be heralded as the essence of art (13:312; 15:562–563).
Hegel writes concerning contemporary readings of Shakespeare:
"Nowadays, however, they make even Shakespeare's characters
ghostlike and suppose that the nullity and indecision in vacillating
and changing, that this rubbish must be just in and of itself interesting. But the ideal consists in this, that the Idea is *real*, and to
this reality the person belongs as subject and therefore as a firm
unity in himself" (13:316; A 244, translation modified).[58] Hegel insists on the distinction between characters who hesitate because
they are confused, weak, and lack identity and those who see a
genuine and irresolvable conflict of goods. "It is already different if
two opposed spheres of life, duties, and so forth, seem equally sac-
rosanct to a self-assured character, and yet he sees himself compelled to align himself with *one* to the exclusion of the other. In
that case the vacillation is only a transitional phase and does not
constitute the nerve of the person's character" (15:563; A 1228–

1229, translation modified). In the worst case, the dramatist wants to suggest: "no character is inwardly firm and self-assured" (15: 563; A 1229).

According to Hegel, Shakespeare does not offer such characters; instead, his heroes are so determined as to border on stubbornness. Macbeth, for example, is ruthlessly committed to his goal: "In the beginning he hesitates, but then he stretches out his hand to the crown, commits murder to get it, and, in order to maintain it, storms away through every atrocity. This reckless firmness, this identity of the man with himself and the end arising from his own decision, gives him an essential interest for us. Not respect for the majesty of the monarch, not the frenzy of his wife, not the defection of his vassals, not his impending destruction, nothing, neither divine nor human law, makes him falter or draw back; instead he persists in his course" (14:200–201; A 578, translation modified). Writing later not only of Macbeth, Othello, or Richard III, Hegel comments: "It is precisely Shakespeare who gives us, in contrast to that portrayal of vacillating and inwardly divided characters, the finest examples of firm and consistent figures who come to ruin simply because of this decisive adherence to themselves and their aims. Without ethical justification, but upheld solely by the formal inevitability of their individuality, they allow themselves to be lured to their deed by external circumstances, or they plunge blindly on and persevere by the strength of their will, even if now what they do they accomplish only from the necessity of maintaining themselves against others or simply because they have reached the point that they have reached" (15:564; A 1229–1230, translation modified; cf. 14:200–202).

Hamlet is the most controversial example. To interpret Hamlet's indecision as a simple inability to act is to transform tragedy into mere suffering. The apparent weakness of Hamlet derives, rather, from the energy of his thought, which recognizes a conflict between the emotional need to act in the face of corruption and indecency and insight into the immoral nature of the contemplated action. Because he is idealistic, conscientious, and sensitive, he hesitates to add to the pollution and sickness of the age; he must first weigh the merits of restoring order and justice through treachery and murder. Thus, he hesitates, disgusted with the world, but tormented in his conscience, weary within himself.

Criticism has been lodged against the Hegelian notion of collision on the grounds that any collision must be provoked by the injustice of a single act; consequently, the two positions are not equally justified (Bungay, *Beauty* 152 and 167–168). Guilt lies on one side and not the other. This may frequently be the case in tragic opposition (such that we must speak—against Hegel—of *some* good on each side and not of an equality of goods), yet what must be clarified, especially in the case of awareness, is that the transgression that triggers the tragic collision need not be subsumed under the two poles of collision. That is, one figure may act in such a way as to create a collision, but the two poles of collision function independently of the catalyst. In Hitchcock's *I Confess*, a work to be analyzed below, the collision is not between Logan and the initial transgressor Keller but between Logan's desire for justice and his adherence to the inviolability of confession. The collision evolves from an act of transgression, but that act does not affect the two poles of collision; whichever path Logan chooses, his action will be just and unjust. Though only partially valid, criticism of Hegel's thesis of an equality of goods does lead to further reflections: if the two poles are unequal, collision tends to break down into self-sacrifice and stubbornness; the more equal the two positions are, the greater the collision, the deeper the tragedy.

Some collisions are equal (certain life versus life situations, for example), and some are unequal even as each side represents a good; as such any choice of the two alternatives remains tragic. The more unequal the goods are, the less tragic is the resulting decision. Some conflicts or decisions are so unequal as to be not truly collisions. Goethe's Clavigo must choose between honesty and betrayal. Because goodness is not on each side, we cannot speak of collision.

Collision seems to invite discussion of tragic situations, yet genuine tragedy, as Hegel knew, demands not just a situation or a constellation of events but also greatness and therefore character. A situation might set a context for tragedy, but the genre also requires a hero who acts consistently and heroically in that situation. Buridan's ass, which starved because it was placed between two bales of hay which attracted it equally such that it could not choose and so ate neither, is not tragic but comic. For tragedy to occur the hero must choose. Shakespeare's Henry VI, for example, does not choose and is thus not tragic; he is a weak and feeble leader who abdicates responsibility and stands idle, lamenting as the battles about him rage. Sophocles' Antigone, in contrast, suffers the consequences of profound choice.

One might ask, how could a neo-Hegelian reading of tragedy place awareness above opposition, when for Hegel the most beautiful of all tragedies, Sophocles' *Antigone*, belongs to opposition (15: 550; 17:133)? We could approach an answer by reflecting on Hegel's assessment that classical art is the most beautiful,[59] whereas romantic art is the highest. Classical art best unites thought and medium, but romantic art, which eventually passes over into philosophy—since it cannot itself fully embody its subject matter— has the highest thoughts. To return to tragedy, we can say that opposition may be the most dramatic form of tragedy, but not the most advanced. Awareness, which gives us a more complex and synthetic content, may, because of the unity of two positions within a single self, become less dramatic than the antithetical subgenres (Brecht's Shen Te, for example, can never meet Shui Ta); on the other hand, it tends to be psychologically and intellectually more differentiated. Awareness allows for richer characterization, a trait Hegel admired in modern drama,[60] and it conduces to a more explicit thematization of tragic essence, that is, the connection between greatness and suffering.

Historical and Transhistorical Collisions

We can recognize different types of collisions by focusing on the relative tenability of the positions in conflict, distinctions which apply to tragic opposition as well as awareness.[61] First, we might consider the collision of two culturally determined aprioris, that is, the collision of two ethical positions determined by the age to be absolute. The conflict is not universal; the positions are not in any logical sense both justified, even if in a historical sense no valid alternative is open to the hero or heroes. If an a priori argument against death as a form of punishment can be presented, then Aeschylus's *Orestia*, for example, must fall in this category even though Aeschylus was not familiar with any such argument. Readers of such texts must think historically. The mode is less universal, but because of its particularity more easily dramatized and potentially more topical. One should be careful not to misread the adjective "culturally determined." All positions have a cultural genesis, but genesis and validity are not one and the same. Because the collision of two culturally determined aprioris presupposes a lower level of knowledge, it arises more frequently in opposition than awareness.

Second, we can note the collision of two culturally determined aprioris in the process of dissolution. This follows the previous pattern except that the drama is aware of the relativity of the positions and points toward their self-cancellation. The untenability is recognized only after the catastrophe, and so this form, however close it comes to the drama of reconciliation, remains tragic. It is particularly frequent in the tragedy of awareness and in the tragedy of opposition insofar as it borders on, or almost passes into, awareness. Kleist's *Penthesilea* and Hebbel's *Agnes Bernauer* (in the figure of Albrecht) are good examples. In general, Hebbel is the master of this form of tragic collision, for he takes as the focus of tragedy the Hegelian insight into ethical substance as relative, one form historically supplanting another.

Third, we can speak of the collision of two genuine aprioris. Here I take apriori in the strict sense. The conflict is universal and not only cultural. Conflicts, for example, of life versus life, of life versus freedom, or of the individual versus the state fit this pattern. Sophocles' *Antigone* is one of the greatest examples. Even if we can justify transgressing one good in order to preserve a higher good, such a transgression remains tragic. This is the highest, because most complex, most universal, and most inevitable form of tragedy.

Recognizing these types of tragedy suggests that the genre can be historically focused, or it can present conflicts of perennial interest. One form does not exclude the other; to see in tragedy only historical situatedness or only metaphysical conflict is to restrict the genre's range.

Tragedy and Contingency

Joachim Maass's little-known radio play *The Ice of Cape Sabine* exhibits a connection between tragedy and historical contingency, yet in so doing paradoxically illustrates the idea that there will always be conflicts of two goods over which we have no control. An errant expedition is in the polar cap for two years beyond its expected stay. The commander of the expedition, Banister, orders a war trial for one of the men, Buck, despite the protestations of others. Buck refused to help others when they were in need and stole from the common rations. After unjustly being attacked as unfair and egocentric (carrying out his will among starving men), Banister administers the trial, makes the final decision, and carries out the death sentence himself. He does so—it is made clear— out of a sense of obligation, also to others. Just before Banister shoots Buck, the audience learns that Buck had once saved Banister's life and that Banister had caught Buck earlier, letting him go unpunished until he watched Buck steal rations from a sick man and could tolerate no more. Banister does not publicly reveal these misdeeds—though it would have justified his position to others. Heroism is often in silence.

Only minutes after the execution of the sentence, the expedition is rescued—under these conditions the death penalty would not have been necessary. Banister had done his duty, which he does not regret, but he does lament the objective conditions that make such actions necessary: "I don't regret it. Regret would a comparatively comfortable feeling. But what a wretchedness of futility! The blindness with which we valiantly blundered into our wrong . . . . The human condition is deplorable. We want the best; but whatever we do, or forbear, or suffer, our efforts, our sacrifices—it's all in vain. What demands are placed upon us? I confess: there are moments in which it is difficult to love God" (123, my translation). This is a much richer tragedy than the simple "tragedy" of being tossed about by fate and not being able to rise to tragic stature. Here, great action nonetheless leads to suffering and doubt about the coherence of the universe. Moreover, we see in this example how even awareness is informed by the category of objectivity, for objectivity is more than naive adherence to an absolute, it is also the world the developed subject must encounter, a world the hero cannot control, however great and just his actions might be.[62]

Self-sacrifice at the Level of Awareness

The tragedy of awareness engenders self-sacrifice, although differently than in the thetic mode. The hero of self-sacrifice need not be the simple hero of an age past, a hero without ambiguities. It is the greater hero still who, though infused with doubts and defects, nonetheless pursues the path she believes to be right. Such a hero moves us in the direction of awareness. If we are willing to accept—as the hero of self-sacrifice usually does—that the spiritual is of more value than the physical, we can argue that self-sacrifice is a relatively simple action. It is, paradoxically, easier for the great individual to sacrifice her life than her principles, as the hero must do in a tragedy of awareness. For Wieland's Lady Johanna Gray to will her death to save her principles was less burdensome than it would have been for her to relinquish her innocence and accept the duties of Queen, which would have led to decisions and riddling guilt. Dora asserts in the final Act of Camus' *The Just Assassins*: "it's easy, ever so much easier, to die of one's inner conflicts than to live with them" (Fre 141; Eng 247).[63] The deepest suffering is moral, not physical.

The self-sacrifice of the thetic mode is in a sense too limited. One should not simply give in to criminals and idiots. Success is important, not only that the individual follow the good but that the good be realized for many. In the tragedy of self-sacrifice, the hero, valuing spirit above nature, gives her life for truth. In the tragedy of awareness, the hero sacrifices her principles. Such self-sacrifice may be viewed as greater than in a tragedy of self-sacrifice, especially if the action ends with the hero's life intact: the hero's suffering will not be erased by the bliss of justification or the consciouslessness of death. Instead of sacrificing her life, the hero of awareness must sacrifice her naive belief in a simple world; she must transgress the good in order to realize the good.

Jean Anouilh's *Antigone* is an excellent example of a conflict between the simplicity of self-sacrifice and the complexity of awareness. The more interesting character in Anouilh's version is Creon; Antigone, on the other hand, is presented as naive and impulsive, without maturity or a sense for the demands of objective spirit. She is a simple hero of opposition, perhaps stubbornness; Creon, in contrast, experiences the inner conflict of tragic awareness.

In her conversation with Ismene, Antigone makes clear her unwillingness to consider alternatives: she argues that "it's best not to think too much," and she affirms that she doesn't want to see "Creon's point of view" (Fre 145; Eng 87). Antigone acts not as an example for others, but as she herself wills and for herself. She doesn't want "to be right," and she doesn't want "to understand" (Fre 146; Eng 88). Antigone resembles Oedipus in her arrogance and stubbornness; in relation to truth and knowledge, however, they are opposites. Oedipus wants to know all, and his search knows no bounds; Antigone seeks no other ideas than those she already has. Instead of arguing against Creon, she simply asserts her stance. After she is caught defying Creon's decree, Creon accuses her of having a vain desire to live a grand and heroic destiny.

Anouilh further undermines Antigone by reducing her motivation. The Sophoclean Antigone could claim that she was upholding a divine order to which the state should also be subservient; here, Antigone defends merely the arbitrariness of her own will. Religious principles and a sense of moral transcendence give way to the blind affirmation of self. Antigone's initial defense, seemingly derived from her brother's act of having once brought her a flower, is destroyed when Creon exposes his betrayal and brutality and explains the unrecognizability of the mutilated corpses (Polynices' body could well be Eteocles'); Antigone's gesture toward burial is ridiculous. Exposing the truth about her brothers, Creon offers Antigone her life. Responding that any life that is not immediately perfect and full is not for her, she insists on death: "But I want everything, now! And to the full! Or else I decline the offer, lock, stock and barrel! I don't want to be sensible, and satisfied with a scrap—if I behave myself! I want to be sure of having everything, now, this very day, and it has to be as wonderful as it was when I was little. Otherwise I prefer to die" (Fre 193; Eng 123). Unwilling to compromise, Antigone demands immediate gratification. Objective norms are for her irrelevant: "What do I care about your politics and what you 'have' to do and all your paltry affairs! I can still say no to anything I don't like, and I alone am the judge" (Fre 182; Eng 114).

Whereas Antigone has traditionally embodied self-sacrifice, Anouilh's Antigone enacts stubbornness: she is less right than her Sophoclean predecessor, but still unwilling to compromise. She has certain moments of the Hegelian "beautiful soul," which lacks the power to endure existence, for it lives always in dread of staining the purity of its inner life: "It lacks the power to externalize itself, the power to make itself into a thing and to endure being. It lives in dread of besmirching the splendour of its interiority by action and existence; and, in order to preserve the purity of its heart, it flees from contact with the actual world and persists in its self-willed impotence to renounce its self, which is reduced to the extreme of ultimate abstraction, and to give itself substantial existence or to transform its thought into being and put its trust in the absolute difference [between thought and being]" (3:483–484; PS 399–400, translation modified). Antigone is the stubborn antithesis both in her negation of knowledge and her refusal of life.

Creon tells Antigone that he, too, once wished to sacrifice everything (Fre 190; Eng 121), but he has grown to a position of weighing alternatives, compromising his own belief in the simplicity of truth and happiness for the sake of political order. He is presented not as an unjust tyrant but as the person most fit to govern: he rules despite not wanting to rule. If Antigone is above all simple and unaware of objective norms, Creon has something of the philosopher-king. He is a sensible king, without ambitions or heroic desires. He must act as he does toward Polynices' corpse for the order of the state.

Creon is forced to kill Antigone; she gives him no alternative. While she has simply renounced her life, he has relinquished a naive vision of the world. Whereas she easily and readily says no to life, he says yes to life in all its complexities, including the assumption of power: "Someone has to say yes. Someone has to steer the ship. It's letting in water on all sides. It's full of crime and stupidity and suffering. The rudder's adrift. The crew won't obey orders—all they're interested in is looting the cargo . . . they think of nothing but their own skins and their own petty concerns" (Fre 184; Eng 115–116). Antigone's response is simple and easy: "I'm not here to understand. I'm here to say no to you, and to die" (Fre 184; Eng 116). It is Creon who is the tragic figure, having to act as he would not like, losing Antigone, his son, and his wife, empty. He has suffered the consequences of not withdrawing.

In Antigone, we see a link between the tragedy of self-sacrifice and the comedy of withdrawal: concern with the rightness of a position but not its realization in life. Creon mocks Antigone's tragic stance as simple: "It's easy to say no! . . . . To say yes you have to sweat, roll up your sleeves, grab hold of life, plunge in up to the neck. It's easy to say no, even if it means dying. All you have to do is keep still and wait. Wait to live. Wait to die, even. It's feeble!" (Fre 184–185; Eng 116). Antigone prefers to sacrifice life rather than her naive vision. Where she has innocence on her side (the child's shovel), Creon must live with bloodstained hands, sacrificing more than his life. One of Creon's final lines—that it would be best never to grow up—is in truth not a gesture toward Antigone's view but a recognition, or lament, of the inevitable suffering his understanding and responsibility have placed on him; were it an affirmation of Antigone, he would have followed her to death; instead he lives, and in this he suffers.

A common view of Anouilh's *Antigone* would have us believe that the play must be read differently. After all, it was allegedly hailed at its Paris premiere in 1944 as expressing solidarity with the French resistance. But the reception in 1944 was more ambiguous than is commonly believed. While some critics viewed the play as an affirmation of Antigone, others felt that Creon's position was stronger and that the play deflated the idea of resistance. Some speculated in fact that it was the work of the German military. A detailed account of the immediate reception of the work is avail-

able in Manfred Flügge (247–304), who notes that for many Creon
was the more significant character and was interpreted as a man
of good will. The resistance was upset by the play's apparent elevation of Creon and even more so by its portrayal of Antigone, the
resister, as a total naysayer and radical skeptic. Flügge summarizes his account: "The resistance didn't recognize itself in this play
and polemicized against it. The myth of *Antigone* as a resistance
play, which was found so frequently after 1945, especially in foreign criticism, and which so greatly influenced the reception after
the war, is based on a misconception" (300, my translation).

If one were to argue in favor of Antigone with any sense of the
text's subtleties, one could not contend that Antigone has the better arguments. The only criticism that could be made of Creon is
that in his pragmatism he tends toward a cynical and patronizing
view of people; he refers to terror and intimidation rather than
education or reform. Instead, one would have to argue that the
play favors Antigone *despite* Creon's arguments. Situating Anouilh
in the context of existentialism, one could argue that—not unlike
Sartre's *The Flies*, where Orestes' revenge is not so much an act of
justice as a (Nietzschean) assertion of freedom and identity—
Anouilh's play heralds will, self-actualization, and irrationalism
over reason. Anouilh himself was reticent concerning the play's reception, but even if we acknowledge that his thematic elevation of
the refusal to be reasonable and his embrace of what has been
called "absurd duty" (della Fazia 38–41) seem to support this reading, we would not need to restrict our interpretation to authorial
intention, for the text itself provides evidence not only for an absurdist and fanatic tragedy of self-sacrifice but also for a complex
and subtle tragedy of awareness or, if we were to remain cautious,
at least a tragedy of opposition—with Creon having as much right
as Antigone does in her "would-be noble" refusal to compromise.
Finally, even the biographical support is complicated and ambiguous, for in his subsequent plays *Romeo and Jeannette* and *Medea*,
Anouilh moved toward an even clearer rejection of childishness
and extremism and a more tolerant view of compromise and acceptance.

Strengths and Weaknesses

The tragedy of awareness, or the conflict of two goods within a
single individual, is philosophically the most interesting form of

tragedy: presenting the boundary cases of ethics, it not only exhibits the good, it portrays conflicts that can in turn give rise to philosophical reflection on the good.[64] The tragedy of collision implies alternatives; the hero of awareness knows of these alternatives. Her choice is conscious, and her act of deliberation brings forth the fullest range of consciousness, the weighing of ends and means, of duties and obligations, the totality of conflicting claims. Traditional definitions of tragedy often stress knowledge and self-recognition; these aspects receive their fullest development in the tragedy of awareness. In addition, any collision of two goods—whether in opposition or awareness—is *in principle* the dramatically richest structure of tragedy.[65] With its recognition of two goods in conflict, awareness best underscores the ambivalence central to the tragic intertwining of greatness and limits, of divinity and nothingness.[66] In giving us the fullest sense of our duplicity, it best engenders the traditional moments of fear and pity. Finally, awareness is formally rich, giving rise to some of the greatest speeches of world drama, monologues and dialogues that presuppose awareness of an ineradicable conflict of goods—among others the powerful formulations of Shakespeare's Hamlet, Kleist's Penthesilea, and Brecht's Shen Te/Shui Ta.

The greatest danger of awareness, beyond the earlier mentioned problem of elevating indecisiveness, would seem to be that awareness might easily become overly schematic and allegorical—an abstract weighing of position x versus position y. If, as we have argued, art is defined by its empirical concreteness and sensuous externality, with which it distinguishes itself from philosophy, and its wholeness and harmony, which it shares with philosophy, the artist should present full and whole and concrete characters, and the artist who presents abstractions—be it Corneille or Racine or Ernst—falls short of the aesthetic ideal. The best tragedies avoid this danger by focusing on character as well as conflict, by presenting strong if complex individuals, and by rendering the conflict not only complex and multifaceted in its ramifications and consequences, but also immediate and existential. Indeed, authors who reach this level of tragedy tend to satisfy audiences in this regard. No one would argue that *Hamlet* or *Penthesilea* or *The Man Who Shot Liberty Valance* lacks the fullness of character, the subtlety and complexity, the irresolvable questions and inevitability of suffering, in short, the mystery and awe critics such as Alan Thompson and Normand Berlin rightly see as essential to tragedy.[67]

The Drama of Suffering

The drama of suffering, which is frequently, but undeservedly, called tragic, elevates the moment of suffering at the expense of greatness.[68] In a drama of suffering the protagonist's position is not necessarily justified, the hero exhibits no formal greatness, and no philosophical conflict arises.[69] What we have is simply the portrayal of a character who suffers.

Suffering at the Expense of Greatness

Suffering is a necessary and important element of tragedy. In Aeschylus' *Agamemnon* we hear the famous line: "Man must suffer to be wise" (178). Sophocles' *Antigone* concludes with the suggestion that wisdom comes to those who suffer (1348–1353). The idea that suffering educates and improves is deeply embedded, manifest even in popular sayings such as "Sorrow draws us nearer to God." For Hegel, suffering may trigger a process of reflection that leads to truth (E § 400). Max Scheler recognizes in the suffering individual a context or disposition in which moral improvement might take place.[70] Suffering creates a disorientation that evokes a variety of possibilities, and it may provide a forum in which the self is challenged. Schelling, drawing on a Stoic concept, suggests: "Only in misfortune is virtue tested, only in danger is bravery tried" (Ger 111; Eng 89, translation modified).[71]

Even if wisdom, then, were to presuppose suffering and suffering were often a catalyst for moral improvement, it does not necessarily lead to wisdom or morality and is hardly a criterion for truth. No logical or immediate connection exists between suffering and wisdom. The statement "I suffer and am therefore wise" is hardly persuasive. Indeed, suffering can lead to numbness, apathy, and indifference or even to the invention of lies and illusions that give us a necessary but merely apparent comfort, as Luka advocates, for example, in Gorky's *The Lower Depths*.[72] In addition, we must ask whether suffering per se is as high a principle in art as is wisdom in suffering. Is the essence of a masterpiece like *Oedipus Rex* the hero's *suffering*, as Nietzsche would have it,[73] or his *greatness* in suffering?

Almost accentuating his critique of Hegel's thesis that tragedy contains a moment of reconciliation, Ludwig Marcuse elevates the modern drama of suffering, which he calls "the tragic tragedy," insofar as suffering is given no meaning, no context, no reason: "The absolute tragic essence of the tragic tragedy is suffering without meaning" (*Die Welt* 17–18, my translation). Marcuse continues his definition: "Modern tragedy is now only a cry of existence; not overcoming, not mitigation of suffering: only a compression and formulation as last and only reaction still possible" (*Die Welt* 20, my translation). Tragedy becomes simple suffering—removed from greatness, from causality, from its position within any overarching narrative.

Recognizing neither an overarching order nor any absolutes that might give meaning to suffering, many contemporary theories of tragedy, like Marcuse's, along with an abundance of contemporary "tragedies," elevate suffering and the irrational, chaotic, and often arbitrary forces that elicit suffering.[74] Suffering becomes the whole of tragedy.[75] The most frequent statement of twentieth-century art is that humankind suffers. Adorno, in part following Nietzsche,[76] goes so far as to embrace suffering as the highest principle of art (*Ästhetische Theorie* esp. 387). Twentieth-century suffering, having become exceedingly self-reflective, is often transformed into self-pity.[77] Though nothing is wrong with self-reflection—Hegel argues that it makes philosophy greater than art—the self-reflection of many modern heroes is directed solely toward their own particularity. It is accidental and of no universal interest. Although many contemporary authors sympathize with their weak and suffering heroes, it is difficult to take seriously the suffering protagonist obsessed with her own particularity. If greatness and a concern for ethical substance belong to tragedy, weak heroes preoccupied with their own particularity and reflecting on their own subjectivity, are better housed in comedies. Woody Allen may be the truth of Max Frisch.

In the drama of suffering we often see a tragic flaw but rarely tragic greatness. In Lillo's *Fatal Curiosity*, the hero returns after seven years' absence to his impoverished parents; so that he might indulge his curiosity and heighten the sense of eventual joy, he does not reveal his identity. In order not to unveil himself unwillingly, he withdraws, leaving in his mother's hands the casket of jewels with which he intends to raise them out of their poverty. Weary of their destitute position and having begun to question divine providence, the parents resolve to kill the stranger in order to steal his wealth. The turn of events is ironic but derives solely from weakness. The structure differs greatly from that of the genuine tragedies discussed above, where the hero is more than the victim of bad luck or arbitrary whims. Camus' *The Misunderstanding*, in the author's words "an attempt to create a modern tragedy" (vii) and a "tragedy" as well in the words of Maria, one of the characters (Act III), has in many respects a similar plot: after twenty years, a son returns home to help his mother and sister, does not reveal his identity, and is murdered for his money. As in *Fatal Curiosity*, the hero dies not of a greatness, but of a weakness and of the arbitrariness and absurdity of fate; the play, profound in its own way, is nonetheless not a tragedy, but a drama of suffering.

The drama of suffering often results from the non-assertion of a tragic stance. In Ibsen's *A Doll's House*, Torvald fails to act out a tragic self-sacrifice (recognizing Nora's love and spiting the world to stand with her—the miracle for which Nora had hoped). The illusion of this possibility is broken, and Nora's hopes for a meaningful marriage disappear. Non-recognition of the other (Torvald treats Nora as a play-toy) is connected to non-recognition of self (Torvald cannot reach into the depths of his potential greatness). The non-experience of tragedy is the direct catalyst for mere suffering also in Hauptmann's *Before Dawn*: Loth is incapable of experiencing a conflict between his scientific beliefs and his love for Helene.

Hegel on Suffering

In analyzing tragedy, Hegel stresses not the hero's suffering, nor even her endurance in suffering,[78] but her relation to the absolute. For Hegel the essence of tragedy is structural conflict, not the effect of suffering. Critics of the Hegelian theory are sometimes led to equate tragedy with suffering and so become proponents, wittingly or unwittingly, of the drama of suffering (see, for example, Israel Knox esp. 115–118). Obviously not all suffering need derive from greatness and not all great heroes need suffer (in this sense Nikolai Tschernyschewskij's critique of Hegel, which asserts that suffering is often contingent, is exceedingly simplistic [127–141, 222, 255]). The richer argument is that some suffering is linked to greatness and some forms of greatness cannot avoid suffering; this specifically organic sphere defines the tragic. Tschernyschewskij's argument shows only that tragedy does not exhaust the sphere of aesthetics: suffering without greatness is generally unaesthetic or

comic, and greatness without suffering leads to the drama of reconciliation.

As should be clear from our earlier discussion of Hegel's theory
of fear and pity, mere misfortune is for Hegel not tragic: "After all,
therefore, we should not confuse interest in a tragic denouement
with the naive sense of satisfaction that a sad story, a misfortune
as such, should claim our interest. Such miseries can befall a person, without his contributing to them and without his fault, merely
as a result of the conjuncture of external accidents and natural
circumstances, as a result of illness, loss of property, death, and so
forth, and the only interest in them by which we should properly be
gripped is eagerness to rush to the person's help. If one cannot
help, then spectacles of wretchedness and distress are only harrowing" (15:526; A 1198, translation modified).[79] Our experience of
tragedy, in contrast, borders more on veneration than pity (15:546).
In the drama of suffering, admiration vanishes. Jeffrey Cox, echoing Marcuse, contends that we no longer need tragic heroes, for
"the world as chaos is tragic enough" (250). But a redefinition of
tragedy as suffering in a meaningless world invites narcissistic
self-pity rather than the expansion of horizons evident in the
Hegelian definition of tragedy. Instead of being ennobled by the
sublimity of a tragic hero, the audience is lowered in the drama of
suffering to feelings of pity for the suffering figure with whom it is
invited to identify.

The link between the drama of suffering and the comic can be
underscored by Hegel's discussion of sensations and feelings, which
relate not to the universal but to the particular. The hero whose
world view is determined by her particular suffering has relinquished the sphere of the substantive and the universal and with
it—though Hegel does not explicitly state this—the sphere of tragedy: "This *natural* subjectivity is not yet a self-determining one,
pursuing its own laws, activating itself in a necessary manner, but
a subjectivity determined from without, bound to *this* space and
this time, dependent on contingent circumstances. Through trans-
position into this subjectivity, therefore, all content becomes contingent and is endowed with determinations pertaining only to this
single subject. It is therefore entirely inadmissable to appeal to
mere sensations. Whoever does so, withdraws from what is common to all, the field of reasons, thought, and the matter at hand,
into his singular subjectivity, in which—since this subjectivity is
essentially passive—what is incomprehensible and what is most
evil is able to intrude as well as what is comprehensible and good"

(E § 400 Z, translation modified). The drama of suffering overlooks philosophical structures and renders the sensations absolute. Hegel gives in his *Aesthetics* a series of arguments against this undue elevation of "Empfindungen" and the attempt to employ them as criteria for great art or for divisions within art (13:52–54). The particularity of suffering and the self-indulgence of feeling are hardly measures of excellence: "For reflection on feeling is satisfied with observing subjective emotional reaction and its particularity instead of immersing itself in the object, the work of art, plumbing its depths and thereby relinquishing mere subjectivity and its states. But in the case of feeling, precisely this empty subjectivity is not only retained but is the chief thing, and this is why humans are so fond of having feelings. This too is why reflection of this kind becomes wearisome on account of its indefiniteness and emptiness and disagreeable by its concentration on tiny subjective peculiarities" (13:54; A 33, translation modified). Humans have feeling in common with animals: "it is the brute, sensuous form" (16:129, my translation). For the true tragic hero, suffering is a consequence of what is primary, the hero's greatness; in the drama of suffering and in comedy the hero's suffering relates instead to the hero's particularity. Moreover, whereas the tragic hero partially overcomes suffering, there is no end to the suffering protagonist's reflections on her own wretchedness, misery, and pain.

According to Hegel, a strong character sees the particularity of emotions as secondary to the universality of substance: "A self-possessed person, a great character, can encounter something conforming to his will without breaking out into the feeling of joy, and conversely he can suffer misfortune without abandoning himself to the feeling of pain. Whoever gives way to such feelings is more or less involved in the vanity of attaching special importance to his particular self, to the fact that he in particular is experiencing happiness or sorrow" (E § 472, translation modified). Comic figures, as we shall see below, extol their suffering not only because they want to claim tragic grandeur but because suffering is an eminently particular sensation, and the comic protagonist is obsessed with the particular at the expense of the universal.

Self-Inflicted and Involuntary Suffering

Distinguishing between two kinds of drama of suffering is useful: self-inflicted suffering and, more frequent, involuntary suffering.

Eboli in Schiller's *Don Carlos* causes her own suffering, as does, for example, Puntila in Brecht's *Master Puntila and His Servant Matti*. Neither figure is formally great; neither suffers of goodness. The figures are more comic than tragic. To distinguish, as Heilman suggests, "kinds of catastrophe—the kind that comes from other persons and other forces and the kind that comes from one's own actions," is not enough (*Tragedy* 288). We must differentiate still further between the kind that derives from one's own weakness—and so belongs to the self-inflicted drama of suffering and to comedy—and the kind that comes from greatness and must be called tragic.

Involuntary suffering represents the extrinsic forces that cause suffering. One thinks of the power of nature and of mythology and fate (from the Greek oracle or curse to the *wêwurt* of the early Germanic *Hildebrandslied* and the daemonic powers that rule the nineteenth-century drama of fate); existential anguish (for example, Sartre's *No Exit*); and social criticism (from a Storm and Stress play like Wagner's *The Child Murderess* to Büchner's *Woyzeck*, naturalist drama, and modern American theater, for example, Arthur Miller's *Death of a Salesman* or Sam Shepard's *The Curse of the Starving Class*, also the linguistic theater of Peter Handke, for example, *Kaspar*). Works of this kind, which portray victims, not heroes, often have tremendous force, and such works uncover important elements of experience such as the power of nature or the injustice of society. The objects of critique in a play such as Masefield's *Tragedy of Nan* range from institutional injustice and perverse social conventions to jealousy, callousness, and greed. The suffering in Toller's *Hinkemann* extends from the physical suffering of war and class to interpersonal weakness, brutality, and even metaphysical disorientation.

Involuntary suffering often sets persons in opposition to natural forces, sickness and physical injury, storms and the power of the sea. Hegel argues that these can be catalysts for tragic heroism, as in Euripides' *Alcestis* or Sophocles' *Philoctetes*, but are not themselves tragic (13:269). The audience focuses its interest not on sickness or misfortune but on these as catalysts for spiritual conflict or the defiance of suffering. Although contingency often engenders a conflict or provides the context for a linkage of greatness and suffering, the fact that contingency affects us is not itself tragic. The context of mere suffering must give rise to a tragic predicament and heroic act—as we see, for example, in Athol Fugard's *Sizwe Bansi is Dead*.

Downfall through uncontrollable passions, as in the plays of Seneca, is likewise difficult to term tragic. Phaedra is driven by passions, instincts, desires over which she has lost control. Her misdirection is contrasted with the almost Stoic restraint of Hippolytus. The most tragic figure in Seneca's version of the Phaedra tale is not the passion-driven and evil Phaedra (who enacts a self-inflicted drama of suffering) or Hippolytus (who is a victim of involuntary suffering) but Theseus, who acts brutally, but justly, with the information he has and is devastated, childless and alone, when truth is unveiled. His lines ("It is the pinnacle of sorrow when / chance makes us wish that we could will away / the very things we so desired to see" 1118–1120) are far more tragic than Phaedra's simple loss of control.

Some works move in both spheres, involuntary as well as self-inflicted suffering, Racine's *Phèdre*, for example: the heroine's misery flows from innocence and guilt; she is victimized by the wrath of Venus and her own weakness. Psychological suffering invariably takes on elements of self-inflicted *and* involuntary suffering. Passions are not only external—insofar as they are driven by the objects of our desire; they also arise from an inner lack of will or control. George Barnwell in Lillo's *The London Merchant*, for example, suffers of his weakness, an inability to control his passion, but also of the seductions and schemes of Millwood.

Chekhov's *The Three Sisters* also combines elements of involuntary and self-inflicted suffering. The Prozorov family is victimized by the ruthless Natasha and the sombering and levelling conditions of provincial life, but the family members themselves succumb to self-pity and occasional willlessness. In contrast to Racine's work, Chekhov's play reflects on the dissolution of more than one individual; it is the decay of a family and, symbolically, that of an entire society. The lack of a strict tragic structure, however, pushes the work—as Chekhov himself argued—into the sphere of the comic.[80] The characters, preoccupied with themselves, believe themselves tragic, while Chekhov's point appears to be that they are precisely not tragic. Checkhov's play ends on a note, unusual for a drama of suffering, of resilience. Although competing events and voices do surface, the forceful suggestion is made that life must be affirmed and meaning may yet be found.

It is difficult to determine whether the drama of involuntary suffering or the drama of self-inflicted suffering is in principle higher. What speaks for involuntary suffering is its ability, in the tradition of satire, to sketch social injustice. Büchner, Strindberg, and Bor-

chert provide diverse examples of this strength. To the extent that
self-inflicted suffering becomes solipsistic and still pretends to be
tragic rather than comic and to the extent that involuntary suffering focuses on causes of suffering, involuntary suffering may appear greater. But self-inflicted suffering, where the cause and the
object of suffering are identical, is more organic. The drama of involuntary suffering lacks dialectical unity: the characters do not
forge their own destinies; the events do not unfold from their actions; rather, the characters are fortuitous victims. Art, however,
should be harmonic and unified, even when it portrays suffering or
its characters are evil—as, for example, in Shakespeare. To the
extent that coherence and organicism are privileged aesthetic categories and prerequisites of excellence, self-inflicted suffering must
stand higher.[81] Comedy, an intellectually more advanced genre
than tragedy, does in fact develop this moment of self-inflicted suffering.

Tragedy at its best includes both undeserved suffering (as in the
tragedy of self-sacrifice, insofar as the good person suffers) and deserved suffering (as in the tragedy of stubbornness, insofar as the
hero wills her suffering). The two moments are united in the conflation of justification and guilt that takes place in any tragedy of
collision. Tragedy cannot be just undeserved suffering (as in the
drama of involuntary suffering, an episodic rather than organic
subgenre) or merely deserved suffering (a danger toward which the
tragedy of stubbornness sometimes tends).[82]

The drama of suffering is not to be equated with Aristotle's account of a tragedy of suffering, that is, a simple plot that derives its
effect not from the structures of reversal and recognition but from
emphasis on painful events, including death, that evoke pity and
fear (XVIII; 1456a). Sophocles' *Ajax*, one of Aristotle's examples, is,
despite the level of suffering and the focus on suicide, an example
of stubbornness: Ajax's suffering derives from greatness. Stubbornness can be simple but organic, that is, it can derive from greatness
but still be without any intricate reversals or recognition. Suffering, meanwhile, can be complex but episodic, that is, it may contain a series of ironic reversals, which, however, are not in any way
connected with greatness.

With Szondi, we can argue that in tragedy reversal is superior to
nonreversal, yet against Szondi we can argue that reversal by itself
is not necessarily tragic. Reversal might involve mere suffering,
albeit unexpected, or even comedy. Szondi's stress on suffering and
reversal at the expense of greatness, including the traditionally or-

ganic relation between greatness and suffering, and his abandonment of harmony can be understood in the context of his non-
Hegelian, non-consequential concept of dialectic. Szondi reduces
the dialectic to the *dialectical*: "In this entire work 'dialectic' and
'dialectical' denote in accordance with Hegel's usage, without, however, the implications of his system, the following situations and
processes: unity of opposites, reversal of something into its contrary, the positing of self-negation, self-differentiation" ("Versuch"
159, my translation). Szondi's theory of tragedy, not surprisingly,
ends in reversal and disaster, and his theory of modern drama ends
in the dissolution of intersubjectivity. He does not recognize in the
genre of tragedy or in the history of modern drama any movement
in the direction of synthesis.

We have considered thus far three catalysts for nontragic suffering. Fate, a form of involuntary suffering, destroys persons by way
of the power of natural elements and the haphazardness of circumstance and luck. It received a great deal of attention in antiquity
and in the modern drama of fate. More consistently important
across the ages have been the social catalysts of suffering: the protagonist is victimized by arbitrary and restrictive social conventions, unjust rulers, brutality, or war. In modernity, with a shift
from tragedy to the drama of suffering and the development of sociology as a distinct discipline, the popularity of this form has increased. Finally, we considered psychological suffering, which can
derive from nature (uncontrolled drives), society (interpersonal
conflicts turned inward), or weakness of will. Its increasing popularity in modernity coincides with the development of psychology
as a science. Not surprisingly, the greatest of American dramatists,
Eugene O'Neill, is a master of this form.

An additional cause of suffering is metaphysical. Not all depres-
sion derives from external fate, social injustice, or psychological
factors, be they interpersonal conflict or chemical imbalance. Grap-
pling with insoluble metaphysical problems demands intellectual
rigor (or greatness) and may evoke frustration and discontent (or
suffering). August Wilhelm Schlegel's almost forgotten theory of
tragedy focuses on the subject's external finitude in relation to an
inner infinity and the infinity of truth.[83] Maurice Maeterlinck successfully presents such spiritual despair in *The Blind*. Nonetheless,
here, too, we should not view all metaphysical suffering as tragic.
Reflection on death, specifically on the particularity of one's own
death, has comic potential—insofar as it suggests an obsession
with particularity. Woody Allen's *Love and Death* presupposes this

insight; so, too, the comic lines from his *Manhattan*: "he spoke of his fear of death, which he elevated to tragic heights when in fact it was mere narcissism."

The self-destruction of humanity does presuppose formal and technological greatness, but tragedy also demands a moment of goodness—something that would be difficult to discern in any such scenario.[84] Philosophical arguments for the ethical and political structures that would make it morally obligatory and politically possible for us to avoid self-destruction do exist (Apel, "The A Priori"). The implementation of this is another matter, as is the fear that implementation will not succeed. Tragedy arises where the hero recognizes a theoretical answer to a crisis but is unable to implement it, or recognizes genuine suffering but cannot overcome it. This social problem has a long philosophical history. Hegel refers to it as the problem of the owl of Minerva, and it was familiar to Plato as well (*Timaeus* and *Critias*). The thinker comes too late, after society is already in a process of decay and dissolution. Even this structure, however, may find its truest expression not in tragedy, but in comedy—as I shall suggest below in my analysis of the comedy of withdrawal.

The Merits of the Drama of Suffering

Although the simple depiction of the suffering individual does not necessarily imply great art and although it lacks the tragic dimensions of nobility, greatness, and conflict, it can serve other purposes. Tragedy may include interesting character studies, including the individual's reaction to pain, and social criticism, in particular, analyses of the social forces that cause suffering; nonetheless, these would seem to be the primary domain of a drama of suffering. The greatness of Eugene O'Neill, for example, lies in his ability to explore the psychology of trust and of suffering and to awaken the emotions of his audience. Having freed himself from the organic link between greatness and suffering, he shifts his focus elsewhere. So, too, the naturalist drama of Europe, which attends far more than traditional tragedy to the social and psychological causes of suffering. Not every depiction of a sick and troubled soul, not every representation of a political and social victim is tragic; suffering that derives from a pathological incapacity or an arbitrary act of oppression hardly derives from greatness. Yet, as we have suggested, it may draw our attention to a range of human activity otherwise overlooked.

Important is that the drama of suffering also allow for a general dimension. The reduction of tragedy to the particular subject's suffering and obsession with this suffering, including a preoccupation with one's own death, would seem to find its fulfillment in comedy. Also important is that the hero of suffering be given some virtue, which, even if in tandem with social injustice, causes the hero's downfall. The suffering in O'Neill's *Long Day's Journey into Night* is particularly intense because each character wants to believe in the other, whether it is a wish for good health, success, or virtue.

The drama of suffering often derives strength from its social import and sympathy for the underprivileged. Intrinsic value does not lie in its general form—which lacks requisite qualities of beauty such as organic unity—though it can sometimes be found in its finite form, for example, the manipulation of language. Neither social import nor linguistic brilliance, however, necessarily results in tragedy. *Richard II* is linguistically one of Shakespeare's greatest plays, but Richard is self-absorbed and not a great individual. The play's structure lags behind its linguistic brilliance. If a work lacks philosophical conflict and includes no great characters, the playwright necessarily falls back on the resources of language; for this reason dramas of suffering often excel rhetorically. Ivan Turgenev's *A Month in the Country* illustrates this moment; the self-sacrifice of Rakitin and Belyaev is clearly subordinate to the play's overarching pathos of suffering. Among German writers, Büchner and Kafka illustrate the frequent conflation of negativity and rhetoric, although in more contemporary works—such as those of Franz Xaver Kroetz—language as a means of effecting suffering often gives way to a dependence on other formal structures, for example, long silences and gestures. Finally, language may also offer a formal, rather than philosophical, transcendence of mere negativity. The artwork as an aesthetically pleasing formal construct overpowers the content of disorder and meaninglessness.[85]

Assuming the drama of suffering does not portray a negativity so bleak as to be unbearable, we could also argue that the drama of suffering is a particularly accessible genre. Self-sacrifice presupposes moral commitment, stubbornness requires formal virtues, opposition and awareness demand complexity of thought. The drama of suffering, on the other hand, merely requires identification with a suffering victim. This accessibility, however, might also be viewed as a vice: the lowering of meaning and action to their lowest and simplest denominators.

The drama of suffering may excel in illustrating the earlier mentioned maxim that suffering can be a vehicle for wisdom, even for greatness. Lear's insights, primarily his humility and ability to distinguish substantial from apparent values, gained on the verge of madness, after he has stopped listening to the flatterers of the court, illustrate this point, as do the insights of Gloucester, which arrive only after he is physically blinded. Tolstoy's Ivan Il-yich can recognize the banality of his life only when confronted with the physical pain and spiritual significance of his own dying.[86] Only through extreme suffering does Maura in Synge's *Riders to the Sea* reach a kind of laconic, but eloquent Stoicism. The connection between suffering and wisdom, however, is contingent rather than necessary. A protagonist such as Miller's Eddie Carbone garners no self-knowledge from his suffering. Though Lear moves out of his shell to recognize the suffering of others (II.iv), many a hero of suffering is consumed by self-pity rather than intersubjectivity.

The strength of the drama of suffering is, as we have seen, not the nobility of purpose, the consistency of character, or the philosophical conflict, but the dramatization of the victim's suffering and the portrayal of forces, whether natural, social, psychological, or metaphysical, that destroy the protagonist. In trying to expand tragedy by extending its range of participants, the drama of suffering unwittingly and paradoxically reduces tragedy to mere suffering. The aesthetically less pleasing aspect of the drama of suffering derives from the lack of a collision and the passive rather than willed nature of the suffering. The value of the genre has a tendency to exhaust itself in its deep exposure of negativity. Euripides is the world's master of this form, his *Trojan Women* a pure drama of suffering.[87] Gerhart Hauptmann is Germany's master of the genre. Shakespeare's *King Lear* could be viewed as the greatest drama of suffering ever written,[88] but its excellence is diminished by critics who overlook those moments that raise it above a mere drama of suffering. Similarly, Ibsen's *Ghosts* could be read as an illustration of involuntary suffering, but it becomes a far more meaningful and significant work when read not simply from the perspective of suffering, in this case, hereditary syphilis, but in the light of opposition (vitality versus duty).

Paratragedy or the Tragedy of Suffering

I noted above the comic potential of the drama of suffering—the drama of self-inflicted suffering as a comedy of reduction and the drama of involuntary suffering as a comedy of negation. I have done so partially because tragedy—especially in this century—is often reduced to the drama of suffering, and stressing the comic implications of a suffering that does not derive from greatness better allows us to recognize the gap between tragic suffering and other forms of suffering. But I have also noted several strengths of the drama of suffering and would caution against transforming all unearned suffering into comedy. First, suffering may be undeserved but nonetheless well-endured, and this endurance may exhibit nobility and greatness. Second, suffering that derives from simple inadequacy may not be comic; a moment of greatness may lie in the hero's genuine efforts, which, if absent, would not have led to such pain and frustration. Third, some involuntary suffering is so extreme that to portray it as comic would be to render it almost harmless. Some pain is so great that it cannot be portrayed in any way but seriously, and if such pain does not derive in any way from greatness, then its only aesthetic outlet is the drama of suffering. Even Woody Allen, who portrays the comic dimensions of certain forms of suffering, is not without moments of genuine melancholy and compassion.

Two of these forms of suffering, which are not easily grasped under the rubric of self-sacrifice, stubbornness, or collision, may still merit the status of tragic suffering, such that we can speak in selected cases not of a drama of suffering but of paratragedy or even of a tragedy of suffering. Consider, first, a suffering whose genesis may be weakness, but which leads to greatness and nobility or to a wisdom that engenders yet more suffering. Second, consider a suffering that is accentuated by a formal virtue, namely, moral sensitivity to suffering.

We must not overlook the importance of a form of suffering that is not caused by greatness but engenders greatness and yet a greatness that comes too late to erase the burden of suffering and the consequences of earlier action. Such a work would preserve a bond—albeit via a reverse connection—between suffering and greatness. We have already cited Scheler's argument that suffering can engender growth and eventual greatness. Unearned suffering leads to greatness in Pseudo-Seneca's *Hercules Oetaeus*. The hero is a victim of his wife's jealousy, anger, and revenge. Recognizing that his robe has been soaked in poison, Hercules reacts with grief and tears; he is delirious. But he regains his composure. Rivalling his twelve labors of greatness, he confronts death calmly, almost joyously, unafraid, defiant. Only in suffering is the magnitude of his self-overcoming apparent.

In a different way, Rowe's *The Tragedy of Jane Shore* evidences suffering that passes over into greatness. The play is primarily a drama of suffering, partially self-inflicted, mainly involuntary; however, in one central scene the heroine wills suffering or, more precisely, further suffering, rather than betray her ideals (IV.170–176). Where Seneca's drama depicts noble defiance of suffering by way of strength and endurance, formal virtues if you will, Rowe's drama transcends mere suffering by integrating a moment of self-sacrifice.

The traditional stress on recognition—which surfaces even in theories that elevate the drama of suffering and which we see, for example, in *Lear*—may derive from an intuitive need to see some form of greatness in the tragic hero. Nikita in Tolstoy's *The Power of Darkness* falls prey to the temptations of evil, which culminate in murder. Finding his life wretched, he finally confesses, indeed to more sins than he himself has committed. A moment of greatness lies in his recognition and willingness to admit sin and accept the consequences; the play, therefore, has a moment of tragedy, even if it is subordinate throughout to the structure of mere suffering. The active and organic structure whereby greatness leads to suffering is preferable to the structure whereby suffering evokes greatness—unless of course that greatness in turn elicits more suffering. This would not be the case with *Hercules Oetaeus*, but it would be with *Lear*.

The definition of tragedy as suffering passing over into greatness and nobility will be familiar to some readers as an essential aspect of Schiller's definition of tragedy. In the Anglo-American world it has been put forward most prominently—and apparently independently of any Schillerian influence—by William O'Connor (esp. 46). It is evident as a moment in almost all great tragedies—whether in art, as in Oedipus, or in life, as in Boethius, but it would be difficult to argue that nobility in suffering is by itself the defining feature of tragedy.

Another way of formulating the reverse relation between suffering and greatness overlaps with one answer—developed by Nicolai Hartmann—to the infamous question, why should we find tragic suffering aesthetically pleasing? The formulation focuses on our *perception* of greatness, what Hartmann calls "the aesthetic magic of tragedy" (*Aesthetik* 384, my translation). He writes: "Every good is most strongly experienced as valuable at that moment when it is stolen or withdrawn: the pain of loss allows it to rise to the highest perceptible value" (*Aesthetik* 384, my translation). A person's virtues are most clearly recognized when they are about to disappear, even when this loss doesn't derive from virtue. The insight is not Hartmann's alone, but is poetically expressed in Shakespeare's seventy-third sonnet: "This thou perceiv'st, which makes thy love more strong, / To love that well which thou must leave ere long."

Many forms of suffering can be experienced only because of the insight and sensitivity of the sufferer. Suffering presupposes certain right categories. Sometimes persons suffer because they are more sensitive to problems—the decay of society, for example, or the possible self-destruction of humankind. To suffer about certain things is a sign of maturity and development, even greatness. Tolstoy's Ivan Ilyich, for example, suffers that he is not remarkable; this is remarkable.

The terms "paratragedy" or "tragedy of suffering" might then also be employed for heroes who want to do well, who desire greatness or even normalcy, but who simply lack the capacity, and yet are not comic. Consider C. F. Meyer's novella *The Suffering of a Young Boy*. The protagonist is a child, "conspicuously untalented" (8, my translation). He is gentle, shy, quiet, trusting, without any concept of deception. The child is eager to please, to be dutiful and helpful, but he lacks the capacity. His ultimate and genuine desire is to lead a heroic life, but he simply does not have the ability. The protagonist not only suffers of not reaching his ideal, he is especially sensitive to pain and disapproval. His suffering is deep, especially when he falls victim to the games of his school comrades and the machinations of a Jesuit teacher. His suffering and eventual death seem arbitrary and so raise questions of the theodicy, but the focus, which is here effective, is more on the victim than the victimizers, who are not all of evil intentions. Serious suffering can thus arise when a hero fails to succeed of his own private limitations. The hero's suffering is sincere; Meyer's novella has little in common with a comedy of reduction.

Serious suffering that is not entirely tragic also surfaces in Hardy's novel *Jude the Obscure*. The young Jude, a victim of the callousness and injustice of society, desires to enter the university, working and studying relentlessly and dreaming, but in vain. The pain of his failure is partly the result of his strong aspirations, but it is also introduced as the consequence of class discrimination and the machinations of Arabella and so includes elements of mere suffering. What makes the suffering so strong is the reader's identification with the character to the extent that he has substantial virtues, even if—and this is what renders it mere suffering—they do not cause his suffering: thus, we think of Jude, seeking wisdom and succumbing to the temptations of Arabella. What also renders Jude's suffering acute is the sense of a loss of potential (what Bradley sees as the essence of tragedy) and the fact that Jude has worked so hard to keep others from suffering: we recall his extraordinary efforts to keep innocent beings—birds and earthworms, for example—free of pain.[89] Finally, we sense suffering as especially severe when the hero has already overcome major obstacles (Jude's orphan status, the disinterest of his aunt, the betrayal of Vilbert) and then succumbs to what could have been avoided.[90]

The suffering of Leni in Ludwig Thoma's *Magdalena* might also be viewed as unearned, but non-comic suffering. Leni was wronged and fell into ill-repute, such that she must constantly battle the hypocrisy, callousness, and self-righteousness of the people of her village. She wants to be accepted, she strives to do well, but the odds against her are too great. Even her father, who abuses her verbally, wants in some sense for her to succeed, but he acts out the callous morality of those around him. Leni is not just the passive sufferer; despite her evident physical weakness, she works hard, and despite being the outsider, she seeks integration. We admire her efforts at resisting a debilitating fate, and we have pity for the pain she feels at this unjust treatment. Greatness does not lead to suffering, but the way Leni suffers awakens in the audience a sense that although she is a victim, she is also more than merely passive. She, too, enacts a tragedy of suffering. While it is true that Leni's oppressors could also have been portrayed satirically as protagonists of a comedy of social negation, it belongs to the richness of art that the emotions aroused by, and insights derived from, a drama or tragedy of suffering can be compelling in their own way.

A work that clearly borders the drama of suffering and the tragedy of suffering is Eugene O'Neill's *The Hairy Ape*. Where in reconciliation we see the fulfillment of spirit, here in suffering we see a reverse movement: technological progress (the steamship), material progress (Fifth Avenue), and democratic progress (the workers' union) contrast with Yank's regression out of the intersubjective sphere and his destruction as a human (Zapf). Yank suffers precisely because he desires the synthesis he cannot have; despite his efforts, he is the object, not the subject, of history. Yank lacks any great intellectual insight, but his pain does derive from a genuine desire to belong. If the hero were simply another mindless worker, he would be indifferent to his identity and position in society. Yank, however, wants to belong, wants to be recognized as a person with dignity, and this genuine longing, as it remains unfulfilled, his genuine efforts, as they are thwarted, lead him ever further into despair. In a sense, every drama of suffering in which suffering is taken seriously offers us a protagonist with a certain sensitivity to pain. The difference may lie in the level of greatness, the measure of sensitivity, and the extent to which the work partakes of the merely melodramatic and the pitiful. Yet in all instances comedy seems far removed.

We cannot help but admire a suffering that arises from a sensitivity to issues and problems callously overlooked by others. The hero who, after a lengthy stay in the Third World, returns to the wealth, extravagance, and waste of her homeland and is unable to bear the contradiction between these two forms of life is indeed tragic. We have argued that stubbornness primarily incorporates strength of will, but greatness in general and formal virtues in particular are so broad as to include also tenderness and depth of feeling and thought. Goethe's Tasso comes to mind; to a certain extent also Hamlet. Tasso is a hero of opposition, Hamlet of awareness, but they partake of formal virtues of this sort and embody a greatness often overlooked in definitions of tragedy that focus on will, action, and endurance in suffering (for an exception, see Volkelt, *System* 2:299–301). In our embrace of courage, discipline, and other such formal virtues, we tend to overlook the formal virtue of sensitivity to suffering. One could introduce a subset of the tragedy of stubbornness that stresses such seemingly non-heroic virtues and speak thus of a tragedy of sensitivity.

Each of the two forms of paratragedy—nobility in suffering and sensitivity to suffering—is a hybrid exhibiting elements of the drama of suffering (the suffering does partially derive from weakness) and elements of tragedy (in one instance suffering leads to nobility or greatness—which generally engenders yet deeper suffering; in the other the formal virtue of sensitivity to suffering, including the suffering of others, intensifies suffering). These tragic elements can be peripherally related to earlier tragic genres: one suffers, although a more cynical view might release one from suffering, such that suffering is a form of self-sacrifice; one has the

formal virtue of moral sensitivity to pain, which engenders the experience of pain as well as the formal virtue of genuinely exerting
oneself to one's limits; or without transgressing a norm oneself, one
is sensitive to the transgression of norms and so suffers vicariously.
Rather than being an autonomous form in the dialectic, the tragedy of suffering is a partial tragedy that contains also significant
moments of mere suffering.

Several levels of suffering exist. On the lowest level is pathetic
suffering: the protagonist suffers needlessly and narcissistically,
and she and others take this suffering seriously. Above this and
more or less on an equal level with one another are serious suffering without greatness, for example, as in the drama of involuntary
suffering, and insignificant suffering presented with wit, the transformation of mere suffering into comedy. The greatness of Chekhov
lies partly in his ability to hover between these two moments—
showing, as for example in *The Cherry Orchard*, sympathy for
weak and suffering characters as well as misdirected persons but
also viewing them with an eye to their inconsistencies and so also
with irony and humor.[91] Higher still is unearned suffering that is
carried with nobility and greatness, and highest of all is tragic or
organic suffering, that is, suffering caused by greatness.

Heuristic Value and Elaboration

I have defined tragedy as an action in which the hero's suffering
derives from greatness, that is, the hero's suffering is not contingent but necessary. Depending on the type of tragedy, the hero's
suffering derives from moral greatness (the tragedy of self-sacrifice), formal greatness (the tragedy of stubbornness), the coupling
of both with an uneradicative conflict (the tragedy of opposition), or
the coupling of both with an uneradicative conflict of which the
hero is aware (the tragedy of awareness). The medieval tradition
defines tragedy as the fall of a great person. Chaucer writes: "Tragedie is to seyn a certeyn storie, / As olde bookes maken us memorie,
/ Of hym that stood in greet prosperitee, / And is yfallen out of
heigh degree / Into myserie, and endeth wrecchedly" ("The Prologue of The Monk's Tale" 3163–3167). The structure also informs
many modern dramas, for example, Grillparzer's *King Ottocar's
Fortune and Fall*. Contemporary tragedies are simpler still: the
suffering of any person. Central to the dialectic of tragedy, however, is the link between the protagonist's virtues and her suffer-

ing.[92] On the basis of such a definition, which presupposes that good art be organic, even if complexly so, the first four forms all hold, but the fifth, the drama of suffering, falls short.[93]

The initial two forms along with the drama of suffering might be viewed as deficient forms of the Hegelian model. In a tragedy of collision one hero will likely exhibit the supremacy of a position by pledging her life for it; another is stubbornly unwilling to compromise, even when the limits of her position are evident; and in the wake of such a collision innocent persons suffer. In their autonomy the forms are deficient. They render individual moments absolute: content at the expense of complexity, form at the expense of content, and suffering at the expense of conflict and greatness. What they gain in terms of focus, they lose in terms of wholeness. The greatest tragedy has all moments: moral goodness, formal strength, complexity, awareness, and suffering. In the tragedy of opposition, we see from the hero's perspective self-sacrifice and from the opponent's perspective stubbornness. In tragic awareness the hero must sacrifice her belief in a simple and just world and knowingly violate a good. The merging of self-sacrifice and stubbornness in opposition, and especially in awareness, is nothing other than the result of the typology's dialectical structure.

Self-sacrifice reaches a peak when it borders on collision, when it is presented as a conflict of goods. This may involve the conflict between the hero's life or well-being and action on behalf of the good, or collision may be underscored insofar as the self-sacrificing hero confronts an already established world, which—as the real representation of ethical life—has a certain formal legitimacy. Likewise, stubbornness fulfills its highest potential when it points toward a collision, the conflict of goodness versus formal virtues or, in a particular variant, the elevation of one virtue at the expense of another. Even as self-sacrifice and stubbornness differ from collision, they find therein their greatest fulfillment. In addition, both self-sacrifice and stubbornness surface more frequently and are more dramatic in periods of conflict, that is, during paradigm shifts, which are in part pushed forward or held back by the tragic heroes.[94] Heroes who are in advance of their time, as are many heroes of self-sacrifice, invite a conflict of values. At times, the herald of the new pursues her course in such a way as to ignore the value of the present or to undermine her own position, thus embodying stubbornness. More commonly, the stubborn hero holds on to the stability or formal greatness of the past and is destroyed by historical developments that transcend her. From a reverse angle, we can say that certain instances of collision contain within them subordinate moments of self-sacrifice and stubbornness.

Heuristic Value

The typology has beyond any internal merit heuristic value. First, and on the simplest level, it provides us with clearer categories in answering inevitable questions such as: "What is tragedy?" or "Is this work a tragedy?" Hegel's highly restricted definition of tragedy can hardly do justice to the diversity of the genre, which is stressed, for example, in Adrian Poole's recent book on Greek tragedy and Shakespeare (1–14, 132).[95] A definition that allows for both diversity and unity by elaborating a limited number of basic structures should be useful not only to the philosopher but to the student of literature as well. The definition allows for precision. We recognize what constitutes tragedy and are able to distinguish its qualities from those, for example, of mere suffering.

Second, in asking the question "What kind of tragedy is this work?" we do more than execute a schoolbook lesson. The typology encourages us to formulate subquestions that penetrate to the core of a dramatic text. Clearer generic conceptions facilitate more challenging interpretive questions.[96] To interpret the meaning of a work is often to understand its genre, and vice versa. In applying the typology to individual works, we are tempted to ask such questions as: Does the hero's suffering (or further suffering) result in any way from greatness? Is the initial cause for suffering internal or external, and if it is internal, does it follow from a moral act? Is the hero in a double bind, which forces her to act as she does, or is the position she chooses untenable and the alternative, which she overlooks, genuine? Is the hero's conflict universal or culturally determined? Is there anything great about the hero that raises her above her contemporaries?

The kinds of questions that derive from the typology can also generate and clarify conflicting readings. Is, for example, Euripides' *Hecuba* a drama of suffering, a tragedy of stubbornness, or both? Is Calderón's *The Constant Prince* a martyr drama or a genuine tragedy of self-sacrifice? Is Shakespeare's *Romeo and Juliet* a tragedy of self-sacrifice (each main character is unwilling to live without the other), a tragedy of stubbornness (in the consequential nature of the characters' passions and suicide), or a drama of involuntary suffering (insofar as chance plays a prominent role in determining the outcome)? Do the surrounding players advance moments of mirroring stubbornness, and if so, how does this tragic structure relate to the conflict of culturally determined aprioris in the process of dissolution, that is, the transition to reconciliation?

Do the mixed sympathies engendered by Thomas Otway's *Venice Preserved* derive from a truly tragic opposition or from inconsistencies in the age and weakness of character, as reflected in the mixed motives of the conspirators and the wavering loyalties of Jaffeir, thus rendering the play at best a tragedy of suffering? What is at stake if we read Grillparzer's *A Fraternal Quarrel in the House of Hapsburg* as a tragedy of awareness, or if we read it as a tragedy of stubbornness or opposition? What evidence speaks for each reading, and which factors are left unaccounted for if we elevate any one reading?

Is Chekhov's *The Seagull* a drama of suffering, as the titular symbol suggests, or does it contain moments of a tragedy of suffering—whether it be Treplev's sensitivity to suffering or Nina's endurance and faith? Is Miller's *A View from the Bridge* a tragedy of stubbornness or a drama of self-inflicted suffering? Is his *Death of a Salesman* a drama of suffering or a tragedy? If we want to argue that the play is a drama of suffering, is Willy's suffering involuntary or self-inflicted or some combination thereof? Is he the victim of his illusions and weaknesses, or does he fall prey to a ruthless system that has only instrumental use for its workers?

A new typology also invites structural comparisons of plays within a particular form, for example, *Oedipus Rex* and *The Deputy*, *Ajax* and *Brand*, *Antigone* and *Agnes Bernauer*, *Hamlet* and *Penthesilea*, *Woyzeck* and *The Curse of the Starving Class*. Such comparisons may shed light not only on the works themselves but also on the typology, which can benefit from detailed analysis of individual works, including comparisons.[97] The typology would also gain through detailed historical analyses, specifically the correlation of different subgenres with specific, in part cyclical and not necessarily linear, periods in which a subgenre is prominent. Historical focus might give us cause to create further differentiation within the individual subgenres. A philosophical study of genre need not ignore historical factors.

Finally, the typology allows us to view the tragic subgenres in a fairly differentiated and complex hierarchy. Different subforms tend to have specific strengths, and the individual subgenres must guard against weaknesses intrinsic to their own forms. Beyond this, there exist in principle higher and lower, more complex and

simpler, subforms. Paul Hernardi has argued that "the better part
of recent genre criticism has . . . tended to be descriptive rather
than prescriptive" (8). This is the natural consequence of a lack of
grounds, as is the widespread hesitation to evaluate works of literature. But even the statement that no objective criteria for evaluation exist assumes a theory of literature; moreover, it presupposes
a theory that, on its own terms, is no better than any other. In
addition, every theory, even the seemingly nonprescriptive theory,
is inherently exclusionary and prescriptive (it excludes the viability of any hierarchy, even as it considers itself *superior* to hierarchical theories). Evaluative criticism of any kind presupposes a
prescriptive method, even if it remains unacknowledged. The contradiction between the proliferation of critical comments on works
and the concurrent tendency to discredit prescriptive theories does
not speak for the coherence of contemporary literary criticism.[98]
Given, then, that prescription is unavoidable, we should do our
best to ground our structures of evaluation. If a theory of literature
is grounded, so too will be its mode of evaluation. If a theory lacks
a ground, its mode of evaluation, whether explicit or implicit, will
be arbitrary.

Time

Tragedy, then, is greatness that leads to suffering, but why doesn't
all greatness lead to suffering? What specific connections link the
two? An important ingredient sometimes overlooked in competing
analyses is time or temporality.[99] For a God, there could be no tragedy—there would always be enough time, always an opportunity to
reorder. For humanity, time is final. In the various spheres of nature and science, time has increasing degrees of importance (Prigogine). In mechanics we see reversible processes, such as the motion of a frictionless pendulum. Chemistry and thermodynamics
are more sensitive to temporality, as, for example, in the irreversible mixing of water and alcohol. In biology as well as in the cultural and social spheres, and thus for humanity, time is especially
crucial, for its processes are consistently irreversible: you cannot
undo death; killing cannot be revoked, nor can certain actions, once
done, be changed or altered. Even their consequences are often permanent. Moreover, unique to the human sphere is consciousness of
time, knowledge of death, and an intimate sense of limits. The hero
seeks the impossible; time grants her only what is possible. The

hero and audience ultimately recognize this. While the tragic hero transcends certain limits in exhibiting greatness, the suffering triggered by this greatness marks an objective limit. Death is disastrous for the human being as natural entity. Nonetheless, to the essence of humanity belongs that its highest purpose transcend nature, thus making possible the reconciliatory moment in tragedy.

Whereas the tragic hero remains solid and stationary in her position, the comic hero changes and adjusts through time. This corresponds to Hegel's assessment of tragedy and space as objective categories and comedy and time as categories of subjectivity. The tragic hero is statuesque, the comic hero fleeting. Time is nonetheless essential to tragedy. The tragic hero's doom derives partly from the necessary temporality of spirit; the stable tragic hero gives way to the history of spirit that transcends her: "World history in general is thus the unfolding of Spirit in *time*, as nature is the unfolding of the Idea in *space*" (12:96–97; PH 75). Iteration is prominent in comedy, but in tragedy we see little repetition: instead the greatness of the hero derives from the originality and uniqueness of her actions, which do not allow for repetition.

In self-sacrifice the hero arrives too early. Her norms are not those of society. Unable to buy time and unable to postpone needs, she persists and is sacrificed by her age. The evil hero of stubbornness, Macbeth, for example, seeks to master time but cannot. The stubborn hero who recognizes goodness does so when it is too late. Her deeds are done; they cannot be undone. She has only to suffer the consequences of her actions. In tragedies of collision, any hero who seeks compromise must suffer the pressing needs of the moment, the lack of time to reconcile conflicting positions. With infinite time all conflicts could be avoided or reconciled. Not surprisingly, then, the tragic hero—of whatever type—reflects on the shortness of time.[100]

In contrast, the comic hero, obsessed with the particular, has no sense of the general brevity of life, of time as it forever shortens her life and limits her possibilities. On the contrary, time unravels events for the good of the hero, as in *Twelfth Night* (II.ii.40), or it brings forgiveness, as in *The Winter's Tale*. Comedy, like the drama of reconciliation, allows for the mitigation of pain. Indeed, built into the structure of comedy—here the genre is less mimetic than tragedy—is that temporal action and probability be interrupted by the parabasis or by self-reflexive asides. In comedy, time is either irrelevant or a force of redemption.

The character Lester, played by Alan Alda, in Woody Allen's

Crimes and Misdemeanors says something more profound than he intends when he asserts that "comedy is tragedy plus time." With more time, tragedy could be avoided; with time pressing, action must be taken. Lester's intention is to focus not on the sharpness and irreversibility of time, but on the distance created through time. Here, too, lies an overcoming of tragedy. Time is the healer of suffering, bringing forgiveness and reconciliation. Not only does the distance of time invite forgiveness, irreversibility encourages repentance. Consider the hero who knows that death is near, that no other time remains, who renounces her deeds and turns to God; we need think only of Hitchcock's *I Confess*. A significant aspect of time is age and the process of aging. If existence in time belongs to the essence and greatness of humanity, then aging and mortality are the painful consequences of this condition. As we age, we have less time to be great; as we near death, we suffer the loss (and essence) of humanity.

The frequent—yet not all-pervasive—tragic motif of the hero's recognition arriving too late, or the hero's just action being delayed, normally occurs within the antithetical modes of tragedy, stubbornness and opposition. In self-sacrifice, heroes act as they should and only rarely do they delay too long; any resulting disaster would be contingent rather than necessary, and it would surely not derive from greatness. The self-sacrificing hero suffers not of belated recognition, but of seeing more of truth than her contemporaries and acting accordingly. Always in stubbornness the hero should have acted differently, and whenever this antithetical form includes a moment of recognition—as with Shakespeare's Othello or Sidney Kingsley's Rubashov—it invariably arrives too late. Rubashov, the hero of *Darkness at Noon*, would have altered his position, had the impetus for meaningful change only arrived sooner. Because the stubborn hero pursues an untenable position with great force, she quickly goes too far. For Macbeth it is too late to turn back: "I am in blood / Stepped in so far that, should I wade no more, / Returning were as tedious as go o'er" (III.iv.137–139). Opposition functions much like stubbornness; but in opposition, even if the hero did gain recognition, she would not be saved.

In awareness the hero already knows of alternatives. Deliberating on them may in some instances prevent the hero from acting until conditions have become worse; Hamlet is a good example. One way to view the contrast between stubbornness and awareness is to suggest that for Othello action is too quick and reflection postponed, whereas for Hamlet reflection lasts too long, thus delaying action until it is too late. Within the tragedy of awareness the sense of belatedness sometimes occurs after the hero suppresses reflection and enacts one pole—that is, for a moment the hero enters the sphere of stubbornness; clear recognition of the erring path arrives after the fact, when it is too late to reverse an action and its consequences. Kleist's *Penthesilea* is a good example. Previous actions, especially when they involve death, are irreversible. However much they add to tragedy, belatedness and the irreversibility of time nonetheless do not suffice as grounds for tragedy; otherwise, we would call plays of suffering such as Lillo's *Fatal Curiosity* or Camus' *The Misunderstanding* tragic. Like the use of *peripeteia*, these temporal structures add force to the drama of suffering (without making it tragic), just as they add power to any tragedy.

Time is essential to tragedy also in the sense of location in time. A paradigm shift, as we have seen, is conducive to every tragic subgenre; the hero may arrive too early, linger too long, or two poles may compete for superiority. If Goethe's Götz von Berlichingen, as Lukács argues, had been situated in an earlier era, even only one generation earlier, Götz would have been a legendary hero; no conflict would have arisen. If he were set in a later period, again perhaps only a generation removed, he would have been a tragicomic Don Quixote (Lukács, *Entwicklungsgeschichte* 83–84).[101] Indeed, we can go further and argue that because Goethe does not portray the bureaucracy positively enough, because the representatives of the modern state are simply evil and weak, the chance for a great tragedy, a genuine collision, is missed. Goethe does not see here, as he does later in *Torquato Tasso*, the necessity of a transition from the age of heroes to the impersonal, bureaucratic power of the modern state. A work that deals with a similar transition, Ford's *The Man Who Shot Liberty Valance*, gives a more balanced presentation of the greatness and limits of the hero and the inevitability of the transition to the modern state, which—despite its weaknesses—has its political necessity and moral legitimacy. The temporal position of the narrative is on the brink of the two eras, and the valuing is more even; thus, the work is rich in its complexity, and the collision is genuinely painful and tragic for each side (Roche and Hösle).

One final respect in which time is essential to tragedy is the time of suffering or death in the life-narrative of the individual or culture. The suffering of tragedy always represents a loss of potential; the great hero must give way. Thus, the decay of a culture before it has ripened, the death of a child before she has blossomed, seems more tragic than the decline of an old culture that is well past its prime or the death of an elderly person who has already lived a full life. In this sense I suggested earlier that Antigone is more tragic than Socrates.

Guilt

In Hegel's analysis of tragedy, a theme as central as time is guilt. Dürrenmatt, having erased the concept of responsibility and thus of tragedy, also eliminates guilt. Dürrenmatt correctly argues that as soon as guilt disappears, so, too, do autonomy and tragedy; witness the non-tragic conclusion of the Judah narrative in Allen's *Crimes and Misdemeanors*. Guilt forms the essence of Hegel's analysis of *Antigone* in the *Phenomenology of Spirit*. In acting, each character must violate one good even as she preserves another; thus, Hegel speaks of the hero as both guilty and innocent (15:545). Moreover, in ancient drama the hero's identity is one with a universal or a cause; thus, the hero's guilt is the guilt of that principle or, we might say, the hero's innocence, for only as an autonomous being can one be guilty. The tragic hero, then, is an individual and is guilty only insofar as she is active and free, more than a puppet of fate. Freedom is for Hegel not indecision followed by arbitrary choice but identification with a cause and action that affirms this identification. The hero is innocent in two respects and guilty in two respects: innocent because the hero adheres to the good and because she acts on behalf of a principle; guilty because the hero must violate a good and because she wills to identify with that principle. Guilt presupposes action for which the hero is responsible; the hero seeks not sympathy or pity but recognition of the substance of her action, including its consequences. Thus Hegel's formulation: "It is the honor of these great characters to be culpable" (15:546; A 1215). Hegel's differentiation of tragedy from mere suffering centers around the question of guilt. After distinguishing from tragedy the merely pitiable and harrowing misfortune caused by circumstance, he continues: "A truly tragic suffering, in contrast, is inflicted on individuals only as a consequence of their own deed, which is both legitimate and, owing to the collision, blameworthy, and for which their whole self is answerable" (15:526; A 1198, translation modified).

No moral principle, however complex in its hierarchy of values, can be an unfailing guide to all possible moral conflicts. Even when the hero is in a moral double bind such that she cannot in any way be legally guilty, she remains morally guilty. Even the hero who knows the necessity of her actions, be it Hebbel's Judith, Anouilh's Creon, or Joffe's Altamirano, must—with true insight into the collision of goods—also experience guilt. Genuine tragedy gives us as much suffering as reconciliation; critics who argue that Hegel overemphasizes reconciliation make a valid point, though they should not underestimate his awareness of the significance and ineradicability of tragic guilt. For Hegel tragedy consists not solely in physical suffering or death but in ethical and psychological suffering, which is especially pronounced in awareness. Guilt is strengthened if the hero recognizes her guilt: objective guilt increases when fewer arguments exist for the hero's transgression, as is the case in stubbornness. This recognition often leads the hero to take her life—a sense that justice must be done to oneself. *Othello* is the greatest example. In self-sacrifice, where duty supersedes interest, we rarely speak of guilt: here, tragedy lies solely in bad fortune and virtue, unless the bad fortune derives from an earlier guilt. Guilt is not universal in tragedy, but it does arise in any transgression of the good, any strictly Hegelian form of tragedy, and it does deepen our sense of tragedy, especially when awareness of guilt arises either when it is too late or when no objective alternative to the hero's destiny is offered.

A mistaken idea of modernism and postmodernism is that if we can free ourselves from guilt and the burden of the past, then all will be well, for guilt and objectivity have only negative consequences. Helpful in this context is Chekhov's masterful story "The Student," which illustrates several important ideas. First, guilt is a freeing experience; a Nietzschean world without guilt and responsibility is in contrast empty. In recognizing guilt, we take ourselves seriously and search for a higher self. Second, suffering is not to be bemoaned or erased, nor to climax in self-pity; rather, it is to be affirmed as a source of insight and, eventually, even joy. Finally, Chekhov's story illustrates the beautiful idea of history as a chain; for an archaic, as opposed to a postmodern, culture, links are present to the past, and characters are able to recognize the problems and greatness of the past as our own. The story of Peter is the story of the present: "The student thought again that if Vasilisa had shed tears, and her daughter had been troubled, it was evident that what he had just been telling them about, which had happened nineteen centuries ago, had a relation to the present—to both women, to the desolate village, to himself, to all people . . .

truth and beauty which had guided human life there in the garden
and in the yard of the high priest had continued without interrup-
tion to this day, and had evidently always been the chief thing in
human life and in all earthly life, indeed" (108). It would be difficult to find a more eloquent argument on behalf not only of the joy
of responsibility and meaning of suffering but also of the value of
measuring texts from different cultures and eras with universal
categories.[102]

Schiller's "Don Carlos"

To illustrate the typology further, I turn now to Schiller's *Don
Carlos*, a complex work that includes moments of all four kinds of
tragedy as well as the drama of suffering.[103] The complex action of
Schiller's eighteenth-century play revolves around the revolutionary desires of Marquis Posa; the support Don Carlos fails to give
Posa as he becomes distracted by his love for his stepmother, the
Queen; and the dilemmas confronting the King, as he contemplates
not only his political power but his relations with those around
him.

In *Don Carlos*, at least two figures illustrate the tragedy of self-
sacrifice: the Queen and, eventually, Don Carlos. The Queen
clearly loves Don Carlos,[104] but she is willing to renounce this love,
initially, for propriety and, eventually, so that Carlos might be free
to fulfill his mission as a liberator. True to the structure of tragic
self-sacrifice the Queen is ethically admirable. In affirming her virtuous and dutiful stance she seems almost to quote from Schiller's
formulation of the sublime: "How great is our virtue, / If our hearts
break in the practice of it!" (I.v, translation modified). The titular
hero undergoes a tragedy of self-sacrifice when he eventually decides to follow the Queen's example; at the end of the play, Don
Carlos sacrifices personal desires for his social mission. He wills to
act out the rhetoric the Queen offered him in the first act: "And
earn the right to rank first in this world / By sacrificing what no
other can!" (I.v). His renunciation of worldly desires is underscored
in the play's final scene by his symbolically being clothed as a
monk and by his tempered body language, which contrasts with his
earlier eccentricity.

More interesting as a tragic hero is the King.[105] Philipp experiences a conflict between his political role as king, which requires
an apparatus of power, hierarchical structures, and strict rules of

interaction, and his human desire for friendship, for intersubjectivity and symmetry.[106] The King is isolated from his son, his wife, and his servants. He is a victim of the master-slave dilemma Hegel was later to articulate in the *Phenomenology of Spirit*. The King wants to be assured of his strength and so must destroy (or at least diminish) the power of others. This also leads to a loss in terms of potentially positive action: the King reacts negatively against the influence of others and so rejects what he might otherwise condone. As a result of his desire for preeminence, valid positions are overthrown, and no equal remains to recognize the King. The various characters are not recognized by the King, and they themselves are *forced* to recognize him: such recognition is worthless. Self-consciousness receives fulfillment only in reciprocal recognition, that is, in the self-consciousness of another. Carlos tempts the King with images of a symmetrical relationship, a solution to this ever present asymmetry:

> If you want love, then here within this bosom
> There is a spring more vigorous and fresh
> Than in those dull and boggy reservoirs
> That Philipp's gold must open first.
> [. . . .]
> How sweet,
> How joyous it can be to find ourselves
> Exalted in another lovely spirit,
> Our joys put color in another's cheeks,
> Our fears cause other hearts to palpitate,
> Our sorrows bring the tears to other eyes! (II.ii)

But Carlos is not equal to the King's demands. Philipp responds "not without emotion": "The happiness / You picture, you would never, ever grant me" (II.ii). The King suffers from his partial divinity; he has no equal,[107] yet he longs for friendship:

> Give me a real person, good Providence—
> You have given me much. Now give me one
> True human being. You—you are alone,
> Your eyes examine what is hidden to me,
> I ask you for a friend; for I am not,
> As you, omniscient. (III.v, my translation)

The King wants friendship, but as the following allusion to classical and Biblical mythology suggests,[108] his thirst for what transcends obedience remains unquenched:

> 'Tis King! And only King
> And King again! Is there no better answer
> Than empty, hollow echoes? Here I beat
> Upon this rock and ask for water, water
> To ease my feverish thirst—and in return
> He gives me gold. (III.ii)

Posa articulates the King's dilemma in III.x, a dilemma that in its
structure borders on a tragedy of collision:

> You still remain yourself a human—
> A being from our Creator's Hand. You
> As mortal have to suffer, to desire;
> *You* need compassion—and before a God
> Human beings can only sacrifice.
> Tremble and pray to Him! Regrettable
> Exchange! Unhappy twist of Nature!—When
> You degraded humankind to your lyre,
> Who then could share your harmony? (my translation)

Philipp's isolation stems from his greatness, and this wretched
knot is what Thomas Mann's Tonio Kröger finds so fascinating and
Mann's Adrian Leverkühn will later embody.[109]

The King's awareness of an alternative that can never be fulfilled—neither by his servants nor by a humanitarian, who must
despise the King's other nature—intensifies his suffering. Momentarily, Posa becomes the King's equal, in the King's words, "the
only person who does not need me!" (III.v, my translation). But the
King is ultimately shaken to hear that Posa thinks so little of him.
The King's famed tears represent, in a reversal of the text's water
imagery, the dissolution of symmetry, but in a different manner
from what the King is used to.[110] Where others look up to the King,
Posa, the one person whose views matter, looks down on him. Posa
destroys the moment of humanity he nurtured in the King. For the
King, Posa was "my first love" (V.ix).

In response to Posa's betrayal the King abandons all reflection
on mutual recognition and withdraws into his role as God: he kills
his son. Inverting the meaning of the cross and the transmission of

Christ to the secular authorities, the King turns his son over to the religious authorities, who are without morality. The King knows that the sun is setting on his reign, but he, a master of formal or secondary virtues, will hold on as long as he can. His humanity having been betrayed, he returns to the only other world he knows. The ruthless consistency of the King's stance is both shocking and perversely admirable:

> [. . .] For
> One evening more the world is mine. I want
> To use it, this one evening, so that when
> I'm gone, no planter for ten generations
> Will harvest anything from this scorched earth. (V.ix)

The King becomes one with the Grand Inquisitor, blind to human qualities. His words of Act IV—"I honor henceforth no moral custom / And no voice of nature and no contract / of nations" (IV.ix, my translation)—become reality. The King is formally great and consistent; however wretched his stance might be, his is a tragedy of stubbornness.

Posa may be the most complex tragic figure in the text. He affirms a good, namely freedom, but his means toward freedom undermine the very goal he seeks.[111] His position is thus untenable.[112] Posa, too, assumes the status of a god. Don Carlos compares him to Christ: "As long as mothers / Have given birth, there is but *one*—just *one* / Who died so undeservedly" (V.iv). Posa compares God to an artist and then views himself in the same terms (III.ix), though he later recognizes his hubris: "Who is the individual who dares / To steer the weighty helm of chance, and yet / Can never claim to be the omniscient one?" (IV.xxi, my translation). Posa's hubris is related not so much to his personality as to the structure of his position and his attempt to preserve freedom by denying freedom. Posa uses the King in the same way that he accuses Philipp of using others. Posa's behavior toward Don Carlos is equally tyrannical:[113] Posa decides that the letter from the King to Eboli must be destroyed and, symbolically significant, he revokes Carlos' autonomy by placing him in jail.

Posa embodies Schiller's definition of the idealist. The idealist is obsessed with the primacy of an idea. Because the idealist is not concerned with individuals, her behavior swings from generosity (she is not concerned with herself) to ruthlessness (she will do anything to realize her ideal). Posa, consistent to the end, sacrifices even his own individuality:[114] "It's past. 'Twas Carlos or myself. The choice / Was quick and frightful. One was to be lost, / And I want to be that one" (IV.xxi). Tragic stubbornness becomes, for a moment at least, tragic self-sacrifice. Schiller depicts in Posa's actions the limits of abstract idealism.[115] Posa's passage from freedom to tyranny shows that the truth of freedom is necessity, even if Schiller depicts this truth in a negative, rather than harmonic, way.[116] In working through this intellectual position, Posa becomes the hero of a tragedy of stubbornness.

Because Posa and the King conflict with one another, we can speak either of mirroring stubbornness or—if we were to stress their submerged moments of goodness—tragic opposition.[117] Owing to the King's ruthlessness, however, such a moment of opposition is minor indeed. Another potential collision would be between Posa and Don Carlos. Each has a different concept of humanity. Don Carlos focuses on individuals and personal relations: thus the text's emphasis on his love for the Queen; his longing for a fraternal relationship with Posa; and his idealistic view of Eboli. It is Carlos who articulates the concept of friendship in a conversation with Posa, Carlos who speaks of Posa and himself as "brothers," and Carlos who stresses the discrepancy between genuine friendship and the lies of social discourse (I.ix). Posa, on the other hand, tends to look past the individual. He thinks of the abstraction *Menschheit*, rather than the individual *Mensch* (Butzlaff 104). Posa's readiness to sacrifice the particular for the universal (in Carlos he would create "a paradise for millions" IV.xxiv) and his stubborn, unrelenting, and inflexible pursuit of a purpose place him in horrifying proximity to the Grand Inquisitor, for whom persons are "just numbers, nothing more" (V.x., my translation; cf. Ernst, *Der Zusammenbruch* 217–218). Unlike Posa, Don Carlos recognizes the value of the individual and, in contrast to the stubborn Posa, appears—at least in principle—capable of change and development.[118] A performance of the play that decides to overlook Don Carlos' comic weaknesses—which I discuss below—would do well to accentuate these elements of opposition rather than present Carlos simply as a protagonist of suffering. A concept of tragic collision delineated in this way would place *Don Carlos* in a line with later works whose structures of opposition also accentuate the conflict of the individual and the whole, for example, Büchner's *Danton's Death* and Weiss's *Marat/Sade*. Don Carlos could be elevated in this regard also as a counterforce to the King. Whereas the King rejects Don Carlos in Act II as weak, more a human being than a prospective ruler, the son represents the undernurtured human side of the King that will trigger his tragedy.[119]

One might at first think that *Don Carlos* contains a tragedy of awareness: Posa is caught between his friendship for Don Carlos and his commitment to political freedom for Flanders. But the play never develops this conflict. Unlike other central characters in Schiller's plays—Karl Moor, Wallenstein, Johanna, Tell—Posa undergoes no serious indecision or self-doubt. Hinrichs claims that Posa experiences a "collision of consciousness" (2:234, my translation), but the collision is more one of principle than of reality; friendship is sacrificed for humanity without any substantive reflections or doubts.[120] From his youth onward, Posa treats Don Carlos not as an end but as a means toward his higher ideals. Posa is not Don Carlos' personal friend: "I stand here not as Roderick, / Not as the playmate of the boy prince—/ A representative of humankind / Embraces you" (I.ii, translation modified). Posa states: "My heart, / though dedicated to just one alone, / Encompassed the whole world!—In Carlos' soul / I created a heaven for millions" (IV.xxi, my translation). The King asserts insightfully:

> [. . .] A Posa does
> Not die for a mere boy. Friendship's meager
> Flame will not fill a Posa's heart. It beat
> For all humankind. His longing was for
> The world with all its coming generations. (V.ix, translation
>   modified)

Posa elevates humanity over the individual also in his unjust treatment of the King, which is never fully reflected in Posa's consciousness. We hear not a word of indecision or remorse about Posa's deception, which alone allows him to make his appeal to the King for just, communicative, and symmetrical relations.

Another potential moment of awareness could be purely strategic. Should Posa work with the King or with Don Carlos? Whose confidant should he be? Posa recklessly wavers between the two, creating doom for the King's better character, which Posa had nurtured, as well as for his friendship with Don Carlos. Yet this indecision and inconsistency are met with little self-reflection. A thematic weakness of this rhetorically powerful play is its inability to develop these potentially interesting conflicts: serving a friend versus serving humankind and the instrumentalization of the one for the purpose of bettering the whole.

The drama of suffering, on the other hand, is clearly present. Eboli exemplifies a self-inflicted suffering. Her flaw is her weak insight: she misreads Don Carlos' love for the Queen as love for her, she assumes Don Carlos knows about the King's advances on her, and she concludes that the Queen loves Don Carlos in such a way that he is justified in expecting a letter from the Queen. Eboli acts according to this false information, suffers, and finally repents, but she is hardly an admirable character—either morally or formally.

Don Carlos, a self-pitying character, could also be said to be the hero of a drama of suffering. His father after all has stolen his bride; but such suffering is neither intellectually nor dramatically interesting. That we as viewers must spend so much time with Carlos' self-absorption and suffering before the playwright presents an almost undeveloped transition to the tragedy of self-sacrifice is a weakness. Carlos' motivation for self-sacrifice is, moreover, suspect. He seems not to have moved beyond the earlier structure of external impetus, even if Posa has replaced the Queen as his inspiration.[121] This weakens the moment of admiration intrinsic to the tragedy of self-sacrifice. Also weak is Carlos' inconsistency. He seems to love the Queen and Eboli. He asserts his purpose early, then abandons it, and the cycle continues after Posa's death. Moreover, he tells the King of Posa's intrigue, a matter he should have kept silent, and despite Lerma's warning that Don Carlos leave immediately, he insists on meeting the Queen. In his portrayal of Carlos, Schiller offers psychological insight into a weak and troubled personality, a theme that quickly wears thin.[122] Even Schiller admits that he lost interest in Carlos (*Letters on Don Carlos*, no. 1). If Carlos exhibits brief moments of self-sacrifice or opposition, he is nonetheless presented most prominently as a weak and vacillating protagonist of suffering. Where Marquis Posa weighs in too far in favor of the universal, Don Carlos is obsessed with the particular. This explains not only general patterns of behavior such as the preoccupation with private desires and the inability to sustain his resolve but also specific incidents, such as his quick transformation before the Queen during his duel with Alba and his unmediated infatuation with Eboli. He is ever distracted by what is before him and, like the comic hero, often succumbs to hyperbole, again the result of his focus on what is present without seeing it in a larger context, as in his elevation of Eboli (II.viii, esp. 1807–1809). Don Carlos' weak behavior explains why critics have been willing to justify Posa's treatment of him.[123]

Don Carlos might have been more successful as a comic figure. Schiller does not succeed in his attempt to have the reader take Carlos' self-absorption seriously. Vittorio Alfieri, in his *Filippo*, has more success in portraying Don Carlos as the hero of a drama of suffering, though his play as a whole is less complex. The King, here too the hero of a tragedy of stubbornness, lacks the grandeur and—with the exception of the play's final lines—the insight of Schiller's Philipp. Modern attempts to bring comedy into the performance of *Don Carlos* have apparently focused not only on the comic weaknesses of Don Carlos, they have also sought—true to the contemporary *Zeitgeist*—to undermine Posa's idealistic rhetoric.[124] The comic elements of *Don Carlos* have also been developed in parodies by Nicodemus Spitel (Silvius Landsberger) and Max Reinhardt.

Every character in the text suffers a drama of involuntary suffering by way of the text's global dramatic irony: everyone is a puppet of the Grand Inquisitor. Ninety years old and blind, the Grand Inquisitor is an inversion of both Sophocles, who died at age ninety, and the blind hero of his final play, the Oedipus of *Oedipus at Colonus*. Instead of the Sophoclean reconciliation that has been called almost Christian, the Grand Inquisitor undermines any sense of hope or harmony. The characters are thus all "tragic" according to critics who equate tragedy with the drama of suffering. This dramatic irony, however, does not undermine the heroism of their individual acts, even as it suggests that at this stage in history protest must inevitably fail. Just as it is not true that those who fail are necessarily good, so is it not true that those who are just will necessarily succeed.

The Queen's tragedy of self-sacrifice is admirable, if somewhat undramatic. The tragedy introduced through the mirroring dialectics of the King's and Posa's tragedies of stubbornness constitutes the core of the play.[125] In portraying Posa, Schiller learned the dangers of his own idealism; in developing the King he learned the dignity and suffering of the other side. The resulting complexity contributed to the aesthetic importance of the two characters. One might be tempted to argue that the moments of truth in Philipp and Posa or Posa and Don Carlos give rise to a skeletal tragedy of opposition—though the play does not itself stress such a structure. Only in brief moments—for example, when the King experiences the schism between the asymmetry of ruling and the symmetry of friendship, or when Posa, approaching death, recognizes his unjust behavior toward his friend—does the play reflect on its potential as a tragedy of awareness.[126] The moments of suffering in Eboli and Don Carlos or the play's dramatic irony hardly ennoble the work; the mere portrayal of suffering does not transform a text into a tragedy. Although *Don Carlos* introduces moments of the various types of tragedy, it does not represent these diverse forms synthetically; this is a final weakness in the play. A work like Sophocles' *Antigone*, on the other hand, is a tragedy of opposition (the individual versus the state) that breaks down into a tragedy of self-sacrifice (Antigone) and a tragedy of stubbornness (Creon).

Bolt's and Joffe's "The Mission"

Antigone, although perhaps the first drama to integrate diverse tragic forms successfully, is not the last. Indeed, a work that won the best film award at the 1986 Cannes Film Festival might be cited as one of the more recent. *The Mission*, written by Robert Bolt and directed by Roland Joffe, is a complex tragedy of collision that integrates moments of the other tragic subgenres.[127] Initially, Father Gabriel (Jeremy Irons) is willing to sacrifice himself as he ascends to what will become the mission of San Carlos. Trusting in love, Gabriel puts his life at risk. Rodrigo Mendoza (Robert De Niro), in contrast, is introduced as a tragic hero of stubbornness: he is strong, courageous, proud, and a skilled fighter, but he is also a mercenary and a slave trader, who in a fit of passion kills his brother. Rodrigo experiences remorse, exhibits the courage of penance, and finds redemption, developing into a centered and just individual, but the film does not turn into a drama of his self-reconciliation. Rodrigo reenters the tragic sphere, and this time, as, too, with Father Gabriel, he confronts a more complex tragic structure.

The two Jesuits' tragedy of awareness is initially prefigured by the Vatican emissary, Cardinal Altamirano (Ray McAnally), sent to South America to quiet European unrest over the power of the Jesuits in Europe and elsewhere. Altamirano faces a choice. If he does what is clearly correct in the immediate situation, that is, let the missions remain a sanctuary for the Guarani Indians, such that they are off-limits to Portuguese slave traders, he will endanger the existence of the very order that has created the missions. If the missions are not turned over to the Portuguese—as had been stipulated by the Treaty of Madrid (1750)—and the Indians not passed on to slave traders, the Jesuits will be expelled from Portugal and, it seems, not only from Portugal. The conflict between an immediate good and the larger good of the preservation of the Jesuit order is mirrored in Mendoza and Gabriel. Mendoza, who has become a Jesuit novice, affirms his vow of obedience when, after justly accusing the Spanish leader, Don Cabeza (Charles Low), of lying about Spanish involvement with the slave trade, he publicly apologizes and does so at the behest of Gabriel. Gabriel has moved beyond a position of self-sacrifice; there is more at stake than his personal adherence to the norms of the order.

Matters become more complex as we move toward the film's central *peripeteia*. Both Gabriel and Mendoza are confronted with Altamirano's command that the mission of San Carlos, located above the Iguassu Falls, be dissolved and that the Jesuits return with him to Asunción. The collision transcends Altamirano himself, for the conflict is with Altamirano not as a person but as an emissary, as a spokesman "for the Church, which is God's will on earth." To preserve itself in Europe, the Church must show its authority over the Jesuits in South America. The very same Church that brought civilization and Christian teachings to the Indians must now, in order to preserve itself and make possible further just acts, turn the Indians over to the ruthless slave traders. Altamirano acts, he says, "as my conscience dictates," and one gets the sense that, however he acts, he will violate his conscience. At conflict is the work of God and the existence of the instrument that will for future generations carry out the work of God. Altamirano's conflict is genuine.[128] He is to be contrasted, for example, to the Portuguese leader, Don Hontar (Ronald Pickup), who is aware that the missions are profitable and for that reason wishes to take them over, and Don Cabeza, who profits directly from the slave trade.[129]

Altamirano's collision is passed on to the two Jesuits, who must decide between their allegiance to the Indians and to the order that brought them to the Indians. Both stay with the Indians; both suffer the consequences of excommunication. The collision now has Altamirano and the Church on one side and the two Jesuits on the other. The collision that was within Altamirano is externalized such that it assumes the outline of opposition.

As the collision increases in intensity, it is externalized even further: the two Jesuits disagree on how to act in the face of the inevitable invasion of the Portuguese. Gabriel, adhering to Christian belief in the supremacy of love, refuses to take up arms and to bless Rodrigo as he prepares for battle. Gabriel is willing to renounce his vow of obedience but not the principle of love. He argues that if Rodrigo fights, he will betray everything they've done at the mission: "You promised your life to God, and God is Love." What might be viewed from Gabriel's perspective as a tragedy of self-sacrifice, is from the larger framework of the film, which thematizes Rodrigo's position and the collective dimensions of sacrifice, a genuine collision. Should we simply suffer injustice, or should we commit injustice ourselves in order to protect what is right? Gabriel opts for the former and asserts his willingness to die for his principles: "If might is right, then love has no place in the world . . . I don't have the strength to live in a world like that, Rodrigo." Gabriel's humble words may appear to show a lack of resolve, but Gabriel could be said—to use his own formulation to Altamirano—to exhibit "the strength and the ·grace to do the good whatever it cost" him.

Nonetheless, Gabriel's act has collective import. If the Indians do not resist, they will become slaves. With this in mind, Rodrigo returns to his role as fighter, but not out of stubbornness, not as an unambiguously evil character. Rodrigo believes that a life with right on its side is worth more than a life without right. Rodrigo fights to the death to preserve the community he has helped to build. As if to stress the complexity of the conflict, the film introduces yet another collision, one which causes Rodrigo's death. Should children be sacrificed so that Rodrigo can destroy a bridge the Portuguese are ready to cross? The answer he gives is no, and this costs him his life. The stubborn hero, who has reached a level of tragic awareness, dies in a moment of self-sacrifice.

Both Jesuits seem right; both seem wrong. Love is an absolute good that should not be transgressed, yet those who would endanger love and harm others must be countered. The unity of (and remaining tension between) the two positions is symbolized in three significant ways: first, Rodrigo's request, unsuccessful though it is, that Gabriel bless him; second, Gabriel's gift of his cross to Rodrigo and the characters' subsequent embrace; and third, the two Jesuits' attempt to near one another just before their death.[130] This externalization of the conflict (Rodrigo versus Mendoza) and the consciousness of individual inadequacy (each is aware of the other's position, each is determined but nonetheless unsure), combined with the desire to reunite, intensifies the tragic collision and blurs the markers between opposition and awareness.

The two Jesuits do not reach one another, for despite their assertions of autonomy their fate has passed into the hands of others. The film introduces a drama of suffering on the level of a massacre.

The Indians, looking for Christian redemption, are met with suppression and annihilation. Their paradise, their garden of Eden, is transformed into a burning hell. The film, which opened with a symbol of Christian martyrdom, concludes with the martyrdom of the Indians—the battle of Caibale (1756). The film's greatest weakness may be its inclusion of a drama of suffering. The Guaranis, presented as joyous and trouble-free, are so clearly the unjust victims of the scheming settlers that we are reminded of the film's ties to Hollywood. Unlike Hochwälder's *Das heilige Experiment* (literally *The Holy Experiment*, but translated as *The Strong Are Lonely*), which also treats the dissolution of the Jesuit missions from a tragic perspective, the Indians are idealized here and so their fall is that much greater, the betrayal that much more brutal (in Hochwälder's play they seek out the missions primarily for material reasons—food and security).[131] The film, however, redeems itself by distancing us, in almost Brechtian fashion, from the action. This is accomplished by virtue of a rift between the portrayal of death and destruction and the harmonic music superimposed on the action.

True to the best dramas of suffering, the focus is less on the moment of pity than on the critique of a society that causes such suffering. Moreover, the drama of suffering is organically related to the film's tragedy of stubbornness: as with the multiple murders in *Medea* or the blood bath at the end of *Macbeth*, the film exhibits the brutal consequences of a particular chain of actions. Fortunately for the work's immanent claim to complexity, the cause of suffering transcends the unambiguously evil settlers. To Don Hontar's suggestion that there were no alternatives ("The world is thus"), Altamirano responds: "No . . . thus have we made the world. Thus have I made it."

Altamirano, having initially thought that he was doing the good, recognizes that his loyalty to the instrument of goodness, even as it betrays its ideals, has led him to an unjust position, to guilt. His tragedy is one of loyalty, of stubbornness. Within this overarching stubbornness, we might nonetheless recognize a moment of self-sacrifice: Altamirano would have liked to give in to his emotions, but he denies them for the sake of the Church. Joffe has acknowledged the complexity of Altamirano's position, stating that Altamirano is "more hamstrung" than other characters: "Because he knows more, he actually finds it that much more difficult to really find a decision that sets with his sense of justice" (Dempsey 6). On a higher level, therefore, Altamirano's dilemma is an instance of tragic awareness. Though infused with doubts and defects, he nonetheless pursues the path he believes to be right. The sacrifice of moral principles, the stubbornness of wrong action, and the collision of two goods are all operative in Altamirano's tragedy.

Unlike Father Gabriel, who in his desire to envisage the good sacrifices his life, the Church is not willing to risk its destruction. The Church, using as its instrument the troubled but resolute Altamirano, compromises itself in its stubbornness. A constitutive element of tragic stubbornness is self-cancellation. Altamirano survives only as a broken man. The self-sacrifice of the Jesuit deserters highlights his stubbornness and may indeed be an elliptical path to the destruction of Altamirano and the policies he follows. The papal emissary recognizes this himself: "So, your Holiness, now your priests are dead, and I am left alive. But in truth it is I who am dead, and they who live."

The film employs a number of visual images to convey these tragic structures. The most dominant spatial image in the film is that of the cross, both in a literal and a figurative sense. The literal portrayal of the cross is frequent from the early image of a priest's martyrdom to one of the last scenes when Gabriel, walking and holding the cross, is sacrificed, and a Guarani raises it from the ground. The film can also be characterized figuratively by its integration of vertical and horizontal images, each of which is related not only to the cross but also to the two most dominant moments of tragedy—the vertical fall from power and grace and the horizontal collision of opposing forces. Vertical images are found, for example, in the image of the priest and the cross descending the falls, Father Gabriel's initial ascent up the cliffs, and the raising of the cross on the new church. As throughout the film, one moment of triumph is contrasted with another element of terror, in this case the ascension of the cliffs by the soldiers and their boats. The complexity of the vertical imagery is also conveyed in the ascent of Rodrigo, as the burden he is carrying is cut loose and falls into the water below; the camera's dwelling on his subsequently ambivalent reaction is one of the most beautiful and powerful images in the history of cinema. With Rodrigo, the audience experiences simultaneously the pain and tears of remorse for an ineradicable offense, the strain of penance, and the laughter of relief and forgiveness. The power of this portrayal is prepared for not only by the many images of Rodrigo carrying his burden, but also by the camera's dizzying hovering around his head after he kills his brother, which evokes his misdirected introspection and symbolically introduces his subsequent isolation and confusion. This wavering of the camera is later contrasted with a steady eye-level shot of Rodrigo's determined face as he reclaims his weapons to defend the Guaranis. This view of Rodrigo reinforces the meaning of horizontal images in the film: the movement on water and land; the firing of arrows, rifles, and cannons; the bridge; and the bodies lying on the ground underscore the viewer's sense of conflict, struggle, opposition.

Two other spatial images, symbolizing remoteness and circularity, must also be integrated into an interpretation of the artwork. The Guaranis are both literally and figuratively isolated. Their mission above the falls serves as a refuge against the settlers, but they have little power to determine the future of this refuge. The Jesuits take part in the Guaranis' isolation not only when they help to create the mission but also when they are "cast out" from the larger order of the Church. Their marginality is reinforced when the Guaranis and the Jesuits are brutally victimized by more powerful forces. The circular structure of the film, insofar as it both opens and closes with Altamirano's narrative, could be said to underscore a kind of aesthetic roundedness or perfection; thematically, however, it symbolizes a lack of linear progress. The Church is preserving itself but not moving forward; it is not progressing in its alleged efforts to realize its ideals on earth.

Insofar as the entire film is presented within the narrative frame of Altamirano's letter to the papacy, the viewer assumes a metaphoric relationship to the Pope, Christ's instrument on earth. By placing the viewer in this vicarious position, the film asks us to reflect on the conditions and actions under which reconciliation might replace tragic collision, without erasing its heroic dimensions. The contemporary viewer's identification with the Pope reinforces the suggestion that the film is making more than an ahistorical statement. Issues such as the instrumentalization of Central America, duplicity in relations between developing and developed countries, the role of priests in relation to political action, the increasing pragmatism of modern politicians, or only remotely historical events such as the Vatican's concordat with Nazi Germany are loosely invoked by way of the film's rhetoric.

The viewer, having been encouraged on the one hand to identify, in traditional fashion, with the oppressed, but then, having been asked, by way of the film's narrative frame, to identify with the oppressor and the papacy, is left with an awareness of suffering (conveyed via the tragedy of self-sacrifice and the drama of suffering) and of those secondary virtues embodied in Rodrigo and employed by the papacy and by virtue of which suffering could, at least in principle, be mitigated. The film—technically and philosophically—encourages active spectatorship. The viewer is left torn, at one and the same time seemingly a tragic victim and a betrayer of truth. Unlike much of contemporary discourse, what is undermined here is not our adherence to absolute values but our abandonment of such values for expediency and pragmatism. Further still, there is not one absolute value, but several, and this leads to the greatest form of tragic collision.

In its portrayal of a tragic conflict of cultures the film does not hesitate to show the irreparable change resulting from the invasion of one culture by another. The Guaranis are forever altered: they do not seek to return to the forest, for their home is now the mission. The Guaranis, it seems, would have been better off had the Europeans never arrived and their lives never been disrupted: the Guaranis do not need to be rescued from any allegedly primitive or backward culture; for them, the transition to the ideal aspects of Christianity is not difficult. The focus in this conflict of cultures, however, is less on the Guaranis (and certainly not on a transformation from primitiveness to reason) than on the contradictions and untenability of the European paradigm.

Rather than attempting to grasp the contingencies that led the Guaranis to sacrifice children (as does, for example, Father Gabriel), the Christian conquerors simply condemn the practice and then brutalize the Guaranis in ways that transcend the comprehension of even the most understanding soul. The Guaranis kill any third child; the limit is one child per parent, for each child needs an adult who can help it flee from enemies, in this case from the Europeans. What on the surface appears to be a simple act of barbarism turns out to be the expression of a deeper logic, perhaps not admirable from a European standard, but certainly not irrational. The inability of the Europeans to grasp the inner logic behind the apparently irrational superstition of the Guaranis is captured in Altamirano's seemingly superficial comment that it is very difficult to tell what the Guaranis are thinking: the problem lies with the Europeans more than the Guaranis.

A contradiction exists between the Europeans' two major exports to the new world: love and slavery. The film reminds us at every turn of their incompatibility. The two moments are symbolically conveyed by the striking images of Europeans lurking within the forests of native lands. Gabriel is discovered in the forest, but he conveys love. Later, the soldiers move through the forest, bringing

violence and slavery. Rodrigo represents both principles: he is seen
in the forest as a mercenary, but later reveals his true essence to
be at one with the highest export of the West. A series of more
specific contradictions reinforces the weaknesses of the Europeans.
The Spanish proclaim that they have no slaves but themselves
profit from the slave trade and clandestinely take part in its every
facet. A contradiction also arises between the Christian elevation
of equality and the opulence and luxury of Altamirano's lifestyle,
with his extensive luggage and the trappings of power, including
servants who scurry about to shield him from the sun with an umbrella. This contradiction is reinforced by the tension between the
early ideals of the Church and the Church's forgetfulness of these
ideals: after hearing that the income at one mission is shared
equally, Altamirano responds, "Ah yes, there is a French radical
group that teaches that doctrine." The missionary's response cuts
to the quick of the Church's contradiction: "Your eminence, it was
the doctrine of the early Christians."

The tragic opposition between the Church and its outcast Jesuits is another manifestation of inner contradiction. The Church
is not at one with itself; its policies are not harmonious. The Guaranis appeal to this contradiction: Gabriel translates for them, "It
was the will of God that they came out of the jungle and built the
mission, they don't understand why God has changed his mind."
The soldiers' prayers before entering the battle and their making
the sign of the cross before burning the mission likewise point to
the contradictions of the Europeans. The contradiction between the
ideals of the Church (the ideals of God) and the reality of the
Church (the work of men) is often expressed in subtle ways. Altamirano is a Cardinal and prominently wears the Cardinal's red,
which is traditionally associated with martyrdom. Here, in a grotesque reversal, he forces others into martyrdom.[132] The Church is
not sacrificed; it sacrifices others. The real red is the red of the
Guaranis and the Jesuits who stay with them.[133]

Tragedy is traditionally defined as more emotional, comedy more
intellectual; tragedy more participatory, comedy more detached
and contemplative. By giving the film an epic frame, its creators
unite the virtues of tragic passion and depth with those of comic
introspection and critique. The characters, as strong as they are,
are complex and not falsely idealized,[134] nor are any of the principal
figures, including Altamirano, simply wrong. The conflicts between
the characters and those within the characters free viewers from
simply immersing themselves in the fate of one figure or the other.

A strength of the film is that it is both illusionistic (we are invited to identify) and alienating (our identification cannot be complete). The audience is to respond both emotively and cognitively, with pleasure and critique.

The fact that *The Mission* is set in the mid-eighteenth century leaves us with ambivalent sentiments. Positive is that a tragedy of collision is being presented as recently as the 1980s; negative is that such a presentation requires us to travel back some 200 years to find a model. But perhaps there is—as Walter Benjamin once said—hope in the past. The film interrupts the narrative, even as it concludes it, with an allusion to contemporaries who continue to risk their lives in the tradition of Gabriel and Rodrigo and also with a verse from John: "The light shines in the darkness, and the darkness has not overcome it."

3

A Study of Comedy

Comedy involves a contrast between contingent particularity and x, whereby the precise content of x varies from one type of comedy to another.[1] By particular I mean that which is aligned with the self's focused attention on itself, its private interests and desires, that which opposes substance and the substantial. The obsession with one's own particularity is comic insofar as it is viewed in contrast to the world and the substantial sphere such particularity tends to overlook. In what I define as the comedy of coincidence, for example, the hero, who lacks any developed consciousness, seeks particular and finite goals that appear to contrast with what is substantial. Behind the hero's back, however, these finite goals end up serving what is in fact substantial. In what I describe as the comedy of reduction, to take a second example, the hero posits valid goals, but because of a variety of weak means, ends up reducing these goals. What is substantial is reduced to what is particular. The audience cannot take seriously the reduction of substance that arises with the hero's focus on his own particularity. The comic protagonist takes seriously that which we find insignificant and overlooks what is crucial. In each form of comedy the contrast between contingent particularity and a more substantial world is operative. The different kinds of contrast generate in turn the various types of comedy.

Hegel on Comedy

The strength of Hegel's discussion of comedy is not his typology, which is both brief and undialectical, but his insight into subjectivity and particularity as the distinguishing features of the genre

135

(15:528–529, 15:534, 15:552–555, and 15:572–574). Hegel was not the first to recognize the link between subjectivity and comedy. Vico, for example, noted that New Comedy is built around private and fictitious personages, who could be fictitious precisely because they were private. This privatization of the genre also explains the elimination of the chorus, whose task was to serve as a civic entity commenting on public matters (Vico 332). Hegel's reflections supersede earlier insights, insofar as he discusses subjectivity in its most philosophical and overarching, rather than merely thematic, aspects. Nonetheless, Hegel's theory of comedy has gaps, and the post-Hegelian elevation of comedy among writers such as Weiße, Ruge, Bohtz, and Vischer can be partially explained as an attempt to fill these lacunae without overlooking Hegel's initial insight. Even a non-Hegelian such as Adolf Zeising follows the neo-Hegelian pattern insofar as he defines "the comic" as "the subjective-beautiful" (130) or "the beautiful in the form of the antithesis" (280, my translation).[2]

Hegel argues not only that comedy requires subjectivity but that subjectivity, especially reflection on particularity, belongs in comedy.[3] Above all in his *Logic* and *Philosophy of Right*,[4] Hegel elucidates the structures of what we might call, using Hegelian practice, false and genuine subjectivity.[5] False subjectivity can be viewed in stages, ranging from a weak subjectivity, in which the hero is unable to reflect on universal values, to a dominant subjectivity, in which the hero mocks the universal and for whom there are no objective values, and finally to a more complex subjectivity, which is developed enough to recognize universal values but nonetheless too weak to realize them. In contrast, there is a genuine subjectivity that comes to itself through its passage beyond false subjectivity, its reflection on universals, its realization of private intersubjective relations such as friendship or love, and its integration into the larger intersubjective sphere of public institutions.[6]

Hegel's typology of comedy is, if briefer, more complex than his typology of tragedy.[7] In his more general reflections, Hegel asserts the importance of subjectivity, contradictions, and the need for a comic resolution. He then discusses three types of comic action. He begins: "On the one hand, *first*, the characters and their aims are entirely without substance and contradictory and therefore they cannot succeed" (15:528; A 1200, translation modified). Hegel elaborates using the example of greed: both the goal and the means to achieve it are "inherently null" (15:528; A 1200). The hero takes the empty abstraction of wealth as the ultimate reality and excludes every other form of contentment. The hero fails to reach his goal but recognizes the untenability of his claims, and so the play ends on a harmonic note. Since the failure stems from worthless values, nothing is lost. The protagonist deserves to fail and in failing recognizes the stupidity of his claims: "Therefore there is more of the comic in a situation where petty and futile aims are to be brought about with a show of great seriousness and elaborate preparations, but where, precisely because what the subject wanted was something inherently trivial, nothing in fact is ruined when his purpose fails; indeed, he can surmount this disaster with undisturbed cheerfulness" (15:529; A 1201, translation modified). Although Hegel doesn't offer an illustration, a good example would be the innkeeper in Goethe's *The Accomplices*. Hegel's description corresponds partially, though not exactly, to a form I define below as the comedy of negation.

In Hegel's second form of comedy the hero's goal is valid, his means, however, limited: "*Second*, the converse situation occurs when individuals plume themselves on their *substantial* characters and aims, but as instruments for accomplishing something substantial, they, as individuals, are the precise opposite of what is required" (15:529; A 1201, translation modified). In this way the hero reduces the substantial to the appearance of what is substantial. The individual is incapable of fully realizing his legitimate goals. The contradiction lies between the noble intention and the insignificant individual who tries to bring this intention to fruition. Hegel names as an example Aristophanes' *Ecclesiazusae*.

A third form of comedy emphasizes the role of chance in bringing about a harmonic conclusion: "A *third* type, in addition to the first two, is based on the use of external contingencies. Through their various and peculiar complications situations arise in which aims and their accomplishment, inner character and external circumstances, are placed in comic contrast with one another and then they lead to an equally comic solution" (15:529–530; A 1201, translation modified). This third Hegelian form corresponds to my initial subgenre, the comedy of coincidence.

The order of my typology differs from Hegel's. In addition, my typology allows for more differentiated subforms than the Hegelian model; it gives a fuller account of those forms Hegel also names; and, finally, it attempts to demonstrate a dialectic within the genre. Hegel begins his typology with an antithetical subgenre, something akin to what I call the comedy of negation.[8] It could be argued that because comedy is itself an antithetical genre, the first comic form should be one in which form (as antithesis) is superior to content (as thesis). The thesis of an antithetical genre would thus be the antithesis. I know of no other sequence in Hegel's work, however, where a similar pattern is employed. Indeed, even if Hegel had introduced this inverse dialectic, it would still be difficult to accept, for one wonders under what principle we would get from the antithesis to the thesis and from the thesis to the synthesis. With this in mind, I would reverse Hegel's thesis and antithesis. Hegel's third form, moreover, is hardly synthetic. It appears to involve an erasure of subjectivity, rather than a synthesis of objectivity and subjectivity; expressed in different terms, the harmony is one of chance, not reason. Hegel's third form will become in my typology the first. As with his typology of tragedy, Hegel excludes dramatic subgenres that must at least be thematized before they are abandoned. Moreover, in his discussion of comedy, unlike his discussion of tragedy, Hegel overlooks not just deficient subgenres but forms that are dramatically and philosophically among the richest.

*

As in tragedy, the increasing level of awareness on the part of the protagonist generates movement from one subgenre to another. In comedy we begin with a lack of consciousness; the hero, knowing little, follows his own particular desires and, led by coincidence and fortune, reaches the good. I call this the comedy of coincidence: the hero achieves harmony through nature and chance not consciousness. This comedy, the comic equivalent of objectivity, passes over into a series of antithetical subgenres: reduction, negation, and withdrawal. In the comedy of reduction the hero has an intuitive grasp of harmony and truth but is unable to reach his goals owing to his own ineptitude and deficiencies. The hero of reduction follows his desires, much like the hero of coincidence, though these desires lead not to the good but to a reduction of the good. The hero of the next form, the comedy of negation, recognizes that a reduced goal is a false goal and so freely seeks evil, albeit with strong (and clever) means. The hero adopts an untenable stance marked by internal incongruities and contradictions; the hero fails but in failing exhibits wit, perseverance, or (at least momentarily) power. The hero's substantial means serve insubstantial ends. The hero of the next form, the comedy of withdrawal, attempts to confront the evils of negation but recognizes only the content of truth, not its means of success. The hero of withdrawal fails mainly because of the inadequacies of society but also because of the hero's unwillingness to grant objectivity, as deficient as it is, its moment of truth. All antithetical forms culminate in a self-cancellation.

These antithetical forms present us with a bow of sorts. In the comedy of reduction the hero initially posits a valid goal, but the weak means reduce the goal. In the most negative form, the hero exhibits strong means toward a clearly false goal, even if the means are in the end self-destructive. In the third form we return toward truth, insofar as a valid goal is again posited; the means, however, are weak, although not as weak as in the comedy of reduction. The bow represents movement away from truth with its reduction, reaching its outer distance from truth in the case of negation, and returning toward truth with the attempt, unsuccessful though it is, of resisting this negation of truth.

The hero of the synthetic genre, finally, unites in himself the objectivity of a valid goal with an awareness of the means necessary to reach that goal. I call this the comedy of intersubjectivity: the hero overcomes contradictions and reaches the intersubjective sphere by virtue of his own reflection rather than mere chance. I also consider a form that is only apparently comic, the comedy of absolute irony, in which the subject's ironic view erases not only all objective values but also the validity of his own erasure of these values.

As in all dialectical progressions, the thesis and the synthesis contain the primary moment, the antithesis the secondary moment: the primary moment in comedy is reconciliation or contingency harmonized; the antithetical moment is the elevation of subjectivity. Recognizing comedy as an antithetical genre, Hegel comments at length on the antithetical elevation of subjectivity. His typological analysis, however, elevates the primary moment. Modern comedies and modern comic theory tend to see the secondary moment as dominant, thus the wealth of modern comedies that fit the antithetical patterns and push them to their limits.

Comedy functions as an aesthetic analogue to Hegel's practice of immanent critique, by which the philosopher seeks to unveil self-contradictory and thus self-cancelling positions. Ruge opens his commentary on the comic by discussing the value of error in the formulation of truth. The comic work takes the hero's position seriously, accepts it, and follows it to the point where it reveals its own absurdity and so destroys itself. According to Ruge, the object of comic negation "cancels itself, it is the negative in and for itself, the self-cancelling" (*Neue Vorschule* 179, my translation). Comedy is "immanent negation" (*Neue Vorschule* 179, my translation). Hegel writes concerning this Socratic technique: "All dialectic allows that which should have value to have value, as if it had value, allows the dissolution inherent in it to come to pass" (18:460; HP 1:400, translation modified). Hegel applies the structure directly to the comic: "The comic is to show a person or a thing as it dissolves itself internally in its very gloating. If the thing is not itself its contradiction, the comic element is superficial and groundless" (18:483; HP 1:427–428, translation modified). Comedy, an antithetical genre, generates a multiplicity of negative and internally contradictory positions.

The Comedy of Coincidence(1)

In the initial comic form, subjectivity is hardly developed; it is subordinate to a more overarching order and viewed as an almost insignificant part of the cosmos. Antirealism and images of nature tend to predominate in works of this kind. Consider Shakespeare's *A Midsummer Night's Dream* or Woody Allen's *A Midsummer Night's Sex Comedy*. Nature and the world of objects are also portrayed dynamically in silent films, especially those of Chaplin and Keaton.[9] The subject is put into his place in a universe where he is not as great as he thinks. By focusing on nature and objectivity, such works delimit the claims of the individual subject.[10] Chance, accident, and coincidence override all subjective plans. Chance wasn't exactly banned from tragedy, but it was limited, insofar as the unconditional firmness of the tragic hero, his allegiance to an idea, determined the dramatic action. In comedies of coincidence the heroes imagine themselves to be the agents of action, but their subjectivity is revealed to be illusory: not the subject, but chance and natural causes are at play; this is cleverly illustrated, for example, in Hitchcock's *The Trouble with Harry*.

The audience tends not to take the protagonist of coincidence very seriously. The multiplicity of marriages with which such works frequently conclude mocks any unnecessary stress on the uniqueness of the individual and exhibits the importance of the overarching order.[11] The broad sphere, what is common not what is particular, is highlighted. What appears contingent and accidental is not the institution of marriage but the subjects entering into it. Institutions have ontological independence; they transcend individuals and generations. The references to procreation, which are frequent in such works, suggest that the individual exists not only for itself but also for the continuation of the species. The individual is subordinate to the whole in the preservation of the genus as well as in the pattern of the genre.

Comic coincidence highlights what the Greeks called *tyche*, the chance or fortune that transcends human actions and intentions. Life is too complex, powerful, and multifaceted to be fully planned. Indeed, as our knowledge increases, so does the complexity of factors influencing the course of events. Coincidence undermines any overconfidence we might have in our capacity to judge or our ability to plan and predict. The unexpected and surprising delimit the hero's claims to knowledge and intentionality. In Menander's *The Girl from Samos*, coincidence both engenders and resolves the problems, such that Demeas' words might be viewed as a motto for the genre to which the work belongs: "Coincidence must really be a divinity. She looks after many of the things we cannot see" (163–165). The prologue of Menander's *The Shield* is spoken by the goddess of chance, who announces that she is controlling and directing events (146–148). Indeed, as in *The Girl from Samos*, she creates both the problem and the solution. As Gregor Vogt-Spira has shown, all of Menander's plays function to a greater or lesser degree under the direction of *tyche*.

In the comedy of coincidence love transcends the autonomy of the individual. The blindness of love, its randomness, irrationality, and mystery, is not only stronger than the contingent beings on whom it exerts its force, it has a logic and grace of its own that transcends mere intellect and conscious choice and may be said to evoke some of the wonder normally reserved for tragedy (Kermode 214–220). Shakespeare's *A Midsummer Night's Dream* displays the blindness of humans controlled by love, people moving subconsciously as if in a dream world, players totally absorbed by a force that leads them hither and yon and finally to their destination. Chance is manipulated by fairies of goodness, themselves allegories—though not just allegories—of the human subconscious. In coincidence, subjectivity is underdeveloped, because the subject is either irrational and following nature or rational and mirroring cosmic law; in either case causality and motivation transcend the self. In such works we laugh not just at good luck—which turns events around—but also at bad luck, for even as we see it heaped on the protagonist, we simultaneously recognize it as a temporary obstacle that will not cause any substantial pain.

In works of coincidence, overarching references remind us that love is not just particular, not just chance and coincidence; it is also a universal love of humanity and nature. The union of lovers often alludes to the mythic image of a sacred marriage (*hieros gamos*) of earth and sky, a motif of harmony that reaches back to Hesiod's *Theogony*. Differentiating references to time and place, to specific identities, give way to a general, even cosmic sense of unity. If a weakness of coincidence is its failure fully to portray individuality and negativity, its corresponding strength lies in its cosmic harmony and freedom from realism, which unburden the imagination and so make possible everything from the supernatural to the improbable.

The comedy of coincidence allows for both probable impossibilities, that is, consistent but magical interference, as in *A Midsummer Night's Dream*, and improbable possibilities, that is, realistic but unlikely events, as in *The Comedy of Errors*. Aristotle preferred the former because of its organic nature. In either case chaos and confusion eventually give way to resolution. Shakespeare, a master of this first comic subgenre, has given us comedies of coincidence that contain magical events and unexpected turns as well as a good deal of physical comedy; verisimilitude is not an issue. Moreover, these plays give rise to as much laughter as reflection. With their bracketing of subjectivity, the agent of morality, such plays tend to exclude moral issues. The focus is on overarching structures, the independent powers that transcend the self, and the gaiety of festivity.[12] The hero's hardships and apparent obstacles are not serious or genuinely dangerous.[13] Even the threat of death with which *The Comedy of Errors* opens must, as the play develops, be taken lightly.

In the comedy of coincidence, identity crises tend to be frequent (it is easy to lose one's identity when one really hasn't any developed sense of self) and superficial (not losing anything substantial, the protagonist cannot really suffer a serious crisis—as he will in the more developed subgenres). Characters are unaware of the significance of their own acts, as, for example, in the ironic developments of Menander's *The Arbitration*. Or, characters are confident of their position and that of others, including the identity of others, only to discover that what they took to be facts were illusions, and they weren't in control of events after all, as, for example, in T. S. Eliot's *The Confidential Clerk*.[14]

Holberg's *Masquerades* illustrates both the irony of coincidence and the importance of symmetry. Two sets of parents have arranged the marriage of a son and a daughter, who have not met since they were children. At a masquerade the night before they are to meet, each falls madly in love with "another person," and so each resists the marriage. Much like Büchner's later *Leonce and Lena*—though here the resolution is positive—each child breaks free of the parents' commands only to fall in love with the very person to whom they were originally engaged. In seemingly breaking free of the engagement, they fulfill it. Like *Leonce and Lena*, the play also relativizes the tragic impulse: Leander says he would rather die than give up his beloved, and Leonora is believed to have drowned herself in despair.[15] Whereas tragedy relies on the exceptional, here similarity dominates. The fates of Leander and Leonora run parallel: each becomes engaged, falls in love with "another," does battle with the parents, and discovers the other's true identity. The fathers' fates are likewise similar: each is frustrated by his child's behavior, each fears the wrath of the other father, and each apologizes to the other. (This symmetry is cleverly portrayed when the two fathers express parallel thoughts on stage not knowing that the other is present.) Symmetry or the exchangeability of roles is central to the idea of coincidence—the sublation of subjectivity and difference. The theme is reinforced by the multiple marriages as well as the idea of the masquerade itself: at the masquerade, with masks veiling everyone's identity, individuality is not expressed; as Leonard states, persons are on equal terms with one another. We see "the natural equality there was in the beginning before pride got the upper hand and one person thought he was too good to associate with another; for, as long as the masquerade lasts, a servant is as good as his master" (II.iii).

George Bernard Shaw's *Man and Superman* can also be considered in the light of coincidence. To be sure, Jack Tanner carries several traits of what I define below as the hero of withdrawal: Tanner's contempt for society, especially expressed through the Don Juan figure of Act III;[16] his desire to flee from Ann, specifically from his role as, first, her guardian, and second, her potential husband; and his elevation of contemplation. Yet as the subtitle tells us, the play is not just a philosophy but also a comedy, and Ann, representing the power of nature, conquers. Tanner recognizes man's impotence in the face of women: "Because they have a purpose which is not their own purpose, but that of the whole universe, a man is nothing to them but an instrument of that purpose" (Act I). Not without irony, Shaw describes on behalf of Don Juan the dissolution of the self in this overarching instinctual force: "my brains still said No on every issue. And whilst I was in the act of

framing my excuse to the lady, Life seized me and threw me into
her arms as a sailor throws a scrap of fish into the mouth of the
seabird" (Act III). Toward the play's conclusion Tanner asserts: "We
do the world's will, not our own. I have a frightful feeling that I
shall let myself be married because it is the world's will that you
should have a husband" (Act IV). Shaw revives a structure of comedy often overlooked in the face of modern subjectivity, and he does
so by following in the tradition of a great debunker of subjectivity
and autonomy, Nietzsche. Shaw's Life Force, modelled after Nietzsche and Bergson's *élan vital*, transcends individuality and generations. The play highlights, moreover, the sense in which chance
and fate overlap; the comedy of coincidence suggests that there is a
certain reason to the world even if the heroes are unsure exactly
what it is.

Finally, Woody Allen's *A Midsummer Night's Sex Comedy* is an
excellent cinematic example of coincidence. The film—like its
Shakespearean model—emphasizes what transcends conscious human intentions and visible reality in general. Isolated shots of nature both early in the film and interspersed throughout stress the
importance of the non-human world, as does the forest setting. Frequent use of wide-angle, distanced shots that diminish the size of
the humans within the landscape reinforce this moment. Dreams
foretell reality. Memories return unaided by human will. The intellectual, Leopold, gives in to his most natural and primitive longings. A pragmatist and skeptic who announces that "there is nothing magical about existence," Leopold doesn't just learn to believe
in spirits, he becomes one. Rather than dying, he is lifted into another dimension. As with Shakespeare, we see the crossing of pairs
of lovers and their eventual union or reunion. Andrew, the Woody
Allen figure, suggests: "Nobody plans these things; they just happen."

The Speculative Structure of Coincidence

At its best the comedy of coincidence is not an insignificant or superficial genre; rather, it contains a highly speculative structure.
Indeed, it might best be understood in the context of Hegel's philosophy of history, which is often brought to bear on his theory of
tragedy,[17] but appears never to have been consulted as a source of
insight into comedy. In fact, comedies of coincidence are generally
regarded as the weakest and most superficial comedies—even by

Hegelians. Friedrich Theodor Vischer, to take one example, strongly favors comedies of character over comedies that stress coincidence or intrigue (6:333–335); he sees in the former a deeper comic element ["eine tiefere Komik"] (6:334). The comedy of coincidence, however, is often deep. It borders on the absurd and the profound, the absurdity of mixed meetings and unexpected recognitions and the profundity of a spirit that directs events toward an ultimate harmony. This form of comedy includes both moments Hegel sees in history: first, the contingencies of natural causes, arbitrary actions, and chance (what we can call external necessity);[18] and second, a higher necessity, a kind of eternal justice or love, which is the goal of history itself (VG 26).[19]

Coincidence shows how the seemingly contingent can be integrated to serve this higher necessity. Chance and necessity are in truth parts of a hidden unity: it is necessary that chance exist; and what happens by chance ultimately serves a pattern of necessity. The study of art, no less than the study of history, presupposes that the object of study follows a rational pattern (12:20), though its details as well as its connections may at times be difficult to discern.[20] There is a pattern to comic coincidence, just as there is reason in world history (12:22). The reason is not the reason of the individual subject—his desires, after all, are often thwarted—but rather an overarching or transcendent reason. Comedy is thus a prolepsis of history. Just as history is not a mere collocation of moments, so the comedy of coincidence brings diverging moments into an overriding pattern.[21] The genre is in its metastructure ironic: it appears to be an innocuous piece about what is insignificant, yet it is at its core serious and substantial. Kierkegaard describes such irony as uncommon: "The most common form of irony is when one says something seriously which is not seriously intended. The other form of irony is when one says something facetiously, as a jest, which is intended seriously, although this occurs more seldom" (*Concept of Irony* 265).

Despite Hegel's emphasis on reason and the universal, he does recognize the validity of personal interests. He also acknowledges that these interests are not necessarily opposed to the universal: "An interest can indeed be entirely particular; but it does not immediately follow from this that it must be opposed to the universal. The universal must enter into reality through the particular" (VG 84–85, my translation). Interests direct one's actions, which can become "the instruments and means of the world spirit" (VG 87, my translation).[22] Another speculative dimension is here apparent.

Not only does the individual serve this higher necessity but the individual in all his contingency is necessary for the larger plan. Even as the individual seems to be erased, he gains a status he might not otherwise have. He participates in, and is necessary for, that greater whole.[23] The individual, unbeknownst to himself, serves the world-spirit. Hegel suggests, "in world history the outcome of human actions is something other than what the agents aim at and actually achieve, something other than what they immediately know and will. They fulfill their own interests, but something further is thereby brought into being, something which is inwardly involved in what they do but which was not in their consciousness or part of their intention" (12:42–43; PH 30).

This is the stuff of the comedy of coincidence,[24] though in comedy the larger harmonic goal may result not from the realization of private pursuits but from the thwarting and redirection of these pursuits.[25] We can speak of a "cunning of the genre." The pursuit of the various particular interests of the characters taken together forms a comic whole. This is generally true thematically, and it is also true in terms of form: one thinks of the *commedia dell'arte*, wherein the collective pursuit of individual parts creates a coherent form.[26] The suggestion seems to be that history and providence work this way as well. Characters on the world stage contribute to progress and the world-spirit by pursuing their own ends. Within this structure we recognize another reason for the prominent role that nature plays in this subgenre. Nature has a teleology without knowledge of a telos. Species continue without the consciousness of the individual representatives that make this continuation possible; the comedy of coincidence elevates this structure of nature to the level of spirit.

The particular interests of finite subjects ultimately serve a harmonic whole. Even as the hero's desires are thwarted, his sentiments proven mistaken, he is, as he contributes to a resolution, revealing an intuitive, subliminal desire for harmony.[27] The importance of music, more dominant in the comedy of coincidence than in any other dramatic genre, can be recognized here as well. The multiplicity of lives has in the long run as much harmony as the multiplicity of individual players and notes in a musical performance or composition. Moreover, the cosmic dimensions of the genre have something in common with celestial harmony, a music of the spheres that is present but unheard. The harmony of coincidence is likewise hidden but present, moved by a hand unseen but felt.

In a little known, but richly insightful essay "On the Apparent Deliberateness in the Fate of the Individual," Schopenhauer speaks of a "transcendent fatalism": a spirit that cannot be localized nonetheless creates visible results that transcend the finite intentions of individuals (Ger 7:224; Eng 204). The hero's desires and intentions—to the degree that they are formulated—are undermined, yet the unexpected result that usurps the desired ends turns out to match a truer desire of which the hero was scarcely aware. Only after the fact does the hero recognize the absurdity of the original intentions. Manipulation by external forces, which could otherwise be tragic, is comic insofar as the hero doesn't get what he thinks he wants but does get what he really or subconsciously seeks. This irony of fate frequently arises in love.[28] Here, we see not only an amusing comic contrast but also the hidden harmony of subjectivity and chance. An especially good example is Howard Hawks's *Bringing up Baby*. As throughout the comic genre, the negative ends in the positive: false intentions are thwarted, and harmony results. A kind of providence is at work: in failing, the hero succeeds. Instead of directly sacrificing ourselves for the universal as in tragedy, we pursue our own particular intentions—and still end up serving the good. The seriousness of the harmony and order may be veiled in the seeming arbitrariness and colorful manifestations of chance, but it is not entirely hidden (Bohtz 185–186).

Art, especially comedy, is the proper forum for Schopenhauer's transcendent fatalism: first, the connections between individual characters or moments cannot be theoretically demonstrated, only concretely imagined—which is not to deny their existence; second, a moment of antirealism is appropriate to a view which suggests that what we take for firm and stable (the moment, the individual, concrete reality) may be transcended by more elusive, if nonetheless more substantial, factors or forces. The magic, nonrealistic aspects of the comedy of coincidence (one thinks of Aristophanes, Shakespeare, or Raimund) need not be underestimated, need not be viewed as being without weight or substance. In this aesthetic transcendence of reality we see a highly speculative moment: comedy sublimates immediate reality and suggests that reality has no absolute claim to reality; the most important elements are those that transcend this reality and reveal its falsity and insignificance. To use Schelling's words: "the *ideal* is the real and is much more real than the so-called real itself" (Ger 35; Eng 35; cf. Hegel 13:22). The comedy of coincidence embodies a self-reflective argument for nonmimetic art, and it is inherently "idealist" as Hegel defines the term in his *Logic*: idealism recognizes the finitude of what is finite (5:172–173). In tragedy the world is serious because the universal is meant to be realized; in comedy we move, reversely, from reality to the universal: the universal (behind finite reality) is to be grasped. Antirealism is not only the formal analogue to this view; it conduces toward it. Thus, Mary Chase's and Henry Koster's *Harvey* ends with a decision to suspend everyday reality in favor of a higher, more harmonic, if nonetheless seemingly inexplicable and supernatural reality.[29]

Comedy integrates the world of fairies, spirits, and pookas not only to suggest a transcendence of restricted definitions of reality or to stress the individual's diminutive role in a larger frame but also to draw attention to the cosmic dimensions of coincidence; not only the individual but the universe is a nexus of coincidence and necessity. The fairies are the mythic representation of a natural causality that serves a spiritual end. The role of fairies and other natural and supernatural forces also functions as a mythic analogue to the revelation that a causal network of forces so extensive and so precise exists that the flight of a bird or the location of the stars or the meeting of persons are all interrelated.[30] We recall Nietzsche's claim that everything is "entangled, ensnared, enamored" (2:557; Eng 435). The idea of connectedness also surfaces in the frequent resurrection of distant relations. Inheritance, which often solves problems for the comic hero, is a product of mere chance: not only that the person dies but also that the recipient's right to the inheritance is natural rather than spiritual, stemming from blood relations, not friendship.

In coincidence, providence and chance, the otherworldly and the secular, complement one another. What appears to be a kind of divine direction is, viewed externally, the chance unfolding of events. Feuerbach notes such a complementarity when he defines grace as religious genius or religious chance: "In relation to the inner life, one can define grace also as *religious genius*; in relation to the outer life, however, as *religious chance*. A person is good or evil by no means only through himself, through his own power, through his own will; rather through that nexus of hidden and evident determinations, which, because they rest on no inner necessity, we ascribe to the power of '*her majesty chance*,' as Frederick the Great used to say. Divine grace is the mystified power of chance" (5:222–23, my translation).[31] Feuerbach asks that more attention be paid to the mysteries and mysticism of chance: "I say: the mysticism of chance; for in reality chance is a mystery, although slurred over and ignored by our speculative religious philosophy, which, because of the *illusory mysteries* of absolute essence, that is, theology, has forgotten the *true mysteries* of thought and life, so also because of the mystery of divine grace or freedom of choice, it has forgotten the profane mystery of chance" (5:223, my translation). To what extent Hegel overlooked chance may be open to question; its importance for comedy, however, is unmistakable.

*

The appearance of unexpected persons and circumstances, which is frequent in comedy, is another way of illustrating the moment of chance or coincidence. The dramatist is given free reign to use his imagination in order to bring about such improbabilities. Yet these accidental and improbable moments are orchestrated in such a way that they help unfold what is ultimately an organic pattern; chance reigns, but it serves a purpose. It enters as a form of the ugly, becomes transformed into an organic pattern, and departs as a form of the beautiful. On the one hand, these moments tend to stress nature, as in the unknown relative whose money the protagonist inherits. On the other hand, these improbabilities are directed toward the universalism of humanity and the interchangeability of characters: thus, for example, the plot of *Bachelor Mother*, where a woman assisting an abandoned child is mistaken for its mother and eventually adapts to the role. Even the finite play of language frequent in these comedies relates to coincidence: the comic effect of a pun, for example, derives from the coincidental linguistic proximity of two different concepts that have in common nothing but the sound, and this is suddenly brought to consciousness.

Whatever form the comedy of coincidence takes, the speculative consciousness of the poet is able to direct language and events in such a way that all comes out fine in the end. The only developed subjectivity we see in the comedy of coincidence is the subjectivity of its creator or that of the "surrogate director," a character who redirects persons from their original intentions and toward an ideal concept of harmony, as, for example, in Shakespeare's final "comedy" *Measure for Measure*, where the Duke remakes reality in order to give it an improbable but happy end, or, to take an example from popular culture, George Stevens's *The More the Merrier*.[32]

Especially interesting are scenarios where the surrogate director's actions appear to get out of control and take on a life of their own, as in Terence's *The Girl from Andros* or Ernst Raupach's *The Converts*, a play Hegel much admired (11:72–82). The surrogate director embodies aspects of negation—he is nimble-witted, clever, full of imagination, and he tries to move other subjects around as pawns on a chessboard; however, he has good, rather than evil, intentions, and true to coincidence, his finite intentions often go awry even as they fulfill expectations. In *The Girl from Andros*, for example, Davos's plotting and counter-scheming get out of control (the vitality and complexity of life cannot be consciously directed) and must be rescued by a *deus ex machina*. Glycerium, whom Pamphilus wants to wed, while his father prefers that he marry Chremes' daughter, Philumena, turns out also to be Chremes' daughter.

The harmony created by the author or surrogate director is more a projection of what *should* be, for already in reduction we see that things don't always work out for the comic character. Coincidence and false subjectivity are for Hegel related terms. Each represents a kind of arbitrariness, the nondevelopment or negation of true substance and necessity. Hegel defines "arbitrariness" as "*contingency* in the shape of will" (R § 15). The introduction of subjectivity in the upcoming subgenres represents not only a difference in relation to the comedy of coincidence but also an overarching similarity, an extension of chance into the sphere of the will.[33] Chance and arbitrary subjectivity fail to satisfy completely, for drives and inclinations can be either good or evil.

The Comedy of Reduction (2a)

The next form of comedy grants subjectivity a greater role. Its expression, however, of the subject's longing for intersubjectivity takes place only at the lowest, most primitive level. In the comedy of reduction the subject has valid goals—at least momentarily—but cannot attain them owing to a lack of insight or will.[34] Intention stands in disproportion to means. The comedy of coincidence appears to be insignificant but is substantial; reduction reverses the process: the protagonist purports to be substantial but reduces substance to the level of insignificance. In each case appearance and reality diverge. The hero of reduction consciously seeks the good but is unconsciously brought down to a level below the good. Intersubjectivity is reduced to a limited move toward recognition of the other, as in Lessing's *The Jews*; purely instrumental relationships, as in Schnitzler's *Anatol*; or forced friendship, as in Brecht's *Master Puntila and His Servant Matti*. Puntila *commands* Matti to be his friend and so cancels the attempt at friendship. We also see Puntila's intuitive desire for intersubjectivity in his collecting brides, but again this act undermines intersubjectivity. Puntila cannot take *each one* as his wife; his attempts at love quickly pass over into possession. Primarily within this subgenre critics speak of a parody of comedy (for example, Berckman), but parody of the happy end is a widespread comic form and not restricted to reduction.

While in reduction we move into the sphere of conscious actions, nature still plays a role. Consider, for example, stuttering, deafness, or clumsiness. Stuttering is in and of itself not comic; potentially comic, however, is the attempt to speak passionately, emphatically, and eloquently, even as one stutters. The nearly deaf person who refuses to acknowledge an inability to hear as well as the misunderstandings on which he bases subsequently ridiculous decisions is also a comic protagonist of reduction. A similar structure surfaces with the clumsy fool who feels adequate to the most complex and daring tasks but is invariably unable to succeed.[35] A protagonist dressed to make a grand impression but unable to control his flatulence also enacts a moment of reduction on the base level of nature. In reduction, the infinite has been rendered finite, the substance of truth reduced. Thus, the genre stresses the material, the sexual, food, digestion, and so forth.

The external nature that predominates in coincidence becomes in reduction internal nature, above all the base inclinations, passions, and drives of the self: sexuality, desire for power, insatiable hunger or thirst. The hero of reduction is far from free, for his actions are determined not by his rationality and universality but by the external world that feeds his desires. Determination by particular drives and interests is in fact the realm of chance: "The contingent is generally what has the ground of its being not within itself but elsewhere" (E § 145 Z). Though we can also call it caprice: "The content of arbitrary choice is given and is known to be grounded, not within the will itself, but in external circumstances" (E § 145 Z, translation modified). Caprice is coincidence internalized: the self moves from one event to another thinking itself its own cause but driven by forces it simply does not comprehend. In coincidence we laugh at the odd circumstances, the high level of chance, as well as at the hero who is, initially at least, the victim of chance. In reduction we laugh at the hero who, of his own accord, has created for himself an absurd situation, a world of chance and arbitrariness he can no longer control. Our laughter and enjoyment is especially pronounced when the hero views this apparent spontaneity, whereby he is in fact driven and determined by chance and arbitrary, finite desires, as the highest expression of freedom (Rosenkranz, *Ästhetik des Häßlichen* 176).

We have argued that subjectivity and particularity are the defining features of comedy. Even the most finite comic moments can be related to these broader categories. A malapropism, spoonerism, or any break of lexicon or grammar that results from the hero's feeble attempt to appear learned and demonstrate erudition represents in nuce the comedy of reduction, that is, good intentions and weak means. So too, for example, the clown who hopes to fend off a blistering rain storm with an umbrella the size of a credit card. Eavesdropping is a reduction of knowledge to curiosity; an even further reduction takes place when the listener is hard of hearing. Another traditional topos of comic reduction is the failure to act according to the tenets of proper behavior despite the hero's efforts—so the comic hero in high society who raises his soup bowl to his face and drinks it dry, remembering thereby to lift his little fingers away from the bowl, or, more simply, the hero perfectly dressed for afternoon tea who immediately drops his cup on his lap.

Among comic heroes of reduction with the most noble intentions and no sense of reality the titular hero of Cervantes' *Don Quixote* comes to mind for his desire to live as a self-sacrificing knight in a world of corruption and decay and his inability to recognize his outdatedness and the inappropriateness of his behavior. He trusts others to hold to his standards and so unwittingly fails to undo wrongs (I.iv); he courageously battles a windmill that he takes to be a giant (I.viii); he believes he is invincible, equal to a hundred men, and so enters battle outnumbered and is immediately drubbed (I.xv); and he frees convicted criminals, taking them for oppressed gentlemen (I.xxii). As Hegel reminds us, Don Quixote is impervious to external pressure (14:218); like most heroes of reduction, he never doubts his cause. This self-confidence only adds to the comedy, for it contrasts with his belatedness. A genuine conflict of paradigms is tragic; return to an earlier paradigm when it is unambiguously past is comic.[36]

The hero of reduction, lacking a clear sense of self, is, despite his outward denials, at the mercy of forces around him. While the protagonist's life is represented by a form of the Hegelian bad infinite,

that is, repetition without progress or completion, the work's form
mirrors this infinity; it is episodic. Many picaresque novels fit the
model of reduction. Thomas Mann's *Felix Krull* is a good example,
especially if we consider the hero's discourse on sexuality and love,
which for all its eloquence and insight is reduced through its context: Krull wants to seduce the recipient of his wisdom. Another
quality of the protagonist of reduction, his inability to deny himself
for the pleasure of others, is illustrated in one of Krull's amusing
conversations with Lord Kilmarnock. When Kilmarnock lets fall
the word "self-denial," Krull reflects: "The word, which I had never
heard before, startled me" (Ger 216; Eng 214, translation modified).[37] Likewise, Schnitzler's Anatol and Brecht's Puntila are incapable of self-denial; they give in to their lowest desires and so trivialize their sense of truth. Krull's intuitive grasp of truth comes to
the fore in his act of writing a confession, a genre in which the
dualism between inner and outer is ideally overcome, yet his confession—and this is Krull's contradiction—is that of a confidence
trickster, and so even this moment of truth is reduced. Krull longs
for unity, the unity of doubles, which would give him the identity
his multiple selves lack and allow him to overcome the dualism
implicit in his many performances, but Krull never realizes unity,
except in the reductive form of the unity of bodies. The desire for
synthesis also manifests itself in Krull's speculative unity with
Venosta. Here, as elsewhere, we see the reduction of a symbolically
ideal unity: Felix Krull is too Protean; Venosta, on the other hand,
too stable, incapable of change and development. Krull, however,
does not realize this unity as an ideal; he continues to dissemble,
fluctuate, and instrumentalize. Krull can control nature with spirit
(as in his performance before the military doctors), a gift alien to
lesser heroes of reduction, but again Krull employs his skills to
achieve goals that satisfy his nature, not his spirit. This is fore-
shadowed early in the novel: debased orgies are what remain of
Olympic revelry. Krull's *Bildung* is also trivialized, resulting in an
ironization more of Krull than of the possibility of *Bildung* itself.[38]

Christopher Hampton's *The Philanthropist* offers us a final example of comic reduction. The play focuses on "a man concerned
above all to cause no offence and be an unfailing source of sweet-
ness and light" (Hampton xi). In many respects a counterpiece to
Molière's *The Misanthrope*, the comedy presents a hero whose
"compulsive amiability" (Hampton xii) is a reduction of the virtues
of tolerance and acceptance: "the basic feature of my character is
an anxiety to please people and to do what they want" (60). Philip

finds something likable in everything and everyone, and he seeks to please everyone—which is not possible, and the play ends with him alone after he has alienated his friends. He refrains from criticizing the most despicable people and so gives them voice, including Braham, a comic hero of negation who revels in his lack of principles; colleagues who allegedly lust after his fiancée; and a seducer to whom he cannot say no. Amusing is also that his desire to praise others is received as a series of ironic insults—by the playwright whose play he abstractly praises or by the writer whose diction he carefully analyzes. Great is the consistency with which he describes his indeciveness and lack of self: "I'm a man of no convictions. (*Longish pause.*) At least I think I am" (52). But the hero is not entirely logical. After he is told that he apologizes too often, he agrees and then apologizes for apologizing too often (57). A hero without character cannot fail to be inconsistent; he is simply the benign counterpart to the hero of negation, who—in Braham's words—revels in holding "opposite points of view with equal conviction. The marvellous thing is that if the internal logic is coherent, I know that even if I'm wrong, I'm right" (26). What is left unsaid is that even if he is right, he is wrong.

Parody of Tragedy

Critics sometimes misinterpret the comedy of reduction as tragic. This misreading derives from two factors: first, critics overlook the extent to which comedy includes the parody of tragedy; second, theoreticians stress not the greatness that leads to tragic suffering but rather the so-called tragic flaw, which in some respects resembles reduction. Heilman, for instance, reads Max Frisch's *The Firebugs* as primarily tragic: Biedermann causes his own destruction, he is divided between actively doing the good and wanting to appease his guests, between recognizing truth and turning away from truth, and he is guilty.[39] In contrast to Heilman, I would argue that the tragic model is evident, but only insofar as it is parodied. The drama of suffering, Biedermann as victim, is mocked, but so, too, is Biedermann as tragic hero: the protagonist is stupid and weak; his conflict is hardly genuine, it is absurd; and he succumbs to a kind of self-pity. His intentions may be good, but his subsequent action is a comic reduction.

Parody of tragedy is polyvalent.[40] It may reduce tragedy to the contradictions of society and evoke a comic world in which fate is

not predetermined; if contradictory social structures or the categories with which the comic figure sees the world were altered, a
seemingly inevitable fate could be overcome.[41] Parody of tragedy
can also involve a critique of a tragic author's presuppositions and
style, as, for example, with Aristophanes' many jabs at Euripides
or Brecht's mockery of Goethe in *Arturo Ui*. It can mock a particular tragic moment, for example, tragic pathos: consider the ironization of near self-sacrifice and suicide in Lenz's *The Tutor* and
Büchner's *Leonce and Lena* or Woody Allen's parody of the hero's
fixation on death in *Love and Death*. At times comedy mocks the
tragic hero's obsession with greatness and inability to compromise,
which leads to a suffering that more balanced individuals might
know how to avoid. The self-sacrificing hero is too impatient, the
stubborn hero unable to compromise, and so forth. The truth of Ajax
is in a sense his insanity; his thirst for greatness can be parodied.

Above all, however, the parody of tragedy targets not the tragic
hero but the comic protagonist who claims for himself tragic stature. The comic protagonist, unstable, inadequate, and without
character, deems his situation noble or tragic. Molière's Arnolphe is
a good example, as when he *threatens* to weep or tear his hair out if
Agnes does not give in to him (*The School for Wives* V.iv); pitying
himself, the hero only adds to his extreme subjectivity. Comedy
thus includes not only a negation of the substance of tragedy but
also an ironization of this negation of substance. In the rhetoric of
the early Hegelians, it includes the ugly as the first, the comic as
the second, negation, whereby the ugly is "nothing but the appearance of false spirit that offers resistance to truth" (Ruge, *Neue Vorschule* 110, my translation; cf. Ruge 60). We laugh not only at comedy's justified mockery of tragic pathos and pessimism but at comic
insufficiency, the unjust erasure of tragic substance.

Lamenting that happiness is illusory, that nothing is secure,
that the forces of the world make chaos of our lives, the hero attempts to justify, from a broader perspective, his self-indulgent despair, his inconsistency, his weakness. The seemingly tragic voice,
however, is spoken not by the great hero who accepts responsibility
for his actions, but by the victim of suffering, such as Euripides'
Polynestor, who lacks tragic grandeur (*Hecuba* 955–960). The comic
hero is not great, and his suffering is not deep. To suffer deeply and
not to speak of it is noble; the comic hero, in contrast, suffers
mildly and speaks obsessively of his suffering. In comedy such parody of tragedy is dominant; this reduction of tragedy mocks the
hero more than it does the pathos of tragedy.

The comic protagonist, preoccupied with his suffering, is unwilling to be hard on himself. Conflict arises not from the hero's greatness but from his limitations, his comic reduction of a true telos. Schnitzler's Anatol longs for permanence, for exclusive and symmetrical relations, but is unwilling to act in such a way as to attain these goals. His seemingly genuine suspicions of infidelity are a reduction of the substantial: first, they are self-contradictory in the sense that Anatol demands fidelity even as he betrays his beloved; second, the stupidest, littlest events give rise to suspicions of infidelity; and third, Anatol reflects not at all on the asymmetrical structures that trigger such infidelity; rather, he is blindly concerned with his own lack of power over the other, who has escaped into the hands of a rival, and his private suffering.[42] Puntila, a drunk who pities himself, likewise lacks the strength and consistency to develop genuine intersubjective relations. We see in reduction a comic inability on the hero's part to transform himself, to learn and to change; there is no evidence of the recognition we often see in the tragic hero or in the comic hero of intersubjectivity.[43] Anatol and Puntila deem their situations tragic, but the audience can hardly take seriously the hero who pities himself and is obsessed with his own suffering.[44]

The embrace of particularity relates also to the motif of death, frequent not only in tragedy but also in the comic parody of tragedy. The tragic hero can face death, for he sees in it only the dissolution of his own finite spirit, a small loss in comparison with his participation in the universal. The comic hero recognizes only what is particular and finite, and so death becomes for him an issue with which he is often, explicitly or implicitly, preoccupied.

Cavalier and Probabilistic Tendencies

Though the hero of reduction has a limited understanding of the good, he does indeed want the good. This evokes two interesting types of action. First, the hero states his goal but fails to reach it owing to weakness. He acts with a bad conscience, though it doesn't trouble him too strongly, for a bad conscience would be incompatible with the protagonist's view of his own invincibility. Where the tragic hero remains consistent and accepts consequences, including guilt, the comic hero gives in, indulges himself, and shifts perspectives. The hero fails to admit his mistakes, and when he does, he imagines that his desire for the good suffices.

Even if the deed was evil, the intention was good. Moreover, the hero's standards shift as easily as do his desires, and so in this respect as well the pains of conscience easily disappear. Conscience, understood as freedom of conscience, something purely subjective, becomes the "principle of moral anarchy" (Scheler, *Formalism* 324; *Formalismus* 327). The hero believes that he is acting consistently, but his concept of himself and his actions contradict one another. Eduard von Hartmann writes insightfully: "To the essence of comedy belongs not only that it is illogical and in the end reveals itself as such and cancels itself, but rather also that it pretends to be a logical entity and poses as such, because it considers itself such" (2:329, my translation).

The hero fails to see the error owing to stupidity or recalcitrance; yet he is conscious enough to think that his position is just. The hero, not the world, is at fault; thus, we watch with approval as he pushes himself to the point of absurdity. Only the absurd consequences of his behavior will teach him his error and sharpen his awareness. What is erroneous unmasks itself as such. In the rhetoric of the nineteenth-century Hegelian, the ugly becomes comic. When a comic hero lies, for example, we enjoy not only the cleverness of the lying but also its consequences, which undo the hero. What differentiates this comic structure and subsequent ones from mere coincidence is the extent to which the hero's subjectivity is responsible for the comic contradiction.

Second, the hero may have an intuitive sense of the good, but he trivializes it and so ends up seeking a reduced goal. The hero, however, is unwilling to recognize that his goal is reduced, and, given his partly developed subjectivity, feels compelled to justify his goal. The hero's capacity for reflection, however, is not so developed that he is aware of first principles and thus of the untenability of his particular goal. Because there are many ways of viewing the world and because every action must have some ground, the hero simply selects or invents a reason for acting as he does. Hegel calls this probabilism. The hero is correct; there should be a ground. Yet the hero sees that there are many grounds and that they are often opposed to one another, and so any action can find its own ground.[45] Again, the hero reduces the absolute. He has an intuitive sense of the good (the need for a reason or ground) but undermines this by recognizing any and all grounds as long as they serve his reduced purpose: seduction, intoxication, whatever. Again, the moment of subjectivity dominates. Objective conditions do not supply the ground; instead, the subject decides, quite arbitrarily, which grounds to pick. The hero, however, doesn't admit this; for him, the reason legitimates the deed. This overlooked moment of arbitrariness subverts the objective order, including religious tradition and society's ethical code.[46]

Related both to the bad conscience and the idea of probable cause is the hero's trivialization of the problem of means and ends. The hero seeks an end, say love, and finds that an appropriate means to this end is seduction. This can give rise to bad conscience (love has been reduced to seduction), which, however, doesn't bother the hero too much, not only because he views himself as invincible, but because nature is for him primary to spirit, or the hero can find probable cause for seduction (for example, the argument that the end justifies the means). Here, however, the means (instrumentalization) undermine the end (the noninstrumentalization inherent in any affirmative symmetrical relationship). The hero has erased not only his freedom but that of the other, for the other is viewed as an object to be used for the satisfaction of the hero's desires. In *The School for Wives*, Arnolphe wants a symmetrical marriage in the sense of the one-to-one correspondence of genuine fidelity, but he would achieve this by breaking the symmetry of subject-subject relations and transforming his bride-to-be into a victim, an object to be manipulated. His goal is partially just, his tactics, however, are brutal; they undermine his purpose.[47] The hero of reduction selects, according to his own probable cause, the various means toward his end, and when confronted with the contradiction is likely to say that all positions are contradictory, a pragmatic contradiction typical for this subgenre.

In the comedy of reduction the hero does not hold his goal high and simply fail to attain it; on the contrary, he reduces his goal and generally sees himself as realizing it.[48] He is like the drunk who decides to pass by the pub without entering and after passing it decides to go in to reward himself for having passed it. The element of dishonesty elicits still further comedy, for the hero spares no imagination in creating fictions and deceptions that serve to justify his reduced existence. Again, the hero of reduction is not consciously or intentionally evil or corrupt. He is simply led to violations of proper behavior by way of his weak reasoning or lack of will. At times the comic deed arises from appropriate reasoning but a false premise. So, for example, the actions of Shakespeare's Malvolio, who has—like many a comic hero of reduction—so high an opinion of himself that he is easily fooled by his vanity.

The hero of reduction expresses his obsession with subjectivity not only by valuing his own greatness but by elevating his eccentricity and uniqueness. The hero, accepting the premises of what Hegel calls *Verstand*, believes that he can assert himself as an individual only by reacting against what is general and common, and he does so with no regard for what is in and of itself valid. Particularity, no longer an element of character, becomes a goal in itself. Schnitzler's Anatol embraces eccentricity, even if it should destroy him.

Aristophanes and Rötscher's Hegelian Analysis

Hegel's central insight into comedy, as we have seen, is his association of comedy with subjectivity. In a work dedicated to Hegel and which Hegel possessed (*Verzeichnis*), Heinrich Theodor Rötscher analyzes Aristophanic comedy by way of the transition from objectivity to subjectivity, from the reliance on tradition and objective values to its dissolution. Rötscher describes the subject matter of Aristophanic comedy as a battle between, on the one hand, "simple moral custom, shame before the law, in short unreflected obedience that recognizes the law and moral custom as ultimate and decisive without needing another authority" and, on the other hand, a "subjectivity for which moral custom and law are no longer the highest authority and which instead draws determination from its own thinking and imagining" (47, my translation). He continues: "Belief in gods, laws, and moral customs are thereby robbed of their former strength and power, since they must first be brought before the forum of reflection and thought in order to receive validation. This battle can thus be characterized abstractly as the opposition of simple moral substance and its objectivity, in which the individual is immersed, and free subjectivity, which renounces the same. This subjectivity dethrones objectivity as such, i.e., as what is immediately valid and decisive . . . and exercises its judgment on it internally" (47–48, my translation).

For Rötscher, the essence of Aristophanes is the development of a subjectivity that reasons and questions and thereby dissolves the objectivity and stability of tradition and state. This reason is not yet the clear reason of freedom, but a reason influenced by nature and the private and arbitrary desires of the self. It is a purely formal capacity of reason and individual will: "The purely formal nature of will, which we call caprice, can choose the lowest as well as the highest, the most moral as well as the most repugnant; it casts

its lot with one or the other according to the contingent constitution of the subject" (48, my translation). The Sophists can be
viewed as the first probabilists: they recognize that even as the
individual seeks private fulfillment, he wants to preserve the appearance of objective right, and so the creativity of his language
replaces the objectivity of truth. Aristophanes attacks the various
intellectual destroyers of the state, Euripides, the Sophists, and
Cleon, who exhibit subjective passions and offer rhetorical defenses
of the same. *The Frogs* most clearly contrasts the objectivity of Aeschylus and the subjectivity of Euripides, but Euripides is a central
figure in two earlier Aristophanic comedies as well, *Acharnians*
and the *Thesmophoriazusae*, and he is parodied in almost all of the
extant plays. For Aristophanes, the language of Euripides is the
language of deception, social disintegration, and evil. *The Clouds*
mocks the subjectivity of the Sophists, including Socrates. Scientific speculation calls into question religious traditions, and rhetoric undermines the previously accepted givens of tradition, including its moral precepts. Socrates, the individual and eccentric
thinker, upsets the commonality of Greek ethical life. Not tradition, but man, indeed the cleverest man, becomes the measure of
all things; not validity, but victory, determines truth. *The Birds*
represents and mocks the dissolution of the state, the emptiness of
the falsely tragic posture, and the baseless ideas of arbitrary spirit.

    As Hegel suggested, Aristophanes' *Ecclesiazusae* is an interest-
ing example of comic reduction. The protagonists' goal is not something particular, as is usually the case in reduction, but something
general, happiness; yet the general is reduced to enjoyment, which
itself depends on the particularity (and arbitrariness) of drives. Enjoyment lies in the vision of the particular subject and is as such no
longer universal. The good intentions within reduction and the formal virtues within negation are essential to the success of the
genres, for we would otherwise react with disgust or boredom.
There must be a moment of substance—however mild, however
levelled, however limited; in Aristophanes' works such a moment is
always present.

    In Rötscher's reading, the women choruses of *Lysistrata* and *Ec-
clesiazusae* express the private desires and passions that serve
only to dissolve the objectivity of tradition, but they also mock
these passions and indirectly recognize the validity of the Athenian
state. In *Lysistrata*, the women openly seek the interests of all
Greece, whereas the men represent only particular interests. While
the women are mocked for their frivolity and elevation of the pri-

vate, the men have a similarly limited perception of what is true and essential, in this case on the level of the state. With Rötscher's analysis we can better grasp why Hegel should tell us that only after reading Aristophanes can we truly know, "how a person can be hoggishly happy [wie dem Menschen sauwohl sein kann]" (15: 553; A 1221, my translation). Not just satire, but gaiety in satire is the essence of Aristophanes. The subjectivity of the characters, whether in the form of reduction or negation, is taken to the extreme and the audience, if not also the characters—as in Rötscher's reading—recognizes its absurdity.

Although Aristophanes' plays are highly episodic, they do not fit the most episodic of comic genres, the thetic genre of coincidence: Aristophanes' plays are too much informed by subjectivity. Withdrawal, on the other hand, presupposes too developed a subjectivity as well as an endorsement of subjectivity, which we do not find in Aristophanes. Instead, his comedies fit the patterns of reduction and negation. His best comedy of negation, *The Clouds*, has, appropriately, the strongest plot line. His comedies of reduction and social negation, on the other hand, are looser and more textured; reduction and social negation seem best to accommodate this style, which is characteristic of Old Comedy as well as much of contemporary comedy.

Rötscher's work represents an essentially forgotten analysis of comedy by one of Hegel's earliest students, more forgotten even than the works of Weiße, Ruge, or Vischer. Unlike works by Hegel's other students, Rötscher's analysis is historical and interpretive; it does not attempt a broadly aesthetic or systematic view of genre. It suggests that Aristophanes can be read and analyzed in the light of a developing subjectivity that assumes the characteristics of what we have called reduction and negation. Greek subjectivity is not as absolutely subjective as modern subjectivity (a Werther, for example, could not have appeared as the hero of a Greek work), but precisely in Aristophanic comedy we see a reflection of the most subjectively oriented developments and expressions of the Greek mind.

*

A danger of the comedy of reduction is that the audience is not disturbed, merely entertained, by the hero of reduction. The audience thus accepts as normal, rather than rejects as untenable, the hero's inadequacies. The viewer who identifies with the protagonist of reduction and finds him genuinely likeable has himself succumbed to the comic. The protagonist is sympathetic in the sense that he does want truth, and we watch him with mildness as he stumbles from this path; but we are also critical, for he does indeed stumble, he does indeed reduce truth.

Coincidence suggests that people are naturally good. Reduction suggests nature alone does not lead to harmony. As we have seen, arbitrary freedom harbors a social dimension; it can, and often does, involve the subjugation of another, the introduction of asymmetrical relations. No such asymmetry exists in true freedom. A purpose of comedy is to encourage reflection on the arbitrariness of natural drives and particular inclinations, on their comic import, and thus to create the mental apparatus for their control.

The Comedy of Negation (2b)

In the comedy of reduction, the hero has valid goals but insufficient means; in the next form, the comedy of negation, we see a reversal. The subject has insubstantial goals and fails, but in failing demonstrates substantial means. The audience, aware of the untenability of the hero's aspirations, is not disappointed to see him fall. Outstanding examples are Aristophanes' *The Clouds*, Johnson's *Volpone*, Molière's *The Miser*, Goldoni's *The Liar*, and Kleist's *The Broken Jug*.[49]

In this subgenre, subjectivity knows itself to be independent of norms of justice and duty. It decides for itself what is just. The hero of negation sees the world as something made by humanity and thus alterable by it. Because the subject is primary, objectivity in the form of *Sittlichkeit*, or ethical substance, is viewed as relative. Subjectivity leads here to a focus on consciousness and self-reflection at the expense of human relations, and within self-reflection an emphasis not on universals but on the particularity of the self. Because the comic hero's subjectivity is all-important, the hero is unwilling to enter into relations with others or to treat them as equals. Instead, the hero unscrupulously seeks his own advantage.

Negation recreates a moment of coincidence insofar as the other is reduced to a contingent element; the other, not recognized in its subjectivity, is treated as an object. The hero of negation doesn't even want the good; he is markedly evil, as in *The Miser*, or a clear hypocrite, as in *Tartuffe*. Nonetheless, the evil hero employs substantial means, and viewers delight in the persistence and resourcefulness, the audaciousness and inventiveness with which a Tar-

tuffe or an Adam cunningly pursues his false goals. The hero, however, is not tragic. A hero whose morality supersedes society's and
suffers for it differs from a protagonist who suspends society's morality, not because he adheres to a philosophically more viable
ethic but because he elevates his private needs and desires. The
former represents the tragedy of self-sacrifice, the latter the comedy of negation.

In *The Broken Jug*, the hero inverts the Socratic (and tragic)
insight that it is better to suffer than to do wrong. The irony here
is that Adam's destructive principle is ultimately self-destructive.
The play is an extended pragmatic contradiction: the hero presides
over a trial that establishes his own guilt. The judge is the criminal
and unveils himself as such in the process of investigating others.
The play demonstrates that the figure who exalts power over justice ("I can administer justice this way or that" 635; my translation) adopts a self-contradictory stance that leads to a philosophical self-cancellation and, on the level of plot, to the hero's demise.
The comedy of negation often uses contrast to undermine the hero.
Adam's corruption and lies contradict the dignity of the court.
Hauptmann's Mother Wolff gives the appearance of moral outrage
when her crimes are reported. It is in the comic protagonist's interest that his lies at least appear true. He thus presupposes (or depends on) precisely what he denies, and this incongruity is comic.

To the extent that the hero of negation himself unveils the absurdity of his position—as when Falstaff's lies, for example, become clearly recognizable as lies—we are not disturbed by the
presence of negation; we know that it will undermine itself. In this
contradiction lies the comic moment. Despite the comic hero's
charm and dazzling intellect, he isn't as strong as he thinks he is.
His lawlessness is not only fascinating but also self-destructive.
Adam's split identity as judge and criminal and the ultimate subordination of his criminality to justice, for example, demonstrate that
the truth of subjectivity is intersubjectivity, here portrayed by justice.

The comedy of negation is often included as a submoment in
comedies where a different structure rules the tenor of the play.
One thinks of Wolf in Raimund's *The Spendthrift* or Madame
Schleyer in Nestroy's *A Man Full of Nothing*. Excluding the main
protagonist from the text's harmonic ending can be harmful to the
expected optimism of the comic genre. Frye writes of "the tendency
of the comic society to include rather than exclude" (*Anatomy* 166).
Moreover, the comedy of social negation, which depicts a plurality

of false subjects, is already implicit in the idea of individual negation. Negative subjectivity generally engenders a plurality of negative subjects. Rarely does an author dwell on a position whose passage to a further one is so obvious.

The Resourceful Protagonist

The comic hero of negation, elevating subjectivity over truth, is often rich in both imagination and rhetoric; this adds to the aesthetic strength of the genre. We see not only a dramatic tension between subjectivity and objectivity, but a subjectivity that is rich in its use of language. The language of the hero is comic, first, because of its cleverness and intricacies; the hero invents, displays, and dissembles with passion and effectiveness. It is comic, second, because of the situation in which it is employed. The hero of negation often finds himself in an interesting dialogical situation, where what he says and the situation in which he says it are incongruous.[50]

Lelio in Goldoni's *The Liar* seeks evil but does so with irrepressible imagination, inventiveness, and self-confidence. He is charming, full of life, and quick of wit. Every chance event is brilliantly transformed into an act of his own intentions. He makes the most of every opportunity—until eventually his lies and deceit come back to haunt him, partly in the form of the persons he has disavowed in word but cannot deny in any objective sense. His statements and the situations in which he makes them are utterly incongruous, culminating in his many assertions—always in the midst of a web of lies—that he has never uttered an untruth.

The formal greatness of Kleist's hero likewise consists in his resourcefulness: Adam knows of the difference between seeming and being, and he cunningly exploits this knowledge with his rhetoric and lies, a form of subjectivity that presupposes a difference between inner and outer. In negation the tension is manifest for the hero and in some cases, in *The Miser* for example but not in *The Broken Jug*, for others.[51] The other characters' lack of knowledge in *The Broken Jug* creates another level of tension, that between the audience who is aware and the characters on stage who are unaware. The hero's knowledge of the situation grants him formal superiority. Adam's ability to spin ever new tales, to adhere to his position consistently, false as it is, further demonstrates his excellence. This formal virtue also endears him to the audience. The hero is clever and exhibits *poneria*. Commenting on the connection between evil and cleverness, Cedric Whitman writes: *"Poneria* in modern Greek indicates not wickedness, but the ability to get the advantage of somebody or some situation by virtue of an unscrupulous, but thoroughly enjoyable exercise of craft. Its aim is simple— to come out on top; its methods are devious, and the more intricate, the more delightful" (30).

In contrast, the heroes of objectivity are dimwitted and easily deceived. Molière's Tartuffe owes his success less to his virtues of persuasion than to the simplicity and blindness of those whom he persuades, above all Orgon, who, until the play's conclusion, might be said to be a bewitched hero of reduction; he wants to do the good but is misinformed as to its content.[52] Similarly, Kleist's play is not only about deception, it is also about blind obedience and faith in authority—comic reduction, if you will (Wittkowski, *"Der zerbrochene Krug"*). In negation, however, the focus is less on the norms of objectivity that are eventually reinstated than on the imagination and comic resourcefulness of the hero who is nonetheless to be dethroned. The moment of truth is there in the hero's words and antics; it must only be uncovered. Adam unconsciously states the truth on many an occasion: "I'm a rogue, if it wasn't Lebrecht" (1205; my translation). The hero of negation does not recognize his superficially tragic predicament. Instead, he busily attempts to skirt it, although he does so in such a way as to arouse laughter in the audience. Consider Tartuffe's avoidance of tragedy when he says to Elmire: "I even resolved to avoid your sight, believing you to be an obstacle to my salvation; but at length I came to realize, O fairest among women, that there need be nothing culpable in my passion and that I could reconcile it with virtue" (III.iii.947–951).

Characters who have formal virtues and are entertaining and partly admirable, such as Adam in *The Broken Jug* or Mother Wolff in *The Beaver Coat*, must be distinguished from those who simply represent untenable positions and fail not because of a hidden dialectic of injustice but because of ineptitude and shallowness. Senden in Freytag's *The Journalists* fits the latter pattern. Müller in Alfred Bäuerle's *The Burghers of Vienna* likewise lacks the wit and verbal dexterity of Kleist's Adam; he exhibits merely a steadfast purpose and the accumulation of wealth, and so the play as a whole suffers in comparison. Similarly, Madame Schleyer in Nestroy's *A Man Full of Nothing* fails to exhibit the formal virtues of Kleist's Adam; she is ultimately more ridiculous than comic. Shakespeare's *The Merry Wives of Windsor* varies the dominant structure of negation insofar as the heroes of everyday life and nor-

malcy are just as clever as the evil hero of negation; yet this levelling of the hero weakens the play. Who would not prefer the comic
Falstaff of *Henry IV, Parts I and II*?

The Victory of Objectivity

Despite the formal virtues of the hero of negation, society, with
correct content and weak form (one thinks not only of characters
such as Orgon but also of Adams's competition, which, with the
exception of the opportunistic Licht, consists of halfwits), still wins
out. Objectivity asserts itself and gains its revenge. Even comedy is
not without its moment of objectivity; indeed, objectivity, which
does battle with the protagonist of negation, eventually gains the
upper hand. Bäuerle's *The Burghers of Vienna* heralds the everyday world of the Viennese *Bürger*: modesty, virtue, honor. The
tyche of coincidence resurfaces in a different guise: as in coincidence, the subject's intentions are thwarted; unlike in coincidence,
however, the intentions are evil, and not the subject, but the opponent, is content with the resolution.

The hero of negation, although clever and manipulative, is ultimately defeated by a naive objectivity that recognizes—often intuitively, rather than intellectually—the hero's sophistry. One is reminded of the story of a witty and charming lover who tries to
seduce a virgin, claiming that he is himself pure and innocent, and
through intercourse, would be able to implant his innocence into
her, thus doubling her purity. The aspiring lover, whose rhetoric
amuses the audience, nonetheless fails. The cleverest comedies of
negation are those defined right from the start by a pragmatic contradiction of this kind. Harpagon wants money he cannot and will
not spend—his desire is insatiable. Adam presides over a trial at
which he is the perpetrator.

In many cases, however, the victory of objectivity also involves
the counter-hero's rising beyond innocence and recognizing duplicity; objectivity passes over into subjectivity (or consciousness) and
only thereby does it defeat a competing (and evil) subjectivity. We
see this, for example, in Garson Kanin's *Born Yesterday*. The punishment of the criminal is a negation of the negation; as such, justice and harmony are restored. Retribution against the comic hero
is generally instituted by the state, whereas in tragedy it is tied to
the individual's personality or desire for revenge (13:242). In trag-

edy the hero defines the law; in comedy heroic subjectivity is replaced by a larger collectivity.

The victory of objectivity in these works lends support to a comic reversal of dialectical logic. Normally, form is viewed as antithetical; thus, content passes over into form. Here, however, form passes over into content. The action demonstrates that being can assert itself, even without knowledge, against purely negative thought. As if fulfilling the words of Goethe's Mephistopheles, the hero of negation would do evil evermore, yet create the good.[53] In this antithetical subgenre heroes who do battle with themselves are frequent. In splitting himself, the hero destroys himself. This issues in hope. Society catches up with the hero. Objectivity claims its place.[54]

The reassertion of objectivity may take many forms, though in every case we recognize an echo of coincidence. The dialectic of calculation and chance is often extremely amusing—especially insofar as it reveals not only a contradiction and an impotence on the part of the hero but also insofar as it grants the comic hero, or, in the case of negation the comic opponent, his deepest wish and grants the audience an experience of poetic justice. The destruction of Molière's Tartuffe, like that of most heroes of negation, is inevitable. Tartuffe depends on justice for his acts of injustice; he relies on his "friend" Oberon and on the justice of the state, and he himself must, in order to carry out his unjust deeds, appear just. Tartuffe's negative position presupposes the positive code of justice he attempts to deny. Yet Molière only hints at this self-destruction.[55] On the level of plot, the King's messenger rescues the day. Though chance is indeed a kind of objectivity, the ultimate truth of negation is neither a reaffirmation of normalcy through chance, nor an objectivity by default, nor, as in a legitimate reading of the conclusion of *The Broken Jug*, a highly elusive harmony, but a higher order that integrates subjectivity into it, an inner resolution. Before we come to this synthesis of content and form, we must first consider a form of negation that represents a false, a merely attempted synthesis, the objectification of dominant subjectivity.

Social Negation

In some comedies negation of the good is not restricted to a single individual but rather permeates an entire society or at least most of that society. The expansion of negation and the subsequent structure of doubling are not only comic, but in a self-reflexive sense predictable: the deceiver is himself deceived. While this multiplicity is not different logically, it creates a new dramatic constellation. Not only the hero is corrupt; the egotistical concerns of the subject are spread over society. The good hero, if there is one, is isolated in his stance against this society. All relationships are now instrumentalized. Subjectivity has become objectified—but in a false way. By virtue of its self-contradictions, such a society is seen to be on the verge of destroying itself.

The expansion of negative subjectivity brings with it, ironically, an undermining of subjectivity. No single hero has a privileged status. While each individual claims a position of strength, the spread of power undermines these claims. Brecht's "Who doesn't think thereby of Richard the Third?" mocks Arturo Ui's distance from this standard (Prologue, my translation).[56] In the face of such a line as "The town is full of types like Ui right now" (sc. 1b, translation modified), the hero of Brecht's play is devastated; he wants to be recognized as a great gangster, a unique hero. Because we see in social negation the paradoxical erasure of individual subjectivity, an irony arises: the most subjective or antithetical of comic forms, social negation, shares a moment with the least subjective, namely coincidence—in each, character and individuality are underdeveloped.

Just as finite analogues exist for the comedy of reduction—stuttering, deafness, and so forth—so too for the comedy of negation. Consider doubling, the principal trigger for the transition to social negation. It is mildly comic when a protagonist peeps through a keyhole to spy on another; it is more comic when whoever is spying is also being spied upon, when two heads move to the keyhole simultaneously. When persons commit adultery in social negation, it invariably involves more than one deception. Congreve concludes *The Way of the World* with the lines: "From hence let those be warned, who mean to wed, / Lest mutual falsehood stain the bridal bed; / For each deceiver to his cost may find, / That marriage frauds too oft are paid in kind" (408). As in coincidence, the object (or other) takes on a life of its own and redirects or thwarts the conscious plans of the subject. In coincidence, chance is the principal counterforce; in negation, deception and intrigue are met by counterdeception and counterintrigue.

Instead of highlighting individual deviance, the comedy of social negation offers a portrait of the age. In many works, as, for example, Brecht's *Mahagonny*, not one character is morally admirable.

The good intentions of reduction are absent, as is the one character of principle we see in withdrawal. When the comedy of social negation does introduce a counter-hero, the character is usually cunning and clever but faces an uphill battle; power lies with the forces of society, and society is not converted at the end. The comedy of social negation is, like the comedy of reduction, a comic form with a muffled happy end. The counter-hero may succeed against society, but society is not cured of its ills. We see in certain plays that belong to this subgenre an affinity to comic withdrawal, as the following lines of misanthropy from Nestroy's *The Talisman* make clear: "I hate you, inhumane humanity. I want to flee from you. Oh, that a deserted place would take me in, I want to be totally alone!" (I.vii, my translation). In withdrawal we see a hero, an intellectual, reject society and withdraw from it; in the comedy of social negation the counter-hero accommodates himself to society, illustrating the absurdity of its tenets.[57] He is at first a victim of a world that treats not only the outsider but its own members asymmetrically. The counter-hero, however, resists this asymmetry through trickery.[58] Such works proffer a spiritual countermodel to the antiquated concept that the comic hero is of lower rank; here, the butt of the comedy is the higher echelon of society, those in power; the hero is the resourceful and tenacious underling.

The structure of the outsider donning the disguise or imitating the actions of the forces to be ruined does more than serve the plot. Works such as Gogol's *The Inspector General*, Nestroy's *The Talisman*, Zuckmayer's *The Captain of Köpenick*, Brecht's *Schweyk in the Second World War*, and Ritt's *The Front* seem to suggest, on either the symbolic or literal level, that these societies are ultimately self-destructive. The outsider who adopts the tricks and techniques of the targeted society merely accelerates its internal decline. The moment is sometimes evident even in the comedy of individual negation. Volpone dons disguises to attain unjust ends (and is thus a hero of individual negation), but his actions also reveal some of the absurdities and contradictions of the larger society.

In the comedy of social negation, society is hierarchically structured; even as the hero ascends, others remain below. Nestroy's *The Talisman* shows, through the figure of repetition, how similar the various stages are. The play also shows how one must push down on those below in order to preserve one's status above them. Finally, with the prop of a wig the play illustrates how arbitrary the exclusive claims of the hierarchy are. One's thoughts or actions are unimportant in comparison with one's external appearance and possessions. Persons are reduced to their function in the hierarchy.

The Ironic Erasure of Subjectivity

Heroes of social negation who ardently seek to elevate their subjectivity are in most cases ironically undermined. We see this structure particularly well in the works of Carl Sternheim and Bertolt Brecht, two of this century's greatest comic artists. Many of Sternheim's comedies fit the pattern of social negation, especially if we read them less according to the author's intention, that is, as a portrayal of middle-class heroes, and more along the—well-accepted—lines of a satire of bourgeois mediocrity and contradictions.[59] In *Burgher Schippel* and *The Snob*, for example, the counter-hero advances into a social structure that remains asymmetrical and corrupt. Integration into the (new) social sphere is everything but an advance. Schippel eventually becomes a *Bürger*, though his path to this position is rocky (owing to his background and the prejudices of others) and farcical (the duel). Less a hero, he is the object of satire. Moreover, the sphere he enters is characterized by arrogance and prejudice. The hero encounters a society that looks down on him, but as soon as he enters it, he acts like one of its members. Asymmetry is not overcome. The victims are merely altered. In *The Snob*, Christian Maske exhibits only secondary virtues, ambition and hard work, and he treats Sybil and his parents as objects (even when he calls for their return, they remain for him "objects of luxury" [II.vi]). But Christian is not the isolated hero; his entire existence is predicated on his becoming part of an aristocratic society, whose main features are arrogance and duplicity.

Identity derives partly from social bonds, but Maske, in seeking his identity solely in society, encounters two problems.[60] First, the aristocratic society that determines his identity is characterized by power and appearance rather than humanity and substance. He enters an instrumental marriage: the partners use each other to gain what they desire. Second, Maske seeks identity by freeing himself from the past. The subjective hero, wanting to define himself autonomously, cannot stand to be limited by what he cannot control—his birth, his origins, his parents. Rather than being grateful for his existence, he tries to escape the past by sending his parents away, in effect buying them off. The hero's subjectivity and

formal virtues of discipline, imitation, and phantasy have here
their limits—that is, until he invents a new past. The subjective
hero denies nature and contingency, what we saw elevated in the
more objective genres; he views his past not as what is handed
down to him, not as something beyond his control, but as something he can invent out of his own subjectivity and something he
can learn from books (for example, the "Who's Who in Nobility"
[II.iii]). Grand is the final scene of *The Snob*, where the wife longs
for the consummation of marriage, and Maske talks obsessively of
himself, his business, his father, and his mother—insofar as he is
their offspring (or, more accurately, the alleged offspring of his
mother and a French aristocrat). To succeed he must deny himself
and his true origins; it is a perverse dialectic. Impromptu and with
the imagination of an Adam, Maske invents a fiction about his
mother's infidelity. Appearance rules, and so Maske rules. He succeeds in the end, because the world of objectivity is absent.

Sternheim's comedies are ambivalent: We admire the discipline
and phantasy of the hero, the secondary virtues that allow him to
succeed (Emrich's heroism thesis). In this sense the heroes fit the
pattern of Lelio in *The Liar* or Adam in *The Broken Jug*. Yet the
heroes go much too far in adapting themselves to society (this is
almost a Leonard Zelig problem). They are satirized for being part
of a corrupt order. To gain identity in the collective, they trample
others and erase their individuality. Maske at one point greatly
mourns that he has recalled his parents only after it is too late—
his mother is dead before his message requesting his parents' return is even written. He loves his mother, and he has hurt her and
lost her in his striving. He must suppress his moments of humane-
ness. Further, the success is ambivalent: he succeeds on the level of
appearances, which alone matter within this society, but in essence
his success remains merely apparent, and his world is the topsy-
turvy world of absurdity.

In *Tabula rasa*, Sternheim offers us a hypocritical, but manipulative and clever hero, who consistently speaks duplicitously; instead of failing, the hero Ständer succeeds at achieving financial
security and autonomy (rather than celebrating commonness, the
final line asserts "What happiness, not to have children!" [my
translation]). Sternheim's elevation of subjectivity and egoism—
rather than its traditional overcoming in the comedy of negation—
may relate to the difficulties of finding individuality and self-iden-
tity in a world of mass movements. Or it may derive from the
increasing dissolution of social norms. Not surprisingly, Franz

Mennemeier sees in *Tabula rasa* a reversal of Hegel: subjectivity is equated with the substantial. This leads Mennemeier to suggest—almost in the spirit of absolute irony—that not the work, but Sternheim himself, is comic, as he fails to see the contradictions in his plays ("Carl Sternheim" 723–724). The verdict is clever and partly true, but it may be too harsh, for Sternheim is aware of at least some of the contradictions of pure subjectivity—even as he continues to elevate it.

Brecht's early play *A Man is a Man* argues that a person has no fixed identity and is determined by his environment. The play suggests not only that we can externally manipulate this raw material ("You can do with a human being whatever you want" sc. 8, my translation), but also that we can transform it internally. It doesn't pay to preserve any identity that holds one back; thus, the self is willing to relinquish its entire past. As Jesse suggests, everything and everyone is relative (sc. 9). This relativity represents the stance of subjectivity, even as its consequence is the erasure of subjectivity and identity. One subverts stability and expands the self only to erase the self. Galy Gay is transformed from a weak individual—by way of lack of resistance (he can't say "no"), bribery, intimidation, and ultimately a shift in desire—into a fierce and successful soldier, "the human fighting-machine" (sc. 11, my translation). What began as Galy Gay's decision to call an old elephant head a pole, and some maps an elephant, a decision that reflects the transformation of essence into function (if he can sell it as an elephant, it is an elephant), ends as a transformation of himself, the erasure of any private essence; he denies his identity so that he can survive (and flourish) as a soldier. In an inversion of Narcissus, he decides it is best not to be attracted to himself (sc. 9). Ironically, those who transform Galy Gay are later subject to his whims.

Brecht's play fulfills the demands of social negation: the institutionalization of asymmetry; loss of individuality; the survival of the self being dependent on the acceptance of the role given to it by society. Simultaneously, it parodies coincidence: persons merely play roles and do not develop their subjectivity, but rather assume the stances society offers them. If, as in coincidence, there is no developed sense of self, if our function in the collective is more important than our individuality, we can be made into whatever the forces of society deem fit. The malleable self can be the instrument (or victim) of an evil, as easily as a harmonic, collective. While identity crises normally originate from a character's obsession with subjectivity, Galy Gay's crisis in *A Man is a Man* stems from his lack of subjectivity and his being nothing but a victim of social manipulation. The tragic motif of heroic consistency, "Mann ist Mann," with the implication "one remains oneself," gives way to the comic motif of ephemerality and manipulation, "Mann ist Mann," with the implication that we are all interchangeable.

The erasure of subjectivity finds its twentieth-century peak in National Socialism. Brecht's *Schweyk in the Second World War*, which thematizes this movement, is another comedy of social negation. The forces in power treat each other and minorities as objects. A hero stands up against this society and fights it—not heroically, but comically—by becoming part of it. In the comedy of social negation, society appears on the verge of destroying itself; in some such comedies this destruction is aided by a hero who resists the society by imitating it to the extreme, thus exhibiting its absurdity. This moment of resistance might even be viewed as a bridge toward the comedy of withdrawal. Schweyk is the witty underdog who knows how to keep afloat. His survival illustrates the incompetence of the regime. The state, in turn, battles with itself; the Gestapo, for example, fights the SS. These contradictions will inevitably lead to self-destruction. A society that is not in harmony with itself, that consists of one entity seeking power over the other and vice versa, will eventually destroy itself.

Tyrants

Lying somewhere between individual and social negation is the individual hero who wields the collective power of the state. Tyrants are comic figures insofar as they pursue private or particular ends, unmotivated by any sense of objectivity. The proximity of tyranny and comedy builds on the comic *senex* of Roman drama as well as the doctrinaire pedants, despotic fathers, and conniving schemers of modern comedy; like these figures, the loathsome dictator is unveiled as grotesquely ludicrous. In individual and social negation alike, the moral law is suspended and arbitrary power is unleashed; probability and substantive intentions vanish and with them constitutive elements of tragedy.

Despite their power, Jarry's Ubu and Witkiewicz's Wahazar could not possibly be viewed as tragic. One even wonders whether Camus' Caligula isn't ultimately comic. Wahazar repeatedly focuses on his own subjectivity: "I have no equals . . . . I alone rule everything, and I'm responsible for everything, and answer only to myself alone" (110). Despite—or because of—this rhetoric of self, Wahazar loses any sense of identity (156, 166). He "transposes" his private "torments into universal values" (118). Comedy must take precedence over the tragedy of stubbornness when the arbitrariness of the hero's pursuits and *false* claims to grandeur are stressed. The comic hero is a performer, who reduces the essence of greatness to mere show. We delight in this charm and performance, but we do not take the character seriously as a substantive hero. Our recognition of this show as show, as illusion, separates the hero from tragedy and us from the followers of any, even mildly, aestheticized politics.

If the tyrant is dethroned and order restored, individual negation is at work. If the tyrant has an array of myrmidons—or if when the power of one tyrant is taken away, it merely passes into the hands of another—we move into the sphere of social negation. The comedy of social negation recognizes that while unjust heroes come and go, the continued arbitrary wielding of power transcends the overturning of any one character. The genre is bleaker in its recognition of evil than the comedy of individual negation, less willing to recognize the positive that arises from a double negation. Being the more pessimistic genre, it has, not surprisingly, gained importance in this century.

Endings

Earlier comedies of social negation, as, for example, Sheridan's *The School for Scandal*, have explicit happy ends. More modern texts tend toward muffled happy ends. First, we may see an isolated happy end where the hero prevails but society remains the same. In Nestroy's *The Talisman*, Titus adopts asymmetrical tactics in order to ascend in society; this can hardly generate a justified happy end. The happy end must be tacked on, through chance, to demonstrate that until society changes (and not that the individual accustom himself to the ways of the unjust society), an earned happy end is mere fiction. Nestroy integrates a moment of coincidence into his comedy of social negation in order to show that a happy end is impossible when society fails to change. In this way an ironic moment of the comedy of coincidence reinforces an argument of the comedy of negation. Second, we may see an ironic happy end where the hero gets his goal only after giving in to the conditions imposed on him by society. We see this in Brecht's *A*

Man is a Man and Zuckmayer's *The Captain of Köpenick*: Voigt receives his longed-for pass, but only after serving a prison term. Third, the work may suggest, at times quite subtly, that society is destroying itself. Schnitzler's *The Green Cockatoo* moves in this direction, as does Brecht's *Fear and Misery of the Third Reich*, whose comic moments hint at the inner contradictions of the Third Reich. In each case the moment of harmony is either ironized or postponed.

*

In the comedy of social negation, we have a plurality of subjects—as in coincidence—but now with incorrect content and a dangerous form of false subjectivity—not a weak subjectivity, as in reduction, but a strong subjectivity, which will reach its goals and create victims before it destroys itself. A plurality of negative subjects, each of which instrumentalizes the other, works against the idea of affirmative intersubjectivity, which is the telos of the entire comic development. Recognition of the untenability of mere negation and awareness of the need for a negation of negativity engenders a genre that pulls us back in the direction of synthesis, the comedy of withdrawal.

The Comedy of Withdrawal (2c)

In the comedy of withdrawal, one figure arises to protest the inadequacies of a corrupt reality. The hero is justified but not yet strong enough that he can have the impact on society he desires. The comedy of withdrawal is the most complex comic genre thus far, yet it falls one step short of portraying a full harmony. Here the subject fails not because he has inadequate means to a true goal, as in reduction, or invalid goals, as in negation, but because the subject, who is more or less correct in his views, cannot accomplish his goals in a world in which invalid goals reign. Heroes of withdrawal fail in part owing to their virtues. The form thus borders on tragedy. One might even be tempted to say that it deviates from tragedy only insofar as no one dies. (*Hamlet* has great affinities to this structure and minus its multiple deaths might well have been a comedy; similarly, Grillparzer's *Fraternal Quarrel*.)

From a more substantial perspective, however, we can argue that the comic structure remains insofar as we recognize a contingent weakness in the subject, specifically a weakness in the form of the hero's actions. The means the hero of withdrawal employs to realize the good are insufficient not because of the difficulties of the situation but because of particular contingencies on the part of the hero; this is comic. A further comic dimension is apparent when the hero of withdrawal exhibits the need to be acknowledged by what he negates. Consistently pointing out to others his independence, the hero only affirms his dependence (on the views of others). The hero pretends to withdraw and negate the world even as he insists on its recognition. He cannot do without the very sphere he negates. Where the tragic hero pursues an end consistently, sacrificing his life for it, the comic hero remains inconsistent, wanting success but neither fully sacrificing himself for it nor recognizing the means necessary for its realization. The comic hero of withdrawal integrates coincidence not only in the criticism of his contemporaries as mere puppets or marionettes but also, unwittingly, in the contradiction between his desire to abandon the world and the reality of his staying.

The Ambiguity of Withdrawal

Some examples will illustrate the ambiguities of this subgenre: the hero is in practice justified; in principle, however, not. Consider Molière's *The Misanthrope*. Alceste's high moral standards lead to his failure in society; he cannot possibly deal with those who are selfish, unjust, and hypocritical. Alceste both seeks and demands a symmetry of inner and outer self. His demand for symmetry in the sense of a one-to-one correspondence in his relationship with Célimène leads to his private unhappiness. Alceste will not compromise. He is in many respects a hero. Yet Alceste lacks tact and with this success, and so he is nonetheless the object of our laughter. Alceste must be candid and outspoken when he might have been elusive or silent.

Moreover, Alceste revels too greatly in his martyrdom; the play parodies, as much as identifies with, the hero's suffering. A fascinating structure of Alceste's misanthropy is that if he loses in his efforts to reform humanity, he can justify his pessimism. To have success would be to deny his position (as misanthrope); there is thus an existential desire for him to fail and so keep his identity intact. After being told that the world laughs at him, Alceste states: "It's a good sign and I welcome it, I find mankind so odious that I should hate to have it approve of me" (I.x.110–113). Alceste's high standards, when contrasted with reality, trigger his misanthropy. The absolute is central to the structure of withdrawal. Bernhard Sorg describes misanthropic individuals as "inspired by the yearning for the unconditional in humanity, which they do not find there" (32, my translation).[61] The reverse side of our admiration for these standards is our sense that the misanthrope's view of humankind is naive.[62] The play's various allusions to the hero's self-deceit reinforce this point, even as they do nothing to undermine the validity of his negation of this society.

We laugh not so much at Alceste's goals as at his failure to achieve them insofar as the failure lies partly within him. The hero of withdrawal lacks the means or the will to realize his ideal; he thus shares moments with the hero of reduction. Alceste is ineffective; he does not change the world. By criticizing failure in this way, the comedy of withdrawal supersedes the tragedy of self-sacrifice. The hero of a tragedy of self-sacrifice is right in sacrificing his life, yet the character is not right enough (it is important to have success for the good of the universal), and that should be shown. A work like *The Misanthrope* ironizes self-sacrifice as insufficient and so moves us in the direction of synthesis.

The titular hero of Schnitzler's *Professor Bernhardi* is correct in his stance; only he mistakenly views his intellectual stance as sufficient. He does not recognize the importance of that sphere which transcends the subject. Bernhardi acts as a particular, not a political, subject. His negation of society appears to represent an advance (the rejection of accepted norms is what pushes history forward), but it becomes an advance only insofar as new norms are realized. The subjectivity of the hero must be objectified.[63] It is at this point that the hero of withdrawal so often falls short.

Bernhardi's decision not to pursue his actions publicly, even when public opinion seems to be on his side, contributes to his failure. The comic hero withdraws—that is his greatness, his consistency, and that is his weakness, his subjectivity. Formally speaking, Bernhardi is not right. He renounces the objective structures of society, in this case the judicial system.[64] He is more interested in the determination of what is valid than in its intersubjective realization. Like Molière's Alceste, Bernhardi wants nothing to do with politics. He is concerned with his own fate, not with the impact an issue might have on society. Bernhardi is ashamed of praise; this sheds light on his preoccupation with himself. He views support as praise directed toward his individuality, not as allegiance on the part of the populace to a general cause. More so than the crowd, Bernhardi takes issues personally. He wants to go so far as to act against his admirers.

That a personal, private action does not suffice is clear in the play's closing passages.[65] Bernhardi asserts: "I simply did what I held to be right in one specific instance" (Ger 6:253; Eng 160). The minister responds ironically that he, too, would have acted like Bernhardi even if it meant he would end up in jail. Yet individual action isn't enough: "It seems much the same to me as trying to solve the social problem by making some poor devil a present of a villa" (Ger 6:253; Eng 160, translation modified). Moreover, doing what is just is not enough; the issue of success should not be ignored. Our principles must be preserved, not for the sake of preservation, but for the realization of norms in society. Although the comedy clearly ironizes the corruption of society, especially that of Flint, the moment of intersubjectivity for which Flint stands needs to be integrated into Bernhardi as well. The hero of withdrawal makes the mistake of not distinguishing between society or the state as it is and society or the state in principle, that is, the logic and meaning inherent in the possibilities of these structures (cf. R § 258 Z). Precisely when society is corrupt, so seems to be the message of many a comedy of withdrawal, society needs those who despise it most.

Finding it absurd to rule over an unjust state, the hero of Dürrenmatt's *Romulus the Great* becomes inactive; he withdraws in order that the unjust state dissolve: "It is my political insight to do nothing" (Ger 76; Eng 89). The situation is an absurd reversal of what one would expect, though within this comedy is a potential element of tragic self-sacrifice. Romulus is willing to sacrifice his life, his power, and the Roman state itself for the good of the world. Romulus fails, however, for the world's corruption and injustice transcend his empire. The future with the Germans is no better than a future with Rome. Odoaker, recognizing injustice in his own empire, announces: "a second Rome will rise, a Teutonic empire, as transitory as Rome and just as bloody" (Ger 109; Eng 113, translation modified). The emperor's withdrawal, a merely negative action, does not suffice even as the emperor appears the greatest, most insightful person of his time. Like Hamlet, Romulus must seek the just course of action in an unjust world; like Creon, his continued living seems worse than death. And yet Romulus remains a comic hero.

Möbius, the hero of Dürrenmatt's later play *The Physicists*, fails like Romulus to recognize the full political repercussions of his withdrawal. Yet his withdrawal is in a sense justified. The world is

not in a position to cope with his wisdom; the hero, however, fails
to counter this situation as best he might, and so even he is ironized. Möbius's negation of the concrete intersubjective sphere is illustrated in his treatment of family members (he must hurt them
to help them forget him) and his murder of Monika (he believes
that he must, for the sake of humanity, destroy the one person who
loves him). His subjectivity is in the interest of the world's salvation and so seems justified. Yet Möbius fails, and he fails it would
seem partially because he has too low an opinion of humanity.

Möbius's withdrawal is futile insofar as his discovery will simply
be made by another: "What Solomon had found can one day be
found also by another" (Ger 70; Eng 345, translation modified). His
skills are thus best utilized in caring for the correct use of his discovery. Yet the point is theoretical; the alternative is not really
open to Möbius, who has no real political power and who recognizes
in the state no overarching ethical concern. Möbius's withdrawal is
empirically justified, even if it is in principle untenable. Yet here
we come to the kind of paradox Dürrenmatt likes to portray; it is
precisely in his withdrawal that Möbius becomes "powerless" (Ger
71; Eng 346). Rendering the structure of thwarted intentions,
which we saw in coincidence, brutal rather than harmonic, Dürrenmatt states in his eighth and ninth theses on the play: "The more
human beings proceed by plan, the more effectively chance may
strike them. Human beings proceeding by plan wish to reach a def-
inite goal. Chance befalls them most severely, when through it
they reach the opposite of their goal: the very thing they feared,
they sought to avoid (e.g., Oedipus)" (Ger 78; Eng 350, translation
modified). Möbius is concerned with the consequences of his science but fails to control the consequences of his action.

Especially interesting in Dürrenmatt's play is the hidden connection between the comedy of withdrawal and the comedy of negation: that is, if the just subject (Möbius) withdraws from the world,
power is released into the hands of the unjust (Doktor von Zahnd);
but in this variation of the comedy of negation there is no happy
end. The forces of subjectivity will destroy not only themselves but
the world. The self-cancellation of injustice becomes universal.

Four types of relations between science and politics are sketched
by characters in the play: Newton is purely scientific, almost aesthetic if you will, and shows no interest in politics; Einstein serves
the politics of a particular state; Doktor von Zahnd serves her own
private interests; Möbius, finally, withdraws from politics for political reasons. All paths are revealed in their weakness. A fifth path,
active engagement with the politics of science for the sake of the

universal, is left as the alternative position not dramatized but invoked by the failure of the others.

Despite the comic hero's withdrawal and contradictions, the greatest critique within this subgenre is directed toward the subjectivity of the world, the false arrogance and biases of the characters in it. Hofmannsthal's *The Difficult Man*, for example, satirizes above all the overpowering self-assurance and unwarranted confidence of Vinzenz, Stani, and Neuhoff. One is tempted, like Hans Karl, to withdraw from a world in which subjectivity reigns so strongly, in which characters are so obsessed with their petty and particular interests.

The ambiguity of the genre must not, however, be lost. As understandable as the hero's withdrawal is, it is equally unjustified. The comedy of withdrawal is the most appropriate medium for portraying the naive idealist who is politically ineffective because he refuses to engage in the art of the possible. Hegel writes concerning the "self-conscious subject, content with itself only in its interiority": "But this subject, which spurns externality, is on its spiritual side not yet the true totality, which has for its content the absolute in the form of self-conscious spirituality; on the contrary, afflicted with opposition to the real, it is a purely abstract, finite, unsatisfied subjectivity" (14:122; A 513, translation modified). The hero of withdrawal is forced into the dualistic relationship of *Verstand*. The other remains other and so limits his perfection and freedom.

If the hero fails not only because of the inadequacies of society but owing to his inability to deal in the best way possible with that society, he is comic. Whereas the philosophy of reverse power positivism argues, "he who fails and suffers is just," the comedy of withdrawal asserts, "he who fails because he is just has nonetheless failed." However the hero's failure is explained,[66] it remains failure and disharmony and is as such for Hegel not yet the pinnacle of art: "But art cannot remain in this discord of the abstract inner disposition and external objectivity without abandoning its own principle. The subjective must be conceived as what is inherently infinite and absolute, as that which, even if it does not let finite reality subsist as the truth, nonetheless does not relate itself to it negatively in mere opposition, but rather proceeds all the same to reconciliation" (14:126; A 516, translation modified).

Withdrawal and Subjectivity

In most comedies of withdrawal the goal is not unconscious or intuitive but rather philosophically justified. Withdrawal represents an advance over earlier forms insofar as the hero, by virtue of his education and developed intellect, can free himself from the immediacy of natural drives and the arbitrariness of subjective preference. In the stages of the antithesis we see an intensification of subjectivity, an increasing internalization. The comic hero of withdrawal is invariably an intellectual;[67] this is his strength (the content is justified) as well as his weakness (the full *realization* of this content beyond the level of *consciousness* is often overlooked or underplayed). It is, one might argue, the comedy of Hegel himself, who, following a focus on subjectivity at the expense of intersubjectivity in his *Science of Logic*, erroneously placed the sphere of philosophy, that is, the realm of absolute spirit, above the realm of objective spirit, that is, normative questions of politics, history, and justice.[68] The story with the owl of Minerva is well-known. Hegel, like his comic counterpart Bernhardi, is better at diagnosis than he is at therapy. The hero of reduction is locked into his own particularity and has little sense of the general. The hero of withdrawal remains within the general and is unable to return to the particular. The particularity of desire gives way to the nonparticularity of reflection.

Stubbornness, or steadfastness, rules the hero's position. Other secondary virtues such as self-sacrifice are also prominent. Indeed, the hero seems to integrate in comic fashion moments of several tragic subgenres: self-sacrifice, stubbornness, and opposition. Surprisingly, the hero's stubbornness and self-sacrifice can be viewed as vices insofar as they represent not only adherence to principle but an unwillingness to enter into relations with a world the hero scorns, a mistrust of the institutions of the world. It is the stance of the early Sophoclean hero. Ajax is a fitting example: the hero's turn against society is concretely justified (society is inadequate, the hero's claims against it are just); nonetheless, the rejection of society is *in principle* unjustified. The comic tone, the emphasis on subjectivity at the expense of substance, and the avoidance of death often bring the play back into the comic sphere. The avoidance of death is not a matter of mere plot; the fact that the hero lives gives rise to comic faith in potential harmony, a faith sustained even in the comedy of negation, a form of comedy that advanced subjectivity to the point where the object, the other, had no value whatsoever.

The hero of withdrawal, rather than actively improving the world, essentially withdraws in order to avoid the displeasure the world gives him. Freud's discussion of forms of suffering and pleasure in the second section of his *Civilization and its Discontents* might aid us here. Freud distinguishes between positive aims, by which he means the experience of strong feelings of pleasure; and negative aims, or the absence of pain and displeasure. Heroes of reduction seek pleasure but fail to achieve it; they lack the proper means. Heroes of negation seek and attain unethical pleasures, which serve only to undermine the hero in the long run and so create displeasure; putting pleasure above morality and caution soon brings its own punishment. The hero of withdrawal, in contrast, seeks to avoid suffering and displeasure. His task is ultimately negative, hence his isolation. The hero of withdrawal seeks refuge in a vision of reality he no longer seeks to realize; instead, he offers it as a solace and an intoxicant to help him forget reality. His happiness would derive from quietude, the negation of instincts, drives, and desires. That the hero has retreated from all pleasure explains not only his withdrawal from human relations, but his frequent chastity as well. Intersubjectivity implies the possibility of betrayal and suffering; the hero of withdrawal sees deceit as inevitable and so refuses to engage in possible or, as the hero would see it, inevitable suffering. When he nonetheless seeks intersubjective relations, a wisdom speaks on behalf of the hero that is greater than his own consciousness.

Often the hero of the comedy of withdrawal loves the most sociable, and as a result often the most superficial, characters. Alceste denounces society but longs for a relationship with its most social member, Célimène. Manly, in Wycherly's *The Plain Dealer*, denounces not only all society but even the woman he cannot help but love; wanting to be free, he is all the more drawn to Olivia. Bernhardi fights for certain values but only to a limited degree. Möbius does not erase his own self but kills another in order to remain a member of even a limited society. This desire for the social may suggest that the truth of the hero's subjectivity may be intersubjectivity, even when the hero denies it. As the heroes become more subjective and withdraw from the world, their desire for the social sphere, even where unfulfilled, only increases.[69] Where coincidence focuses more on action, withdrawal concentrates more on character and with this on actions contemplated but not executed. The hero's longing for, and intuitive elevation of, humanity is inconsistent with his withdrawal and vice versa. But this inconsistency is typical of someone defined, as in comedy, by inner contradictions. Célimène describes Alceste precisely in this manner.

*

The inwardness of withdrawal is linked to the possibility of evil. The hero of withdrawal transcends objectivity and establishes norms in opposition to the status quo. His position presupposes a negation of the existing ethic. The idea of a negation of the objective order is common to both the antithetical possibility of evil, that is, an unjustified negation of order, and the nearly synthetic negation of antithesis. That the earliest Hegelians viewed comedy as the transformation of the ugly makes sense, for in the Hegelian system the aesthetic concept of the ugly is analogous to the ethical concept of evil, which Hegel defines as false subjectivity, and which is also the central category in his analysis of comedy.[70] Evil and morality have for Hegel a common genesis: the negation of the existing order by virtue of adherence to subjective standards: "Conscience, as formal subjectivity, consists simply in the possibility of turning at any moment to evil; for both morality and evil have their common root in that self-certainty which has being for itself and knows and resolves for itself" (R § 139).[71] The difference lies in the means for establishing the new standards: the embrace of one's own arbitrary subjectivity or adherence to values the subject knows to be universal.[72] The affirmation of arbitrary subjectivity led in earlier forms to evil, which Hegel defines as "the most intimate reflection of subjectivity itself in opposition to the objective and universal, which it treats as mere sham" (E § 512, translation modified). The contradiction of the hero of withdrawal—his affirmation of the universal by way of reflection and his negation of the order in which the universal has yet to be realized—and his frustration at his inability to enact the universal reflect his continued immersion in the antithesis. Just as the heroes of reduction and negation have withdrawn from truth, so does the hero of withdrawal withdraw from intersubjectivity, which is the highest truth. Structurally, synthesis is now possible; the hero of the comedy of withdrawal, however, owing to his contingent weakness, has yet to realize it.[73]

The Comedy of Intersubjectivity (3)

In the synthetic form of comedy, the subject begins with an untenable stance but is led to alter his position in the course of the play. The hero is as much obsessed with subjectivity as in the antithetical forms (2) but eventually reaches the content sketched in coincidence (1). The union here, however, has been earned; it thus provides evidence against Walter Kerr's claim, which would reduce comedy to a lower, inorganic form of art: "in comedy all endings

must be contrived" (72). For Northrop Frye, comic action is invariably "twisted to fit the demands of a happy ending" (*Anatomy* 206),
but this description does not apply to the comedy of intersubjectivity. In many works of literature the happy end is unearned and
gives a sense of false accomplishment. But the abuse of the happy
end is, as Ernst Bloch argues, no argument against it. In fact,
Bloch goes so far as to claim: "As long as no absolute In-Vain (triumph of evil) has appeared, then the happy end of the right direction and path is not only our pleasure, but our duty" (Ger 1:518;
Eng 446).

Outstanding examples of the comedy of intersubjectivity from
the British tradition are Shakespeare's *Much Ado About Nothing*
and Goldsmith's *She Stoops to Conquer*, from the German tradition
Raimund's *The King of the Alps and the Misanthrope* and Grillparzer's *Woe to the Liar*!. Students of cinema may want to think of
Capra's *It Happened One Night* or Cukor's *The Philadelphia Story*,
works that belong to the Hollywood comedy of remarriage, a genre
defined by Stanley Cavell and itself a subset of the comedy of intersubjectivity.

Intersubjectivity as Synthesis

Coincidence is a subordinate genre precisely because of the individual's lack of autonomy: subjectivity is philosophically a higher category than chance or luck. The harmony of coincidence also lacks
stability: the individuals are not knowledgeable; thus, they could
easily be led astray. The synthesis is stronger than the thesis, for it
arises as a result of the act of thinking through the antithesis.
Whereas the objectivity of 1 is subject to chance, the objectivity of 3
is made by the knowing subject.[74] The harmony of coincidence is, in
Hegelian terms, only abstractly positive. It is a harmony of unreflected naiveté that has yet to differentiate the negative from the
positive and so cannot resist the powers of negativity. Its optimism
is not, as later in intersubjectivity, earned by way of the refutation
of alternatives. The subject develops truth and harmony out of itself, knows it, and acknowledges its validity. Elder Olson's definition of comedy as "the imitation of a worthless action" (46–47) does
not cover the highest form of comedy, for the comedy of intersubjectivity is the *overcoming* of worthless action, or the overcoming of
particularity.

Just as a false and a true subjectivity exist, the first ruled by chance and caprice, the latter by reason, so are there for Hegel parallel forms of false and genuine objectivity (R § 26 Z). The comedy of intersubjectivity represents objectivity or *Sittlichkeit* at a higher stage, after the hero has passed through subjectivity or *Moralität*. Whereas intersubjectivity evokes freedom, in coincidence we see only chance, that is, dependence on external and arbitrary factors. This corresponds to the proximity of coincidence to nature: "nature exhibits no freedom in its existence, but only *necessity* and *contingency*" (E § 248). Because the development in the synthesis is controlled rather than coincidental, the plot tends to be organic rather than episodic—another dimension in which intersubjectivity supersedes coincidence.

The comedy of intersubjectivity is superior not only to the thesis but also to the antithesis, for it has overcome and integrated negativity. Intersubjectivity blocks the destructive power of negativity and so better assures harmony and stability. Once beyond 1, the hero has a choice of good or evil. He *can* choose evil but is not obligated to do so. The highest comic form must include the possibility of evil, for only with this possibility are arguments recognized that negate negativity, only then can harmony be assured. Hegel suggests: "*only* the human being is good—but only in so far as he can also be evil" (R § 139 Z). Intersubjectivity argues that nature may follow a rational plan, as in coincidence, but that spirit is higher than nature insofar as it *knows* this plan and knows of plans that transcend nature.[75] Chance plays a lesser role in spirit than in nature. I suggested the significance of chance and arbitrariness for subgenres such as reduction and negation, but the audience that *recognizes* this arbitrariness is itself *capable* of transcending it. Intellect can overcome the arbitrariness of nature and natural drives. Just as in the Hegelian system the purpose of nature is to bring forth spirit, so—in comedy—is the truth of coincidence the higher structure of intersubjectivity. The victory of unconscious objectivity we saw in negation is here superseded by conscious action. The temporary success of the hero of negation lay not only in his verbal dexterity but also in the stupidity of his listeners; the moral obligation to fight evil, and not be duped by it, is only here fully developed.

The cooperative, intersubjective dimensions of the synthesis recreate a moment of the thesis and supersede a moment of the antithesis: in the antithesis, the self elevates itself and sees itself as the catalyst for action; in the thesis, as again in the synthesis, the self recognizes the limits of the self and works with others for common goals. The moment of chance in the comedy of coincidence, which limits the self, is transformed in the comedy of intersubjectivity into recognition of forces beyond the self, including the activities of other persons. What was objective becomes intersubjective; collectively, chance is brought under (at least partial) control. Although the self has knowledge of absolute duties, he is a small part of the cosmos, even of the community of spirits: a moment of coincidence is thereby integrated into intersubjectivity. In earlier comic forms (with the partial exception of withdrawal) other characters are means to the hero's ends; for the hero of intersubjectivity, who recognizes not only his own subjectivity but that of others as well, people are ends in themselves.

Thus, a moment frequently stressed in the comedy of intersubjectivity is equality—between classes, genders, and individuals. Thomas Dekker's *The Shoemaker's Holiday* overcomes the arbitrary schisms between classes: "Dost thou not know that love respects no blood, / Cares not for differences of birth or state?" (xxi.104–105). This genre of equality also upsets gender hierarchy. Women assume a strong role in determining events; a variety of examples comes to mind, ranging from Lessing's *Minna von Barnhelm* and Goldsmith's *She Stoops to Conquer* to the roles Katharine Hepburn assumes in a number of films, most notably *Adam's Rib*.[76]

Love that has passed through obstacles is deeper than the superficial and primitive love that reaches its goals without any hindrances. The partners' ironic revelation of unknown depths of the self—which are complexly and slowly uncovered—hinders immediate gratification and simple love but eventually evokes a greater fullness. Thus, intersubjectivity eclipses coincidence, which offers only natural hindrances, as well as any non-aesthetic and immediate gratification. Intersubjectivity also surpasses the infinite deferment of an endlessly ambiguous or ironic relation. The purpose of irony is complex revelation, not simply deferment. Without any revelation of the true self, meaningful and fulfilling relations are impossible. True intersubjectivity cannot be grounded in the bad infinite.

Unlike in reduction and withdrawal, the union in 3 is realized. Subjectivity passes over into intersubjectivity; paradoxically, this passage into intersubjectivity allows the subject to overcome its identity crisis. The self comes to itself by recognizing another self. Difference and individuality are not dissolved; on the contrary, intersubjectivity is possible only on the basis of difference. Although individual subjectivity is contingent, this contingency is necessary and must be preserved if intersubjectivity is not to be swallowed up by an empty universality. One could even argue that intersubjectivity, with its symmetrical relations, brings difference and subjectivity to their fullest potential; the difference within the identity of marriage, for example, is central to the richness of the unity. Only in intersubjectivity do we see the full complexities of love. Not the mere bonding of coincidence, love is a speculative activity in which the contradictions of identity and difference are first introduced and then resolved in a higher unity (R § 158 Z). The unity of marriage can be viewed on yet another level as the free and conscious choice of two individuals who have met by chance and coincidence.[77] As such, it represents the speculative unity of chance and necessity already nascent in 1.

In the comedy of intersubjectivity true content is reached (the intersubjective realms of love, friendship, and the public sphere), and ultimately the hero's virtues bring him there. Although subjectivity represents a necessary step toward intersubjectivity, it is also often the greatest danger to it, as in Shakespeare's *Much Ado About Nothing* or Grillparzer's *Woe to the Liar!*. Comedy teaches us the need for subjectivity but also the need for the transcendence of subjectivity: only in freeing oneself from obsessive self-reflection does one really come to oneself. The self is something exclusive, yet all other human beings are selves. Hegel writes: "'I' is the universal in and for itself . . . . All other humans have this in common with me" (E § 20). The self finds itself (or comes to itself) only in another self. Intersubjectivity culminates not only in love but in self-knowledge; the two are seen to be related insofar as each is achieved via a kind of mirroring—seeing oneself as other or seeing the other as oneself. Recognition of the other leads to the identity of the self.[78] Hegel discusses friendship and love as the realization of freedom: "Here, we are not one-sidedly within ourselves, rather we willingly limit ourselves with reference to an other, but know ourselves in this limitation as ourselves" (R § 7 Z, translation modified). To acknowledge someone as a subject is to see that person simultaneously as other and as the same as oneself: "In love the separate does still remain, but no longer as something separate, rather as something united, and life experiences life" (1:246; ETW 305, translation modified). In another passage Hegel suggests: "The true essence of love consists in relinquishing the consciousness of oneself, forgetting oneself in another self, yet in this surrender and erasure having and possessing oneself for the first time" (14:155; A

539–540, translation modified). Freedom, as Hegel liked to say, is realized not through defiance of the objective spirit or the negation of otherness (7:15). Instead, freedom is "being at home with oneself in one's other" (E § 24 Z2). One has freedom and self-consciousness in the freedom and consciousness of the other.

The freedom of intersubjectivity is a true freedom, not the false freedom of caprice sketched in reduction or negation, where the hero is determined by nature and chance: "Caprice, to be sure, is often equally called freedom; but caprice is only non-rational freedom, choice and self-determination issuing not from the rationality of the will but from fortuitous impulses and their dependence on sense and the external world" (13:136; A 98, translation modified). True freedom is not the liberty to do what one arbitrarily chooses. The freedom of arbitrariness is, to Hegel, a contradiction, for "it is inherent in arbitrariness that the content is not determined as mine by the nature of my will, but by *contingency*; thus, I am just as much dependent on this content . . . . The common man believes that he is free when he is allowed to act arbitrarily, but this very arbitrariness implies that he is not free" (R § 15 Z, translation modified). The evil of negation is a formal advance that arises with the expansion of subjectivity, but its content is nature, natural drives and inclinations. As such, it is not yet the sphere of freedom. True freedom is linked not with comic particularity and caprice but with the universal concepts of morality and necessity.

The Sublation of Earlier Forms

Depending on the play or the moments we stress in reading a play, the comedy of intersubjectivity can often be read as the overcoming of any of the previous comic subforms. Duty as freedom, for example, is freedom from dependence on chance and natural drives, from the stifling effects of mere intention, and from the chaos of no standards. Just obligations restrict arbitrary, that is, false subjectivity, not genuine subjectivity (R § 149). Whereas love as inclination is ruled by nature and chance, marriage transforms this inclination into a necessity that transcends ephemerality, moodiness, and mere subjectivity. Chance may lead to marriage but is in marriage overcome (R § 161–164). Thus we see not only in 3 the fulfillment of 1 but in 1 a prolepsis of 3. To sketch another example of sublation, comic resolutions are often brought about by those who refuse to fall into self-pity or let themselves be brought down to the level of others' self-pity. One thinks of Dorine's chastening words to Marlane in the second act of Molière's *Tartuffe* or Minna's venturesome ridicule of Tellheim's self-absorption in Lessing's play. The comedy of intersubjectivity is often the direct overcoming of qualities found in the protagonist of reduction.

The comedy of intersubjectivity must, if it is the truth of the previous genres, contain both the possibility of the weaknesses of the other genres and their moments of truth. The theme of coincidence, of other powers guiding our lives, often recurs in intersubjectivity where persons act as agents; for T. S. Eliot in *The Cocktail Party*, the forces of spirit are the guardians, who assist others in finding themselves. Interestingly, even the guardians admit that they are moved by powers they do not quite grasp (Act II).[79] Harpagon's miserliness in Molière's play is a particular form of subjectivity: the desire to turn everything he sees as valid into *his* property. Yet this moment of subjectivity contains a seed of truth: true subjectivity is reached when it desires to possess not material things but knowledge of the world and its structures, such that one can act according to proper values, and knowledge of the world as one with oneself, such that one can experience true freedom. Hegel writes: "Freedom and reason consist of my raising myself to the form of I = I, of my apprehending all as *mine* . . . of my grasping each object as a member in the system of what I am myself. In short, they consist of my possessing *self* and the *world* in *one and the same* consciousness, of finding myself again in the world, and conversely in my possessing in my consciousness that which *is*, that which has *objectivity*" (E § 424 Z, my translation). The identity of subject and object intrinsic to such possession leads in truth to a recognition of the object as subject, that is, the transformation of subject-object relations into subject-subject relations or intersubjectivity. Similarly, the self-consciousness of withdrawal, in which subject and object are identical, finds its truth in the recognition that if subject and object are identical, the truth of their relation is the structure of subject-subject relations. Earlier subforms include moments of 3; this sheds light not only on intersubjectivity. Without the possibility of overcoming, the earlier forms would be locked into a purely stagnant negativity.

The comedy of intersubjectivity may be realized in either of two ways, the second being more frequent. According to the first model, the hero begins as a *weak* subject who attempts to find himself by erasing his self and immersing himself in the whole. The hero eventually finds that he can come to himself by resisting the temptation of self-surrender and by entering into a singular intersubjective relation. Coincidence and reduction are sublated as mere stages. Excellent cinematic examples are Billy Wilder's *The Apartment* and Woody Allen's *Zelig*. Zelig represents at an initial stage a ridiculous form of intersubjectivity (bordering between coincidence and reduction) that eventually passes over into a substantial intersubjectivity.

According to the second model, the hero begins as a *strong* subject who attempts to realize himself by negating other individuals (or withdrawing from them) and by mocking either the universal or the inability of others to reach the universal. The hero eventually finds that he can come to himself by overcoming an obsession with his own particular interests or desires, whether they be of pride or prejudice, and by recognizing the validity of intersubjective structures. Negation and withdrawal are overcome as options. Good examples would be *The King of the Alps and the Misanthrope* and *The Philadelphia Story*. The hero reverses his standards or tactics, what Molière's Alceste, for example, is unable to do.

In some works, justified moments of earlier genres, for example withdrawal, are integrated into the final harmony even as they are overcome.[80] At the center of Herb Gardner's *A Thousand Clowns* is Murray Burns, a witty and comic "Alceste" who appears destined to fail, owing to contemporary complacency, stupidity, and bureaucracy. In the end, however, Murray decides to play the game, motivated by love for his nephew Nick, whom he will lose if he continues to mock, and only mock, other people. In this harmony, however, Murray's (and the play's) insights into false objectivity are not lost. Nick retains elements of Murray (including his intolerance of stupidity and, symbolically, Murray's name, which he now adopts as his own), just as Murray appropriates traits of Nick, which indeed allow him to remain Nick's guardian. Similarly, though with a different focus, Capra's *Mr. Deeds Goes to Town* presents us with an intractable hero seemingly destined to fail in a world of corruption, deceit, and manipulation. The hero overcomes his justified recalcitrance only when he recognizes moments of goodness in the world from which he is determined to withdraw.

Grillparzer's *Woe to the Liar!* successfully illustrates the ways in which a comedy of intersubjectivity integrates, even as it overcomes, earlier comic subforms. The play may appear to be a comedy of coincidence. Three moments are relevant here: first, the Bishop's elevation of nature over spirit insofar as nature is true, insofar as it represents a harmony of being and seeming, of being and obligation; second, Edrita as a child of nature and a privileged character; third, the series of "miracles" that help Leon along his path, above all the initial flash of lightning, his discovery of the key, the assistance of the ferry man, and the transference of Metz from the Saxons to the Christians.

Each of these moments, however, is best reinterpreted in the light of intersubjectivity. The Bishop's analysis of truth begins with nature but ends with a paean to friendship, love, and trust. The very symmetry in nature that the Bishop elevates may be evidence of nature's low-level status; nature cannot extend itself. Human beings experience ruptures not only because they fail, but because they project norms that should be realized. Consciousness of what should be, as opposed to what is, makes possible intersubjectivity, yet it also brings with it, as the Bishop notes, the dangers of subjectivity: arrogance, deception, discord. Nature is not the highest stage. Indeed, it is this sphere of subjectivity and intersubjectivity toward which Edrita, a child of nature, strives. She has an intuitive longing for intersubjectivity: first, for conversation and spiritual love, in particular with Leon (713–714, 721); and second, for the religion of intersubjectivity, Christianity (1151–1170, 1741–1749). Further, the play's various religious miracles can be demythologized and understood in human or intersubjective terms. The Bishop describes Leon's first otherworldly vision as intellectual insight ("The spirit of goodness shone within" 381, my translation). In the legend on which Grillparzer bases his play, the gates open with the help of God; in Grillparzer's version, Edrita supplies the key. Leon's dependence on others is reinforced here, as it is later with Atalus's digging and Edrita's erasure of the footprints. The assistance of the ferry man is not a miracle but the simple result of Leon's revelation of truth and the self-destruction of Kattwald's injustice. Finally, the transference of Metz to the Christians only reinforces our sense that Leon depends on forces beyond his own self. The miracle is a human act. Coincidence finds its truth in intersubjectivity.

During the course of his development Leon appears to act out a comedy of reduction, as when he sees, initially, the telling of truth and, then, Edrita as obstacles to his mission, whereas they in fact become two of the guiding forces and dominant goals of his journey. Also of interest is the comic reduction of spirit to its letter. Edrita tells Leon: "Even if you always spoke the truth / (laying his hand on his heart) / Nonetheless, I feel here that you have deceived me" (1137–1138, my translation). Drawing on the structure whereby one figure, usually a servant, literally tells the truth but pretends that it is a trick or a lie, prominent in Terence (for example, *Andrea* sc. 4 and *Heautontimorumenos* sc. 3), Leon succeeds in dissembling even as he adheres to the Bishop's command not to lie. This form of reduction is, however, merely a phase for Leon.

Kattwald exhibits moments of negation. He is powerful but unjust, and, as in many comedies of negation, his injustice leads to a self-cancellation: his unjust acts toward the ferry man lead to his undoing; they motivate the ferry man to turn to the other side.

The Bishop adopts a stance of withdrawal at the play's outset. He is a man of principle, not action. His stance is potentially tragic. Leon asserts in response to the Bishop's elevation of principle over pragmatism: "Then no other choice remains except: we tell the truth, / And he stays where he is" (331–332, my translation). The Bishop, like other heroes of withdrawal, lacks power.[81] A strength of Grillparzer's play is that it ironizes both the Bishop's lack of action and Leon's absence of principles, just as it elevates the Bishop's principles and Leon's pragmatism, suggesting that truth lies in a synthesis of the two. Indeed, it would not be difficult to show that the Bishop moves in the direction of Leon (recognizing that he cannot free Atalus alone and that compromise is necessary) and that Leon moves in the direction of the Bishop (recognizing limits to his subjectivity, eventually overcoming his instrumentalization of others, and becoming an advocate of principle and truth).[82] The Bishop will now, as he did not before, ask the King for a favor, and he will strive to raise his nephew well; Leon becomes more reticent and reflective before expressing his personal needs, and he recognizes the importance of the communal whole. Edrita and Atalus develop as well, and if harmony is still not complete, and certain characters tend to occupy one side of what should be a unity, the unifying pattern is still clear. The lack of *realized* perfection, moreover, is a precondition of further development: only with a break between being and perfection is further development possible; because, therefore, a gap between what is and what ought to be should exist, we can see from a higher vantage point that everything indeed is as it ought to be (cf. Roche, *Dynamic Stillness* 46–47).

Grillparzer's play recognizes the limits of a merely theoretical knowledge (the Bishop's withdrawal and negation of activity) and a merely instrumental activity (Leon, a cook by trade, tends to treat others as objects along his path). Neither a subjectivity that withdraws from the objective world nor a subjectivity that manipulates the objective world is sufficient. Instead, the play elevates the reciprocity of subject-subject relations. Moreover, insofar as Leon, without unduly compromising his principles, brings about a happy resolution, a potential tragedy (of collision) is averted. Christian self-sacrifice, to which Edrita alludes in one of her reflections, is also transcended. Where the play begins with Leon announcing a duel, it ends with his marriage to Edrita. Although Kattwald and his cohorts are not integrated into the final harmony, they are treated as subjects ("There's no coercion here" 1728, my translation), and the path across the river to Christianity and intersubjectivity has been opened to them by Edrita's example.

Unsublated Moments

Although intersubjectivity sublates moments of the earlier comic genres, it is also possible to recognize unsublated moments of the earlier comic genres in 3. Not only in Grillparzer's *Woe to the Liar!*, as we have seen, but also, for example, in Lessing's *Minna von Barnhelm*, the hero's recognition of otherness is embedded within a society that on a larger scale continues to act like a subject obsessed with its own subjectivity.[83] *Minna* reflects on the fact that the extension of subjectivity to friendship and love is far from universal; the final lines address the issue of continuing wars. It is just that this moment of nonclosure be stressed. For a comedy to fulfill all the demands of intersubjectivity it would have to end in something like the world state.[84] Because reaching harmony in a broader universal sphere is harder, the comedy of intersubjectivity frequently focuses on private and individual relations, whereas reduction and negation often delve into the realm of the public and the political; thus, the Old Comedy of Aristophanes hardly fits the model of intersubjectivity. Yet comedies of intersubjectivity sometimes integrate the wider sphere by exhibiting a model of harmony on a small scale together with the need for yet more harmony on a broader scale. Lessing's and Grillparzer's comic plays share a virtue with Aristophanes' political comedies: they integrate the fullest dimensions of objective spirit into comedy and do not stop with marriage. Marriage could also represent withdrawal from a broader responsibility: Alceste's desire to marry *and* withdraw in *The Misanthrope* is a good illustration. It is a skillful writer who can exhibit the restricted, comic particularity in what is otherwise taken to be the universal.

The accomplished writer also overcomes the false dualism of perfection and despair. Cukor's *The Philadelphia Story* achieves its resolution precisely when the heroine recognizes that perfection is not intolerant of deprivation, when Tracy (Katherine Hepburn) transforms from "goddess" to "human," accepts her former husband in a new way, and recognizes that desire (and thus imperfection) belong as moments to perfection (or what we might call the most desirable state). In the comedy of intersubjectivity, truth is realized, yet not exhausted; it is "what is absolutely accomplished and is ever accomplishing itself [das an und für sich Vollbrachte und stets sich Vollbringende]" (13:82; A 55).

Obviously, levels of reconciliation, harmony, and acceptance exist. Robert Heilman spends a great deal of time on a comedy characterized by acceptance of the second best. While this answers the failures of withdrawal, it falls short of the utopian dimensions of intersubjectivity. I view the weaknesses of the world as they are integrated into 3 as simultaneously negated—in their specificity—and accepted—as the necessary element that keeps the world dynamic rather than empty. Hegel suggests: "The good ought to be realized; we have to work at this, to bring it forth, and the will is simply the good that is self-activating. But then if the world were as it ought to be, the result would be that the activity of willing would disappear. Therefore the will itself also requires that its purpose not be realized . . . . This agreement between is and ought is not rigid and unmoving, however, since the final purpose of the world, the good, only *is*, because it constantly brings itself about" (E § 234 Z, translation modified). I do not view intersubjectivity as mere acceptance: it is both utopian and inclusive of negativity. Shakespeare's *As You Like It*—to name one example among many—shows how a play can include moments of mockery and satire without undermining the substance of reconciliation. Part of perfection is the very movement toward perfection without which there would be emptiness; as such, this movement is itself a kind of perfection, a state beyond which perfection would lapse into emptiness.[85] The formation of a new society may mean progress, but it is not a final closure. We laugh at the finite with the intention of overcoming the finite; laughter passes over into a resolution, but the new resolution will always allow for more laughter. The comic thrust is to negate whatever becomes recalcitrant or subjective; to paraphrase Hegel, comedy recognizes the rights of the world-spirit vis-à-vis the status quo (VG 148).

Humor

The comedy of intersubjectivity has much in common with the concept of *Humor*, as defined, for example, by the most prolific of post-Hegelian aestheticians, Friedrich Theodor Vischer.[86] Vischer and others have been vigorously attacked for their (apologetic) elevation of *Versöhnung* or reconciliation, but this is unwarranted.[87] First, the hero's turn to intersubjectivity may not represent an embrace of the *existing* society but, as a simple thinking through of the comedy of withdrawal, the work may represent an affirmation *in principle* of the social sphere and so illustrate social consciousness at its best. Second, the resolutions depicted in any comedy of intersubjectivity worthy of the name are earned and genuine. Vischer prefers humor to satire because, and justly so, a *true* reconciliation is higher than, because it has passed through, satire. The hero has, in the realm of art, worked through contradictions; he has not skirted them. Third, one must recognize the differences between art and life. A mimesis theory cannot account for the proleptic moment in art, which the comedy of intersubjectivity represents. Humor is an *aesthetic* ideal, whose function is the representation of the unity of truth and sensuousness and as such preparation for the unity of truth and history. According to this view, humor is neither escapist nor self-indulgent. To adopt yet another perspective on the matter, negative endings may conduce to the indulgence of self-pity, and open endings may appeal to the interpreter's false sense of autonomy and power. The critique of closure, generally viewed as an embrace of openness, tolerance, and negative capability, can also be viewed as feeding narcissism—to have closure, in contrast, is to recognize an objectivity, a shape or form that exists independently of oneself and one's power as interpreter (Sennett 335).

Finally, in response less to Marxist critics and more to the poststructuralists,[88] we can recognize the priority of intersubjectivity as a consequence of the ontological and logical priority of the positive over the negative, the resolution of contradictions over the embrace of contradictions. Though Hegel himself seeks contradictions as the necessary path to truth, he would resolve them: "the power of life, and still more the might of the spirit, consists precisely in positing contradiction in itself, enduring it, and overcoming it" (13:162; A 120). Elsewhere, he writes: "The highest truth, truth as such, is the resolution of the highest opposition and contradiction" (13:137; A

99–100).[89] Intersubjectivity, including the privileged moment of love, can be a central catalyst in this process: "Love is both the production and the resolution of this contradiction" (R § 158 Z).

The Comedy of Absolute Irony and the Hermeneutics of Interpretation

In the comedy of negation, the protagonist abandons all norms and seeks to exploit others for private gain. Despite the negativity present in the genre, norms are still presupposed as a measure against which we can recognize negativity as negative. In the comedy of absolute irony, all norms have been abandoned. Everything, including even the unstated norms of measure we saw in the comedy of negation, is ironized.

Absolute irony is unlikely to surface in any culture that views art as an expression of absolute spirit, that sees art as embodying the generally valid ethical substance of the age. In modern culture, however, with a breakdown in universals and with the subject expressing his own particularity, art often evokes ironic and reflexive structures, playful and clever forms that negate, rather than affirm, traditional norms and in some cases negate the idea of norms as such.

Hegel and Absolute Irony

The comedy of absolute irony resembles what Hegel calls Romantic irony, first, because the irony is all-pervasive, and second, because it transcends the work's object-level and relates to its meta-level.[90] For a variety of reasons, however, I would like to avoid the term "Romantic irony." First, Romantic irony is a multivalent concept. To some critics, Romantic irony is simply transcendental art, a self-reflective art aware of itself and of the conditions of the possibility of its existence; romantic irony integrates philosophical self-reflection into the sphere of art (cf. Szondi, "Friedrich Schlegel"). To others, for example, Friedrich Schlegel, Romantic irony is the recognition of an absolute that cannot be realized in the present. This represents for Hegel the inadequacy of the bad infinite, but it is hardly the position Hegel means when he speaks of Romantic irony as rendering absolute the individual subject and its arbitrary whims, even if the two are indirectly connected.

Second, comedies that draw on Romantic irony are not works whose irony is all-pervasive and all-destructive, as Hegel seems to imply. In comedies of Romantic irony, the author's subjectivity is pronounced; he can enter the scene and negate his creation. The individual characters are not taken seriously, and the illusion of verisimilitude is often broken,[91] but the Romantic artist's destructive acts, rather than turning on the author or negating his creation, often make the work what it is. Tieck's *Puss in Boots*, for example, develops its argument by breaking the illusion of verisimilitude and showing how the audience within the play reacts to the play within the play. As a satire of reduced audience expectations, the work illustrates reduction.[92] Its ironic stance toward the individual also evidences moments of coincidence.

Third, the term "Romantic irony" suggests a historical entity whose time is past. The call for the all-encompassing ironic stance, however, is with us today as never before.[93] We would have to go back to the Sophists to find as vigorous arguments against truth as are offered by postmodernists. The concept "absolute irony" captures the transhistorical dimension of this phenomenon. Finally, in its transhistoricism it can assume various manifestations. Although Hegel locates Romantic irony in the autonomous self, an equivalent form of destructive irony can arise in the larger world-order, as, for example, in Kafka's *The Trial*.

The comedy of absolute irony is a comedy of negation taken to the nth degree and applied not only to the work's content but to the work as such. Because the principle of destruction applies to "everything inherently excellent and solid, it follows that irony as this art of annihilating everything everywhere, like that heart-felt longing, acquires, at the same time, in comparison with the true ideal, the aspect of inner inartistic lack of restraint. For the ideal requires an inherently substantive content" (13:211; A 160). In its most brutal forms, absolute irony is the negation of art. One is tempted to situate here the Theater of the Absurd, which assaults all systems of values, including the value of the medium to which it would belong. According to Hildesheimer, the Theatre of the Absurd not only confronts its audience "with the unintelligibility, the dubiousness of life" (173, my translation), it "acknowledges the helplessness of theater to purify humans and employs this helplessness as a pretence for theater" (178, my translation). Not surprisingly, such plays are on their own terms anti-drama or non-art; Ionesco subtitles his *Bald Prima Donna* "An Anti-Play." We recognize in the comedy of absolute irony the negation of plot, character, message, and form, a disenchantment with not just the world but itself.

The Theatre of the Absurd has been elevated not only for its rhetorical power and formal innovativeness but also for its modesty (Esslin 402). Writers, no longer adhering to a system of values, do not pretend to know any absolute or clear truths; they merely express their subjective vision. But the relativization of the absolute, which we see with any absurdist position, inevitably leads to the absolutization of the relative: if the absolute is silent, the highest authority is the individual self: "By placing the divine essence beyond our knowledge and human things in general, one secures the convenience of indulging one's own notions. One is freed from having to relate one's knowledge to the divine and true; on the contrary, the complacency of this and subjective feeling have for themselves complete justification; and the sanctimonious humility, by keeping knowledge of God distant from oneself, knows full well what it gains thereby for its own caprice and vain activities" (12: 27, my translation; cf. 16:180–183, 16:348–349, and 18:168). A hidden arrogance lies behind the alleged modesty of the absurdist authors.[94]

If the ironist's negation of substance were to succeed, the sphere of the comic would be missed, for Hegel—quite rightly—cannot accept as comic a destruction of what is itself substantial: "For, as true art, comedy, too, is obliged through its presentation to bring the absolutely rational into appearance, not at all as what is internally inverted and collapsing, but on the contrary as what assigns neither victory nor permanence to folly and unreason, to false oppositions and contradictions" (15:530; A 1202, translation modified). Absolute irony, however, involves the arbitrary and all-encompassing negation of genre and art, of substance and objectivity: "It is not the object [die Sache] that is excellent, but I who am so; as the master of law and object alike, I *simply play* with them as with my own caprice, and in this ironic consciousness in which I let the highest of things perish, I *merely enjoy myself*. This type of subjectivity not only substitutes a *void* for the whole ethical *content* of rights, duties, and laws—and so is evil, in fact evil through and through and universally—but in addition its form is that of *subjective* vanity [Eitelkeit], in that it knows itself as this emptiness [Eitelkeit] of all content and, in this knowledge, knows *itself* as the absolute" (R § 140, translation modified). The objectivity of the world is dissolved by the subjectivity of creation. The principal activity of the subjective artist "through the power of subjective insights, flashes of thought, and striking modes of interpretation, consists in destroying and dissolving everything that proposes to make itself objective and win a firm shape for itself in reality or that seems to have such a shape already in the external world. In this way every autonomy of objective content and the fixed connection of form, which is given by the subject matter, is annihilated in itself, and the presentation is a mere sporting with the topics, a derangement and perversion of the material as well as a rambling to and fro, a criss-cross movement of subjective expressions, views, and attitudes, whereby the author sacrifices himself and his topics alike" (14:229; A 600–601, translation modified).

Romantic irony elevates the subject to the position of creator of the world. If subjectivity transcends and creates the world, the subject is free to negate it: "Whatever is, is only through me, and what exists through me I can equally well annihilate again . . . . Letting it pass or canceling it depends wholly on the pleasure of the *self*, which is already absolute in itself simply as *self*" (13:93–94; A 64–65, translation modified). The artist creates ironic distance toward his characters and work, because he can no longer believe that they carry meaning. "Irony," viewed by Hegel's contemporaries as "the pinnacle of art," elevates contradiction and the destruction of human value: "It should consist in the fact that everything that begins as beautiful, noble, and interesting later destroy itself and seek its opposite; real enjoyment would be found in the discovery that goals, interests, and character are *nothing*" (11:80, my translation).

This loss of meaning becomes unwittingly comic as the writer's only topic remains the difficulties of writing. The ironist finds everything null, ultimately even himself, empty and devoid of substance.[95] Nothing is to be taken seriously: "In that case I am really not at all in *earnest* either with this content or with its expression and actualization. For genuine earnestness enters only by means of a substantial interest, a matter of intrinsic worth, truth, ethical life, and so forth, by means of a content which as such already counts for me as essential, so that I only become essential myself in my own eyes insofar as I have immersed myself in such a content and all my knowing and acting is in accord with it. When the self that sets up and dissolves everything out of its own caprice is the artist to whom no content of consciousness appears as absolute and independently real, but only as a self-made and destructible show, such earnestness can find no place, since validity is ascribed only to the formalism of the self" (13:94–95; A 65, translation modified).

The stance is one of great arrogance, though not the justified arrogance we see in tragedy: "Whoever has reached such a standpoint of divine originality, looks down from on high at all other persons, who are pronounced narrow-minded and dull, inasmuch as justice, ethical substance, and so forth still count for them as enduring, binding, and essential" (13:95; A 66, my translation). At the extreme antithetical point of comedy, the hero and author view everything with irony. By viewing all as one, the purely comic or ironic consciousness has no grasp of what is irreversible and what is genuinely evil; though claiming insight and power, the stance is in truth blind and impotent.

The doubling of the negative we see in the comedy of absolute irony engenders a self-cancellation: "The supreme point of the *phenomenon* of will, sublimating itself to this absolute vanity—to a goodness, which has no objectivity but is only sure of itself, and a certainty which involves the nullification of the universal—directly collapses into itself" (E § 512, translation modified). Negativity ultimately negates itself. In the context of irony Hegel speaks of "the immediate inversion and annihilation of itself" (E § 512, my translation). The ironist sees nothing whatsoever of value except itself, yet even the self, the author, is ultimately without value:[96] "If the self remains at this standpoint, everything appears to it as null and vain, except its own subjectivity, which therefore becomes hollow and empty and itself mere *vanity*. But, on the other hand, the self cannot, contrariwise, find satisfaction in this self-enjoyment and instead must become inadequate to itself, so that it now experiences thirst for the constant and the substantial, for determinate and essential interests" (13:96; A 66, translation modified).

The hero, or author, enters into a contradictory position whereby, one, he tries to find value outside himself where he had just negated all value and, two, he recognizes, or refuses to recognize, that his negation of external value derives from an internal source that is itself without value, thus the negation is no longer tenable. The negation of value itself lacks validity and so cancels itself. Value and objectivity are reinstated as a consequence of the self-cancellation of false subjectivity. The comedy of absolute irony claims to be self-reflexive, but it also purports to present negativity as permanent rather than as self-reflexively self-negating. Negation and self-reflection, however, transcend the particular intentions of the author and so restore harmony. Absolute irony is never a final stage. Hegel separates comedy and irony (13:97; 13:211), for the comic as the negation of what is itself nugatory can contain the ironic, while the ironic cannot contain, or negate, the comic, or any other substantive position, without cancelling itself. Absolute irony negates the substantive and so cancels itself.[97] The logic of the genre argues against the creation of art; not surprisingly, the genre itself contains few examples. It is a world view that taken on its own terms must self-destruct.

Absolute Irony and Interpretation

The comedy of absolute irony then is a genre that is itself impossible or, more precisely, a genre that is the negation of itself. Works belong to it only insofar as no determinate message is garnered from them. Thus, plays such as Beckett's *Waiting for Godot* or Handke's *Offending the Audience* belong to either the comedy of absolute irony or another subgenre depending on whether one can salvage something from them other than a mere self-cancellation. For such works the question of interpretation is partially one of performance. We could imagine a performance of *Waiting for Godot* as a serious portrayal of self-absorbed misery, such that it becomes a drama of suffering, or a representation in which the meaninglessness of the work itself is stressed and in which the audience is mocked for thinking the play might contain some discreet message. In this case, it would become a comedy of absolute irony. The best performance, however, would likely develop the work as a comedy of reduction, mocking the attitude that waiting, bored reflection, and the creation of imaginary meaning in order to pass discontinuous moments in time are enough for humanity or as far as humans could extend themselves. As such, the work would hardly be a revelation of nonmeaning.

Just as a postmodern critic might argue that one can improve a seemingly coherent and positive narrative by unravelling it into a drama of suffering or a comedy of absolute irony,[98] so can we argue, more coherently, I believe, that a comedy of absolute irony becomes a greater text if it is seen to be a hidden negation of itself, something more than a comedy of absolute irony. From this perspective, one lowers a work by interpreting it as a drama of suffering or a comedy of absolute irony when it is potentially more than that. The argument that works that make evident the illusory nature of all reality and truth claims are somehow truer and more insightful than competing texts is self-cancelling.

The structure by which a work that appears to be an example of the comedy of absolute irony but is, on closer analysis, an example of an earlier genre and thus, despite our initial belief, not non-art but art, is evident, for example, in Pirandello's *Each in His Own Way*.[99] In this play, we seem to find an undermining of not only the reader's views but also the author's intentions. I suggested that the comedy of absolute irony might be viewed as an extension of the comedy of negation. In the comedy of negation we see on the object-level, the level of action, the pursuit of a false goal. In the comedy of absolute irony, the pursuit of a false goal takes place on the meta-level.[100] The author purports to write a work about nothing. Comedy is the genre of subjectivity and thus the genre of reflection.[101] The comedy of absolute irony views a false goal reflexively. It takes itself seriously enough to create a work, not just a character or set of characters, that embodies negativity and purposelessness. Pirandello's play would seem to be not only a play about absurdity but a play about the absurdity of a play, and as such an absurd play or non-play.

Just as the comedy of negation turns on itself, exhibiting the self-destruction of the hero's false goals, so does the comedy of absolute irony turn on itself. Intentionally perhaps a work of absolute irony, Pirandello's play is in effect, and behind the author's back, a work more of intersubjectivity than of absolute irony.[102] In trying to say there is no meaning or truth, the artist ends up making a great artwork. A moment of coincidence, whereby a spirit works through the author even as he is unaware, resurfaces here, transforming negation into hidden harmony. Absolute irony does what it intends not to do, although it does what spirit really wants. To make matters more complex, we might ask whether the act of literary creation as a form of the negation of meaning does not itself seek to be proven false by an audience that is able to meet the author's challenge and reinterpret, question, or refute the author's bitterly ironic and nihilistic views (Guthke, *Modern Tragicomedy* 170–171).

Each in His Own Way is openly self-reflexive. The play-within-a-play format allows for interpretations of the play from within the play itself. Among these interpretations are direct references to the meaninglessness and absurdity of Pirandello's plays. As in Romantic irony, the author is directly named. The play, which is broken off before the third act, seems to be a play about the impossibility of a play, in the words of one character, the play is "a joke on the audience! What's it all mean? No one knows what it means! No one can make head or tail to it!" (Ita 4:180; Eng 316), or in the words of another, the play is "Nonsense! Just plain damn nonsense" (Ita 4:181; Eng 317).

Despite the apparent intention of producing a comedy of absolute irony (the play even opens with a discussion of the relativity of all views), the drama has a highly speculative structure. The play's suggestion of the end of art derives not, as it seems, from art's anarchic self-destruction but from its fulfillment. The play is about the relation of life and art, and the artwork, as it turns out, is a prolepsis of life, preparing the words and images for a reconciliation between warring parties.

The play parodies a tragic world view, in particular the inescapability of tragedy. An apparent tragedy of collision arises when two characters each recognize the validity of the other's position and thus change roles, eventually attacking their earlier stances: "Why, here the two of them were on opposite sides of the same question. They both changed their minds at the same time, each coming around to the view of the other. Naturally, they collided in the process" (Ita 4:191; Eng 328). Rather than suggesting inevitable conflict or an "anything goes" mentality, the split indicates the potential for recognizing the validity of another stance, the stance originally negated, as well as a contingent inability to recognize the instability of each position as it is embraced. This structure of reversal, if applied self-reflexively, may imply that the negation of art and meaning is, behind its own back, an affirmation of art and meaning.

The structure is dialectical, and the play is sprinkled on the finite level with precisely such dialectical insights: that refusing to have an opinion is a way of having one (Ita 4:150; Eng 279); that talking about why one shouldn't talk is still talk (Ita 4:151; Eng 280); that the claim that nothing is true derives from a deeper presupposition of truth (Ita 4:169; Eng 305). In each case, a negative position passes over into the object of its own negation. The audience articulates this point, although it does so critically: "Nobody knows what it's all about! / First it's this, and then it's something else! / First they said one thing, but now they say the opposite! / It's a joke on the audience!" (Ita 4:180; Eng 316). Pirandello shows that reality, or what we take to be reality, is not fixed, which is not to say that everything is illusion (cf. Ita 4:183; Eng 321 and Ita 4:194; Eng 332). Instead, reality can be transformed by illusion; in that sense reality is not fixed; in that sense what was taken to be illusion can become reality.

Art, rather than being mere illusion or the illusion of an illusion,

is the norm by which life rises to a position of symmetry and intersubjectivity, as is demonstrated in the fulfillment of Act 2 in the
Second Interlude.[103] Delia Moreno and Baron Nuti break through
their mask of hatred and embrace one another. Illusion is pierced
by reality but a reality prepared for by illusion. The play does not
end in disruption and chaos; that is mere illusion. It ends, rather,
in fulfillment and harmony. Although the heroes earlier reacted
with rage at seeing their lives mirrored before them (they object to
accusations of ignorance and immorality), they do not leave the
theater. This suggests a structure by which the heroes want to see
themselves mirrored, yet they want the mirror to lead them to a
better, not a weaker, reality. Art's imitation of life is scorned; but
life's imitation of art is embraced.

Intention and Reception

Most important in interpreting a literary text are not the author's
intentions but the structures at work in a text. A naive position
reduces the structures of meaning in a work to the consciousness
that created it and seeks to grasp only what the author intended.
Recognition of an author's intentions always has a certain *historical* interest, but it is a sign of the reduction of aesthetics to history
in contemporary literary culture that we have become preoccupied
with intentionalism and the history of reception at the expense of
aesthetic and logical analyses, which should have priority (Roche,
Gottfried Benn 75–79). If a work expresses more than personal
opinion, if it attempts to grasp what is valid and true, then we
should be interested in more than the author's self-interpretation.
We must be attentive to the often unintentional meanings that surface in the richness of a text's layers. This is not to suggest that
anything can be read into or out of a text; far from it, it is to argue
that the text is the highest authority—as illuminated by its inner
logic.

The most interesting works of absolute irony are not those that
end in nonsense, nothingness, or despair, but those that unwittingly lead to a form of affirmation, derived from the ironization of
irony or the negation of negativity. We can distinguish between
these two forms by speaking of the *non-art of absolute irony* on the
one hand and the *metacomedy of absolute irony* on the other.[104]
Every comedy of absolute irony is by definition, as we discussed
above, a comedy of negation on a metalevel; thus, every comedy of

absolute irony is a metacomedy. The metacomedy of absolute irony, however, is self-reflective in a greater sense. It is not just a negation of negativity on the level of self-reflection; it negates negativity within the metalevel of reflection. It is, therefore, a more complex version of the other antithetical comedies.

To summarize, then, the non-art of absolute irony negates all meaning and ends in nonsense and ultimate despair. The work's status as non-art may derive from authorial intention, a strongly deconstructionist reading, or both. The metacomedy of absolute irony suggests that a layer of meaning lies hidden in the work. In some cases, the author has created an extraordinarily complex work, whose affirmative moments are not easily discernible; in other cases, the moment of affirmation is unveiled against the author's intentions by way of the reader's attention to the work's independent dialectical structures. The distinction between the two terms often results only *after* careful and elaborate analysis, whereas the *possibility* of the work's belonging to absolute irony is readily apparent, thus the advantage of a single or overarching term, even as we recognize its variations.

We could take the extreme view that there is no such thing as the *non-art* of absolute irony. Every negative position cancels itself, such that the irony of absolute irony can always be recognized. Pirandello's anti-Pirandellism is always visible. But this may place too much emphasis on the work; we should not ignore the history of its interpretations. Our readings determine whether a work will be read this way or that. Interpretation determines which subform applies or—in the case of an especially complex work such as Kleist's *Amphitryon*—which genre applies. Thus, though readings of works as non-art, that is, as the negation of all meaning, may be wrong, they do exist, and so I leave open the question of whether absolute irony is always comic or at times non-art. In principle it is always comic; in practice it often becomes comic only unwittingly in the hands of the interpreter who would render it non-art, even as he seeks to elevate it to the highest form of art.

Elaboration

Studying forms of subjectivity in comedy has significant value. As above with our discussion of tragedy, we arrive at clearer categories, challenging subquestions, new structural comparisons, insights into strengths and weaknesses of individual subgenres, and a hierarchy of forms that is valid in principle and allows us to better use our critical, rather than merely interpretive, tools. In addition, a study of comic subjectivity may shed light on subjectivity itself, including the sometimes somber contemporary reflections on the dissolution of the subject. Preoccupation with subjectivity may find its truest expression in comedy. Finally, types of comic characters are as important for the tradition of comedy and the inventiveness of comic authors as are myths to the tragedian (Warning 289; cf. Salingar). The better we understand the various forms of comedy, the paradigms, the better we grasp comic tradition and possibilities, the shifts within and against earlier forms.

Other Typologies of Comedy

Most discussions of comedy, especially in the English-speaking world, delineate subgenres inductively. We speak of situation and character comedy, of the comedy of humors, manners, intrigue, and ideas, satiric comedy, romantic comedy, farce, low comedy, and high comedy. Although the various terms have explanatory power, a comprehensive and systematic account of comedy that can subsume and organize these distinctions should be privileged. By themselves, these designations cannot be systematically or coherently related, for they address in varying ways emphasis, types of character and action, technique, topic, quality, and so on. In contrast, the subgenres articulated in this study are all related to the overarching categories of objectivity, subjectivity, and intersubjectivity.

Moreover, the subgenres discussed above allow for finer distinctions than terms such as situation and character comedy. Is Kleist's *The Broken Jug*, for example, a situation or a character comedy? Clearly it is both, and neither concept helps us grasp the play in its specificity. But recognizing that the play is a comedy of negation and not, for example, a comedy of coincidence or a comedy of intersubjectivity tells us a great deal about the work, both thematically and formally. Each subgenre has a defined realm of action, introduces different types of characters, and makes varying philosophical statements.

Farce, the comedy of errors, and *commedia dell'arte* generally belong to the initial comic form, the comedy of coincidence; here, situation and plot override the autonomy and development of individual subjects. In the comedies of reduction, individual negation, and withdrawal, character becomes increasingly important. In social negation, character is generally overridden by intrigue, the result of a multiplicity of false characters. When villains and dissemblers conspire endlessly against one another and the innocent, as in Congreve's *The Double Dealer*, negation and intrigue become inseparable. When the action moves quickly and ironically and no single character is in control, intrigue can resemble coincidence.

A number of traditional forms overlap with the antithetical subgenres. The comedy of manners normally fits either reduction or negation, though in some cases it may overlap with withdrawal. The comedy of humors likewise allows for a wide range and could fit, depending on the particular humor, either reduction, negation, or withdrawal. Satiric comedy also belongs to all the antithetical subgenres, though it exhibits an especially strong affinity to the comedy of social negation. Comedies of ideas generally, though not necessarily, belong to withdrawal; Goethe's Wagner, to cite an exception, is a comic protagonist of reduction; so, too, is George in Stoppard's *Jumpers*.

Sentimental and romantic comedy, finally, fit either coincidence or intersubjectivity, depending on the ironies of plot and the development of the characters who reach harmony. Northrop Frye's typology of comedy, surely the most discussed in recent times, is directed primarily toward Romantic comedy. In his *Anatomy of Criticism*, Frye offers an illuminating discussion of comedy that stresses the crystallization of a new society around the young hero and heroine who overcome obstacles in their path toward fulfillment and resolution (43–52 and 163–186). Frye's definition of comedy, however insightful, is essentially restricted to the forms I describe as coincidence and intersubjectivity.[105] But comedy allows for greater variety than is permissible in a definition that demands a happy end, a "comic resolution" (171).[106]

Strengths and Weaknesses of the Comic Subgenres

The individual subgenres, each of which contains the comic contrast between contingent particularity and the substantial, can be analyzed for their strengths and weaknesses. The primary weakness of coincidence is that it may remain a lower form of art, not substantial but silly, not organic but episodic. The series of events, not set in motion by any one developed character, may seem arbitrary; the events happen one after the other, but may not appear to flow one out of the other. The genre can be thoroughly entertaining and delightful, but its intellectual import is sometimes limited.[107] The comedy of coincidence is the purest form of comedy in its focus on aesthetic experience rather than ethical intention; it is there for its own enjoyment. However, the comedy of coincidence may also contain elements of a speculative philosophy of history and so evidence more substance than is immediately apparent. As a subgenre that delimits subjectivity and confers a spiritual dimension upon nature, coincidence seems almost out of place in modernity, yet like other genres that contest, rather than mirror, their age, it does surface in this era. Often the performance as much as the work will determine where the play stands on a spectrum between the merely entertaining and the speculative, between arbitrariness and hidden necessity.

Reduction is among the most successful and popular of subgenres. It raises significant issues by way of the character's unsuccessful attempts to recognize and realize truth. Unlike in withdrawal, we see here a stress on action as well as character; unlike in negation, the hero's actions are relatively harmless—there are no brutalized victims. Unlike in intersubjectivity, reduction will never risk the danger of an unearned happy end. Moreover, here more frequently than in other genres—with the possible exception of coincidence—we see a moment Hegel viewed as essential to comedy: not only the audience but the characters themselves laugh at their inadequacies (15:552 and 15:569).[108] Though not always present in reduction, this moment does allow for a more amusing and less brutal atmosphere.[109]

The primary danger of reduction is that the audience, depending on the performance, may identify with the protagonist rather than recognize his inadequacies. The problem is common to all antithetical subgenres. The structures of the antithetical forms may or may not be received as comic in the sense of a negation of the negation. The observer of such comedies plays a central role, for the hero is comic only if the observer can distance himself from the hero and recognize the absurdity of his actions. Thus, if the first negation, the negation of substance, takes place on stage, the second negation, the recognition of the comic as comic or absurd, takes place in the consciousness of the audience. The extent to which the object is viewed as comic varies, because the values of different spectators vary as well, although the play can in its argument, its *reductio ad absurdum*, encourage the viewer to *change* his values. Nonetheless, the viewer may well be content with the appearance of the hero as he is and fail to recognize his absurdities. Because we do not take the hero seriously, we are lulled into a relaxed, indulgent view and are tempted to identify with the first negation.

The comedy of individual negation functions much like the tragedy of stubbornness; the action is highly dramatic because of the stress on formal virtues. Due to the extraordinary demands placed on ingenuity and the author's language as well as the actor's performance, the genre is relatively rare; when it succeeds, the hero's cleverness and wit raise the work to great heights.

The comedy of social negation is generally filled with tendentious themes and a critical-satirical spirit, with the forms of negativity portrayed ranging from frivolousness to brutality. This subgenre is most removed from art as an end in itself. To the extent that it becomes polemical, it is privileged by those who equate literature with social criticism and disparaged by those who view art as autonomous. If coincidence is weakened when it becomes all form and no substance, social negation is endangered insofar as it becomes all message. An interesting dialectic surfaces in this genre: the more extreme the characters' inadequacies are, the clearer the message; to the same degree, however, the less likely the audience is to recognize its own weaknesses in the action. The danger of comedy's passing over into propaganda is immanent in each antithetical subgenre, but most pronounced in social negation, which tends to border on satire and the grotesque. Plays of this subgenre are most successful when they stress not the victimization of a character but the comic contradictions in a society that victimizes itself. Lubitsch's *To Be or Not to Be* is a good illustration of this virtue; it renders evil aesthetic by playing with the comic artifice of intrigue and counter-intrigue.

While I do not share Hegel's assertion that comedy requires "an infinite light-heartedness and confidence felt by someone raised altogether above his own inner contradiction and not bitter or miserable in it at all" (15:518; A 1200),[110] clearly the more a comedy focuses on the absurdity of contradictions and less on the victims of these contradictions, the more it will aspire to a comic ideal and distance itself from the mere drama of suffering. Taking pain seriously awakens sympathy, not laughter or joy. If comedy addresses alienation by focusing on the victim rather than the victimizer and his contradictions, the audience experiences the emotions of suffering and tragicomedy, not those of comedy.[111]

The main value of withdrawal is intellectual, the thematization of what borders on a tragedy of opposition. The reduction of plot will disappoint those who prefer the liveliness of coincidence, and the poet is often forced to rely on sharpness of language and successful staging. Here no less than in the other comic subgenres, however, we see inconsistencies and contradictions that can be dealt with playfully and contribute to what is often called comic spirit. Whereas in negation the hero's claims are demolished, in withdrawal—because the hero shares more in truth—his position is only mildly ironized. The latter form is more subtle, even to the point of springing the boundaries of what is traditionally considered comic. The rarity of the genre appears to derive from its complexity and from its being on the edge of the genre.

Intersubjectivity runs the danger of failing to develop a conflict before its resolution, not presenting the conflict as substantial, or introducing an early resolution without developing the path toward this resolution, that is, without motivating the character's growth. Under certain circumstances, intersubjectivity could appear escapist or evasive. Some problems cannot easily be resolved. Thus, Lessing's *The Jews* ends with a moment of enlightenment (the Baron recognizes exceptions to the rule that Jews are evil) and a moment of reduction (the Baron fails to see that he should abandon his rule entirely). The comic critique, with a reconciliatory sentiment expressed only indirectly and ex negativo, may have been the best message for an age not inclined to accept marriages across racial and religious boundaries (Hinck, "Vom Ausgang" 150). While intersubjectivity is in principle the highest form, this insight must be tempered with recognition of particular themes and contexts; in many an instance reduction or negation may be the most compelling comic form.

The comedy of intersubjectivity may appear to be a subgenre where audiences tend not to laugh, though this is in no way necessary. The difficulty seems to arise, first, from the seriousness of the conflict, second, from the resolution of the contradictions. Philosophers and psychologists have developed essentially three theories of laughter: contrast, superiority, and festivity.[112] The latter two can be subsumed under the first.[113] When we laugh at another because of our superiority over him, we laugh at the implied contrast between what the comic character is doing and what he should be doing or what we imagine we would have done. Festive and communal laughter, laughter as celebration, arises from a moment of overcoming, the contrast between expectation and accomplishment, between the dualism of real and ideal and the harmony of real and ideal.[114] The superiority theory is especially supported by coincidence (where the audience knows more than the protagonist, who misapprehends his situation) and the antithetical subgenres (where the protagonist deviates from the good). The laughter of festivity is prominent in both coincidence and intersubjectivity.

Incongruities, however, are found in every subgenre. The best comedies—from the perspective of technique—have the greatest contrast between contingent particularity and substance. We have already argued that the best comedies—from the perspective of their participation in truth—overcome this contrast. Thus, the best comedy in every respect presents us with an extreme contrast that is nevertheless organically overcome. In 2a through 2c, contrast, in the form of contradictions, is prominent and laughter is pronounced, unless, as in 2b, the conflict becomes serious and victimization realistic. Ideally, intersubjectivity integrates these contradictions, allowing for moments of laughter and tension, but also overcoming them and ending on a note of festivity.

One can argue that a particular comedy is weak by pointing to a lack of tension between substance and particularity: the greater the tension, the greater the comedy, both in terms of laughter or drama and from the perspective of import and meaning. The possible lack of tension in coincidence and intersubjectivity, and the potential for superficiality or evenness, makes these forms far more difficult to conceive successfully. The clear schisms in the antithetical forms, on the other hand, open these works to diverse and extensive comic manipulation. Nonetheless, to the extent that intersubjectivity includes earlier moments, it becomes the liveliest of all subforms, for it is the unity of the most diverse and as such the richest genre of all.

In the comedy of intersubjectivity, the identifying audience passes beyond mere negativity. The action on stage portrays the consequences which in the antithetical forms the audience must draw for itself. The danger here is that the audience, not having to work to find an answer, may not have immersed itself enough in the negative and may have reached for itself a rather unstable harmony.[115] Chance, as dependence on the external, can resurface here as well. Not unrelated to this issue is the Socratic elevation of ironic knowledge, knowledge that has passed through negativity. It is an absolute knowledge, and in some senses a comic knowledge, that contains, via negation, its own finitude and is as such no longer susceptible to the outside influence of finitude.

The comedy of absolute irony, finally, is always either a meta-comedy of absolute irony, and as such overlaps with one of the

212 Tragedy and Comedy

other comic forms, or a work that transcends the boundaries of art. Absolute irony fulfills to the nth degree the antithetical position of the genre insofar as it is characterized by subjectivity. Comedy has a tradition of suspending limits, mixing styles and categories, and experimenting with diversity.[116] This revision of expectations—despite certain mechanical formulas—is made possible by comedy's highly self-reflexive mode, its self-reflection being concurrent with its subjectivity, which is most pronounced in absolute irony. The greatness of absolute irony is its complexity, its limits lie in its highly cerebral nature, which can weaken comic spirit, and its tendency toward nihilism.

A difficulty of the comic as such is the balance between frivolity, encouraging the audience to exhaust itself in the comic eccentricities of the hero, and pedantry, driving home the negation of the negation at the expense of the genuine entertainment value of the comic. Neither extreme is tenable: the first destroys the intellectual, the second the sensuous moment of art. Art becomes non-art, "a mere game of entertainment or a mere means of instruction" (13:77; A 51, translation modified). The greatest comedies, in contrast, make their moral arguments and ethical statements in the very act of amusing and delighting the audience.

Death and Cruelty

Comedy often ends in marriage, while tragedy ends in death. Death is viewed as anathema to the comic spirit. Nonetheless, death (as well as pain and cruelty) can occur in comedy. First, it is possible in coincidence, when the setting is magical and death is viewed as part of the life of the cosmos. Consider the death of Leopold in Woody Allen's *A Midsummer Night's Sex Comedy*: death is comic when the dead person becomes a friendly spirit—and it is especially comic when the person who becomes a spirit announces before his death that he does not believe in spirits.

Another possibility for comedy is a death that is contemplated or attempted but not realized. Also workable—if in a slightly different, yet related way—is a death that is non-real and diffused because it is surreal. Any pain that is so extreme or grotesque that we cannot take it seriously is comic. Consider the portrayal of death in Allen's *Love and Death* or the comic dimensions of the cripple in his *Everything You Always Wanted to Know About Sex (But Were Afraid To Ask)*: a cripple whose condition results from a

four-hour orgasm cannot be other than comic. Caliban's misfortune
in Shakespeare's *The Tempest* is likewise placed in bizarre and ridiculous settings, thus undermining the seriousness of his suffering. We laugh because the character's suffering is not real; we are
not met with the gravity and finitude of tragedy. The widespread
use of the surreal and grotesque in the comedy of negation—also
as a means of rendering pain and death comic—reintegrates a significant moment of coincidence, antirealism. The non-realism of
death and even murder are also conveyed when murder is discussed, but never shown, especially when it is talked about in such
a bizarre and absurd way as in Capra's *Arsenic and Old Lace*,
where two happy and otherwise amiable aunts view murder matter-of-factly and as a form of charity. Another example of the audience's suspension of reality, which allows it to laugh at brutality, is
the comic technique in silent cinema whereby shots are taken at
normal speed but accelerated on the screen; here, too, pain is rendered surreal.

Cruelty can also be comic when we are aware of the artifice of
the story, either because the story is already familiar to us and the
comic presentation differs from reality or because of messages conveyed to us by the actors. We laugh at an apparent danger we
know is not serious. At the end of Aristophanes' *The Clouds*, Strep-
siades sets Socrates' house on fire and Socrates cries out in desper-
ation, but the audience knows that the real Socrates did not die in
this way. Finally, we become aware of the artifice of cruelty when
the actors give us messages that make clear to us the fiction—as
when the comic actor is whacked on the seat of his pants with a
broom and waits five seconds before saying "Ouch!" Causality is
suspended, and the action becomes irreal and aesthetic. We laugh
at the comic representation of a cruel act, not the cruel act itself.[117]

When a cruel act is not framed in one of these ways—as sometimes arises in social negation—the hero's pain breaks the frame of
comedy. The most consistently challenged aspect of Hegel's theory
of tragedy has been the assertion that tragedy includes a moment
of reconciliation. His theory of comedy, being less well-known, has
not suffered the same level of critique. Yet a parallel moment in his
theory of comedy has been at odds with the development of modern
comedy and most theories about it: the related claims that comedy
include a moment of lightness, that the comic hero not suffer real
pain, and that he somehow be beyond his situation. With the modern development of comedy, especially that of social negation, and
thus the transformation of comedy into satire and the grotesque,

the genre has become as dark vis-à-vis Hegel's theory of comedy as modern tragedy has become vis-à-vis his theory of that genre.

Hegel, however, is not alone in making these arguments. In the fifth chapter of the *Poetics*, Aristotle views the comic defect as "not painful or destructive" (5.1) and adds that "the comic mask is ugly and distorted, but does not imply pain" (5.1). Johann Stephen Schütze, a precursor of Hegel, likewise argues for the limits of comic negation: "The comic is concerned not with error that destroys the world, but rather only with error that may exist with it and also eternally exist; and if the poet should choose to destroy his play himself, then he does so only in order to allow a more beautiful harmony to emerge" (114, my translation).[118] Karl Überhorst, a nineteenth-century aesthetician, adds to his definition of comedy the stipulation that the comic experience not awaken in us any vehemently unpleasant feelings.[119] Despite shifts within comic theater, a number of modern theorists share this Aristotelian-Hegelian view. Nicolai Hartmann, for example, writes: "obviously comedy stops where serious suffering and bitter pain begin" (*Aesthetik* 422, my translation). A literary danger of the modern comedy of negation is that the comic heroes' transgressions are so severe as to surpass the limits of the comic: pain and suffering are indeed evident; even murder is not beyond the bounds of the modern comedy of negation. There may be a metacomedy in the audience's disinterest in such works. The objectivity of the audience takes its revenge on the illicit intentions of the authors who are so obsessed with transgressing generic boundaries. No country has developed this dark comic tradition greater than Germany, and no country has more difficulties convincing world audiences of the value of its comic tradition.

Iteration

The privileged moment of particularity unleashes various comic structures of which we have long been aware. One such elemental and philosophical structure is iteration. Iteration as a form of coincidence—a series of unexpected meetings, for example—illustrates the subject's powerlessness in a world of complex relations that transcend his grasp. We also see in iteration the logical extension of particularity, not one particular but many particulars. This multiplicity within the antithetical mode of difference suggests, however, that if x, y, and z are all different, they all share the quality of difference and so are in principle not only different but also similar. The comic protagonist, moreover, who is reduced to the level of nature and instinct, finds that he does not progress. As the human sphere of progress eludes him, he falls back into the natural cycle of repetition, an infinite regress.[120] The protagonist continually reduces his goal, making the same mistake over and over. We see a finitization of the infinite and thus the bad infinite of continually reducing or withdrawing from truth.

The dialectic might be illustrated more closely by another look at Schnitzler's *Anatol*. In this play we see the permanence of Anatol's impermanence; there is something static about his many relations. Comedy represents in a sense the inability to transcend the finite. Thus, repetition takes over insofar as every attempt to overcome one barrier leads only to the next and so forth ad infinitum. Change is unveiled as a form of stasis. The episodic but repetitive character of Anatol's relations also has speculative import. His frequent change of partners, the result of his longing for independence, has at its core the same basic structure throughout. Changing constantly, Anatol is locked into the sameness of change. Although in a state of *flux*, he *remains* in a state of flux. Hofmannsthal speaks quite rightly of the Medusa-like qualities in *Anatol* (797). The relationships become formal and mechanical. These structures of comic reduction refute the claim that "everything about comedy confirms the possibility for change" (Corrigan 9).

In Brecht's *Master Puntila and His Servant Matti*, we see a similar pattern. Puntila is drunk, then sober, then drunk, then sober again. There is a permanence to this impermanence, but it is at a nonconscious level. The action demonstrates in the most primitive way the dialectic of constancy and inconstancy. Impermanence absolutized is permanence, or to use a Hegelian expression, the truth of inconstancy is constancy. Anatol and Puntila, however, realize the speculative idea of a oneness in multiplicity or a permanent impermanence at the lowest possible level.

The dialectic of iteration extends beyond reduction. In the comedy of negation we see the consistent inconsistency of the hero as he tries to hide his crimes; one thinks of the repetitive deceptions of Goldoni's Lelio or Kleist's Adam. We also recognize the repetitiveness of injustice when its particular manifestations are multiplied through society, as, for example, in Zuckmayer's *The Captain of Köpenick*. In the comedy of withdrawal we see the hero continually make the same mistake of tact; Alceste is a good example. Repetition of this kind clashes with human value. Intersubjectivity often begins with iteration, but only in order to surmount it, as in Allen's *Zelig* or Ramis's *Groundhog Day*; when a comedy of intersubjectivity closes with iteration, it is often a gesture to coincidence and represents as such a delimiting of subjectivity.

One form of iteration is circularity, which takes on different aspects depending on the subgenre: in coincidence, it relates to the cyclical aspects of nature and the human wheel of fortune; in reduction, it represents the repetition of inadequacy (constant inconstancy, for example), in negation, the repetition of evil scheming (the hero duped by his own schemes or by the mirror image of his duplicity), and in withdrawal, the back and forth dialectic with society; in intersubjectivity, it is normally the repetition of coincidence on a higher level, a spiral, if you will.

Identity

The question of sameness and difference penetrates to the core of subjectivity and comedy. Difference after all is *the* category of any antithesis. Sameness and difference within the subject manifest themselves in frequent crises of identity, which arise either from a lack of self-knowledge (the hero pursues a goal at odds with his own nature) or from a difficult situation (the hero would prefer to remain himself but in pursuing a just goal must contradict himself or disguise himself).[121] Identity crises need not be limited to the crisis of an individual self. Northrop Frye speaks of singular identity (an individual hero comes to know himself in a way he did not before); dual identity (the unification and new identity of lovers); and social identity (the crystallization of a new harmony of selves or the formation of a new society) (Frye, *A Natural Perspective* 78). Each crisis and resolution involves a transition from false subjectivity to true subjectivity and intersubjectivity.

Because identity crises can also be tragic, the question arises, what makes an identity crisis specifically comic? I would argue that it is the playful context in which the crisis is embedded. In coincidence and intersubjectivity, the hero is self-confident—beyond the crisis, if you will. Unlike a tragic hero, the comic hero does not take the crisis seriously; he overlooks it—this is amusing. In the antithetical genres, the crisis often revolves around a trivial matter, and the hero takes it too seriously. Contingent particularity overrides all substantial considerations, just as in coincidence and intersubjectivity an overridingly confident subjectivity shields us from any substantial questions. The hero searches for an identity by reflecting only on his own self and not also on the extent to which identity presupposes identification with universal norms.

The theme of twins or doubles is a particular manifestation of iteration, the search for identity, and the question of sameness and difference.[122] Doubling is an essentially comic structure, insofar as it relates to subjectivity and the doubling of particularity, as, for example, in Plautus's *Menaechmi*, Shakespeare's *A Comedy of Errors* and *Twelfth Night*, Raimund's *The King of the Alps and the Misanthrope*, or Woody Allen's *Zelig*, but the structure also allows for tragic overtones. The division of the self may represent a rupture of unity and harmony, as, for example, in Kleist's *Amphitryon* or Brecht's *The Good Person of Sezuan*. Whenever the doubles are reunited in the same person, representing thereby the unity of unity and difference, as, for example, in Preston Sturges's *The Lady Eve*, intersubjectivity and reconciliation reenter the stage. The importance of doubling and difference in comedy also helps explain the frequency of double plots, as, for example, in Terence and Shakespeare, and the mirroring of characters, for example, masters and servants.

A related theme is that of mistaken identities (as opposed to internal identity crises) and the swapping of roles. These moments can be seen in the light of coincidence (we are all interchangeable) or intersubjectivity (we are all of equal worth). Of particular interest here is the swapping of roles between master and servant, which generally suggests either that the servant is, despite external appearances, the real mover of events or that a deeper equality exists behind the facade of rank. Although unsublated master-servant relations are frequent in the antithetical comedies, more harmonic works such as Plautus's *The Prisoners* or Lessing's *Minna von Barnhelm* stress equality and symmetry.

Role Playing

A variation of the double and identity crisis theme is the structure by which a character is given a role (or seeks one) that he then fulfills; the character appears to satisfy his own desires, those of society, or both. Characters in coincidence and reduction pass from one role to the next because they lack control over their own fate or are unable or unwilling to develop a sense of character, stability, and identity. One thinks of Anatol, Felix Krull, or the early Leonard Zelig.[123]

Characters in reduction may also trivialize their roles, in effect reducing what is substantial. The comedy of Frisch's *The Firebugs* consists in Biedermann's attempt to be the trusting and tolerant person the arsonists tell him he is. Herr Biedermann wants the arsonists to like him not only so they don't burn down his house but because they've challenged him to be a generous, kind, just human being. Biedermann, however, lacks insight, cannot recognize evil, and so fails. Although Biedermann is not already convinced of the greatness of his own subjectivity, he is so obsessed with pleasing others and thus becoming an admired subject that he consistently acts according to the most absurd principles. In this way, the play satirizes passivity and conformism in the face of collective acceptance and evil. The hero answers his identity crisis by becoming what others want even when that is absurd and ridiculous. Biedermann's extreme role playing also introduces, however, some great comic moments, as when Biedermann asks, is it really true that the containers the arsonists have placed in his attic contain gas, to which the arsonists respond, "Don't you trust us?" (sc. 4, my translation).

A third form of role playing occurs in negation, where the hero undergoes a split between what he appears to be and what he is. This duplicity arises from the frequency with which the hero of negation lies, and it results in the erasure of the hero's true essence. Good examples for this would be Sternheim's *The Strongbox* and *Tabula rasa*. A fourth form, likewise evident in negation, occurs when the hero is given a role by society and fulfills it, but the new position hardly leads to the hero's inner fulfillment. The hero becomes what society dictates.[124] We find this structure in plays such as Nestroy's *The Talisman*, Horváth's *Stories from the Vienna Woods*, Brecht's *A Man is a Man*, and Zuckmayer's *The Captain of Köpenick*.

Finally, the comedy of intersubjectivity allows for the structure by which the hero is given an admirable role, a calling so to speak, which he then fulfills as he fulfills his greatest potential. The figure by which the hero is viewed as x and so becomes, or tries to become, x often encourages development and may lead to a happy end. In Freytag's *The Journalists*, for example, the Oberst rises to the label given him by those who want him to become forgiving and gracious. A contemporary example of characters becoming the role they are playing is Weir's *Greencard*, which is also an excellent example of intersubjectivity as the deepening of coincidence. The acquisition of a role has a self-reflective dimension that is particularly fitting for comedy; theater after all is defined by actors playing the roles of others. Allen's *Play it Again, Sam* illustrates both the self-reflexive structure of role playing and its progressive, intersubjective possibilities. Role playing can also relate to the theme of doubles. In Raimund's *The King of the Alps and the Misanthrope*, the hero sees himself in an untenable, rather than admirable, role and consequently frees himself from his weaker self.

Appearance and Reality

Contingent particularity as opposed to substance also parallels the appearance-reality dualism characteristic of European comedy. Comic figures view appearance and reality as identical when they are different or vice versa. Characters preoccupied with the external, whether titles, formalities, or position, as, for example, in Kotzebue's *The German Small Town Folk*, reduce substance to its lowest dimension. Overlooking what is essential, characters become entrenched in the contradictions of particularity and contingency. They occupy themselves with trivial customs, the particularity of gossip, and the superficialities of social rank. In reduction the hero unwittingly mistakes appearance for reality; in attempting to outwit his opponents, the hero of negation consciously substitutes appearance for reality. At times, the hero takes this play with appearances to be of greater significance than reality itself, thus creating an overlay of negation and reduction, as, for example, in Mann's *Felix Krull*. Insofar as comedy deflates substance and greatness, including the mirage of greatness in the work itself, we recognize a link to the breaking of the illusion of verisimilitude, which culminates in absolute irony. Here too, appearance is unveiled as appearance.

Self-Reflection and Reception

Subjectivity also explains the traditional emphasis within comedy on self-reflexive structures, including the breaking of the illusion of verisimilitude and the development of an immanent aesthetics. These structures pervade comedy from Aristophanes through the German Romantics to Pirandello and modern cinema and are not restricted to absolute irony. On occasion, self-reflexivity is used to parody tragedy, as in Aristophanes' *The Frogs*, or to affirm the value of comedy, as in Sturges's *Sullivan's Travels*. More often, it is used to mock the feigned tragic pathos of the comic hero, as in Schnitzler's *Professor Bernhardi* or Allen's parodies of his own figures and works. In all instances, self-reflection tends to engender laughter and so enhances comic spirit.

A central structure in both tragedy and comedy is self-cancellation. The tragic hero's greatness leads to his demise; the comic hero's obsession with contingency leads to his demise. Thus, the formal structure of self-cancellation can be tragic or comic. It can even be tragicomic, as, for example, in Shakespeare's *The Merchant of Venice*, where Shylock, mediating between tragic stubbornness and comic particularity, loses his position owing to the self-cancellation of his own claims for justice.

One difference between tragic and comic self-cancellation lies in the distinction between greatness and particularity, which in turn creates different possibilities of viewing the world. In tragedy we identify with the hero's efforts and subsequent suffering. This identification represents a commitment to finitude. We experience suffering and concern, thereby recognizing the need for action; tragic reception is oriented toward praxis and reality. In comedy we contemplate the hero's weaknesses and distance ourselves from him; this can lead to coldness. Ironically, the reception of tragic greatness engenders a commitment to finitude and particularity, whereas the reception of comic contingency engenders a theoretical attitude beyond particularity.[125] We adopt a sovereign perspective—not unlike, but not going as far as, that of the ironist. Both attitudes are important and could be said to complement one another.

Comedy, the most subjective genre, also requires the most active audience; the viewer must act out mentally the complex structure of the negation of negativity. He must negate the object as the mere appearance of objective beauty in order to arrive at true beauty within his consciousness. Comic enjoyment requires "the sublation [Aufhebung] of the object in the subject" (Zeising 136, my translation). The least subjective reception in drama takes place in the objective or thetic subgenre of tragedy, itself aligned with objectivity, the tragedy of self-sacrifice; little distancing or reflection is necessary. The most subjective reception takes place in the most subjective or antithetical subgenre of comedy, itself aligned with subjectivity, the comedy of absolute irony, where there is only distancing and a tremendous intellectual effort is asked of the viewer.

This structure would seem to correspond to a historical development whereby the tragedy of self-sacrifice is prominent in the beginning of a culture, the comedy of absolute irony during its decline.

The elevation of subjectivity in comedy explains the author's playfulness. Whereas tragedy is an objective (or serious) portrayal, comedy is subjective (or playful). The subjectivity of the author is central: because he doesn't take things too seriously, pain is generally absent. In coincidence, he manipulates events; in reduction, he mocks the hero; in negation, he has the hero attempt all kinds of heinous acts but has him fail; and in withdrawal, he playfully stresses the hero's contradictions. The playfulness of the comic author helps explain why Romantic irony is comic rather than tragic. Comic spirit, finally, is also informed by the history of a genre's conventions and by elements ranging from diction to the choice and development of minor characters.

Instrumental Relations and Their Transcendence

In the comedies of reduction and negation, the hero's instrumentalization of others is criticized. The hero manipulates the other as an object rather than recognizes him as a subject, and the hero, who ultimately fails, is ironized or comically undermined. The heroes are not justified in their transgressions, and their purposes are illicit. In the comedy of social negation one character strategically instrumentalizes another who has himself manipulated others, demonstrating by a kind of symmetrical instrumentalization or double negation the untenability of instrumentalization. One thinks of works by Hauptmann, Sternheim, and Brecht. The hero of withdrawal, wanting to treat everyone with utmost honesty and respect, does not act strategically, yet this non-strategic thinking contributes to the hero's failure.

In the comedy of intersubjectivity we see the synthesis of strategic and communicative action. A character manipulates an other in order to realize an end that will benefit the manipulated other; the other will recognize the benefit and so in the end be grateful for the instrumentalization.[126] A good example would be the deceit of Miss Hardcastle, which brings out the true love of Marlow in Goldsmith's *She Stoops to Conquer*. The synthesis of strategic and communicative action corresponds to the maieutic structure of education as well as the ironic or playful elements of love. The good teacher doesn't force a lesson on a passive student, but works indirectly, which is to the student's benefit; the student eventually recognizes this. The beloved uses irony to exhibit the depths and resources of the self that the lover might otherwise underestimate.

Coincidence and intersubjectivity sometimes overlap in benevolent instrumental relations. Consider the instrumentalization of the other in order to achieve an end that will benefit the other and which the other will recognize, though the other never recognizes the actual process of instrumentalization and manipulation. Theodor's direction of events so as to bring about Jaromir's turn from false subjectivity to intersubjectivity in Hofmannsthal's *The Incorruptible One* is a good example. Coincidence occurs here on a metalevel as well: though Theodor arranges events, he may himself be the instrument of something higher.[127]

One of the few contemporary thinkers who consistently defends a transcendental approach to instrumentalization and other ethical issues is Karl-Otto Apel, whose essay "The A Priori of the Communication Community and the Foundations of Ethics" offers not only an outstanding modernization of the categorical imperative but a sound answer to a contemporary dilemma which states that a universally valid system of ethics is both necessary and impossible (*Transformation der Philosophie* 2:358–435). Drawing on the transcendental conditions of discourse, Apel sketches a twofold imperative: first, that we not destroy our *real* community of discourse, that is, that we work for the preservation of the human race (by not eliminating ourselves through nuclear war, environmental destruction, or philosophical-political disintegration); and second, that we enrich the community of rational beings by projecting the goal of an *ideal* community of discourse and that we work to realize this goal. The first imperative is the necessary condition of the second, which in turn gives meaning to the first, a meaning that is anticipated in every dialogue.

It may have to do with the symmetry of transcendental arguments that Apel's imperatives can be viewed against the backdrop of this typology of comedy and vice versa. The comedy of coincidence portrays Apel's first imperative: a community exists and thrives. It is not a richly differentiated or necessarily enlightened community, but a community it is. Its natural existence, its transcendence of the merely individual, and its continued preservation are all central ingredients. The goal of an ideal community is presented ex negativo in the antithetical comic subgenres, where the reduction, negation, and nonrealization of an ideal are thematized.

Further, the focus of the antithetical genres, subjectivity, is precisely what Apel wants to overcome in his arguments against Kant
and others: a transformation of the transcendental philosophy of
subjectivity into a transcendental philosophy of *intersubjectivity*.
The equality that would be reached would address all spheres of
life, economic and social as well as intellectual, asymmetries of all
kinds, in short, the infinite focus of antithetical comedy. Finally,
the realization of the ideal community, the development of richer
intersubjective relations, is central to the comedy of intersubjectivity, our synthetic genre.[128]

The progression toward intersubjectivity can also be viewed
from the perspective of sexual ethics. In coincidence, with the focus
on ritual, fertility, and the multiplicity of marriages, procreation is
dominant. In reduction and negation, sex is essentially hedonistic.
The focus is not on the development of a third out of a dialectic of
unity (indeed, little is said of children at all in these comedies).
Where coincidence, with its lower claims, harmlessly embraces fertility, reduction and negation portray, but also negate, hedonism,
often through a complex *reductio ad absurdum*. Withdrawal occu-
pies a unique position. The focus on reflection transcends the natural theme of procreation, and the moral stance overrides the hedonistic theme of desire; yet, the hero's standards, withdrawal, or
arrogance prevent him from entering a love relationship.[129] Intersubjectivity, finally, sublates procreation (the sphere of mere objectivity) and hedonism (the sphere of false subjectivity) and raises
sexuality to the level of love (the sphere of intersubjectivity, which
includes true subjectivity). The relationship is not just natural and
pleasurable, it is also spiritual, and it is affirmative and symmetrical, not negative and asymmetrical. Marriage integrates the moment of nature without letting it dominate over spirit. The essence
of spirit is oneness: "the *inherently* indissoluble that stands out as
exalted above the contingency of the passions and particular transient caprice" (R § 163, translation modified).

In coincidence we have symmetry without substance, a kind of
indifference, for Hegel the categories of Being. Truth is in itself but
not for itself. Relationships are scarcely mediated. An atmosphere
of indeterminacy reigns. The dominant categories of antithetical
comedy, if not comedy as such, are those of the logic of Essence:
appearance and essence, identity and difference, origin and reflection, the positive and negative, chance and necessity, oppression
and victimization. The two relata negate one another and are in
that very respect dependent on each other. They stand in a deter-

minate relation. Identity and difference, for example, are each the opposite of the other but are incomprehensible without the other. The hero of withdrawal finds his identity in a negation of society (he stands in absolute opposition to it), but his would-be independence from that society depends on the existence of the society he would negate (he is connected to that society, for his withdrawal has meaning only in relation to it). This is displayed dramatically in the fact that the hero remains preoccupied with the society he says he wants to have nothing to do with.

Only in intersubjectivity do we reach, and in some ways transcend, Hegel's logic of Concept. Relations are symmetrical and substantive, and they suggest that the truth of subjectivity is intersubjectivity. In Hegelian terms, truth is in itself and for itself, or for one another. The two selves are not simply related to one another, they are constituted by this relation and constituted as subjects, not objects. In the thetic and synthetic forms of tragedy, the hero sacrifices himself for another person or a universal. In comic reduction and comic negation, the hero abandons the universal and uses other persons as the means toward an end. Only in the comedy of intersubjectivity is the intersubjective "we" dominant, such that a supportive symmetry sublates both sacrifice and instrumentalization.

*

As we have seen, however briefly, such comic topics as the particularity of the subject, iteration, identity crises and doubles, role playing, self-reflexivity, and the instrumentalization of the other can be subsumed under a philosophical definition of subjectivity. Related to this structure as well as the issue of historical and systematic definitions of genre discussed in the introduction is the inability of critics, even as they focus on both tradition and function, to unite the two elements. Comedy is defined as the multiplicity of comic motifs (doubles, reversals, appearance-reality, and so on) and as, let's say, the negation of norms; no attempt is made to relate the one to the other. But as Aristotle suggests, a definition should not be enumerative, it should be a unity not by virtue of its being a string of words connected together but by virtue of its being one object (*Metaphysics* 8:6, 1045a). A definition of comedy as contingent particularity in contrast to one or another form of substance provides us with this unity, even as it generates subgenres and implies various manifestations of related themes.

Hofmannsthal's "The Difficult Man"

Some comedies show signs of more than one subgenre—either by including several protagonists, each of whom fits a different pattern, or by introducing a complex character or action, such that elements of different subgenres are united in a highly complex fashion. This is especially frequent in the synthetic subgenre, the comedy of intersubjectivity.

An illustration of the way in which the comedy of intersubjectivity crowns any hierarchy of comic forms is the extent to which it sublates, whether through integration or mockery or both, other forms of comedy. Hofmannsthal's *The Difficult Man* is a good example. One of the most famous and urbane comedies in the German language, Hofmannsthal's play depicts aristocratic Viennese society at the time of World War I. The hero, Hans Karl, is the difficult character, seemingly unwilling to enter into relations with others, including the delightful Helene Altenwyl, with whom he eventually becomes engaged. He is also difficult in the sense of being indecipherable, misread by some characters because of their self-confidence, such as Cresence and Stani, and by others, such as Agatha and Neugebauer, because of their insecurities.

The play introduces the reigning motif of the comedy of coincidence, the elevation of the universal over the individual, in several ways.[130] Consider the self-deprecatory manner of Hans Karl, who argues for the value of the institution of marriage in the face of individual importance. At one point he goes so far as to suggest that it doesn't matter whom Helen marries, just that she marry (II.xiv). Helen, too, recognizes the insignificance of the individual; she relates it to an overabundance of superficial rhetoric: "if all people knew how unimportant they are, not one of them would utter a word" (II.xiv, translation modified). Hans Karl, like Helen, is aware of the eternal, not the moment, the universal, not the particular. He invokes the eternal with his belief, "that everything has long since stood forth somewhere already completed and only suddenly becomes visible" (I.xviii, my translation). Helen states: "For me the moment simply doesn't exist" (II.xiv). Hans Karl's lack of intentions and his openness for mystical insight also contribute to an erasure of the self in the light of a greater whole. Hans Karl sees the insignificance of the individual, including himself, through the category of chance: "Then someone came along—by chance—it was I" (II.x, translation modified). He continues: "Everything that happens is effected by chance. We can't fully conceive how much we are creatures of chance, and how chance brings us together and drives us apart, and how anyone could set up house with anyone, if chance willed it" (II.x, translation modified). Hans Karl, who wants least to be the director of events, is placed in that role. Throughout the play the conscious intentions of individuals, including those of Hans Karl, are either thwarted or redirected. As we shall see, most of these moments, which seemingly represent coincidence, are further developed so as to fall ultimately in the realm of intersubjectivity.

The comedy of reduction is widespread in Hofmannsthal's play: Stani is the most prominent representative, but Cresence, Hechingen, Antoinette, Altenwyl, Edine, the famous man, and Neugebauer fit the model as well. Stani has absolutely no doubts as to his own greatness. Indeed, his sense of self in the first act has no match in German literature outside of Mann's Felix Krull.[131] The praise he extends to Hans Karl is really directed toward himself; he considers himself a mirror image of Hans Karl, but without his faults. To cite one example, Stani states: "It was only because she [Antoinette] thinks me wonderfully like you that I had any chance with her in the beginning. For instance, our hands. She goes into ecstasies about your hands" (I.viii). The stage directions add: "He looks at his own hand" (I.viii, my translation). Stani desires Antoinette and Helen, but he trivializes his relationships with these women. His decision to marry Helen, for example, occurs on the stairwell: "I am resolved to marry Helen . . . . I thought it all through. On the way up the stairs between here and the third floor" (I.xvi, my translation).[132] This is probabilism personified.[133] Stani is utterly content with himself. He constantly uses phrases like: "That's of course why women are so enormously impressed with me" (I.xvi, my translation). Hans Karl asks him: "Ah, you're always absolutely satisfied with the way you act?" Stani responds without hesitation: "Yes, if I weren't, then I would of course have acted differently" (I.viii, my translation).

Cresence's and Stani's repeated visits to Hans Karl, their movements to the exit and their many returns in the first act are comic not only as repetitions but also as illustrations of their self-importance. What they have to offer is so momentous, they must absolutely say it. This sense of self-worth leads not only to the overuse of language but to misunderstandings. Many of the play's confusions arise not from the supposed incommensurability of language but from the characters' inability or unwillingness to consider any perspective other than their own. Stani confidently insists he knows the other, for the other is for him an object, not an autonomous subject; to Hans Karl he states: "I know you through and through" (I.xvi). He asserts that no one may take Hans Karl literally just after Hans Karl insists that what he says he does mean literally (I.x). Stani reads every ambiguous statement or gesture in the light of his own greatness and personal intentions. Cresence, like Stani, is not only sure of herself, she is confident of what others mean, whether she is wrong—as is frequently the case—or, as when she affirms to Hans Karl, "When you say in general you mean something in particular" (I.iii), she is in fact correct. Meanwhile, Cresence fails to read not only Hans Karl's infrequent words but also his gestures, for example, his fiddling with the desk drawer. Extending the pattern, Cresence tries to direct Hans Karl's thoughts and conversations: "You should back me up, Karl . . . . Do back me up, Karl! [Der Kari soll sagen, daß er mir recht gibt . . . . Sag, daß du mir recht gibst, Kari!]" (II.i). Stani, Cresence, and Antoinette create confusions by their readings of events even when no words are spoken. Antoinette misreads gestures in II.v, Cresence in II.xii and II.xiv, and Stani in III.vii. Hans Karl develops with Hechingen a privileged moment of intersubjectivity, namely friendship, but Hechingen continually misunderstands Hans Karl (I.xv and III.xiii) even as he remains convinced that he understands Hans Karl's words intuitively, before Hans Karl even speaks.[134]

Cresence is interested in the coupling of characters, but the idea of getting together interests her more than the substance of any relationship. The symmetrical matching of partners is less important to her than that she be fulfilled in her desire to see an engagement; she has worked herself into the mood for one: "Kari, with you one never gets away from shilly-shallying. And just when I've worked myself into the mood for an engagement!" (III.xii, translation modified). Like Cresence, Antoinette lives for the moment. Though she can see through the play's arch-villain Neuhoff, she remains superficial and a flirt, thereby undermining her relationships.

Altenwyl speaks out in favor of dialogue and witty discussion: "In my view, conversation is an art that no one knows anymore: it consists not in pouring out words oneself, like a waterfall, but in giving the other a cue . . . . In my time conversation had quite a different set of values. We thought highly of a witty repartee: we used to lay ourselves out to be brilliant" (II.i, translation modified). But Altenwyl trivializes his ideal of discourse by suggesting that the exchange of ideas is designed to further one's own interests and appearance: "In my time one used to say: with my guest I must manage the conversation so that when his hand is on the door-latch, he'll feel that he has been brilliant, then on the way down-stairs he'll think me brilliant" (II.i). Altenwyl's dialogue is under-mined: first, by its latent self-directedness; second, by its artificial nature, which may block genuine communication; third, by its non-adherence to its own claims for validity (his lament is highly un-conversational); and fourth, by the comically repetitive way in which he tries to underline his point.[135] Yet another elliptical (and aesthetic) critique might derive from Altenwyl's prominent use of the phrase "on the way downstairs [auf der Stiegen]" (II.i), which after Stani's "I've thought it all through. On the way up the stairs between here and the third floor [Ich habe alles durchgedacht. Auf der Stiege von hier bis in den zweiten Stock hinauf]" (I.xvi), cannot help but have a comic effect.

Edine trivializes intellectual discourse and the sacred with her symbolic misreading of Brücke and Brückner. Edine's confusion has symbolic resonance: she turns from her conversation with Brücke to the game of bridge, which is the English translation of the professor's name. Unwittingly, Edine is unable to bridge a transition to the world of intellect and is sent back to the world of games. No bridge exists between her and the professor or vice versa: the signifier does not correspond to any substance. Edine is further ironized by her unabashed question about Nirvana. She seeks to be transported "away from banality" and is herself banal (II.i). The famous man is a reduction of the philosopher's ideal in-fluence on society; all he cares about is prestige and form. In a sense, the two characters mirror one another. Edine seeks to tran-scend the social for the intellectual world; the famous man wants as an intellectual to be recognized in the social world. Both of them fail comically. Neither finds a bridge. Indeed, Brücke cannot even satisfy his desire to meet Hans Karl, let alone impress him. Neu-gebauer, finally, is ironized for his false sense of honor and resigna-tion (a minor parody of tragedy).

The comedy of negation applies to Neuhoff and Vinzenz. Neuhoff is the outsider who has no regard for Austrian society. He speaks of the powerless and willless Austrians (II.xiii).[136] He is two-faced to-ward Hans Karl, and he is utterly inconsistent, quickly passing from Helen to Antoinette. Neuhoff is the opposite of Hans Karl on the axis of discretion. Consider his analysis of knowing ["kennen"] in the first act. Neuhoff views everything from his own perspective, for example, his analysis of Hans Karl's platoon commander (I.xii). We are reminded of one of the attributes Hofmannsthal ascribes to the Prussian individual: "an inability to think oneself into the other's position" ("Preusse," my translation). True to the structure of negation, Neuhoff fails. He falls hard before the viewers' eyes when Antoinette, in dismissing him, unwittingly cites Neuhoff's own rhetoric. Neuhoff had said the Viennese are "nothing but shadows [nur mehr Schatten]" (II.ii), and in the light of his own Prussian superiority he asserted without success his right over Helen: "So we meet as equals and yet not as equals, and out of this inequality has grown my right over you [So stehen wir gleich zu gleich und doch ungleich zu ungleich, und aus dieser Ungleichheit ist mir mein Recht über Sie erwachsen]" (II.xiii, translation modified). Antoinette's crushing line is in response to Neuhoff's "One could read in your face everything that has ever happened to you [Man könnte diesem Gesicht alles entreissen, was je in Ihnen vorgegangen ist]" (III.iv). Antoinette responds: "Could one? Perhaps— if one had a *shadow* of *right* to do so [Man könnte? Vielleicht— wenn man einen *Schatten* von *Recht* dazu hätte]" (III.iv, my emphasis, translation modified). Neuhoff is not only wrong in his reading of Antoinette, not only immodest, he exhibits here his lack of loyalty to Helen.[137]

Vinzenz, like Neuhoff, is convinced of his own greatness, lacks any sizeable virtues, and his legitimacy as a comic figure derives from contradictions of which he is unaware. Vinzenz constantly speaks of his own intentions and assumes similar attitudes in others; everything is for him instrumentalized. Like Neuhoff, he wants to control the world. He imagines that he will soon have Hans Karl wrapped around his finger and views him in the rhetoric of a false marriage: "In a month's time I'll be winding him round my little finger . . . he himself has resolved to live an old bachelor's life with me. That's just what I thought would happen" (I.xx, translation modified). Vinzenz is precisely when he is most confident most wrong. He is busy dominating conversation, and he expects Lukas to *tell* him all he needs to know. He fails to observe Hans Karl and does not react to his needs.

In attempting to instrumentalize the world, Neuhoff and Vinzenz employ language as the tool of their will; speaking at length and only of their own intentions, these comic figures evoke a will of domination, not of ethical action. As is common in negation, each loses out in the end: Vinzenz is fired, Neuhoff rejected. As in reduction the characters with strong intentions fail—either because they are inept or because they lack insight into the higher order according to which events unfold (Söhnlein 77). They cannot see the telos because they lack any sense for intersubjectivity: Neuhoff, for example, ignores Helen's reactions and signals in conversation and persists with his attempts to win her hand, going so far as to command her to marry him (II.xiii); similar is his failure with Antoinette (II.iv). Both Neuhoff and Vinzenz represent comic negation less for their formal virtues, which exist only in their imagination, than for their illicit goals.

Hofmannsthal's play portrays aristocratic society at the end of the Austro-Hungarian empire. The strong appearance-reality dualism and the widespread, almost all-pervasive, disregard for any interests other than one's own (consider the plurality of figures who embody 2a and 2b) suggest that the comedy might also be read in the light of social negation. True to its own dialectic, individual negation has become multiple or social negation. The play is ruled by self-absorbed impostors.

Hans Karl has difficulties coping with a world of characters obsessed with their own importance. The constant refrain in the stage directions, "Hans Karl says nothing," illustrates this point. Hans Karl must come a long way psychologically, if not philosophically, before he becomes engaged to Helen. His early "I dislike being tied down [ich binde mich so ungern]" (I.iii) refers to the simple act of accepting an evening's invitation. We wonder how he could possibly commit to the eternity of marriage. Indeed, his continuing resistance and distancing are evident even in III.viii. Though Stani is ironized, he does have a moment of truth over against Hans Karl, who seems incapable of action.[138] Stani's assertion concerning his marriage to Helen proves incorrect, but it does exhibit his resolve: "I never thought of it! And yet, in the very moment when I do think of it, I bring it to an end" (I.xvi). Stani analyzes Hans Karl's lack of pragmatism: "You, Uncle Karl, are *au fond*, excuse me for saying it, an idealist: your thoughts fly off to the absolute, to some ideal of perfection. That's a very elegant way of thinking, but it can't be realized" (I.xvi, translation modified). Hans Karl has difficulties acting because he is aware of complexities. Stani never hesitates, for he simplifies the world. Hans Karl's more perceptive and complex view of the world (he states his awareness of "contradictory obligations interfering with each other" I.viii) makes it difficult for him to act.

Hans Karl is an elusive character and a perfect embodiment of withdrawal, for we are never sure whether his hesitation stems

from philosophical collision or psychological weakness. In a mirroring way, we wonder whether the characters' adoration of Hans
Karl—his aura increases to the same degree he withdraws—is
genuinely founded or a sign of decadence and misjudgment.[139]
Moreover, despite the general adoration of Hans Karl we do hear
criticism of him. While we sense from Hans Karl's gestures and
reactions that he would prefer to be alone, he openly criticizes not
others, but himself; this is endearing to the audience. Others,
meanwhile, Stani, for example, or Neuhoff, criticize Hans Karl
rather than themselves and do so in such a way that we question
their perspectives more than we do Hans Karl's. In this complex
drama, however, some truth is found in the claim that Hans Karl
has inadequacies we should not overlook.

Hans Karl views speech as a manifestation of self-importance,
a pragmatic contradiction that hints at the inadequacies of his
stance, as justified as it may appear in a world of subjectivity and
superficiality. Hans Karl has been in parliament for more than a
year and a half and has yet to open his mouth. Even at the end of
the play he expresses his unwillingness to do so. The themes on
which he refuses to voice his ideas again suggest that his withdrawal is, if understandable, unjustified: "I am supposed to stand
up and make a speech about peace among peoples and the united-
ness of nations . . ." (III.xiii). The comments, which contain one of
Hans Karl's central tirades against language, are also undermined
by virtue of their origins. Hans Karl speaks with Hechingen only in
order to avoid Altenwyl. He introduces his views with the suggestion that they speak "as if we were settling some important matter"
(III.xiii) and ends, again motivated by external considerations,
with the simple line, "He's gone." Hans Karl's speech on the absurdity of language is parodied by way of not only its internal contradictions and social irresponsibility but its external context as well.
The conversation, along with the tirade against conversation, serves
merely the practical purpose of eluding Altenwyl and thus lacks
substance. The very speech that addresses the absurdity of having
interests is itself spoken only because speech here serves ulterior
intentions. In a complex way, the speech does what it says speech
should not do.[140] Because here and throughout the play Hans Karl
acts in defiance of his intentions (he goes to the party after having
decided not to; after doubting the powers of language he speaks on
behalf of Hechingen; he leaves the party only to return; instead of
winning Helen for Stani, he himself becomes engaged to her, and
so forth), we wonder whether, after having entered the intersubjec-

tive sphere in a limited sense, he may indeed be in a position to expand his sense of world and speak at parliament. His marriage does after all bind him to the larger society, and Hans Karl knows that Austria is not entirely without dignity (I.xii). Further, his use of language as subterfuge and his attention to the play of language throughout the text suggest that he is aware of language's positive potential as an instrument.

While the drama generally portrays language as the sphere of subjectivity (characters try to manipulate others and express their own intentions), silence is equally a form of subjectivity. Only with language can we truly objectify subjectivity and reach the inter-subjective sphere.[141] Only with language can the claim that one's thoughts are deep actually be measured. Hegel writes with insight and clarity: "It is, however, equally absurd to regard thought as defective and ill-fated on account of its being bound to the word, for although precisely the inexpressible is commonly regarded as most excellent, this view, fostered by vanity, has no basis, for the truth is that the *inexpressible* is merely a turbid fermentation, which only becomes clear when it is capable of verbalization. It is, there-fore, the word which endows thought with its worthiest and truest determinate being" (E § 462, translation modified).

Finally, Helen and Hans Karl are able to transcend the super-ficiality of this society. Each is self-effacing, each is discreet, each reacts to the attitudes and intentions of the other. Hans Karl artic-ulates this principle on behalf of Furlani: "All the others are driven on by some purpose and look neither right nor left—indeed, they hardly even breathe—until they've achieved what they set out to do . . . . But he seemingly does nothing on purpose—he always acquiesces in the intentions of others. He wants to do whatever the others are doing, he's so full of good will, he's so fascinated by every single bit of their performance" (II.i, translation modified). True to the comic focus on reflection, the allusion to Furlani appears also to be a self-reflective allusion to the genre of comedy and to the reading or viewing process itself. The reader is encouraged to view the artwork with a minimum of prejudgment, to let the comedy work on the reader, to allow for a reciprocity between text and reader. Helen, who listens to Hans Karl, can offer him recognition. Furlani speaks to Hans Karl. Similarly, the text should be able to speak to the reader or viewer willing to be enriched. Intersubjec-tivity is possible with subjects willing to hear the other.

Despite the overarching theme of linguistic frustration, commu-nication is possible; Hans Karl tells Helen in the second Act:

"You're a wonderfully understanding person [Man versteht sich mit Ihnen ausgezeichnet]" (II.xiv). In the third Act, he asserts: "How well you know me!" (III.viii).[142] Hans Karl speaks not of universal misunderstandings but of misunderstandings that derive from particular characters: "But there are people who can't help distorting every nuance" (I.xiii). The communication between Helen and Hans Karl succeeds partially beyond words, but also with words. Despite her linguistic skepticism, she reveals in language her love for Hans Karl; without her words—however much they represent a self-overcoming—union would not have been possible. Helen, though willful, is not—as are other characters in the play—manipulative or deceitful.[143] Between the two is a great trust. Knowing Hans Karl, Helen gives him the words that allow him to speak of what is meaningful to him, as when she opens a discussion, "You like Furlani so much, do you? [Sie haben ihn so gern, den Furlani?]" (II.i). The relationship between Lukas and Hans Karl also succeeds. Lukas straightens paintings, for he knows Hans Karl's preferences; he can read his moods from his gestures; he correctly interprets, for example, Hans Karl's reaction to Crescence's insistence that Hans Karl go to the party. The viewer of the play is invited to read gestures in a similar way.[144]

Hans Karl makes a strong case for the institution of marriage, and Hofmannsthal carefully avoids sentimentalizing his presentation by having someone who is normally reticent present it by proxy to someone who is a skeptic.[145] The elevation of the institution of marriage over the individual self mentioned in correlation with comic coincidence really belongs to intersubjectivity, for it is one of Hans Karl's major insights that marriage is an institution of necessity, not chance: "And so humanity found the institution that transforms what has happened by chance and is impure into what is necessary and permanent and valid: the institution of marriage" (II.x). Comradeship is a similar necessity: "there is also a necessity . . . . Without that there would have been nothing you could call a life at the front but only men dying in heaps like brute beasts. And the same necessity runs between men and women as well" (II.x).[146] Hans Karl affirms "constancy . . . permanence" (II.x). The catalysts for this necessity are not always intellectual. Hans Karl's reflections normally prevent him from acting, and his unconscious brings him back to the party to see Helen. Yet this necessity is not blind—the result of merely external factors—it is consciously willed and affirmed. The engagement between Hans Karl and Helen takes place partially without words, but also with words and as a result of Helen's conscious action and Hans Karl's recognition of love, which is also a self-recognition.

The play's final embrace—directed by Stani, the master of proper form—excludes Helen and Hans Karl: their relationship is too substantive to be reduced to generic and formal considerations—mere coincidence or mere necessity—and too substantial to be included in the play's final parody of form. Yet their exclusion also suggests the limits of their harmony. Although the play ends on a note of intersubjectivity, it is restricted. The play's recognition of the pervasiveness and power of subjects preoccupied with themselves remains even at the end. The moment of intersubjectivity is an island in a sea of subjectivity, but an island that gives hope and suggests that the voices of humanity, though they are in danger, may yet avoid being drowned out entirely.[147]

I have not tried to give a comprehensive or detailed reading of *The Difficult Man*. Nonetheless, the attempt to illustrate forms of comedy within this complex play has led to insights that add different nuances to the critical consensus. First, the theme of chance and its overcoming is not unique to Hofmannsthal or the aestheticism of early twentieth-century Vienna but is a comic theme in its own right and a structure of universal interest.

Second, the many misunderstandings in the play have their origin not in the intrinsic inadequacies of language (an argument we see in critics as diverse as Emil Staiger and Benjamin Bennett) but in the proliferation of false forms of subjectivity. The modernity of the structures lies not in the linguistic confusion itself—which has a long tradition—but in a linguistic confusion that stems not from objectively confusing circumstances—as with the misunderstandings generated by the twins in Plautus' *Menaechmi*—but from views of reality colored by the characters' subjectivity. Moreover, the barriers of language and subjectivity, though widespread, are capable of being broken. Although many great comic scenes in this play and elsewhere are based on language games and categorical misunderstandings, on language that comically draws attention to its own misuse, we need not conclude that language is in principle incommensurable. After all, we do *recognize* the comic aspects of communication.[148] This moment of self-consciousness would seem to cancel the seemingly necessary confusions of language. *The Difficult Man*, often taken to be primarily about the incommensurability of language, is equally about alternative forms of communication that break free of societally conditioned language games.[149]

I do not want to erase the problems of language in Hofmanns-

thal, but I do want to see them in a broader and more differentiated context. The difficulties of language in the "Letter of Lord
Chandos," for example, stem, first, from the experience of unity
and nondifferentiation, whereas language categorizes and differentiates; and second, from the experience of individuality, whereas
language is abstract and general. These difficulties differ radically
from the dominant cause of linguistic frustration in *The Difficult
Man*: false intentions and obsession with one's own self. Genuinely
mystical moments arise in *The Difficult Man* (Hans Karl's soul has
depths he cannot easily articulate, and as soon as he attempts to
do so, miscommunications arise), but this is not to suggest that
nothing true can be revealed through language. Nor does it imply
that all miscommunication stems from language itself or that potential miscommunication cannot be overcome—as between Helen
and Hans Karl. Too often in Hofmannsthal criticism, the different
forms of linguistic frustration are overlooked, as is their possible
overcoming.

Third, intentions—albeit intentions for others—are not universally discredited: this is clear from the fact that Hans Karl's unity
with Helen is the result, ironic though it may be, of his coming to
the party with intentions for Stani and from the fact that Helen is
instrumental—in true comic tradition—in helping Hans Karl come
to himself (intersubjectivity reintegrates not only the erasure of
self in 1 but also the subjective calculus of 2).

Finally, Hans Karl is not an unambiguously ideal character (cf.
Yates, "Der Schwierige" 12); his negation of society, if it does remain constant, is in principle unjustified: either Hans Karl exhibits a particular weakness in his withdrawal, or his withdrawal
is not as complete as is sometimes believed.

More Difficult Cases

Having illustrated the individual subgenres with examples and
having sketched a play in which every subgenre takes part, I would
like to discuss a variety of works that are seemingly difficult to
place because they border or combine subgenres.[150] Mixed genres
within comedy appear to be more frequent than in tragedy. Comedy, the more complex genre, has a larger number of subforms,
thus allowing for a greater variety of combinations. Moreover,
while comedy draws on the flexibility of characters (and thus their
shifts between subgenres), tragedy demands consistency. Finally,

as I suggested earlier, self-sacrifice and stubbornness often unite in a single action; tragic unity is generally simple rather than complex.

Shakespeare's *Love's Labor's Lost* successfully integrates a variety of moments, even as one subgenre, reduction, dominates. We see in the play several elements of coincidence. The men's original intentions are thwarted, and their more genuine longings are developed. Some of the characters are virtually interchangeable—although the courtiers' conventional language and inability to recognize individuality are also mocked as reductions of true love. The courtship is fourfold, true suffering occurs only via a messenger at the end of the play, and most of the characters have undeveloped personalities.

Reduction, however, is more prominent. The learnedness of the four men and their desire to attain immortality by withdrawing from the world are unveiled as a reduction of true knowledge and a perversion of life. Moreover, they do not have the stamina to hold on to their promises and pact. Their first attempts at courtship are unveiled as folly and in essence impersonal, if not antisocial: they substitute signs for persons ("The ladies did change favors, and then we, / Following the signs, wooed but the sign of she" [V.ii.469–470]). Because love is reduced to "acting love and talking love" (Barber 93), we are not disappointed to see the courtiers fail. Love's labor is lost; "Jack hath not Jill" (V.ii.865). As might be expected in reduction, the sincerity of the lovers is questioned. Their earlier inconstancy makes any new vow suspect: "If love make me forsworn, how shall I swear to love?" (IV.ii.104). Holofernes is a prototypical hero of reduction: he uses language and rhetoric, whether Latin phrases, synonyms, or alliteration, in the most tedious and pointless way and so reduces true learning to pedantry. Mirroring the courtiers, he uses language as a province for cleverness, not a means for communication. Mote comments in an aside: "They [Holofernes and Nathaniel] have been at a great feast of languages and stolen the scraps" (V.i.36–37). Dull's malapropisms evidence reduction on a slightly lower level: the dull-witted wants to speak with the learned and fails.

Berowne and the other courtiers eventually recognize that verbal excess and wit should be banished in favor of natural expression and truth, whence a development toward intersubjectivity. The men's deceit is met by counterdeceit, and their loose rhetoric by literal-mindedness, which in turn leads to their abandonment of deceit: "There's no such sport as sport by sport o'erthrown" (V.ii.

153). The play seeks a reconciliation of nature and art, and it points toward a union of immediate affection and enduring commitment. Berowne and Rosalind almost prefigure the feisty love relationship of Beatrice and Benedick, just as Dull anticipates Dogberry. Precisely because the play functions for the most part on the lighter side of comic coincidence and reduction (the message of the death of the King of France shatters this lightness), its evocation of synthesis and intersubjectivity can take place only on a meta-level—which focuses on the author's linguistic and dramatic artistry, his use of symmetry, and his balancing of opposites—or in the future at which the play's ending hints. Because intersubjectivity is evident only elliptically in the self-conscious allusions to art and in a future beyond the play ("a twelvemonth and a day . . . that's too long for a play" V.ii.867–869), reduction remains dominant. The play is unusual among Shakespeare's comedies, as most of the comedies more fully endorse coincidence or intersubjectivity and are more joyous than satiric. *Love's Labor's Lost*, in contrast, questions these conventions, as indeed it questions all conventions—even as it partakes of them (Leggatt 63–88). Nonetheless, its connection to the other works is sustained in the strongly Shakespearean (and Hegelian) idea that true love demands its moments of struggle.

William Wycherly's *The Plain Dealer* begins as a comedy of withdrawal. The hero, Manly, prefers the sea to land so as to be free of civilization; when he is on land, he has his servants guard his door so that he will not be disturbed by unwanted visitors. Manly detests and openly denounces the corruption, deceit, and flattery of the world, but his behavior, at least at first, elicits only the laughter of those he scorns. He grossly misjudges the two characters he adores, his one friend, Vernish, and his love, Olivia. The play mocks the hero almost as much as it does the characters Manly rightly denounces and those who betray him. In such a corrupt world the honest hero seems unable to succeed. The viewer both admires Manly for his moral principles and recoils from him for his surly and indecorous behavior.

Yet the play does not end on a note of withdrawal or failure. The hero uses his wit to manipulate the characters around him, as when he convinces a greedy lawyer to accept a pauper's brief and so rids himself of a nuisance. The hero, after finally recognizing the genuine love of Fidelia, will not leave the world and appears to have the cunning to survive in even the most hypocritical of environments. Preferring honesty to guile, the plain dealer still recognizes that cunning is not without its moment of virtue and that total scorn brings with it nothing but self-destruction. The play is a comedy of social negation insofar as it mocks the deceit and corruption of the social sphere; a comedy of withdrawal insofar as Manly reviles a world he cannot change; and a comedy of intersubjectivity insofar as the hero, unlike Molière's Alceste, eventually learns the value of cunning and finds genuine, if restricted, love.[151]

A combination of subforms sometimes works to the detriment of a play. Goethe's *The Accomplices* might initially be read as a comedy of coincidence. The plot is full of convoluted situations and misunderstandings; the action as well as the incongruities between the pragmatic speaking situation and the alexandrine verse transcends the probable. The vicissitudes of gambling are a major theme. The work, originally a one-act play, contains farcical elements. Yet the play introduces two serious conflicts (Alceste's idea of love and his experience of it; and Sophie's dutiful adherence to the institution of marriage and her love of another) that work against the silliness of the plot and the simplicity of the conclusion. Moreover, the development of Stöller, about whom Sophie expresses the wish that he now live "truly polite, tranquil, and loyal" (III.10, my translation), is not motivated. The resolution of conflict and the development of the self-absorbed character demand the intricacies of a comedy of intersubjectivity or a drama of reconciliation. Once negativity has entered the play, the conditions for a resolution change. In other words, the seriousness of the moral crises destroys the farcical tone. The play suffers from this disharmony, which is all the more unfortunate given the independent success of the farce and the selection of such substantial moral dilemmas.[152]

Georg Büchner's *Leonce and Lena* is one of the most complex comedies in the German tradition. This complexity may derive from the integration of diverse, seemingly contradictory, comic strategies. One prominent moment in the play is coincidence. The hero and heroine flee their respective roles and kingdoms after being told that they are to enter into an arranged marriage; in flight each meets the other and, unaware of each other's identity, the two characters fall in love. The integration of coincidence mocks the mechanical and automatic nature of 1 especially when viewed in connection with the final scene, an apparent marriage in effigy, that is, a marriage for purely formal purposes, a marriage in which the identity of the partners is irrelevant. It is a *reductio ad absurdum* of a symmetrical relationship that is devoid of substance, a common figure in coincidence.

The comedy of reduction arises by way of King Peter, a philosopher-king who forgets his people and whose territory reaches about as far as the eye can see. Lena, who is compared to Christ, likewise represents a reduction: Christ willingly and genuinely suffers; Lena does so unintentionally and superficially. Finally, Leonce strives for a meaningful occupation, but with the assistance of Valerio, a cross between Falstaff and Mephistopheles, Leonce forever reduces his ideals.

The mocking portrayal of the King is part of a general satire directed toward the court. The peasants are given a mere whiff of roast and are told precisely how to act; Leonce behaves sadistically toward Rosetta; and Valerio scorns all meaning, though with the wit of a fool. This broader ridicule fulfills many facets of negation.

Because neither Leonce nor Valerio consider any activity meaningful, they essentially retreat, yet their withdrawal is entirely negative and appears to illustrate less the comedy of withdrawal than the comedy of reflexive negation or absolute irony. If we view the nihilistic statements of Leonce and Valerio as one with the message of the text, a number of difficulties arise. First, harmonic coincidence becomes fatalistic despair; and the play's seemingly utopian conclusion becomes pure satire, an illusory happy end. Second, if there is no meaning, the play's satire becomes insignificant, a mere joke. The play's onion metaphor, which is originally applied to the emptiness of politics, becomes, on a metalevel, a metaphor for the emptiness of any critique of politics. Third, the play's nihilism, insofar as it undermines all content, passes over into pure formalism: language is employed not for communication but for rhetorical play (we recall the play's abundance of puns and meaningless oxymorons); thought becomes reduced to the empty rules of formal logic (King Peter's "either-or" and "if-then" or Valerio's empty "because"); people, having no substance, are unwritten texts and mere automatons; and the happy ending is motivated by formal considerations of genre and these alone. Here, negativity passes over into absolute irony. The play is not only a mockery of meaning but a mockery of the mockery of meaning. Just as the characters have nothing meaningful to say to one another, so does the play become itself a meaningless play on words. This self-reflective dimension is thematized throughout the text, most especially in I.iii and III.iii.

Conflicting readings of this play arise from the isolation of its individual moments—satire, nihilism, and formalism. The play's satire, which becomes impotent if the play's nihilism and formalism are not themselves satirized, is too powerful to be undermined, but it is not the only moment in the text. Although much of life may be absurd, frustrating, even meaningless, Leonce's despair is mocked, and he himself genuinely seeks, even if he fails to find, meaning. His inability to "see the top of his head" may symbolize an incapacity to recognize the self-cancellation of his own nihilism (I.i). If everything is meaningless, then so, too, the insight that everything is meaningless.[153] Though rhetoric is essential to the play's sensuous and linguistic brilliance, its intertextual satire of contemporary literary ideals, and its self-reflection, the pure autonomy of rhetoric is itself nihilistic. Moreover, it could not even present itself as a theory (since it undermines all content).

Individual images and passages are best seen as implying all three readings. For example, the wedding in effigy is, first, a satire of the court insofar as the court ignores individuality and fails to acknowledge the genuine death (and hunger) in its midst; second, a nihilistic jab at the emptiness of human relations; and third, a parody of literary expectations and a self-reflexive reference to literature as a form of effigy. Likewise, the prominent onion motif not only refers to a satire of tiny, if not empty, principalities; it also suggests a nihilistic ontology of emptiness and artificially induced tears (a kind of parody of tragedy), which parallels the artificially induced pleasure of the peasants (their whiff of the roast) and may even suggest a mockery of the play's apparent claims to satire, nihilism, and art.

Even the play's preface or motto ("Alfieri: 'And fame? [E la fama?]' / Gozzi: 'And hunger? [E la fame?]'") implies all three readings: first, a satire of the contemporary concern with fame rather than hunger; second, a nihilistic suggestion that there are questions but no answers, that the two questions cancel one another, or that our hunger for knowledge is as yet unfulfilled; and third, a simple play on vowels and an intertextual reference that has no greater significance than its idle form.

From the opening to the play's conclusion the complexity of readings is visible: Is the final image a utopian complement to the play's reigning satire, a sarcastic and nihilistic representation, or a formal appeal to genre expectations, a playful and absurd joke on the audience? These and other passages could surely be developed in such a way as to show that the play's seemingly absolute irony reinforces its other moments. Büchner's play is a comedy of absolute irony that, aware of its own irony, overcomes itself without fully spelling out alternatives. When the play is read in this light, the motifs of coincidence, reduction, and negation all take on newer, more complex forms.

Nestroy's *A Man Full of Nothing* integrates a series of comic subgenres and culminates in intersubjectivity. Herr von Lips, a rich man whose life is without meaning or adventure, decides to do something original: he chooses to make a choice *unconditionally* but *arbitrarily*. Mocking decisionism before its time, Nestroy unveils the emptiness of choice for the sake of choice. Lips's decision to marry the next woman he sees is hardly an expression of freedom (even if it does incorporate a moment of truth in its unconditionality) but rather a reduction to chance and coincidence. Equating freedom and originality with arbitrariness, Lips selects without recourse to any rational norms and is thus determined by the chance events of his environment. Like a character in a comedy of reduction Lips is obsessed with his suffering (in comic and paradoxical fashion he suffers because he does not suffer), and he desires intersubjectivity, in this case marriage, but he perverts his goal. Gluthammer mirrors Lips in his desire for marriage coupled with his initial inability to recognize the unfitness of his partner (or, in the case of Lips, to act according to this insight). Gluthammer's blind trust—a mirror image to Lips's extreme skepticism—provides us with another instance of reduction. Important elements of the comedy are iteration and symmetry: Lips and Gluthammer each thinks he has killed the other, one after another surfaces after having been taken for dead, and the one follows the other below the trap door.

Madame Schleyer, whose goals are invalid, fails to succeed, is excluded from the final harmony, and so enacts a comedy of negation. Nestroy's play, by its use of contradictions, includes satiric elements directed toward the widespread injustices in society. Lips's would-be friends dissemble in order to gain his favor. Interesting is that they lack any individual touches; their behavior echoes one another. (Gluthammer in turn reveals his stupidity by repeating himself.) Also they are duped by the very technique they employ; Lips dissembles in their presence and so comes to the truth behind their appearances. The appearance-reality scheme so important for comedy runs throughout the play.

Lips, unable to develop symmetrical relations in a corrupt society where others please him in order to take advantage of his wealth, thereby abusing the concept of friendship, is tempted to withdraw from this society and occasionally becomes misanthropic. Early in the play he leaves his party; in the third act he longs to abandon the world. Even nature has no meaning for him. In a parody of tragedy, the hero decides not to kill himself, for if he were to die, his money would pass into the hands of his friends, who are of course not his friends. Lips's initially quick transition from generosity to misanthropy has shades of Shakespeare's *Timon of Athens*, though unlike Timon, Lips eventually develops a less extreme, more differentiated view of humanity.

Finally, the play becomes a comedy of intersubjectivity insofar as Lips finds a symmetrical partner, Kathi. Through his experiences of fear and guilt, work, and finally love, Lips grasps the inadequacies of his earlier obsession with fullness and the boredom that resulted from his false conception of self. The language at the end of the play addresses the need for genuine wholeness. Earlier, Lips lacked the sense of a lack, a recognition of need; thus he was without hope, without expectation. He had no direction, or—more precisely—arbitrary and fickle direction, as is evidenced by the anaphor in his first song. Lips later finds a wholeness outside of himself; he recognizes that he himself is incomplete but can be made whole. Paradoxically, only in suffering, despair, or frustration does Lips experience hope and a sense of youth. The play's ironization of marriage and friendship is not a simple attack on intersubjectivity but a complex ironization of the way in which people, including the early Lips, treat the intersubjective sphere.[154] Lips's development is a bit quick, as much slapstick as it is serious internalization, and so the play has never achieved world fame. Diverse comic structures, however, are present, and the play's clever puns and comic paradoxes and incongruities are extraordinarily rich. Moreover, the play integrates despair and *Angst* not by revelling in it but by working through it.

Reflection on the extent to which various subgenres are integrated within a single work also leads to diverse possibilities of performance. Productions of Grillparzer's *A Fraternal Quarrel in the House of Hapsburg*, for example, might interpret the work as a tragedy of stubbornness, a tragedy of awareness, a drama of suffering, or even—against the grain—as a submerged comedy, which is why I include it among my examples of more difficult cases. Grillparzer undoubtedly intended his work to be a substantive tragedy, most likely a tragedy of awareness. Rudolf is critical of action, for he believes that it is always motivated by self-interest. He refuses, therefore, to act; instead he would preserve—or restore—the order of his empire by exhibiting an exemplary stillness, which itself attempts to imitate the harmony of the divine sphere. All tragedy presupposes that the world is not already as it should be; thus, action is necessary. The paradox of Rudolf II is that the world is not as it should be because of action; thus, non-action becomes the ideal, but insofar as Rudolf resists action, his power is diminished. Grillparzer's play is partly about the absence of clear norms, the problem of giving content to the absolute; Rudolf does not know the truth and so cannot act according to it (I.418–422). Even the one abstract truth he does recognize—"Not I, only God" (III.1221, my translation)—offers no guidelines for specific action and is itself corrupted in the light of the religiosity and view of God assumed by a figure such as Ferdinand.

One might stress Rudolf's withdrawal as a form of idealistic stubbornness, an action or inaction taken of good will but clearly untenable, or as a form of reduction—he seeks to preserve a truth that is incompatible with the contingencies of his age. Rudolf's strength—his sense of the whole, his insight, his attachment to repose—which would seemingly predestine him for legitimate and potentially great rule, makes him incapable of acting, and thus of ruling, and forces him into withdrawal and solitude, thus setting up his demise. Although Rudolf does not know *how* to act, it is clear *that* he should act. In a world where no substantive absolutes are asserted, power passes over into the hands of the power positivist (Klesel) or the fanatic (Ferdinand). Though Klesel and Ferdinand are Rudolf's opposites, Rudolf's inaction makes these positions possible; his inactivity and stubbornness necessarily pass over into—because they allow for—relativism and fanaticism.[155] Symbolically significant, Rudolf is the father of the ruthless and passionate Don Cäsar. In fact, Rudolf treats Don Cäsar with arbitrary abandon. In this reading, Rudolf's inaction and occasionally ruthless action are well-intentioned, but untenable; Rudolf is a hero of stubbornness.

Evidence for a drama of suffering might also be noted. Rudolf is a self-pitying character, the victim of historical events and the machinations of his subjects. Yet this drama of suffering might be viewed more productively as partially comic—if not as an implicit comedy of self-inflicted suffering, then as a comedy of reduction or, even more so, of withdrawal. Grillparzer's play does contain a significant number of comic scenes: Rudolf's paranoia with regard to his servants; his long speeches, in effect monologues embedded within dialogues, which continue even after his listeners have departed and which contrast comically to the urgency of the political situation (IV.2392–2394); the fact that Julius must disguise himself to gain audience with Rudolf; Rudolf's locking himself into the closet to avoid an encounter with Leopold; the lack of objective evidence for Rudolf's withdrawal (we have principally Rudolf's insistence that the world is corrupt, whereas in works such as *Hamlet* or *The Misanthrope* the world's corruption is unambiguously evident); Rudolf's unrelenting self-reflection and his necessarily unsuccessful (and partially comic) attempts to overcome reflection with reflection—Rudolf *argues* against reflection (III.1640–1652); and, of course, the repetition of Rudolf in Mathias. Other elements independent of Rudolf carry with them comic traces as well, for example, the stupidity of Mathias toward Klesel in Act III.

Grillparzer's play exhibits characteristics of various tragic and comic subgenres. This is part of the drama's complex appeal. Yet one imagines that a successful performance would allow one or the other of these diverse generic possibilities to become dominant; the dramaturge's intimate knowledge of the subgenre to which he or she ascribes the work could only help in the development of an imaginative and internally consistent production.

Hauptmann's *The Beaver Coat* has left critics in a quandary partly because it mixes two forms of comic negation. Wolff, with her larceny and lies, acts according to the comedy of individual negation. Wolff is a complex character, whose diligence, energy, boldness, cleverness, and even moments of goodness (for example, her affection for Dr. Fleischer's child or her desire to improve her daughters) arouse a certain sympathy, but critics, expecting the play to follow the model of *The Miser* or *The Broken Jug*, are understandably surprised or disappointed not to see her fall. Readers are bothered not just because the play deviates from a norm, but because there is reason to the norm. The negative protagonist is normally given free reign only when the audience knows that he will ultimately destroy himself. For Wolff, justice is whatever serves her particular purpose; the good is what succeeds. She is indignant when she hears of a theft (but it is always she who has done the stealing)—a comic contradiction that underscores the asymmetry of inner and outer. We appreciate Wolff's secondary virtues and the ironies vis-à-vis Krüger and Wehrhahn (especially at the end of Acts III and IV) but are critical of Wolff's lack of primary virtues, her failure to place her cleverness in the service of goodness. Thus, we can be at one and the same time outraged and amused.

The twist in Hauptmann's plot derives from the play's integration of social negation. Wolff survives because the structures of jus-

tice in this society, as represented by Wehrhahn, are inadequate to
their task. Wehrhahn is unfair and his values false (he pursues
Fleischer, for example, at the expense of looking for the thief), he is
blind toward Wolff, and he ignores the clues offered to him for solv-
ing the crimes. Wehrhahn considers his position of great importance but trivializes it in his execution. Enmeshed in contradictions, society as the other to the comic hero lacks simple objectivity
and resilience. Wolff seems hardly more evil than the society
around her; thus the traditional ending is altered.

Oscar Wilde's *The Importance of Being Earnest* might be viewed,
from the perspective of plot, as a comedy of coincidence. The play
concludes with an array of improbabilities and embraces. The characters, however, are brighter and wittier than in most comedies of
coincidence. The play contains comic elements of reduction (the
characters' concerns with appearances and trivialities) and negation (the dishonest and manipulative antics of Jack and Algernon).
The multiplicity of negation is especially developed in Act II when
Jack and Algernon mirror one another not only in supposedly being
Ernest but in voicing a series of symmetrical sentiments (297; Act
II). The play beautifully illustrates a central element of negation:
the characters, though unconcerned with truth, are exceedingly
clever and witty. Moreover, like other highly developed comedies of
social negation, the play reintegrates moments of coincidence:
characters are interchangeable, meaning is hidden behind what is
seemingly absurd, and the trivial becomes important.

Or, to view the play more from the perspective of the author, we
could say that, like Pirandello's *Each in His Own Way*, *The Importance of Being Earnest* is a would-be comedy of absolute irony,
mocking and levelling society, art, everything imaginable, including even its own cleverness (270; Act I), but this mockery contains
a kernel of hidden and not only negative wisdom. The play that
seems to elevate wit for the sake of wit alone engages—almost behind its own back—such substantial issues as class, education,
property, marriage, domination, insensitivity, decay, and identity.
Behind even the most manipulative, mocking, and nonsensical behavior, a spirit of truth surfaces.

Ray Cooney's popular British farce *Run for Your Wife* very much
belongs to the comedy of coincidence—owing to the hero's lack of
self-consciousness, the thematization of chance and coincidence,
the introduction of character-types, and the play's self-acknowl-
edged irreality. Yet the play also exhibits elements of reduction and
negation: the hero's subjective desires, his split-identity, his imag-

inative lies, and his polygamy. Because of the presence of the antithetical genres, the simple happy end of coincidence is blocked. The play suffers from this schizophrenia. Despite many hilarious moments—surely the secret of its success—the end fizzles, and the play lacks any organic structure.

A good work may fulfill a genre form as it is; it may stretch or overreach it. Both seem possible. One thinks, for the former, of Molière's *Tartuffe*, for the latter, of Hauptmann's *The Beaver Coat*. Neither purity of genre, that is, the claim that a work belong to one and only one genre, nor the breaking of generic norms, that is, the claim that a work transcend at least one genre, is an appropriate criterion for great art.[156] If we accept the view of art that I delineated in the introduction, then greatness derives from the validity of the work's idea, from its successful form, and from the interrelation and coherence of the two. A complex idea may be successfully realized in a combination of genres; the only requirement is that the form be appropriate to the idea. A coherent idea in the wrong form is weak, as is any contradictory idea, which cannot save itself, even by borrowing from more than one genre.

These reflections suggest that though the forms I have proposed are not always realized in a pure way, the categories nonetheless can be employed, as heuristic devices, to help us better grasp the intersecting structures of individual plays and to recognize, in a complex way, the strengths and weaknesses of individual works.

4

On the Drama of Reconciliation

In my introduction I suggested four ways to improve on Hegel's aesthetics: expanding brief insights; integrating recent advances in art; recognizing and correcting misapplications of valid logical insights; and uncovering and revising flawed logical structures. With the drama of reconciliation, every method applies, though the second least of all: relatively few dramas of reconciliation have been written since the time of Hegel. Beyond the brevity of Hegel's comments on the drama of reconciliation, we also recognize the lack of an application of strictly dialectical and speculative structures to drama and the difficulties that arise from Hegel's neglect of intersubjectivity.

Tragedy, Comedy, Reconciliation

Like a tragedy, the drama of reconciliation portrays, in a serious manner, substantial conflicts. The two genres differ in their endings: where tragedy culminates in catastrophe, usually death, the drama of reconciliation presents on stage, and not simply in the consciousness of the audience, a reconciliation of opposing forces. Whereas the tragic hero is one-sided and preoccupied with her position's exclusive validity, the reconciliatory hero sees the limits in her position and recognizes what is valid in the other. The drama of reconciliation ends like a comedy of intersubjectivity. It can be defined either as an initially tragic conflict that ends in reconciliation or as a comedy whose conflict is substantial, rather than superficial, and also resolved. The drama of reconciliation synthesizes the firm principles of tragedy with the yielding spirit of

247

comedy: the hero is strong but recognizes and cooperates with the other; the hero adapts but does so with the good in mind.

In tragedy, with the exception of the tragedy of stubbornness, the subject identifies with objective values. In comedy, as in the tragedy of stubbornness, a split occurs; we recognize either objectivity without subjectivity (the comedy of coincidence) or subjectivity without objectivity (the antithetical subgenres). Only with the comedy of intersubjectivity and the drama of reconciliation are objectivity and subjectivity reunited and only here does the identity of the subject with objectivity also include the subject's survival.

Conflict in drama can be serious or playful. If it is serious, it can end in catastrophe (as in tragedy) or in resolution (as in the drama of reconciliation). If it is playful, it can end in resolution (as in the thetic and synthetic subgenres of comedy) or in nonresolution (as in the antithetical subgenres of comedy). As a serious conflict that is resolved, the drama of reconciliation is thus closest to tragedy and the thetic and synthetic genres of comedy; it is furthest removed from the drama of suffering and the antithetical subgenres of comedy, the forms of drama that dominate today.

Speculative Drama

The supremacy of the drama of reconciliation corresponds to Hegel's argument that we should not remain "at the merely negative result of the dialectic" (E § 81 Z 2). Tragedy, with its portrayal of the eclipse of one-sided, if substantive, positions, and comedy, with its negation of one-sided and clearly untenable positions, both point toward the positive: in the case of tragedy, the absolute that is preserved in the instance of death; in the case of comedy, the positive position that follows from the negation of negativity. This common thread links Hegel's theories of tragedy and comedy; not surprisingly, Hegel offers one of his most lucid definitions of tragedy when criticizing Solger's reading of irony and comedy (R § 140). He argues that the essence of tragedy is not destruction but triumph of the good. The truth of comedy meanwhile is not negation as such but the negation of an untenable stance and thus movement toward a positive position. In the drama of reconciliation, this moment of harmony becomes explicit.[1]

The structure of Hegel's *Logic*, with its dynamic differentiation of pure being, has distinctly dramatic qualities (Desmond, *Art and the Absolute* 30–31). The various categories or definitions of the absolute assume the stage, do battle with one another, enter into reversals, self-cancellations, completions, and take part in a grand narrative culminating in the harmony of the absolute Idea. To view the *Logic* as a philosophical analogue to the drama of reconciliation would not be unwarranted. Like the *Logic*, the drama of reconciliation overcomes the dualisms of *Verstand* and is ultimately not dialectical or "negatively rational," but speculative, "positively rational" (E § 79).[2] Like Hegel's dialectical categories, the drama of reconciliation does not erase negativity or pretend that its resolution will halt history; it portrays, rather, a harmony that includes the possibility of tension and further progress.

Moreover, the transitions in dialectical logic parallel the generating structures of reconciliation. Each side of an opposition is true, for the validity of each presupposes the validity of the other, but each is true only insofar as it erases its extreme claims to exclusive validity and recognizes its own truth in a higher unity together with its other. The speculative shows that the (partial) truth of each is only in recognition of the (partial) truth of its other. This movement toward the speculative is analogous to the movement from tragedy and comedy to reconciliation. The isolation of one pole is tragic stubbornness or, if you will, the comic position that sees truth only in the particular and thus imagines that each particular viewed for itself is valid, when the truth is that they are valid only as parts, a position that is positively reached only in the drama of reconciliation—or, to invoke once again the analogue, in a valid logical transition to a higher synthesis.

The drama of reconciliation, like each higher term in Hegel's *Logic*, is not something new but simply the thinking through (and thus the truth) of its antecedents. For Hegel, the transition from one category or genre to the next takes place without external impetus. Hegel writes: "producing and apprehending the *positive* content and result which it contains" is "not an *external* activity of subjective thinking, but the *very soul* of the content which puts forth its branches and fruit organically" (R § 31, translation modified; cf. E § 379 Z). The limits of tragedy and comedy are thus limits not only from our point of view; the limits lie in the material and the genres themselves, in their inability fully to grasp the absolute.

The drama of reconciliation is a necessary genre, and its necessity derives from the inadequacies of tragedy and comedy. It is better if truth arises without the destruction of the individual, who is all too frequently a woman,[3] and it is better if truth is realized on stage (or in reality), that is, intersubjectively, and not merely in consciousness—as in tragedy or the comedy of withdrawal. Comedy is intellectually a more advanced form than tragedy, but it is not the most advanced. The drama of reconciliation, which integrates the virtues of each, the absolutes of tragedy with the negativity of comedy, is the highest.

The drama of reconciliation is highest not only philosophically or thematically but ideally from an artistic perspective as well. Art is not simple unity, not mere struggle, but a complex unity that includes struggle as a moment. It is a harmony of opposites, ultimately the harmony of thought and sense, but in terms of content, the harmony of opposition and reconciliation. Great art then is formally what the drama of reconciliation is thematically: a unity of opposites.

Melodrama, the Problem Play, and the Drama of Reconciliation

We can better understand the drama of reconciliation not only by analyzing it philosophically or by comparing it with tragedy and comedy but also by viewing it beside two other genres with which it forms a dialectical progression: melodrama (with a happy end) and the problem play.[4] Melodrama, the problem play, and the drama of reconciliation move in the direction of the speculative and realize moments that point beyond tragedy and comedy.

Melodrama is the more objective, thetic form. A clear black and white conflict dominates the work. Evil tempts goodness or overpowers it and momentarily gains the upper hand; goodness, however, triumphs—by converting evil or overpowering it. Psychologically and morally simplistic, melodramas present us with archetypes of good and evil; the characters are clearly contrasted and for the most part unchanging. Melodrama tends to idealize both primary and secondary virtues, integrity and courage, justice and patriotism; correspondingly, it creates clearly recognizable and unambiguous villains. The work is substantial and generally serious, it does not end tragically, and yet we hesitate to call the work a drama of reconciliation: we find it trite and unnuanced in its presentation of evil, the characters' psychologies are underdeveloped, the logic of the plot is at times artificial, and the denouement tends to be irrational or sensationalist. The work appeals more to our emotions than our intellect. It is as much propaganda or entertainment as it is refined art. It is unaware of a potential tragic tension within the good itself and relies on a harmony triggered either by the objectivity of events or the simplicity of naive and straightforward language.

Peter Brooks sees in melodrama the "logic of the excluded middle" (15, 18): right versus wrong, not a sense of the nuances by which two polar positions imply one another and move toward each other dialectically. In melodrama, we see the victory of one side rather than the development of all sides or a speculative synthesis. The clear conflicts of melodrama can be read as belonging to the realm of objectivity or a bankrupt subjectivity longing to return to objectivity. The content of the good is merely willed, affirmed, stated; it is not earned or shown. The result of virtue's triumph is not a higher integration but a reaffirmation of objectivity.[5] We do not see compromise or gradual development, but rather polarization and the complete undoing of evil or its utter conversion.

The conservative Austrian Max Mell has written a number of reconciliatory dramas that might be said to illustrate melodrama for a twentieth-century audience. Mell's highly allegorical works clearly contrast good and evil. In *The Play of the Guardian Angel*, a guardian angel gives as penance to a haughty girl the humbling command to ask everyone who enters church to marry her, and she agrees to marry the derelict who accepts her proposal. Her honesty is rewarded when the derelict reveals that he is in truth her guardian angel and brings to the altar her true love. In *The Play of the Apostles*, a young girl imagines how she would receive the apostles if they were still alive. Two wanderers arrive, whom she takes for apostles; planning to rob her and her grandfather, they play along. She teaches them, unwittingly, about Christ's suffering; and, shamed by her trust and goodness, they leave the cabin. *The Play of the Imitation of Christ* takes place during the crusades. The lord of a castle is crucified by Turks, but is then rescued. He wants to pardon the criminals, but his elevation of grace is overridden by the concept of justice advanced by the captain who rescued him. The lord of the castle asks God for a miracle, and he dies, like Christ, to free the criminals from their sins; the captain pardons them. Despite some interesting structures, such as the hero's coming to recognition in *The Play of the Guardian Angel*, the conversion of evil in *The Play of the Apostles*, and the conflict of secular and religious authority in *The Play of the Imitation of Christ*, the characters remain psychologically unnuanced, the structures appear somewhat artificial and forced, and the contrasts are for the most part simple and naive.

The antithetical work within this broad structure of serious drama is the problem play. In the problem play, the moment of reconciliation is either bitter, coming at an extreme price that mitigates the extent of reconciliation; partial, lacking either fullness or stability; or suspect, not fully earned, but artificial and so undeserved. The subject questions the order into which she is integrated and seems also to stand outside it. Problem plays are invariably intellectual puzzles that set limits to any desire for synthesis even as they coyly point toward it. The resolution, being partial or arbitrary, is called into question, as are the characters and institutions that appear to guarantee harmony. The reader or viewer is also led to question the portrayal: problem plays generally invite multiple—and often conflicting—readings. A good example would be Shakespeare's and Fletcher's *The Two Noble Kinsmen*. What is attained comes at such a price that the resolution is questioned ("O cousin, / That we should things desire which do cost us / The loss of our desire! that nought could buy / Dear love but loss of dear love!" V.iv.109–112). What triggers the resolution in this play, moreover, is at best arbitrary (the answer to the dilemma which of the two cousins should have the beautiful Emilia is the one who saw her first). A problem play whose resolution is not bitter like *The Two Noble Kinsmen*, but artificial, unearned, and seemingly mocked is Shakespeare's *All's Well That Ends Well*.

The drama of reconciliation contains the clear triumph of goodness we see in melodrama but also the complexity associated with the problem play. Because it is the most speculative genre, it is as affirmative as melodrama and as complex and dialectical as the problem play. The triumph of good within melodrama survives in the drama of reconciliation but only insofar as it is deepened by the psychological, rhetorical, and aesthetic complexity of the problem play and only insofar as a moment of non-completion is integrated, rather than excluded, from the reconciliation. Any would-be drama of reconciliation that completely suppresses a distinction between the ideal and the real would easily fall back into melodrama. A more detailed study would likely have little trouble developing the dialectic of the three forms: melodrama in relation to objectivity (and tragedy, especially the tragedy of self-sacrifice, the most objective of tragic genres, with which it shares much—though of course not the ending); the problem play in relation to subjectivity (and comedy, especially the most subjective, that is, the antithetical, forms, including absolute irony, with which it shares a suspicion of closure); and the drama of reconciliation, which is informed by intersubjectivity.

Not only do melodrama, the problem play, and the drama of reconciliation stand in a dialectical relation, the three works function together as the heuristic categories by which we grasp to what extent a work is or is not an example of the synthetic genre. A work may have some of the structures of the drama of reconciliation but be too undifferentiated or simple (and so melodramatic), or it may be too riddled with unresolved issues, the resolution being weakened or so ambiguous as to fall short of reconciliation (and so it is a problem play).

Our evaluation of individual artists and works may rest on such interpretive efforts. Today the rhetoric of literary criticism has unequivocally elevated the problem play over the drama of reconciliation. Thus, the more ambiguities one can find in an apparent reconciliation, the greater the play, the more modern and revolutionary the author. Goethe's *Iphigenia*, which is unquestionably a drama of reconciliation, might all too easily be dismissed as naive, while Kleist's *Prince Friedrich* is reinterpreted as a problem play and elevated for that very reason.

In considering the terms heuristically, we might take as an example the works of Frank Capra. Primarily four films by Capra might be considered in the light of melodrama or reconciliation: *Mr. Deeds Goes to Town*, *Mr. Smith Goes to Washington*, *Meet John Doe*, and *It's a Wonderful Life*. In each case a naive, yet idealistic hero is confronted by self-doubt or political manipulation, but in the end he triumphs over the forces of evil. The central questions become: Is the threat to the hero genuine? Is the portrayal of evil nuanced? Is the development of the hero differentiated? Different answers are possible, but the questions—which parallel the typology—are central to the evaluation of each film. One could argue, for example, that in *Mr. Smith Goes to Washington*, the hero's mastery of complex political and rhetorical devices is hardly differentiated or realistic, and so one could speak of melodrama. The work simplifies and appeals primarily to our emotions. Yet one could also argue that the vulnerability of naive and good-natured people to the machinations of power politics is thoroughly presented, the hero is not simple but ravaged with doubt and conscious of his shortcomings, and the villain is not only destroyed but intellectually disturbed and finally converted; in this way, one could try to build a case for the drama of reconciliation. I seek not to answer these questions here, merely to propose them.

A paradigmatic example of a play that borders on the problem play and the drama of reconciliation is Shakespeare's *Measure for Measure*. Outwardly, the play exhibits the essential features of reconciliation: instead of mere error repentance, instead of self-righteousness forgiveness, grace following sin, strict justice and technical application of the law passing over into mercy and love, and instead of death the emergence of new unions. The theatricality of the Duke's endeavors reminds us of the playwright's freedom to change and better the lives of his characters. Yet it might be countered that the play lacks the fullness of reconciliation. The Duke manipulates characters in an arguably unnecessary way that appears to satisfy gamesmanship and curiosity, perhaps also a secret desire for instrumentalization. Angelo's pardon and marriage seem degrading to women. The inner conflicts of the characters and the play's images of disease and portrayal of "vice" do not appear fully answered by the artificiality of the Duke's machinations or "craft" (III.ii.270). The Duke's ordering and arranging is not without problems even on the level of efficacy: Lucio, for example, is not brought into the fold; and Isabella's response to the Duke is unstated (and for that reason has been interpreted variously). Above all, the realism of conflict is in disproportion to the artificiality of resolution, including the quick rehabilitation of Angelo and the Duke's undeveloped courtship of Isabella. The initial problem of the play—vice rampant because of a lack of strict measures—may seem scarcely answered by the accumulation of further leniency and tolerance of human weakness. The analyses of Rosalind Miles and Ralph Berry chronicle the shifting fortunes of the play at the hands of interpreters and directors; the work cannot easily be classified either as a problem play or as a drama of reconciliation. Indeed, even beyond this one example, the distinction between problem play and drama of reconciliation is sometimes very fine, for not every problem play is without moments of reconciliation, and every drama of reconciliation has moments that hint at further development.

The distinction between problem play and drama of reconciliation is not unique to modern drama. A central debate of classical scholarship revolves around the Euripidean *deus ex machina*. Is Euripides' use of this device in his late plays religious, involving epiphany and illumination, as Andreas Spira, for example, argues, or is it ironic, as Wieland Schmidt, for example, contends? If the *deus ex machina* is employed ironically, the works are problem plays. If it is religious, then the extent to which the divine epiphany is integrated into the play will determine whether the work is a problem play (not as intentionally ironic but as artificially constructed) or a genuine drama of reconciliation. The viability of the terms problem play and drama of reconciliation as heuristic devices for works ranging from Euripides to Shakespeare and modern cinema speaks for their transhistorical relevance, even if each interpretation must draw on historically specific factors and the nuances of the individual work.

Melodrama, most popular in everyday culture, carries with it the seeds of great art and should be recognized both as a danger to the drama of reconciliation (it gives it a bad name) and contrary to its further development.[6] The problem play has been heralded as the greatest of modern speculative genres, but one might ask whether this antithetical moment could not be integrated into a more overarching, more complex synthetic genre.

Neighboring Terms, Forms, and Issues

Tragicomedy

Although the drama of reconciliation unifies other genres, tragedy and comedy as much as melodrama and the problem play, it does so not in the same way as tragicomedy. In English and American criticism the term "tragicomedy" sometimes means precisely what I understand by the drama of reconciliation: the transcendence of tragedy, the resolution of conflict (Bentley, *Life* 319; cf. Guthke, *Modern Tragicomedy* 7–22; and McCollom, *Divine Average* 45–46). This usage of the term is primarily a vestige of its meaning in the seventeenth century. But the more frequent contemporary meaning of tragicomedy is comedy with an unhappy ending; it is this definition with which I want to contrast the drama of reconciliation, and the frequency with which this definition is applied to the word "tragicomedy" encourages me to seek new expressions such as "drama of reconciliation" or "speculative art."

Hegel does not adhere to classical arguments for the purity of genres, as voiced by Cicero, Quintilian, Horace, Racine, Gottsched, or—closer to Hegel's own era—Heydenreich. For Hegel, that would represent the either-or mentality of *Verstand*, but neither does he see truth in an arbitrary mix of genres. He prefers the drama of reconciliation to tragicomedy. The drama of reconciliation is not a double or alternating plot, one serious and the other comic, nor is it an ambivalent work that seems simultaneously comic and tragic, nor can it be a play that ends tragically. Instead, it is a serious (and thus potentially tragic) conflict that ends harmoniously. It is a synthesis, not a juxtaposition or simple mixture, of the two genres. Where tragicomedy more often than not turns comedy into tragedy, the drama of reconciliation is more often than not the reverse movement from tragedy to comedy. Shakespeare's *Cymbeline* might be taken as a paradigmatic example. Beginning not unlike *Othello* or *King Lear*, the play ends in a threefold harmony: within marriage, within the state, and between states.

The focus of my study is, first, the possibilities and limits of the tragic, second, the possibilities and limits of the comic, and third, the truth of the two genres in the drama of reconciliation. The tragicomedy as a nonsynthetic mix of tragic and comic moments has for the most part been bracketed. In the rhetoric of this work, tragicomedy corresponds to: first, the antithetical forms of comedy, including the comedy of absolute irony, insofar as the finite comic moment of laughter is underplayed, the resolution, that is, the self-cancellation of the untenable position, is withheld, or the moment of suffering is at least partially genuine; and the drama of suffering, insofar as its comic potential is only modestly developed.

For research on tragicomedy with special attention to German literature, Karl Guthke's studies are of particular interest.[7] Guthke gives a rich, if not widely accepted, definition of tragicomedy as an ambiguous work that integrates tragic and comic moments simultaneously and in tension with one another. Whereas most studies of tragicomedy speak of a loose mix, or even a succession, of tragic and comic elements, Guthke's rigorous definition allows us to recognize a distinct genre characterized by its internal ambiguities: the tragic and comic are not juxtaposed; they are identical. Although this discussion of tragicomedy as the simultaneity of the tragic and comic appears to suggest that tragicomedy is a truly speculative genre, Guthke's understanding of the tragic component is too reduced to be in any way speculative. Guthke speaks of tragicomedy as in essence a drama (or tragedy) of suffering with a comic angle: echoing Dürrenmatt, Guthke at one point suggests that the tragicomic hero finds herself in a chaotic and meaningless world but is somehow able to endure this meaninglessness (*Modern Tragedy* 134). There is thus a simultaneity of suffering and comic absurdity, a simultaneity I have likewise privileged in my discussion of the drama of suffering, but not a synthesis of tragedy and comedy as defined by Hegel or as developed in this study. Moreover, by not distinguishing the drama of suffering from trag-

edy, Guthke sometimes mistakes comic parody of tragedy for tragicomedy and misreads the unwittingly comic dimensions of suffering as genuinely tragicomic. Critics speak too frequently of tragedy
within comedy, not recognizing, first, the *parody* of tragedy, and
second, comedy's ability to integrate substantive and *serious* themes
(in their contrast to comic particularity and in their eventual fulfillment via intersubjectivity). The best comedies are not always
the funniest.[8]

Romance and the Drama of the True Infinite

A common term for the drama of reconciliation is "romance." Above
all the term is associated with Shakespeare's final plays. Also important—at least in the German tradition—is Lukács's designa-
tion of non-tragic drama as "romance" ("Das Problem" 32). I prefer
"drama of reconciliation" to "romance" for three reasons. First, the
term is close to the Hegelian rhetoric of *Versöhnung*. Second, romance often implies overly idealized characters and "static conditions" that are transcended in the drama of reconciliation (Scholes
and Klaus 43); the drama of reconciliation, insofar as it integrates
negativity, is a dynamic, not a static, work of art. Third, romance
generally includes magical, fairy-tale moments that run counter to
what I stress in the drama of reconciliation, not an external *deus ex
machina*, as, for example, in Euripides' *Alcestis*, where Heracles
brings Admetus' wife back from death, but rather internal development.[9]

Tragedy derives from a contrast between greatness and suffering, the absolute and the finite; its emphasis—and this is why I
exclude the drama of suffering from tragedy—is on the greatness
of the absolute even as we deviate from it. Comedy, which also
contrasts the particular and the substantial, focuses more on the
particular—which is why I suggest that the truth of the drama of
suffering is comedy. Tragedy and comedy are each characterized by
finitude. Tragedy is a falling away from the absolute into finitude;
comedy is a negation of the hero's stagnation in finitude.

The drama of reconciliation might be thought of in terms of the
infinite. The hero transcends her finitude and enters a sphere beyond this, without, however, leaving her life or identity behind.[10]
We can thus speak of an infinite that includes the finite. Likewise,
the perfection or reconciliation gained in a drama of reconciliation
does not negate time, history, or future development. The contem-

porary rejection of all resolution or reconciliation as illusionary or imaginary, as a betrayal of truth or a kind of wish fulfillment, derives from a simplistic *Verstandesdenken* that, even as it denies dualisms, holds on to the dualism of closure and non-closure. True perfection does not exclude imperfection; otherwise it would lack something, namely imperfection, and would not be perfect. One is almost tempted to adopt a privileged and complex category of Hegel's and so rename the drama of reconciliation the "drama of the true infinite." The drama of reconciliation or the drama of the true infinite recognizes the unity of poles: that negativity is a part of harmony; that progress belongs as a moment to perfection; that a rich unity requires the articulation and resolution of contradictions; that greatness can be realized and the particular elevated. Hegelian reconciliation is so complete as not to exclude conflict or opposition.

Adorno, Brecht, and Redemption

Theodor Adorno and Bertolt Brecht seemingly present obstacles to the vocabulary and concept of reconciliation. Adorno was an opponent of any form of redemption from his *Habilitationsschrift* on Kierkegaard to his later *Aesthetic Theory*. Considering the current popularity of Adorno among literary theorists, one may find a certain rhetorical disadvantage in using the term "reconciliation," or *Versöhnung*, which to some ears carries the negative associations of extortion and abuse. Unlike Lukács's notion of *Versöhnung*, which Adorno criticizes in "Extorted Reconciliation," the Hegelian form suggests a unity of the ideal not with the real outside of art but with the real portrayed within art. Ideally, art would harmonize with the reality outside of art, but if such reality deviates from the ideal, the portrayal of reconciliation in art serves as a countermodel to reality. The Hegelian concept of *Versöhnung* thus need not imply a counterfeit or false reconciliation.

Important to the drama of reconciliation is that it not falsify conflict, that it not promise too much or present unearned resolutions. The greatest danger to a drama of reconciliation today is that it simplify complex conflicts, by either bordering on melodrama or becoming heavy-handed and didactic. The moral issues must be nuanced, the hero must be psychologically differentiated, the strategies must be complex, and the aesthetic presentation of reconciliation must be both earned and subtle. The viewer must barely recognize the genre. Pseudo-Longinus' view that a figure is best when its figuralness is concealed may be taken to the macro-level of structure: if the portrayal is subtle and the resolution earned, the construct of genre is scarcely visible (*On the Sublime* 17.1–17.2).

Brecht's theory of drama is likely the most influential in this century, and its relation to my typology and to the drama of reconciliation in particular should be noted. First, distinguishing his theory from his works, we can deal with his plays independently of his intentions. We can discuss Brecht's works as illustrations of the tragedy of self-sacrifice (*The Exception and the Rule*), the tragedy of stubbornness (*Mother Courage*), the tragedy of opposition (*The Measures Taken*), and the tragedy of awareness (*The Good Person of Sezuan*), and, more frequently, as types of comic texts, primarily the comedy of reduction and the comedy of social negation.

Second, Brecht bases his evaluation of epic theater on the thesis that we should not identify with the heroes presented on stage. My privileging of the drama of reconciliation runs counter to this central tenet. If beauty is in principle one with truth, then art should present not only the negation of untenable positions (as Brecht would argue) but also (and owing to the privileging of the speculative, this next group is in principle superior) positive and admirable, though nevertheless complex, positions, with which viewers are encouraged to identify. If these positive positions are reached via the passage through negativity and if they do not mask social inequities, I should think that Brechtian resistance to this theory would be only slight. Indeed, some of Brecht's works, for example, *The Yeasayer and the Naysayer* and *The Caucasian Chalk Circle*, border on the drama of reconciliation. Moreover, there is no a priori reason as to why we should distance ourselves from, rather than identify with, characters on stage. In fact, the same argument that says our identification with characters is an escape from reality that blinds us to the nonideality of life could be employed to suggest that our experience of negativity in the theater is a substitute for reality, such that, if negation is realized in the theater, it needn't also be enacted in reality.[11] Further, non-resolution need not imply Brechtian didacticism and social criticism. Non-closure can easily be debased into the idea that no solutions are possible, thus endorsing not active engagement but skepticism, laziness, and the status quo. In addition, works prepared strictly according to the Brechtian maxim, among which I would not necessarily include works by Brecht, tend to weigh in overly on the side of the intellect. The sensuous moment in general and the moment of sensuous harmony in particular are lacking. That a work without full pleasurable allure will fail to reach a broad audience almost goes without saying. Finally, it is a spurious assumption that intellect, rather than passion, motivates good deeds. Although Hegel is correct in arguing that passions cannot be a measure of what is good, they can help us realize the good. Hegel's comments on Kant might be redirected, *mutatis mutandis*, toward Brecht: "Nothing great has been accomplished without passion, nor can anything great be accomplished without it. It is only a dead, too often, indeed, a hypocritical moralising that inveighs against the form of passion as such" (E § 474, translation modified). Brecht's negation of emotions in art may bring him further from the goal that appeared to justify this negation.

Following Brecht and Ernst Bloch in their critique of fatalistic literature, especially drama, Walter Hinck elucidates a genre he calls the "theater of hope" (*Theater der Hoffnung*). While it has some affinity to the drama of reconciliation (among his prized illustrations are Lessing's *Nathan* and Goethe's *Iphigenia*), Hinck sees its origin primarily in the Enlightenment (though he also includes the Baroque martyr drama), and he includes works that gesture toward hope even as the situation remains tragic, as in Schlegel's *Canut* or Brecht's *The Good Person of Sezuan*, or works of comic reduction, as in Lenz's *The Tutor*. Works fulfilling this genre offer enlightenment and are generally optimistic; instead of encouraging fear and sympathy, they awaken defiance and hope, which are the ingredients of emancipation. Ranging over tragedy, comedy, and the drama of reconciliation, the theater of hope is less an independent genre than a moment of enlightenment that could surface in any number of genres.[12] Hinck's analysis shows a possible proximity of Brecht to the idea of (dramatic) reconciliation, which becomes more pronounced the more we recognize the schism between epic theater and the fatalism of the drama of suffering.

Film, Prose, and Poetry

Because drama is overwhelmingly characterized by tragedy, comedy, and tragicomedy, many speculative works are found outside drama, where these (potentially limiting) categories no longer predominate. Reconciliation, for example, is often evident in film, as, for example, in most of Hitchcock, arguably in Capra, as well as in

Ford's *Young Mr. Lincoln*, Cukor's *The Philadelphia Story*, Chaplin's *Limelight*, Kurosawa's *Ikiru*, and Lumet's *Twelve Angry Men*. Consider also lyrical works such as Goethe's "The Divine," "Nature and Art," and "Reunion," Schiller's "The Security," and Hölderlin's "The Rhine," "Celebration of Peace," and "Patmos," or narratives such as Wezel's *Herrmann and Ulrike*, Goethe's *Wilhelm Meister*, Hölderlin's *Hyperion*, Chamisso's *The Wondrous Tale of Peter Schlemihl*, Hoffmann's *Princess Brambilla* and *Master Flea*, Keller's *Pankraz, the Pouter, Frau Regula Amrain and Her Youngest Son, Clothes Make the Man, The Architect of His Own Fortune, The Misused Love Letters, Hadlaub,* and *Green Henry* (second version), Stifter's *Brigitta* and *Indian Summer*, Ebner-Eschenbach's *The Child of the Parish*, or Schnitzler's *Blind Geronimo and His Brother*. Not all these works immerse themselves in negativity as deeply as is desirable, yet the fact that writers turn to film, poetry, and narrative to portray a serious harmony tells us something about the relationship between aesthetic theory, tradition, and creativity, specifically the extent to which tragedy, comedy, and tragicomedy serve as categories influencing dramatists. As a final illustration of the anomalous position of reconciliation in drama, consider Lessing's generic formulation for his non-tragic, non-comic *Nathan the Wise*, "A Dramatic Poem."

Religion and Reconciliation

Although not all dramas of reconciliation are religious,[13] a religious framework frequently allows for and encourages mansuetude, reconciliation, and atonement, especially when it is informed—as is the religious thought of figures such as Origen, Lullus, Cusanus, Lessing, Schleiermacher, and Hölderlin—by the harmony of diverse religions.[14] The intersubjective structures found in sacraments such as communion, confession, and marriage exhibit similarities to drama's most speculative genre,[15] and religion in its broadest sense tends toward the harmonic combination of humility and greatness.[16] Hegel's student Carl Ludwig Michelet sees the synthesis of tragedy and comedy in drama as the pinnacle of art; moreover, he views the combination of inner reconciliation and recognition of an objective universal, the overcoming of the dualism of subjectivity and objectivity without destruction of either the subjective or objective order, as a transition to the sphere of religion, whose focus is the harmony of the absolute and the subject.[17]

The drama of reconciliation suggests—whether in general or by way of its integration as a moment into more tragically structured works—that reconciliation, by way of confession, conversion, and forgiveness, can come very late. Lateness of reconciliation is evident in religious works of this genre, from Hartmann's *Gregorius* and the conciliatory plays of Hrotswitha of Gandersheim to Hofmannsthal's *Everyman* and Hermann Hesse's *Siddhartha*.[18] Even a writer such as Voltaire embeds the drama of reconciliation within a religious framework, as, for example, in *Alzire*, where he elevates Christian forgiveness over the principle of vengeance. The forgiveness of reconciliation renders the consequences of action partly reversible; the future and present reshape the burden of the past. Indeed, reconciliation reintroduces the harmony of coincidence insofar as the hero recognizes that her errors, though errors, were in fact the hidden agency of her newly reconstituted self.

The strongest dramas of reconciliation exhibit hope not just in the transcendent realm but in this world; religion conduces to the highest reconciliation when it is immanent, as, for example, in pantheism. Lukács in fact has noted an affinity between the drama of reconciliation and pantheism ("Das Problem" 233). God is in the world and does not, as in tragedy, transcend it. This may be yet another reason for the importance of the drama of reconciliation during the age of Goethe.

The argument we shall consider more fully below, namely, that the incarnation, resurrection, and redemption make Christian tragedy an impossibility, can be used here to support the proximity of Christianity and the drama of reconciliation.[19] Adolf Zeising calls the highest genre of tragedy "Christian tragedy" and means thereby the drama of reconciliation. Although Zeising recognizes moments of this structure in the *Eumenides*, *Philoctetes*, and *Oedipus at Colonus*, the full realization of tragic reconciliation comes only with the Christian idea that divinity stands not in conflict with humanity but rather infuses humanity with itself. In this sense, both pantheism and the Christian idea of incarnation support the drama of reconciliation.

Finally, we might consider the relation of the drama of reconciliation to a religious (or philosophical) view that stresses not the infusion of divinity in the world as much as the transcendent import of religion which allows us to recognize the particularity of suffering in this world as belonging to a greater whole, of which it is only a small part. In a sense this is the technique Hegel himself employs to recognize reconciliation within tragedy. Tragedy is overcome—at least to a degree—when we reflect on the universal and view life *sub specie aeternitatis*. This, for example, is the perspective of the astronomer Ternowski in Andreyev's first play *To the Stars*. Ternowski's view of celestial harmony and the wholeness of life gives him an extraordinary equanimity and allows him to put particularities in perspective.[20]

The Difficulty of Reconciliation

The technical difficulties involved in creating a great artwork that is conciliatory rather than simply negative are extraordinary. To portray a third position is very difficult. The fear of closure, the desire to avoid sentimentality, the hesitancy to obscure the negative, all play a role here. Nonetheless, these obstacles should serve as a challenge.

Walter Jens argued already in the 1960s in "A Plea for the Positive in Modern Literature" that the avoidance of any portrayal of goodness on the part of seemingly talented authors might appear to speak against them: "Who, however, can portray not only anxiety, but also happiness, which is artistically far more difficult? . . . . Goodness is no prerogative of mediocrity; morality no resting place for chanting philistines; we cannot wish that today moral customs and decency become tabu, only because the ability of the writers does not suffice to portray morality" (1074, my translation). According to Jens, modern poets rip apart human potential, placing it in a kind of inferno, and they reduce the sphere of beauty to that of the ugly. By seeing in the avoidance of reconciliation a possible weakness of talent, Jens turns the tables on the modern artist: "An unhappy love is easy to portray; a happy love—already more difficult; a happy marriage, however: here a genius of Hofmannsthal's rank is necessary if the poet does not want to idle in sentimental preaching" (1073, my translation).[21] Jens calls for a higher unity that would integrate the depth of Western European art with the optimism of Eastern European art: "But are not we in the West very often inclined, against noble tradition, to underestimate the pedagogical-formative aspect of literature to the same extent that it is overemphasized in the East at the price of artistic development . . . . Whoever wants to prevent the disintegration of the world must not only stand up to the totalitarian political forces and reject all one-sidedness, he must also—in the literary arena—defend himself against every attempt to achieve a canonization of the one at the expense of the other" (1075, 1077, my translation). Jens sees—in an almost Hegelian way—the need for today's art to become once again comprehensive and inclusive, to become richer and more complex than mere negativity permits.[22]

Hitchcock's "I Confess"

Alfred Hitchcock's *I Confess*, one of the greatest religious works of this century, is a drama of reconciliation that invites detailed analysis.[23] Technically and formally outstanding, it is also a film with many speculative structures. The hero of the film, Father Logan (Montgomery Clift), enacts for the greatest part of the film a tragedy of collision (the divine justice of preserving the inviolability of confession versus the earthly justice of apprehending and sentencing a self-confessed murderer). The collision overlaps with a tragedy of self-sacrifice: Logan himself is tried for the murder committed by his confessee, and although he is resolved to act according to the good, he is not without temptation; in one telling scene, he imagines the police apprehending Keller, the murderer. But Logan does persevere; he adheres to the confidentiality of confession. The greatness of his act, however, leads to his suffering. During the trial the Crown Prosecutor (Brian Aherne) accuses Logan of being unable to control his passions (and thus capable of murder), but the film audience, unlike the courtroom audience, knows that Logan's reticence derives precisely from his controlled passions and thus his ability to preserve the sanctity of confession. At his noblest moment of self-sacrifice and adherence to virtue, the crowd taunts Logan most strongly. The courtroom hisses after he is declared not guilty. Voices cry out in scorn: "Take off that collar!" and "Preach us a sermon, Logan!" Eventually, intellectual ridicule shifts to physical abuse.

Logan suffers not only a tragedy of self-sacrifice, he undergoes various forms of collision. Because Logan is unwilling to betray the sacrament of confession, Ruth (Anne Baxter) is in essence forced to reveal her love for Logan. In conflict throughout the film are the claims of secular justice and the demands of professional and religious confidentiality. The collision reaches its deepest point when not only Logan's life but also the lives of others are in danger. Keller murders his wife and then in flight kills a hotel worker. Knowing that Inspector Larue (Karl Malden) has given orders that the police not shoot (Larue wants above all to know the truth about

Vilette's murder and so wants Keller left alive even if this should mean endangering innocent persons), the priest still refuses to betray the sacrament of confession. The one-sidedness of Logan's position is reinforced when it is necessary for earthly justice (the police) to shoot Keller and so save the priest's life. The higher principle may be divine justice, but the divine needs the assistance of the earthly powers. (In this externalization of collision we see an overarching unity of awareness and opposition.)

Just before Keller is shot, he draws a comparison between himself and Logan: both are isolated and alone. The parallel invites further reflection. Logan has been associated with Christ: he has willingly agreed to suffer in order to pay for the sins of another, and he has been taunted by a crowd unaware of his holiness. A series of shots reinforces this association: the early portrait of Logan looking for Keller, in which Logan emerges from an image of the crucified Christ; the shadow on Logan's forehead in the shape of a cross during Keller's confession; the powerful shot of Logan down below on the street and behind a silhouette of Christ carrying the cross; and finally, the close-up of Logan as he is testifying, which includes a symbolic icon of Christ on the left of the screen. Logan suffers the solitude of holiness.[24] Keller is Logan's counterpart, even to the point of his association with the devil. When the cameras show him whispering into Logan's ear, it is as if they were capturing the temptations of the devil. Keller imagines that Logan will tell the police of his crime: "You told them about me . . . . You are a coward after all. You are frightened . . . . Perhaps you'll tell them." Keller's temptation is symbolic of the devil's temptation of Christ (Matthew 4), which Logan, like Christ, is able to resist without himself turning to deception. The association is wittily reinforced by the fact that Logan skips his breakfast the morning after Vilette's murder and turns himself in to Larue without having eaten lunch. Logan has not succumbed to the devil's temptations to satisfy his hunger.

Moreover, a psychological as well as theological (or philosophical) structure is at work here. The greater Logan becomes in the eyes of Keller, the more diabolically Keller acts. The devil is driven crazy by the holiness of Christ's servant. Beginning with their first conversation, Keller is obsessed with Logan's goodness. For his own survival, Keller does not want Logan to betray the sacrament. Yet the priest's infinite goodness makes Keller appear to wish that he would speak. Keller wants the priest to fail, to share in his mediocrity. Like the mob, but even more so, Keller wants to bring

Logan down to his level. A consensus of criminality would make his crime more bearable. If the priest betrays his secret, a standard or norm of justice will blur or disappear. Keller is directed by a kind of resentment. He wants to view himself as equal with the person he values, Logan. His consciousness of self-value derives from comparison, and he recognizes that he is not as good as Logan. In this act of comparison Keller constitutes his values. Rather than aspiring to elevate himself to Logan's position, Keller would erase his inferior value by levelling out the value-difference in a negative way, by dragging Logan down to his level. This explains Keller's continuous suspicion, and hidden desire, that Logan has turned him in. Perversely, though with an inner logic, Keller would prefer to equal Logan's values (by seeing Logan weakened) than to see himself a free man and a figure whose values and integrity society does not question.[25] In the end Keller admits his crime, assuming, in a wishful way, that the priest has weakened. "So, the priest talked . . . . How kindly he hears my confession. And then, a little shame, a little violence, that's all it takes to make him talk. It was too much for you . . . . You are a coward like all other people, aren't you? A hypocrite." Keller, like Logan, is also isolated, but Keller suffers the isolation of evil. In Plato's *Symposium* Alcibiades argues that those whom we love most, we also hate (216b–c). It is those we respect or admire before whom we are most easily ashamed, and an inner desire arises to remove the source of that shame.[26] The devil hates God in part owing to his love for him.

At the film's conclusion, Keller's underlying love for Logan, the devil's recognition of God, is stressed. As his wife did earlier, Keller asks the priest's forgiveness: "Oh, Father, help me . . . . Vergib . . ." Logan has redeemed Keller. The devil recognizes God and is so reintegrated into the holy. It is an early Christian teaching to which Hitchcock here returns,[27] a teaching we also find at the beautiful conclusion of Carl Orff's contemporaneous opera, *Comoedia de Christi Resurrectione*. The reconciliation Hitchcock portrays is a consummation not only of Keller's hidden longing but of the priest's holiness, for Logan's position is not self-righteously exclusive or condemning, but spiritually inclusive and forgiving.

The drama of reconciliation is structured such that Logan's self-sacrifice and collision are not final. Given the superiority of intersubjectivity over subjectivity, it is important that the priest's deed be recognized, that the crowd be sparked by his heroism. We see this beautifully through the figure of Ruth, who initially belongs to a drama of suffering. Ruth is introduced to us—in her own words—as "selfish," unfair to her husband and unable to recognize Logan's vocation. Her description of Logan's departure for war illustrates her self-directedness: "I was selfish even then . . . . It was our last night together . . . . I thought the world was coming to an end. I suppose there were millions of people feeling the same way that night. You don't think of millions of people. You think of yourself and the one you're in love with." Ruth's self-centeredness persists until she finally recognizes in the nobility of Logan's act, the priest's self-denial and nonbetrayal of the sacrament, that his vocation is indeed sacred. Her simple and subtle departure with Pierre ("Pierre, take me home.") represents recognition of Logan even as she now binds herself in a new way to her loving husband.[28] Ruth is ennobled by Logan, just as Keller's wife is earlier. Likewise, Larue is ennobled. His first gaze at Logan is directed downward from Vilette's window, and, as the camera suggests, the vision is of one eye only, a merely partial perspective (Brill 100). Larue's final gaze is upward and is one of admiration and clarity. One might even add that Logan appears ennobled; the end of the film presents above all not release but self-recognition, which should make Logan even stronger.

While the film portrays at its two poles Logan and Keller, the middle is occupied by the mediocrity of the crowd. As in a wealth of other films by Hitchcock, the untenability of a consensus theory of truth is revealed.[29] The crowd is mediocre in its opinions and attitude toward Logan. It does not want to be humbled before a hero. Its callousness is particularly evident in the shot of the woman onlooker who eats an apple as she watches Logan being abused. That we as film spectators are asked to identify with the crowd as much as with Logan is less an affront than a challenge to our consciousness. At the upper end of the crowd is Ruth, always attracted to Logan but nonetheless not able to recognize the legitimacy of his vocation. If Ruth represents the best, Alma Keller represents, at least until her final confession, the crowd's worst potential. As Ruth humbles herself in an attempt to free Logan, Alma long remains silent.

During the investigation and trial, the forces of evil predominate. The skewed shots of churches leaning and almost falling illustrate this, as does the contrast between high angle, distanced shots of Logan, minimizing his power, and low angle shots of Keller, as his face dominates the screen. The film's conclusion, however, does not leave us with this negativity. Alma overcomes a temporary collision (protecting an unjust husband as opposed to an innocent other), and she, like her husband, eventually asks forgiveness. Confession had earlier been a means of escape for Keller and the catalyst for Logan's suffering; this institution, whose sacredness Logan has preserved, becomes at the film's conclusion a tool of salvation. Keller's confession both opens and closes the film, but this symmetry is representative less of a static circle than a progressive spiral, a movement from darkness (the church confessional) to light (the hotel room where Keller asks forgiveness).[30] Where at the film's opening Keller asserts, "No one can help me," the film closes with his genuine plea for help.

Logan's one-sidedness has two facets. First, he adopts a religious perspective that denies the claims of secular justice, thereby allowing Keller to kill two additional persons and endanger even more. It is almost as if Logan lives in a transcendent sphere, beyond the concerns of other humans. Second, even as Logan adheres to a religious and moral code, he finds it difficult to adapt to the needs of others, primarily Keller and Ruth, and so convince them of his position without first causing more suffering than seems necessary. Logan, with his eyes transfixed on the divine, has difficulties approaching other human beings as individuals. His imperative to Keller is clear: Keller must turn himself in, but when Keller asks further questions and desires to speak with him again, to be counselled in his fear and experience Logan's sympathy, the priest curtly asserts that he has nothing more to add. Logan does not seek out ways to assist Keller; he can't fully adapt to his weaknesses. We both admire Logan for this and see it as one-sided. His very greatness, his excess of moral virtue, is also a weakness: he cannot sympathize with the weaknesses of others. An excess of one virtue means the neglect of another, and this one-sidedness has negative repercussions. In his unwavering insistence on truth and morality, Father Logan bears a certain similarity to the tragic hero of stubbornness who abstractly pursues a moral ideal, leaving victims in his wake.

When Logan meets with Ruth on the ferry, he denies the existence of any love between them and abruptly counsels her to stop hurting herself. He speaks openly and directly, but without great tact. She is offended by his apparent condescension, and the scene concludes with Ruth and Logan turning away from one another. As with Keller, here, too, we see that Logan has trouble dealing with others intimately. This isolation gives him strength for his moral code but takes him away from others. A less tragic character would not only be right, he would know how to work with Keller and how to gain Ruth's acceptance of his calling. Logan eventually gains both, but only after Ruth is disoriented and humiliated and Keller has suffered alone and hurt others; it is a drama of reconciliation won at a great price.[31] The black and white of the film formally underscores the black and white morality of Logan, who cannot easily deal with the shades in between (which is, ironically, precisely where Canadian law briefly places him—innocent but only because of insufficient evidence). Yet a reconciliation is gained because Logan's god-like stature finally earns the admiration of Keller and Ruth.

At the film's conclusion, confession is preserved as a valid institution; the consistency of Father Logan's character is likewise maintained. Logan acts out the consequences of his emotional and intellectual commitment to the office of priest. In this sense, *I Confess* provides a positive countermodel to both *Rope* and *Strangers on a Train*. The first film shows the consequences of a philosophical position beyond good and evil, according to which superior persons may claim the right to destroy weaker individuals. The second film argues that the mere thought that we would like to be rid of another can have consequences beyond our intentions. The issue from a larger frame is not whether we should act according to a principle or an emotion but which principle, which sentiments, should be selected and privileged.

I Confess is a good illustration of the way in which a formally successful artwork ruled by dialectical categories can convey in its reception the privileged emotions of sympathy, admiration, and joy, perhaps even awe and wonder. Hitchcock offers his audience not merely an intense but also a significant experience. Like Ruth, the audience is to be ennobled. The film avoids sentimentality, first, by its clear account of negativity (the reconciliation is earned), and second, by its inclusion of brief comic structures, for example, the repetitively falling bike of Father Benoit (not all priests are Christ figures).[32]

It is a telling truth that Hitchcock can in the contemporary world still create a drama of reconciliation. It is even more telling that the film has always been underrated.[33] Yet in Father Logan we see a remarkable character, a figure before whom the self-absorbed heroes of most contemporary art pale. Indeed, many of our contemporary heroes would scarcely reach beyond the level of Ruth at the beginning of the film. Hitchcock was not unaware that his admiration of Logan's courageous adherence to an absolute would cast him against the grain of secular modernism. This is symbolized in

Hitchcock's cameo appearance: at the film's opening, Hitchcock confidently walks across the screen as one-way traffic signs point in the opposite direction. The self-reflective connection between Hitchcock and the signs is further underscored by the repetition of the word "DIRECTION."

Contradictions in Aristotle and Hegel

Not only the contemporary world gives short shrift to the drama of reconciliation. Aristotle's and Hegel's theories of tragedy, the two most widely quoted, suffer from the failure to sufficiently distinguish tragedy from the drama of reconciliation. In his analyses of *peripeteia* and *hamartia*, Aristotle criticizes tragedies with a reversal from bad fortune to good. Euripides, who portrays the passage from good fortune to bad, offers us the most appropriate endings: "The change of fortune should be not from bad to good, but, reversely, from good to bad . . . . A tragedy, then, to be perfect according to the rules of art should be of this construction. Hence they are in error who censure Euripides just because he follows this principle in his plays, many of which end unhappily. It is, as we have said, the right ending" (13; 1453a). However, in his subsequent discussion of *anagnorisis* along with combinations of action and inaction, knowledge and ignorance, Aristotle argues for the superiority of the plot in which the hero is about to commit a horrible deed, in ignorance, and then before acting discovers his error; the evil act is averted, rather than performed. This sequence is privileged over action with knowledge, for example, *Medea*; action, in ignorance, that is discovered only afterwards, for example, *Oedipus Rex*; and action, in knowledge, that is, however, never perpetrated, for example, Haemon's threatening Creon in *Antigone*. The fourth case is "when someone is about to do an irreparable deed through ignorance, and makes the discovery before it is done . . . . The last case is the best, as when in the *Cresphontes* Merope is about to slay her son, but, recognizing who he is, spares his life. So in the *Iphigenia*, the sister recognizes the brother just in time" (14; 1454a). After favoring the plot that represents a reversal from good fortune to bad, Aristotle then elevates the plot that averts disaster. Could it be that Aristotle's contradiction stems from a failure to distinguish the truest tragedies from the best plays, which in turn are not tragedies at all?

For Hegel, as we have seen, tragedy portrays the conflict of two particular positions that should be united in a higher third. Tragedy illustrates with the death of the hero the one-sidedness of a position. The moment viewed as an absolute by the hero is taken as what it is, a moment, and the whole is restored. The tragic action portrays contradiction; the resolution remains the work of the audience. In his discussion of tragedy, however, Hegel alludes to another form of drama ("the deeper mediation of tragic and comic conception") in which resolution is achieved on stage: "Instead of acting with comical perversity, the subjectivity is filled with the seriousness of solid relations and strong characters, while the tragic consistency of will and the depth of the collisions are so far mollified and smoothed out, that there can emerge a reconciliation of interests and a harmonious unification of individuals and their aims" (15:532; A 1203, translation modified). Hegel mentions in this context Aeschylus' *Eumenides* and Sophocles' *Philoctetes* as well as Goethe's *Iphigenia*, which Hegel elevates even higher than the Greek plays insofar as its resolution is unambiguously organic, flowing as it does directly from the action. In his lectures on the philosophy of religion, Hegel returns to this elevation of resolution, arguing again for a transcendence of tragedy: "The higher reconciliation would be that the attitude of one-sidedness would be overcome [aufgehoben] *in the subject* . . . and that it renounce injustice in its mind" (17:134, my translation).[34]

That a nondualistic philosopher like Hegel should announce a third, a synthetic, form of drama, is natural, especially when we consider that Hegel consistently views art in connection with the speculative. He claims, for example, that the either-or mentality of *Verstand* cannot grasp the unity of art (13:152) and that poetic, as opposed to prosaic, consciousness represents the literary equivalent of the speculative (15:240–245). Unfortunately, Hegel never fully develops his brief discussion of the drama of reconciliation, and when he does return to it his comments are as frequently derogatory as they are laudatory. The form is "of less striking importance" (15:531; A 1202). It runs the danger of not fully developing a conflict (15:533). The hero who alters his position may appear to lack character (15:550). Such changes may diminish the determination and pathos of his position (15:568). Finally, harmonic resolutions are frequently unearned (15:569). Most of these points we have already recognized as dangerous; they can weaken a drama of reconciliation, but they do not belong to it in principle. Hegel himself seems unsure whether these characteristics are contingent or necessary elements of the drama of reconciliation.

We can relate Hegel's limited and ambivalent reflections on the drama of reconciliation to his view of comedy and in turn to his philosophy of subjectivity. Hegel presents three historical phases of art: symbolic, classical, and romantic. The romantic is characterized by subjectivity, and with comedy, the genre of subjectivity, Hegel's aesthetics closes.[35] The fact that comedy is free to turn any chance event into art means for Hegel the near dissolution of art (14:220–222 and 15:572–573). The arbitrary content of comedy no longer serves truth. Hegel's view reveals a failure fully to appreciate comedy as the negation of the negation, a point on which the early Hegelians scored better than Hegel himself.[36] If comedy is the negation of a negation, the first negation must include as its possibility all forms of particularity.[37] Only when the second negation fails is art, which requires a moment of truth, dissolved. Here, as is the case elsewhere, Hegel's *Realphilosophie* is determined by a logic of subjectivity. The drama of reconciliation, the drama most characterized by intersubjectivity, is, like the comedy of intersubjectivity, left silent, when comedy, as the ultimate genre of subjectivity, leaves the stage.

Post-Hegelian Discussions of the Drama of Reconciliation

The drama of reconciliation is the overlooked genre of drama, neglected by dramatists and theorists alike.[38] The early Hegelians are among the few theorists ever to address the topic. This is not surprising: Hegel is the perfect thinker to inspire reflection on the drama of reconciliation, for he is both the philosopher of negativity, who addresses "the seriousness, the suffering, the patience, and the labour of the negative" (3:24; PS 10), and the philosopher of the speculative, whose writings have as their telos synthesis, recognition, and harmony. Though Hegel's contemporary Christian Weiße does not speak of a third genre, he does characterize modern drama in general by the unity of the unity and difference of tragedy and comedy, and he terms this unity "the highest calling of dramatic art" (2:333, my translation; cf. 2:344–346). Friedrich Theodor Vischer briefly reflects on the issue of a third genre but comes to the conclusion that all dramas are either comedies or tragedies (6:314–316). In addition, he states his preference for negative tragedies, finding them deeper than dramas of reconciliation (what he calls positive tragedies), for the former stress the moments of motion, battle, and partiality, which are somehow truer to history and life (6:326–328). Carl Ludwig Michelet, in contrast, does speak of a third form, but unfortunately his analyses are even shorter than Hegel's (Michelet, *Geschichte* 784 and *Das System* 3:444 and 3: 453–454). The only nineteenth-century Hegelian to discuss the drama of reconciliation at any length is Moriz Carriere, who speaks in his *Aesthetics* of tragedy, comedy, and the drama of reconciliation and in *The Essence and Forms of Poetry* of tragedy, comedy, and "the play of reconciliation or freedom [das Schauspiel der Versöhnung oder der Freiheit]" (293, my translation). Carriere's discussions are not as systematic or helpful as one might like, although he does note examples of the genre in Lessing, Goethe, Schiller, and Kleist (*Das Wesen* 291–304 and *Aesthetik* 2:611–616).

The writer and aesthetician Adolf Zeising, not a Hegelian but writing with a knowledge of the Hegelian tradition, discusses something akin to the drama of reconciliation when he analyzes what is in his vocabulary the highest form of tragedy: a work that recognizes the finitude of the finite insofar as the finite destroys itself in its conflict with the absolute; the absolute thus enters the world of appearances (341–347). After initially treating the *Eumenides*, *Philoctetes*, and *Oedipus at Colonus*, however, Zeising then limits his discussion to moments of reconciliation within genuine tragedy, for example, the role of the prince in *Romeo and Juliet* or of Malcolm in *Macbeth*. He gives less of an argument for the drama of reconciliation than he does for a moment of reconciliation within tragedy itself.

The next thinker to reflect on the concept, albeit only briefly, is Paul Ernst, a dramatist and student of German Idealism, who speaks of some of his own works as "dramas of redemption [Erlösungsdramen]" ("Tragödie"). Paul Kluckhohn, coming from a non-Hegelian framework and proposing a typology of drama, analyzes what he calls the "Lösungsdrama," which he divides into dramas with external solutions ("Gnadendrama") and internal solutions ("Läuterungsdrama") [see esp. 247–252]. The difference is, if you will, that between Euripides' and Goethe's treatment of the Iphigenia theme. While crediting Kluckhohn with modern critical revival of the drama of reconciliation, we might also point out that he views the genre as just another form in a multiplicity of dramatic types. We see in Kluckhohn's otherwise helpful analysis an inflation of categories and little attempt to relate the diverse forms systematically. The contemporary Hegel scholar Vittorio Hösle has most recently reflected on the drama of reconciliation in his analysis of Greek drama (*Vollendung der Tragödie*), which culminates in a discussion of *Philoctetes* and *Oedipus at Colonus*. Another source of theoretical insight into the genre would, as I suggested above, include generically structured interpretations of the Shakespearean romances, such as those by Robert Hunter.

Critics who attempt a restrictive definition of tragedy rarely discuss different types of non-tragic works. Oscar Mandel, for example, lumps together as examples of "paratragedy" such diverse works as *The Trojan Women* and *Oedipus at Colonus* (26–30). The current study has the advantage of distinguishing types of "paratragedies," for example, the drama of suffering and the drama of reconciliation. The only other critics to adopt such an approach are Heilman, whom I discussed at length above, and Ekbert Faas. Faas employs the term "anti-tragedy," by which he means purposeless suffering and absurdity. The concept bears some similarity to what I call the drama of suffering and the comedy of absolute irony—though Faas includes as examples not only *King Lear* but also *Hamlet*. In addition, Faas speaks of "post-tragedy," or the transcendence of tragedy, which partly overlaps with the drama of reconciliation and which he illustrates primarily via Shakespeare's romances and *Faust II*. Although the prefix for anti-tragedy effectively captures the negative and parasitic tendencies of the first genre, Faas unfortunately refers to the speculative genre with another negative (and extremely vague) prefix. After defining tragedy as suffering that leads to wisdom and meaning and anti-tragedy as random and meaningless suffering, he then speaks of the post-tragic as any glimpse of hope within suffering, thus reducing the post-tragic to the tragic and illustrating it with Beckett's *Waiting for Godot*, of all texts. The drama of reconciliation seems so foreign to contemporary theory and art that even its advocates unwittingly reduce it.

Varieties of Sublation

An interesting question for any detailed study of the drama of reconciliation would be which tragic or comic subforms are best—or in an empirical variant of the question, most often—employed as subplots in the drama of reconciliation. We could analyze, for example, numerous dramas of reconciliation for the ways in which they overcome particular subgenres of tragedy. Sophocles' *Oedipus at Colonus*, for example, transcends a tragedy of self-sacrifice. Shakespeare's *The Tempest* overcomes a potential tragedy of stubbornness ("Yet with my nobler reason 'gainst my fury / Do I take part. The rarer action is / In virtue than in vengeance" V.i.26–28). Some works overcome opposition: the hero or heroine recognizes the truth of the other, thus eliminating a collision unto death, as in Corneille's *The Cid*. Goethe's *Iphigenia* transcends a tragedy of awareness, and Shakespeare's *The Winter's Tale* overcomes a self-inflicted drama of suffering.

Some works surmount an entire series of possible tragedies. Consider the forms of tragedy overcome in Calderón's *Life is a Dream*: for Rosaura, the victim of Astolfo's callousness, a drama of involuntary suffering; for Clotaldo, with his conflicting ties, first, to the King and Rosaura, then, to Rosaura and Astolfo, a tragedy of awareness; for Basilio, the collision between Poland's future and that of his son; and finally, for Segismundo, first, as the victim in the tower, a drama of suffering; second, as the powerful but unjust king in Act II, a tragedy of stubbornness; and third, a tragedy of self-sacrifice, represented by his renunciation of Rosaura in Act III, which, however, is soon transformed into a reconciliation from which suffering virtually vanishes. The play ends in an all-encompassing harmony that is void of neither heroism nor individuality.

Dramas of reconciliation sometimes sublate comedies. Some of Shakespeare's dramas of reconciliation might be interpreted as a deepening of the comedy of coincidence.[39] *Cymbeline* and *The Tempest*, for example, contain many of the accidental, magical, and natural moments of the earlier comedies, though they are enriched by developed characterization, suffering, and forgiveness.[40]

In the most complicated dramas of reconciliation, several subforms, for example, the tragedies of opposition and awareness and the comic focus on subjectivity, are transcended in the final resolution. Consider such diverse plays as Sophocles' *Philoctetes*, Schiller's *William Tell*, and Kleist's *Prince Friedrich von Homburg*. In *Prince Friedrich*, for example, each of the opposing figures acknowledges the other to be in the right. The state, in the figure of the Elector, becomes milder with the state's subject and acknowledges the right of the individual to act freely, which in effect leads the Prince to a recognition of forces beyond his subjectivity.

In Kleist's play, the hero is imprisoned; he is later freed, and a tragic outcome is avoided. This dialectic is also evident in the ancient satyr play, which to a degree resembles the drama of reconciliation (15.531). The satyr play, as reconstructed from Euripides' *Cyclops* and other fragmentary evidence, has tragic elements (the subject matter of myth, a tragic predicament involving possible suffering, and authorship by a tragedian) as well as comic aspects (obscenity, hilarity, and a joyful resolution).[41] In one of the most frequent plots a villain or monster threatens an innocent wayfarer, who succeeds, through trickery, in defeating the abusive host. Also common is the dialectic of bondage and escape. These archetypal plots surface in several ancient dramas of reconciliation, including *Iphigenia at Tauris* and *Helen*. The bondage and release motif also arises in the modern drama of reconciliation, not only in Kleist but also, for example, in Calderón's *Life is a Dream* and Hitchcock's *I Confess*. The proximity of satyr play to the drama of reconciliation is further evident in Euripides' *Alcestis*, which was written in place of a satyr play as the final play in a tetralogy.

One comedy of intersubjectivity, Freytag's *The Journalists*, shows, through the very moments it overcomes, in what ways tragedy and comedy find their truth in the drama of reconciliation. On the one hand, we see the tragic subordination of individual relationships to general concerns, as with Oldendorf and Bolz; on the other hand, we see a character obsessed with his own subjectivity, a character who blocks his own happiness and that of others by embroiling himself in contradictions, the Oberst. Adelheid, through her cunning, overcomes both problems. She thinks pragmatically and so is able to overcome tragic resignation and defeatism, and she, like Lessing's Minna, can develop the educational context that leads the comic blocking character to self-knowledge.

Some works could be studied as partial dramas of reconciliation. Racine's *Bérénice* is a tragedy of awareness that borders on the drama of reconciliation. Though suffering is real and though the play culminates in gestures of sacrifice and renunciation, the conflict is resolved. Resolution is achieved in fact without the death of either hero. Although Goethe's Iphigenia overcomes the collision of honesty and gratitude versus the lives of her brother and his friend, the somewhat milder, but still tragic, situation of Thoas remains: his generosity leads to the suffering of isolation and a kind of tragic renouncement. A particularly modern combination seems to be the drama of suffering that ends with a nod toward reconciliation, a gesture that makes for more than a problem play but something less than full reconciliation; a good example would be Tennessee Williams's *The Night of the Iguana*.

A work that begins as a drama of suffering but clearly ends as a drama of reconciliation is Akira Kurosawa's *Ikiru*. The hero, Kanji Watanabe, who has lived a mundane, almost lifeless existence as a city clerk, learns that he has stomach cancer. After despair and self-pity, Watanabe follows an almost Faustian path through drinking and revelry with a Mephistophelean companion, infatuation with a young woman, and eventually the reclaiming of land. Watanabe almost singlehandedly arranges for a park to be built in a poor section of the city otherwise barren and a sewer problem. The hero, facing death, turns his life around by finding meaning in doing something valuable for others. The film is more a drama of reconciliation than one of suffering, for the hero dies a happy man; tragedy is further transcended by his family's and co-workers' belated recognition of his greatness. Kurosawa's formally masterful film is a wonderful example of an earned and subtle reconciliation.

Finally, to reflect on precisely what kinds of action prevent reconciliation would be interesting. The riddle is raised, for example, by Schlegel's *Canut*, where the titular hero goes out of his way to seek reconciliation with Ulfo, first, after Ulfo's rebellion, then after Canut hears of Ulfo's deceit toward him and his sister, yet again after the duel between Ulfo and Godewin, and finally after Ulfo tries to dethrone Canut. Canut does all he can to help Ulfo and keep from having to sentence him to death. Yet Ulfo is unbending in his refusal to express remorse and so in the end cannot be pardoned.

Tragedy Versus Reconciliation

The final question that arises in the context of the drama of reconciliation is, how is tragedy possible in a Hegelian universe where all conflict is in principle solvable? Why doesn't the possibility of the drama of reconciliation eliminate the reality of tragedy? Aren't, as Otto Pöggeler suggests, Hegel's dialectical-teleological reflections in the long run incompatible with tragedy? Hegel does not himself raise these questions. But his suggestion that in tragedy two goods are *equally* justified does appear to conflict with the reconciliatory spirit of his own philosophy.

Perhaps one can answer in the following way. First, according to Hegel, already in tragedy a moment of reconciliation surfaces—though this reconciliation comes at a price (the hero's death) and is generally visible only to the audience. Second, tragedy can in many cases be overcome. Either under alternative conditions or from the perspective of the universal many conflicts are in principle solvable. Even the collision of two goods can often be resolved by the argument that in a conflict of aprioris, one good can and *should* be violated on the basis of another good whose value is greater and in the interest of whose preservation the violation of the lesser good is demanded. Hegel, who speaks of "a *right of necessity* (not in equity, but as a right)" (R § 127), differs from Kant in this regard.[42] From this perspective tragedy can be overcome, but this is not the entire picture.

In some instances, tragedy is not only possible, it is *unavoidable*. That is, even if it is possible to justify the morality of violating one good in favor of a higher good, we still transgress a good.[43] Such a violation is tragic, even when it is justified, even when it is inevitable, even when it alone leads to the preservation of the higher good.[44] One must recognize the importance of contingency for Hegel. If, from the perspective of the universal, tragic failure and comic particularity are frequently overcome, from the perspective of the real world such transcendence is rare. Moreover, only in the particular, in history is the universal realized; tragedy is indispensable for the realization of spirit in history. Here, Hegel would agree with Hölderlin's stimulating reflection that in tragedy the universal comes to itself through the particular, as sacrifice. When faced with a collision of goods, the great and tragic hero does not simply choose the higher good and feel she has made the correct choice, she senses also the loss of the lesser good, which is indeed still a good. She chooses with regret and remorse, if also with necessity. Duke Ernst in Hebbel's *Agnes Bernauer* knows how he must act, but this does not erase his guilt. Moreover, even if we recognize history as generally progressive, at any given moment there exist both individual conflicts engendering tragedy and broader conflicts, shifts between paradigms, that create inevitable collisions. As we argued above, human time is neither reversible nor infinite. Even when a reconciliatory future beckons, a tragic present holds firm; even when an alternative lies on the horizon, the hero either stubbornly holds on to the past or seeks a more immediate realization of that alternative and is willing to sacrifice her life for it.

In addition, conflicts exist where there is no Hegelian *Aufhebung* whatsoever (certain life versus life collisions, for example, or the unexpected conflict of two substantial promises). No hierarchy of values can solve the hero's dilemma. The crisis resists systematic resolution. Which is higher in a conflict between freedom and life? Is it life, which might be rephrased negatively as subservience, or is it freedom, which might be rephrased negatively as foolish bravado? The answer is not so simple, for, whereas freedom is the ideal meaning of life, life is the necessary condition of freedom; conflicts between the two are in many cases irresolvable. The drama of reconciliation thus supplements, rather than replaces, tragedy. As Nussbaum cogently argues in *The Fragility of Goodness*, there are moments that prevent us from harmonizing ethical alternatives.[45] As we saw in Maass's radio play, circumstances do not always allow us to harmonize ethical conflicts. Again in contrast to Dürrenmatt, we could argue that the complexity of modern life and its unpredictability only increase the chances for unforeseen moral dilemmas. Such tragic collisions and encounters leave us less with a concept of reconciliation than with an immersion in contradiction, even if such contradictions do not lead to ultimate despair or absurdity.

Finally, however, it is important to recognize that not all conflicts are of this type.[46] Comedy and the drama of reconciliation illustrate this point: comedy by its parody of false tragedy, the drama of reconciliation by allowing for a union in which tragedy is not dominant, but merely a moment.

5

The Dialectic of Genre—or: Transitions and Interrelations

In this chapter, I correct the common misconception that tragedy is for Hegel the highest form of drama, attempt to grasp the factors that motivate the movement from tragedy to comedy as well as transitions between the individual subgenres, and consider a variety of ways in which the tragic and comic subgenres relate to one another philosophically and formally.

Comedy as the Truth of Tragedy

We might expect a hierarchy of dramatic forms to mirror social convention; thus, tragedy with its elevated heroes supersedes comedy with its low characters. Hegel upsets this hierarchy. Tragedy with its affirmation of the substantive is a thetic genre; comedy, in its negation of tragedy, is an antithetical genre and in this sense more advanced. Yet the erroneous claim that Hegel views tragedy as the highest of dramatic forms is widespread and still current. Consider, for example, Werner Koepsel, who calls tragedy "the highest genre in Hegel" (216, my translation); Leon Rosenstein, who writes that for Hegel tragedy is "the highest form of art" (521); or Clayton Koelb, who asserts, "tragedy is in Hegel's view the highest form of drama" ("Tragedy" 72). Even Werner Schultz, who clearly recognizes the importance of reconciliation in Hegel's thought, asserts that "tragedy" is for Hegel "the highest artform" (96, my translation).[1] For Hegel, however, comedy is philosophically (and also historically) a later genre.[2] In comparison with the more advanced genre of comedy, tragedy may be viewed as unreflective and naive.

Vischer, too, recognizes at least one sense in which comedy is more advanced than tragedy; it is more reflexive and in that sense more expansive: "That first of all comedy is in a certain sense higher follows for us in principle from the most inner essence of the comic . . . . The comic has shown itself to be an act of the pure freedom of self-consciousness, which engenders and dissolves in infinite play the contradiction with which everything sublime is afflicted. It therefore contains in itself the absolutely great, which is the tragic, as a moment of its process, has thus more, is beyond it. . . . Comedy thus belongs to the later age of human ripeness, which developed calm and serenity out of storm, is brought out of balance by no power of experience and with clear and cheerful insight grasps the great and small as the inseparable sides of one world essence [als die ungetrennten Seiten Eines Weltwesens]" (6:345–346, my translation).[3]

In another sense, comedy transcends tragedy, though my analysis, which has bracketed the theatrical, has not mentioned it until now. Comedy, because it deals, unlike tragedy, primarily and directly with the finite,[4] is easier to visualize and thus in a sense a better genre for the stage than tragedy.[5] In comedy, particularity dominates, and with this particularity come the manifold and the multifarious—both in thought and externalization; thus, realistic portrayal reaches its height not in tragedy but in comedy.[6]

In tragedy the goals of the hero are substantial, the conflict serious, and the characters strong. In comedy the hero's goals are on the whole trivial or trivialized, the conflict need not be taken seriously, and the hero's weaknesses are manifest.[7] Tragedy sacrifices the individual for truth; comedy suspends truth for the benefit of the individual. Tragedy is the genre of principle, comedy the negation of principle or, more precisely, the negation of the negation of principle. The comic does not destroy the positive; it negates it, but this negation is itself negated, thus leading to a resurrection of the positive. The sense in which comedy is the negation of tragedy is manifest not only in the reduction of absolute values to the trivial and material, but also in the widespread comic motif analyzed above of the parody of tragedy.

In comedy, unlike tragedy, the hero frequently surmounts obstacles. This opens up the possibility of harmony. Not all comedies, however, sketch resolutions. Often a reconciliation can be achieved only in the mind of the viewer, who sees the ironization of the comic hero's untenable stance as a negation of negativity, a preformulation of synthesis. Such a synthesis is found in the highest comedy, the comedy of intersubjectivity, which, as I have suggested above, is also a form of the drama of reconciliation.

Transitions

Within Tragedy

The various types of tragedy can be viewed dialectically.[8] The tragedy of self-sacrifice, with its simple affirmation of the good (and its nonrecognition or nonintegration of opposing positions), is essentially thetic. A simple goodness that does not include negativity as a moment must itself pass over into negativity.

The tragedy of stubbornness, with its enactment of evil and its elevation of form over content, is the initial antithetical subgenre. The hero has regressed in terms of content but gained on the level of form. In the second antithetical form, opposition, we advance in the direction of synthesis. The hero enacts a tragedy of stubbornness insofar as he transgresses the good, but he also effects a tragedy of self-sacrifice insofar as he adheres to the good. The collision falls to disparate individuals (or institutions), who are unaware of their inadequacies. They stubbornly adhere to their own definition of the good, despite its limits. The hero, in negating the other position, also destroys a moment within himself.

The synthetic form, the tragedy of awareness, draws on the seeds in opposition of this inner conflict. The hero unites a collision within himself; he is aware of a conflict of goods. By introducing a triadic (or more precisely tetradic) structure to a post-Hegelian theory of tragedy, we are in a sense merely spelling out what is already implicit in the Hegelian model. This link to Hegel is even more prominent when we consider that self-sacrifice can be viewed as the submerged collision of doing the good versus preserving one's life and stubbornness as the submerged collision of good content versus formal virtues. Moreover, self-sacrifice and stubbornness seem strongest when set within periods of paradigm shifts, that is, within eras of collision.

The tragedy of self-sacrifice tends to exclude complexity and dramatic tension, the tragedy of stubbornness the element of correct content, a just goal, and the tragedy of opposition the hero's awareness of the extent of his collision. The tragedy of awareness synthe-

sizes and transcends the previous forms: the hero acts according to
the good even as he negates it, and he is aware of the complexity of
two-sided issues and conflicts. The synthetic form of tragedy is the
complex unity of the unity and difference of the previous genres.
Because the individual hero in a tragedy of awareness has transgressed the whole, he must, ironically, renounce his position by
adhering to it unto death; in the wake of the hero's passage, so the
Hegelian reading, the whole is restored.

From Tragedy to Comedy

Vischer argues that the resolution of tragedy is only apparent (the
realization of unity is an idea, not a dramatic reality); the necessity
of a passage to comedy thus derives from beauty's desire to recon-
struct the unresolved contradiction between dramatic reality and
the truth of the idea (1:358–359). What is in tragedy conceptual
and in the receiver's mind must, in order to become a purer harmony, be moved onto the stage itself.

Tragedy culminates in the dissolution of the subject: on the one
hand, the hero sacrifices himself; on the other hand, the hero is
aware of the division within truth and in the subject who would
adhere to truth. Correspondingly, comedy opens with a subgenre in
which the autonomous subject has essentially been dissolved, and
the legitimacy of the individual self (in its difference from the
whole) is still in question. The restitution of the absolute that
arises in tragedy with the demise of the one-sidedness of the individual's position realizes itself in a cosmic and comic harmony
in which the individual is subordinate to the whole. We arrive at
the first comic subgenre by a kind of linear extrapolation.[9] The
comic protagonist is "the cheerful soul that is absolutely reconciled
within itself" (15:552, my translation).

As we move toward the antithesis, the transition can be recognized as dialectical. Because the tragic hero's ideal is not realized,
the particular is no longer viewed as a vessel of the ideal, as an
entity whose value derives from its connection to an entity beyond
itself. The particular becomes what it truly is, particular, independent of the ideal and shorn of greatness. This, too, contributes to
the transition from tragedy to comedy, from the particular as a
moment within the ideal to the particular as the particular. The
particular and external are now free to be taken as such. In comedy, unlike tragedy, the finite as finite comes to its full glory.[10]

We have thus three overlapping perspectives on the transition from tragedy to comedy: first, the recognition of a contradiction insofar as unity is not yet a dramatic reality (and thus not truly whole); second, the dissolution of the subject and the resulting concept of a unity without subjectivity; and third, the detachment of the particular from the ideal and thus recognition of the particular as particular. The first argument explains the need for movement in principle beyond tragedy; the second motivates a transition to the comedy of coincidence; and the third justifies passage to the regnant categories of comedy, particularity and subjectivity.

Within Comedy

In the transition from the first to the second comic form, from coincidence to reduction, the subject imagines itself at one with the cosmic order; it is confident, sure of itself, and has no doubts about its fitness. The self is convinced of its great destiny, which it derives partly from its good fortune, partly from its increasing sense of self. Its self-reflection, however, is only partial, for the self is unaware of its potential inadequacies.

The rarity of the comedy of coincidence suggests that a different and more direct transition from tragedy to the comedy of reduction may exist.[11] Indeed, Arnold Ruge assumes precisely this position in his *New Introduction to Aesthetics*. I have suggested that tragedy leads to an erasure of self and thus to a union of self and world; in this way I have argued for a transition to the unconscious harmony of coincidence. Ruge views the matter differently. He sees the tragic as a subform of the sublime, which he defines as transcendence of the finitude of the self and movement in the direction of the absolute and eternal. But this transition presupposes as its origin the finitude of the self and implies therefore the possibility of a return to finitude.[12] Indeed, in Ruge's reading the finite stance, the position of failed tragedy or return from tragedy, is more common. Ruge reflects here on the finite as separate from the infinite and on its desire to assert its own particular validity. It negates the true without negating itself and holds on to contradiction. Ruge calls this form the ugly.[13] I would suggest that the form is comic in the sense that the comic protagonist, in the antithetical forms, fails to recognize the contradictions in his behavior and the untenability of his elevation of false subjectivity; the moment of beauty arises, however, through the poetic transformation of the ugly: the character is negative, but the work negates the character and is as such a double negation or affirmation of the beautiful.

The probabilism of reduction, which allows for any goal, even a contradictory one, generates a passage to negation. It is a short step from the subtle relativism of 2a to the open power positivism of 2b.[14] If all positions are contradictory and thus equally false (or equally true), then I can select whatever position pleases my subjectivity, even if it means the destruction of other subjects. The hero arrogantly believes that no objective standards exist; order is whatever I make it. We are in the realm of bad Romantic irony and utter brutality, the domain of evil made possible by the introduction of subjectivity. Order is not the highest; I as subject am the ultimate authority.

If comedy originates with the unity of self and other in tragedy, it progresses toward ever more subjectivity, the consequence of which is a dethroning of the gods, an abandonment of absolutes, the opposition of self and other. In reduction the goal is valid but the means insufficient. Negation reverses this structure: the formal means are adequate to an end that is itself invalid. The formal virtues of the comic hero often have something perverse about them: the hero exhibits, for example, not parsimony but miserliness, not courage but bravado. The comic heroes of 2b have no regard for the world of objectivity and do not hesitate in their attempts to destroy it. Negation of this kind presupposes a formal intelligence and level of discipline that surpasses that of earlier heroes. The heroes of negation are powerful, clever, and rhetorically gifted.

Negation represents a material regression vis-à-vis reduction but a formal progression. The hero of negation in his strongest form—particularly as he evidences shades of stubbornness—exhibits a capacity for realizing the good even as he seeks evil. Such a hero is determined less by natural drives, hunger or lust, for example, and more by a vision of self that counters the moral law. Thus, we recognize the middle stage between an inability to follow the moral law (reduction) and a justifiable reaction to contingent morality (withdrawal). Negation is an unjustified reaction to the moral law but—insofar as it is subjective and intellectual—an advance in the direction of freedom (from nature).

The comedy of negation also opens up the possibility of a widening of subjectivity to the extent that an entire society views itself as an object. Subjectivity as a reigning force becomes, by logical necessity, a multiplicity of reigning subjects. This explains why some works, for example, Jonson's *Volpone* or Sheridan's *The School for Scandal*, though focused primarily on a single character, also portray a multiplicity of unjust persons. In the comedy of social negation, asymmetrical relations, including the mishandling of other subjects, become the dominant feature of an entire society. Comedy approaches satire, and the author portrays the contradictions of society as comically incongruous. The society, although it often remains victorious, exhibits the seeds of its own destruction, a self-destruction that befalls any attempt to make a negative position absolute, be it relativism, injustice, or whatever. The negation of all norms must consequently include a negation of its own negation of norms. This doubling of the negative brings us back in the direction of the positive.

Negation depicts a world full of contradictions; against such a world the hero of withdrawal asserts himself. He opposes the societal elevation of arbitrary subjectivity. The hero who occasionally asserted himself in negation could do so for the most part only by becoming one with the false order. In withdrawal, resistance excludes integration. Here, we have a return to content and form, yet the hero, despite reflecting on a universal ethic, which leads to his negation of the false order, has yet to shake the reduction of subjectivity to self-centeredness and withdrawal. The hero is so close to synthesis, he integrates not only aspects of the earlier antithetical comic forms, he also combines in himself moments of the first three tragic subgenres: the hero sacrifices himself in his defiance (though he does not die); he stubbornly adheres to his position without recognizing the validity of the other; and he faces a collision of two goods, in which he sees an absolute confrontation of his position with that of the world. The hero remains a finite subject in opposition to the world.

The earlier antithetical comic forms are, we might say, withdrawals from truth. While the hero of withdrawal may appear to stand for truth, he withdraws from the public sphere, from intersubjectivity, which is inseparable from truth. In a sense, his act, even in its difference, is an explication of earlier forms. The hero suffers a contradiction between outrage at injustice and withdrawal from any action that would rectify injustice. In this sense, the hero's withdrawal can be viewed partly as a complex form of reduction, a reduction of the good. The advance consists in the hero's negation of the false order. The truth of subjectivity, however, is not the negation of order and institutions, but the grounding of correct positions, even if they are not yet realized in the current order and in existing institutions. Unable to realize his vision in the present order, the hero ultimately fails. Between the two poles of 2 we see the transition from an intuitively and vaguely experienced goal of intersubjectivity to the philosophical justification of that goal. This philosophical elevation derives from the awareness of evil represented in negation and brings with it a clear perception of the good and the strength with which to adhere to one's position. The hero, however, is faced with characters unable to reach his level of insight or discipline and so appears to be involved in a futile struggle with forces that would, were he to act on their behalf, seemingly bring him down to their level. The hero justifies in this way his negation of a world in which the absolute could only be debased.

The comedy of intersubjectivity reasserts the conflict of subject and other but allows for the adjustment and flexibility of the subject along with the development of the objective world, a development brought about by the sublation of its contradictions. Negation and withdrawal attempt in different ways to universalize subjectivity. Negation does so by imposing its arbitrary order on the world, and withdrawal does so by weighing as valid only its own subjectivity and so erasing the significance of what is other. Each represents a merely formal and inadequate attempt to objectify, or universalize, subjectivity. The comedy of intersubjectivity is likewise an objectification of subjectivity but a subjectivity that treats other subjects as subjects. Intersubjectivity passes through the extreme subjectivity of earlier genres; the hero encounters a society ruled by contradictions, but he works with this society to recognize its potential; finally, the hero reenters the harmonic sphere not through coincidence, as earlier, but through the hero's awareness of the validity of the other or society's acceptance of the individual or both. The comedy of intersubjectivity reintegrates tragic awareness and brings it to its moment of truth.

Interrelations between Tragic and Comic Subgenres

Reflections on interrelations between the two genres suggest that the symmetry of tragic and comic subgenres is not restricted to the tragedy of awareness and the comedy of intersubjectivity. The following reflections encourage us to consider parallel works as well as in tragedy hidden moments of comedy and in comedy hidden moments of tragedy. To cite a few examples: we might compare

Richard III and *Volpone*, *Hamlet* and *The Misanthrope*, *Woyzeck* and *The Captain of Köpenick*. Guthke's definition of tragicomedy as a simultaneity of tragic and comic moments could be productive here. Unfortunately, although critics sometimes speak of a hidden identity of tragedy and comedy (Spivack), their comments are generally on a very abstract level. We might profit by comparing types of tragedy with types of comedy. Such comparisons could also shed light on the subgenres themselves, for generic insights are enhanced when we grasp a genre more fully in its relation to others.

The thetic position within the tragedy typology, the tragedy of self-sacrifice, shares much in common with the thetic position within comedy, the comedy of coincidence. The thetic categories are the least complex on the scale of both characters and issues. In each, the individual is subordinate to a higher, more general entity. In the tragedy of self-sacrifice, the hero sacrifices himself for a greater whole, for a principle that transcends his self, even as he incorporates that principle. In the comedy of coincidence, the self is likewise subordinate to an institution, community, or principle that supersedes the self, even as he takes part in that greater whole. Differences arise from the level of greatness reached by the tragic hero; from the more dramatic thrust of the comic work, which elevates action above character; and from the obvious difference in outcome. The comic hero survives in the order that recognizes him as a part. In addition, the form of contradiction differs, as it does in every distinction between tragedy and comedy. In tragedy the content is an organic relation between greatness and suffering; in comedy we see a discrepancy between the pursuit of insubstantial and particular goals and the ironic outcome of these pursuits.

The tragedy of self-sacrifice also shares elements with the comedy of withdrawal: in each case the hero does the good and acts according to a rigidly applied standard, even as he knows that he will suffer for it, even when it means the hero's death or ostracization. Progress normally arises through a hero's assertion of subjective morality, or *Moralität*, in the face of an immoral objectivity, or *Sittlichkeit*. Yet the truth of *Moralität* is its introduction into a revised *Sittlichkeit*, the objectification of subjectivity.[15] At this point the hero of withdrawal falls short. If the hero were to assert his position in the face of a retaliating objectivity, the situation would be tragic. The major shift in the comic mode is that the hero's adherence includes not only an erasure of his integration into the social sphere but a negation of the social sphere as such, yet the comic hero's negation, although extreme, is not complete. Alceste's scorn for the world, for example, is not so great that he kills himself. In contrast, tragic consistency culminates in death. Shakespeare's *Timon of Athens* is in this sense a tragedy, though the general problematic of the play (wherein an overly generous hero falls victim to a greedy and unfeeling world, which he finally recognizes and consequently abandons, becoming a cursing misanthrope) has affinities with withdrawal and might have been more successful had its comic potential been exploited; the play's unfinished form may well be the consequence of an unresolved generic dilemma. The confusions experienced by the comic character relate to his scorn for a world in which he wants to continue to take part, if at times only on its fringe. Here, we see another example of the contradictoriness of the comic hero. Whereas in tragedy withdrawal is necessary and complete, in comedy it is partial and contradictory.

The comedy of withdrawal, owing to the ambiguities of the hero's action, is a richer dramatic form even as it erases the image of the perfect hero, and the hero fails to reach a high moral level. This richness allows us to recognize in the hero of withdrawal also a certain element of stubbornness. The hero of Nossack's *The Testament of Lucius Eurinus* enacts a kind of withdrawal, though he remains consistent, becoming thus a tragic hero of stubbornness. Correspondingly, in the stubborn hero, in Coriolanus, for example, we sometimes see potential for comic treatment. Heroes of stubbornness and protagonists of withdrawal can be profitably compared. Indeed, there may be hidden meaning in a letter Goethe wrote to Zelter in July of 1828, wherein he brings together Faust and Alceste (*Briefe* 806–810).

The tragedy of stubbornness can also claim obvious parallels to the comedy of negation. In each subgenre the hero adopts an untenable position but displays an array of secondary virtues: for the tragic hero, loyalty, bravery, and ambition; for the comic hero, cunning, rhetoric, and steadfastness of ill purpose. Each breaks out of the objective norm: in tragedy, the hero dies of this, in comedy, objectivity reasserts itself, and the hero is merely banished. In both cases, the hero falls, and ethical life is reaffirmed. Each form demands for its success excellence in language and acting. Its strength arises from the medium and the structure of a negation of the negation, not any positive or synthetic message.

Moreover, we encounter in each a related problem. How is it that we admire and even identify with the evil hero? In real life the acts of a Medea or an Adam would elicit abhorrence; in the ideal world of art we attend less to their transgression of ethics than to their passionate motivation (in the case of tragedy) or their clever justifications and alibis (in the case of comedy). The difference lies not only in the varying kinds of formal virtues (tragic courage or loyalty versus comic wit or consistency of ill purpose), but also in the level of passion and the direction of their pursuits: the comic hero seeks money or a fast and easy life; the tragic hero seeks a new world order. The comic hero hopes to satisfy private material desires; the tragic hero longs for recognition and greatness. The difference thus lies with the difference between tragedy and comedy in general, that is, the distinction between substance and particularity. The hero of the tragedy of stubbornness wants something substantial, something general: Ajax seeks objective recognition, Schiller's Phillip desires to preserve the state, Posa hopes to universalize freedom. In comedy the justness and generality of the goal differ. Moreover, in the tragedy of stubbornness senses are not primary; they are subservient to false, but nonetheless abstract, goals. In comedy sensual gratification reigns. Finally, the comic hero undermines only himself, whereas in tragedy the stubborn hero destroys both himself and others. In this sense, tragedy is the more realistic of the genres, for it is certainly true that while negativity must overturn itself, it also often destroys—in the short run at least—the good as well. One must speak with Weiße of a half-theodicy: the bad must suffer, but the good do not always succeed (2:328).

The tragedy of stubbornness that highlights a hero with good intentions who pursues them relentlessly and with evil consequences, as we saw, for example, in Schiller's *Don Carlos*, Ibsen's *The Wild Duck*, or Lean's *The Bridge on the River Kwai*, has certain parallels with the comedy of reduction, although the tragic hero is more grand and consistent, and the consequences of his action are more brutal. Nonetheless, one could rethink the very same structures from a comic perspective. Not only the tragic hero of stubbornness with good intentions but also—if to a lesser degree—the tragic hero of stubbornness who mistakes or overreads what is valid has an affinity to reduction. Macbeth's ambition, for example, is a distortion of the idea that greatness deserves a crown; Othello's jealousy is a perversion of the desire for affirmative symmetrical relations. Behind the stubborn hero's irrational obsession we may even find hidden comic elements, as Robert Norton shows in his reading of Lessing's *Philotas*. Finally, the tragic hero of stubbornness who isolates one virtue, as in Ulfo's elevation of fame in Schlegel's *Canut*, could also be portrayed as a comic hero of reduction. Indeed, Dürrenmatt's *The Marriage of Mr. Mississippi* takes an array of potential tragic heroes of stubbornness and transforms them into comic heroes of reduction.

Even as the comedy of reduction and the tragedy of stubbornness share common features, the comedy of reduction and the satiric comedy of social negation correspond most precisely to the drama of self-inflicted suffering and the drama of involuntary suffering respectively. In the drama of self-inflicted suffering, the hero fails because of ineptitude, immorality, or weakness in character. I suggested above that the truth of the drama of self-inflicted suffering is comedy; more precisely, the comedy of reduction. In reduction the hero fails for similar reasons, but the audience refrains from taking seriously the weak hero obsessed with his suffering and believing in his own greatness.

The comedy of social negation can be viewed as a comic counterpart to the drama of involuntary suffering. It is the least specifically comic form, since the serious satire and the presentation of the hero as victim mitigate against the laughter and gaiety of comedy; nonetheless, works that present asymmetrical structures in society tend to be aware of their comic potential. Consider, for example, the thematization of comic contradictions in Fontane's *Effi Briest*.[16] Whereas the drama of suffering focuses on the hero as victim, recording his reactions to the powers of fate in whatever form they appear, its comic counterpart ironizes those very forces. It shows less their power than their absurdity, their smallness, their contradictions, their nearness to their own self-created abyss. When it presents a hero, it is the victim turned into a cunning trickster who outwits those powerful, but stupid, imitations of fate.

The drama of suffering also shares a moment with the initial comic form, the comedy of coincidence: in each, we see the power of nature, whether as fate or as providence, also in each a focus on the physical and material, rather than intellectual, catalysts of suffering or resolution. Indeed, one is tempted to rename the two forms, respectively, the tragedy and comedy of the elements. Not only do the natural elements play a role in each, so too whatever transcends the power of the self. We see in each subgenre the role of chance encounters and mistaken identities—in comedies by Menander, Terrence, and Shakespeare, for example, and in dramas of suffering by Lillo, Werner, and Camus. In each subgenre the hero's original intentions are thwarted by the complexity of coincidence and events: the differences lie in the quality of each goal and the consequences of the hero's being thwarted. Where in coincidence we see lotteries won or wealth inherited, we encounter in the drama of suffering a pessimistic wheel of fortune, including even— as in O'Casey's *Juno and the Paycock*—legacies promised, but withdrawn. An interesting silent film that combines the two genres is Murnau's *The Last Laugh*: the film is a drama of suffering embedded within a comedy of coincidence.

Those dramas of suffering that lack value even as political criticism and instead lament the universal, all-pervasive, and chaotic suffering of the world border on the comedy of absolute irony, which likewise fails to specify the cause of suffering; suffering and inadequacy are deemed universal.[17] Viewed from another angle, comedies of absolute irony negate substance, orientation, and meaning, thus leaving characters in a state of misfortune, into which they appear to have been thrown. Their misery is not as in a tragedy but rather as in a drama of suffering.[18] Seen in this light, the difference between the drama of suffering and such comedies of absolute irony becomes one more of form than of content. Does the play focus on despair as the result of nonmeaning and injustice or on nonmeaning as that which elicits, among other things, despair and injustice? Viewed from a different angle, the two subgenres may intersect by way of the social criticism implicit in some of the less extreme examples of the Theatre of the Absurd, which reveal the grotesque aspects of current inauthentic existence, rather than the absurdity of existence as such. The two subgenres, however, may also radically differ. One thinks, for example, of those dramas of suffering that view suffering as produced by humans under specific historical conditions vis-à-vis those comedies of absolute irony that see suffering as universal and irresolvable.[19]

As suggested above, the two most synthetic subgenres, the tragedy of awareness and the comedy of intersubjectivity, share the portrayal of a substantial and ambiguous conflict. Whereas in tragedy the two colliding forces must give way, the comic genre allows for moments of development, recognition, and forgiveness and so realizes the drama of reconciliation.

What separates the tragedies of opposition and awareness from the drama of reconciliation links them with an earlier comic subgenre, the comedy of withdrawal. In this subgenre, the hero is in practice justified, in principle, however, not. That is, as in any tragedy of collision, the hero's position is partly justified, partly untenable. The hero cannot possibly act in the corrupt world, but nor can he fail to act. The proximity of the two structures explains, I believe, the comic implications of *Hamlet* or *Fraternal Quarrel* and the tragic tone of *The Misanthrope* or *The Difficult Man*. What helps preserve the tragic spirit of *Hamlet* and *Fraternal Quarrel*, beyond the brutal consequences of the action, is the fact that they are tragedies of awareness. The comedy of withdrawal corresponds more closely to tragic opposition than awareness, for a certain nonrecognition is common to both forms.

In tragedy the subject dies even as he transcends objectivity; the hero is equal to his task but must perish. In the first four comic forms, the subject lives but the sphere of objectivity transcends the inadequacies of the subject; though the hero survives, he is not equal to his task. In the final comic form, as in the drama of reconciliation, subjectivity and objectivity harmonize; the hero is equal to his task, and he survives. Even when the festive moment of comedy excludes a hero (as in *As You Like It* or *Twelfth Night*), the excluded hero does not die. In tragedy, on the other hand, death excludes the hero's possibility of reentering intersubjectivity.

In comedy, objectivity is never so strong as to crush the individual. Even in the comedy of negation, in works such as *Tartuffe* or *The Broken Jug*, the subject survives. The self-destruction of the negative hero is essential; we need to be reassured that goodness triumphs. Yet the hero's survival is equally important; we need to be reminded that goodness is strong enough to allow for reintegration of the negative. The implications of this structure reach into the philosophy of punishment. If the sphere of objectivity were to destroy the individual, we would have either the tragic philosophy of retribution or the finality of general deterrent. The fact that the subject survives implies an affirmation of special deterrent or rehabilitation. The individual lives on, and the possibility of his integrating himself back into the objective sphere remains. The truth of the comic genre is this possibility of intersubjectivity, just as, logically speaking, the truth of subjectivity is intersubjectivity.

*

Great potential exists for grasping the interrelatedness of diverse genres by way of individual works. With the aid of the categories developed above, a text can be interpreted as partly tragic, partly comic. Consider the proximity of tragic stubbornness and comic reduction in Renoir's film about different forms of love at the end of the aristocratic era, *The Rules of the Game*. Each of Christine's suitors embodies a moment of love. Andre is sincere, absolute, and passionate in his love. A hero, Andre is willing to risk all for love, and he does indeed die young. Andre, however, is also narcissistic; his love knows no bounds even when, unfulfilled, it borders on self-pity. Moreover, he understands little of the social dimensions of love and speaks indiscreetly of his torments. Christine's husband, Robert, in contrast to the passionate Andre, is almost mechanical in his love. We see this, symbolically, in his hobby of collecting mechanical dolls and making toy birds, also in his face, which has a doll-like character to it. Moreover, Robert is weak in contrast to the heroic Andre. Nonetheless, Robert grasps love in its institutional dimensions; unlike Andre, he understands its formal rules, its etiquette, its social aspects. Octave's love, to take the third figure, represents an avuncular dimension of love; he is the confidant with whom Christine can relax and be herself. His love develops from friendship and has substance; yet, unlike Andre, Octave is a coward and, unlike Robert, he lacks any social foundation: his life is without stability or permanence. We can add to this list of reduced manifestations of love the misdirected sincerity of Schumacher: perfectly loyal to Lisette, he demands the same from her; and he is willing to shoot and kill for the sake of this love.

All these figures are in a sense comic. The film borders at times on farce, and its comic dimensions are accentuated by the deception and decadence of the social strata portrayed. Yet it would be cruel to laugh at every one of these characters. Robert, who announces that he does not like to suffer, is never truly sincere in his suffering and would seem to be the most comic. Schumacher, on the other hand, who is the most superficially comic, suffers perhaps more than any other and must be viewed as tragic, if not exclusively tragic. Andre and Octave place similar, if less extreme demands, on the viewer.

Each character, although representing a comic reduction of love, also enacts a moment of tragic stubbornness. Andre is a truly absolute and heroic lover, a throwback to an earlier era in his commitment to one person. Robert has the formal virtue of mastering the rules of social interaction, an ability that is dying out in the transition to a more modern world. Whereas Robert's love for play as play allows him to continue after a loss of love, Andre has no such alternative. He puts everything into love and is manifestly tragic. Octave has the virtue of sensitivity to others, and Schumacher the virtue of absolute loyalty, which leads him to kill another person. Although Schumacher is a comic reduction, he is also genuinely tragic, and our sympathy for him is deep. Much the way *Rules of the Game* hovers between comic reduction and tragic stubbornness, other works could be understood and interpreted in the light of the ways they reveal the tragicomic interrelatedness of diverse tragic and comic subgenres.

6

Tragedy and Comedy Today

I f tragedy and comedy are more than just literary structures, a focus on their contemporary fate should bring insight not only into tragedy and comedy but also into today's world.

The Disappearance of Tragedy

By focusing on the four forms of tragedy and the drama of suffering, we can shed light on the apparent disappearance of tragedy. Self-sacrifice has met its principal resistance by way of the contemporary overvaluation of subjectivity; few today are willing to identify with heroes who sacrifice themselves for the universal. The idea of self-sacrifice, implying some sort of self-denial, does not easily harmonize with a cultural elevation of individualism and the idea that what is good is what is good for the self. This is related to the problem of what Richard Sennett in his insightful book has called "the fall of public man": the public sphere, the realm of social action, has lost prestige and been partially replaced by individuals reflecting on their private psyches and unable to transcend a "tyranny of intimacy," that is, a life ruled by singularities, particularities, and self-absorption. In a world where public life is reduced to a merely formal obligation, where self-knowledge has become an end in itself, not a means for the betterment of others, the passionate and dignified act on behalf of what is public and universal is rare indeed. Even those ostensibly concerned with the public are often viewed or view themselves not by way of their impersonal relation to substance but by way of their emotions, style, and personal intentions. Such characters border on the comic. As the self becomes unsure of its nature, as it becomes problematic, it becomes an obsession—all this at the expense of the sphere in which it is embedded, the sphere of public responsibility and social cohesion.

Further, a contemporary skepticism exists toward secondary virtues, which were partly discredited in the Third Reich and which accompany not only stubbornness but also self-sacrifice. This skepticism is falsely grounded. The validity of secondary virtues such as discipline, courage, or loyalty depends on the ends they serve. Although secondary virtues can be abused, they are necessary, and the possibility of abuse is no argument against them. Indeed, to locate the problem in secondary virtues is false, when it really lies in the disintegration of primary virtues, which should be their end.

Christianity has also affected tragic self-sacrifice. Religious individuals may be motivated to do the good not because it is good but because of promised rewards in the afterlife. The fourth tempter in T. S. Eliot's *Murder in the Cathedral* cleverly thematizes this moment, even as Becket overcomes it in his Christmas sermon. If the tragic act becomes a means rather than an end, the element of sacrifice is annulled (everything is gained and nothing lost).[1]

The tragedy of stubbornness is in jeopardy for a variety of reasons as well. First, anti-elitist tendencies argue against the portrayal and idealization of formally powerful characters. The tendencies are unfortunate. Certainly, many modern works extend the range of our sympathy to characters earlier not treated in tragedy, but this is no argument against traditional tragedy or a more innovative modern tragedy. We must distinguish the arbitrary convention of the superiority of rank from the legitimate elevation of moral worth and formal strength and the just recognition that even a humble person can be the carrier of extraordinary virtues. Likewise, realistic drama in the formal sense, drama without verse, is entirely compatible with tragedy.

Second, Hegel argued that the strength of any one individual is limited by ties to the existing order. After discussing justice, morality, and law, he writes: "The individual is now no longer the vehicle and sole actualization of these powers as was the case in the heroic age" (13:255; A 194). "Universal ends," he argues in another passage, "cannot be accomplished at all by one individual in *such a way* that others become his obedient instruments; on the contrary, such ends prevail by their own force, partially with the will of the many, partially against it and without their knowledge" (15:558; A 1224, translation modified; cf. R § 93 Z and 12:45–46). In "Problems of the Theater," Dürrenmatt extends Hegel's reflections, per-

suasively arguing that the individual in today's complex, bureaucratic, and decentralized society has even less chance to assert
power and assume responsibility. The development Hegel and Dürrenmatt describe makes responsibility more complex, power more
difficult to wield; it does not, however, eliminate the two.[2]

Interestingly, where Dürrenmatt sees in the modern world the
devolution of the individual and hence the disappearance of tragedy, Paul Ernst observes in this same process something akin to
the Greek notion of fate and, with this, tragic potential: "The development and extension of the monetary economy has created a universal and very close relationship of all members of society to one
another, as never before existed, indeed in such a way that the
individual is thoroughly dependent on this relationship. The relationships are created, however, neither for the purposes of the individual nor do they follow a rational direction; instead, they develop
according to their own laws: they represent for the individual blind
fate" (*Der Weg zur Form* 130–131, my translation). Beyond this,
however, Ernst does lament a lack of conflict, arguing that conflict
presupposes resistance (rather than mere passivity) and freedom
(rather than all-consuming necessity). In short, the elements Dürrenmatt sees as transforming tragedy into comedy Ernst views as
part of a potentially tragic frame—as long as this overpowering
organization and heteronomy does not *fully* obliterate moments of
resistance and responsibility.

Also contributing to the modern trivialization of tragedy is the
transformation of admiration for (potentially tragic) heroes to a
(comic) preoccupation with celebrities, persons known for their
"well-knownness," rather than their deeds, their success rather
than their performance (Boorstin 57). This, too, relates to a comic
focus on the contingent and non-substantial, what is easily and
quickly forgotten. Americans are very fickle about their heroes,
and fickleness conduces to comedy, not tragedy. On the American
stage, celebrities replace heroes, and we begin to forget what greatness is. This shift has been facilitated by many factors, including
the media and the proliferation of "pseudo-events," but the process
is hardly irreversible.

Another anti-tragic dimension is the tendency to shift values in
new circumstances, to abandon, rather than hold on to, a position
in a time of crisis. We conclude after all that there is no transhistorical validity to matters of right and wrong; our historical
framework conditions all our claims to truth. The intellectual analogue to this is an unwillingness to think positions through. We are

extremely inconsistent in our stances. If relativism, or the claim that truth and justice are illusions, were thought through, it would not be difficult to see that it passes over into power positivism, or the reduction of truth and justice to power: if all positions are illusory, we cannot argue against any one position; we are thus free to assume force in order to advance our positions at the expense of others. This transition is rarely recognized. Ironically, the extreme relativists or power positivists are actually less relativistic than the moderate relativists, for the extreme relativists recognize the law of consistency and become power positivists (or at least recognize the validity of this transition).[3] The moderate relativists, on the other hand, are more relativistic, for they aren't even consistent. Not following their stance to its conclusion, they fail to become candidates even for a tragedy of stubbornness.

Turning now to the two forms of Hegelian collision, opposition and awareness, we again recognize the problem of the disintegration of the absolute. The relativism of all values has become in the wake of Nietzsche and most recently as a consequence of postmodernism the dominant theme of the age. We can only laugh at those who take their positions seriously and do not recognize the inability to ground first principles—and thus the relative arbitrariness of all standpoints. A tragedy of awareness, or for that matter of opposition, is impossible in a society that recognizes no aprioris, that sees morality as contingent, a matter of convention. In my analysis of the tragedy of awareness, I mentioned the possible conflict of culturally determined aprioris. While such aprioris can conflict, tragedy is not possible if the culturally determined aprioris are viewed, as they are today, as culturally determined, that is, as contingent. Tragedy arises when the cultural determination or contingency of absolutes is not recognized or not viewed as relative, even though the tragedy may end with a recognition of this relativity, as does Kleist's *Penthesilea*. A related reason—not often articulated—for the disappearance of tragedy may be that we no longer have faith in a genre that purports to express permanently valid truths about the human condition. Meanwhile, the few who have recognized permanent truths have tended to transform every tragedy into a drama of reconciliation, either by recognizing the inevitability of salvation (as in Christianity) or by envisaging the end that justifies the means (as in Marxism).[4]

Nietzsche's suggestion that faith in reason has destroyed tragedy is untenable not only for purely descriptive reasons—our faith in reason seems almost past[5]—it fails on its own terms. Aprioris can conflict. Moreover, adherence to absolute principles of virtue can endanger lives. Not despite, but because of, his affirmation of reason (and thus virtue), Socrates was condemned to death.

Finally, I turn to the drama of suffering. Lionel Abel has documented the rise of metatheater over tragedy. Pursuing a line of thought begun by Hegel, Abel asserts that self-conscious and indecisive heroes have replaced the blind and willful heroes of earlier days. Much criticism can be lodged against various aspects of Abel's reading of modern drama and of *Hamlet* in particular. Moreover, despite his focus on subjectivity and self-reflection, Abel has very little to say about comedy. Nonetheless, his general point is well-taken: self-conscious, self-reflective heroes preoccupied with their own subjectivity and weak in character populate many of our modern narratives and dramas. If Hegel is right on this (15:527–530), and I think he is, most such characters belong in comedies, not tragedies—yet another factor in the dissolution of contemporary tragedy. In addition, as I suggested above, plays of mere suffering, despite a popularity that appears to derive primarily from the genre's confrontation with nothingness and meaninglessness and its assertion of the failure of all rational structures, can hardly be called tragedies. Heroes who are determined by historical or even psychological forces are no longer active agents of history or persons whose suffering stems from greatness. The tragic hero is neither a self-pitying victim nor an irresponsible character whose weakness causes his misery.

The thesis has also been put forward that the inability to write tragedies in the present is itself the greatest tragedy and marks profound insight into the illusions of the world and the suffering of modern generations. Absolute irony thus becomes the center of tragedy, much as Nietzsche argued that the greatest tragedy is comedy infinitely extended (Roche, "Laughter"). I oppose this view for several reasons: first, it broadens tragedy to mean any significant failure, regardless of its cause—thus breaking down the useful distinction between tragedy and simple suffering; second, it reduces the greatness of the tragic tradition by calling such tragedies illusions and elevating what is more of an unintentional parody of tragedy; third, it implies the objectivity of a world view that denies objectivity and is as such internally contradictory.

What then is the outlook for tragedy? I would suggest that our literary works have become increasingly conscious of the social, rhetorical, and psychological conditions that cause suffering, but at the price of transforming virtually all heroes into victims,[6] and that comedy may be the most promising genre for an age immersed in the finite, an age like ours that refuses to recognize any absolutes. Second, our fear of secondary virtues must be overcome and the self-cancellation of relativism and power positivism needs to be more broadly recognized—philosophically or intuitively—before we shall see any extensive resurfacing of the tragedy of stubbornness. Third, in order to allow for the tragedies of self-sacrifice, opposition, and awareness, we must again learn to recognize normative values, and we must embrace more than the value of our own identities or our own subsystems of values. The overarching claim that tragedy is dead should perhaps be seen as a stage in a cycle of history that has occurred before. Not every age is capable of tragedy, yet tragedy has resurfaced at various times. Until such a change occurs, the genre will remain merely historical and distant, performances of great tragedies will focus on the mere fact of suffering, contemporary dramatists will have only a reduced sphere of subject matter and forms, and audiences will be kept from experiencing the aesthetic emotions unique to great tragedy.[7]

Dürrenmatt's *The Visit* illustrates some of the difficulties contemporary authors have in dealing with a potentially tragic theme. In this drama Claire Zachanassian offers the people of Güllen increased wealth under the condition that they execute one of their citizens, Alfred Ill, who had seduced Claire long ago and at that time denied the parentage of her child. The obvious choice the citizens of Güllen have is to act according to a philosophically coherent notion of justice, to let Ill live, and to suffer the consequences, in short to enact a tragedy of self-sacrifice. But this is not possible for them. The citizens of Güllen, having lost transcendent values, give in to their material longings. Justice is reduced to personal conscience, which can legitimate nothing and everything, and consensus, which gives the majority the freedom to suspend minority rights. The citizens of Güllen treat Ill not as a subject but as a means to an end. Dürrenmatt introduces to the play a comic angle that brings into focus the appearance-reality dualism of the people of Güllen, the schism between their rhetoric and their actions, and eventually the citizens' fickleness and blindness. The people of Güllen convince themselves that their collective murder is in the service of an ideal form of justice.

Ill may appear to be in a position to raise a drama of suffering to a tragedy of self-sacrifice. Like Oedipus, Ill is the one obstacle to the seeming health and prosperity of his community, which suffers not from the plague but from economic plight; like Oedipus, Ill is charged with an earlier crime and comes to recognize his guilt. Although Ill does not sentence himself, he does refrain from fleeing, and he does prevent the teacher from telling the press of Zachanassian's unorthodox conditions. But Ill is not an Oedipus. Any dignity he achieves is undermined by the absurdity of its context.[8] His death, that of a scapegoat, is not an act of defiance or a willful assertion of truth; it gives the citizens of Güllen material prosperity at the expense of human values. Ill's self-sacrifice is neither mythic nor purposeful. Here, the sacrifice of one individual for the whole is not a cleansing process but the introduction of yet more moral decay.

Claire Zachanassian represents a reduction of tragic stubbornness. The teacher compares her to Medea, as does Dürrenmatt (102), but this strikes me as parody. To be sure, Zachanassian was wronged, but not in the same way as Medea. Indeed, Ill's breach of loyalty is matched by her fast-paced array of empty marriages. She exhibits consistency of ill purpose and power but she is entirely without recognition, and rather than enacting—according to the laws of retribution—a false, but firm, notion of justice, Claire's revenge is as much against the citizens of Güllen as against Ill; she extends the level of corruption and injustice and so proves her cynicism.

Not only does the play parody the tragedies of self-sacrifice and stubbornness, not only does it ironize the drama of suffering by transforming it into a comedy of negation with a grotesque happy end, even including a chorus that affirms material prosperity, the idea of a collision of goods is nowhere thematized. When, as in much of the modern and postmodern world, a single absolute is missing, the conflict of two absolute goods is even further removed. I have argued above that the comic can best deal with this elimination of the absolute, and it is through the comic, which is itself not simply a negation, but a negation of the negation, an ironization of untenable positions, that we can overcome the mere drama of suffering and return to the absolute.

Comedy, Despair, Finitude

Despair can arise from a substantive conflict and be portrayed as tragic. It can also arise from a focus on the self and its particularity. Dwelling on our own dolorous finitude as a pretext for ignoring more substantial intersubjective issues is a comic theme, in particular material for the comedy of reduction. Though some forms of *Angst* and despair may belong in tragedy (we could despair, for example, of seeing the good but not being able to realize it), most forms, particularly those that relate to the contingent weaknesses of the subject, would be better treated in comedy than in the serious and somber literature of *Angst* (I'm thinking of Kafka, when he is not read comically, Benn, Trakl, Heym, Camus, Beckett, Thomas Bernhard, excluding the comedies, Heiner Müller, and others). While the literature of *Angst* wallows in despair, comedy seeks to do something about it.[9] To deal effectively with *Angst* or despair is not to feel it or be in it but to *know* about it and thus to be in a position that will lead to its overcoming. Comedy affirms its superiority over the literature of despair in the way that consciousness asserts its preponderance over simple being; comedy brings to light the causes of despair and negates negativity, preparing then alternatives as well.

I have argued that the truth of the drama of suffering is comedy: the hero obsessed with his own particular suffering should not be taken seriously, and the significance of the drama of involuntary suffering is in most cases less the victim and more the (contradictory) forces that create victims. Although I recognized exceptions to this rule, works in which we have genuine compassion for the simple and suffering protagonist, the general insight still holds. After having argued that the highest dramatic form is the drama of reconciliation, I also questioned whether this is always the most suitable genre. For an age preoccupied with its own subjectivity, an age that questions all universals as the (false) realization of arbitrary subjectivity, comedy may be the most appropriate genre. Because we have lost belief in transcendent meaning, stable values, and even the concept of a self, comedy, along with the hybrid tragicomedy, has more or less usurped the heroic genre of tragedy. This has a certain inner logic. The loss of absolutes makes tragedy impossible, and it must be replaced by the negative genre of comedy.

The increase in comedy, in particular antithetical comedy, with its frequent doses of hedonism, may correlate not merely to the theoretical questioning of absolutes, but to actual decline. The hedonistic impulse—contrary to a popular conservative view—may be less the cause than the result of decay: when we are discontent, we are disposed to supplant our despair with pleasure. This is evident not only in the comedy of reduction, with the individual hero's diminishing of truth, but in the comedy of negation as well, with the possibility of far-reaching destruction. Insofar as negativity be-

comes the regnant attitude of society, the number of means designed and employed to satisfy pleasures increases, including of
course means of possession and instrumentalization. A contradictory element here is that an insistence on pleasure presupposes
its loss, that is, the disappearance of a spontaneous joy of life.
Pleasure—which is by definition immediate—is now mediated by
thought and is as such no longer possible. The hero's longing for
pleasure cannot be fulfilled; this has tragic (Faustian) as well as
comic (reductive) potential.

Comedy as a negation of the finite is appropriate for an age that
has absolutized finitude. An age, however, that absolutizes the finite tends not to recognize the finitude of the finite. Comedy may
flourish as the negation of particular instances of the finite without
negating finitude. One negates this or that behavior, this or that
policy, but one doesn't laugh about the finite as such. Because one
has nothing transcendent, but only what is finite, one can't negate
the finite. Absolute irony is desperately attracted to what it negates because that's all it has;[10] for absolute irony no positive alternative exists. Although comedy is capable of showing the finitude
of the finite, it seems today to be locked in a negation not of finitude but of particular manifestations of the finite. Like the many
heads of the Hydra, an individually finite moment is undermined
only to reappear in a variety and multiplicity of equally finite appearances. Comedy of this sort will not return us to what was lost
with the dissolution of tragedy, nor will it move us forward to the
harmony of speculative art. In an age of absolute finitude, where
no alternatives are spelled out, comedy can reign and yet do nothing.

Comedy and the Negation of Negativity

The finitude of comedy taken as finite points toward the infinite,
that is, the stable values seemingly lost with the dissolution of
tragedy. Instead of negating one manifestation of the finite in favor
of another, true comedy negates finitude as such and invokes the
logical necessity and empirical possibility of the infinite, or absolute and normative positions. Comedy evokes via negation the
values sketched in tragedy, as the unspoken standards against
which we measure the comic hero's follies. Hegel writes insightfully that in comedy the reduced reality "is brought into portrayal
in *such* a way that it destroys itself from within, so that precisely

in this self-destruction of the right element, the true can display itself in this reflection as a fixed, abiding power, and the face of madness and unreason is not left with the power of directly contradicting what is inherently true" (14:120; A 511, translation modified). Socrates' statement on the hidden unity of tragedy and comedy is perhaps best understood in this spirit. Seemingly lost values are recognized after we pass through their negation. Comedy makes explicit for the audience, it objectifies, the errors of the age and so helps society's efforts to transcend them. The comic negation of the various forms of negativity—indulgence, nonmeaning, frivolity, brutality, monotony—leads to truth. Knowledge of error as error frees us from the compulsion to continue to err. Hegel writes concerning one of the functions of art: "For then the person *contemplates* his impulses and inclinations, and while formerly they carried him away without his reflecting, he now sees them outside himself and already begins to approach them in freedom, for they face him in their objectivity . . . . Art by means of its representations, while remaining within the sensuous sphere, liberates us at the same time from the power of sensuality" (13:74–75; A 48–49, translation modified).

The view that comedy negates negativity, which was clearly recognized by early Hegelians such as Christian Weiße, Arnold Ruge, and Karl Rosenkranz, has been forgotten or denied in most contemporary theories of comedy.[11] The early Hegelians went to great lengths to show that comedy integrates negativity, but only by sublating it. If tragedy endorses value even as it is limited, comedy ridicules limits insofar as they deviate from value. Rosenkranz, in his *Aesthetics of the Ugly*, views the ugly, the aesthetic counterpart to evil, as a necessary, but subordinate, moment that is ultimately sublated in comedy:[12] "The ugly contrasts with the beautiful and contradicts it, while the comic can be at the same time beautiful, beautiful not in the sense of simple, positive beauty, but in the sense of aesthetic harmony, the return from contradiction to unity. In the comic, ugliness is posited as the negation of the beautiful, which, however, it negates in turn" (53, my translation).[13] The ugly, according to Vischer's somewhat earlier definition (1:362), is an appearance in opposition to an idea (we could say an act of reduction, negation, or withdrawal). The comic then is the formal treatment of the ugly in such a way as to present it as a nullity. To view the matter in a related but different way we can say with Weiße that what is immediately beautiful can never be comic; comedy requires negation (2:344).

In contrast, the late twentieth century, even more so than the early nineteenth century, may be deserving of Weiße's comment that the contemporary age tends to equate the ugly with the beautiful (1:175); it fails to see the ugly as subordinate and deserving of negation.[14] Weiße is surely correct in demanding that art and aesthetics deal with the ugly (he calls for "watchful immersion in the contradiction itself" 1:176, my translation). Only a merely thetic position would want to exclude the ugly from art, yet it is an antithetical and self-canceling position that equates the ugly with beauty or even elevates the former above the latter.

As these critics demonstrate, classical aesthetics can deal with the ugly, the disjointed, and the asymmetrical; in fact, it deals with these negative categories more consistently than most modern and postmodern aesthetic theories by dealing with them as negative.[15] The comic, in short, is not the negation of substance but the negation of the negation of substance or the negation of the ugly as the reduction of truth. In comedy we laugh at contradictory positions; we don't take them as the final truth. Showing the nullity of that which is null and nugatory, comedy does not cancel what is substantial. In his *Aesthetics of the Ugly*, Rosenkranz treats obscenities, for example, as belonging to the sphere of the comic (235–246); a function of the comic is to present them in their absurdity and as such negate them: "This whole sphere of sexual vulgarity can only be aesthetically freed through the comic" (246, my translation). The presentation of obscenities indirectly serves a moral purpose. This is the case with Aristophanes, Jonson, Grabbe, even Woody Allen, all of whom, in their unique ways, are masters of the *reductio ad absurdum*.[16] We recognize in their portrayals the mere appearance of freedom, that is, the negative freedom of libertinage, and the mere appearance of true subjectivity, that is, self-assertion without true intersubjectivity. As Weiße suggests, the focus on audience reception, its recognition of the negation of a negation, reintegrates true subjectivity into the ideal, even as false subjectivity, or the mere appearance of true subjectivity, is ridiculed and erased (1:227).

The antithetical forms of comedy share elements with the overarching contemporary desire for openness over closure, the claim that the purpose of art is to shock and decenter the viewer. Though the subversion of untenable positions is a necessary moment in any dialectic, we need not view it as the ultimate moment (Booth 60–70). Even a critique of closure depends on certain set—or closed—value judgments, for example, that openness is a higher value than

closure. Moreover, to suggest that a position is untenable is to presuppose a contrasting standard which the untenable stance fails to
attain; a critique is strengthened if the unspoken standards are
given explicit shape and a full defense. Finally, it is not self-evident that recipients are in need of shock. Perhaps disoriented and
postmodern readers most need a center. Only a center would move
us beyond the elevation of all-pervasive irony. What may be needed
after intense immersion in negativity is the self-reflexive negation
of mere negativity.

Comic Harmony and Cooperation

As a negation of negativity, comedy leaves viewers with no firm
orientation, no articulation of norms (merely a mockery of their
present positions); it is, therefore, particularly destabilizing: once
subjectivity has been reached, one cannot return to the simplicity
of objectivity. Rötscher uncovers this principle as the paradox of
Aristophanes' comedies, which mock the subjectivity that has freed
itself from objective *Sittlichkeit* and which seek in the viewer a
consciousness of this transition; thus, comedy presupposes what it
endeavors to negate, subjectivity (365–377; cf. Hegel 15:555). In a
sense, this paradox renders the greatest comic artist a tragic figure. *Recognition* of the enemy as enemy presupposes defeat of the
naive ethos. The only logical path is to move forward to a higher,
less arbitrary, concept of subjectivity, as in the comedy of intersubjectivity or the drama of reconciliation. If all reconciliatory genres
are—for whatever reason—to be avoided, the next best structure
would at least evoke recognition of the possibility of change and
exhibit some of the forces that could lead to change.

Despite the danger of disorientation, comedy is appropriate for
some audiences and clearly superior to tragedy, which is incomprehensible (except in the reduced form of a drama of suffering) to
an audience that has abandoned normative values. Comedy is also
superior, as I suggested above, to the literature of *Angst* and despair, which offers a kind of wallowing in negativity. Whereas comedy focalizes its negation, the literature of *Angst* refuses to explain
suffering, perhaps so as not to obviate its moment of self-pity. The
reductio ad absurdum of the antithetical comic genres does exhibit
for the audience the absurdity of an immersion in finitude, particularity, and negativity. If, as suggested above, however, a comedy
of intersubjectivity does contain moments of the earlier, more ex-

plicitly negative subgenres, it, too, may be capable of reaching a contemporary audience and would in fact be preferable, for it leaves the audience with speculative affirmation, not just the dialectical negation of negativity.[17]

Finally, we should consider epistemological arguments against the comedy of intersubjectivity and the drama of reconciliation. The postmodernist might be inclined to view the drama of reconciliation as a falsification of life's absurdity and meaninglessness; yet, if—as the postmodernist argues—there is no truth, to view the drama of reconciliation as a *falsification* of anything, least of all life, is contradictory. In fact the postmodernist could not consistently make such a claim (that is, a position is false, *because* . . .), even if it were true, for the grammar of "because" presupposes the transcendental principle of causality, which belongs to an overcome metaphysics of wholeness and presence.[18]

The study of genre and history need not be restricted to the ways in which historical circumstances engender the need for, or the dominance of, one genre or another. Of equal interest is the question, whether certain historical figures or subjects demand a particular genre.[19] In this case there appears to be not a dominance of history over genre but a symmetry of the two. In addition, the power of genre over history arises, the idea that art can partially transcend history by presenting new models and modes of thinking or feeling. Art is sometimes able to shape its time, genre able to influence history. Hans Robert Jauß speaks of art's *"socially formative* function" (*Literaturgeschichte* 207; *Toward an Aesthetic* 45). Art satirizes what is untenable, sketches solutions to unresolved problems, and presents utopian models. Here, too, is a counterargument to the postmodernist's hidden elevation of mimesis, the reduction of art to the chaos of the age. The beauty and harmony of great art represent in a sense an analogue of the ideal society or state in which the private interests of its citizens are in perfect harmony with the overarching interests of the state as a whole. Unfortunately, most contemporary artists and theorists merely replicate, and so perpetuate in art, the conflict, strife, and disharmony that are already present in contemporary politics and culture; for this reason I call postmodernist art mimetic rather than progressive.

The most interesting facet of the contemporary disappearance of the hero, which takes us beyond the simple transition from tragedy to comedy, is the need for intersubjective cooperation, which in turn may lead to a particular form of comedy, the comedy of intersubjectivity. The development by which the individual's autonomy is weakened can also be viewed as positive. The desire for political and economic independence is the result of atomistic and isolationist thinking. Political and economic interdependence requires cooperation; so, too, the levels of scientific knowledge that transcend the capacity of any one person. If comedy is what is possible, what is necessary is the comedy of intersubjectivity, in which the hero recognizes the value of communal cooperation and collective efforts. In the increasing importance of cooperation, a structure that has both historical and generic dimensions, we can recognize the complex interaction of history and art. Historical development toward an increasingly complex and less individualistically determined world may lead to a partial eclipse of tragedy. Yet the aesthetic response, initially reactive, can surpass history, sketching, before its historical realization, an ideal of cooperation, whether on the local level or, even more coherently, on the level of the cooperation of nations and ultimately on the level of something like the world-state—as it is now beginning to evolve with regard to human rights, telecommunications, financial markets, and the environment.[20]

7

Afterword

This book has attempted to shed light on tragedy, comedy, and the drama of reconciliation by offering a constructive and immanent critique of Hegel's discussion of these genres. Hegel can be made productive for the present even as we note his inadequacies. In developing Hegel's initial insights, I have drawn not only on the Hegelian system but also on the early Hegelians and modern literary critics, but these have been only sporadic guides, for despite the wealth of literature on Hegel and the multitude of studies on tragedy and comedy, this book is the *first* comprehensive analysis and critique of Hegel's theories of these genres.

Chapter 1 opened with reflections on contemporary approaches to genre, recognizing weaknesses in diverse historical and systematic approaches. The chapter argued that we should approach antecedents by focusing on immanent critique, and it defended a systematic method based on transcendental principles, which derive from the self-cancellation of competing views. Taking Hegel as a starting point, I argued for the need to expand the dualism of objectivity and subjectivity by adding intersubjectivity. Tragedy is dominated by the category of objectivity, comedy by subjectivity, and the drama of reconciliation by intersubjectivity, although the sequence objectivity-subjectivity-intersubjectivity can be found within each genre. I then defined art in relation to philosophy, took account of the roles of truth and emotions in art, and argued for an understanding of tragedy and comedy that transcends drama alone.

Hegel's theory of tragedy has suffered the paradoxical fate of being next to Aristotle's the most quoted and studied theory of tragedy while being almost universally discarded for its sundry

311

weaknesses. One problem is his assertion that all tragic collisions contain poles of equal value. My revision of Hegel in Chapter 2 integrates this criticism: I discuss different kinds of collisions, some of which are uneven, as in self-sacrifice and stubbornness. The second major criticism is directed toward Hegel's claim that tragedy always contains a moment of reconciliation. Partly concurring with this criticism, I separate tragedy from the drama of reconciliation. Recognizing a moment of truth in Hegel's analysis, however, I separate tragedy also from the drama of suffering, which eschews not only the reconciliatory moment but also the organic link between greatness and suffering. The final overarching criticism of Hegel is that his theory applies to only a handful of plays; my expanded definition covers more plays than does Hegel's, and the heuristic value of the categories is applied to a large range of works. In addition, I distinguish two types of Hegelian tragedy, opposition and awareness, which contain different philosophical, psychological, and dramatic structures.

The greatness of Hegel's theory of comedy is his insight into subjectivity and particularity as the defining features of the genre. Beyond this insight, Hegel's theory is greatly lacking. His sequence of comic genres is illogical, he neglects a multiplicity of comic forms, and he underestimates comedy—much as he does other antithetical genres. The analysis in Chapter 3 of the comedy of coincidence draws not only on Hegel's aesthetics, but also on his philosophy of history. The discussion of antithetical comic forms is primarily inspired by his *Logic* and the *Philosophy of Right*. The analysis of the comedy of intersubjectivity, a genre Hegel never considers, develops his diverse reflections on the speculative moment in the dialectic.

Chapter 4 views the drama of reconciliation in relation to melodrama and the problem play as well as in the context of tragedy and comedy. We can resolve Hegel's as well as Aristotle's contradictory reflections on various aspects of tragedy by distinguishing between tragedy and the drama of reconciliation. Hegel's ambiguous reflections on the drama of reconciliation are sorted, weighed, and developed.

The dialectical logic of dramatic genres—a deduction Hegel never considers as closely as do his first followers and critics—is the subject of Chapter 5. The chapter also elicits reflections on parallel, complementary, and polar structures of different genres.

Chapter 6 argues that the categories developed in this study

help us understand the disappearance of tragedy and the promi-
nence of comedy in the modern world.

An Invitation for Further Work

Although my book has focused on the universal principles that govern tragic and comic structures, I do not thereby deny the individuality of art works or the variants of the models in different ages
and cultures. Indeed, my book invites further work in a variety of
areas: on the drama of reconciliation; on individual works in the
light of their proximity to, or difference from, these models; on a
delineation of non-formal types within the typology; on the relationship between the structures I have thematized and historical
developments within the literatures of individual cultures; on the
interrelation of logic and form either in principle, in the development of art, or in individual works; and on the application of the
generic categories to tragic and comic structures in the real world.

The *drama of reconciliation* has been addressed only fleetingly
by Hegelian and non-Hegelian critics. When discussed, it has been
given various names ranging from "comedy of forgiveness" to "post-
tragedy," yet no single term has emerged as dominant.[1] We lack a
full theoretical analysis of the genre as well as histories of the theory of the genre and of the genre itself. A history of the theory of
the genre would want to draw on Hegelian aesthetics; criticism of
the Shakespearean romances; and isolated theoretical reflections,
as they have arisen in interpretations of reconciliatory works by
Sophocles, the German classical dramatists, and a small number of
others.

A history of the genre itself would want to pursue questions concerning the relation of the drama of reconciliation not only to other
genres but also to diverse historical periods, broad literary developments, and the maturation of individual authors. Why, for example, is reconciliation often the work of an older artist, as in Shakespeare's *The Tempest*, Goethe's *Faust*, or Chaplin's *Limelight*?[2] And
how do the themes of these dramas of reconciliation relate to earlier works by the same artist, for example, the smooth abdication
in *The Tempest* that contrasts so visibly with *Lear* and which represents Shakespeare's final words? Finally, the drama of reconciliation might be analyzed more closely from a systematic perspective,
not only its relation to melodrama and the problem play, but also

the ways in which it sublates traditionally tragic and comic moments, be they reversal, recognition, subjectivity, or contradiction.

The lenses developed in this study should help readers ask questions that uncover previously overlooked facets of *individual works*. Close readings of specific works, more detailed studies of subgenres, and questions concerning the relationship between individual works, subgenres, and the historical development of national literatures could be developed and would likely reinforce one another.

The categories I employ are on a certain level formal. An analysis of the *content intrinsic to different genres* could also be imagined. One could delineate the kinds of conflicts that enter into opposition or awareness, conflicts, for example, of family and state, of justice and expediency, of conscience and duty. Basic spheres of conflict could be systematically developed along with the possibilities of their combination. This would give richer material filling to our understanding of tragedy. Self-sacrifice and stubbornness could be analyzed in similar ways and also refined formally; for example, distinguishing between an excess of will, feeling, or intellect might lead to differentiation within stubbornness.

Distinctions could also be made among material types of comic conflicts. The three types of relations in the traditional *oikos*—husband/wife, parent/child, and master/servant relations—which are consistently underscored in comedies, could be examined in the light of the various subgenres I have delineated. Diverse master/servant relations, for example, could be related to the typology sketched above—servants who complement their masters, masters who mistakenly think they treat their servants justly, masters who are outspoken tyrants, servants who are smarter than their masters and who scheme for or against them, and masters who would elevate their servants to freedom and friendship.

Various comic themes and conflicts could be viewed not only systematically, but also historically. Consider the popular plot in which a father resists a marriage—successfully developed, for example, by Menander, Shakespeare, Molière, and Raimund; such a plot would seem to be less appropriate today, at least in the United States. Adultery is comic, especially when both partners are adulterous and both are upset; but in a society where adultery is not a crime, a comedy about adultery cannot succeed. Works about gender identity, to take a second example, would tend to succeed more in certain eras than in others; the theme of gender identity is less central, for example, in an age that endorses equal rights and accepts homosexuality.

Further inquiry into *historical developments within the subgenres* would also be welcome. An entire work could be written on pre-Christian, Christian, and post-Christian forms of self-sacrifice. The identity crises that are central to comic subjectivity could also be viewed by way of their historical genesis. The ancient self merely plays with his identity crisis, for his identity is in the polis, the ethos, the family; the hero remains sovereign. In modern cultures, the comic hero often survives by shifting perspectives; in archaic cultures the comic hero draws on a fundamental resource that transcends the ephemeral: his identity is deeply rooted. In the post-Cartesian world, identity is dissolved from tradition; it rests on the self in its individuality and its more or less successful relations with others. One is defined not by one's relation to tradition but by one's own experiences and choices. In Kleist, for example, identity is sought in human relations that are not embedded within broader institutions, relations without a common structure, and this inevitably leads to failure. In the modern world, as intersubjectivity breaks down even further, identity crises become almost inseparable from suffering. Whereas in Menander the causes of identity crises are external (abandoned children seek to discover their relatives and so their true identity), in modern drama the causes are generally internal or psychological: the hero, recognizing no transindividual bonds, turns inward but cannot quite determine the role or function of the self. Moreover, in the ancient world, where the self is fully embedded within his sphere, the kinds of identity crises we see, for example, in Sternheim, where heroes move from one class to another, are unthinkable.

Any transhistorical typology would be enriched if we analyzed in detail the historical development of subthemes that are central to a genre. Antiquity, not as developed as modernity in its conception of subjectivity, does not know the misanthrope theme in its richness as does modernity—despite Menander's *Dyskolos* or Lucian's *Timon, or the Misanthrope*. The dissolution of the polis and the increasing stress on subjectivity contributed to this shift. Another turning point lay with the development of Christianity: its transcendent telos has nurtured negation of the world. Entirely new in modernity is, moreover, a development that begins with Molière's Alceste: the misanthrope's need for love and communicative rationality, which stems from the increasing importance of strategic thinking and thus the greater need for its contrary. In their accounts of the misanthrope theme, neither Gerhard Hay nor Bernhard Sorg recognizes the love interest as a historical shift, but Sorg does acknowledge that the misanthrope develops into the artist and vice versa, a process that mirrors modernity's elevation of subjectivity and self-reflection and its increasing discontent.[3] These and other historical transitions could be developed with the help of the categories employed in this study.

Numerous broad questions of genre and history also remain as yet unexplored. A difficult question such as why so few great dramas exist from the period of German realism may be easier to answer if we divide the question into subquestions, generated from the typology outlined in this study. The drama of reconciliation, an idealizing rather than mimetic form of art, is obviously incompatible with any strict definition of realism. Hebbel, for example, was a vehement critic of reconciliation (2776 and 4150). Tragedy, with its idealizing moments and focus on great characters, is also hardly compatible with such tenets of realism as mimesis and broad, many-layered portrayals, as was evident already to the early Lukács ("Metaphysics of Tragedy" 229). Of tragic subgenres, the tragedy of collision is most in harmony with realism: it is less idealizing than self-sacrifice and more complex and comprehensive than the other tragic forms. The drama of suffering also shares elements of realism. In this light we might consider Hebbel and Büchner, whose works at times appear to fulfill a concept of realist drama. Certain elements of comedy also appear to conflict with realism: the magical elements of coincidence; the idealizing resolutions of coincidence and intersubjectivity; the self-reflexivity of absolute irony; and, to a degree, the exaggerated flaws found in most heroes of the antithetical subgenres. Nonetheless, among the most realistic of dramatic genres are the antithetical subgenres of comedy, especially negation, with its focus on societal contradictions; and withdrawal, with its subtlety of portrayal. Not surprisingly, Sternheim and Schnitzler, not realistic authors but very adept at mirroring the society of their day, experimented with these subgenres.

Numerous correlations could be developed: Enlightenment and the comedy of intersubjectivity; Storm and Stress and the tragedy of stubbornness; German *Klassik* and the drama of reconciliation; Romanticism and the comedy of absolute irony; naturalism and the drama of suffering. In addition, we might examine the ways the genres relate to one another during various periods and in eras of transition. Why, for example, do the drama of suffering and the comedy of social negation appear to surface and dominate simultaneously or in close succession to one another?

Even if we were to assent to the historical claim that pure tragedies (or comedies) have disappeared, we could still argue for further analysis of these forms, for they continue to live in performance; moreover, any development of new or mixed genres tends to build on earlier foundations even as it extends or combines, modifies or inverts them.[4] We must know what is being modified in order to grasp the new. In this sense, modern dramas of suffering and tragicomedies can be studied in relation to earlier tragic and comic archetypes: this, too, is a wide field of inquiry.

When reflecting on historical developments within genres, we should not ignore typological considerations. A precise knowledge of subgenres can help us delimit misleading historical claims. In his book on fin-de-siècle comedy, Peter Haida asserts: "The positive ending is a constitutive element of comedy, its condition" (19, my translation). He then shows how modern works, beginning with Hauptmann's *The Beaver Coat*, shift this genre expectation, creating problematic, rather than harmonic, endings: "This suggests that one speak not of a final stage or abdication of comedy but rather of an evolution of the genre. This further development follows from a loosening of the principle 'positive ending,' which had been constitutive of the genre, and its replacement by a negative ending. Precisely this subversion points to the continuing membership of plays within the genre, which thereby is newly defined" (156–157, my translation).[5]

A historical shift does indeed occur, but we overstress it if we fail to distinguish the comedy of negation, which had previously been harmonic, from the comedies of reduction and withdrawal, which evidence a long tradition of less harmonic endings. To cite *Anatol* and *Professor Bernhardi* as examples of this historical shift is to overstate the case insofar as these works belong to subgenres with problematic endings that reach back, for example, to Lessing's *The Jews* and Molière's *The Misanthrope*. We would do better to isolate what is genuinely new, for example, an increase in the writing and performance of non-harmonic comedies, such as those of reduction and social negation, and the virtual disappearance of comedies of intersubjectivity.

Haida's historical, but untypological, study also errs when it argues that the more traditional genres have lost aesthetic appeal: "To be sure, the old form continues to exist alongside the new, but it loses all meaning as an artistic possibility of expression. It becomes trivialized and serves only the purpose of entertainment" (157, my translation). Do all modern comedies of intersubjectivity (or contemporary performances of older comedies of intersubjectivity) have merely entertainment value? Changes in aesthetic taste are not as exclusionary as Haida's limited definitions suggest. Moreover, to argue that good comedy necessarily lacks harmony is to be as arbitrarily restrictive as the eighteenth-century aestheticians were in arguing exclusively for the contrary view. In general, the modern stipulation that all good art is open-ended is no less spurious and dogmatic a genre restriction than the eighteenth-century imperative for closure.

The tragic and comic categories developed in this study could be expanded from literature onto *life*. We might view Martin Luther King, Jr., for example, as a tragic hero of self-sacrifice who risked his life protesting the injustices of his age; or Mikhael Gorbachev as a tragic hero of awareness who tried to find the balance between too much reform, which might, by creating a backlash, undermine his power to continue reforms, and too little reform, such that progress might become unjustly stalled. Comic reduction is evident in certain aspects of political correctness, for example, Actor's Equity's failed efforts in the Summer of 1990 to dictate the racial composition of the cast for *Miss Saigon*. The categories of tragedy and comedy can aid us in comprehending dramatic conflict in the world.

*

If art is the unity of philosophical truth and sensuous representation, a typology like my own cannot exhaustively elucidate the sphere of the beautiful. The typology can explain, deductively, why the drama of reconciliation is in principle better than the drama of suffering, but it cannot fully explain how a particular example of one subgenre is better or worse than another instance of the same genre. The typology cannot fully explain. for example, why a particular tragedy of awareness is a poor work. Each subgenre has better and weaker representatives. We can speak of a superior tragedy of stubbornness and a poor drama of reconciliation. Indeed, a particular tragedy of stubbornness may be more beautiful than a particular drama of reconciliation. Some dramas of reconciliation, even as they transcend melodrama, are not quite as psychologically differentiated, linguistically sharp, or socially oriented as we might prefer. Büchner's *Woyzeck*, though read here as a drama of suffering, is surely greater than all of Paul Ernst combined. We must recognize that strength in form can outweigh philosophical weaknesses. In the reception of every art work—less so in literature, more so in film—are elements that have to do with anthropology, biology, and physiology; these cannot be deduced a priori. Rational beings with completely different sensuous organs might be unable to enjoy our greatest films—even if their subjective sense of time were to deviate by only a fraction of a second.

The philosophical structures articulated in this book are essential to the evaluation of art. They alone, however, do not allow us to value art appropriately or to comprehend the history of art in its finite details. Specific formal aspects must also be taken into consideration: in literature, sound and syntax; in film, color and editing; in theater, staging and acting. In short, while a philosophical typology based on a priori principles is essential to the evaluation of art, it leaves us with structures that need to be complemented by detailed immersion in the finite dimensions of individual works; we must not neglect those aspects that elicit a sensuous response.[6] Precisely this split between abstract structure and finite detail allows us to understand how a work like *Woyzeck* can be great and still have weaknesses. Art cannot be exhausted by isolated analyses of either its philosophical or its sensuous structures; nonetheless, just as I have argued that literary critics can benefit from the application of philosophical structures to art, so too could they benefit from deeper immersion not only in the traditional tools of rhetoric but also in the sciences of anthropology, physiology, and biology. Hegel's general argument that the philosophy of spirit must also be understood with the assistance of the philosophy of nature, which it presupposes, seems especially true for the philosophy of art, whose object, beauty, is the synthesis of spiritual content and sensuous form.

APPENDIX A
TRAGEDY

Tragedy is an action in which the hero's greatness leads inexorably to suffering. Enumeratively stated, the hero's suffering derives from moral greatness (the tragedy of self-sacrifice), formal greatness (the tragedy of stubbornness), the coupling of both with an ineradicable conflict (the tragedy of opposition), or the coupling of both with an ineradicable conflict of which the hero is conscious (the tragedy of awareness).

1. The Tragedy of Self-Sacrifice

The hero acts according to the good even as she knows she will suffer for her actions. Selected examples:[1] Aeschylus, *Seven against Thebes* (though this also includes moments of stubbornness); Sophocles, *Oedipus Rex* (Oedipus valiantly seeks the murderer—despite the obstacles placed in front of him by the external world—and does not waver when the search comes back to himself) and *Antigone* (Antigone); Euripides, *Hippolytus* (in the sense that the hero refuses to save himself by breaking his oath of silence); Gryphius, *Catharina von Georgien* and *Papinianus*; Lessing, *Emilia Galotti* (Emilia wills death to preserve her purity); Klinger, *Medea in the Caucasus* (Klinger enriches the structure of tragic self-sacrifice by transforming a former hero of stubbornness, Medea, into a hero of self-sacrifice and awareness; Medea overcomes her disgust with humankind and relinquishes her powers in order to preach goodness. That Medea fails with all but two individuals reinforces her earlier expectations of the majority but does not diminish the tragic greatness of her sacrifice); Schiller, *Don Carlos* (the Queen, eventually Posa, later also Don Carlos) and *Wallenstein* (Max);

Hölderlin, *Empedocles*; Goethe, *Faust I* (Gretchen, though only partially);[2] Dumas, *Camille*; Hebbel, *Agnes Bernauer* (Agnes wills her death to preserve the sanctity of love); Dickens, *A Tale of Two Cities* (Sydney Carton); Kaiser, *The Burghers of Calais*; Dreyer, *The Passion of Joan of Arc*; Eliot, *Murder in the Cathedral*; Dieterle, *The Life of Emile Zola* (though the tragedy is followed by strong moments of reconciliation); Hemingway, *For Whom the Bell Tolls*; Brecht, *Mother Courage* (Kattrin) and *Master Puntila and His Servant Matti* (Athi); Rossellini, *Open City*; Ford, *The Fugitive*; Miller, *The Crucible* and *Incident at Vichy*; Bergman, *The Seventh Seal*; Bolt, *A Man for All Seasons*; Hochhuth, *The Deputy*; Weiss, *The Investigation* (Lili Tofler); Duigan, *Romero*; and Zwick, *Glory*.

2a. The Tragedy of Stubbornness

The hero adopts a clearly untenable position but displays outstanding secondary or formal virtues. Selected examples: Sophocles, *Ajax* and *Antigone* (Creon); Euripides, *Medea* and *Hecuba* (though the latter is also in part a drama of suffering); Seneca, *Medea*; Shakespeare, *Richard III* (though principally a melodrama, it partakes of stubbornness), *Othello* (insofar as one stresses Othello's strong, but misdirected, trust; his absolute love that can tolerate no doubt; the consistency of his final actions; and his sense of justice that knows no flexibility or pardon), *Macbeth*, *Timon of Athens*, and *Coriolanus*; Lessing, *Philotas*; Schlegel, *Canut*; Goethe, *Götz von Berlichingen* and *Faust I* (Faust, though subordinate moments of opposition and awareness need not be overlooked); Leisewitz, *Julius von Tarent*; Schiller, *The Robbers* (Karl Moor), *Fiesko*, and *Don Carlos* (Posa and Philipp); Kleist, *Michael Kohlhaas*; Grillparzer, *Medea* and *A Fraternal Quarrel in the House of Hapsburg* (in a particular reading); Büchner, *Danton's Death* (Robespierre); Ludwig, *The Hereditary Forester* (though the play also includes the opposition of Stein and Förster as well as two forms of justice and elements of suffering, including improbable coincidences and misunderstandings); Hebbel, *The Niebelungs* (Hagen and Kriemhild) and *Herodes and Marianne*; Ibsen, *Brand*, *The Wild Duck*, and *John Gabriel Borkman*; Barrie, *The Admirable Crichton*; Pirandello, *Henry IV*; O'Neill, *Mourning Becomes Electra*; Camus, *Caligula*; Zuckmayer, *The Devil's General* (though moments of self-sacrifice and awareness surface as well); Thomas Mann, *Doctor Faustus*; Ford, *Fort Apache*; Lean, *The Bridge on the River Kwai*; Dürrenmatt, *The Promise*; Nossack, *The Testament of Lucius Eu-*

rinus; Fassbinder, *The Marriage of Maria Braun*; Jelinek, *Clara S.*; and Sheridan, *The Field*.

2b. The Tragedy of Opposition

This is the Hegelian form of tragedy, the collision of two goods, insofar as the colliding parties, whether individuals, institutions, or principles, do not recognize the intrinsic goodness of the positions they oppose. Selected examples: Aeschylus, *The Persians*, *Prometheus Bound* (though it also evidences moments of stubbornness), and *The Choephori*; Sophocles, *Antigone* (Antigone versus the state); Euripides, *Hippolytus* and *Bacchae*; Shakespeare, *Julius Caesar* and *Antony and Cleopatra* (though the drama is not exhausted by this one subgenre); Schiller, *Intrigue and Love* (in the limited sense of a collision between the rights of individuals and the [historical] rights of class), *Wallenstein* (Wallenstein versus Octavio and the Kaiser), and *Maria Stuart* (though Maria tends toward self-sacrifice, the more complex Elizabeth exhibits stubbornness and even flashes of awareness); Goethe, *Torquato Tasso* (though the play hints, however slightly, at reconciliation); Grabbe, *Don Juan and Faust*; Büchner, *Danton's Death* (assuming one can make a case for Danton as a tragic hero and not simply a protagonist of suffering); Hebbel, *Judith* and *Gyges and His Ring*; Grillparzer, *Libussa* (even as it includes reconciliatory moments that transcend opposition, for example, the riddles about wholeness and the marriage of Libussa and Primislaus); Ibsen, *Emperor and Galilean* (though Julian is ultimately portrayed as a hero of stubbornness) and *Ghosts* (vitality versus duty); Storm, *The Rider on the White Horse*; Fontane, *Effi Briest* (though the novel ends with moments of recognition); Toller, *Man and the Masses* (though Sonja Irene L., in trying to mediate between the official and the nameless person, might be viewed in the light of awareness); Shaw, *Saint Joan*; von Sternberg, *The Blue Angel*; Brecht, *The Measures Taken*; Ford, *The Man Who Shot Liberty Valance*; Joffe, *The Mission* (though it contains moments of all tragic subgenres); and Gurney, *Another Antigone* (though we also recognize a parody of tragedy).

3. The Tragedy of Awareness

This is the Hegelian form of tragedy, insofar as the collision takes place within a single individual, who is aware of the conflict and recognizes the validity and untenability of each alternative. Selected examples: Aeschylus, *The Suppliants* (Pelasgus, though the suppliants' drama of suffering tends to overshadow his moment of awareness); Sophocles, *Antigone* (Haemon, though he is less an active hero of awareness than he is the victim of tragic opposition); Euripides, *Iphigenia at Aulis* (although the play ends with a miracle that partially dissolves the tragedy); the *Song of Hildebrand*; the *Song of the Niebelungs* (Rüedeger's promise to avenge Kriemhilt's suffering and the obedience of the vassal collide with the loyalty of friendship and the sacredness of hospitality); Shakespeare, *Hamlet*; Racine, *Bérénice*; Schiller, *The Maid of Orleans* (Johanna's humanity and love versus the divine command to spare no enemy and renounce love, though her final resolve borders on self-sacrifice); Kleist, *Penthesilea* (though the play also contains moments of awareness, insofar as Penthesilea embodies the central conflicts within her own psyche); Grillparzer, *Sappho*, *The Argonauts*, and *The Waves of Sea and Love*; Hebbel, *Agnes Bernauer* (Ernst); James, *The Princess Casamassima*; Melville, *Billy Budd, Foretopman*; Thomas Mann, *Death in Venice*; Anderson, *Winterset* (though the play is not without moments of simple suffering and the hint of reconciliation); Anouilh, *Antigone*; Brecht, *The Good Person of Sezuan*; Hitchcock, *Shadow of a Doubt*; Camus, *The Just Assassins*; Maass, *The Ice of Cape Sabine*; Hochwälder, *The Holy Experiment* (above all for the Provincial); and Endo, *Silence* (Rodrigues betrays his creed so that others will not be sacrificed; whether this action is evidence of tragic greatness or a sign of inconsistency and weakness cannot be answered unambiguously).

The Drama of Suffering

In the drama of suffering, the protagonist's suffering does not derive from adherence to a morally justified stance, formal virtues, or a philosophical conflict. The character suffers of her own weaknesses (self-inflicted suffering) or external forces (involuntary suffering). The genre appears to be tragic but is not. Selected examples: Euripides, *Trojan Women*, *Hecuba* (in its earliest parts), and *Andromache*; Shakespeare, *Othello* (insofar as Othello is the victim of jealousy, the rhetoric of Iago, and a society that treats him as an outsider and alien, thereby diminishing his self-respect and confidence); Lillo, *The London Merchant* and *Fatal Curiosity*; Gerstenberg, *Ugolino*; Wagner, *The Child Murderess*; Klinger, *The Twins* (though some critics might want to see in Guelfo a tragedy of stubbornness); Schiller, *Don Carlos* (Don Carlos initially and Eboli); Goethe, *The Natural Daughter* (though the drama ends in partial reconciliation); Grillparzer, *King Ottocar's Fortune and Fall* and *The Jewess of Toledo*; Grabbe, *Duke Theodor von Gothland*; Büchner, *Woyzeck*; Strindberg, *The Father* and *Miss Julie*; Maeterlinck, *The Blind*; Pinero, *The Second Mrs. Tanqueray*; Gorky, *The Lower Depths* and *Summer Folk*; Masefield, *The Tragedy of Nan* (the dominant motif is involuntary suffering, even though the work culminates in a moment of stubbornness); Hauptmann, *Before Dawn*, *The Weavers*, *Drayman Henschel*, *Rose Bernd*, and *Before Sunset*; Wedekind, *The Awakening of Spring*; Toller, *Hinkemann*; O'Casey, *Juno and the Paycock* (though one could argue that Juno reaches a tragedy of suffering with her refusal to despair and ability to survive—in contrast to the almost comic as well as weak [and selfish] figure of Boyle); Hitchcock, *Easy Virtue*; Cocteau, *The Infernal Machine*; O'Neill, *Long Day's Journey into Night*; Sartre, *No Exit*; Camus, *The Misunderstanding*; Anouilh, *Romeo and Jeannette*; Williams, *A Streetcar Named Desire*; Miller, *Death of a Salesman*; Albee, *The Zoo Story*; Pinter, *The Caretaker*; Frisch, *Andorra*; Handke, *Kaspar*; Mailer, *The Deer Park*; Rudkin, *Afore Night Come*; Kroetz, *Homeworker* and *Farmyard*; Fassbinder, *The Merchant of Four Seasons*; Shepard, *The Curse of the Starving Class*; Strauss, *Big and Little*; Lee, *Do the Right Thing*; and Mamet, *Oleanna*.

Paratragedy, or the Tragedy of Suffering

In paratragedy, or the tragedy of suffering, the hero's suffering does not initially derive from greatness; nonetheless, suffering eventually engenders a form of greatness. Selected examples: Pseudo-Seneca, *Hercules Oetaeus*; Shakespeare, *King Lear* (in a particular reading); Webster, *The Duchess of Malfi*; Calderón, *The Mayor of Zalamea*; Rowe, *The Tragedy of Jane Shore*; Meyer, *The Suffering of a Young Boy*; Tolstoy, *The Power of Darkness* and *The Death of Ivan Ilyich*; Synge, *Riders to the Sea*; Thoma, *Magdalena*; O'Neill, *The Hairy Ape* and *Desire Under the Elms* (Abbie also evidences elements of stubbornness); Ford, *The Informer*; Camus, *The Plague*; Hansberry, *A Raisin in the Sun*; and Sheridan, *In the Name of the Father*.

Appendix B
Comedy

Comedy is an action in which we see a contrast between contingent particularity and x, whereby the content of x is variable. In the thetic and, to a greater degree, the multiple antithetical forms, the contrast remains even at the work's conclusion. Only in the synthetic mode is the contrast fully overcome.

1. The Comedy of Coincidence

The hero follows his own particular desires and, led by coincidence and fortune, reaches the good. Selected examples: Menander, *The Girl from Samos* and *The Arbitration*; Terence, *The Girl from Andros*; Shakespeare, *The Comedy of Errors*, *A Midsummer Night's Dream*, and *Twelfth Night, or What You Will* (with some restrictions); Holberg, *Masquerades*; Raimund, *The Peasant as Millionaire* and *The Spendthrift*; Nestroy, *The Girl from the Environs* and *The Matchmaker* (though the two works also contain distancing, almost satiric, reflections on the very form to which they belong); Shaw, *Man and Superman*; Chaplin, *The Gold Rush*; Zuckmayer, *The Merry Vineyard*; Conway, *Libeled Lady*; Hawks, *Bringing up Baby*; Kanin, *Bachelor Mother*; Koster, *The Bishop's Wife* and *Harvey*; Hitchcock, *The Trouble with Harry*; Ashby, *Being There* (though it also contains elements of a comedy of negation); and Allen, *A Midsummer Night's Sex Comedy*.

327

2a. The Comedy of Reduction

The hero has an intuitive desire for truth, which is then reduced to its lowest level. The hero's inadequate means reduce, and thus falsify, an originally substantial goal. Selected examples: Aristophanes, *Acharnians*, *Lysistrata* (the comic reduction of love to lust, however, also points toward an expansion—lust as symbolic of friendship and union—and so the play ends harmonically), and *Ecclesiazusae* (though victories are gained, they include comic reductions); Shakespeare, *Love's Labor's Lost*; Cervantes, *Don Quixote*; Gryphius, *Absurda Comica or Mr. Peter Squentz* (a reduction of the desire to produce beautiful art); Molière, *The School for Wives*; Lessing, *The Jews* and *The Young Scholar* (the play entails a reduction of wisdom, though this is not the full focus of the play); Lenz, *The Tutor* (Major von Berg and Wenzeslaus—though for different reasons); Kleist, *Amphitryon* (Sosias—he would sacrifice his goals rather than himself, and is thus comic rather than tragic); Keller, *The Fool of Manegg*; Schnitzler, *Anatol*; Hofmannsthal, *The Difficult Man* (Stani, Cresence, Hechingen, Antoinette, Altenwyl, and Edine); Musil, *The Enthusiasts*; Keaton, *Our Hospitality* (a partial comedy of reduction and unusual in the sense that, rather than focusing on weak means, the work stresses the comic implications of a strictly defined—and thus reduced—concept of goodness); Wilder, *Heaven's My Destination* (though moments of withdrawal surface as well); Brecht, *Master Puntila and His Servant Matti*; Frisch, *The Firebugs*; Merz and Qualtinger, *Der Herr Karl*; Hampton, *The Philanthropist*; and Bernhard, *The World Reformer*.

2b. The Comedy of Negation

The hero's goals are invalid and egotistical, but the hero nonetheless displays limited secondary virtues, for example, wit, discipline, or power of persuasion. Substantial means are employed to serve an insubstantial end, which the hero does not reach. The comedy of negation can be loosely divided into the comedy of individual negation and the comedy of social negation. In the comedy of social negation, subjectivity is not isolated. We see a plurality of dominant subjects, all serving insubstantial ends and undermining not only themselves but each other. Selected examples of the comedy of individual negation: Aristophanes, *The Clouds* (though the force that defeats injustice is itself unjust); Jonson, *Volpone*; Molière, *Tartuffe* and *The Miser*; Goldoni, *The Liar*; Kleist, *The Broken Jug*; Bäuerle, *The Burghers of Vienna*; Raimund, *The Spendthrift* (Wolf); Nestroy, *A Man Full of Nothing* (Madame Schleyer); Hauptmann, *The Beaver Coat* (though the play deviates in its conclusion from the expected pattern); Wedekind, *The Marquis of Keith* (though the play also contains a protagonist of reduction, Scholz, and its moments of genuine suffering push it in the direction of tragicomedy); Hofmannsthal, *The Difficult Man* (Neuhoff and Vinzenz); and Witkiewicz, *Gyubal Wahazar*.

Selected examples of the comedy of social negation: Aristophanes, *The Birds* (the perfect state suffers from human imperfections—continued interest in power and demagoguery—though one could also recognize in the play a comedy of reduction); Congreve, *The Double Dealer*; Sheridan, *The School for Scandal*; Gogol, *The Inspector General* (though this could also be read in the light of reduction—the desire to identify with a higher principle); Nestroy, *The Talisman*; Schnitzler, *The Green Cockatoo* and *The Vast Domain*; Hauptmann, *The Red Rooster*; Heinrich Mann, *The Untertan*; Sternheim, *The Trousers, The Strongbox, Burgher Schippel*, and *The Snob*; Chaplin, *Sunnyside*; Brecht, *A Man is a Man, The Three Penny Opera* (which includes a parody of coincidence), *The Rise and Fall of the City of Mahagonny* (though we might also view the work as a reduction of contentment to the physical and to the purchasability of justice), *Fear and Misery in the Third Reich, The Resistible Rise of Arturo Ui*, and *Schweyk in the Second World War*; Fleißer, *Pioniers in Ingolstadt*; Horváth, *Stories from the Vienna Woods*; Zuckmayer, *The Captain of Köpenick* (though subordinate moments of reduction surface as well, for example, in Hoprecht and Obermüller); and Genet, *The Balcony* (though one might prefer to see the play as a reduction of ritual and myth or as a work of absolute irony that denies meaning and rejects all institutions).

2c. The Comedy of Withdrawal

The hero tries to stand up against a world dominated by unjust subjectivity and fails, primarily owing to the weaknesses of society, but also because of the hero's inflexibility or callousness or withdrawal. Selected examples: Molière, *The Misanthrope*; Schnitzler, *Professor Bernhardi*; Dürrenmatt, *Romulus the Great* and *The Physicists*; and Ionesco, *Rhinoceros*.

3. The Comedy of Intersubjectivity

The hero reaches intersubjectivity, and thus true subjectivity, after passing through false subjectivity or negativity. Selected examples: Plautus, *The Pot of Gold* (as far as fragmentary evidence indicates) and *The Prisoners* (though this also contains strong moments of coincidence); Terence, *Adelphoe*; Shakespeare, *Much Ado About Nothing*; Dekker, *The Shoemaker's Holiday*; Wycherly, *The Plain Dealer* (though until the end it fits the pattern of withdrawal—we both admire Manly for his moral principles and recoil from him for his surly and indecorous behavior); Lessing, *Minna von Barnhelm* (with some restrictions); Goldsmith, *She Stoops to Conquer*; Raimund, *The Peasant as Millionaire* (though the play includes significant moments of coincidence as well), *The King of the Alps and the Misanthrope*, and *The Spendthrift* (though the play is not without moments of coincidence and negation); Grillparzer, *Woe to the Liar!*; Nestroy, *A Man Full of Nothing*; Freytag, *The Journalists*; Hofmannsthal, *The Difficult Man* (Hans Karl and Helen, though substantial questions remain) and *The Incorruptible One*; Capra, *Mr. Deeds Goes to Town* and *You Can't Take It With You*; Lubitsch, *The Shop Around the Corner*; Sturges, *The Lady Eve*; Cukor, *The Philadelphia Story* and *Adam's Rib*; Gardner, *A Thousand Clowns* (which overcomes a well-developed comedy of withdrawal); Allen, *Play it Again, Sam, Broadway Danny Rose*, and *Zelig*.

The Comedy of Absolute Irony

As in the comedy of negation, subjectivity dominates, but in the comedy of absolute irony no measures exist against which to recognize valid as opposed to invalid positions. Everything is ironized, including the act of ironization. Two possibilities follow: the non-art of absolute irony, in which we see nonsense and the self-cancellation of all positions, including even the claim that the work is art; and the metacomedy of absolute irony, in which the negation of negativity leads to a hidden and complex affirmation. Selected examples of the non-art of absolute irony: Ionesco, *The Chairs* (in a particular reading); Beckett, *Endgame* (in a particular reading); Hildesheimer, *The Delay* and *Nocturne*; and Handke, *Offending the Audience* (in a particular reading). Selected examples of the metacomedy of absolute irony: Grabbe, *Jest, Satire, Irony and Deeper*

Significance (though it also has moments that transcend this subgenre); Büchner, *Leonce and Lena* (though it, too, contains a wealth of subgenres); Wilde, *The Importance of Being Earnest*; Pirandello, *Right You Are (If You Think You Are)* and *Each in His Own Way*; Kafka, *The Trial*; and Beckett, *Waiting for Godot.*

APPENDIX C
DRAMA OF RECONCILIATION

In the drama of reconciliation, the conflict is serious and substantial but ends harmonically. The genre encompasses initially tragic works whose resolutions take place on stage and not in the consciousness of the audience as well as comedies of intersubjectivity. The genre includes moments of melodrama and the problem play even as it transcends them. Selected examples, not including works listed under the comedy of intersubjectivity: Aeschylus, *Eumenides*; Euripides, *Helen*; Sophocles, *Philoctetes* and *Oedipus at Colonus*; Kālidāsa, *Shākuntalā*; Roswitha of Gandersheim, *Abraham* and *Pafnutius*; Hartmann von Aue, *Gregorius*; Marston, *The Malcontent*; Shakespeare, *Henry V* (though one could focus on the brutal path toward peace and overlooked contradictions, thus arguing against inclusion within the drama of reconciliation),[3] *Measure for Measure* (though the text might arguably be called a problem play), *Cymbeline*, *The Tempest*, and *The Winter's Tale*; Calderón, *Life is a Dream*; Corneille, *The Cid* and *Cinna*; Gryphius, *Cardenio and Celinde or Ill-Fated Lovers*; Racine, *Esther*; Steele, *The Conscious Lovers*; Voltaire, *Alzire* and *The Orphan of China*; Lessing, *Nathan The Wise*; Goethe, *The Siblings, Iphigenia at Tauris*, and *Faust II*; Kotzebue, *Misanthropy and Regret* (although the drama is not completely free of melodramatic moments); Schiller, *William Tell*; Kleist, *Prince Friedrich von Homburg*; Grillparzer, *A Loyal Servant of His Master* (though the drama contains strong, if subordinate, moments of tragic self-sacrifice [Erny] and stubbornness [Bancbanus]); Ibsen, *The Lady from the Sea*; Hirschfeld, *The Mothers* (though minor elements of the problem play surface as well); Strindberg, *Easter*; Maeterlinck, *The Blue Bird*; Hofmannsthal, *Everyman*; Ernst, *Ariadne at Naxos* and

Prussian Spirit; Marcel, *The Broken World*; Hitchcock, *Murder!*, *Young and Innocent*, *Spellbound*, *The Paradine Case*, *Under Capricorn*, *I Confess*, *Rear Window*, *North by Northwest*, and *Marnie*; Brecht, *The Yeasayer and the Naysayer* and *The Caucasian Chalk Circle*; Renoir, *Grand Illusion*; Ford, *Young Mr. Lincoln*; Capra, *Mr Smith Goes to Washington*, *Meet John Doe*, and *It's a Wonderful Life* (though the extent to which Capra's works transcend melodrama is open to debate); Werfel, *Jacobowsky and the Colonel*; Curtiz, *Casablanca* (whether the film is melodramatic or reconciliatory is arguable); Rapper, *Now, Voyager*; Hawks, *Red River*; Chaplin, *Limelight*; Kurosawa, *Ikiru*; Johnson, *The Man in the Gray Flannel Suit*; Lumet, *Twelve Angry Men*; and Breuer, *The Gospel at Colonus*.

NOTES

Preface

1. For the latest statement on what issues the new edition must confront, see Gethmann-Siefert, "Ästhetik oder Philosophie der Kunst."

Chapter 1: Introduction

1. The descriptive approach need not be restricted to the past; it can be a non-evaluative description of what is current, as in Olsen esp. 34.

2. On the interdependence of philosophical system and generic classification, see Szondi's discussion of the affinities between German Idealism and genre theory in "Von der normativen zur spekulativen Gattungspoetik" esp. 10, 12, and 17.

3. Koelb draws this conclusion with regard to tragedy, arguing that because tragedy is an institution that changes through time, any attempt to define it is to attempt "the impossible" ("Problem" 252); the use of tragedy in anything other than a restricted (historical) frame "is of no use whatsoever; on the contrary, it is a positive hindrance to rational inquiry" ("Problem" 264). A typical illustration with regard to comedy is Haberland, who, after offering a description of comic theory from Plato to Jean Paul, concludes: "there is no one definitive explanation or theory of the comic, for the comic spirit alters with time and place" (127).

4. For a discussion of contemporary resistance to genre, including a parade of quotations along these lines, see Rosmarin esp. 6–8. Though the resistance can be related to the contemporary elevation of difference, it does have a history. Croce had argued that genres do not exist (32–38), although, contradicting himself, he also suggested that all works transgress the boundaries of a particular genre (37). Peter Szondi and Tzvetan

Todorov, two of the greatest European literary critics of this half-century, were deeply involved in genre criticism despite the fact that more recent and arguably less interesting critics view genre criticism as passé. The most sustained contemporary defense of genre criticism is Fowler's, though his defense does not extend to systems of genres. See also Ralph Cohen, who defends the study of genre specifically against its postmodern critics.

5. Apel and Habermas argue that a consensus theory of truth refers to an ideal consensus, not the real consensus of the present; however, because no material norms follow from the ideal consensus, even the most demanding theory of consensus can lead to incoherent positions.

6. I do not want to disparage historical studies, which have a value and fascination of their own, but I find it hard to believe that anyone might seriously claim that the essence of comedy is captured by, for example, Schrimpf's account of the *history* of the words *Komödie* and *Lustspiel*, yet many genre studies offer no systematic or aesthetic perspective beyond the merely historical.

7. Cf. Olson (*Tragedy* 31) and Hans Wagner 36. A unity is obligatory, although one might want to argue in favor of a loose or imprecise unity, along the lines of a Wittgensteinian "family of resemblances" (67), aspects of genre, including texts, grouped together for conceptual convenience. Though we do not find something common to all the texts, we do see similarities and relationships between them. Fowler, for example, advocates this view (40–44). But it would not be difficult to see in such a theory, even as it seemingly contains the virtue of unity, the deficiencies of historicist and inductive genre-theorizing. Family resemblances easily dissolve into non-distinctions: How do we distinguish tragedy from a plane crash? How do we argue the distinction between comic negation and lying? What method allows us to separate slapstick from the speculative structures of coincidence? If only resemblances and loose similarities define the genre, how can the genre become exclusive in any meaningful sense? By what means can we assert with confidence that Kleist's *The Broken Jug* is not tragic, but comic? If rigor disappears from genre criticism, then any theory can claim validity—resemblances are infinitely loose, infinitely extendable, and infinitely probabilistic. In arguing that what all tragedies have in common is that they are tragedies, the Wittgensteinian is close to the nominalist who argues that what all tragedies have in common is only that they are called tragedies. She is far removed from the realist (or objective idealist) who argues that all tragedies have in common the property x. Not surprisingly, Fishelov notes that advocates of the family resemblance the-

ory often contradict themselves in their practical criticism by referring to the necessary conditions of a genre (57–61).

8. For a succinct introduction to basic terms and issues in contemporary genre criticism, see Hernadi esp. 1–9. For a more detailed introduction, see Hempfer.

9. In North American literary criticism this appears to derive from a longstanding preference for empiricism. Consider, for example, Kerr, who wittily asserts: "I would rather lose a definition than a tragedy" (87). Even a critic such as Frye, who is interested in archetypal patterns, unabashedly confesses his preference for induction (*Anatomy* 6–7). In Germany, where we might expect a more systematic approach, the influence of Viëtor's empiricism still reigns. See, for example, Trautwein 88.

10. Under the pragmatic method I also include approaches that purport to "intuit" the elements of a genre. Viëtor speaks of "a divining intuition of generic elements from the poetically most significant representatives of the genre" (308, my translation). The riddle of how a critic such as Viëtor can be both inductive and pragmatic is solved as soon as we remember that pure induction is impossible.

11. Skeptics unwilling to recognize a correspondence theory of truth frequently endorse a consensus theory. Simon, however, has unravelled the irony that consensus presupposes correspondence—not of subject and object but of subject and subject. See 1–34.

12. Rosmarin calls her method deductive, but rather than developing it from systematic philosophy, she derives it from her pragmatic purpose, from a premise that is not itself deduced. The lack of reflexive justification suggests that it has little in common with a deductive approach that starts with first principles.

13. Henry Schmidt's analysis of drama endings is an example of a pragmatic approach that so assiduously avoids the stigma of systematization that its randomness and its shifts between different types of defining categories diminish its value. Critics today are extraordinarily precise in their historical inquiries but completely unambitious as far as systematization is concerned, even as reflection on systematic issues remains unavoidable.

14. For an illustration of an earlier version of pragmatic aesthetics, complete with political ramifications, see Rosenberg.

15. Though the deductive approach is viewed here as superior, it is best coupled, as I suggest below, with the strengths of induction.

16. When I use the concept "arbitrary" in this text, I do not necessarily mean unrestricted and unsupported, but I do mean subject to one's individual choice and unsupported by self-reflexive principles. One would do well to think of probabilism, the idea that a reason can be found to support almost any position. For further discussion of probabilism, see my analysis below of the comedy of reduction.

17. For a critique, from a different vantage point, of theorists (and non-theorists) who think that systematic and logical analyses are incompatible with historical specificity and the uniqueness of literary texts, see Ellis 1–23 and 211–232, esp. 3–6.

18. After reeling off a list of acclaimed anti-foundationalists, Stanley Fish, an adherent of a consensus theory of truth, calls anti-foundationalism "the *going* argument" (68).

19. Though the number of generic studies since Hegel remains high, not a single non-inductive, non-pragmatic theory of genre has, to my knowledge, been proffered since the time of the early Hegelians. The view of one of Germany's most influential theoreticians of genre, Karl Viëtor, may be taken as representative: "Where does poetics get the concept of genre? Most certainly from the history of the genre itself; one cannot think up a genre, there is also no apriori, no innate idea of it . . . one extracts the literary type of genre by studying all the individual works that belong to the genre" (302, my translation). For a skeletal history of anti-Hegelianism in aesthetics, see Gethmann-Siefert, "Die Ästhetik in" 127–132. This skepticism toward absolute grounds has led admirers of Hegel to suggest that Hegel did not himself attempt to present any foundational arguments. See, most recently, Pinkard, *Hegel's Dialectic* esp. 176 and 231.

20. Hypothetical norms, in contrast, are normally accepted: *If* someone wants to oppress others, *then* he must accumulate power. The categorical norm—in this case "oppression of others is wrong"—is considered an axiom, which cannot itself be rationally proved.

21. Hans Albert refers to this as the Münchhausen trilemma; see 16–21, esp. 18.

22. See, for example, Otto Mann esp. 327–330, where we also encounter the self-contradiction implicit in any argument for description: according to Mann, we should not evaluate texts but merely describe them in their historical context; if this is true, then by what right does one *criticize* theoretical texts that take an opposing view?

23. Walter Benjamin's widely received study of the Baroque *Trauerspiel* attempts a seemingly unorthodox critique of the deductive approach

to genre. For a refutation of Benjamin's arguments, reached by way of the figure of self-cancellation, see Kany 195–213, esp. 201–203.

24. The position has been revived by contemporary philosophers such as Apel and Hösle, from whom I freely borrow in my attempt to rephrase transcendental arguments for the present.

25. American Hegel critics commonly contest that the thesis-antithesis-synthesis model has anything to do with Hegel. See, for example, Mueller, Kaufmann, "Hegel: Contribution" 165–168 and *Hegel* 167–175, and Allen Wood xxvii and xxxii. Whether or not Hegel used precisely these terms, a glance at either Hegel's use of triadic structures both on the microlevel—as in the finite, the bad infinite, and the true infinite—or on the macrolevel—as in the logic, the philosophy of nature, and the philosophy of spirit—should convince the reader that this tendency in Hegel criticism misses the mark. It has been justly criticized by Merlan, and the importance of the triad is underscored by Hegel's programmatic analysis of the dialectic in paragraphs 79–82 of the *Encyclopedia* and his philosophical and methodological elevation of the triad in the concluding section of the *Science of Logic*, "The Absolute Idea" (6:553–573). One should note, however, that the antithesis is never added arbitrarily to the thesis but is an extension of the thesis, its self-cancellation or truth—more on this anon.

26. For a cogent analysis of Hegel and the law of non-contradiction, see Hösle, *Hegels System* 156–179.

27. Commenting on Kant's antinomies of pure reason, Hegel writes: "The main point to notice here is that the antinomies are not confined to the four special objects taken from cosmology: rather, they appear in *all* objects of every kind, in *all* representations, concepts, and ideas. To be aware of this, and to know objects in this property of theirs, is one of the most essential aspects of philosophical reflection; this property constitutes what will further be determined as the *dialectical* moment of logic" (E § 48, translation modified).

28. McCollom, for example, speaks of types of tragic heroes and types of tragic situations but does not reflect on their systematic interrelation. See McCollom, *Tragedy* 43 and 58–61. For examples with regard to comedy, a genre for which critics are more inclined to discern subforms, see Kindermann, Rommel, and Tener.

29. The contradiction often becomes comic: I once heard an esteemed literary critic attack a more traditional approach with the argument, "Don't you see that the most progressive literary criticism undermines notions of *Bildung* and of progress?"

30. Even a subschool of Hegel criticism that refuses to take his foundational and necessitarian claims seriously nonetheless finds extraordinary value in Hegel's theory of categories as an explanatory enterprise or an account of logically possible explanatory options, indeed the best account from the perspective of conceptual coherence and explanatory power. See the works of Klaus Hartmann, Pinkard, and Bole, along with the two anthologies edited by Hartmann's students, Koch and Bort and Engelhardt and Pinkard.

31. The abandonment of earlier thinkers might also be considered in the light of psychological, as well as scholarly, motivations: the desire to simplify tradition and thus free ourselves from the burden of deciphering precisely what is of value and what is not; the conceit that we are far beyond all earlier and naive thinkers; and an obsession first and foremost with what is new and original rather than with what has value.

32. Hegel employs this technique himself in various external reflections designed to illuminate structures whose being is initially logical. See, for example, 12:134–135.

33. Hegel takes these meanings of subjectivity and objectivity partially from his reading of Kant. See esp. E § 41 Z 2.

34. Much more could be said about these structures, but to do so would be to focus on their philosophical import, and we are concerned here with art, not philosophy, even as we recognize that art cannot be entirely divorced from questions of logical structure.

35. The best discussions in English of Hegel's philosophy of art are Bungay and Desmond. The strength of Bungay's work is its consistent attention to the systematic claims of Hegel's aesthetics. (A synopsis of Bungay's book-length analysis is also available in German.) The strength of Desmond's *Art and the Absolute* lies in its argument that Hegel's philosophy of art can be made productive for the present. Winfield has in two very recent contributions added force to the relevance of Hegel's aesthetics today. Because our studies do not greatly overlap in terms of subject matter, it would take me too far afield to evaluate any of his claims in detail. However, two general comments are in order: Winfield's contributions have the advantage of seeking to evaluate, not merely paraphrase, Hegel and the disadvantage of being far removed, unlike Hegel, from drawing connections to particular works of art. The best comprehensive discussion of Hegel's philosophy of art in German is still Szondi's "Hegels Lehre von der Dichtung," even if Szondi's analysis excels more in clarity than critique. Important systematic insights can also be gained from Hösle's analysis

(*Hegels System* 589–638). In addition, for the student of Hegel's aesthetics with a particular interest in the plastic arts, Schüttauf is helpful.

36. Hamburger attempts to defend precisely this position (135–145). Hamburger's claim derives from her view that interpretive multiplicity and singular truth are incompatible. But the questions "Is this interpretation commensurate with the text?" and "Are the propositions I have presented as illustrative of the text's meaning logically coherent?" should be kept separate. Hamburger undermines her thesis by citing a Paul Celan text as illustrative of the propositions she develops in her book. That Celan could be interpreted differently does not affect Hamburger's claim that Celan's text speaks a truth.

37. A fuller formulation reads: "The beautiful is the Idea as the immediate unity of the concept with its reality, the Idea, however, only in so far as this its unity is present immediately in sensuous and real appearance" (13:157; A 116).

38. Though my investigation is confined to literature and film, I presume—with Hegel—that even those forms of art that are not propositional, as, for example, architecture or instrumental music, mirror the categories of dialectical logic and thus also truth, though such a claim would be more difficult to prove.

39. For various defenses of literature as propositional, see Graff 156–163 and Juhl 153–195.

40. The call for an ironic attitude toward all content, even substantive and ethical content, is for Hegel the worst form of irony. Where art tries to ironize what is substantive, it itself becomes a nullity. The position is by the way self-contradictory: if the only worth lies in recognizing that everything is worthless, then worth, as the negation of worth, negates itself, and so affirms worth. Comedy avoids this self-contradiction by negating only what is itself a nullity. Indeed, a proper subject for comedy, as we shall see below, is precisely the stance of absolute negation implicit in absolute irony.

41. Two levels of form are at play here: form as the general structure (or plot) of a work and form as the finite concretization of language and other sensuous media. Though I am interested in both (and though I see in each a relation to content), this study focuses on the more general meaning of form.

42. For Hegel, art is "one way of bringing to consciousness and expressing the *divine*, the deepest interests of humanity, and the most comprehensive truths of spirit" (13:21; A 7, translation modified). The function

of art is to realize truth in sensuous form; therefore, art does not run counter to a philosophy of art that operates logically. Cf. 13:28–29.

43. Schelling's discussion of art and beauty as the complete interpenetration of the ideal and the real, the unity of the universal and the particular, can also be integrated into this framework. See esp. 25–27, 55, and 118–119. To argue that this view died with the German Idealists would be mistaken; witness George Steiner's *Real Presences*, which speaks— albeit more intuitively than argumentatively—for a view of art as a formal expression that opens up a sense of transcendence.

44. For some brief reflections from a materialist perspective on aesthetics as being concerned with "the relation between particular and universal" and thus "a matter of great importance to the ethico-political" (413), see the final pages of Eagleton's *The Ideology of the Aesthetic*, which argues for the revival of dialectical thought and appeals to the complex viability of concepts such as reason and truth.

45. I do not mean that individual characters should not present untenable claims; rather, the work as a whole should not present an untenable "statement." Hölderlin is helpful on this point: "The poet must . . . often say something untrue and contradictory, which, however, must of course be resolved in truth and in harmony within the totality in which it is presented as something transient" (6:344, my translation).

46. Cf. Hegel: "This right form is so far from being indifferent with respect to content, however, that, on the contrary, it is the content itself. A work of art that lacks the right form cannot rightly be called a work of art, just for that reason. It is not a true work of art. It is a bad excuse for an artist as such to say that the content of his works is certainly good (or even excellent) but that they lack the right form. The only genuine works of art are precisely the ones whose content and form show themselves to be completely identical" (E § 133 Z).

47. The superiority of the affirmative does not negate the validity of avant-garde art immersed in negativity; it merely requires of such art that its telos be more than negative, even if this telos is not portrayed. Thus, the works of predominantly negative artists such as George Grosz and Franz Kafka are aesthetically true insofar as the thrust of their art is the negation of negativity, the exposure of untenable positions.

48. For a convincing view of the history of philosophy as partly cyclical, see Hösle, *Wahrheit und Geschichte*.

49. Ellis also argues along these lines, suggesting that there "is no reason why works originating from the same time should always be compa-

rable, nor why works from widely different points of time should not be; the continuing similarity and variety of human nature is a far more important factor in generalizing about literary texts than any set of local historical circumstances" (227). For another at least tentative affirmation of universality, in this case with regard to tragedy, see Hamlin 164–165.

50. An overvaluation of genesis can also be seen in meta-reflections on the critical enterprise—along the lines that every statement is historically conditioned, thus relative, or that any attempt to define aesthetic terms as universal is to document a "cultural bias" (Henry Schmidt 30). One can counter that the metaargument—that all universal claims document a cultural bias—itself documents a cultural bias; the reduction of all transcendent truth-claims to historicity is self-cancelling.

51. Hösle, like Wandschneider, succeeds in making the structures of Hegel's *Logic* fruitful for contemporary developments in *Realphilosophie*. Since logic is in principle capable of a priori truth and since the laws of this logic also apply to the real world, Hegel criticism would do well to refine the logic both in its macrostructures and its fine details and to relate this logic to issues of relevance in, among other areas, the natural sciences, psychology, political philosophy, and aesthetics. My book attempts to follow this pattern by using Hegelian structures to refute—or expand, if you will—Hegel's typology of dramatic genre.

52. See Hösle, *Hegels System* 130–154, 344–346, 424–462, 590–611. For an attempt to build on Hösle's revision of Hegel and a detailed account of the systematic relation of the parts of intersubjective spirit, see von Werder, who argues for a tetradic—and dialectically developed—division, at least within the normative part of intersubjective spirit (which follows the universal and historical sections), containing religion as the thesis; art and philosophy as the antithesis; and a synthesis consisting of an objective spirit modified by the normative insights of philosophy, not just the communication, but the realization, of philosophy in the world.

53. A paradigmatically historical or sociological study of genre such as John Orr's *Tragic Drama and Modern Society* complements, rather than contradicts, the systematic approach of this work. Even as Orr analyzes the diverse geographical and temporal manifestations of what he calls the "tragedy of social alienation" during the period from 1880 to 1960, he presupposes a universal definition of tragedy as the portrayal of human alienation and the experience of irreparable loss. (Orr's definition, by the way, is a good formulation for what is involved in tragedy *and* the drama of suffering, though it does not differentiate between the two, as I do below.) To imagine that some differentiation of types will be more systematic,

others more historical, is both commonsensical and philosophically sound. The elevation of the historical seems to be simply a matter of bias; in any case, I have not seen it defended in any systematic way.

54. Despite the continuing reign of postmodernism, the concept of "transhistoricality" has received recent support from some unexpected quarters. See, for example, Eagleton 410.

55. After working through this study, one might also be encouraged to view with the aid of universal categories artworks *as* particular works, whereas within the confines of this study I shall be concerned with artworks primarily as representative of universal categories and less as particular works, though in three detailed analyses below I attempt to do both.

56. To offer a brief and limited response: the comedy of withdrawal, which elevates subjectivity to the nth degree, was barely known to the Greeks and in the one example, Menander's *Dyskolos*, was not developed with the same depth as in modernity.

57. For Hegel's answer to this question, see 15:498–499 and 15:545.

58. Exemplary in its analysis of a shift in historical consciousness as bringing about a shift in views of what is comic and tragic is Auerbach's account of Saint Peter (40–49). According to antique tradition, Peter should be viewed as comic, the servant who thinks he knows more than the master. The fact that he is wrong is predictable; the servant doesn't know. The Gospels, however, do take Peter seriously: he is not simply the outcome of his role, and he is in a sense tragic. This tragic view requires an entirely new, and Christian, consciousness.

59. Most of the recent work written in English on German tragedy has been prepared not by germanists but by comparatists: Faas, Cox, and Bouchard, for example. Aesthetic and generic considerations have all but disappeared owing to the germanists' focus on the socio-historic dimensions of literature; a recognition of the one-sidedness of the sociological approach, especially the extent to which it is unable to render transparent what makes art uniquely art and not just a product of specific historical and ideological structures, would be warranted. When approaching genre, germanists tend to dissolve overarching aesthetic structures into historical difference. Again, comparatists offer a different view, as, for example, Berlin, who writes almost matter-of-factly that he is "interested less in tragedy's changing form than its enduring substance" (x).

60. My response to this particular form of production aesthetics will bring me to my focus on artwork aesthetics, in particular, the coherence of

the text's ideas rather than the conditions of its genesis; as I have suggested above, such a focus need not be viewed as a denial of history.

61. The only nineteenth-century Hegelian to reflect at some length on the emotions is Carriere, though his analysis remains by modern standards primitive. See Carriere, *Aesthetik* 1:1–73 and 1:248–288. Hegel's restricted view of emotions and desires figures prominently in Willett's critique.

62. Hegel, who focuses on conflict, and Szondi, who elevates *peripeteia*, are the only major figures in the tradition to take a different path. Partially because I value their analyses more than others, my detailed criticisms are most often directed against these two thinkers. Schelling and Hölderlin, who are less frequently cited in contemporary studies of tragedy, also focus on tragic structure rather than tragic effect.

63. In non-scholarly debates we tend to evaluate art in emotive—which is to say, subjective—terms: a work is exciting or boring, interesting or dull. In each instance, the stress is not on the work but on the individual's relation to the work. The claim that every view is colored by subjectivity frees us, first, from our responsibility to the work itself, and second, from systematic reflection, as, for example, in the postmodern view, "If someone calls it art, it's art."

64. The field is hardly exhausted by scholastic discussions of whether emotions engendered by artworks are distinct from ordinary emotions.

65. Scheler argues, in contrast to Kant, that ethics must be "both absolute *and* emotional" (*Formalismus* 260; *Formalism* 254).

66. This is not to say that emotions are preferable to reason; obviously only a combination provides the strongest resistance to the threefold assault of sophistry, misguided emotions, and weak will.

67. Recognizing the value of emotions for ethics, our disagreement with Kant, is central to one's evaluation of tragedy, one's estimation of sympathy as a morally relevant ground of willing.

68. I also bracket most questions of performance. Although Greek tragedy and comedy are very much linked to the cultic setting and much discussion of tragedy in particular, taking the lead from Aristotle, has focused on audience reception, I have chosen to focus more on the basic structures of tragedy and comedy and issues of artwork rather than reception aesthetics. Nonetheless, the alert reader will often recognize in my readings of individual plays arguments for and against particular types of performances. My interpretation of Schnitzler's *Anatol*, for example, im-

plies that a performance that is too serious or brooding will miss the parody of tragedy, while one that is too comic or lighthearted will miss Anatol's genuine longing for intersubjectivity. Performance is central to the Hegelian idea of beauty as the unity of body and spirit.

69. See Reichert, "More than Kin" 66–70. My terms transcend literature as well; though without overlooking what is specifically literary or dramatic, I try to turn this to an advantage. There are two reasons for wanting to understand the individual work of literature: first, for the aesthetic experience; second, because literary categories are relevant for life. If this holds true, then we should be attentive to both the literary and transliterary dimensions of literature.

70. My suggestion that the tragic and comic transcend drama is not without precedent—many theorists, regardless of the specifics of their theories, speak of tragedy as applying to life, and one of the most recent introductions to comedy, Nelson, makes a point of including fiction and film.

71. Film studies would benefit from a more philosophical approach to genre. One now speaks empirically of Westerns, film noir, science fiction, and so forth. No attempts are made, as far as I know, to relate diverse subject matter to basic structures of conflict. Again, this is not to suggest that inductive analyses are without value. Gerald Mast's account of comic film, including his typology, is highly suggestive.

72. For similar reasons, Hegel elevated opera as the highest of dramatic forms. Gethmann-Siefert quotes one of the anonymous and unpublished manuscripts of Hegel's *Lectures on Aesthetics*: "If then drama in all its facets becomes a complete artwork, then it is opera; opera appears as the perfectly developed artistic drama" ("Welt und Wirkung" xlii, my translation).

73. Bibliographical information on Hegel's *Aesthetics*, including his theory of drama, can be found in Henckmann; Helferich; Steinkraus and Schmitz 239–249; and Steinhauer and Hausen. A survey of modern criticism on Hegel's *Aesthetics* is available in Gethmann-Siefert, "Zur Begründung." For publications after 1957, the annual bibliographies in the *Hegel-Studien* are an additional resource. Finally, *The Owl of Minerva*, the journal of the Hegel Society of America, should be consulted for its sections on "new books" and "dissertation abstracts."

74. Transcendental propositions can be refuted only by arguments not by experience. Aesthetics draws on transcendental arguments, but itself combines transcendental and contingent factors. New media, even new works, encourage us to refine, or even revise, our categories. Thus, art-

works can themselves influence an aesthetic system, even if it is initially grounded not in the works but in transcendental logic. Aesthetics as an application of the transcendental to the contingent lacks the stability of the former, but it gains on the side of richness and complexity. Nonetheless, without a transcendental moment an approximation of norms (or, for that matter, even a denial of norms) would be impossible. The not-merely-but-nonetheless-also transcendental nature of art is clearly elucidated by Lukács in "Die Kategorie der Besonderheit." See esp. 230–231 and 260.

75. For this reason as well, my study does not attempt to delineate the stages of evolution in Hegel's thinking on tragedy; for commentary on this topic, as well as a close reading of Hegel's discussion of *Antigone*, see Steiner, *Antigone* 19–42. The most thorough general account of the development of Hegel's thinking on art is Gethmann-Siefert (*Die Funktion der Kunst*), which includes some reflections on tragedy (198–204, 216–230, 356–359, and 364–366). See also Schlunk 9–23, Pöggeler, Jamme, and Schulte.

76. Readers interested in previous attempts to define the tragic would do well to turn to Szondi ("Versuch"), Kaufmann, or Hans Wagner. Extensive information on the history and theory of comedy, including bibliographical information, can be found in Rommel; Pfister, "Bibliographie"; Haberland; Heilman, *Comedy* 254–278; and McFadden.

77. The only recent literature on the aesthetics of an early Hegelian are Oelmüller's studies of Vischer, from the late 1950s. The analyses, being paradigmatic illustrations of the expository approach, are of biographical and historical rather than philosophical interest. They detail what Vischer thought, focusing on his doubts about the validity of objective idealist aesthetics in a world of contingency and alienation. They do not attempt to weigh the tenability of Vischer's arguments. The lack of genuine interest in the systematic aesthetic claims of the Hegelians is also manifest in Pfister, who opens his introduction to drama with the lapidary assertion that normative-deductive theories have nothing to tell us about modern drama (18–19).

78. The trilogy tragedy, comedy, and drama of reconciliation partially mirrors the sequence from epic objectivity and substance to lyric subjectivity and particularity and, finally, to drama, whose essence is intersubjectivity and whose highest form is, correspondingly, the drama of reconciliation.

79. The position I defend is especially alienating to the historicist critic who views the structure of genre as absolutely inseparable from its history.

80. Sengle ("Vorschläge") is justified in his suggestion that discussion of only three forms—epic, lyric, and dramatic, or within drama, simply of tragedy and comedy—fails to grasp literary genre in the richness of its detail. Whether this multiplicity of forms means that poetics can no longer be systematic—as Sengle also believes—is a different question.

81. Consensus and usage are for Hegel no grounds for legitimation. Karelis takes Hegel to task for suggesting that beauty is essential to art, that works we tend to call bad art are not really art at all (xlviii–l); but from a Hegelian standpoint, which argues for the priority of norms, the position is legitimate. Similarly, just because most people call a particular dramatic work a tragedy does not make it a tragedy, not even a bad tragedy.

82. See esp. 13:29–40. In his lecture on Hegel, Szondi speaks with admiration of "the extraordinary capacity of his thinking, in the abstract dialectic of thought not, let's say, to dissolve the concrete but rather first and foremost to make it transparent" (445, my translation). A disadvantage of many philosophic approaches to genre—Heilman notes as examples Feibleman, Monro, and Swabey—is the lack of examples and in particular the paucity of references to drama (*The Ways of the World* 256); I hope to avoid this common error.

83. One of the few contemporary critics to employ Hegel's theory of comedy as a heuristic tool is Watson, who reads Shakespeare's problem comedies in the light of Hegel's argument that subjectivity is central to comedy. In contrast to comedy, the Hegelian theory of tragedy has had tremendous influence. Moss has argued in a fascinating article that Hegel's impact reaches so far that many contemporary analysts of tragedy, often ones openly critical of Hegel, "employ a Hegelian terminology yet are unaware of their source" (91). Gellrich's recent study of tragedy suggests that Hegel's emphasis on tragic *conflict* was a central, if not fully recognized, turning point in the history of tragic theory.

84. For discussions of Hegel's use of the term "subjectivity," see Düsing, "Hegels Begriff" esp. 201–202 and *Das Problem*; Braitling; Bykova; and Findlay.

85. Yet another explanation for the lack of a universal theory of comedy is that comedy, being bound to the particular and the local, is forever variable (Beare 4). Such a view, not recognizing that there may be a form of unity that remains a unity even amidst plurality, encourages an expository approach to the study of comedy, as is illustrated, for example, in Beare's own historical and descriptive account of comic themes.

86. On the contemporary avoidance of evaluation, see Barbara Smith 17–24. Smith's answer to the problem differs from mine and is, despite her proleptic denials, either self-refuting or, as she sometimes implies, a nonargument, and thus self-erasing. For a helpful discussion of the nature of evaluation and its legitimacy, see Reichert, *Making Sense* 173–203.

87. Wayne Booth in *The Company We Keep* has reintroduced to literary criticism the argument that literature has an ethical component, that it can act as nourishment or as poison, and that authors, readers, and critics have therefore certain responsibilities. One needn't agree with all the particulars of Booth's study or the more recent attempt by Nussbaum (*Love's Knowledge*) to argue for the ethical nature of literary texts in order to accept their most overarching points.

88. This critique of *Woyzeck* does not imply that we should ignore the work's virtues. On the contrary, a weakness in one respect, for example, genre, can be offset by strengths in other respects, for example, originality of conception, rhetoric, or socio-historic importance.

Chapter 2: A Study of Tragedy

1. Hegel's theory of tragedy contains a dialectic insofar as it applies to the Greeks, the movement, namely, from an undifferentiated and ahistorical totality to necessary division within the absolute, and finally to the finitude of what is essentially finite, that is, to the death of the hero and the overcoming of one-sidedness. See esp. 15:522–523 and 15:540–543. Without necessarily denying the validity of this structure, I suggest a more specific dialectic among the subgenres of tragedy.

2. I use the qualifier "affirmative," for symmetry, which in its privileged forms is higher than asymmetry, nonetheless can be negative and abusive—symmetrical hate, for example, or symmetrical instrumentalization. In Edward Albee's *Who's Afraid of Virginia Woolf?* George and Martha torture one another verbally; though not affirmative, the action is symmetrical.

3. A classic, and still useful, introduction to Hegel's theory of tragedy, especially for students of English literature, is Bradley, "Hegel's Theory." For commentary on Bradley's theory (in its divergence from Hegel's), see LeBlanc.

4. As a contrasting example, consider Orson Welles's *Citizen Kane*. Though a formally great work and rich from psychological and political

perspectives, it suffers thematically from its failure to introduce a tragic knot, to unite Kane's power and greatness with his isolation and suffering: nowhere does the film show that one necessarily follows from the other. The film is sad, but not tragic, its plot accidental rather than organic.

5. Most tragedies of self-sacrifice end in death, but not all. Some forms of suffering are worse than death. Oedipus, for example, suggests that he has sinned such sins as hanging could not punish (*Oedipus Rex* 1375–1376). Consider, similarly, Sophocles' Creon, Grillparzer's Medea, or Hebbel's Judith.

6. The concept of moral resistance to suffering, which bears a certain resemblance to the structure of self-sacrifice, is the essence of Schiller's definition of tragedy. Schiller's plays, however, transcend this definition, and in one paragraph of "On the Pleasure Derived from Tragic Objects," which has been overlooked in comparative discussions of Schiller's and Hegel's theories of tragedy, Schiller explicitly addresses the topic of tragic collision. The paragraph begins: "But there are cases where moral pleasure is obtained only through moral pain, and this happens whenever a moral duty must be transgressed in order to act more in accordance with a higher and more universal duty" (20:143, my translation). Although Schiller, unlike Schelling and Hegel, views tragedy primarily from the perspective of the *Affektenlehre*, rather than metaphysics—as Borchmeyer rightly emphasizes (243), he does speak here of collision. True to Schiller's focus on reception, a primary purpose of the collision is to create a combination of "Lust" and "Unlust" or "pleasure" and "aversion" in the viewer.

7. *Oedipus Rex* culminates in self-sacrifice, but a comprehensive reading of the drama might also recognize moments of stubbornness (Oedipus' initial hubris) and opposition (divine oracles and prophecy versus human enlightenment and autonomy) as well as suffering (the arbitrariness of fate).

8. Divine beings can reach the highest form of love, self-sacrifice for another, only as human or finite beings; this structure helps to illuminate the incarnation as well as a number of modern texts, including popular—if less beautiful works—such as *The Bishop's Wife* or *Wings of Desire*.

9. The willingness to die for a cause is in a sense grand, especially if that death means the loss of extraordinary potential. Often the potential resurfaces in a transfigured way; the deaths of Romeo and Juliet, for example, inspire reconciliation among their families.

10. Heroes of stubbornness tend to be figures of the past, though there are exceptions, for example, Schiller's Marquis Posa. The issue of

whether the tragic hero ideally represents the past or the future has greatly interested Marxist critics. See, for example, Lukàcs, "Hegels Äs-thetik" 50 and Marcuse, "Die marxistische Auslegung." In Marx's non-aes-thetic writings, tragic self-sacrifice (the willingness to risk one's life for the cause of human emancipation) shows the individual's readiness to over-come the kind of egotistical behavior that informs the capitalist spirit. The tragedy of stubbornness and comedy, in contrast, exhibit individuals caught in the contradictions of decaying political, ideological, or economic systems, characters unable to adjust. But in comments directly addressing tragedy, Marx argues that the tragic hero always arrives too early. He would have preferred for Ferdinand Lasalle in his historical tragedy *Franz von Sickingen* to have made the early revolutionary Thomas Münzer, not the late knight von Sickingen, the hero of his tragedy. See Marx's letter to Lasalle of April 19, 1859.

11. Many tragedies contain several heroes, whose actions fit differ-ent forms of tragedy. The works are not pure but mixed. Indeed, mixed works are sometimes the richest and most complex. In such cases the task of the genre critic as interpreter is to show how the different subgenres interrelate.

12. That tragedy is viewed as the exception is also clear from a play such as Brecht's *The Exception and the Rule*.

13. For a reading of tragedy that stresses—against Hegel's contrast-ing focus on the reemergence of the whole—the immensity and unre-peatability of the singular that is lost, see Desmond, *Perplexity* 27–54. While Desmond's reading is a useful counterweight to Hegel's universal-ism, it is important to remember that the identity of the hero is as much aligned with the universal as it is with the singular: both moments are requisite for tragedy (and reflection on tragedy).

14. For recent discussions of Socrates' fate as tragic, see Versényi 160–168 and MacDonald 178–195. Philosophers of tragedy as diverse as Fritz (21, 97–98) and Kohlberg (387) have argued, however, that Socrates is not a tragic figure. Even if we were to contest the complete disap-pearance of tragedy in Socrates, we would nonetheless see a weakening of tragedy vis-à-vis the more painful variants of self-sacrifice. The strongest argument for Socrates as a tragic figure places justice (and thus tragedy) also on the side of his opponents. Hegel himself speaks of a collision of naive or objective *Sittlichkeit*, which as the ethos of the state has a formal justification, versus the subjective principle of *Moralität*, a moral con-sciousness or knowledge whose content is more valid (18:446–447 and 18:514). Interesting would be a drama that associates tragedy less with

Socrates than with Athens itself; it would, I imagine, be a tragedy of stubbornness.

15. For an insightful discussion of Brecht's play as tragic, see Sokel, "Brecht's Split Characters" esp. 127–131.

16. *Oedipus Rex* is a great work and an exception within self-sacrifice partly because Oedipus's process of recognition is itself dramatic, and his consequential action leads not to release but to even greater suffering.

17. *Don Carlos* IV. xxi.

18. *Agnes Bernauer* V.vi.

19. *The Crucible* Act IV.

20. *The Deputy* V.ii and V.iii. Fontana's hesitation and subsequent affirmation of his role recall Sienkiewicz's *Quo vadis?*, which recounts St. Peter's intended departure from Rome and subsequent return after he recognizes that Christ, having seen his deputy abandon him, was himself on his way to Rome (ch. 59). Affirmation of a position after reflecting on its abandonment is always more powerful and more dramatic, for it contains its negation within itself. Cf. Roche, *Dynamic Stillness* 96–98.

21. This is not to suggest that the tragedy of self-sacrifice is necessarily without drama or variety. Not only do the internal and external causes of death vary, so too do the emotions with which one affirms self-sacrifice, as a simple glance at Rodin's masterpiece "The Burghers of Calais" attests. Tragic self-sacrifice can also be strengthened by showing the diverse means of deception employed by the forces of evil, as, for example, in Schiller's *Intrigue and Love*.

22. Plato's *Crito* and *Phaedo* are good examples; the works serve philosophical rather than dramatic purposes. Plato does not want us to suffer with Socrates; he wants us to admire him in the spirit of eventual emulation. The former stance would make us, under similar circumstances, vulnerable to weak, unassertive, and unvirtuous self-pity. Aristotle, on the other hand, argues that through identification and catharsis tragedy cleanses us of an emotion such as pity. The third alternative, after avoidance and identification, is the comic one: undermining self-pity and other unvirtuous emotions or acts via comedy and the argument ad absurdum.

23. Blissful martyrdom is particularly evident in Baroque drama, for example, in Gryphius's *Catharina von Georgien* (IV.305–08, IV.335–336, IV.347–355; V.31–336, V.51, V.121–123).

24. See Hösle, *Vollendung der Tragödie* 63. The appeal to victimization as a means of grounding one's morality is common in contemporary society. On this topic see especially Hughes.

25. That steadfastness, resolve, and intransigence belong to even those tragic heroes who transcend the specific subgenre of stubbornness is effectively illustrated—for the plays of Sophocles at least—in Bernard Knox's account of "the Sophoclean hero" (1–61).

26. The informed reader may wonder why I list courage, one of the four cardinal virtues, as a secondary virtue. While I am sympathetic to Plato's arguments, that all the virtues are interrelated and ultimately one and that courage is truly courage only when it serves a just end and is chosen wisely, I nonetheless recognize, with others, that what we call courage can often be employed in the service of an apparent, rather than a real, good or even in the service of evil. In this sense, even as courage is not without its intrinsic value and even as it is ideally understood as a form of justice, it is more often than not the means to an end rather than an end in itself.

27. The critics who come closest to recognizing something like the tragedy of stubbornness are Vischer in his discussion of "The Sublime Nature of Evil Intent" (1:276–281) and Volkelt in his analysis of "The Tragic Nature of the Criminal Act" (*Ästhetik* 182–195), though major differences still exist. Cf. also isolated reflections in Rosenkranz's discussion of "The Criminal" (*Ästhetik des Häßlichen* 325–337).

28. Virtue and power are etymologically connected: the word "virtue" has as its root "power," "might," or "potency."

29. The ancient tragedy of stubbornness that best illustrates this externalization of suffering is *Medea*; not surprisingly, Euripides is the Greek tragedian most at home with the drama of suffering.

30. In *The Wild Duck* is a subtle moment of opposition: Relling's suggestion that stability and happiness require a life-lie versus Gregers's demands for truth at all costs.

31. One might want to counter that Macbeth, precisely because he is not fully autonomous (he is partially the pawn of Lady Macbeth's aspirations), is less of a tragic hero. In being not purely evil, however, Macbeth is more aware, more doubtful of his actions, even as he finally acts as his own agent; this moral awareness makes him the more complex, the greater tragic hero.

32. The transition from honor (among enemies) to deception (for a cause or for friends) is prefigured in Renoir's great war film *Grand Illusion*.

33. Cf. Grimm, "Komik und Verfremdung" and Arntzen, "Komödie und episches Theater." For a more critical view of the connection between comedy and epic theater, see Warning 311–316. The issue is also weighed in Giese's lengthy study of Brecht and comedy.

34. Postwar Germany's most intriguing tragedy of stubbornness, Fassbinder's *The Marriage of Maria Braun*, is highly Brechtian. Not only does the hero destroy herself without reaching any self-knowledge, the film also introduces various devices of alienation: the interplay of radio and conversation; the use of mirrors; the role of incongruities and humor; and the appearance of Fassbinder himself.

35. Unusual is the reverse movement from self-sacrifice to stubbornness. It does occur, at least in a loose sense, in Grillparzer's *The Golden Fleece*, where Medea sacrifices her inner self (as well as her father) for love and, finding herself betrayed, seeks extreme vengeance.

36. This structure surfaces in other works as well, for example, Curtiz's *Angels with Dirty Faces*. A parallel structure can be seen in those tragedies of stubbornness that pass over into reconciliation only at the last moment, usually at the point of death, as, for example, in Sidney Kingsley's *Detective Story*.

37. Egmont's tragedy of character could be viewed from other angles as a tragedy of self-sacrifice: he does not compromise his views, and he dies for an ideal of freedom. Egmont's irreflexive character, however, delimits his self-sacrifice: he does not act knowing that he will suffer; rather, he acts unknowingly, if also honestly.

38. If the forces Stockmann does battle against were less evil, he might have been developed as a comic hero—not unlike an Alceste.

39. See esp. 15:522–524. Hegel limits this dialectic when he comments, in his discussion of the chorus, that romantic art tends not to portray the division of an original absolute (15:543).

40. Cf. also Nussbaum, *Fragility* 63–67, who, by agreeing with this statement, acknowledges that Hegel's reading is, if not without flaws, at least fundamentally sound. An enlightening account of the historical reception of Hegel's reading of *Antigone* is available in Donougho esp. 70–77.

41. Israel Knox overlooks the element of critique implicit in the Hegelian view that each position is one-sided when he contends that Hegel's theory of tragedy justifies "the socio-political and the historico-cultural *status quo*" (109). If both the individual and the institution are undermined, then it does not follow, as Knox thinks it does, that the individ-

ual is doomed, but the "majesty and sovereignity of the institution remain sacred and inviolable" (110).

42. Goethe gives an unusual reading of Aristotle when he argues that catharsis is an element of action, not of reception. See "On Interpreting Aristotle's *Poetics*" (12:342–345).

43. For further elaboration of this point, see below. Bremer argues that Hegel's theory of tragedy is most strongly influenced by Aeschylus's *Orestia*, the model of Greek tragedy as reconciliation: it alone survives as the complete articulation of what all Greek tragedy ultimately included, a final or reconciliatory moment.

44. Donougho has recently claimed that for Hegel tragedy does not end in reconciliation (87–88), but I fail to recognize a coherent argument for this anomalous position. For a non-Hegelian focus on reconciliatory moments in tragedy, or tragic relief in its broadest sense, see Guha.

45. On this last criticism, see Volkelt, *Ästhetik* 98–99 and *System* 306; Dixon 160–169; Lucas 42–45; Greene 96; Welleck 333; Pöggeler; Michel, *The Thing Contained* 157; Kurrik 249–250; Draper 32; Wittkowski, "Die Aufspaltung Gottes"; Barbour 26–27; Nussbaum, *Fragility* 67–69; Oudemans and Lardinois 116; Gellrich xii–xiii, 32–33, and 69–71; and May 58. The criticism is generally a modern one. In the nineteenth century, the Hegelian concept of reconciliation in tragedy was so pervasive that one aesthetician, Adolf Zeising, himself a non-Hegelian, argued for tragedy as art's most synthetic genre (135). Rare, however, is the modern reading of tragedy, such as that by Weisinger, which sees—with Hegel—a "sense of assurance, achieved through suffering, of rational order" (266), or Krüger, who argues that every genuine tragedy ends "in essence reconciliatory" (15, my translation). For one of the few defenses of Hegel's idea of reconciliation within modern Hegel literature, see Schlunk 63–65, who stresses that the moment of reconciliation is situated not in the immediacy of the action but in the audience's reflection, as it accompanies and follows the action. See also Sengle ("Vom Absoluten"), whose entire focus is the element of reconciliation behind the catastrophe, and Ellis-Fermor, who argues that tragedy demands a moment of "affirmation" or "balance" (139; cf. 127–147). Often overlooked—especially by critics who accuse Hegel of oversystematizing art—is the opinion of one of Hegel's contemporaries, in certain respects an antiphilosophical mind, Goethe, who writes: "a reconciliation, a solution is indispensable as a conclusion if the tragedy is to be a perfect work of art" (12:343; "On Interpreting" 198). Finally, Dilthey and Scheler address the need in tragedy for both suffering and reconciliation; see Dilthey 162–63 and Scheler, "Zum Phänomen" 292.

46. Lenson indirectly defends Hegel by arguing that balance and the equality of antagonists allow us to separate tragedy from pathos (15).

47. Among modern critics of Hegel, Jaspers offers a balanced view. He justly argues that Hegel renders tragedy overly harmonic (79), yet he recognizes the validity of the Hegelian definition of tragedy as collision (57, 95) and skillfully deflates the anti-Hegelian view that there is nothing but tragedy and within tragedy nothing but ambiguity and despair (80–87, 97–101).

48. See Hösle, *Vollendung der Tragödie* 97. This does not mean that every conflict between an unjust ruler and an individual is a tragedy of opposition. The ruler must mean well and identify with the apparent justice of the state. Lessing's *Emilia Galotti*, for example, is hardly a tragedy of opposition.

49. Cf. Hegel: "For the first principle of a state is that there is no reason, conscience, righteousness, or anything else higher than what the state recognizes as such" (18:510; HP 1:443, translation modified).

50. Heilman uses the related terms "division" and "dividedness" to define *all* tragedy: "I have proposed that the identifying mark of the tragic character is dividedness: that he is caught between different imperatives each of which has its own validity, or that he is split between different forces or motives or values. In other words, his nature is dual or multifold, and the different or competing elements are present at the same time, are operative in the dramatic situation, and are known to us as realities that have to be reckoned with" (*Tragedy* 89). Heilman's discussion of kinds of division deals not with levels of consciousness (my opposition and awareness) but addresses rather the differences between imperatives (or obligations) and impulses (or passions). Heilman's study could be paralleled to some degree with my own, perhaps along the following lines: an imperative triumphing over an impulse = self-sacrifice or awareness; an impulse triumphing over an imperative = stubbornness or awareness; the conflict of imperatives or the conflict of impulses = awareness. It is, I believe, an advantage of my study that it differentiates kinds of "impulses," for example, love and ambition, and stresses substance and greatness rather than impulse, which is often comic. Further, my definition allows for tragic collision, or a dividedness between, rather than within, characters, what I call opposition; Heilman, in contrast, does not recognize a conflict of goods between individuals. In general Heilman tends to restrict tragedy to the private and individual sphere (see *Tragedy* esp. 99–101), whereas substance demands objective causes and concerns—again unlike comedy. Heilman also has no category for a drama of good and evil, wherein the good hero

does not triumph, but suffers, and does so by an act of her own will; Heilman falsely reduces the tragedy of self-sacrifice to the drama of suffering or victimization, in his terminology the drama of disaster. In addition, Heilman measures tragic greatness only by dividedness. But commitment to an ideal in the face of potential suffering is often as great or as tragic as uncertainty and extreme self-consciousness. Finally, it is astonishing that in two substantive books on tragedy that at times sound as if they were written by Hegel, Heilman never once mentions the philosopher. Even if, as seems apparent, Heilman developed his theory independently of Hegel, a discussion of similarities and differences vis-à-vis a theory that is not only close to his own but generally regarded as one of the most important would seem warranted.

51. Volkelt's discussion of "The Tragic Nature of Equal but One-sided Opponents" in his *Ästhetik des Tragischen* bears some resemblance to my category of opposition; it is, however, scandalous that Volkelt does not recognize a connection to Hegel, even as he elsewhere criticizes Hegel's theory of tragedy.

52. The overlap of self-sacrifice and stubbornness can surface even outside the tragedy of opposition. Consider Barrie's *The Admirable Crichton*: Crichton embodies courage, consistency, and loyalty; he is, even as a servant, a master of secondary virtues. His loyalty, however, ultimately leads to an act of self-sacrifice (his setting off the flares).

53. For an enlightening discussion of similarities between Caesar and Brutus, see Rabkin.

54. Note especially the language of unity in V.iii.

55. Brutus is a particularly complex character who experiences awareness as well as opposition; in contemplating his love for Caesar vis-à-vis his loyalty to Rome, he compares his soul to a kind of battlefield (II.i.61–69).

56. It is incorrect to criticize Hegel's theory of tragedy, as does Volkelt (*Ästhetik* 28–32 and 300), with the argument that tragedy portrays particular individuals, not metaphysical ideas. The two are not mutually exclusive. To stress the metaphysical at the expense of the psychological is of course possible, but that is in no way the necessary result of a Hegelian approach.

57. A distinction between antithetical opposition and synthetic awareness is very much in the spirit of Hegel's enterprise. In his discussion of the symbolic artform, Hegel notes that in Zoroastrianism different gods represent contrasting principles: "The substance of the divine . . . is

not this one God who in itself, as this one, has the negative as its own determination necessarily belonging to its concept" (13:449; A 347, translation modified). A significant transition occurs when the negative is viewed as part of one's identity, such that "the true God appears as the emerging negation [Negativwerden] of *itself* and therefore has the negative as its own immanent determination" (13:449; A 348, translation modified). The transition represents, in Hegelian terminology, the movement from abstraction to the concrete or from understanding to reason, in our vocabulary the transition from opposition to awareness.

58. The most thorough study of Hegel and Shakespeare, though it suffers from an overabundance of quotation and paraphrase, is Wolff. See also the important Shakespeare readings of Bradley, which are partially informed by Hegelian concerns.

59. Hegel's elevation of classical art applies to drama as well, as when he writes of the development of the tragic and comic in Greece: "After these opposed ways of looking at human action had been firmly separated and strictly distinguished from one another, first tragedy, then comedy, developed organically and attained the summit of perfection, of which, finally, Roman dramatic art gives us only a pale reflection" (15:538; A 1208, translation modified).

60. For a discussion of Hegel that stresses his positive evaluation of post-classical drama, see Paolucci, "Bradley."

61. Hegel discusses forms of conflict in 13:266–283. His subdivisions, which present a hierarchy moving from natural to spiritual conflicts, cover more than just the tragedy of collision.

62. Another work that successfully captures the crumbling of heroic action in the face of a contingency the hero cannot control is Dürrenmatt's magisterial story *The Promise*.

63. Dora and Kaliayev seek self-sacrifice as a release from awareness, which they can scarcely bear; in contrast, the simple, but extreme, ideology of Stepan, whose position is one of ruthlessness and stubbornness, fails to reach the tragic heights of awareness. Camus' play illustrates the complexity of awareness vis-à-vis both self-sacrifice and stubbornness.

64. The question of moral collision, which has received much recent attention, has benefited from illustrations derived from literature. See esp. Gowans, which contains a selection of essays, as well as Cunningham and Morris. On tragedy and ethical reflection, see also Barbour.

65. The theater of ideas, even when it is not tragic, tends to draw on the structure of collision, as, for example, in Shaw's *Major Barbara*, which contrasts ineffectual goodness with immoral power.

66. On paradox and ambivalence as central to tragedy, see Napieralski and Cole. Modern theory supposedly elevates concepts such as ambiguity and ambivalence, but in dismissing tragedy and with it the moment of greatness in the protagonist, it unwittingly becomes reductionist and one-sided.

67. Also stressing the moment of wonder beyond intelligibility that tragedy evokes is Georgopoulos.

68. Readers interested in my analysis of the drama of suffering will also profit from Heilman's discussion of what he calls the "drama of disaster," (*Tragedy* esp. 3–73 and *Iceman*). I was well into this study when I discovered Heilman's use of this term for works in which the protagonist is a victim. Like Heilman, I insist that tragic suffering must be organic, it must derive from the hero's action, but I prefer *suffering* to *disaster*, for the term *disaster* suggests a level of calamity often lacking in dramas of suffering, especially those focusing not on the "disaster" itself but on the protagonist's self-pity, that is, her suffering. Further, Heilman excludes from his definition of "disaster" all self-inflicted suffering, but some non-tragic suffering is self-inflicted, deriving from weakness, rather than greatness.

69. I explore the drama of suffering after analyzing the four forms of tragedy not in order to suggest a logical progression in this direction but because I can concisely discuss the genre's weaknesses only after the categories of tragedy have been articulated.

70. See Scheler (*Formalismus* esp. 346–354; *Formalism* esp. 344–353). Kierkegaard can also be read with profit here if we keep in mind his distinction between misfortune, which is generally rendered external, accidental, and meaningless, and suffering, which is necessarily inward, organic, and paradoxically blessed. See his *Concluding Unscientific Postscript* esp. 386–410.

71. Cf., for example, Seneca, *De providentia*, 2.4 and 4.6.

72. On suffering leading to indifference, see Moravia. Vickers also argues that suffering need not lead to moral improvement (52– 99, esp. 64–70).

73. For Nietzsche's description of tragedy as unmotivated suffering, horror, and absurdity, see esp. section 7 of *The Birth of Tragedy*. For a

comparison of Hegel and Nietzsche on tragedy, including an enlightening critique of Nietzsche, see Houlgate, *Hegel* 182–220, esp. 213–220.

74. See, for example, Vickers, who attempts to strengthen his position with the psychological argument that those who do not see suffering as the center of tragedy are unwilling to "face the real horror of tragedy" (595). An exception among contemporary critics is Ruprecht. Likewise influenced by Hegel, he draws on the distinction between (unwilled) fate and (willed) destiny to separate mere suffering from tragedy. See esp. 65 and 90–91.

75. There are exceptions. One reason for the success of the American television series *The Fugitive* in the 1960s appears to have been that it took a potential drama of suffering (an innocent person, wronged by circumstances and by failures in the system, is now isolated and alone) and raised it to the level of self-sacrifice (virtually every episode portrays the hero risking his life, that is, risking being caught, in order to do the good). The series places greatness in suffering above suffering and, deviating from the tragic model, also allows for the possibility of reconciliation.

76. As I suggested above, the drama of suffering shares certain elements with Nietzsche's concept of tragedy. Nietzsche argues that if we strip away life's serene appearance of happiness, we uncover the horror of suffering, the vacuity of meaning. What most dramas of suffering lack from the Nietzschean standpoint is the experience of this horror as nonetheless somehow joyful.

77. Some convincing arguments for viewing involuntary suffering as not tragic are proffered by Heilman (*Tragedy* 18–28), who also argues for the connection between modern victimization and self-pity and stresses that completeness of understanding, insight into human division, and an awareness of human excellence as well as human inadequacy have been diminished by the contemporary over-elevation of simple suffering. Within such a framework, we have a reduced sense of moral predicaments and less genuine self-awareness. But Heilman does not take the next step of suggesting how comic such self-pity really is.

78. Hegel does not overlook the hero's endurance in suffering (see, for example, 13:536), but he does not stress it, as do, for example, the Stoics (Marcus Aurelius 11.6) or Schiller. A focus on collision and a focus on endurance in suffering are not in principle incompatible.

79. Cf. Schelling 338. For a recent and independent formulation of this idea, see Olson, *Tragedy* 249–250.

80. The comic implications of such a drama of suffering resurface in a play that owes much to Checkhov, Shaw's *Heartbreak House*.

81. The lack of interest in such causal relations may derive from a postmodernist distrust even of causality. Earlier thinkers, in contrast, viewed organic causality and self-determination as the keys to tragedy. See, for example, Heubaum, who sees in "every tragic effect" a "necessary precondition of a *causal* relationship between the character of the person and his suffering" (244, my translation).

82. Precisely the idea that tragic suffering is partly needless or undeserved is at work when we say that a youth's death in a car accident is tragic. To capture a moment, however, is not to grasp the whole; thus, we can be critical of this usage, suggesting instead terms such as pitiful or disastrous. Similarly, when we say that the loss of a beautiful forest is tragic, we elevate the moment which says that loss, in order to be tragic, must be of great value—what is necessary for tragedy is taken to be sufficient.

83. Schlegel's theory is not, however, one of simple despair or suffering but has been successfully compared to Keats's concept of "negative capability," the ability to live with uncertainties (Reavis 105–106). The sublime hero capable of this is in truth beyond tragedy, such that Schlegel, like Hegel, if in a different way, sees the truth of tragedy in the transcendence of tragedy.

84. While the scenario has a moment of comic potential—the collective suicide of an egoistic humanity would be the ultimate return to a subject-free, inorganic objectivity (what I shall later define as an element of the comedy of negation)—it lacks entirely the comic moments of resilience and lightness.

85. Bentley 293 and 350. The argument in its broadest strokes may be traced to Hume, who tried to solve the riddle of tragic pleasure by arguing that a tragedy (or any work that expresses suffering) is pleasing insofar as it is eloquently and beautifully expressed. The most recent discussion of tragic pleasure is Packer, who would dissolve the paradox by arguing that different causes, on the one hand the misfortunes of the individual character, and on the other the depth and sophistication of the play's meanings as well as the aesthetic structure and form in which they are embedded, simultaneously trigger distinct emotions, pain and pleasure.

86. In such dramas of suffering, the association with tragedy is reinforced by the sense of belatedness. Suffering triggers insights that cannot be fulfilled.

87. Consider also, to name the most obvious, *Andromache* and the initial parts of *Hecuba*.

88. Such a split view of *Lear* is not as unusual as it might sound. Arguing from a different set of categories, Bradley discusses the work's weaknesses as a drama and its merits in terms of imaginative effects (*Shakespearean Tragedy* 198–230).

89. We experience more deeply the suffering of any hero who is sensitive to the suffering of others, especially innocent others, such as animals. Besides Jude, consider, for example, Toller's Hinkemann.

90. Jude's suffering is complex enough to contain other aspects as well. A moment of self-sacrifice surfaces insofar as Jude, honoring Sue's aversion to physicality, does not touch her, thereby renouncing his desires. We can also see in Jude a tragedy of stubbornness: he is generally misguided and confused, but his efforts are extraordinary, as is his ability to survive and endure; his passion for Christminster, center of learning, remains even after he unambiguously becomes an outsider. The overarching tragic structure of the novel, however, is of collision: instinct, pleasure, and self-realization versus convention, duty, and self-abnegation, or Greek joy versus Christian self-denial. Jude and Sue suffer this tragic collision as they push each other to the extreme.

One reason why the categories of tragedy and comedy are more readily applied to dramas than novels is that whereas dramas tend to have clear structures, novels are often so complex, interwoven, and multifaceted as to escape these categories. Yet precisely this complexity, coupled with the specificity and range of subgenres, allows us to employ subgenres heuristically when analyzing a novel.

91. One need think only of Trofimov, who waxes eloquently of the need to work and chastises those who live off the costs of others, even as he lies idle for months on end and lives at the expense of the debt-ridden Ranevskaya.

92. The organic structure of tragedy is not recognized by a critic such as Brereton, who takes his definition of tragedy from normal usage and writes, "the death of a great man in an air-crash qualifies for tragedy unequivocally" (18). See also Nicolai Hartmann, *Ästhetik*, who defines tragedy rather simply as "the downfall of human greatness" (383, my translation).

93. Even readers who insist that the drama of suffering is *tragic* would still benefit from recognizing it as a different *kind* of tragedy.

94. In this context consider Hölderlin's theory of tragedy. The culminating moment of self-sacrifice, as in *Empedocles*, derives from a metaphysical collision of divine and human, of what Hölderlin calls the aorgic (or a kind of boundless life-force) and the organic (or a structuring and forming principle). Such self-sacrifice occurs only in eras of historical transition and results in the reestablishment of metaphysical unity. The proximity to Hegel, despite differences in detail and emphasis, cannot be overlooked. For a comparison see Düsing, "Die Theorie der Tragödie."

95. On Shakespeare's proximity to, and distance from, the Greeks, see also Söring esp. 193–213. Readings that acknowledge both transhistorical similarities and historical differences are often the most convincing and balanced.

96. For general reflections on the interrelation of generic conception and interpretation, see Hirsch esp. 71–77.

97. Logic and experience, transcendental and contingent concerns, should combine in aesthetics. Precisely in what way, however, is not clear. To this most difficult of aesthetic questions Hegel himself presents no satisfactory answer.

98. For a defense of prescriptive genre criticism, see Fowler 26–32.

99. Unusual in its insight into time is Gruber, who indirectly sheds light on tragedy by arguing that the suspension of time and tragic destiny is a fundamental comic norm that transcends the ages.

100. As one example for many, see Hemingway, *For Whom the Bell Tolls* 168–169, 291–292, and 379–398. Socrates combines optimism and tragedy when he argues that had there been enough time, he would have convinced the judges of his innocence (*Apology* 37a–b).

101. The structure of the hero's being out of his time and thus comic also surfaces in John Osborne's *Look Back in Anger*. The drama has elements of tragic conflict (Jimmy sees through the staleness and hypocrisy of contemporary Britain), but in his hyperbole and rudeness he is himself undermined. Jimmy is seen as being "born out of his time . . . he thinks he's still in the middle of the French Revolution," and not surprisingly, this is recognized as "slightly comic—in a way" (III.ii).

102. Fortunately, if J. Hillis Miller is to be believed, the Russian elevation of absolute and universal values in literature appears not to have dwindled, as it has in the United States, where we see, rather, "the mindless celebration of difference" (Gates 38), an example of which is Miller's own laudation of an American diversity that is, ironically, *common* in its negation of universals.

103. The literature on *Don Carlos* has dealt principally with the play's genesis, Marquis Posa's unorthodox behavior, the question of the play's unity (or lack thereof), and the complexities of discreet passages. The question of tragedy has been mentioned only fleetingly. Among those who do address this issue are: Fricke and Ebstein, who downplay the work's tragic dimensions; von Gronicka, who sees Posa's ruthless idealism as a tragic flaw; Finger, who relates the play to Schiller's definition of tragedy (as the expression of will despite already annihilating circumstances); Koopmann, who argues from the perspective of authorial intention and views the play as a *Familientragödie*; Müller, who speaks rather loosely of a fourfold tragedy (of friendship, trust, humanity, and tyranny) (108–123); and von Wiese, who focuses primarily on Posa's tragedy as the inevitable failure of an idealist in an imperfect world and the King's tragedy as an erasure of the humanity toward which he strives (191–202).

The one study from the perspective of Hegel is Pillau, who analyzes *Don Carlos* in the light of Hegel's discussion of modern drama, noting thereby Don Carlos's subjectivity and the private motivations of his action and Posa's self-reflection, rhetorical appeals, and calculating action, which contrast with the objectivity and immediacy of the ancient hero.

104. The Queen's love for Don Carlos is developed throughout the play; see esp. I.v, IV.xxi, and V.xi.

105. Some of the more successful *Don Carlos* productions of this century have focused on the King; the greatest example is the Hamburg production of 1962, directed by and starring Gustaf Gründgens.

106. The best reading of Philipp as a tragic figure is Beyer, who develops precisely this collision.

107. Even Don Carlos, a prospective King, suffers from his exceptional stature (I.ii).

108. The passage alludes, on the one hand, to Midas, and, on the other, to the Book of Exodus: the water of life from the rock of Horeb contrasts with the misdirected worship of the golden bull.

109. See the first section of "Tonio Kröger." In *Doctor Faustus*, the hero's greatness and isolation stem from intellect, not power.

110. Water, one of the most polyvalent images in world literature, assumes the meaning of symmetry in another German drama about asymmetrical relations, Lessing's *Minna von Barnhelm* (III.vii).

111. One of the most recent, if also longest enduring, debates on *Don Carlos* focuses on Posa's manipulation of means in order to reach a valid

end. Malsch ("Moral und Politik"), for example, defends Posa, stressing, first, the differences between the despotism of Posa and that of the King and, second, Schiller's belief that evil means are justified in the service of a regulative idea. Kufner and Wittkowski ("Höfische Intrige") view Posa's actions as morally reprehensible. Though Posa differs from the King and though circumstances arise where evil means may be justified, Posa's actions are not clearly justified in this way and, more importantly, the play does not thematize his appropriation of evil means as a (moral or tragic) collision. Critics tend to simplify matters by labelling Posa either the pure herald of freedom or a warning against any and all machinations. For a history of the criticism on Posa, see Malsch, "Robespierre ad Portas?"

112. My reading of Posa is partly, if not completely, in harmony with Schiller's interpretation of Posa in his *Letters on Don Carlos*. The strongest defense of *Schiller's Letters* stems from Polheim.

113. Crawford, who stresses the eternal friendship of Posa and Don Carlos, rightly argues that Posa needs Don Carlos for his political goals and that their friendship is partly based on their mutual dedication to these goals, but this does not mean that for Posa politics is not primary to friendship or that Posa does not instrumentalize Don Carlos when Carlos fails to live up to Posa's standards.

114. What I have elsewhere called "the Don-Carlos-conflict" (the mutual exclusion of concrete intersubjective relations and commitment to the universal) is common to all four characters. Don Carlos, the Queen, the King, and Posa. The intellectual-historical significance of this structure resides primarily in its influence on Hölderlin. See Roche, *Dynamic Stillness* 80.

115. Schiller's reflections on idealism are complex. An obsession with idealism can lead to its undermining; idealism easily passes over into despotism, as with Posa or, for example, Kleist's Michael Kohlhaas. We see in both instances a tragedy of stubbornness. Idealism may, on the other hand, remain absolutely pure and untarnished, but in this case it fails, for it lacks that moment of reality (and success) that ideally belongs to the ideal. Here, we see the tragedy of self-sacrifice. Schiller unites idealism with realism near the end of *On Naive and Sentimental Poetry* and thus moves in the direction of the drama of reconciliation. *Don Carlos*, however, does not present this third alternative.

116. A positive reading of the dialectic of freedom and necessity argues that freedom fulfills itself in adherence to a priori laws.

117. The concept of mirroring stubbornness—illustrated by Posa and the King or by other pairs such as the families in *Romeo and Juliet* or the brothers in Leisewitz's *Julius von Tarent*—is worthy of closer analysis.

118. Vaughan, for example, stresses Carlos's capacity for development (203).

119. Note the association of Don Carlos with tears in both II.ii and V.iii.

120. Wittkowski ("Höfische Intrige") has also seen that Posa not only acts unethically toward Don Carlos (and the King) but lacks ethical scruples, ethical reflections or hesitation, in doing so.

121. Cf. I.vii: "Flanders must be saved. / It is her [the Queen's] wish—that is enough for me" (translation modified).

122. Hansgünther Heyme centered his 1979 Stuttgart production of *Don Carlos* on Carlos as a victimized and screaming psychopath. The portrayal of Carlos as a sufferer whose language has become unintelligible was in my estimation a misguided failure, a reduction of the work to a weak drama of suffering.

123. No less a critic than Thomas Mann writes of Posa's relationship to Carlos: "He sees the future King in him and is justly horrified to find, at his return, instead of a youth conscious of his mission one broken by cursed infatuation. That he expresses this *grande passion* as a trifle, in comparison with the great things at stake, is his perfect right" (*Briefe* 232–233, my translation).

124. See the collection of newspaper reviews of the performances in Munich 1985 (dir. Alexander Lang) and Cologne 1988 (dir. Siegfried Bühr), which are available at the Deutsches Literaturarchiv in Marbach.

125. Harrison notes symmetrical structures (centering on III.vii and IV.xxi) that reinforce my reading of the play as dominated by Philipp's and Posa's tragedies of stubbornness. Also the recent discovery of Schings—that Posa incorporates elements of the Freemasons, which Schiller criticizes—appears to support this reading: the latent dogmatism of Posa mirrors the manifest dogmatism of the King.

126. Another moment of potentially tragic awareness is Don Carlos's recognition that his love for the Queen cannot and should not be fulfilled (I.ii and I.v), but the play quickly transforms this into self-pity. Development of these potential elements of tragic awareness might have resulted in the unity for which critics have long searched but have been unable to locate or substantiate.

127. As yet, only one substantial study of *The Mission* exists, namely McInerney, which places *The Mission* in the context of Bolt's other works.

128. The threat, like the conflict, was real, and it is a painful dramatic irony that despite Altamirano's efforts, rumors of Jesuit machinations persisted, and in 1759 the Portuguese minister of foreign affairs, Carvalho, who is introduced in Bolt's novel version, exiled all Jesuits from Portugal and its overseas possessions. As suspected, Portugal was not alone. The Jesuits were subsequently expelled from France (1764), then Spain (1766), and Naples (1767), followed by Parma (1768). In 1773, Pope Clement XIV dissolved the order. Forty-one years later it was restored worldwide by Pope Pius VII.

129. The film's fictitious Altamirano is far more complex than the ruthless historical Altamirano, whose high-handed maneuvers are detailed in Caraman 235–255.

130. As Berrigan points out, Gabriel's "going forth" from the church implies that his nonviolence means not withdrawal but a desire to counter the world, actively, with a different and ideal path (26).

131. Common to Hochwälder's *The Holy Experiment* and *The Mission* are the following tragic moments: the missions are dissolved precisely because of their success; individual Jesuits must choose between preserving the missions by resisting with force and obeying the commands of their order, whose existence in Europe is endangered by the missions in Paraguay; and the sense of despair and emptiness on the part of at least some of those who contribute to the dissolution of the missions.

132. We see a similar reversal in *Don Carlos*: the tragic heroes of self-sacrifice are victimized by Domingo and the Grand Inquisitor, who aspire to—or actually wear—the Cardinal's red; they force others into martyrdom, rather than act as martyrs themselves.

133. The Jesuits were the Church's most liberal order in mediating between the universality of the Church and the particularity of local cultures. This is here symbolized in the Jesuits' decision in favor of the Guaranis. With the Church's conservative decisions in the Chinese rules controversy and the Malabar rules controversy and the eventual suppression of the Jesuit order, the Church's missionary activities were damaged. The other orders, such as the Dominicans and Franciscans, were not as responsive to indigenous customs. The conflict between a universal Church and accommodation to the particular practices found in multicultural societies is one of the film's most contemporary moments; finding the right balance is not always without its tragic dimensions.

134. It is difficult to understand why a film that provides as many questions as answers should be accused of simplicity, self-righteousness, and smugness, as was the case in two of the film's early and most critical reviews. See Canby and Schickel. The movie's simple and righteous solutions are primarily those of the self-sacrificing Gabriel—in Bolt's novel version, Altamirano reflects to himself concerning Gabriel, "The man must be a simpleton unless he is some sort of saint" (242)—but the film does not identify with Gabriel alone.

Chapter 3: A Study of Comedy

1. Comedy is an abstract structure that often evokes laughter, though laughter is neither a necessary nor a sufficient condition of comedy; depending on the subgenre, laughter can easily be subordinate to sympathy, mild amusement, ridicule, or joy. Other genres, including tragedy, may contain scenes that make us laugh without being transformed in our eyes into comedies. Whether laughter inevitably accompanies the most successful comedies is a separate, and complex, question. In any case, the study of laughter within the comic should analyze not only what excites laughter but also what is worthy of laughter. On this distinction of fact and value, see Swabey, who writes, "the perception of the comic, besides involving emotional and physiological responses, requires logical and metaphysical comprehension, a normative intellectual insight which grasps what is worthy of laughter, what in a state of affairs is laugh*able* and not merely what makes us as organic creatures laugh" (823).

2. Although Zeising insightfully analyzes comedy as antithesis and recognizes the important role subjectivity plays in the reception of comedy, his analysis of comedy otherwise lags behind his commentary on tragedy and the drama of reconciliation.

3. Galligan (119–148) argues that obsession with the self is anathema to the comic vision and thereby overlooks many comedies that focus on identity crises, self-adoration, self-pity, stubborn withdrawal, and so forth. In contrast, I side with Hegel and argue that subjectivity is central to the comic vision but only insofar as it is mocked or overcome.

4. For the structures of false and genuine subjectivity, see, besides the *Logic*, § 138–40 of the *Philosophy of Right*, the *Philosophy of Religion* (16:180–183), and E § 400.

5. Hegel speaks at least once of a false subjectivity (E § 147 Z). For Hegel, false or bad is whatever is "not in accord with its concept or its

determination" (E § 213 Z, my translation). As we have seen, truth is the correspondence of reality with its concept, for example, an infinite that by not excluding the finite is truly infinite.

6. For an analysis of the superiority of this Hegelian notion of self-hood over the Kierkegaardian, in which the self attempts to come to itself through difference alone, see Taylor, *Journeys to Selfhood* esp. 271–276.

7. Anne Paolucci ("Hegel's Theory") offers an intelligent paraphrase of Hegel's theory of comedy. The one reservation I have is with her comment that Hegel's theory is "empirical and inductive" (106) even as she admits that, like Hegel's theory of tragedy, it relates to the general structures of the Hegelian system.

8. Hegel's movement directly to the antithesis could be explained in two ways. First, the culmination of tragedy is genuinely ambiguous: it could mean the dissolution of the hero's onesidedness and thus the erasure of the self in the reconstitution of the whole (thus providing a transition to the comedy of coincidence); it could also mean the dissolution of the moral order, the disintegration of a unified, universal spirit, such that the individual subject determines the truth even as he fails to reach it (thus providing a transition to the antithetical subgenres of reduction, negation, and withdrawal). Second, Hegel's neglect of intersubjectivity might have led him to mistake the mere objectivity of the comedy of coincidence for a synthetic form.

9. On "determination by the other" as a structuring force in comedy, see Stierle, who suggests that in comedy subject-object relations often become object-subject relations: the external world—whether natural or mechanical—takes on a life of its own.

10. One is almost tempted to suggest that Schelling would have done well to write a comedy of coincidence as part of his critique of Fichte.

11. The multiplicity of marriages also symbolizes the role of the broader intersubjective sphere, in which marriage, otherwise taken as a whole, is only a part; however, the broader sphere, society and ultimately the state, helps guarantee, through its norms and laws, the stability of marriage, even as society transcends it.

12. Barber has analyzed Shakespeare's comedies from *Love's Labor's Lost* to *Twelfth Night* in the light of their festive celebrations, which include—true to the structure of coincidence—a "heightened awareness of the relation between man and 'nature'—the nature celebrated on holiday" (8).

13. For some critics, for example, Nevo, this would serve as a description of all comedy.

14. Eliot's work, however, cannot be restricted to coincidence. Of particular interest are Mrs. Guzzard, who enacts on the margins of the play a significant and complex tragic self-sacrifice, and the moments of understanding gained in the course of the play, which suggest at least the possibility of intersubjectivity.

15. To my knowledge, *Leonce and Lena* has not been interpreted in the light of Holberg's play—despite the similarity in overall plot, the common parody of tragedy, the importance of masks, the similarities in the roles of the servants, and the obvious aural proximity of Leonce and Lena to Leander and Leonora.

16. Consider the Devil's statement: "Beware of the pursuit of the Superhuman: it leads to an indiscriminate contempt for the Human" (Act III).

17. The most important figure is the German dramatist Hebbel; for more recent reflections along these lines, see Calarco 121–126 and 135–139, Galle 9–18, Gellrich esp. 36–42, and Schulte.

18. Chance and external necessity are the same for Hegel in the sense that each has its cause outside itself (VG 29).

19. By showing that the gaiety of coincidence can be linked to reason, I would like to counter the *Verstandesdenken* of critics such as Greiner who see an absolute difference between the "comedy of pleasure" and the "comedy of reason" (246).

20. Philosophy, according to Hegel, differs; it does not presuppose, it proves, the existence of rational patterns.

21. In its attempt to realize a panorama of forces, the comedy of coincidence shares certain elements with the epic, a genre that is likewise defined by the overarching category of objectivity.

22. The necessity of 2 consists partly in the fact that private interests do not *necessarily* serve the greater whole.

23. Woody Allen's *Zelig* mocks the comedy of coincidence in the sense that it mocks the individual who all too freely and willingly would gain identity by absorbing his self into a greater whole. An excellent German example of this structure is Musil's story "The Giant Agoag," a comedy of reduction in which the hero seeks identity in something greater than himself—an omnibus.

24. It is also, in its negative repercussions, the stuff of tragedy. Hegel's philosophy of history is rich enough that it can be read in relation to both tragedy (the world-historical individual, the collision of paradigms, the demise of individuals and nations on the altar of history) and comedy (the hidden reason of chance, the ironic redirection of particularity, and the triumphs of spirit).

25. Cf. Plautus: "Such is chance—/ More good is often done in ignorance / Than by design" (*The Prisoners*, 44–45).

26. The *commedia dell'arte* also includes the possibility of (social) negation, intrigues that blend "to a conspiracy of nearly all against all" (Hinck, *Das deutsche Lustspiel* 7, my translation); yet even here the focus is on not morality or immorality but the optive effect of the performance. True to coincidence is an element of amorality, derived from the presentation of types rather than individuals.

Also important for the success of the *commedia dell'arte* was the self-abnegation of the actors who could not overindulge their own roles but had to hold back in order to let the other roles develop as well (Ducharte 30–32). Thematically the comedies mocked various forms of subjectivity; the actors' personal restraint formally mirrored this content. Improvisation succeeded only to the extent that the actors cooperated. Moreover, the players thematized in their works the idea of inevitable events and did so by improvising in a way that appeared as if all were prearranged—though it was not.

27. The comedy of coincidence appears to be the least psychological of comic forms; the subject after all is not fully developed. Hidden psychological elements are nonetheless present: the thwarting and redirecting of unconscious drives and the transformation of passions into virtues bear at least some similarity to Freud's theory of sublimation. If we wanted to develop this psychological moment in the light of the speculative structure sketched above, Vico would be a good link, for he argues that we should redirect, rather than negate, the passions. Moreover, for Vico providence is a guiding category (130; cf. 5, 335, 630, and 1109).

28. The structure can also be tragic if the fulfilled desire also leads to destruction; consider, for example, Aschenbach's not leaving the hotel in Thomas Mann's *Death in Venice*.

29. Grand in this film are the scene in which Elwood P. Dowd recalls meeting Harvey (Dowd would like to call him Harvey and by coincidence that is his name) and Harvey's decision to stay with Dowd rather than Dr. Chumley, who would instrumentalize Harvey for his private interests and whose intentions clash with the film's critique of instrumental rationality.

30. The evocation of the supernatural within tragedy, as for example in *Macbeth*, serves a mirroring purpose proper to that genre—it symbolizes and accentuates the essential course of tragic events.

31. Unfortunately, the translation of *The Essence of Christianity* currently in print (New York: Harper, 1957) is extremely misleading. Updating this translation would be a service to the profession.

32. Not every comedy of coincidence has a surrogate director. In Shakespeare's *The Comedy of Errors*, nobody oversees the multiple confusions; even the audience is stripped of its superior knowledge (its subjectivity) when the Abbess is unveiled as the wife of Egeon and the mother of the twins.
Interesting would be a study of the differing role of the surrogate director in tragedy and comedy: in each we see the irony of thwarted intentions, though with differing results.

33. Frank Wagner speaks of "the conceptual proximity of arbitrariness, particularity, and subjectivity, which one notes everywhere in Hegel" (151, my translation). The combination has particular import for the study of comedy.

34. Elder Olson excludes the kinds of plots I have called reduction, not to mention withdrawal, when he writes that in comedy the hero "succeeds or fails according as he has good or bad intentions" (*The Theory of Comedy* 90). Certain variations of the comedy of negation also challenge the efficacy of Olson's model.

35. On the other hand, the clumsy comedian who inadvertently succeeds after seemingly creating chaos and disaster is a hero of coincidence: Buster Keaton comes to mind.

36. The folly of *Don Quixote*, however, is more than one-sided; the society in which the hero fights his battles fails to recognize him not only because he deceives himself and remains ineffective, but also because this mundane and prosaic world lacks a sense for the greatness of the heroic era (Hegel 15:411). Don Quixote's chivalric code is outdated, and so he is a comic hero of reduction, but the materialistic society around him can view idealism and nobility only as madness and is thus satirized as well.

37. Previously overlooked is the allusion to Plato's *Gorgias*, where Callicles is baffled by the term "self-mastery" and appears to be unfamiliar with the concept (491d).

38. Kern rightfully recognizes the trickster figure as a central ingredient of what she calls the absolute comic, but she fails to see that the butt

of the joke is not only those fooled by the trickster but often the trickster himself. Many tales, proverbs, jokes, and even cartoons rely on this structure. A contemporary version of the trickster being tricked is Joseph Mankiewicz's *Sleuth*; the structure is as old as Aristophanes' *The Clouds*.

39. Heilman sees *The Firebugs* as dominantly tragic, partially melodramatic, and only in the "Afterpiece" comic (*Iceman* 195–199).

40. The comic topos of the parody of tragedy is worthy of a monograph, which—to my knowledge—has yet to be written. The only major study is Rau, which is restricted to the parody of tragedy in Aristophanes. Such a work might begin with the ancient satyr drama, which was designed to parody tragedy, less, however, to mock tragedy or the tragic hero or to satirize the comic protagonist who elevated himself to tragic stature, than to provide comic relief from the burdens and terror of tragedy (Sutton), a motif successfully integrated into some of the greatest modern tragedies, including those of Shakespeare.

41. Comedy sharpens our eyes for contradictions. In this light, note Brecht's comments on Hegel: "He had the makings to be one of the greatest humorists among philosophers; only Socrates, who had a similar method, could compare . . . Hegel's book 'The Greater Logic' is one of the greatest comic works of world literature . . . I have yet to meet anyone without a sense of humor who understood the dialectic of Hegel" (14:1460–1462, my translation).

42. I make only a few isolated references to *Anatol* in this chapter. For a fuller reading of *Anatol* as a comedy of reduction (though in this earlier essay I call it a comedy of "underdeveloped intersubjectivity"), see Roche, "Schnitzler."

43. Stolnitz, who also notes the comic hero's frequent lack of progress, unfortunately extends this trait to all comic heroes, thus overlooking the comic hero of intersubjectivity.

44. I disagree with Sokel's reading of Brecht's play as in many respects tragic. The play rather integrates the central comic theme, familiar in works from Aristophanes to Woody Allen, of the parody of tragedy.

45. Hegel links probabilism with sophistry when he speaks in the *Encyclopedia* of the invention of grounds or reasons that serve illicit purposes and the dependence of grounds on the individual's whim to select them. He continues with reflections that seem to apply to our age as well: "In our time, which is rich in reflection and given over to abstract argumentation, someone who does not know how to advance a good ground for everything, even for what is worst and most perverse, cannot have come

very far. Everything in the world that has been corrupted has been corrupted on good grounds" (E § 121 Z, translation modified).

46. Probabilistic arguments will also surface in negation, but here the hero is not himself deceived; instead, he attempts to dupe others, so, for example, Tartuffe's attempts to seduce Elmire (IV.v.1487–1496).

47. *The School for Wives* is a comedy of reduction that borders on negation (Arnolphe's treatment of Agnès and Horace is not only manipulative but brutal) and withdrawal (society is full of coquettes and cuckolds).

48. Überhorst doesn't see that essential to the comic is not just the deviation from virtue but the desire to claim for oneself a virtuous position even as one deviates; this is true not only of reduction but of negation and withdrawal as well. Not surprisingly, the positivistic researcher misses the complexity of the comic structure.

49. Though the details of our analyses differ, students of Olson's *Theory of Comedy* will recognize in the comedy of negation the plot of cleverness (as opposed to folly) in which the wit has bad intentions (as opposed to good intentions).

50. A desideratum in comic theory is an analysis of the contradictoriness of the comic hero, including his pragmatic contradictions. The historical dimension of such a study might begin with the relationship between content and dialogical structure in the early Socratic dialogues, where the interlocutors pretend to be more than they are. It might well conclude with some of the often overlooked contradictions in contemporary theory.

51. In Molière's *The Miser*, the world knows of Harpagon's unjust activities, but Harpagon is still able to manipulate the world—by virtue of his power.

52. Reduction and negation sometimes overlap; a good way to distinguish them is to think of Orgon and Tartuffe. The hero of negation is generally more evil and cleverer than the hero of reduction.

53. It does not take a great deal of imagination to see Mephistopheles as a comic hero of negation. At this point it should be clear that such a suggestion is not meant reductionistically, as an attempt to file a play into its corresponding drawer. Instead, I seek to employ genre labels as a kind of shorthand: in describing a character as a hero of reduction, negation, withdrawal, or whatever, I invoke a wide variety of concepts and possibilities. Moreover, as we consider a work within the rubric of a genre, our understanding of that genre is enriched; new possibilities are brought to our attention.

54. The victory of objectivity and normalcy dominates in McCollom's reading of comedy as "the divine average." Cf. similarly Cook.

55. The internal destruction of the comic hero is at times only metaphorical; as such the nonmimetic or antirealistic moment of coincidence, what Kern describes as the absolute comic, is reintegrated. Those who were not expected to win do. We also see the moment in social negation whenever the meek hero unexpectedly triumphs over those in power.

56. The comparison with Shakespearean heroes is not uncommon in the parody of tragedy, or more precisely in the mockery of the comic hero who claims for himself tragic status. Besides Brecht's play, consider, for example, Tellheim's equation of himself with Othello in *Minna von Barnhelm* or Söller's comparison of himself with Richard III in Goethe's *The Accomplices*.

57. In some cases the two moments are combined: in *Modern Times*, Chaplin wants to be part of society, and his efforts illustrate the absurdity of urban life and modern technology; in the end, he decides to abandon the city and withdraw.

58. Anyone wanting to develop the theme of the *comic hero*, a figure who acts with vitality and resourcefulness often against an oppressive society, might turn with profit to Torrance esp. 1–11. The counter-hero within social negation reasserts the vital impulse of coincidence without developing it so fully that he is able to tame his nemesis, the corrupt or depersonalized society.

59. For an introduction to this debate in Sternheim scholarship, with further bibliographical references, see Myers.

60. Sternheim's heroes recognize that they must become part of society in order to gain an identity (and so they do not suffer the contradictions of withdrawal). In their pursuit of a social identity they exhibit moments of reduction; their most distinguishing features, however, are those of negation: the reckless imagination and freedom with which they seek conformity and identity.

61. Comic withdrawal is complex only when the hero's disdain can be viewed as justified. A figure such as Adrast in Lessing's *The Free Spirit* unjustly criticizes others and so is simply a comic hero of reduction.

62. Plato argues that the misanthrope lacks a "critical understanding of human nature" (*Phaedo* 89e).

63. Cf. Hegel: "at first this end is only *subjective* and internal to me, but it should also become *objective* and throw off the deficiency of mere subjectivity" (R § 8 Z). Cf. R § 33 Z.

64. Not surprisingly, many comedies operate with the themes of law and justice, that is, the objective sphere that forms a counterpoint to the comic hero.

65. Unlike Lessing's Nathan, with whom Bernhardi shares the problem of confronting forms of discrimination, Bernhardi, a modern and individualistic figure, is unable to recognize a normative or universal ethic with which to confront his opponents. Further, where Nathan personifies the principles of dialogue and education, Bernhardi is often reduced to brief interjections and aposiopesis. His withdrawal, which is partly the consequence of modern subjectivity, functions even on a linguistic level.

66. The hero of the comedy of withdrawal might be contrasted with Hegel's world-historical individual who follows his passions, which are one with the universal, in such a way as to arouse others and change history (12:45–49). The comic hero lacks this emotional, rhetorical, or formal quality.

67. Berenger in Ionesco's *Rhinoceros*, which includes significant elements of withdrawal, is, despite his strong moral stance, intuitive, not intellectual, but the exception here derives from the fact that the intellectuals in Berenger's society, for example, Dudard, are convinced that all values are relative, a question of personal preference, and that there is no such thing as absolute right; such characters offer no resistance to the processes of dehumanization. According to Ionesco, the intellectual might be more corrupt than the intuitively good figure. The nonintellectual knows less and has fewer refined categories, but that also means, in a misguided age, that the nonintellectual has fewer wrong categories. This reinforces for us the importance of the thesis within the comic sequence. For related reasons intellectuals within coincidence are often upstaged by life-affirming heroes or heroines, as in Shaw's *Man and Superman* or Hawks's *Ball of Fire*.

68. The parallel between Hegel and the comedy of withdrawal has further significance. The comedy of withdrawal, which includes reflection on matters of ethics, follows the dissolution of practical ethics sketched in reduction and negation. This shift from practical disintegration to philosophical reflection has a historical analogue. Hegel himself speaks of philosophy's having arrived too late. More recently, Max Scheler has argued that the attempt to ground ethics in first principles "is always connected with processes of disintegration in an existing ethos" (*Formalismus* 312; *Formalism* 308). The comedy of intersubjectivity, however, will argue that the truth of philosophical ethics is its communication and realization. Though the owl of Minerva has always come too late, history does not rep-

resent future necessity. Intellect has, in principle, the power to redirect and redesign the pattern of history. To this end art can contribute.

69. This moment is also sometimes visible in the tragedy of stubbornness, where the hero longs for the intersubjective sphere even as he negates it. See, for example, Adrian Leverkühn's relations with Rudi Schwerdtfeger in Thomas Mann's *Doctor Faustus*.

70. The proximity of the comic and the ugly finds its first formulation in Aristotle (*Poetics* 5).

71. Cf. E § 511–512: "This pure self-certitude, rising to its pitch, appears in the two forms that directly pass over into one another, *conscience* and *evil*. The former is the will of *goodness*, which, however, in this pure subjectivity is the *non-objective*, non-universal, the unutterable and over which the subject is conscious that *he* in his *individuality* has the decision. *Evil* is the same awareness of the single self as decisive insofar as the single self does not remain in this abstraction but takes up the content of a subjective interest contrary to the good . . . . *Evil* as the most intimate reflection of subjectivity itself in opposition to the objective and universal, which it treats as mere sham, is the same as the *good sentiment* of *abstract* goodness, which reserves to the subjectivity the determination thereof:— the utterly abstract *appearance*, the immediate inversion and annihilation of itself" (translation modified).

72. The theme is historically reflected in Aristophanes' and Plato's evaluations of Socrates: for Aristophanes, Socrates' subjectivity is reduced to the negativity and relativism of the Sophists; for Plato, it is elevated as the path toward self-grounding and normative knowledge.

73. In Hegelian terms, the transition from withdrawal to intersubjectivity might be said to parallel the historical transition from an emerging Christianity (as inward spirituality) to Christianity's actualization in the modern state. See 12:138–141 and R § 357–360.

74. It speaks for an opera like Puccini's *The Girl of the Golden West* that the full reconciliation takes place not after chance (the gambling that concludes Act II) but after recognition and forgiveness (Act III).

75. If the artist Schelling had written a comedy of coincidence to counter Fichte, Hegel would have done well to upstage Schelling with a comedy of intersubjectivity.

76. According to Carlson, the welcoming of women's power in comedy is not without complexities and restrictions—at least in traditional British comedy. Women come to power, according to Carlson, by an inversion of the

status quo. This alternative world has an atmosphere of farce or fantasy, which prevents us from taking it seriously, or it is not as richly alternative as it might seem. Moreover, it is only temporary, for comedy generally ends in a reversal of the reversal, such that women are ultimately reined in by conventional social limitations, including marriage.

Although much of Carlson's argument is convincing, a few aspects might be called into question: one wonders, for example, whether Carlson is working with a notion of liberty rather than freedom (to use Locke's distinction, 2.22 and 2.57), which will not allow her to see bonds as fulfilling; whether some marriages—a good example would be that of Hans Karl and Helen in Hofmannsthal's *The Difficult Man*—do not dilute female strengths; and whether it is mistaken to assume that comedies produced in a "patriarchal society" must by definition endorse patriarchy.

77. Cf. R § 164. Symptomatic of increasing subjectivity is that twentieth-century comedy focuses on the failure to reach the speculative moment of marriage; consider the popularity of comic reduction and the so-called parody of comedy. Yet the truth of reduction is the negation of the negation of substance. Schnitzler's *Anatol* and *The Round Dance* mock less the institution of marriage than attitudes toward this institution. Even in the tradition, poor unions or marriages tend to ridicule not the institution as such but the players in it.

78. For a discussion of Hegel's concept of recognition that includes some passing references to his theory of comedy and especially tragedy, see Williams, *Recognition*.

79. The guardians are presented as the play's surrogate directors; on a metalevel their comments indicate that the work's author recognizes the extent to which art transcends the creator's intentions.

80. *Minna von Barnhelm* is not only as a variant of the comedy of intersubjectivity a synthesis of general forms of comedy (coincidence, withdrawal, and so forth), it also unites, according to Wicke (109–122), the historically specific types of comedy prevalent during the Enlightenment. Strohschneider-Kohrs argues in a similar vein, recognizing in *Minna* a dialectical synthesis of *comédie gaie* and *comédie sérieuse* ("Die überwundene Komödiantin" esp. 196). A legitimate area of inquiry would be to what extent the synthetic forms of drama (tragedies of awareness, comedies of intersubjectivity, and dramas of reconciliation) also unify historically specific forms or themes.

81. The Bishop lacks real power but has a strong charismatic authority, an interesting moment in many dramas. Leon is attracted to the natural authority of the Bishop; his eyes are as windows onto the heavens.

Similar, for example, is Kent's attraction to Lear or the aura of Schiller's Wallenstein.

82. McFadden's theory of comedy as "a characteristic maintenance-as-itself, despite the implicit threat of alteration" (25) may capture the antithetical forms of comedy but fails to account for the comedy of intersubjectivity, as illustrated, for example, by Leon and the Bishop. This limitation parallels McFadden's inability to appreciate the value of Frye's analysis of comic recognition, movement, and rebirth (159–173). Finally, McFadden's definition exhibits a common and serious deficiency: it could just as easily apply to tragedy and so misses the *differentia specifica* of comedy.

83. The argument that a family or state can also be viewed as an individual is a traditional and well-justified topos in Hegel. See, for example, 12:26 and 12:73.

84. The world-state is an analogue of 3 insofar as it sublates negativity (conflict, lack, crime, and so forth) within itself; it does not need the negative in the form of another, potentially warring state.

85. Cf. Roche, *Dynamic Stillness* esp. 46–47 and 86–89. Sound reflections on a wholeness that mediates between incompleteness and closure can also be found in Desmond, *Art* esp. 77–101 and *Desire* esp. 77–84. Though many postmodernists pride themselves on overcoming binary oppositions and illusory dualisms, their either-or thinking still pervades such distinctions as closure/non-closure and synthesis/non-synthesis; unwittingly they fall back into the realm of *Verstand*. See, for example, Kuzniar.

86. The concept of "humor" has a messy history. Preisendanz (*Humor*) has shown how complex and nuanced Hegel's concept of humor is, but the post-Hegelians are basically uniform in defining humor as a sense of reconciliation that is nonetheless aware of still unresolved tensions in reality; it is tolerant of human foibles and inadequacies, for it views them *sub specie aeternitatis*. Thus, for authors such as Kuno Fischer, Friedrich Theodor Vischer, Karl Rosenkranz, Moriz Carriere, or Adolf Zeising, it signifies a kind of harmony, whereas for a contemporary American critic such as Lang it represents an undermining of the notion of representation and immersion in ambiguities and aporias, the priority of the signifier over the signified. For Lang, humor is, in the language I have introduced, absolute irony, irony as an end in itself. The contradictions of such a position are sketched below and do not disappear even if we view absolute irony with affirmation and joy rather than despair. See Lang 69 and 195. The post-Hegelian elevation of "humor" can also be seen among later German humanists, whose orientation is not in any literal way Hegelian. See, for ex-

ample, Eduard von Hartmann esp. 2:391–425; Lipps esp. 261–264; Volkelt, *Das System* esp. 2:529; Hermann Cohen esp. 2:114–117; Kutscher esp. 1:158–161; and Maier. The elevation is so widespread that Jünger feels compelled to argue against a modern overvaluation of humor and a subsequent weakening of our insight into comic incongruity (83–95). The major exception is Kirchmann, who argues against the elevation of humor in Hegel and his students, because—of all things—it represents a holding on to, rather than an overcoming of, contradiction (2:65–66).

87. For criticism of the post-Hegelians see, for example, Baum, *Humor* and "Der widerspruchsvolle Charakter" 208 and 251–252; and Grimm, "Kapriolen" and "Comic Reversal." Heise, who reduces all comic conflict to class struggle, locates the apologetic nature of humor already in Hegel (816–819). Baum indirectly recognizes the validity of intersubjectivity and humor when she concludes her long critique of post-Hegelian theories of comedy by calling for recognition of "the propelling role of humor, supportive of development in a positive sense" (*Humor* 177, my translation). In the end, Baum objects not to the principle of humor or synthesis but its false and apologetic applications.

88. Frederic Jameson, arguing from a Marxist perspective and informed by the apparent aporias of negative hermeneutics and negative dialectics, argues in the conclusion of *The Political Unconscious* that literature and criticism should attempt to reintegrate a utopian element (see esp. 291–299). Critique implicitly invokes an ideal against which we measure the inadequacies of what is current; it is essential that this ideal be made explicit and that we present arguments for it. Interesting is Jameson's stress on the collective dimensions of utopia, though he himself admits that a theory of the collective utopia—as the transcendence of the merely subjective or the merely negative—has yet to be written (294). One need not view utopia as "libidinal gratification" (73) or as "the liberation of desire" (167), that is, as irrational and an outlet for the id, to appreciate Jameson's formal concern with the utopian. (For a critique of the content of Jameson's utopia, including its refusal to recognize any role for sublimation, see Seaton 137–142.) A discussion of utopian structures would benefit from attention to, first, the arguments of objective idealism, and second, the genres I designate as the comedy of intersubjectivity and the drama of reconciliation.

89. In another passage, Hegel states: "Reason is indeed able to endure the contradiction, yet also, it is true, able to resolve it" (17:436, my translation). See also 17:230–231.

90. For a comprehensive study of Romantic irony—in theory and practice—see Strohschneider-Kohrs, *Die romantische Ironie*. That Hegel's concept had little to do with the historical phenomenon of Romantic irony—a point recognized very early (see, for example, Bohtz 112–114)—supports an application to later authors who fit the pattern Hegel describes. My reading of Hegel's critique of romantic irony as extendable to the present is shared by Desmond, *Art* 114–120 and *Beyond Hegel* 292–300, and Houlgate, *Freedom* 148–153 and 170–171.

91. The supernatural moments of coincidence contrast with the magic of absolute irony. In authors such as Aristophanes, Shakespeare, or Raimund, the fairies represent a moral order; in Tieck and Grabbe, on the other hand, unreal events are presented either as mere play or as illustrations of authorial subjectivity.

92. For an excellent analysis of the play's satire of the audience, see Brummack.

93. Richard Rorty makes the most recent case for all-pervasive irony but is no more consistent than the Romantic ironists Hegel condemns. Rorty insists that the ironist "has radical and continuing doubts about the final vocabulary she currently uses" (73), but Rorty exhibits little (self-reflexive) irony toward contingency and irony, his principal antifoundationalist terms. Not only does the ironist dogmatically, if indirectly, affirm the lack of foundations; having denied the existence of any objective criteria to adjudicate differences, the ironist is free to privilege whatever position he wants: he can become a dogmatist while claiming to be an ironist.

94. The undermining of traditional standards is often progressive, but the claim that we are free to remake *all* truths has tyrannical possibilities. Alfred Rosenberg, the philosopher of National Socialism, was one of the most strident relativists of the twentieth century. He merely drew the consequences: according to Rosenberg, if the absolute is relativized, we may freely absolutize the relative—including, for example, race. See Roche, "National Socialism."

95. Works of absolute irony must be distinguished from works in which all characters are ironized but in such a way that norms are still evoked (as in the comedy of negation) and in which *levels* of irony and acceptance can be measured. In Thomas Mann's *The Magic Mountain*, for example, irony is all-pervasive, but Settembrini is still preferable to Naphta.

96. Contemporary comedy tends toward the tragicomic partly because the portrayal of selves seeking, but lacking, coherence or identity is viewed not as a form of reduction but as an extension of the world as it is.

97. We can view the self-cancellation of the comedy of negation, alternatively, on a more direct level, by way of the self-cancellation of injustice or power positivism, which, despite its claims to the contrary, presupposes internal cooperation, dialogue, and an objective order of recognized justice. See Roche, "Plato."

98. Gardner has some compelling reflections on our tendency to impoverish great works by reading them in the light of our anxieties and sense of meaninglessness ("Religion" 117–118). An ideology that denies us access to what is other about these works along with a methodology that elevates what is marginal over what is dominant adds justification to this tendency.

99. My analysis of Pirandello's play builds on an earlier study. See Roche, "Kafka, Pirandello, and the Irony of Ironic Indeterminacy." Significant passages of that study have been incorporated here and are used with the gracious permission of the Kafka Society of America.

100. Absolute irony can be viewed not merely as a self-reflexive intensification of comic negation, but also as a complex form of reduction. Where reduction mocks deviation from a variety of ideals or norms, absolute irony delights in the deliberate subversion of all ideals and norms. The subversion of unjust norms and standards is valid; the negation of all norms is a *reduction* of this ideal, which undermines itself.

101. One critic who consistently stresses the self-reflexivity of comedy, at least from the formal perspective of the play within a play, is Martini (*Lustspiele*).

102. This dialectical strategy could be applied to other works by Pirandello, for example, his splendidly complex *Right You Are (If You Think You Are)*. The play may mean to parody busybodies and superficial certainty-seekers, and to an extent it does, but it also mocks Laudisi's laziness (if there is no truth, why search for it), his callousness, and, taken self-reflexively, the titular view that there is no truth: if any position is right, then so, too, the stance that rejects the position that any position is right. The text means more than its apparently reliable spokesman Laudisi thinks it means. The noncommittal ironist is more concerned with demonstrating that truth does not exist than with averting the pain of the Ponza-Frola family (Oliver 35–46). Absolute irony, as illustrated by the play's title and its advocate Laudisi, is not only intellectually self-destructive, it

is ethically damaging. Laudisi, unable to persuade other characters and ineffectual at preventing further insensitive inquiries, only *seems* to come into his own; by a series of dialectical inversions, the position he advocates is actually undermined. This dialectic is missed in the more straightforward readings of the play from Vittorini 120–128 to Biundo 123–140.

103. The structures of intersubjectivity are prepared for earlier, as, for example, when Diego states: "We all yearn to marry, and for our whole life long, some one particular soul" (Ita 4:163; Eng 297).

104. If art is the sensuous appearance of truth, bad art is weakly sensuous (for example, poorly executed or cliche-ridden) or barely truthful (for example, shallow or simply silly). Non-art, on the other hand, is whatever lacks a spiritual moment (for example, certain instances of "found art"), whatever is blatantly false (for example, the statements of absolute irony), or whatever is not sensuous (for example, certain examples of "conceptual art" and much of philosophy). For illuminating reflections on non-art, see Fowkes.

105. Within this definition Frye allows for a multiplicity of subforms, "a sequence of stages in the life of a redeemed society" (*Anatomy of Form* 185). These represent the movement within comedy from the ironic to the romantic, from the earliest to the latest stages of comic society. In addition, Frye allows for a moment of comic negation, the *alazon* figure, yet such a figure is ultimately subordinate to the new order, that is, to the portrayal of characters as they realize coincidence or intersubjectivity.

106. Frye is not alone in assuming that all comedies end happily. For additional examples, taken almost at random, see Nevo 331 and Shershow 17.

107. Cf. Hegel: "Were a comedy, however, to forgo seriousness completely, then it would indeed sink to the level of farce and lower still . . . . If it were a matter of locating authorities for what in comedy transcends the merely cheerful, then I would cite above all Aristophanes, in most of whose works, at least those approaching farce, simultaneously the most bitter seriousness, that is to say the *political* . . . constitutes the main interest" (11:74, my translation).

108. Buster Keaton is absolutely comic in the fact that he never laughs. Paradoxically, he fulfills the Hegelian moment.

109. In terms of authors, rather than genres, the moment Hegel admired is particularly pronounced in Aristophanes and Shakespeare, for example, in the Falstaff plays. In the German tradition one thinks of

Nestroy. In the contemporary era selected works of Woody Allen come to mind, especially his earlier films.

110. I thus share with Baum a critique of Hegel's reluctance to consider as comic the mere negation of a negation, that is, the critical portrayal of an untenable position that does not result in any kind of reconciliation. Hegel's concept of the comic in this passage is reduced to what Germans generally understand by *Humor*. Two modern critics who share Hegel's belief that comedy should be joyous and ultimately affirmative are Martens and Amur. A question worthy of detailed investigation would be why the province of what is called comic has become increasingly expansive such as to include what would otherwise be classified as satire, grotesque, and so forth, and what precisely the historical steps in this expansion have been.

111. Hegel, as Friedmar Apel notes (152), does not integrate alienation into the sphere of the comic; instead, Hegel stresses the subject's self-assurance. The trick would seem to be not to ignore alienation but to render it comic—either by focusing on its excesses (self-inflicted suffering as comic) or its catalysts (involuntary suffering transformed into the comedy of negation).

112. The laughter of contrast has been articulated by Jean Paul, Schopenhauer, and Kierkegaard, among others, the laughter of superiority by Hobbes, Vico, and Baudelaire, among others, the laughter of festivity above all by Bakhtin. Rephrased as liberation, psychic relief, or release from restraint, the third form can also be attributed to Spencer and Freud. Many theorists (for example, Kant and Bergson) focus on particular kinds of contrasts. Monro anomalously discusses a fourth theory of laughter, the ambivalence theory: "we laugh whenever, on contemplating an object or a situation, we find opposite emotions struggling within us for mastery" (210). I consider this definition another variant of the incongruity theory, a particular kind of contrast, though here in the viewing subject, not in the object.

113. I view contrast or incongruity as a necessary though not sufficient condition of the comic. For intelligent discussions of this issue, see Elder Olson, *Comedy* esp. 3–24 and Schaeffer esp. 3–33. Great diversity exists within laughter and what is often called humor—as Apte and Lewis, for example, have argued; but a definition that encompasses both unity and diversity need not be accused of overgeneralization. Morreall also tries to combine the three theories into an overarching definition that favors incongruity; his definition reads: "laughter results from a pleasant psychological shift" (39).

114. For Bakhtin and his modern interpreter Kern, laughter arises from the contrast between previous standards and their momentary dissolution in the carnivalesque situation.

115. It is surely in part with such ideas in mind that Brecht preferred to write comedies of reduction and comedies of social negation.

116. Peter Pütz suggests: "Since the beginning of European theater comedy has been more suited than tragedy to play around with aesthetic precepts and prohibitions and otherwise to suspend meticulously respected limits . . . . It has to do with the basic function of comedy that bonds are relaxed, boundaries are opened, things and styles that are far removed from one another according to the ruling aesthetic ontology are brought together and liberated from their mutual rigidity: banal realities and highest ideals, counts and figaros, formed characters and herd-like beings . . . . With its tendency toward reversal, shift in perspective, and discovery of new latitude, comedy is, despite its apparent dramaturgical mechanics, a constantly experimenting, genre-expanding form of art, which prefers to move on the margins of its own enterprise, thereby transcending through poetic self-reflection . . . precisely these margins" (61–62, my translation). On comedy as a genre that dissolves boundaries, see also Greiner, *Die Komödie*.

117. The relation between cruelty and comedy is a rich topic—with historical (why does cruelty within comedy increase in modernity?), dramaturgical (how do we present cruelty on stage as comic?), psychological (what needs are here relieved?), and ethical (what are the limits and dangers of comic cruelty?) ramifications that have yet to be explained. One of the few critics to broach the topic is Blistein 42–76.

118. Hegel apparently did not own Schütze's work on comedy, but he was familiar with the author: he owned, for example, his *Versuch einer Theorie des Reims nach Inhalt und Form* (Magdeburg: Keil, 1802). See *Verzeichnis*.

119. "A sign of an unfavorable characteristic of another person appears to us as comic, if we are not conscious of the same unfavorable characteristic in ourselves and it provokes no virulently unpleasant feelings in us" (Überhorst 2–3, my translation).

120. Grimm discusses repetition and circularity as central to much of modern drama, thus in a sense highlighting not only a structure of comedy but a comic tendency of modern drama in general ("Pyramide"). See also Klotz, *Geschlossene und offene Form*.

121. Identity crises can also be tragic, especially within the rubric of awareness. Ransom Stoddard in Ford's *The Man Who Shot Liberty Valance* is one example among many. A full analysis of identity crises in comedy is a desideratum. Filling it might also shed light on some of the unwittingly comic aspects of the contemporary preoccupation with self-reflection.

122. Although diverse thematic studies of doubles exist (Tymms, Rank, Hildenbrock), an analysis of doubles and genre appears to be a desideratum.

123. The hero's cure in *Zelig* begins when another person mirrors his role back to him; Zelig becomes in a sense self-conscious, but self-conscious via the help of an other, who is one and the same with himself.

124. The proximity of the drama of involuntary suffering to the comedy of social negation, a point to be developed in a later chapter, might be noted here, specifically by alluding to the similar function of role playing in Frisch's *Andorra*, a drama of involuntary suffering.

125. In *On Naive and Sentimental Poetry*, Schiller, too, recognizes that tragedy is more related to the practical and passionate, comedy to the theoretical.

126. The related technique by which a good hero must act disingenuously in order to defeat an antagonist occasionally surfaces in the drama of reconciliation. Good examples would be Euripides' *Helen* and Marston's *The Malcontent*.

127. For a more complex account of types of comic instrumentalization, see Roche, "Apel and Lessing." Instrumentalization can also be tragic, as, for example, in *Medea* or *The Wild Duck*.

128. In his most recent reflections, Apel recognizes the need for strategic action as long as there is a break between the real and the ideal; this could be further related to our comic reading of the non-strategically inclined hero of withdrawal. See Apel, *Diskurs und Verantwortung* esp. 141–153.

129. The antithetical forms could also be analyzed in the light of their psychological facets. In reduction, sexuality is common, in negation, aggression, and in withdrawal, conscience or the internalization of aggression. In each case a loss of balance and measure is ironized. Whether these Freudian concepts mirror a logical sequence and whether they can enrich in detail the investigation of comedy would be worthy of study.

130. A review of the secondary literature on *The Difficult Man* would demand a book-length study in and of itself. The readings most in spirit

with my own are Wittmann, Guidry, and Söhnlein. Bennett focuses on the role of chance in the play (*Hugo von Hofmannsthal* 168–229), Greiner stresses the revelations of the unconscious ("Die Rede"), and Cohn compares the play with Molière's *The Misanthrope*, thereby underscoring the play's relation to the comedy of withdrawal.

131. Stani could also be compared with Grillparzer's Ferdinand, another confident nephew in Austrian literature. Ferdinand realizes the tragic potential of stubborn self-confidence; true to the comic mode, however, Stani is relatively harmless and in his own way delightful.

132. Stani is ironized for his categories, and one could imagine a metaphoric critique of my reading of the play, whereby I, too, make categories. To which I can only respond that such a critic must have two categories himself: those who have categories and those who don't, and the critic, by necessity, is in my camp. Conclusion: What is important is the arbitrariness of certain categories and their possible misuse, not the application of categories per se.

133. Wittmann, in describing Stani as rational (138–139), fails to see in Stani's thought processes the reduction of reason. The target of the comedy is Stani and the misuse of reason, not reason itself.

134. The miscommunication in Act I, however, stems partly from a modern apparatus, the telephone, that hides as much as it reveals.

135. I disagree here with Guidry, who views Altenwyl in an entirely positive light. Similarly, Greiner sees in Altenwyl's ideal of conversation a delimiting of subjectivity or "ein Außer-Kraft-Sein des Selbst" ("Die Rede" 242) and so overlooks the hidden self-directedness of the model. Altenwyl not only repeats his point, his very view of conversation is the repetition of a traditional view advanced, for example, by La Bruyère (*Les caracteres*, "De la societe et de la conversation" 16). Surprisingly, critics elevate Altenwyl as if he were proposing a new intersubjective ideal, when he is in fact adhering to a traditional rhetorical and strategic concept. Though it contains a moment of truth, it also represents a reduction.

136. The play's mockery of Neuhoff's adoration of will appears to be a hidden critique of Nietzsche, especially insofar as Neuhoff speaks in Nietzsche's voice: Neuhoff's "You belong to no one and to everyone!" (III.iv) echoes the title page of *Thus Spoke Zarathustra*. However, the play's reading of Nietzsche, which has never been fully developed, is complex. In its discussion of eternity and the momentary, the play appears to embrace Nietzsche's complex reading of *Faust* in the last book of *Zarathustra*. In addition, Hans Karl speaks of something like eternal recurrence (I.xviii),

and his suggestion that necessity chooses us is likewise Nietzschean (II.x). For a general discussion of Nietzsche and Hofmannsthal, see Del Caro.

137. Wittmann mistakenly views Neuhoff as tragic (140); see also Söhnlein 90. Failure does not necessarily imply tragedy—as the drama of suffering and the various antithetical comedies illustrate. Hechingen, who suffers of his genuine love for his wife and his willingness to grant her the freedom she abuses, may at first glance appear tragic, though his stupidity, weakness, and overriding concern for his own particularity push him ultimately into the sphere of the comic.

138. A parallel structure surfaces in Schnitzler's *Professor Bernhardi*: Flint, despite his obvious inadequacies, does represent a moment of truth in relation to the reclusive Bernhardi.

139. One could say that there are two kinds of power. One is intentional and signifies the ability to get what one wants; the other is unintentional and involves a moment of grace. In the latter, the self brings about events owing to an unintentional charisma, an exemplary life that draws others to it—Goethe's Egmont and Grillparzer's Bishop have elements of this. For the characters in Hofmannsthal's play, Hans Karl appears to embody just such a charismatic power. Some people succeed precisely because they appear not to have intentions; if they were to have intentions, others might react negatively.

140. One could also undermine Hans Karl's stance from an intentionalist perspective. In clear contrast to the reticent Hans Karl, Hofmannsthal spoke out in February 1919 in his open letter to Henri Barbusse for understanding, peace, and comradeship between nations.

141. The elevation of language cannot be reduced to a Eurocentric bias. One could never, for example, *argue* that dance is higher than language (one would have to dance such an argument). The strength of language appears to derive from its breadth, clarity, and reflexivity.

142. I would disagree with Dorrit Cohn, who limits *The Difficult Man* to the comedy of withdrawal, when she writes that for Hans Karl "language is *always* an impediment to sincerity" (296). The above quotes seem to prove otherwise.

143. To draw a comparison with another major comic heroine in the German tradition: Helen is willful, like Lessing's Minna, but not manipulative, and in this sense unlike Minna.

144. See Thomas Heine for a helpful discussion of understanding as mediated by gestures and the unconscious.

145. In retrospect, Antoinette, the skeptic, is correct: Hans Karl—at least unconsciously—does have Helen in mind as he elevates the concept of marriage. He articulates more than he knows. On critics' general under-valuation of Antoinette's insights, see Lubich, who fails, however, to grasp the validity of Hans Karl's arguments on behalf of stable relations.

146. Recognizing a positive moment within a structure that is other-wise evil is not one and the same with embracing that structure. The ele-vation of comradeship is equally evident, for example, in Remarque's *All Quiet on the Western Front*, a decidedly anti-militaristic work. Mauser overestimates the play's elevation of war. Moreover, if Hofmannsthal had wanted to embrace war, we needn't read the play as fulfilling these expec-tations. Plays offer their readers meanings that often transcend, and some-times even conflict with, the author's intentions.

147. Greiner reads the restrictions on final harmony as a means of underlining its aesthetic status as a mere prolepsis of reality that the viewer must complete: "For the observer the discovery of the answering you is brought back into the sphere of signs, it is an evocation, unreal, aesthetic pre-lumination [Vor-Schein], which must still become reality" ("Die Rede" 244, my translation). Söhnlein adopts a more historical ap-proach, viewing marriage as a middle path between pure isolation and questionable integration into a dying society, "a hold in a world in which traditional categories of value have suddenly lost their meaning" (116, my translation).

148. The structure is not restricted to the theme of language: Act I of Ionesco's *Rhinoceros* mocks the Logician, but only insofar as we see that the Logician himself transgresses the laws of logic, which remain intact. An overarching issue is at stake in one's interpretation of such passages. Comedy immerses itself in disarray and incongruities not in order to cele-brate the irrational, as Gurewitch, for example, contends, but in order ei-ther to show a hidden element of reason behind the disorder of farce or to shed light on the incongruous as incongruous, as untenable. The reason behind the irrational is more, not less, comic than the irrational itself.

149. Fred Robinson's *The Comedy of Language* exhibits some of the confusions of linguistic skepticism. Robinson couples the comedy of lan-guage with a metaphysics of negativity: our concepts, expressed through the abstractions and fixities of language, fail to grasp the flux of reality. Bergson's laughter, which occurs when something mechanical is encrusted on the living, is transformed by Robinson into a linguistic framework and then universalized: "language is impotent to describe reality" (Robinson 20). But if Robinson is correct, he is wrong; the statement cancels itself

and is comic in a different way than he envisaged. Just as the contemporary focus on comedy's negativity does not take the moment of negativity far enough, so are studies on comic language frequently unable to recognize language as the essence not of impotent nonrecognition, but of recognition, not of an isolated and subjective consciousness, but of intersubjective relations.

150. One could develop newer, more complex metagenres based on the appearance of different genres and subgenres within individual works, though my intuitive sense is that in systematizing at this level, one would quickly reach a point of diminishing returns.

151. On differences between *The Misanthrope* and *The Plain Dealer*, see Friedson.

152. For similar evaluations of the play's disharmony, including discussion of Goethe's different versions, see Martini 105–149 and Preisendanz, "Das Schäferspiel."

153. A more obvious and equally legitimate way to limit a nihilistic reading would be to historicize the characters' nihilism and recall their privileged positions within society.

154. Nestroy criticism does not frequently recognize the harmonic moments of his works. For an exception, see Katann, who writes: "Even if satire has a negative, condemning, castigating, critical nature, it nonetheless, as has been unrecognized in the case of Nestroy, does not forgo the positive, and precisely Nestroy's *A Man Full of Nothing* is living proof that the poet has positive ideals: true friendship along with love and marriage in their moral, purifying effect stand sublimely there at the end of the play; in the course of the drama the deep meaning of need or want for the moral purification of character is elucidated" (93, my translation).

155. The complexities of *Fraternal Quarrel* have something in common with Shakespeare's *Henry VI*, with which it has to my knowledge not been compared—not even by a critic such as Yates (*Grillparzer*), who is otherwise sensitive to connections between Grillparzer and Shakespeare. In each play we see a critique of the age (in *Henry VI*, for example, the consistent breaking of oaths) and a complex philosophical and dramatic evaluation of a ruler more given to religious and contemplative pursuits than to action. In each work a power vacuum is created by a noble but weak and melancholic ruler who refuses to wield power and whose commentary on the action around him functions almost like that of a chorus. Rudolf's power is transferred to the power positivistic Klesel and the fanatic Ferdinand; the Thirty Years' War lies on the horizon. The inactive

Henry relinquishes power to an arbitrary, ruthless, and anti-intellectual mob (the murderers of Suffolk, Jack Cade and his followers) and sly traitors (York, Edward, and eventually Richard III). Anarchy, civil war, and tyranny fill the vacuum of power. Not unlike what we see in Grillparzer's play, it is a world of moral decay, political chaos, and social disintegration.

156. Jauß views the breaking of generic norms, "the alteration of the horizon of the genre" (*Toward an Aesthetic* 94), as the criterion for great art, but I see no reason why the unique fulfillment of a genre, especially a superior one, should not also suffice as a criterion for greatness. Genres after all do allow for diversity. It belongs to the beauty of art that one masterpiece does not exclude another.

Chapter 4: On the Drama of Reconciliation

1. One might think that harmony should not be portrayed in art—it is too direct and overbearing. But a complex harmony transcends a complex negativity by virtue of the logical and ontological superiority of the positive. (Whereas negative positions cancel themselves, positive ones do not.) Moreover, a negative work can be as direct, and as a result just as unaesthetic, as a work that depicts a false harmony. Clara Park, one of the few contemporary critics to embrace something like the drama of reconciliation, makes a strong case for the validity of what she calls *"earned happy ends"* (61) and disparages thereby the almost automatic tendency in contemporary letters toward final negativity. Helen Gardner also assumes this anomalous position in criticizing "the distrust so widely expressed today in the power of art to present images of human life that strongly engage our sympathies and give pleasure: the pleasure arising both from that concord of ends and beginnings that makes the work a whole and from the truth of what is shown or told to our own experience of living" ("Happy Endings" 42).

2. Bennett interprets two German dramas of reconciliation, Lessing's *Nathan the Wise* and Kleist's *Prince Friedrich von Homburg*, as uniting reason and freedom, "opposites which are irreconcilable in logic" (*Modern Drama* 94; cf. 95 and 148). Such a logic, however, is merely the subordinate logic of *Verstand*; Bennett unfortunately does not add to his historical study the contemporary philosophical discussions, above all the analyses of Hegel, which make this claim so repeatedly.

3. A long tradition—from which Hegel is not excluded—renders man the public being and woman the private being (Elshtain and Loraux). Within this paradigm the woman is frequently viewed—also by women—

as the sacrificial (or expendable) figure on the altar of male-dominated politics. *Agnes Bernauer* is the classic example within the German tradition. The problem of women being sacrificed for the goals of men has only partially abated in the twentieth century, as is evident, for example, in Dürrenmatt's *The Physicists*. The predominance of the sacrifice of women, especially in tragedy, may explain the contemporary idealization of the tragic counterstrand exemplified by Medea. Jelinek's *Clara S.* works with both models, the sacrificial and the revengeful woman.

4. I am speaking here only of pure melodrama or melodrama with a happy end, what James Smith calls the "melodrama of triumph" (15); the term "melodrama" has also been used for works without a positive resolution.

5. With the help of this analysis we can see how self-sacrifice and stubbornness when furthest removed from integrating a true collision tend to border on the melodramatic.

6. A question to which probably only a subtle answer can be given is whether melodrama (which still contains within it the truth of objectivity) is in principle greater or weaker than a drama of suffering that is artistically more differentiated but intellectually a purely negative work.

7. The tragicomic combination is not a twentieth-century invention. Schelling had already written, "the *combination of opposites*, and thus primarily that of the tragic and comic, is the principle upon which modern drama is based" (Ger 362; Eng 267). See also Hegel 15:532, who implies that the genre derives from tragedy combined with the modern focus on subjectivity. As the modern world begins to equate the substantive with the subjective, tragedy and comedy move closer together. Such observations do not argue against a study of genre that discusses tragedy and comedy primarily in their difference. In fact, detailed readings of tragicomedies might gain by looking at the types of tragic and comic structures integrated; in this light see my discussion below of interrelations.

8. For a defense of comedy as integrating serious themes without thereby passing over into tragedy or tragicomedy, see Arntzen, *Die ernste Komödie*.

9. The magical moment is present but subordinate in some works. The magical dimension of Raimund's *The King of the Alps and the Misanthrope* simply triggers the hero's internal development.

10. An exception to this structure is the hero's death in Chaplin's *Limelight*. Calvero's death, however, comes at a moment of ripeness, and the film stresses throughout the connections between death and life. The

hero will live on in the heroine whose life he has saved and who will continue to occupy the limelight. Though the players change, the vitality of life and the greatness of art remain. If a hero survives in memory or in culture, death is less tragic—as is visible already in *Oedipus at Colonus*.

11. The argument also applies, though it must be taken to a meta-level, to performances of Brecht's works outside the theater, for example, in factories. The point is not that Brecht's technique is ill-advised, but that it is not necessarily the right method and not the only viable method for his aims.

12. Hinck contradicts himself when he includes as examples of the theater of hope such works as Gryphius's *Catharina von Georgien*, Schlegel's *Canut*, and Goethe's *Egmont* and, differentiating his view from Hegel's discussion of the reconciliatory moment of tragedy, writes: "In contrast reconciliation in the theater of hope does not demand the human sacrifice of tragedy, its perspective is: salvation in defiance of guilt" (180, my translation). Symptomatic of both the selective reading of Hegel and a general neglect of early Hegelian theorizing about the drama of reconciliation, Hinck makes it a point to distance his theater of hope from the moment of reconciliation in Hegel's theory of tragedy (180), but he does not mention Hegel's comments on the drama of reconciliation or the writings of the early Hegelians that share some of Hinck's concerns and from which he might have attempted to differentiate his position or from which he might have learned. Why, for example, does the genre commence with the Christian martyr drama or in the eighteenth-century Enlightenment? Was there no enlightenment in ancient Greece? Does Sophocles' *Philoctetes* not exhibit hope or the overcoming of tragedy?

13. Krook, one of the few modern writers to recognize the unique features of a tragedy that ends in redemption, devotes several pages to what he calls not the drama of reconciliation but "religious tragedy" (253–271). The term is telling, insofar as it highlights the parallels between the drama of reconciliation and structures of religious redemption, but not *all* dramas of reconciliation are to the same degree religious or even religious at all.

14. The concept of *Versöhnung* is prominent in Hegel's discussion of religion. See esp. 17:203, 17:269–274, 17:320, and 17:342. The model for this is the language of reconciliation in the *New Testament* doctrine of atonement, as expressed, for example, in 2 Corinthians 5.17–21.

15. Of interest is the development within the Catholic Church to substitute the word "reconciliation" for "confession."

16. The connection between religion and reconciliation allows for various shades of emphasis. Williams ("Theology and Tragedy") defends Hegel's view of reconciliation by stressing its dialectical relation to opposition and suffering and comparing it with less complex views of Christology.

17. "We have passed through the entire circle of the beautiful, from the most external objectivity of the same, to the freest embodiment of the subjectivity that knows itself as the absolute. This subjectivity does not just succumb, as in tragedy, to the higher power, does not merely know itself as master of this in comedy; rather, insofar as the subject knows itself to be at peace in the harmonious denouement of serious drama, it simultaneously recognizes the higher power as one that exists objectively, with which it knew itself to be in conflict, but is in the end reconciled, without either surrendering or destroying itself. This opposition of both sides, the absolute and the subject, with which we began, in order finally to arrive at reconciliation,—that is the religious standpoint, which we must now portray" (Michelet, *Das System* 3:454, my translation).

18. Calderón takes this structure one step too far when in *The Devotion of the Cross* he allows for a confession of sins after death. The idea, though valid, is lost in the execution. The work contains the kind of weakness we noted above in Euripides' *Alcestis*.

19. Interesting from the perspective of religion and genre, the drama of reconciliation has played a significant role for a number of Catholic artists: Calderón and Hofmannsthal are among the most prominent examples. Also, when most of Europe's intellectuals were obsessed with negativity and fragmentation, one of the most earnest writers of reconciliatory drama was the Austrian Catholic Max Mell. Finally, it seems more than chance that the three greatest American directors to give us a wealth of speculative films were all immigrant Catholics: John Ford, Alfred Hitchcock, and Frank Capra.

20. *To the Stars*, however, cannot be read simply as a drama of reconciliation. It offers a tragic collision, contrasting even at its conclusion Ternowski's celestial and eternal perspective with a passionate and unmitigated view of present and individual suffering on earth.

21. The issue of capability which Jens stresses differs from the focus of Emil Staiger's "Literatur und Öffentlichkeit" and the ensuing *Züricher Literaturdebatte*, where the emphasis is less on what one can write and more on what one should write. Though we can easily object to aspects of Staiger's position, it is difficult to deny his claim that the positive and reconciliatory are for contemporaries forbidden territory.

22. Interesting in the context of Jens's insights are Hölderlin's wondrous lines: "For heavy is the bearing of / Misfortune, but fortune weighs yet more" ("The Rhine," my translation). Hölderlin speaks here of happiness as heavier (and more difficult) because in order to be genuine, happiness must include not only itself but also its opposite, unhappiness. Pain must be affirmed as a part of beauty. Hölderlin's lines might also be read metaphorically as invoking the aesthetic difficulties that Hölderlin himself was not unwilling to confront in writing such reconciliatory works as *Hyperion*, "Celebration of Peace," and "The Rhine" itself.

23. My analysis of Hitchcock's film builds on an earlier study. See Roche, "Hitchcock's *I Confess*." Significant passages of that study have been incorporated here and are used with the gracious permission of *Post Script*.

24. Logan's isolation might be viewed as an extreme case of what belongs intrinsically to his vocation as priest, though there is a difference. Logan's misdeeds appear so great that he can no longer cloak himself in the holiness and righteousness the office of priest might normally grant him. Indeed, Logan's holiness, even when Logan is viewed as a false priest, tells us, as Brill insightfully suggests (108), that it is not the institution that protects the individual from evil but the individual who protects the institution. This is one of the great insights of Hochhuth's *The Deputy*. The recalcitrance of evil in Hochhuth's drama, however, renders that work tragic rather than conciliatory.

25. Nevertheless, the fact that Keller would compare himself with Logan and not with common man represents an intuitive desire on Keller's part for greatness, indeed for goodness.

26. In his interview with Truffaut, Hitchcock refers to this idea as well. Commenting on *Shadow of a Doubt*, Hitchcock states: "You destroy the thing you love" (111). Hitchcock cites as his source Oscar Wilde, a reference to "The Ballad of Reading Gaol."

27. I'm thinking primarily of Origen's concept of the *apokatastasis panton*, a final consummation or restoration of all, including earlier negativity and evil; according to Origen, even Satan will freely acknowledge God's excellence and so return to Him. See especially I.6.1–4 and III.6.1–9. The doctrine, also espoused by St. Gregory of Nyssa, Didymus the Blind, and Evagrius Ponticus, but much opposed in the later development of Christian thought, was in fact condemned by Anastasius at the turn of the fourth century and by Vigilius and Emperor Justinian at the Council of Constantinople II in 553. For one of the most prominent examples of oppo-

sition, written between the two papal declarations of heresy, see Augustine, *The City of God* 21.17.

28. The beauty of this scene is missed by Robin Wood, for example, who writes: "Anne Baxter's final withdrawal with her husband, leaving the man she loved in a situation of extreme peril, showing neither concern nor interest, is very awkward and indeterminate in aim" (39–40).

29. *See Murder!, The 39 Steps, Young and Innocent, The Lady Vanishes, Foreign Correspondent, Saboteur, Spellbound, Rear Window, To Catch a Thief, The Man Who Knew Too Much* (version of 1956), *The Wrong Man, North by Northwest,* and *Frenzy.* The predicament of the hero who knows or wishes to uncover truth, despite the consensus against her, is, I would suggest, one of Hitchcock's two major themes, the other being the difficulties of achieving absolute certainty in intersubjective relations. For the latter moment, *Rebecca, Suspicion, Shadow of a Doubt, Lifeboat,* and *Stagefright* come immediately to mind, though the structure is visible in virtually all of Hitchcock's works.

30. On the film's circular structure, see also Spoto 223. During the first confession, the grated slats of the confessional give Keller the appearance of being behind bars or in prison. This suggests that where confession should mean release (the unveiling of one's false subjectivity in an intersubjective forum), Keller abuses the sacrament and thus imprisons, rather than frees, himself. Nonetheless, Keller's intuition, the need for confession or intersubjectivity, is valid, even if it is here reduced.

31. Some dramas of reconciliation originate out of tragedy, others out of comedy. Those that derive from tragedy and contain tragic suffering are in most cases furthest removed from the accusation of superficial and unearned harmony. *I Confess* belongs to this group.

32. Hitchcock himself spoke of the film's regrettable "lack of humor" (Truffaut 149). The film may have fewer comic moments than other serious Hitchcock films, but it is not entirely without humor.

33. Of the almost two dozen Hitchcock critics who have discussed *I Confess*, only two offer substantially positive comments on the theme: Rothman, who sees the film's depiction of courage and despair in the face of persecution and scorn as "a thinly veiled allegory of McCarthyism and the blacklist" (248); and Brill, who argues that the film clarifies "the analogies between the secular films and Christian doctrine" (97). The film's formal technique has been given somewhat better reviews.

34. Cf. 17:135. In Hegelian terms, tragedy portrays the transcendence of one-sided positions through death, thus offering an "objective rec-

onciliation [objektive Versöhnung]." The drama of reconciliation, in contrast, exhibits a shift of consciousness; the warring forces give way, thus creating a subjective or "inner reconciliation [innerliche Aussöhnung]" (15:550–551; A 1218–1219).

35. In his final discussion of drama, Hegel treats the genres in the sequence tragedy, drama of reconciliation, comedy (15:555–574). The newly discovered transcription of Hegel's lectures on aesthetics from the Winter Semester 1820/21 also ends with comedy. See Schneider.

36. Hegel's view of comedy may be brief and undeveloped as well as skewed in part because Hegel tends to underestimate the role of negativity in art, and comedy is the dramatic genre of negativity. This thesis could be reinforced by Schüttauf's claim that Hegel shortchanges the role of negativity in the plastic arts, for example, in undervaluing the loss and pain in the passion and pietà motifs (168–170 and 179–181). Modern art and theory insofar as they underestimate reconciliation are no less one-sided; indeed, it could be argued that Hegel recognizes more of negativity than modern art does of reconciliation.

37. To an extent, Hegel's argument is on track. The purpose of art is not just immersion in the contingencies of reality. Indeed, one of its principal purposes is precisely the transcendence of mere particularity and fragmentation, the suggestion that what is generally taken for reality is not as real as the ordering structures of thought. Thus, it is essential that the nugatory dimensions of particularity and negativity, of false reality, be brought to light. Hegel overlooks this latter moment, and his analysis is weakened by this oversight. Nonetheless, Szondi errs when he criticizes Hegel's aesthetics as inadequate for modern art insofar as modern art is immersed in the particularities and antagonisms Hegel wanted to overcome ("Hegels Lehre" 414–416). First, it is not self-evident that modern art, even as it deals with dissonance, is itself ultimately only dissonant. Second, it is not self-evident that dissonance doesn't represent an attempt to expand the dialectical whole in order to make it more whole. Third, it is not self-evident that all dissonant art is great art, or that it is great by virtue of its dissonance. A dose of Hegel might be appropriate for a culture that sees greatness not in the sublation of particularity but in particularity itself. I do not contest that Hegel may have misjudged the importance of particularity for modern art. I do question the claim that the particularity of modern art precludes a modified Hegelian view of that art.

38. Even dramatists who write dramas of reconciliation will often refer to their works, theoretically, as tragedies, so, for example, Voltaire, who in his preface to *The Orphan of China* calls the work a "tragedy."

39. Without using these terms or stressing Shakespeare's concern with ideas, Frye stresses the extent to which Shakespeare's romances develop the techniques of the earlier comedies (*A Natural Perspective*).

40. In his analysis of Shakespeare, Hunter coins the term "comedy of forgiveness." The concept is telling and Hunter's analysis instructive, but the genre remains a subset of the drama of reconciliation, which allows for reconciliation not only by the forgiveness of another but also by the development of the self. That the two moments are often united does not diminish the importance of the distinction.

41. Good introductions to the satyr play can be found in Seaford and the works of Sutton.

42. Kant refuses to acknowledge the existence of any tragic conflicts: "*A conflict of duties* (collisio officiorum s. obligationum) would be that relationship between them in which one would (wholly or partially) cancel the other. But since duty and obligation in general are concepts which express the objective practical *necessity* of certain actions, and since two opposite rules cannot be necessary at the same time, then if it is a duty to act in accordance with one of them, it is not only not a duty, but contrary to duty, to act in accordance with the other. It therefore follows that *a conflict of duties* and obligations is inconceivable (obligationes non colliduntur)" (*The Metaphysics of Morals* 8:330; Eng 24). See also his essay "Über ein vermeintes Recht aus Menschenliebe zu lügen" (8:637–643).

43. This process of justification does not lead to relativism; on the contrary, only on the basis of a *normative* hierarchy of values can such decisions be justified. See Bockelmann esp. 21–55, who derives his arguments partially from R § 127; and, more recently, Hösle, *Hegels System* 516–520.

44. Herman Shumlin's *Watch on the Rhine* illustrates this point particularly well.

45. Nussbaum cites this view as an apparent refutation of Hegel (*Fragility* 167–179), but the possibility of a drama of reconciliation does not mean that it is in every instance realizable. The possibility of mediating some tragic conflicts even as others remain insoluble is the focus of Hook's discussion of tragedy. See also Ricoeur esp. 323.

46. A legitimate critique of Hegel that stresses the idealist tendency to overlook unsublated and irreducible moments does not justify abandoning sublation in those instances where sublation is legitimate. For an attempt to rescue the Hegelian dialectic, even as some moments are acknowledged to be beyond the reach of dialectic, see Desmond's *Desire, Dia-*

lectic, and Otherness; *Philosophy and Its Others*; and *Beyond Hegel and Dialectic*. In a discussion of what has a certain affinity to intersubjectivity, Desmond calls for an open dialectic or the category of the "metaxological": a unity that is not void of otherness, a unity for which art is particularly suited.

Hegelian prolepses for this structure exist, though they may be in need of further articulation. Consider, for example, the element of openness without which the true infinite would be reduced to mere finitude or the argument that contingency is necessary—not only as a logical category but also in nature as well as in spirit, insofar as spirit presupposes (in its genesis) nature. Although Hegel had a tendency, first, to try to deduce too much from reason and thus to overlook what is indeed contingent and, second, to underestimate the role of contingency in the generation of ideas (Hösle, *Hegels System* 79–99), the framework for a recognition of contingency is nonetheless present in the *Logic*.

Chapter 5: The Dialectic of Genre—or: Transitions and Interrelations

1. See also Gearhart 76; Henry Paolucci 201; Anne and Henry Paolucci, "Introduction" xxiv; Axelos 655–656; and Nicolai Hartmann, *Die Philosophie* 376. The error appears to be a modern one. The superiority of comedy within the Hegelian system was clear to nineteenth-century thinkers attuned to Hegel's dialectic, even those who were decidedly anti-Hegelian, as, for example, Eduard von Hartmann 1:418.

Hegel elevates tragedy in such a way as to make it appear superior only in his Jena essay on natural law, where he defines comedy as either a plot without a conflict or a plot without substance and elevates tragedy for containing both: "the absolute relationship is put forth in tragedy" (2:499, my translation). In the *Phenomenology* and the *Aesthetics*, comedy has an unambiguously later (and superior) position. Though Hegel may have had a stronger emotional attachment to tragedy, the systematic position of the two genres is beyond question.

2. A variety of moments comes into play here. First, tragedies, originally presented as trilogies, were normally followed by a satyr play. Second, comedy did not receive official standing in Greece until 486 B.C., almost fifty years after tragedy. Third, if Hegel is to be believed, comedy, not unlike philosophy, reaches its peak in periods of social dissolution (15:555).

3. Vischer—Hegelian that he is—notes also that every advance comes at a price: "But progress is also loss; levity and freedom themselves

become on closer inspection one-sided . . . . Comedy contains the sublime, the tragic in itself, but only in order to grasp it in its one-sidedness before it develops and to transform it with a sudden reversal into its opposite . . . . The levity is therefore bought at the price of taking too lightly what forms the great content of serious drama" (6:346, my translation).

4. The classic analysis of this point is Schelling 360–361. Heine draws the distinction on behalf of Aristophanes and Molière: "But for Aristophanes as well as Molière reality, the actual world, always serves as the ground of their portrayals . . . . Comedy, therefore, has its source in the world that surrounds the poet, and it adheres, much closer than tragedy, to the external facts of reality" (4:288, my translation). For an engaging and insightful modern discussion of comedy and finitude, see Kerr.

5. As a result, while tragedy runs the risk of becoming too philosophical and not visual enough, comedy faces the danger of becoming too sensuous and not intellectual enough. But this is a danger of comedy, not its essence, which as the realization of true art is necessarily a unity of thought and sensuousness.

6. Occasionally in this chapter I use the term "comedy" and mean thereby all forms of comedy except the comedy of intersubjectivity, which is admittedly on a different level and in truth a subset of the drama of reconciliation.

7. Hegel writes that in comedy, as opposed to tragedy, we see "only shadows of clashes or mock battles" or "only shadows of self-determination and absoluteness" (2:496; NL 105). In this early analysis Hegel equates the former with ancient comedy, in particular Old Comedy, the latter with modern comedy, suggesting that earlier comedies do not present serious conflicts or genuine schisms in the ethical substance. Hegel later modifies this view, arguing that the conflicts are sometimes serious and substantial, though, unlike modern comedy, the characters are able to distance themselves from them. See, for example, 11:74. Anticipating this idea as well as Bergson's analysis of laughter, Hegel writes already in 1803 that ancient comedy gives us particularly lively characters, whereas much of modern comedy proffers automatic, mechanical characters who appear to embody a principle of "non-animation" (2:496, my translation).

8. Because the drama of suffering isn't tragic, we needn't consider it in a dialectic of tragedy. Were one to attempt to embed the drama of suffering within a sequence on drama, arguments speak for placing involuntary suffering, insofar as it has natural causes, before tragedy—in analogy to farce as a precomic form in which nature also plays a significant role. Self-inflicted suffering and involuntary suffering insofar as it has human cau-

sality might be viewed as raw material for antithetical comedy, primarily reduction and negation. What I have called paratragedy or the tragedy of suffering appears to belong within the sphere of antithetical tragedy.

9. The difficulties in formulating the exact transition from tragedy to comedy may have to do with the fact that the most difficult transitions in the dialectic generally are those between a completed synthesis and a new thesis; on this problem, see Wandschneider, "Dialektik."

10. This moment has certain affinities to Hegel's discussion of the "realistic" moment within what he calls romantic art: "External appearance can no longer express the inner life, and if it is still called to do so, it has only the task of demonstrating that the external is an unsatisfying existence and must point back to the inner, to mind and feeling, as the essential element. Precisely for this reason, however, romantic art leaves externality for its part to go its own way again freely and independently and in this respect allows any and every material to enter the representation without hindrance, down to flowers, trees, and the commonest household instruments, even in the natural contingency of existence" (14:140; A 527, translation modified).

11. Independently of Ruge's position discussed below, one could argue that the tragedy of awareness, which culminates in a form of subjectivity, albeit a subjectivity aware of an intersubjective conflict, creates a transition to a genre, namely comedy, whose dominant category is subjectivity, and in whose synthesis subjectivity will not only recognize intersubjective conflicts but also harmonize them.

12. The major problem I have with Ruge's account is that it fails to explain how comedy, if it represents a return, is also an advance and why it shouldn't then be the first genre.

13. Unlike Ruge, I view the ugly as a moment within the comic rather than as an entity in itself. The value of Ruge's distinction is that it highlights the complexity of the comic genre. Comedy is not just a negation of tragedy but a negation of the negation of tragedy; it is not just a portrayal of finitude but a negation of the absolutization of finitude.

14. While the transitions from 1 to 2 and 2 to 3 are dialectical (objectivity, subjectivity, intersubjectivity), the transitions within the antithesis are of a different order. They are merely linear: they represent an elaboration of what comes earlier without necessarily containing the earlier forms. 2c, for example, is not the synthesis of 2a and 2b, whereas 3 is the synthesis of 1 and 2.

15. Hösle sensibly argues for two distinct forms of *Sittlichkeit* (*Hegels System* 476).

16. Unable in her particular situation to reconcile passions and obligations, Effi is forced into what the narrator calls a hidden game of deception, "ein verstecktes Komödienspiel" (169). More importantly, Innstetten finds that his ideals are illusory and that he is acting out a meaningless role, living a contradiction, what he himself calls a comedy (243). *Effi Briest*, however, also exhibits structures of the tragedy of opposition, indeed one in which each hero (Innstetten and Effi) eventually recognizes the validity of the other's position. The tragic and comic structures are also evident in the work's hidden allusions to Goethe's *Faust*, which in the Gretchen-Effi comparison are tragic and in the Faust-Innstetten comparison primarily comic.

17. One way to categorize subforms of the drama of suffering is to distinguish works that imply that suffering can be overcome by a change in social structure (taken to the extreme, the drama of suffering as propaganda play) and works that imply, cynically, that suffering can in no way be remedied (taken to the extreme, the drama of suffering as medium for the pessimistic world view). Like Hegel's theory of tragic collision, the greater work would seem to have moments of each, the desire for change that presupposes guilt and the sense of ineradicable suffering that belongs to the essence of humanity.

18. The pun in Mark Taylor's *Tears* (in the sense of ripping and crying) suggests that connections between absolute irony and suffering are not only systematically justified but are at the center of contemporary ideology.

19. Cf., similarly, Heidsieck, who uses the terms *grotesque* and *absurd* to designate a parallel distinction. The grotesque, in the form of the drama of suffering or the comedy of absolute irony, can be rationally analyzed and in principle remedied; it seeks enlightenment, if often via the most shocking means. The absurd, in the form of unsublated absolute irony, gives way, on the other hand, to arbitrary decisionism or irrational fatalism. Heidsieck's intelligent contribution has, unfortunately, not made its way into the mainstream of modern drama criticism.

Chapter 6: Tragedy and Comedy Today

1. The greatest modern affirmation of an ethics beyond reward and punishment is Kant's moral imperative, which indirectly endorses tragic self-sacrifice.

2. As Dürrenmatt expressed his resigned insights in a Europe turned inward toward self-reflection, America rejoiced in Westerns and the works of Frank Capra, the focus of which is the power of the individual to shape history. The cultural-historical difference is also evident in drama: Miller's *Incident at Vichy*, for example, insists on the individual's responsibility and power to break through the system and so deflates the idea that "there are no persons anymore" (54).

3. To state this with more differentiation and in the light of Plato's paradigmatic analysis in *Gorgias*, the relativist draws the consequence of becoming a hedonist (Polus) or a power positivist (Callicles); hedonism, however, is an ephemeral stage, for the hedonist is ineffectual at resisting the greater rhetorician.

4. On the tension between Christianity and tragedy, see esp. Niebuhr's *Beyond Tragedy*. Cf. also Michel, "The Possibility" and Steiner (*Death of Tragedy*), whose otherwise admirable presentation is weakened by his nondifferentiation of tragedy and the drama of reconciliation. If in Steiner's system the drama of reconciliation is a form of tragedy, then the emergence of Christianity cannot account for the disappearance of tragedy. "Tragedies" such as *The Eumenides, Helen, Philoctetes*, and *Oedipus at Colonus* have long since existed in harmony with notions of progress, salvation, and the transcendence of catastrophe. I direct this critique less against Steiner's association of Christianity with the transcendence of tragedy than against his system of generic classification.

For different views of tragedy as at least partially compatible with Christianity, see Eberhart; Henn esp. 288–291; Gardner, "Religion"; Drewermann; Brueck; and, to a degree, Scott. The most reasonable reading of the issue strikes me as the following: Christianity's promise of an afterlife does diminish the finality of tragedy; Christianity thus offers a less tragic world view than many competing perspectives. Nonetheless, any person can encounter a tragic situation regardless of the particularity of his world view, and indeed such tragic involvements often befall persons precisely in their Christianity, as, for example, in Hochhuth's *The Deputy* or Joffe's *The Mission*.

On the modern dissolution of tragedy in general, see, besides Steiner: Abel; Harris; Gassner; Olson, *Tragedy* 237–260; Gardner, "Religion"; Heilman, *Iceman* 3–21; Kaufmann, *Tragedy* 204–211 and 371–377; Karl Reinhardt 107–114; Klapp; Kerr 263–308; and Ahuja 174–186.

5. More precisely stated, our recognition of value rationality and our adherence to coherence and correspondence theories of truth seem past, not our dependence on instrumental reason.

6. The social-political thrust of recognizing victims often backfires, leading to either self-pity or fatalism (the disappearance of strong characters mirrors the belief that society cannot change).

7. Vischer observes in reference to the discussion at the end of Plato's *Symposium* that it would be easier for the tragic poet to write comedies than for the comic poet to write tragedies (1:525). His conclusion follows from the Hegelian insight that comedy follows tragedy: the movement from tragedy to comedy is easier than the reverse movement from comedy back to tragedy (Vischer 6:346).

8. I do not share Dürrenmatt's view, expressed in his afterword, that in death Ill finds greatness: "a simple man in whose mind something slowly dawns, by the agency of fear and terror, something highly personal; a man who in recognizing his guilt lives out justice and who, in death, achieves greatness" (Ger 102; Eng 107). Dürrenmatt's view has been adopted and developed in criticism, as, for example, in Guthke, *Geschichte und Poetik* 386–388; Heilman, *Iceman* 223–224 and 320; and Berlin 137.

9. In his work on contemporary realism, Lukács asks whether *Angst* ought to be taken as an absolute or overcome, and he arrives thereby at a number of interesting, if controversial, conclusions. He does not, however, see comedy as an alternative means of dealing with despair and subjectivism.

10. Analogous with this arise fear of old age and death, valorization of youth, and fascination with the present at the expense of tradition.

11. For an example, taken at random, see Mast 338–342. Completely independent of the Hegelian tradition, one astute twentieth-century literary critic does define comedy along the lines of a double negation: "*Comedy*, then, *consists in the indirect affirmation of the ideal logical order by means of the derogation of the limited orders of actuality*" (Feibleman, *In Praise of Comedy* 178–179). Feibleman's work was first published in the late 1930s and does not appear to have had much impact, especially on recent, postmodern theories of comedy. For further elaboration of the definition, see Feibleman, *Aesthetics* 81–98. An interesting facet of the similarity with the Hegelian school is that Feibleman, an anti-idealist, also views comedy as a progressive and revolutionary genre.

12. Unfortunately, because Rosenkranz's topic is the ugly, he doesn't explain exactly how comedy fulfills this function.

13. For similar formulations see 8–10. Weiße, one of the first critics to address the ugly, also speaks of comedy as "*superseded ugliness*, [die *aufgehobene Häßlichkeit*] or . . . the *reconstitution of beauty out of its abso-*

lute negativity, which is the ugly" (1:210, my translation). My main contention against the early Hegelians is that they define comedy as the self-cancellation of the ugly: while this may cover negation and absolute irony, it surely does not encompass coincidence, reduction, or withdrawal, where we see, rather, the self-cancellation of particularity. Moreover, modern art shows us how the ugly can be integrated into art without necessarily becoming part of the comic.

14. For a description of "Taking Pleasure in the Ugly," which likewise has relevance today, see Rosenkranz, *Ästhetik des Häßlichen* 52.

15. Beyond a critique of the inherent contradictions in any stance that elevates negativity and alienation as principles of artistic excellence, we might also consider the following: in an age where the beautiful is defined as what alienates and where alienation has become a dominant form of art, it follows that what must really alienate is the harmonic. Similarly, if we are to take seriously the postmodern elevation of the marginal and if we recognize the dominant position of marginalism in recent conventions and publications, then the only consequential stance would seem to be to become truly marginal and speak out on behalf of transcendental norms.

16. Extrafilmic developments may lead the reader to question whether Woody Allen's portrayals of obscenities are negations of negativity rather than ends in themselves, but we must keep separate the structures of meaning at work in a text and the consciousness that created them. For a discussion that tries to take some of these ambiguities into account, see Roche, "Justice and the Withdrawal of God."

17. Changes in aesthetic taste seldom arise independently of art; when the types of art that are produced change, the feelings of those who enjoy art adapt to the aesthetic values of the new art. The argument that because people do not want (even a genuine) reconciliation, the drama of reconciliation cannot survive, strikes me as ill-conceived.

18. The erasure of causality brings with it an erasure of responsibility (and thus of tragedy); responsibility is possible only within a world of causality.

19. With Hegel I would argue that a particular content demands a particular form. Peter Szondi shares this insight and develops it, shedding light on the dissolution of form in twentieth-century drama (*Theorie des modernen Dramas*). Szondi stresses the historical dimensions of this sequence, but the historical merely realizes what the systematic-logical has already shown theoretically. Whether the loss of intersubjectivity, which Szondi sees as engendering the dissolution of dialogue and thus of classical

dramatic form, will become self-reflexive and turn into a double negation, opening the way for the historical reemergence of a systematically superior genre, the drama of reconciliation, remains as yet an open question.

20. Hegel concludes his *Philosophy of Right* not by discussing the world-state, as does his student Michelet (*Das System* 3:346), but by affirming wars between nations (R § 321–340). Hegel believes that nations form themselves against other nations and that war is therefore both necessary and productive: "Every nation constitutes for itself a totality different from and opposed to another. If they become enemies, no ethical bond is snapped, nothing absolutely valid is violated, no necessary whole is split up; on the contrary, it is a battle for the undamaged preservation of such a totality and its right to exist" (15:352; A 1061, translation modified). At the end of his *Philosophy of Right*, Hegel falls back into the categories of Being ("Etwas" *gegen* "Anderes") when he should be concluding with categories taken from the logic of the Concept (internal differentiation, the unity of opposites, and so forth).

Chapter 7: Afterword

1. The diversity of terms is symbolized in the terminological gap between Golden's "heroic tragedy" (56) and Maier's "cheerful drama" (vi). Golden's term applies only to the harmonic drama of Greek antiquity; Maier does not separate out lower forms of comedy and so seeks to find a term for any drama with a happy end.

2. Cf. Ellis-Fermor, who sees a movement toward reconciliation and harmony in the late works of Aeschylus, Euripides, Shakespeare, and Ibsen ("Spätwerke").

3. Similarly, Hay sees the importance of the misanthrope theme for the eighteenth-century *Genie* (117–135).

4. Todorov discusses the emergence of new genres in a similar light: "Where do genres come from? Quite simply from other genres. A new genre is always the transformation of an earlier one, or of several: by inversion, by displacement, by combination" (*Genres* 15; cf. 13–26). Cf. Hirsch 105.

5. For a broader historical view of the happy end in comedy and the related issue of poetic justice, including its devolution in modernity, see Zach.

6. The two moments are not mutually exclusive. Indeed, certain formal tendencies derive from the logical structures of works, for example,

the formal superiority of collision over self-sacrifice or the need for the drama of suffering to compensate for its lack of philosophical structures with social concerns or linguistic brilliance. Recognizing the importance of content and form, this study acknowledges its limits. A reductive analysis would argue that either content or form alone is sufficient. If, however, form alone is not sufficient, then this study—or another like it—is essential to the comprehension and evaluation of art. Though not complete, a focus on truth in art is indispensable.

Appendices

1. The examples listed here and throughout my three appendices are only illustrations and not meant to be exhaustive. Moreover, not every reader will agree with every example. As I mentioned above, debate on individual cases often leads to new and concrete insights into the works themselves. In this light, see Roche, "Areas of Expertise."

2. *Faust I* is a tragedy of opposition (intellectual greatness versus love) split into stubbornness (Faust) and self-sacrifice (Gretchen); though Gretchen's unwillingness to flee represents self-sacrifice, her death is also execution for murder and seemingly the only form of punishment that will free her for salvation. Early in the play Gretchen suffers a collision of love and morality.

3. For the most consistently reconciliatory reading of the play, however, see Reese 317–332.

WORKS CITED

Abel, Lionel. *Metatheatre: A New View of Dramatic Form*. New York: Wang, 1963.

Adorno, Theodor W. *Aesthetic Theory*. Trans. C. Lenhardt. London: Routledge, 1984.

———. *Ästhetische Theorie*. Frankfurt: Suhrkamp, 1970.

———. "Extorted Reconciliation: On Georg Lukács' *Realism in Our Time*." *Notes to Literature. Volume One*. Trans. Shierry Weber Nicholsen. New York: Columbia UP, 1991: 216–240.

Aeschylus. *The Oresteian Trilogy*. Trans. Philip Vellacott. New York: Penguin, 1959.

Ahuja, Chaman. *Tragedy, Modern Temper, and O'Neill*. Atlantic Highlands, N.J.: Humanities, 1984.

Albert, Hans. *Treatise on Critical Reason*. Trans. Mary Varney Rorty. Princeton: Princeton UP, 1985.

Alexander, Peter. *Hamlet: Father and Son*. Oxford: Clarendon, 1955.

Allen, Woody, dir. *Crimes and Misdemeanors*. Orion, 1989.

———. *Manhattan*. United Artists, 1979.

———. *A Midsummer Night's Sex Comedy*. Orion, 1982.

Amur, G. S. *The Concept of Comedy: A Restatement*. Dharwar, India: Karnatak U, 1963.

Anouilh, Jean. *Antigone. Nouvelles Pieces Noires*. Paris: La Table Ronde, 1946: 131–212.

———. *Antigone*. Trans. Barbara Bray. *Five Plays*. London: Methuen, 1987: 77–137.

Apel, Friedmar. "Komische Melancholie, lustige Entfremdung: Zur Struktur der Komik im neueren Lustspiel." *Sprache im technischen Zeitalter* 70 (1979): 145–170.

Apel, Karl-Otto. *Diskurs und Verantwortung: Das Problem des Übergangs zur postkonventionellen Moral*. Frankfurt: Suhrkamp, 1988.

409

———. *Transformation der Philosophie*. 2 vols. Frankfurt: Suhrkamp, 1973.

Apte, Mahader L. *Humor and Laughter: An Anthropological Approach*. Ithaca: Cornell UP, 1985.

Aristotle. *Poetics*. Trans. S. H. Butcher. New York: Wang, 1961.

Arntzen, Helmut. *Die ernste Komödie: Das deutsche Lustspiel von Lessing bis Kleist*. Munich: Nymphenburger Verlagshandlung, 1968.

———. "Komödie des Irrtums: Zur heutigen Rezeption von Sternheims Stücken 'Aus dem bürgerlichen Heldenleben.'" *Drama und Theater im 20. Jahrhundert. Festschrift für Walter Hinck*. Ed. Hans Dietrich Irmscher and Werner Keller. Göttingen: Vandenhoeck, 1983: 92–104.

———. "Komödie und episches Theater." *Der Deutschunterricht* 21.3 (1969): 67–77.

Auerbach, Erich. *Mimesis: The Representation of Reality in Western Literature*. Trans. Willard R. Trask. Princeton: Princeton UP, 1968.

Marcus Aurelius. *Meditations*. Trans. Maxwell Staniforth. New York: Penguin, 1981.

Axelos, Christos. "Zu Hegels Interpretation der Tragödie." *Zeitschrift für philosophische Forschung* 19 (1965): 655–667.

Baird, Jay W. *To Die for Germany: Heroes in the Nazi Pantheon*. Bloomington: Indiana UP, 1990.

Bakhtin, Mikhail. *Rabelais and His World*. Trans. Helene Iswolsky. Cambridge: MIT Press, 1968.

Barber, C. L. *Shakespeare's Festive Comedy: A Study of Dramatic Form and its Relation to Social Custom*. Princeton: Princeton UP, 1959.

Barbour, John D. *Tragedy as a Critique of Virtue: The Novel and Ethical Reflection*. Chico, Cal.: Scholars Press, 1984.

Baum, Georgina. *Humor und Satire in der bürgerlichen Ästhetik: Zur Kritik ihres apologetischen Charakters*. Berlin: Rütten, 1959.

———. "Der widerspruchsvolle Charakter und der historische und gesellschaftliche Inhalt des Komischen in der dramatischen Gestaltung." *Wesen und Formen des Komischen im Drama*. Ed. Reinhold Grimm and Klaus L. Berghahn. Darmstadt: Wissenschaftliche Buchgesellschaft, 1975: 206–252.

Beare, Mary. *Die Theorie der Komödie von Gottsched bis Jean Paul*. Bonn: Rhenania, 1927.

Benjamin, Walter. *Ursprung des deutschen Trauerspiels*. Frankfurt: Suhrkamp, 1978.

Bennett, Benjamin. *Hugo von Hofmannsthal: The Theaters of Consciousness*. Cambridge: Cambridge UP, 1988.

———. *Modern Drama and German Classicism: Renaissance from Lessing to Brecht*. Ithaca: Cornell UP, 1979.

Bentley, Eric. *The Life of Drama*. New York: Atheneum, 1967.

Berckman, Edward M. "Comedy and Parody of Comedy in Brecht's 'Puntila.'" *Essays in Literature* 1 (1974): 248–260.

Bergson, Henri. *Laughter*. In *Comedy*. Ed. Wylie Sypher. Baltimore: Johns Hopkins UP, 1980: 61–190.

Berlin, Normand. *The Secret Cause: A Discussion of Tragedy*. Amherst: U of Massachusetts P, 1981.

Berrigan, Daniel. "The Mission Diary." *American Film* 12.2 (1986): 20–26, 65–67.

Berry, Ralph. "*Measure for Measure*." *Changing Styles in Shakespeare*. London: Allen, 1981: 37–48.

Beyer, Karen. "Staatsraison und Moralität: Die Prinzipien höfischen Lebens im *Don Carlos*." *Schiller und die höfische Welt*. Ed. Achim Aurnhammer, Klaus Manger, and Friedrich Strack. Tübingen: Niemeyer, 1990: 359–377.

Biundo, James V. *Moments of Selfhood: Three Plays by Luigi Pirandello*. New York: Lang, 1990.

Blistein, Elmer M. *Comedy in Action*. Durham: Duke UP, 1964.

Bloch, Ernst. *The Principle of Hope*. Trans. Neville Plaice, Stephen Plaice, and Paul Knight. Cambridge: MIT Press, 1985.

———. *Das Prinzip Hoffnung*. 2 vols. Frankfurt: Suhrkamp, 1959.

Bockelmann, Paul. *Hegels Notstandslehre*. Berlin: de Gruyter, 1935.

Bohtz, August Wilhelm. *Über das Komische und die Komödie: Ein Beitrag zur Philosophie des Schönen*. Göttingen: Vandenhoeck, 1844.

Bole, Thomas J, III. "Contradiction in Hegel's *Science of Logic*." *Review of Metaphysics* 40 (1987): 515–534.

Bolt, Robert. *A Man for All Seasons*. New York: Random House, 1962.

———. *The Mission*. New York: Penguin, 1986.

Boorstin, Daniel. *The Image: A Guide to Pseudo-Events in America*. New York: Atheneum, 1961.

Booth, Wayne C. *The Company We Keep: An Ethics of Fiction*. Berkeley: U of California P, 1988.

Borchmeyer, Dieter. *Tragödie und Öffentlichkeit: Schillers Dramaturgie im Zusammenhang seiner ästhetisch-politischen Theorie und die rhetorische Tradition*. Munich: Fink, 1973.

Bradley, A. C. "Hegel's Theory of Tragedy." *Hibbert Journal* 2 (1903–04): 662–680. Rpt. in *Oxford Lectures on Poetry*. London: Macmillan, 1909: 69–95.

———. *Shakespearean Tragedy: Lectures on Hamlet, Othello, King Lear, Macbeth*. London: Macmillan, 1966.

Braitling, Petra. *Hegels Subjektivitätsbegriff: Eine Analyse mit Berücksichtigung intersubjektiver Aspekete*. Würzburg: Königshausen, 1991.

Brecht, Bertolt. *Gesammelte Werke in zwanzig Bänden*. Frankfurt: Suhrkamp, 1967.

———. *Life of Galileo*. Trans. John Willett. Vol. 5, pt. 1 of *Collected Plays*. Ed. John Willett and Ralph Manheim. 8 vols. London: Methuen, 1980.

———. *Man Equals Man*. Trans. Gerhard Nellhaus. Vol. 2, pt. 1 of *Collected Plays*. Ed. John Willett and Ralph Manheim. 8 vols. London: Methuen, 1979: 1–76.

Bremer, Dieter. "Hegel und Aischylos." *Welt und Wirkung von Hegels Ästhetik*. Ed. Annemarie Gethmann-Siefert and Otto Pöggeler. Bonn: Bouvier, 1986: 225–244.

Brereton, Geoffrey. *Principles of Tragedy: A Rational Examination of the Tragic Concept in Life and Literature*. Coral Gables, Fla.: U of Miami P, 1968.

Brill, Lesley. *Hitchcock Romance: Love and Irony in Hitchcock's Films*. Princeton: Princeton UP, 1988.

Brooks, Peter. *The Melodramatic Imagination: Balzac, Henry James, Melodrama, and the Mode of Excess*. New York: Columbia UP, 1985.

Brueck, Katherine T. *The Redemption of Tragedy: The Literary Vision of Simone Weil*. Albany: SUNY, 1995.

Brummack, Jürgen. *Satirische Dichtung: Studien zu Friedrich Schlegel, Tieck, Jean Paul und Heine*. Munich: Fink, 1979.

Büchner, Georg. *Leonce and Lena. Complete Works and Letters*. Trans. Henry J. Schmidt. Ed. Walter Hinderer and Henry J. Schmidt. New York: Continuum, 1986: 163–198.

———. *Leonce und Lena. Ein Lustspiel*. Ed. Otto C. A. Zur Nedden. Stuttgart: Reclam, 1985.

Bungay, Stephen. *Beauty and Truth: A Study of Hegel's Aesthetics*. Oxford: Oxford UP, 1984.

———. "Der Entwurf einer kategorialen Ästhetik bei Hegel." *Kategorie und Kategorialität: Historisch-systematische Untersuchungen zum Begriff der Kategorie im philosophischen Denken. Festschrift für Klaus Hartmann zum 65. Geburtstag*. Ed. Dietmar Koch and Klaus Bort. Würzburg: Königshausen, 1990: 195–210.

Butzlaff, Wolfgang. "Die Schlüsselwort-Methode—Grundlagen und Beispiele." *Der Deutschunterricht* 6.1 (1964): 93–120.

Bykova, Marina. "Das Problem der Subjektivität bei Hegel und sein realer und aktueller Inhalt." *Hegel-Jahrbuch* (1991): 405–414.

Calabresi, Guido, and Philip Bobbitt. *Tragic Choices*. New York: Norton, 1978.

Calarco, N. Joseph. *Tragic Being: Apollo and Dionysus in Western Drama*. Minneapolis: The U of Minnesota P, 1968.

Camus, Albert. *Caligula and Three Other Plays.* Trans. Stuart Gilbert. New York: Vintage, 1958.

———. *Les Justes: piece en cinq actes.* n.p.: Gallimard, 1950.

Canby, Vincent. "Screen: 'The Mission,' With De Niro and Irons." *The New York Times* (31 October 1986): C13.

Caraman, Philip. *The Lost Paradise: The Jesuit Republic in South America.* New York: Seabury, 1975.

Carlson, Susan. *Women and Comedy: Rewriting the British Theatrical Tradition.* Ann Arbor: U of Michigan P, 1991.

Carriere, Moriz. *Aesthetik: Die Idee des Schönen und ihre Verwirklichung im Leben und in der Kunst.* 3rd ed. 2 vols. Leipzig: Brockhaus, 1885.

———. *Das Wesen und die Formen der Poesie: Ein Beitrag zur Philosophie des Schönen und der Kunst. Mit literarhistorischen Erläuterungen.* Leipzig: Brockhaus, 1854.

Cavell, Stanley. *Pursuits of Happiness: The Hollywood Comedy of Remarriage.* Cambridge: Harvard UP, 1981.

Charney, Maurice. *Comedy High and Low: An Introduction to the Experience of Comedy.* New York: Oxford UP, 1978.

Chaucer, Geoffrey. *The Works of Geoffrey Chaucer.* Ed. F. N. Robinson. 2nd ed. Boston: Houghton Mifflin, 1961.

Chekhov, Anton. *Anton Chekhov's Short Stories.* Ed. Ralph E. Matlaw. New York: Norton, 1979.

Cohen, Hermann. *Ästhetik des reinen Gefühls.* 2 vols. Berlin: Cassirer, 1912.

Cohen, Ralph. "Do Postmodern Genres Exist?" *Genre* 20 (1987): 241–258.

Cohn, Dorrit. "The Misanthrope: Molière and Hofmannsthal." *Arcadia* 3 (1968): 292–298.

Cole, Susan Letzler. *The Absent One: Ritual, Tragedy, and the Performance of Ambivalence.* University Park: Penn State UP, 1985.

Congreve, William. *The Comedies of William Congreve.* Ed. Eric S. Rump. New York: Penguin, 1985.

Cook, Albert. *The Dark Voyage and the Golden Mean.* Cambridge: Harvard UP, 1949.

Corneille, Pierre. *Polyeuctus.* Trans. John Cairncross. New York: Penguin, 1980.

Corrigan, Robert W. "Introduction: Comedy and the Comic Spirit." *Comedy: Meaning and Form.* Ed. Robert W. Corrigan. 2nd ed. New York: Harper, 1981: 1–13.

Cox, Jeffrey N. *In the Shadows of Romance: Romantic Tragic Drama in Germany, England, and France.* Athens: Ohio UP, 1987.

Crawford, Ronald L. "Don Carlos and Marquis Posa: The Eternal Friendship." *Germanic Review* 58 (1983): 97–105.

Croce, Benedetto. *Aesthetic as Science of Expression and General Linguistic*. Trans. Douglas Ainslie. New York: Macmillan, 1922.

Cukor, George, dir. *The Philadelphia Story*. MGM, 1940.

Cunningham, Anthony P. "The Moral Importance of Dirty Hands." *The Journal of Value Inquiry* 26 (1992): 239–250.

Dekker, Thomas. *The Shoemaker's Holiday*. Ed. Anthony Parr. New York: Norton, 1990.

Del Caro, Adrian. "Hofmannsthal as a Paradigm of Nietzschean Influence on the Austrian *fin de siècle*." *Modern Austrian Literature* 22 (1989): 81–95.

della Fazia, Alba. *Jean Anouilh*. New York: Twayne, 1969.

Dempsey, Michael. "Light Shining in the Darkness: Roland Joffe on *The Mission*." *Film Quarterly* 40.4 (1987): 2–11.

Desmond, William. *Art and the Absolute: A Study's of Hegel's Aesthetics*. Albany: SUNY, 1986.

——. *Beyond Hegel and Dialectic: Speculation, Cult, and Comedy*. Albany: SUNY, 1992.

——. *Desire, Dialectic, and Otherness: An Essay on Origins*. New Haven: Yale UP, 1987.

——. "Hegel, Art, and History," *History and System: Hegel's Philosophy of History*. Ed. Robert L. Perkins. Albany: SUNY, 1984: 173–193.

——. *Perplexity and Ultimacy: Metaphysical Thoughts from the Middle*. Albany: SUNY, 1995.

Dilthey, Wilhelm. "Die Einbildungskraft des Dichters. Bausteine für eine Poetik." Vol. 6 of *Gesammelte Schriften*. Leipzig: Teubner, 1924.

Dixon, Macneile W. *Tragedy*. London: Arnold, 1924.

Donougho, Martin. "The Woman in White: On the Reception of Hegel's *Antigone*." *The Owl of Minerva* 21 (1989): 65–89.

Draper, R. P. "Introduction." *Tragedy: Developments in Criticism*. Ed. R. P. Draper. London: Macmillan, 1980: 11–38.

Drewermann, Eugene. *Das Tragische und das Christliche: Von der Anerkennung des Tragischen—oder: gegen eine gewisse Art von Pelagianismus im Christentum*. Schwerte: Katholische Akademie, 1981.

Duchartre, Pierre Louis. *The Italian Comedy: The Improvisation Scenarios, Lives, Attributes, Portraits, and Masks of the Illustrious Characters of Commedia dell'Arte*. Trans. Randolph T. Weaver. New York: Dover, 1966.

Dürrenmatt, Friedrich. *Der Besuch der alten Dame: Eine tragische Komödie*. Zürich: Arche, 1956.

——. *The Physicists*. Trans. James Kirkup. *Four Plays*. New York: Grove, 1965: 287–351.

————. *Die Physiker: Eine Komödie*. Zürich: Diogenes, 1985.

————. "Problems of the Theatre." Trans. Gerhard Nellhaus. *The Marriage of Mr. Mississippi and Problems of the Theatre*. New York: Grove, 1958: 7–39.

————. *Romulus the Great: An Historical Comedy without Historic Basis in Four Acts. Second Version 1957*. Trans. Gerhard Nellhaus. *Four Plays*. New York: Grove, 1965: 41–119.

————. *Romulus der Große. Eine ungeschichtliche historische Komödie in vier Akten. Neufassung 1980*. Zürich: Diogenes, 1985.

————. *The Visit: A Tragi-Comedy*. Trans. Patrick Bowles. New York: Grove, 1962.

Düsing, Klaus. "Hegels Begriff der Subjektivität in der Logik und in der Philosophie des subjektiven Geistes." *Hegels philosophische Psychologie: Hegel-Tage Santa Margherita 1973*. Ed. Dieter Henrich. Bonn: Bouvier, 1979: 201–214.

————. *Das Problem der Subjektivität in Hegels Logik: Systematische und entwicklungsgeschichtliche Untersuchungen zum Prinzip des Idealismus und zur Dialektik*. Bonn: Bouvier, 1976.

————. "Die Theorie der Tragödie bei Hölderlin und Hegel." *Jenseits des Idealismus: Hölderlins letzte Homburger Jahre (1804–1806)*. Ed. Christoph Jamme and Otto Pöggeler. Bonn: Bouvier, 1988: 55–82.

Eagleton, Terry. *The Ideology of the Aesthetic*. Oxford: Blackwell, 1990.

Eberhart, Carl Johannes. "Von der Möglichkeit christlicher Tragödie in dieser Zeit." *Das Goldene Tor* 6 (1951): 22–29.

Ebstein, Frances. "In Defense of Marquis Posa." *Germanic Review* 36 (1961): 205–220.

Eichenbaum, Boris. "Die Theorie der formalen Methode." *Aufsätze zur Theorie und Geschichte der Literatur*. Frankfurt: Suhrkamp, 1965: 7–52.

Eliot, T. S. *The Cocktail Party*. New York: Harvest, 1978.

Ellis, John M. *The Theory of Literary Criticism: A Logical Analysis*. Berkeley: U of California P, 1974.

Elshtain, Jean. *Public Man, Private Woman: Women in Social and Political Thought*. Princeton: Princeton UP, 1981.

Emrich, Wilhelm. "Vorwort." Sternheim, Carl. *Dramen I*. Berlin: Luchterhand, 1963: 5–19.

Engelhardt, H. Tristram, Jr., and Terry Pinkard, ed. *Hegel Reconsidered: Beyond Metaphysics and the Authoritarian State*. Dordrecht: Kluwer, 1994.

Ernst, Paul. "Tragödie und Erlösungsdrama." *Die neue Literatur* 33 (1932): 337–341.

————. *Der Weg zur Form: Abhandlungen über die Technik vornehmlich der Tragödie und Novelle*. Munich: Müller, 1928.

Esslin, Martin. *The Theatre of the Absurd.* 3rd ed. New York: Penguin, 1988.

Euripides. *The Medea.* Trans. Rex Warner. *Euripides I.* Ed. David Grene and Richmond Lattimore. Chicago: The U of Chicago P, 1955.

Faas, Ekbert. *Tragedy and After: Euripides, Shakespeare, Goethe.* Montreal: McGill- Queen's UP, 1984.

Feibleman, James. *Aesthetics: A Study of the Fine Arts in Theory and Practice.* New York: Duell, 1949.

———. *In Praise of Comedy: A Study in Its Theory and Practice.* New York: Russell, 1962.

Fergusson, Francis. *The Idea of Theater: A Study of Ten Plays. The Art of Drama in Changing Perspective.* Princeton: Princeton UP, 1949.

Feuerbach, Ludwig. *Werke in sechs Bänden.* Ed. Erich Thies. Frankfurt: Suhrkamp, 1976.

Findlay, John. "Hegel's Conception of Subjectivity." *Hegels philosophische Psychologie: Hegel-Tage Santa Margherita 1973.* Ed. Dieter Henrich. Bonn: Bouvier, 1979: 13–26.

Finger, Ellis. "Schiller's Concept of the Sublime and its Pertinence to 'Don Carlos' and 'Maria Stuart.'" *Journal of English and Germanic Philology* 79 (1980): 166–178.

Firmat, Gustavo Pérez. "The Novel as Genres." *Genre* 12 (1979): 269–292.

Fischer, Kuno. *Diotima. Die Idee des Schönen. Philosophische Briefe.* Pforzheim: Flammer, 1849.

Fish, Stanley. "Anti-Foundationalism, Theory Hope, and the Teaching of Composition." *The Current in Criticism: Essays on the Present and Future of Literary Theory.* Ed. Clayton Koelb and Virgil Lokke. West Lafayette, Ind.: Purdue UP, 1987: 65–79.

Fishelov, David. *Metaphors of Genre: The Role of Analogies in Genre Theory.* University Park: Penn State UP, 1993.

Flügge, Manfred. *Verweigerung oder Neue Ordnung: Jean Anouilhs 'Antigone' im politischen und ideologischen Kontext der Besatzungszeit 1940–1944.* Rheinfelden: Schäuble, 1982.

Fontane, Theodor. *Effi Briest.* Frankfurt: Ullstein, 1974.

Fowkes, William. "A Hegelian Critique of Found Art and Conceptual Art." *Journal of Aesthetics and Art Criticism* 37 (1978): 157–168.

Fowler, Alastair. *Kinds of Literature: An Introduction to the Theory of Genres and Modes.* Cambridge: Harvard UP, 1982.

Freytag, Gustav. *Die Journalisten: Lustspiel in vier Akten.* Stuttgart: Reclam, 1977.

———. *Die Technik des Dramas.* 1863. Darmstadt: Wissenschaftliche Buchgesellschaft, 1965.

Fricke, Gerhard. "Die Problematik des Tragischen im Drama Schillers." *Jahrbuch des Freien Deutschen Hochstifts* (1930): 3–69.

Friedländer, Saul. *Reflections on Nazism: An Essay on Kitsch and Death.* Trans. Thomas Weyr. New York: Avon, 1984.

Friedson, A. M. "Wycherly and Molière: Satirical Point of View in *The Plain Dealer.*" *Modern Philology* 64 (1967): 189–197.

Frisch, Max. *Biedermann und die Brandstifter. Ein Lehrstück ohne Lehre.* Frankfurt: Suhrkamp, 1980.

Fritz, Kurt von. *Antike und moderne Tragödie: Neun Abhandlungen.* Berlin: de Gruyter, 1962.

Frye, Northrop. *Anatomy of Criticism: Four Essays.* Princeton: Princeton UP, 1957.

———. *A Natural Perspective: The Development of Shakespearean Comedy and Romance.* New York: Columbia UP, 1965.

Fubini, Mario. "Genesi e storia dei generi letterari." *Critica e poesia: Saggi e discorsi di teoria letteraria.* 2nd ed. Bari: Laterza, 1966: 127–228.

Galle, Roland. *Tragödie und Aufklärung: Zum Funktionswandel des Tragischen zwischen Racine und Büchner.* Stuttgart: Klett, 1976.

Galligan, Edward L. *The Comic Vision in Literature.* Athens: U of Georgia P, 1984.

Gardner, Helen. "Happy Endings: Literature, Misery, and Joy." *Encounter* 57 (1981): 39–51.

———. "Religion and Tragedy." *Religion and Literature.* New York: Oxford UP, 1971: 13–118.

Gassner, John. "The Possibilities and Perils of Modern Tragedy." *Tulane Drama Review* 1 (1957): 3–14.

Gates, Henry Louis, Jr. "Pluralism and Its Discontents." *Profession* (1992): 35–38.

Gearhart, Suzanne. *The Interrupted Dialectic: Philosophy, Psychoanalysis, and Their Tragic Other.* Baltimore: Johns Hopkins UP, 1992.

Gellrich, Michelle. *Tragedy and Theory: The Problem of Conflict Since Aristotle.* Princeton: Princeton UP, 1988.

Georgopoulos, N. "Tragic Action." *Tragedy and Philosophy.* Ed. N. Georgopoulos. New York: St. Martin's, 1993: 104–122.

Gethmann-Siefert, Annemarie. "Die Ästhetik in Hegels System der Philosophie." *Hegel: Einführung in seine Philosophie.* Ed. Otto Pöggeler. Freiburg: Alber, 1977: 127–149.

———. "Ästhetik oder Philosophie der Kunst: Die Nachschriften und Zeugnisse zu Hegels Berliner Vorlesungen." *Hegel-Studien* 26 (1991): 92–110.

———. *Die Funktion der Kunst in der Geschichte: Untersuchungen zu Hegels Ästhetik.* Bonn: Bouvier, 1984.

———. "Welt und Wirkung von Hegels Ästhetik." *Welt und Wirkung von*

Hegels Ästhetik. Ed. Annemarie Gethmann-Siefert and Otto Pög- geler. Bonn: Bouvier, 1986: V–XLVI.

———. "Zur Begründung einer Ästhetik nach Hegel." *Hegel-Studien* 13 (1978): 237–289.

Giese, Peter Christian. *Das Gesellschaftlich-Komische: Zur Komik und Ko- mödie am Beispiel der Stücke und Bearbeitungen Brechts*. Stutt- gart: Metzler, 1974.

Godlen, Leon. "Aristotle, Frye, and the Theory of Tragedy." *Comparative Literature* 27 (1975): 47–58.

Goethe, Johann Wolfgang. *Briefe der Jahre 1814–1832*. Ed. Christian Beutler. *Gedenkausgabe der Werke, Briefe und Gespräche*. Ed. Ernst Beutler. Vol. 21. Zürich: Artemis, 1951.

———. *Goethes Werke*. Ed. Erich Trunz. 10th ed. 14 vols. Munich: Beck, 1974.

———. "On Interpreting Aristotle's *Poetics*." *Essays on Art and Literature*. Trans. Ellen and Ernest H. von Nardroff. Ed. John Gearey. Vol. 3 of *Goethe's Collected Works*. Ed. Victor Lange, Eric Blackall, and Cyrus Hamlin. 12 vols. New York: Suhrkamp, 1986: 197–199.

Gowans, Christopher, ed. *Moral Dilemmas*. New York: Oxford UP, 1987.

Graff, Gerald. *Literature Against Itself: Literary Ideas in Modern Society*. Chicago: U of Chicago P, 1979.

Greiner, Bernhard. *Die Komödie. Eine theatralische Sendung: Grundlagen und Interpretationen*. Tübingen: Francke, 1992.

———. "Die Rede des Unbewußten als Komödie: Hofmannsthals Lustspiel 'Der Schwierige.'" *German Quarterly* 59 (1986): 228–251.

Grillparzer, Franz. *Sämtliche Werke*. 4 vols. Ed. Peter Frank and Karl Pörnbacher. Munich: Hanser, n.d.

Grimm, Reinhold. "Comic Reversal: A Tendency in the Development of Modern Aesthetics." *Imperial Germany*. Ed. Volker Dürr, Kathy Harms, and Peter Hayes. Madison: U of Wisconsin P, 1985: 149– 160.

———. "Kapriolen des Komischen. Zur Rezeptionsgeschichte seiner Theo- rie seit Hegel, Marx und Vischer." *Zwischen Satire und Utopie: Zur Komiktheorie und zur Geschichte der europäischen Komödie*. Ed. Reinhold Grimm and Walter Hinck. Frankfurt: Suhrkamp, 1982: 20–125.

———. "Komik und Verfremdung." *Strukturen: Essays zur deutschen Liter- atur*. Göttingen: Sachse, 1963: 226–247.

———. "Pyramide und Karussell: Zum Strukturwandel im Drama." *Nach dem Naturalismus*. Kronberg/Ts.: Athenäum, 1978: 3–27.

Gronicka, André von. "Friedrich Schiller's Marquis Posa: A Character Study." *Germanic Review* 26 (1951): 196–214.

Gruber, William E. "The Polarization of Tragedy and Comedy." *Genre* 13 (1980): 259–274.

Guha, P. K. *Tragic Relief.* London: Oxford UP, 1932.

Guidry, Glenn A. "Hofmannsthal's 'Der Schwierige': Language vs. Speech Acts." *German Studies Review* 5 (1982): 305–314.

Gurewitch, Morton, *Comedy: The Irrational Vision.* Ithaca: Cornell UP, 1975.

Guthke, Karl S. *Geschichte und Poetik der deutschen Tragikomödie.* Göttingen: Vandenhoeck, 1961.

———. *Die moderne Tragikomödie: Theorie und Gestalt.* Göttingen: Vandenhoeck, 1968.

———. *Modern Tragicomedy: An Investigation into the Nature of the Genre.* New York: Random House, 1966.

Haberland, Paul M. *The Development of Comic Theory in Germany during the Eighteenth Century.* Göppingen: Kümmerle, 1971.

Haida, Peter. *Komödie um 1900: Wandlungen des Gattungsschemas von Hauptmann bis Sternheim.* Munich: Fink, 1973.

Hamburger, Käte. *Wahrheit und ästhetische Wahrheit.* Stuttgart: Klett-Cotta, 1979.

Hamlin, Cyrus. "Tragedy and Modernity: Hölderlin, Hegel and the Theory of Modern Tragedy." *Tragique et tragedie dans la tradition occidentale.* Ed. Pierre Gravel and Timothy J. Reiss. Montreal: Determinations, 1983: 151–165.

Hampton, Christopher. *The Philanthropist and Other Plays.* London: Faber and Faber, 1991.

Hardy, Thomas. *Jude the Obscure.* Ed. Patricia Ingham. Oxford: Oxford UP, 1985.

Harris, Mark. *The Case for Tragedy: Being a Challenge to Those Who Deny the Possibility of a Tragic Spirit in the Modern World.* New York: G. P. Putnam's Sons, 1932.

Harrison, R. B. "'Gott ist über mir': Ruler and Reformer in the Twofold Symmetry of Schiller's 'Don Carlos.'" *Modern Language Review* 76 (1981): 598–611.

Hartmann, Eduard von. *Aesthetik.* 2 vols. Leipzig: Haacke, n. d. [1887].

Hartmann, Klaus. "Hegel: A Non-Metaphysical View." *Hegel: A Collection of Critical Essays.* Ed. Alasdair MacIntyre. Notre Dame: Notre Dame UP, 1976: 101–124.

———. "Die ontologische Option." *Die ontologische Option: Studien zu Hegels Propädeutik, Schellings Hegel-Kritik und Hegel's Phänomenologie des Geistes.* Ed. Klaus Hartmann. Berlin: de Gruyter, 1976: 1–30.

Hartmann, Nicolai. *Aesthetik.* Berlin: de Gruyter, 1953.

————. *Die Philosophie des deutschen Idealismus. II. Teil: Hegel*. Berlin: de Gruyter, 1929.

Hay, Gerhard. *Darstellung des Menschenhasses in der deutschen Literatur des 18. und 19. Jahrhunderts*. Frankfurt: Athenäum, 1970.

Heath, Malcolm. *The Poetics of Greek Tragedy*. London: Duckworth, 1987.

Hebbel, Friedrich. *Tagebücher*. 3 vols. Ed. Karl Pörnbacher. Munich: DTV, 1984.

Hegel, G.W.F. *Aesthetics: Lectures on Fine Arts*. Trans. T. M. Knox. Oxford: Clarendon, 1975.

————. *Early Theological Writings*. Trans. T. M. Knox and Richard Kroner. Chicago: U of Chicago P, 1948.

————. *Elements of the Philosophy of Right*. Trans. H. B. Nisbet. Ed. Allen W. Wood. Cambridge: Cambridge UP, 1991.

————. *The Encyclopaedia Logic, with the Zusätze: Part I of the Encyclopaedia of Philosophical Sciences*. Trans. Theodore F. Geraets, W. A. Suchting, and H. S. Harris. Indianapolis: Hackett, 1991.

————. *Introduction to the Philosophy of History*. Trans. Leo Rauch. Indianapolis: Hackett, 1988.

————. *Lectures on the History of Philosophy*. Trans. E. S. Haldane and Frances H. Simson. 3 vols. New York: Humanities, 1955.

————. *Natural Law: The Scientific Ways of Treating Natural Law, its Place in Moral Philosophy, and its Relation to the Positive Sciences of Law*. Trans. T. M. Knox. Philadelphia: U of Pennsylvania P, 1975.

————. *Phenomenology of Spirit*. Trans. A. V. Miller. Oxford: Clarendon, 1977.

————. *Philosophy of Mind*. [Part Three of the Encyclopedia of the Philosophical Science.] Trans. William Wallace. Oxford: Clarendon, 1894.

————. *Philosophy of Nature: Being Part Two of the Encyclopedia of the Philosophical Sciences*. Trans. A. V. Miller. Oxford: Clarendon, 1970.

————. *Science of Logic*. 2 vols. Trans. W. H. Johnston and L. G. Struthers. Ed. H. D. Lewis. 3rd ed. New York: Macmillan, 1961.

————. *Die Vernunft in der Geschichte*. Ed. Johannes Hoffmeister. Hamburg: Meiner, 1970.

————. *Werke in zwanzig Bänden*. Ed. Eva Moldenhauer and Karl Markus Michel. Frankfurt: Suhramp, 1978.

Heidsieck, Arnold. *Das Groteske und das Absurde im modernen Drama*. Stuttgart: Kohlhammer, 1969.

Heilman, Robert Bechtold. *The Iceman, the Arsonist, and the Troubled Agent: Tragedy and Melodrama on the Modern Stage*. Seattle: U of Washington P, 1973.

————. *Tragedy and Melodrama: Versions of Experience.* Seattle: U of Washington P, 1968.

————. *The Ways of the World: Comedy and Society.* Seattle: U of Washington P, 1978.

Heine, Heinrich. *Sämtliche Schriften.* Ed. Klaus Briegleb *et al.* 6 vols. Munich: Hanser, 1968–76.

Heine, Thomas. "The Force of Gestures: A New Approach to the Problem of Communication in Hofmannsthal's 'Der Schwierige.'" *German Quarterly* 56 (1983): 408–418.

Heise, Wolfgang. "Hegel und das Komische." *Sinn und Form* 16 (1964): 811–830.

Helferich, Christoph. *Georg Wilhelm Friedrich Hegel.* Stuttgart: Metzler, 1979.

Hemingway, Ernest. *For Whom the Bell Tolls.* New York: Macmillan, 1968.

Hempfer, Klaus W. *Gattungstheorie: Information und Synthese.* Munich: Fink, 1973.

Henckmann, Wolfhart. "Bibliographie zur Ästhetik Hegels 1830–1965." *Hegel-Studien* 5 (1969): 379–427.

Henn, T. R. *The Harvest of Tragedy.* London: Methuen, 1966.

Hernardi, Paul. *Beyond Genre: New Directions in Literary Classification.* Ithaca: Cornell UP, 1972.

Heubaum, A. "Ueber das Tragische." *Die Wahrheit* 8 (1897): 239–249.

Hildenbrock, Aglaja. *Das Andere Ich: Künstler, Mensch und Doppelgänger in der deutsch- und englischsprachigen Literatur.* Tübingen: Stauffenburg, 1986.

Hildesheimer, Wolfgang. *Theaterstücke. Über das absurde Theater.* Frankfurt: Suhrkamp, 1976.

Hinck, Walter. *Das deutsche Lustspiel des 17. und 18. Jahrhunderts und die italienische Komödie.* Stuttgart: Metzler, 1965.

————. *Theater der Hoffnung: Von der Aufklärung bis zur Gegenwart.* Frankfurt: Suhrkamp, 1988.

————. "Vom Ausgang der Komödie. Exemplarische Lustspielschlüsse in der europäische Literatur." *Zwischen Satire und Utopie: Zur Komiktheorie und zur Geschichte der europäischen Komödie.* Ed. Reinhold Grimm and Walter Hinck. Frankfurt: Suhrkamp, 1982: 126–183.

Hinrichs, H. F. W. *Schillers Dichtungen nach ihren historischen Beziehungen und nach ihrem inneren Zusammenhange.* 3 vols. Leipzig: Hinrichs, 1837–1839.

Hirsch, Jr., E. D. *Validity in Interpretation.* New Haven: Yale UP, 1967.

Hitchcock, Alfred, dir. *I Confess.* Warner Brothers, 1953.

Hofmannsthal, Hugo von. "An Henri Barbusse, Alexandre Mercereau und ihre Freunde." *Gesammelte Werke in zehn Einzelbänden. Prosa III*. Frankfurt: Fischer, 1952: 436–440.

———. *The Difficult Man*. Trans. Willa Muir. *Selected Plays and Libretti*. Ed. Michael Hamburger. New York: Bollingen Foundation, 1963: 633–823.

———. *Gesammelte Werke in zehn Einzelbänden*. Frankfurt: Fischer, 1979.

———. "Preuße und Österreicher: Ein Schema." *Gesammelte Werke in drei Bänden*. Berlin: Fischer, 1934: 3:61–62.

———. "Über Schnitzlers 'Anatol.'" *Neue Rundschau* 82 (1971): 795–797.

Holberg, Ludvig. *Four Plays By Holberg*. Trans. Henry Alexander. Princeton: Princeton UP, 1946.

Hölderlin, Friedrich. *Sämmtliche Werke. Große Stuttgarter Ausgabe*. Ed. Friedrich Beißner. 8 vols. Stuttgart: Kohlhammer, 1946–85.

Höllerer, Walter, ed. *Der Zürcher Literaturstreit: Eine Dokumentation*. *Sprache im technischen Zeitalter* 22 (1967): 83–206.

Hook, Sidney. *Pragmatism and the Tragic Sense of Life*. New York: Basic Books, 1974.

Hösle, Vittorio. *Hegels System. Der Idealismus der Subjektivität und das Problem der Intersubjektivität*. 2 vols. Hamburg: Meiner, 1987.

———. *Die Vollendung der Tragödie im Spätwerk des Sophokles. Ästhetisch-historische Bemerkungen zur Struktur der attischen Tragödie*. Stuttgart-Bad Cannstatt: Frommann-Holzboog, 1984.

———. *Wahrheit und Geschichte. Studien zur Struktur der Philosophiegeschichte unter paradigmatischer Analyse der Entwicklung von Parmenides bis Platon*. Stuttgart-Bad Cannstatt: Frommann-Holzboog, 1984.

Houlgate, Stephen. *Freedom, Truth, and History: An Introduction to Hegel's Philosophy*. New York: Routledge, 1991.

———. *Hegel, Nietzsche and the Criticism of Metaphysics*. Cambridge, Cambridge UP, 1986.

Hughes, Robert. *Culture of Complaint: The Fraying of America*. New York: Oxford UP, 1993.

Hume, David. "Of Tragedy." *Tragedy: Developments in Criticism*. Ed. R. P. Draper. London: Macmillan, 1980: 92–98.

Hume, Robert D. "Some Problems in the Theory of Comedy." *Journal of Aesthetics and Art Criticism* 31 (1972): 87–100.

Hunter, Robert Grams. *Shakespeare and the Comedy of Forgiveness*. New York: Columbia UP, 1965.

Ibsen, Henrik. *The Plays of Ibsen*. Trans. Michael Meyer. 4 vols. New York: Washington Square Press, 1986.

Jameson, Frederic. *The Political Unconscious: Narrative as a Socially Symbolic Act*. Ithaca: Cornell UP, 1981.

Jamme, Christoph. "Liebe, Schicksal und Tragik: Hegels 'Geist des Christentums' und Hölderlins 'Empedokles.'" *"Frankfurt aber ist der Nabel dieser Erde." Das Schicksal einer Generation der Goethezeit.* Ed. Christoph Jamme and Otto Pöggeler. Stuttgart: Klett, 1983: 300–324.

Jaspers, Karl. *Tragedy is Not Enough.* Trans. Harald A. T. Reiche, Harry T. Moore, and Karl W. Deutsch. Boston: Beacon, 1952.

Jauß, Hans Robert. *Literaturgeschichte als Provokation.* Frankfurt: Suhrkamp, 1970.

———. *Toward an Aesthetic of Reception.* Trans. Timothy Bahti. Minneapolis: U of Minnesota P, 1982.

Jens, Walter. "Plädoyer für das Positive in der modernen Literatur." *Deutsche Reden.* Ed. Walter Hinderer. Stuttgart: Reclam, 1973: 1067–1077.

Joffe, Roland, dir. *The Mission.* Warner Brothers, 1986.

Juhl, P[eter]. D. *Interpretation: An Essay in the Philosophy of Literary Criticism.* Princeton: Princeton UP, 1980.

Jünger, Friedrich Georg. *Über das Komische.* 3rd ed. Frankfurt: Klostermann, 1948.

Kant, Immanuel. *The Metaphysical Principles of Virtue: Part II of The Metaphysics of Morals.* Trans. James Ellington. New York: Bobbs-Merrill, 1964.

———. *Werkausgabe.* Ed. Wilhelm Weischedel. 12 vols. Frankfurt: Suhrkamp, 1968.

Kany, Roland. *Mnemosyne als Programm: Geschichte, Erinnerung und die Andacht zum Unbedeutenden im Werk von Usener, Warburg und Benjamin.* Tübingen: Niemeyer, 1987.

Karelis, Charles. "Hegel's Concept of Art: An Interpretative Essay." *Hegel's Introduction to Aesthetics.* Trans. T. M. Knox. Oxford: Clarendon, 1979: xi–lxxvi.

Katann, Oskar. *Gesetz im Wandel: Neue literarische Studien.* Innsbruck: Tyrolia, 1932.

Kaufmann, Walter. "Hegel: Contribution and Calamity." *From Shakespeare to Existentialism.* Garden City, N.Y.: Anchor, 1960: 163–174.

———. *Hegel: Reinterpretation, Texts, and Commentary.* Garden City, N.Y.: Doubleday, 1965.

———. *Tragedy and Philosophy.* Princeton: Princeton UP, 1979.

Kermode, Frank. "The Mature Comedies." *The Early Shakespeare.* New York: St. Martin's, 1961: 211–227.

Kern, Edith. *The Absolute Comic.* New York: Columbia UP, 1980.

Kierkegaard, Søren. *The Concept of Irony with Constant Reference to Socrates.* Trans. Lee M. Capel. New York: Harper, 1965.

──────. *Concluding Unscientific Postscript to the Philosophical Fragments*. Trans. David F. Swenson and Walter Lowrie. Princeton: Princeton UP, 1941.

Kindermann, Heinz. "Grundformen des komischen Theaters." *Wesen und Formen des Komischen im Drama*. Ed. Reinhold Grimm and Klaus L. Berghahn. Darmstadt: Wissenschaftliche Buchgesellschaft, 1975: 93–126.

Kirchmann, Julius Hermann von. *Ästhetik auf realisticher Grundlage*. 2 vols. Berlin: Springer, 1868.

Klapp, Orrin E. "Tragedy and the American Climate of Opinion." *Tragedy: Vision and Form*. Ed. Robert W. Corrigan. 2nd ed. New York: Harper, 1981: 252–262.

Kline, George. "The Use and Abuse of Hegel by Nietzsche and Marx." *Hegel and His Critics: Philosophy in the Aftermath of Hegel*. Ed. William Desmond. Albany: SUNY, 1989: 1–34.

Klotz, Volker. *Bürgerliches Lachtheater: Komödie, Posse, Schwank, Operette*. Darmstadt: Wissenschaftliche Buchgesellschaft, 1984.

──────. *Geschlossene und offene Form im Drama*. 10th ed. Munich: Hanser, 1980.

Kluckhohn, Paul. "Die Arten des Dramas." *Deutsche Vierteljahrsschrift für Literaturwissenschaft und Geistesgesschichte* 19 (1941): 241–268.

Knox, Bernard M. W. *The Heroic Temper: Studies in Sophoclean Tragedy*. Berkeley: U of California P, 1964.

Knox, Israel. *The Aesthetic Theories of Kant, Hegel, and Schopenhauer*. New York: Columbia UP, 1936.

Koch, Dietmar, and Klaus Bort, eds. *Kategorie und Kategorialität: Historisch-systematische Untersuchungen zum Bergiff der Kategorie im philosophischen Denken. Festschrift für Klaus Hartmann zum 65. Geburtstag*. Würzburg: Königshausen & Neumann, 1990.

Koelb, Clayton. "The Problem of 'Tragedy' as a Genre." *Genre* 8 (1975): 248–266.

──────. "'Tragedy' as an Evaluative Term." *Comparative Literature Studies* 11 (1974): 69–84.

Koepsel, Werner. *Die Rezeption der Hegelschen Ästhetik im 20. Jahrhundert*. Bonn: Bouvier, 1975.

Kohlberg, Lawrence. *Essay on Moral Development*. New York: Harper, 1981.

Koopmann, Helmut. "Don Karlos." *Schillers Dramen: Neue Interpretationen*. Ed. Walter Hinderer. Stuttgart: Reclam, 1979: 87–108.

Krook, Dorothea. *Elements of Tragedy*. New Haven: Yale UP, 1969.

Krüger, Manfred. *Wandlungen des Tragischen: Drama und Initiation*. Stuttgart: Freies Geistesleben, 1973.

Kufner, Stephanie. "Utopie und Verantwortung in Schillers 'Don Carlos.'" *Verantwortung und Utopie. Zur Literatur der Goethezeit. Ein Symposium.* Ed. Wolfgang Wittkowski. Tübingen: Niemeyer, 1988: 238–255.

Kurrik, Maire Jaanus. *Literature and Negation.* New York: Columbia UP, 1979.

Kutscher, Artur. *Stilkunde der deutschen Dichtung.* 2 vols. Bremen-Horn: Dorn, 1951.

Kuzniar, Alice A. *Delayed Endings: Nonclosure in Novalis and Hölderlin.* Athens: The U of Georgia P, 1987.

Lang, Candace D. *Irony/Humor: Critical Paradigms.* Baltimore: Johns Hopkins UP, 1988.

Lean, David, dir. *The Bridge on the River Kwai.* Columbia, 1957.

LeBlanc, Gisèle Marie. "Bradley's Misreading of Hegel's Theory of Tragedy." *Frontenac Review* 3 (1985): 71–83.

Leggatt, Alexander. *Shakespeare's Comedy of Love.* London: Methuen, 1974.

Lenson, David. *Achilles' Choice: Examples of Modern Tragedy.* Princeton: Princeton UP, 1975.

Levin, Harry. *Playboys and Killjoys: An Essay on the Theory and Practice of Comedy.* New York: Oxford UP, 1987.

Lewis, Paul. *Comic Effects: Interdisciplinary Approaches to Humor in Literature.* Albany: SUNY, 1989.

Lipps, Theodor. *Komik und Humor: eine psychologisch-ästhetische Untersuchung.* Hamburg: Voss, 1898.

Locke, John. *Two Treatises of Government.* Ed. Peter Laslett. Cambridge: Cambridge UP, 1989.

Loraux, Nicole. *Tragic Ways of Killing a Woman.* Trans. Anthony Forster. Cambridge: Harvard UP, 1987.

Lubich, Frederick Alfred. "Hugo von Hofmannsthals *Der Schwierige*: Hans Karl Bühl und Antoinette Hechingen unterm Aspekt der Sprache und Moral." *Monatshefte* 77 (1985): 47–59.

Lucas, F. L. *Tragedy in Relation to Aristotle's Poetics.* New York: Harcourt, 1928.

Lukács, Georg. *Entwicklungsgeschichte des modernen Dramas. Werke.* Vol. 15. Ed. Frank Benseler. Darmstadt: Luchterhand, 1981.

———. "Hegels Ästhetik." *Sinn und Form* 5/6 (1953): 17–58.

———. "Die Kategorie der Besonderheit." *Die Eigenart des Ästhetischen.* 2 vols. Neuwied: Luchterhand, 1963: 2:193–266.

———. *The Meaning of Contemporary Realism.* Trans. John and Necke Mander. London: Merlin, 1963.

———. "Metaphysics of Tragedy: Paul Ernst." *Soul and Form.* Trans. Anna Bostock. Cambridge: MIT Press, 1974: 152–174.

————. "Metaphysik der Tragödie: Paul Ernst." *Die Seele und die Formen: Essays*. Neuwied: Luchterhand, 1971: 218–50.

————. "Das Problem des untragischen Dramas." *Die Schaubühne* 7 (1911): 231–234.

————. *Die Theorie des Romans: Ein geschichtsphilosophischer Versuch über die Formen der großen Epik*. Neuwied: Luchterhand, 1971.

Lyotard, Jean-François. *The Postmodern Condition: A Report on Knowledge*. Minneapolis: U of Minnesota P, 1984.

Maass, Joachim. "Das Eis von Cape Sabine." *Die Stunde der Entscheidung: Drei Dramen*. Basel: Desch, 1965: 49–123.

MacDonald, Michael Hugh. "Hegel and Tragedy." Diss. University of Washington, 1975.

Maier, Karl. "Untersuchungen zur Struktur des höheren Humors im deutschen Lustspiel: Unter besonderer Berücksichtigung der Stücke 'Minna von Barnhelm' von Lessing und 'Der Schwierige' von Hofmannsthal." Diss. Tübingen 1957.

Malsch, Wilfried. "Moral und Politik in Schillers 'Don Karlos.'" *Verantwortung und Utopie. Zur Literatur der Goethezeit. Ein Symposium*. Ed. Wolfgang Wittkowski. Tübingen: Niemeyer, 1988: 207–237.

————. "Robespierre ad Portas? Zur Deutungsgeschichte der *Briefe über Don Karlos* von Schiller." *The Age of Goethe Today: Critical Reexamination and Literary Reflection*. Ed. Gertrud Bauer Pickar and Sabine Cramer. Munich: Fink, 1990: 69–101.

Mandel, Oscar. *A Definition of Tragedy*. New York: New York UP, 1961.

Mann, Otto. *Poetik der Tragödie*. Bern: Francke, 1958.

Mann, Thomas. *Briefe 1948–1955*. Frankfurt: Fischer, 1965.

————. *Confessions of Felix Krull Confidence Man: The Early Years*. Trans. Denver Lindley. New York: Knopf, 1955.

Marcuse, Ludwig. "Die marxistische Auslegung des Tragischen." *Monatshefte* 46 (1954): 241–248.

————. *Die Welt der Tragödie*. Berlin: Schneider, 1923.

Martens, Rolf Wolfgang. "Über das Komische und den Witz." *Zeitschrift für Ästhetik und allgemeine Kunstwissenschaft* 15 (1921): 459–467.

Martini, Fritz. *Lustspiele und das Lustspiel*. Stuttgart: Klett, 1974.

Mast, Gerald. *The Comic Mind: Comedy and the Movies*. 2nd ed. Chicago: U of Chicago P, 1979.

Mauser, Wolfram. "Österreich und das Österreichische in Hofmannsthals *Der Schwierige*." *Recherches Germaniques* 12 (1982): 109–130.

May, Keith M. *Nietzsche and the Spirit of Tragedy*. London: Macmillan, 1990.

McCollom, William G. *The Divine Average: A View of Comedy*. Cleveland: P of Case Western Reserve U, 1971.

————. *Tragedy*. New York: Macmillan, 1957.

McFadden, George. *Discovering the Comic*. Princeton: Princeton UP, 1982.

McInerney, John. "The Mission and Robert Bolt's 'Drama of Revolution.'" *Literature/Film Quarterly* 15 (1987): 70–77.

Menander. *Plays and Fragments*. Trans. Norma Miller. New York: Penguin, 1987.

Mennemeier, Franz Norbert. "Carl Sternheims Komödie der Politik." *Deutsche Vierteljahrsschrift für Literaturwissenschaft und Geistesgeschichte* 44 (1970): 705–726.

————. "Drama." *Moderne Literatur in Grundbegriffen*. Ed. Dieter Borchmeyer and Victor Zmegac. Frankfurt: Athenäum, 1987: 89–101.

Merlan, Philip. "Ist die 'These-Antithese-Synthese' Formel unhegelisch?" *Archiv für Geschichte der Philosophie* 53 (1971): 35–40.

Meyer, Conrad Ferdinand. *Das Leiden eines Knaben*. Stuttgart: Reclam, 1965.

Michel, Laurence. "The Possibility of Christian Tragedy." *Thought* 31 (1956): 403–428.

————. *The Thing Contained: Theory of the Tragic*. Bloomington: Indiana UP, 1970.

Michelet, Carl Ludwig. *Geschichte der letzten Systeme der Philosophie in Deutschland von Kant bis Hegel*. Vol. 2. Berlin: Duncker, 1838.

————. *Das System der Philosophie als exacter Wissenschaft enthaltend Logik, Natur- und Geistespilosophie*. 3 vols. 1876–78. Brussels: Culture et Civilisation, 1968.

Migne, Jacques Paul, ed. *Patrologiae cursus completus, seu bibliotheca universalis, integra, uniformis, commoda, oeconomica, omnium ss. patrum, doctorum scriptorumque ecclesiasticorum, sive latinorum, sive graecorum* [. . .] Series Graeca. 167 vols. Paris 1857–66.

Miles, Rosalind. *The Problem of Measure for Measure: A Historical Investigation*. London: Vision, 1976.

Miller, Arthur. *The Crucible*. New York: Penguin, 1987.

————. *Incident at Vichy*. New York: Penguine, 1985.

Miller, J. Hillis. "Literature and Value: American and Soviet Views." *Profession* (1992): 21–27.

Molière. *The Misanthrope and Other Plays*. Trans. John Wood. New York: Penguin, 1959.

————. *Oeuvres completes*. Ed. Georges Couton. 2 vols. Paris: Pleiade, 1971.

Monro, D. H. *Argument of Laughter*. Notre Dame: U of Notre Dame P, 1963.

Moravia, Alberto. "The Sterility of Suffering." *The Yale Review* 47 (1957): 175–180.

Morreall, John. *Taking Laughter Seriously*. Albany: SUNY, 1983.

Morris, Michael K. "Moral Conflict and Ordinary Emotional Experience." *Journal of Value Inquiry* 26 (1992): 223–238.

Moss, Leonard. "The Unrecognized Influence of Hegel's Theory of Tragedy." *Journal of Aesthetics and Art Criticism* 28 (1969–70): 91–97.

Mueller, Gustav E. "The Hegel Legend of 'Thesis-Antithesis-Synthesis.'" *Journal of the History of Ideas* 19 (1958): 411–414.

Müller, Joachim. *Das Edle in der Freiheit*. Leipzig: Koehler, 1959.

Myers, David. "Carl Sternheim: Satirist or Creator of Modern Heroes?" *Monatshefte* 65 (1973): 39–47.

Napieralski, Edmund A. "The Tragic Knot: Paradox in the Experience of Tragedy." *Journal of Aesthetics and Art Criticism* 31 (1972): 441–449.

Nelson, T. G. A. *Comedy: An Introduction to Comedy in Literature, Drama, and Cinema*. Oxford: Oxford UP, 1990.

Nestroy, Johann. *Gesammelte Werke*. Ed. Otto Rommel. 6 vols. Vienna: Schroll, 1948–49.

———. *A Man Full of Nothing. Three Comedies*. Trans. Max Knight and Joseph Fabry. New York: Ungar, 1967: 28–93.

Nevo, Ruth. "Toward a Theory of Comedy." *Journal of Aesthetics and Art Criticism* 21 (1963): 327–332.

The New Oxford Annotated Bible with the Apocrypha. Ed. Herbert G. May and Bruce M. Metzger. New York: Oxford UP, 1973.

Niebuhr, Reinhold. *Beyond Tragedy: Essays on the Christian Interpretation of History*. New York: Scribner's Sons, 1941.

Nietzsche, Friedrich. *Thus Spoke Zarathustra. The Portable Nietzsche*. Ed. and Trans. Walter Kaufmann. 1954. New York: Penguin, 1985: 103–439.

———. *Werke*. Ed. Karl Schlechta. 6th ed. 3 vols. Munich: Hanser, 1969.

Niven, William John. *The Reception of Friedrich Hebbel in Germany in the Era of National Socialism*. Stuttgart: Heinz, 1984.

Norton, Robert E. "'Ein bitteres Gelächter': Tragic and Comic Elements in Lessing's *Philotas*." *Deutsche Vierteljahrsschrift für Literaturwissenschaft und Geistesgeschichte* 66 (1992): 450–465.

Nussbaum, Martha C. *The Fragility of Goodness: Luck and Ethics in Greek Tragedy and Philosophy*. Cambridge: Cambridge UP, 1986.

———. *Love's Knowledge: Essays on Philosophy and Literature*. New York: Oxford UP, 1990.

O'Connor, Wiliam Van. *Climates of Tragedy*. New York: Russell, 1965.

Oelmüller, Willi. *Friedrich Theodor Vischer und das Problem der nachhegelschen Ästhetik*. Stuttgart: Kohlhammer, 1959.

———. "Das Problem des Ästhetischen bei Friedrich Theodor Vischer." *Jahrbuch der Deutschen Schillergesellschaft* 2 (1958): 237–265.

Oliver, Roger W. *Dreams of Passion: The Theater of Luigi Pirandello.* New York: New York UP, 1979.

Olsen, Lance. *Circus of the Mind in Motion: Postmodernism and the Comic Vision.* Detroit: Wayne State UP, 1990.

Olson, Elder. *The Theory of Comedy.* Bloomington: Indiana UP, 1968.

———. *Tragedy and the Theory of Drama.* Detroit: Wayne State UP, 1966.

O'Neill, Eugene. *Three Plays.* New York: Vintage, 1959.

Origen. *On First Principles.* Trans. G. W. Butterworth. New York: Harper, 1966.

Orr, John. *Tragic Drama and Modern Society: Studies in the Social and Literary Theory of Drama from 1870 to the Present.* London: Macmillan, 1981.

Oudemans, Th. C. W., and A. P. M. H. Lardinois. *Tragic Ambiguity: Anthropology, Philosophy and Sophocles' Antigone.* Leiden: Brill, 1987.

Packer, Mark. "Dissolving the Paradox of Tragedy." *Journal of Aesthetics and Art Criticism* 47 (1989): 211–219.

Paolucci, Anne. "Bradley and Hegel on Shakespeare." *Comparative Literature* 16 (1964): 211–225.

———. "Hegel's Theory of Comedy." *Comedy: New Perspectives.* Ed. Maurice Charney. New York: New York Literary Forum, 1978: 89–108.

Paolucci, Anne, and Henry Paolucci. "Introduction." *Hegel on Tragedy.* New York: Harper, 1962: xi–xxxi.

Paolucci, Henry. "The Poetics of Aristotle and Hegel." *Review of National Literatures* 1 (1970): 165–213.

Park, Clara Claiborne. "No Time for Comedy." *Comedy: Meaning and Form.* Ed. Robert W. Corrigan. 2nd ed. New York: Harper, 1981: 58–64.

Pfister, Manfred. "Bibliographie zur Gattungspoetik. Theorie des Komischen, der Komödie und der Tragikomödie (1943–1972)." *Zeitschrift für französische Sprache und Literatur* 83 (1973): 240–254.

———. *Das Drama: Theorie und Analyse.* 6th ed. Munich: Fink, 1988.

Pillau, Helmut. *Die fortgedachte Dissonanz: Hegels Tragödientheorie und Schillers Tragödie. Deutsche Antworten auf die Französische Revolution.* Munich: Fink, 1981.

Pinkard, Terry. *Hegel's Dialectic: The Explanation of Possibility.* Philadelphia: Temple UP, 1988.

———. "Hegel's Idealism and Hegel's Logic." *Zeitschrift für philosophische Forschung* 23 (1979): 210–225.

Pirandello, Luigi. *Opere.* 6 vols. Milan: Mondadori, 1956–60.

————. *Naked Masks: Five Plays by Luigi Pirandello.* Ed. Eric Bentley. New York: Dutton, 1952.

Plato. *The Collected Dialogues including the Letters.* Ed. Edith Hamilton and Huntington Cairns. Princeton: Princeton UP, 1978.

Plautus. *The Pot of Gold and Other Plays.* Trans. E. F. Watling. New York: Penguin, 1965.

Pöggeler, Otto. "Hegel und die griechische Tragödie." *Heidelberger Hegel-Tage 1962.* Ed. Hans-Georg Gadamer. Bonn: Bouvier, 1964: 285–305.

Polheim, Karl Konrad. "Von der Einheit des 'Don Karlos.'" *Jahrbuch des Freien Deutschen Hochstifts* (1985): 64–100.

Poole, Adrian. *Tragedy: Shakespeare and the Greek Example.* New York: Blackwell, 1987.

Preisendanz, Wolfgang. *Humor als dichterische Einbildungskraft: Studien zur Erzählkunst des poetischen Realismus.* Munich: Eidos, 1963.

————. "Das Schäferspiel 'Die Laune des Verliebten' und das Lustspiel 'Die Mitschuldigen.'" *Goethes Dramen: Neue Interpretationen.* Ed. Walter Hinderer. Stuttgart: Reclam, 1980: 11–22.

Prigogine, Ilya. *From Being to Becoming: Time and Complexity in the Physical Sciences.* San Francisco: Freeman, 1980.

Pütz, Peter. *Die Leistung der Form: Lessings Dramen.* Frankfurt: Suhrkamp, 1986.

Rabkin, Norman. "Structure, Convention, and Meaning in *Julius Caesar.*" *Journal of English and Germanic Philology* 63 (1964): 240–254.

Rank, Otto. *The Double: A Psychoanalytic Study.* Trans. Harry Tucker, Jr. Chapel Hill: U of North Carolina P, 1971.

Rau, Peter. *Paratragodia: Untersuchung einer komischen Form des Aristophanes.* Munich: Beck, 1967.

Reese, M. M. *The Cease of Majesty: A Study of Shakespeare's History Plays.* New York: St. Martin's, 1961.

Reichert, John. *Making Sense of Literature.* Chicago: U of Chicago P, 1977.

————. "More than Kin and Less than Kind: The Limits of Genre Theory." *Theories of Literary Genre.* Ed. Joseph P. Strelka. University Park: Penn State UP, 1978: 57–79.

Reinhardt, Karl. *Die Krise des Helden und andere Beiträge zur Literatur und Geistesgeschichte.* Munich: DTV, 1962.

Reinhardt, Max. *Schall und Rauch.* Berlin: Schuster, 1901.

Ricoeur, Paul. *The Symbolism of Evil.* Trans. Emerson Buchanan. Boston: Beacon, 1969.

Robinson, Fred Miller. *The Comedy of Language: Studies in Modern Comic Literature.* Amherst: U of Massachusetts P, 1980.

Roche, Mark W. "Apel and Lessing—or: The Ethics of Communication and the Strategies of Comedy." *Lessing Yearbook* 25 (1993): 41–54.

———. "Areas of Expertise, Proleptic Interpretation, Penultimate Drafts: Three Ideas for the Graduate Seminar in Literature." *Die Unterrichtspraxis* 20 (1987): 261–268.

———. *Dynamic Stillness: Philosophical Conceptions of Ruhe in Schiller, Hölderlin, Büchner, and Heine.* Tübingen: Niemeyer, 1987.

———. *Gottfried Benn's Static Poetry: Aesthetic and Intellectual-Historical Interpretations.* Chapel Hill: U of North Carolina P, 1991.

———. "Hitchcock and the Transcendence of Tragedy: *I Confess* as Speculative Art." *Post Script: Essays in Film and the Humanities* 10.3 (1991): 30–37.

———. "Justice and the Withdrawal of God in Woody Allen's *Crimes and Misdemeanors.*" *Journal of Value Inquiry* 29 (1995): 547–563.

———. "Kafka, Pirandello, and the Irony of Ironic Indeterminacy." *Journal of the Kafka Society of America* 18 (1994): 42–47.

———. "Laughter and Truth in *Doktor Faustus.* Nietzschean Structures in Mann's Novel of Self-cancellations." *Deutsche Vierteljahrsschrift für Literaturwissenschaft und Geistesgeschichte* 60 (1986): 309–332.

———. "National Socialism and the Disintegration of Values: Reflections on Nietzsche, Rosenberg, and Broch." *Journal of Value Inquiry* 29 (1992): 367–380.

———. "Plato and the Structures of Injustice." *Inquiries into Values: Conference Proceedings of the 1988 Inaugural Meetings of the International Society for Value Inquiry.* Ed. Sander Lee. Lewiston, N.Y.: Mellen, 1988: 279–290.

———. "Schnitzler's *Anatol* as a Philosophical Comedy." *Modern Austrian Literature* 22 (1989): 51–63.

Roche, Mark W., and Vittorio Hösle. "Vico's Age of Heroes and the Age of Men in John Ford's *The Man Who Shot Liberty Valance.*" *CLIO* 23 (1994): 131–147.

Rommel, Otto. "Die wissenschaftlichen Bemühungen um die Analyse des Komischen." *Wesen und Formen des Komischen im Drama.* Ed. Reinhold Grimm and Klaus L. Berghahn. Darmstadt: Wissenschaftliche Buchgesellschaft, 1975: 1–38.

Rorty, Richard. *Contingency, Irony, and Solidarity.* Cambridge: Cambridge UP, 1989.

Rosenberg, Alfred. *Der Mythus des 20. Jahrhunderts: Eine Wertung der seelisch-geistigen Gestaltenkämpfe unserer Zeit.* Munich: Hoheneichen, 1943.

Rosenkranz, Karl. *Ästhetik des Häßlichen.* 1853. Darmstadt: Wissenschaftliche Buchgesellschaft, 1979.

————. Rev. of *Vorlesungen über die Aesthetik*. Vols. 2 and 3. By G. W. F. Hegel. Berlin: Duncker, 1838. *Jahrbücher für wissenschaftliche Kritik* 47/48 (1838): 363–390.

Rosenstein, Leon. "Metaphysical Foundations of the Theories of Tragedy in Hegel and Nietzsche." *Journal of Aesthetics and Art Criticism* 28 (1970): 521–533.

Rosmarin, Adena. *The Power of Genre*. Minneapolis: U of Minnesota P, 1985.

Rothman, William. *Hitchcock—The Murderous Gaze*. Cambridge: Harvard UP, 1982.

Rötscher, H. Theodor. *Aristophanes und sein Zeitalter: Eine philologisch-philosophische Abhandlung zur Alterthumsforschung*. Berlin: Vossische Buchhandlung, 1827.

Ruge, Arnold. *Neue Vorschule der Ästhetik. Das Komische mit einem komischen Anhang*. 1837. Hildesheim: Olms, 1975.

Ruprecht, Louis A., Jr. *Tragic Posture and Tragic Vision: Against the Modern Failure of Nerve*. New York: Continuum, 1994.

Salingar, Leo. *Shakespeare and the Traditions of Comedy*. London: Cambridge UP, 1974.

Schaeffer, Neil. *The Art of Laughter*. New York: Columbia UP, 1981.

Scheler, Max. *Formalism in Ethics and Non-Formal Ethics of Values: A New Attempt toward the Foundation of an Ethical Personalism*. Trans. Manfred S. Frings and Roger L. Funk. Evanston: Northwestern UP, 1973.

————. *Der Formalismus in der Ethik und die materiale Wertethik: Neuer Versuch der Grundlegung eines ethischen Personalismus*. 6th ed. Bern: Francke, 1980.

————. "On the Tragic." *Tragedy: Vision and Form*. Ed. Robert W. Corrigan. 2nd ed. New York: Harper, 1981: 17–29.

————. "Zum Phänomen des Tragischen." *Abhandlungen und Aufsätze*. Leipzig: Verlag der weissen Bücher, 1915: 1:275–315.

Schelling, Friedrich Wilhelm Joseph von. *Philosophie der Kunst*. 1859. Darmstadt: Wissenschaftliche Buchgesellschaft, 1960.

————. *The Philosophy of Art*. Ed. and Trans. Douglas W. Stott. Minneapolis: U of Minnesota P, 1989.

Schickel, Richard. "Up the Creek." *Time* (10 November 1986): 111.

Schiller, Friedrich. *Don Carlos, Infant von Spanien*. Stuttgart: Reclam, 1979.

————. *Don Carlos*. Trans. A. Leslie and Jeanne R. Wilson. *Plays: Intrigue and Love and Don Carlos*. Ed. Walter Hinderer. German Library 15. New York: Continuum, 1983: 103–303.

————. *Schillers Werke: Nationalausgabe*. Ed. Julius Peterson and Hermann Schneider. Weimar: Böhlaus, 1943– .

Schings, Hans-Jürgen. *Die Brüder des Marquis Posa: Schiller und der Geheimbund der Illuminaten.* Tübingen: Niemeyer, 1996.

Schlunk, Wolfgang. "Hegels Theorie des Dramas." Diss. Tübingen 1936.

Schmidt, Henry J. *How Dramas End: Essays on the German Sturm und Drang, Büchner, Hauptmann, and Fleißer.* Ann Arbor: U of Michigan P, 1992.

Schneider, Helmut. "Eine Nachschrift der Vorlesung Hegels über Ästhetik im Wintersemester 1820/21." *Hegel-Studien* 26 (1992): 89–92.

Schnitzler, Arthur. *Das dramatische Werk.* 8 vols. Frankfurt: Fisher, 1979.

———. *Professor Bernhardi. A Comedy in Five Acts.* Trans. Hetty Landstone. 1913. New York: Simon, 1928.

Scholes, Robert, and Carl H. Klaus. *Elements of Drama.* New York: Oxford UP, 1971.

Schopenhauer, Arthur. "On the Apparent Deliberateness in the Fate of the Individual." Vol. 1 of *Parerga and Paralipomena: Short Philosophical Essays.* 2 vols. Trans. E. F. J. Payne. Oxford: Clarendon, 1974: 199–223.

———. *Zürcher Ausgabe. Werke in zehn Bänden.* Zürich: Diogenes, 1977.

Schrimpf, Hans Joachim. "Komödie und Lustspiel: Zur terminologischen Problematik einer geschichtlich orientierten Gattungstypologie." *Zeitschrift für deutsche Philologie* 97 (1978): 152–182.

Schulte, Michael. *Die 'Tragödie im Sittlichen'. Zur Dramentheorie Hegels.* Munich: Fink, 1992.

Schultz, Werner. "Die Bedeutung des Tragischen für das Verstehen der Geschichte bei Hegel und Goethe." *Archiv für Kulturgeschichte* 38 (1956): 92–115.

Schüttauf, Konrad. *Die Kunst und die bildenden Künste: Eine Auseinandersetzung mit Hegels Ästhetik.* Bonn: Bouvier, 1984.

Schütze, Johann Stephan. *Versuch einer Theorie des Komischen.* Leipzig: Hartknoch, 1817.

Scott, Nathan A., Jr., ed. *The Tragic Vision and the Christian Faith.* New York: Association Press, 1957.

Seaford, Richard. Introduction. *Cyclops.* By Euripides. Oxford: Clarendon, 1984: 1–60.

Seaton, James. "Marxism Without Difficulty: Fredric Jameson's *The Political Unconscious.*" *Centennial Review* 28/29 (1984–85): 122–142.

Seneca. *Phaedra.* Trans. Frederick Ahl. Ithaca: Cornell UP, 1986.

Sengle, Friedrich. "Vom Absoluten in der Tragödie." *Deutsche Vierteljahrsschrift für Literaturwissenschaft und Geistesgeschichte* 20 (1942): 265–272.

———. *Vorschläge zur Reform der literarischen Formenlehre.* 2nd ed. Stuttgart: Metzler, 1969.

Sennett, Richard. *The Fall of Public Man: On the Social Psychology of Capitalism*. New York: Vintage, 1978.

Shakespeare, William. *The Complete Works of William Shakespeare*. Ed. David Bevington. 6 vols. New York: Bantam, 1988.

Shakespeare, William, and John Fletcher. "The Two Noble Kinsmen." *The Riverside Shakespeare*. Ed. G. Blakemore Evans. Boston: Houghton Mifflin, 1974: 1639–1681.

Shaw, Bernard. *Man and Superman. A Comedy and a Philosophy*. Ed. Dan H. Laurence. New York: Penguin, 1985.

Shershow, Scott Cutter. *Laughing Matters: The Paradox of Comedy*. Amherst: U of Masschusetts P, 1986.

Simmel, Georg. "Der Begriff und die Tragödie der Kultur." *Philosophische Kultur. Gesammelte Essais*. Leipzig: Klinkhardt, 1911: 245–277.

Simon, Josef. *Wahrheit als Freiheit: Zur Entwicklung der Wahrheitsfrage in der neueren Philosophie*. Berlin: de Gruyter, 1978.

Šklovskij, Victor. "Literatur ohne 'Sujet.'" *Theorie der Prosa*. Trans. Gisela Drohla. Frankfurt: Fischer, 1966: 163–185.

Smith, Barbara Herrnstein. *Contingencies of Value: Alternative Perspectives for Critical Theory*. Cambridge: Harvard UP, 1988.

Smith, James L. *Melodrama*. London: Methuen, 1973.

Söhnlein, Heike. *Gesellschaftliche und private Interaktionen: Dialoganalysen zu Hofmannsthals 'Der Schwierige' und Schnitzlers 'Das weite Land'*. Tübingen: Narr, 1986.

Sokel, Walter. "Brecht's Split Characters and His Sense of the Tragic." *Brecht: A Collection of Critical Essays*. Ed. Peter Demetz. Englewood Cliffs, N.J.: Prentice Hall, 1962: 127–237.

Soll, Ivan. *An Introduction to Hegel's Metaphysics*. Chicago: U of Chicago P, 1969.

Sophocles. *Antigone*. Trans. Elizabeth Wyckoff. *Sophocles I*. Ed. David Grene and Richmond Lattimore. Chicago: U of Chicago P, 1954: 157–206.

Sorg, Bernhard. *Der Künstler als Misanthrop: Zur Genealogie seiner Vorstellung*. Tübingen: Niemeyer, 1989.

Söring, Jürgen. *Tragödie: Notwendigkeit und Zufall im Spannungsfeld tragischer Prozesse*. Stuttgart: Klett-Cotta, 1982.

Speidel, E. "Brecht's 'Puntila': A Marxist Comedy." *Modern Language Review* 65 (1970): 319–332.

Spira, Andreas. *Untersuchungen zum Deus ex machina bei Sophokles und Euripides*. Kallmünz: Lassleben, 1960.

Spitel, Nicodemus. *Dum Carlos, der reitende Infanterist von Spanien, oder: Die schrecklichen Folgen der Trunkenboldigkeit. Ein dramatisches Ungeheuer nach den besten carnevalistischen Quellen, nach dem Punch, Kladderadadtsch, etc. etc.* Erfurt: Bartholomäus, n.d.

Spivak, Charlotte K. "Tragedy and Comedy: A Metaphysical Wedding." *Bucknell Review* 9 (1960–61): 212–223.

Spoto, Donald. *The Art of Alfred Hitchcock: Fifty Years of his Motion Pictures*. New York: Hopkinson, n.d.

Staiger, Emil. "Hugo von Hofmannsthal: 'Der Schwierige.'" *Hugo von Hofmannsthal*. Ed. Sibylle Bauer. Darmstadt: Wissenschaftliche Buchgesellschaft, 1968: 402–433.

Steiner, George. *Antigones*. Oxford: Clarendon, 1984.

———. *The Death of Tragedy*. New York: Knopf, 1961.

———. *Real Presences*. Chicago: U of Chicago P, 1989.

Steinhauer, Kurt, and Gitta Hausen. *Hegel Bibliography: Background Material on the International Reception of Hegel within the Context of the History of Philosophy*. New York: Saur, 1980.

Steinkraus, Warren E., and Kenneth I. Schmitz. *Art and Logic in Hegel's Philosophy*. Atlantic Highlands, N.J.: Humanities, 1980.

Stern, J. P. *Hilter: The Führer and the People*. Berkeley: U of California P, 1988.

Sternheim, Carl. *Der Snob: Komödie*. Darmstadt: Luchterhand, 1981.

———. *The Snob. Scenes from the Heroic Life of the Middle Classes: Five Plays*. Trans. M. A. L. Brown, M. A. McHaffie, J. M. Ritchie, J. D. Stowell. London: Calder, 1970: 145–193.

———. *Tabula rasa: Ein Schauspiel*. Stuttgart: Reclam, 1978.

Stierle, Karlheinz. "Komik der Handlung, Komik der Sprachhandlung, Komik der Komödie." *Text als Handlung: Perspektiven einer systematischen Literaturwissenshaft*. Munich: Fink, 1975: 56–97.

Stolnitz, Jerome. "Notes on Comedy and Tragedy." *Philosophy and Phenomenological Research* 16 (1955): 45–60.

Strohschneider-Kohrs, Ingrid. *Die Romantische Ironie in Theorie und Gestaltung*. Tübingen: Niemeyer, 1960.

———. "Die überwundene Komödiantin in Lessings Lustspiel." *Wolfenbütteler Studien zur Aufklärung* 2 (1975): 182–199.

Sutton, Dana Ferrin. *The Greek Satyr Play*. Meisenheim am Glan: Hain, 1980.

———. "Satyric Elements in the *Alcestis*." *Rivista di studi classici* 21 (1973): 384–391.

———. "Satyric Qualities in Euripides' *Iphigenia at Tauris* and *Helen*." *Rivista di studi classici* 20 (1972): 321–330.

———. "Satyr Plays and the *Odyssey*." *Arethusa* 7 (1974): 161–185.

Swabey, Marie C. "The Comic as Nonsense, Sadism, or Incongruity." *Journal of Philosophy* 55 (1958): 819–833.

Szondi, Peter. "Friedrich Schlegel and Romantic Irony, with Some Remarks on Tieck's Comedy." *On Textual Understanding and Other*

Essays. Trans. Harvey Mendelsohn. Minneapolis: U of Minnesota P, 1986: 57–73.

———. "Hegels Lehre von der Dichtung." *Poetik und Geschichtsphilosophie I.* Ed. Senta Metz and Hans-Hagen Hildebrandt. Frankfurt: Suhrkamp, 1974: 267–511.

———. "Theorie des modernen Dramas (1880–1950)." *Schriften I.* Ed. Jean Bollack. Frankfurt: Suhrkamp, 1978: 11–148.

———. "Versuch über das Tragische." *Schriften I.* Ed. Jean Bollack. Frankfurt: Suhrkamp, 1978: 149–260.

———. "Von der normativen zur spekulativen Gattungspoetik." *Poetik und Geschichtsphilosophie II.* Ed. Wolfgang Fietkau. Frankfurt: Suhrkamp, 1974: 8–183.

Taylor, Mark C. *Journeys to Selfhood: Hegel and Kierkegaard.* Berkeley: U of California P, 1980.

———. *Tears.* Albany: SUNY, 1990.

Tener, Robert L. *The Phoenix Riddle: A Study of Irony in Comedy.* Salzburg: Institut für Anglistik und Amerikanistik, Universität Salzburg, 1979.

Thompson, Alan Reynolds. "Melodrama and Tragedy." *PMLA* 43 (1928): 810–835.

Todorov, Tzvetan. *Genres in Discourse.* Trans. Catherine Porter. Cambridge: Cambridge UP, 1990.

———. *The Fantastic: A Structural Approach to a Literary Genre.* Trans. Richard Howard. Ithaca: Cornell UP, 1975.

Toller, Ernst. *Man and the Masses.* Trans. Louis Untermeyer. New York: Doubleday, 1924.

———. *Masse Mensch.* Stuttgart: Reclam, 1979.

Torrance, Robert M. *The Comic Hero.* Cambridge: Harvard UP, 1978.

Trautwein, Wolfgang. "Komödientheorien und Komödie: Ein Ordnungsversuch." *Jahrbuch der Deutschen Schillergesellschaft* 27 (1983): 86–123.

Truffaut, François. *Hitchcock.* New York: Simon and Schuster, 1967.

Tschernyschewskij, Nikolai Gaurilowitsch. *Die ästhetischen Beziehungen der Kunst zur Wirklichkeit.* 1853. Berlin: Aufbau, 1954.

Tymms, Ralph. *Doubles in Literary Psychology.* Cambridge: Bowes and Bowes, 1949.

Tynjanov, Jurij. "Das literarische Faktum." *Russischer Formalismus: Texte zur allgemeinen Literaturtheorie und zur Theorie der Prosa.* Ed. Jurij Striedter. Munich: Fink, 1971: 393–431.

———. "Über die literarische Evolution." *Russischer Formalismus: Texte zur allgemeinen Literaturtheorie und zur Theorie der Prosa.* Ed. Jurij Striedter. Munich: Fink, 1971: 433–461.

Überhorst, Karl. *Das Komische: Eine Untersuchung.* 2 vols. Leipzig: Wigand, 1896–1900.

Vaughan, C. E. *Types of Tragic Drama.* London: Macmillan, 1908.

Versényi, Laszlo. *Socratic Humanism.* New Haven: Yale UP, 1963.

Verzeichnis der von dem Professor Herrn Dr. Hegel und dem Dr. Herrn Seebek hinterlassenen Bücher-Sammlungen. Berlin: Müller, 1832.

Vickers, Brian. *Towards Greek Tragedy: Drama, Myth, Society.* London: Longman, 1973.

Vico, Giambattista. *The New Science.* Trans. Thomas Goddard Bergin and Max Harold Fisch. Ithaca: Cornell UP, 1984.

Viëtor, Karl. *Geist und Form: Aufsätze zur deutschen Literaturgeschichte.* Bern: Francke, 1952.

Vischer, Friederich Theodor. *Ästhetik oder Wissenschaft des Schönen.* 2nd ed. Ed. Robert Vischer. 6 vols. 1846–1857. Hildesheim: Olms, 1975.

Vittorini, Domenico. *The Drama of Luigi Pirandello.* Philadelphia: U of Pennsylvania P, 1935.

Vogt-Spira, Gregor. *Dramaturgie des Zufalls: Tyche und Handeln in der Komödie Menanders.* Munich: Beck, 1992.

Volkelt, Johannes Immanuel. *Ästhetik des Tragischen.* Munich: Beck, 1897.

———. *System der Ästhetik.* 3 vols. Munich: Beck, 1905–14.

Wagner, Frank Dietrich. *Hegels Philosophie der Dichtung.* Bonn: Bouvier, 1974.

Wagner, Hans. *Ästhetik der Tragödie von Aristoteles bis Schiller.* Würzburg: Königshausen, 1987.

Wandschneider, Dieter. "Die Absolutheit des Logischen und das Sein der Natur. Systematische Überlegungen zum absolut-idealistischen Ansatz Hegels," *Zeitschrift für philosophische Forschung* 39 (1985): 331–351.

———. "Dialektik als antinomische Logik." *Hegel-Jahrbuch* 1991: 227–242.

———. *Grundzüge einer Theorie der Dialektik: Rekonstruktion und Revision dialektischer Kategorienentwicklung in Hegels 'Wissenschaft der Logik.'* Stuttgart: Klett-Cotta, 1995.

———. "Nature and the Dialectic of Nature in Hegel's Objective Idealism." *Bulletin of the Hegel Society of Great Britian* 26 (1992): 30–51.

———. "Das Problem der Entäußerung der Idee zur Natur bei Hegel." *Hegel-Jahrbuch* 1990: 25–33.

———. *Raum, Zeit, Relativität. Grundbestimmungen der Physik in der Perspektive Hegelscher Naturphilosophie.* Frankfurt: Klostermann, 1982.

Warning, Rainer. "Elemente einer Pragmasemiotik der Komödie." *Das Ko-*

mische. Ed. Wolfgang Preisendanz and Rainer Warning. Munich: Fink, 1976: 279–333.

Watson, Shawn. "Shakespeare's Problem Comedies: An Hegelian Approach to Genre." *Drama and Philosophy.* Ed. James Redmond. Cambridge: Cambridge UP, 1990: 61–71.

Weisinger, Herbert. *Tragedy and the Paradox of the Fortunate Fall.* East Lansing: Michigan State College P, 1953.

Weiße, Christian Hermann. *System der Ästhetik als Wissenschaft von der Idee der Schönheit.* 1830. Hildesheim: Olms, 1966.

Welleck, René. *A History of Modern Criticism: 1750–1950. The Romantic Age.* Vol. 2. New Haven: Yale UP, 1955.

Werder, Annette von. "Philosophie und Geschichte: Das historische Selbstverständnis des objektiven Idealismus bei Hegel und bei Hösle." Diss. Aachen 1993.

Weyl, Hermann. *Symmetry.* Princeton: Princeton UP, 1952.

White, Hayden. "Ideology and Counterideology in the *Anatomy.*" *Visionary Poetics: Essays on Northrop Frye's Criticism.* Ed. Robert D. Denham and Thomas Willard. New York: Lang, 1991: 101–111.

Whitman, Cedric H. *Aristophanes and the Comic Hero.* Cambridge: Harvard UP, 1964.

Wicke, Günter. *Die Struktur des deutschen Lustspiels der Aufklärung. Versuch einer Typologie.* Bonn: Bouvier, 1965.

Wiese, Benno von. *Die deutsche Tragödie von Lessing bis Hebbel.* 5th ed. Hamburg: Hoffmann, 1961.

Wilde, Oscar. *Plays.* New York: Penguin, 1985.

Willett, Cynthia. "Hegel, Antigone, and the Possibility of Ecstatic Dialogue." *Philosophy and Literature* 14 (1990): 268–283.

Williams, Robert R. *Recognition: Fichte and Hegel on the Other.* Albany: SUNY, 1992.

———. "Theology and Tragedy." *New Perspectives on Hegel's Philosophy of Religion.* Ed. David Kolb. Albany: SUNY, 1992: 39–58.

Winfield, Richard Dien. *Stylistics: Rethinking the Artforms After Hegel.* Albany: SUNY, 1996.

———. *Systematic Aesthetics.* Gainesville: U P of Florida, 1995.

Witkiewicz, Stanislaw Ignacy. *Tropical Madness: Four Plays.* Trans. Daniel and Eleanor Gerould. New York: Winter, 1972.

Wittgenstein, Ludwig. *Philosophische Untersuchungen.* Frankfurt: Suhrkamp, 1971.

Wittkowski, Wolfgang. "Die Aufspaltung Gottes oder das Ende der deutschen Tragödie bei Hebbel und Büchner." *Sprachkunst* 13 (1982): 231–243.

———. "Höfische Intrige für die gute Sache. Marquis Posa und Octavio

Piccolomini." *Schiller und die höfische Welt*. Ed. Achim Aurnhammer, Klaus Manger, and Friedrich Strack. Tübingen: Niemeyer, 1990: 378–397.

———. *"Der zerbrochene Krug*: Juggling of Authorities." *Heinrich von Kleist Studies*. Ed. Alexej Ugrinsky *et al*. New York: AMS, 1980: 69–79.

Wittmann, Lothar. *Sprachthematik und dramatische Form im Werke Hofmannsthals*. Stuttgart: Kohlhammer, 1966.

Wolff, Emil. "Hegel und Shakespeare." *Vom Geist der Dichtung: Festschrift für Robert Petsch*. Ed. Fritz Martini. Hamburg: Hoffmann, 1949: 120–179.

Wood, Allen W. "Editor's Introduction." Hegel, G. W. F. *Elements of the Philosophy of Right*. Cambridge: Cambridge UP, 1991: vii–xxxii.

Wood, Robin. *Hitchcock's Films*. 2nd ed. New York: Barnes, 1969.

Yates, William Edgar. "Der Schwierige: The Comedy of Discretion." *Modern Austrian Literature* 10 (1977): 1–17.

Zach, Wolfgang. *Poetic Justice: Theorie und Geschichte einer literarischen Doktrin: Begriff-Idee-Komödienkonzeption*. Tübingen: Niemeyer, 1986.

Zapf, Hubert. "O'Neill's *Hairy Ape* and the Reversal of Hegelian Dialectics." *Modern Drama* 31 (1988): 35–40.

Zeising, Adolf. *Aesthetische Forschungen*. Frankfurt: Weidinger, 1855.

INDEX

Individual artworks are listed only in cases where I have given a detailed reading or where an author had enough entries to warrant subheadings; in order to hold the index to a reasonable length, such works are listed only as subheadings under their authors and not also independently. For the same reason, authors mentioned in passing and works cited simply as examples have not been included. Critics are listed only when their work is discussed rather than simply noted.

Names Index

Subjects Index